TREATIES AND ALLIANCES
OF THE WORLD

TREATIES AND ALLIANCES
OF THE WORLD

3rd Edition

A Keesing's Reference Publication

Compiled and written by
Henry W. Degenhardt
General editor: Alan J. Day

TREATIES AND ALLIANCES OF THE WORLD

1st Edition 1968
2nd Edition (revised and updated) 1974
3rd Edition (substantially revised and rewritten) 1981

Published by Longman Group Limited, Longman House,
Burnt Mill, Harlow, Essex CM20 2JE, United Kingdom

Distributed exclusively in the United States and possessions,
Canada and Mexico by Gale Research Company,
Book Tower, Detroit, Michigan 48226, USA

ISBN 0 582 90250 9 (Longman)
     0 8103 1602 1 (Gale)

Library of Congress Catalog Card Number: 81-83479

First published 1981

British Library Cataloguing in Publication Data
Degenhardt, Henry W.
   Treaties and alliances of the world. — 3rd ed. — (Keesing's reference publications).
   1. Treaties — Collections
   I. Title   II. Day, Alan J.
   341'.026   JX171

ISBN 0 582 90250 9

Printed and bound in Great Britain by
William Clowes (Beccles) Limited, Beccles and London

Contents

Maps

Tables and Diagrams

Introduction

Since the publication of the second edition of this book in 1974 (by Charles Scribner's Sons of New York) considerable changes have taken place in the pattern of alliances, treaties and agreements concluded between the states of the world. The present volume covers all major new developments in this field up to the end of 1980 and also contains expanded coverage of earlier international agreements, including fuller treatment of relevant basic documents and texts.

The trend towards mutual understanding and détente between East and West, begun in the early 1970s, continued in the latter half of the decade, a major landmark being the signature in 1975 of the Helsinki Final Act on security and co-operation in Europe. However, the terms of the Helsinki agreement have not been interpreted equally in East and West, while more recently new international tensions arising from the Soviet intervention in Afghanistan raise the possibility of a return to cold-war attitudes in the 1980s.

The principal change reflected in this edition, however, is the emergence of North-South antagonisms—between developed or industrialized countries on the one hand and the developing third-world countries on the other. Attempts to bridge this gap are described in some detail, especially in the section on international economic co-operation.

A wide network of cross-connexions arising from treaties, alliances and agreements in force throughout the world has now become apparent. Only few countries, such as South Africa and Taiwan, appear to have been left more or less outside international mutual obligations under the ever-increasing incidence of bilateral and multilateral links involving most states of the world.

Thanks for various kinds of assistance with the compilation of the present volume are due to the editorial staff of *Keesing's Contemporary Archives,* and in particular to Richard German for the index.

Bath   HWD
June 1981   AJD

1. Early International Agreements and their Later Expansion

Early international agreements and their later expansion dealt with in this section comprise (i) the various 19th and 20th century agreements on the conduct of war, notably the Geneva and Hague Conventions; (ii) various conventions safeguarding intellectual property by means of copyright and patent arrangements; (iii) Concordats and other agreements entered into by the Roman Catholic Church; and (iv) certain treaties and agreements concluded after World War I which are still in force.

Agreements on the Conduct of War

The Declaration of Paris of 1856

The Congress of Paris, attended by representatives of the leading European powers, in 1856 adopted the Declaration of Paris designed to assimilate the provisions of the maritime law of individual states in the event of war. After being signed by Austria, Britain, France, Prussia, Russia, Sardinia and Turkey, the declaration was eventually adhered to by all civilized states except Bolivia, the United States, Uruguay and Venezuela.

The declaration provided for:

(*a*) The continued prohibition of privateering (i.e. warfare by privately armed vessels under a commission from the state);

(*b*) acceptance of the principle that a neutral flag covers enemy goods except contraband of war, and that neutral goods—again except contraband of war—are not liable to confiscation under an enemy flag; and

(*c*) the principle that blockades, in order to be binding, must be effective—i.e. maintained "by forces sufficient to prevent access to the enemy coast line". (This provision on blockades was repeated in the Declaration of London of February 1909, which was, however, never ratified.)

The Geneva Conventions of the International Red Cross

EARLY CONVENTIONS

First Geneva Convention. The first Geneva Convention, signed by delegates from 16 European countries in Geneva in 1864, established the principle that sick and wounded combatants in war should be respected and cared for irrespective of their nationality; that the personnel caring for them, as well as buildings, equipment and transport used for their care, should be protected, and that a distinctive emblem—the Red Cross (to which the Red Crescent for Moslem countries and the Red Lion and Sun in Persia (Iran) were added later)—should be the symbol of their immunity. This protection was to be claimed only in respect of medical personnel, buildings, equipment and transport operating as part of the medical services of the armed forces of the belligerents.

Second Geneva Convention. The second Geneva Convention of 1906 extended the above principles to maritime warfare and included shipwrecked persons among those to be protected.

Third Geneva Convention. The third Geneva Convention of 1929 contained amendments to the earlier conventions arising out of experiences during World War I and incorporated provisions from a Prisoners of War Convention of the same year. This provided for information bureaux in the belligerent countries to circulate information on prisoners of war, and to safeguard their interests through a neutral power, whose representatives were allowed to visit prisoner of war camps and to question prisoners.

At the outbreak of World War II the Geneva Conventions had not been signed by a number of states, including Japan and the Soviet Union.

1948 CONVENTIONS

Further conventions were drafted at an International Red Cross conference in Stockholm held on Aug. 23-30, 1948. These included:

1

(1) Convention on the Protection of Civilians in Wartime. This convention was to apply not only in circumstances of war declared between states but also in interstate conflicts where one of the belligerents did not recognize the existence of a formal state of war, including civil, colonial and religious wars.

The convention (*a*) recommends the immediate designation in peacetime of "security zones" (which will be recognized by signatory belligerents in wartime) for the wounded, children under 15, pregnant mothers and mothers with children under 7, and persons over 65, without discrimination on racial, national, religious or political grounds;

(*b*) provides, in addition, for the setting up of "neutral zones" in actual fighting areas to which the sick and injured, as well as all non-combatant civilians, may be removed;

(*c*) grants special protection from attack to civilian hospitals marked with the Red Cross sign, as well as to transports of sick and injured;

(*d*) prohibits the sending of "protected persons" (i.e. all those who in the case of war or occupation come under the rule of a power whose nationality they do not possess, or those who in the case of civil war do not take part in hostilities) to, or their retention in, areas subject to warlike actions; their misuse for the safeguarding of certain areas or military operations; physical or mental torture and similar practices to obtain information; collective punishment, reprisals, and the destruction of property if not necessitated by military operations; and the taking of hostages;

(*e*) prohibits also, in the case of occupation, deportations, evacuations not required for military reasons, and conscription of "protected persons" for combatant units or auxiliary forces, or their voluntary recruitment, and allows conscription for work only to safeguard public services, as well as laying down specific rules concerning labour conditions, hygiene and sanitary measures, the prevention of epidemics, etc., in occupied countries;

(*f*) makes the occupying power in wartime responsible for feeding the civilian population, prohibits the removal of food if there is any shortage, and likewise prohibits the transfer of part of the occupying power's own civilian nationals to occupied territory;

(*g*) grants analogous protection to aliens in belligerent countries, who are given the right to return to their home country unless a special court set up to examine these cases orders their retention for cogent security reasons, the court having also to make a decision as to whether the alien concerned is to be placed under supervision or to be detained, all proceedings being subject to the ordinary guarantees of law;

(*h*) provides, as far as civilian internment camps are concerned, that internees must be grouped according to nationality, language and habits, that family members should not be separated and parents be entitled to have their children with them, that internment and P.O.W. camps must be separated, and that internees must not be forced to work unless they choose; detailed provisions also deal with housing and sanitary conditions in such camps, protection against air attack and war operations, feeding, postal communications, receipt of gift parcels, censorship, etc.;

(*i*) empowers the representatives of the Protecting Power to visit any place where there are "protected persons" and to talk to them personally without observers;

(*j*) lays down that the free passage of medical supplies and, in the case of children and pregnant mothers, of food and clothing, must be allowed by belligerents even if destined for civilians of an enemy country.

(2) Convention on the Treatment of Prisoners of War. This amends the 1929 convention to enable prisoners of war to receive collective relief assignments; pledges signatories to give them adequate rations to keep them in good health (instead of "rations equal to those of their captors", as previously); and extends the application of the 1929 convention to include not only members of the armed forces and civilians openly bearing arms in defence against enemy forces, but also members of military organizations or resistance movements fighting an occupying power, provided they wear armlets or other visible signs and carry arms openly (the existing requirement of a uniform being dropped).

(3) Convention on Relief of the Wounded and Sick in Armies of the Field.

(4) Convention adapting the principles of the Geneva Convention of 1906 to maritime warfare.

These conventions were approved in Geneva on Aug. 12, 1949, by the representatives of 58 countries—although only a minority of these signed all of them.

1977 ADDITIONAL PROTOCOLS

An international Diplomatic Conference on Humanitarian Law Applicable in Armed Conflicts adopted, on June 10, 1977, two protocols additional to the 1949 Geneva Conventions.

Protocol I. Article I of this protocol contained a statement to the effect that "the people's struggle against colonial domination, against occupation by a foreign power and against racist regimes in accordance with their right of self-determination and the Charter of the United Nations" should be regarded as an "armed international conflict". In Article 42, dealing with conflicts involving national liberation movements recognized by the Organization of African Unity or the Arab League, it was laid down that armed combatants should be given protection equivalent to that accorded to prisoners of war even if such combatants did not comply with the conditions of wearing armlets or other visible signs and carrying arms openly.

In other articles mercenaries were declared not to be entitled to the status of combatants or prisoners of war; "war crimes" were listed as including attacks on the civilian population by target area (or "carpet") bombing, the destruction of nuclear power stations, dams, food supplies and water installations indispensable to the survival of civilians, and also "inhuman and degrading practices . . . based on racial discrimination".

Protocol II. This set out a "humanitarian minimum" of provisions relating to internal conflicts, in particular for the protection of the sick, the wounded and medical personnel; the obligation to protect objects and installations essential to the survival of the civilian population; the prohibition of forcible deportation; the privileged treatment of children; and the prohibition of starvation of the civilian population as a method of combat.

These two protocols were signed on Dec. 12, 1977, by ambassadors of 42 countries, including almost all Western states (except France), those of Eastern Europe and several Latin American states, but almost none in Africa or Asia.

The Hague Conventions of 1899 and 1907

1899 Conventions. At an international conference held at The Hague in 1899 on the initiative of Czar Nicholas II of Russia and attended by representatives of 26 nations (which included the USA and Mexico), a number of conventions were adopted, and declarations issued, limiting methods of warfare and providing for peaceful settlement of disputes.

The first of the conventions adopted concerned the laws and customs of war. In this connexion the conference issued three declarations prohibiting (a) the discharge of projectiles from balloons; (b) the use of asphyxiating gases; and (c) the use of expanding bullets.

Further, a *Convention for the Pacific Settlement of International Disputes* established the Hague Permanent Court of Arbitration, the forerunner of the International Court of Justice.

1907 Conventions. A second international conference, held at The Hague from June 15 to Oct. 18, 1907, and attended by representatives of 44 countries, revised and renewed the 1899 conventions (though without renewing the declarations on asphyxiating gases and expanding bullets).

In a *Convention on Prisoners of War* it laid down rules, largely already in practice, on their treatment.

In accordance with this convention, prisoners of war must be humanely treated, protected from violence, not subjected to reprisals, and supplied with reasonable nourishment as well as medical and sanitary facilities. They are regarded as being in the power of the Government of the captors, and not in that of the captors themselves; their personal belongings (other than arms and military papers) remain their own; they may not be detained in a convict prison; the captor state may utilize their labour, except in the case of officers, with payment according to rank and ability, but they may not be engaged in excessive work or any tasks relating to military operations.

Prisoners of war need not give any other information than their true name and rank, but these they must give under penalty of losing normal prisoner of war advantages. The convention also provides for exchange procedure.

The conference also adopted 10 new conventions, notably a *Convention respecting the Limitation of Force for the Recovery of Contract Debts*. The nine others dealt with (a) the need for a declaration of war, i.e. "previous and explicit warning, in the form either of a reasoned declaration of war or of an ultimatum with a conditional declaration"; (b) the rights and duties of neutrals in war on land; (c) the status of enemy merchant vessels at the outbreak of war; (d) the conversion of merchant vessels into warships; (e) the laying of automatic submarine contact mines; (f) bombardment by naval forces; (g) the right of capture in maritime war; (h) the setting-up of an international prize court; and (i) the rights and duties of neutral powers in maritime war.

The Geneva Protocol

A protocol prohibiting the use in war of asphyxiating, poisonous and other gases, and of bacteriological methods of warfare, was signed at Geneva on June 17, 1925. Twenty-nine countries signed the protocol originally, the Soviet Union adhering in 1928. Although the United States had adhered to the protocol in 1925, the US Senate did not ratify it until December 1974, whereafter President Ford signed the instrument of ratification on Jan. 22, 1975. By Dec. 31, 1979, the protocol was adhered to by 108 countries.

Other Agreements on the Conduct of War

Kellogg Pact. A treaty on the renunciation of war as a means of settling international disputes—the Kellogg Pact—proposed by the United States was signed in Paris on Aug. 27, 1928. It was accepted by 15 Governments and subsequently ratified by 63 states; it came into force on July 24, 1929.

This pact consisted of two paragraphs as follows:

"**Art. 1.** The high contracting parties solemnly declare in the name of their peoples that they condemn recourse to war for the solution of international controversies, and renounce it as an instrument of national policy in their relations with one another.

"**Art. 2.** The high contracting parties agree that the settlement or solution of all disputes or conflicts of whatever nature or of whatever origin they may be, which may arise among them, shall never be sought except by pacific means."

The Kellogg Pact was binding only upon the parties to it.

Submarine Warfare. A protocol (to a London naval treaty of 1930) on rules of submarine warfare was signed on Nov. 6, 1936, by France, India, Italy, Japan, the United Kingdom and Dominions, and the United States; it required submarines to conform to the law of prize, which forbade the sinking of merchant ships before passengers and crews had been saved. By Dec. 31, 1979, it was adhered to by 46 countries.

Conventions for Protection of Intellectual Property*

The Convention of the Union of Paris for the Protection of Industrial Property

This convention, approved in Paris on March 30, 1883, and revised at The Hague (on Nov. 6, 1925), in London (on June 2, 1934), in Lisbon (Oct. 31, 1958) and in Stockholm (on July 14, 1967), gave inventors' patents protection in foreign countries by providing that patent applications in the other member countries should apply from the same date as the patent application in the inventor's home country. By 1980 a total of 88 countries were parties to these conventions; they included the Soviet Union but not China.

European Patent Conventions

European Patent Convention. A *Convention on the Grant of European Patents*, which had been approved by representatives of 21 European countries and signed by 14 of them in Munich on Oct. 5, 1973, provided for 20-year "European patents" to be valid in all acceding states (but in most cases subject to the patent laws of each state), with these patents being available from a European Patent Office (which was opened in Munich on Nov. 2, 1977). The agreement first became effective on Oct. 7, 1977, for Belgium, France, the Federal Republic of Germany, the Netherlands, Luxembourg, Switzerland and the United Kingdom, and by Dec. 31, 1979, it was also in force for Austria, Italy and Sweden. A **European Patent Organization**, headed by an Administrative Council, was constituted on Oct. 19, 1977, to implement the 1973 Munich convention.

European Community Patent Convention. A Community patents convention, signed in Luxembourg on Dec. 15, 1975, by the nine member states of the European Communities, provided for the harmoniza-

tion of patent laws within the European Communities, with the latter becoming a uniform bloc within the framework of the broader 1973 Convention on the Grant of European Patents.

Copyright Conventions

1886 Berne Convention. The Berne Copyright Convention of 1886 was adhered to by 41 countries (mostly European, with only Brazil and Canada from the western hemisphere), and was revised in Paris in 1896, in Berlin in 1908, in Rome in 1928, and in Brussels in 1948.

The Brussels revision of 1948 extended the protection previously given to authors of works of literature, art, and music to the spheres of film, radio, television and allied arts, and laid down that disputes between countries on the interpretation or application of the convention were to be submitted to the International Court of Justice.

The convention was further amended at the 1967 Stockholm Conference on Intellectual Property by a protocol (proposed by Sweden) giving preferential rights to those developing countries which are members of the Berne Copyright Convention.

This protocol authorized these countries: (*a*) To translate into their own language and publish, without permission by its author and immediately after publication of the original, "any book to be used for teaching, study and research in all fields of education"; (*b*) to translate and publish literary and artistic works similarly three years or more after their original publication (though reprinting of such books in the original language remained subject to the existing copyright regulations); and (*c*) to pay, in all these cases, royalties to authors in accordance with the developing countries' own rates.

The protocol was applicable only against a country of origin which had agreed to its

---

* See also World Intellectual Property Organization, page 38.

provisions. Of the developing countries, India is the most prominent member of the Berne Convention, while most other developing countries are not members.

The protocol was adopted without dissent, but with Britain abstaining, and the British Government did not sign it.

Pan-American Conventions. Several Pan-American conventions have also been signed between western hemisphere countries, the most important being the Buenos Aires Convention of 1910 with 15 adherents, including the USA.

Universal Copyright Convention. Under the auspices of UNESCO, a conference held in Geneva from Aug. 25 to Sept. 7, 1952, resulted in the signing by representatives of 35 countries of a *Universal Copyright Convention*, the principal provisions of which were:

(1) Each signatory country undertakes to give to foreign works the same copyright protection as that given to works of its own nationals. The terms of protection will be not less than the life of the author and 25 years after his death.

(2) All existing formalities of registration and legal deposit will be eliminated, and will be replaced by a simple system under which the letter "C" will be imprinted within a circle on each copy of the works protected, accompanied by the author's name and the date of the first publication.

(3) Translation rights will also be covered, and during a minimum period of seven years authors will have the exclusive right to publish translations of their works, or to authorize the making and publication of such translations.

By Dec. 31, 1979, the Universal Copyright Convention had been ratified by 72 countries. The Soviet Union acceded on May 27, 1973. The convention does not supersede the Berne Convention, which remains binding upon its members.

1971 Revision of Universal and Berne Copyright Conventions. The Universal Copyright Convention was revised at a conference of 46 countries—the contracting parties to the convention—in Paris on July 5-24, 1971, by the addition of three new articles:

(1) Defining "non-industrialized countries" and the period of preferential treatment to be granted to them for their needs in teaching, scholarship and research;

(2) reducing the seven-year period for authors' exclusive rights to translation of their work [see (3) above] in the case of editions to be used for teaching, scholarship or research to three years for works published in a widely-used language, and to one year in the case of a little-used language—subject to a ban on exports of such translations; and

(3) enabling any national of a contracting country to obtain a licence, under certain conditions, for reproduction, for the purpose of "systematic instructional activities", of a work of which the first issue had not been distributed within a specified period.

At the same time the Berne Convention of 1886 was modified so as to give non-industrialized countries the same advantages as they had under the Universal Convention.

Agreements entered into by the Roman Catholic Church

Concordats

Concordats are treaties concluded between the Pope, as head of the Roman Catholic Church, and secular governments on matters concerning the interests of Roman Catholic citizens, especially in education, and property of the Catholic Church.

Among over 20 such Concordats signed since the end of World War I were the following:

Lateran Treaty. The Lateran Treaty, signed by the Cardinal Secretary of State of the Vatican and Benito Mussolini, then head of the Italian Government, on Feb. 11, 1929, embodied recognition by the Government of Italy of the sovereignty of the Vatican City State, and provided for compensation by the Italian state for Church property seized in 1870.

Bavarian Concordat. A Concordat concluded with Bavaria in 1924 was expressly reaffirmed in the 1946 Constitution of the *Land* of Bavaria.

Concordat with Nazi Germany. The Concordat concluded with Nazi Germany on July 20, 1933, was ruled by the German Federal Constitutional Court in 1957 to be still in force though not binding on *Länder* (i.e. federal units of the Federal Republic of Germany) in regard to school legislation.

Lower Saxony Concordat. A new Concordat was subsequently concluded between the Vatican and the *Land* (state) of Lower Saxony on Feb. 26, 1965, covering provisions for the establishment and maintenance of Roman Catholic schools, a grant-in-aid towards salaries of ministers of religion, and the setting up of a Roman Catholic Theological Faculty at the *Land*'s university in Göttingen.

Portuguese Concordat. The Concordat with Portugal, signed on May 7, 1940, included an acknowledgment by the state of the intangible character of church marriage, as well as provisions confirming the Church's possession of property and the appointment of bishops by the Pope with their formal nomination by the head of the state.

The validity of the 1940 Concordat was confirmed in a protocol which was signed on Feb. 15, 1975, but which recognized the legal right of couples married in church (and not only, as hitherto, of those Catholics who had contracted civil marriages, and of non-Catholics) to obtain a civil divorce, while reaffirming the doctrine of the Church on the indissolubility of marriage.

Other Agreements of the Roman Catholic Church

Agreement with Spain. Under an agreement signed in Rome on July 28, 1976, the King of Spain renounced the right—as granted to him in a Concordat signed on Aug. 27, 1953—of proposing bishops and archbishops for appointment, and the Vatican renounced the right of priests and nuns not to be tried by civil courts without authorization by their Church superiors. Instruments of ratification of these agreements were exchanged on Aug. 20, 1976.

The 1953 Concordat with Spain was re-placed by four agreements signed on Jan. 3, 1979, specifying that (i) the Spanish Government recognized the Roman Catholic Church and its activities, the inviolability of its places of worship and the full civil effects of marriage under canon law, while rulings of the ecclesiastical court (on nullity) would be subject ultimately to state law in the case of civil marriages; (ii) the state would phase out its annual direct subsidy to the Roman Catholic Church and instead raise a "religious levy" so that the Church would receive a percentage of the state's income and wealth tax revenue; (iii) religious instruction would be a non-compulsory part of the school syllabus; and (iv) guidelines were laid down for clerics carrying out military service.

Hungarian Agreement. Other agreements concluded by the Catholic Church and a secular government have been entered into by church leaders in their respective countries. These include the agreement concluded between Archbishop Grosz of Kalocsa and the Hungarian state on Aug. 30, 1950, by which the bishops undertook to "recognize and support the Constitution and state order of the Hungarian People's Republic".

Treaties and Agreements concluded in the Wake of World War I

Among treaties concluded in the aftermath of World War I and still in force are the following:

The Svalbard Treaty (or Treaty of Spitsbergen)

As a result of work by a commission under the auspices of the Versailles peace conference, this treaty was concluded on Feb. 9, 1920, and was eventually adhered to by 41 countries (including Norway as well as China, France, Germany, the Soviet Union, the United Kingdom and the United States). It entered into force on June 14, 1925.

The treaty granted Norway "full and absolute sovereignty" over the Svalbard archipelago (of which Spitsbergen is the main island) while economic activities such as fishing, hunting and mining were open to nationals of all the contracting states on a footing of absolute equality. At the same time Svalbard was made a demilitarized area not be be used for war purposes. (The only countries economically active in Svalbard have been Norway and the Soviet Union.)

Under an agreement signed in Oslo on March 7, 1974, the Soviet Union was granted landing rights and other rights for civil air-craft at an all-year airport to be built on West Spitsbergen.

The Aaland Islands Convention

A convention on the demilitarization and neutralization of the (Finnish) Aaland Islands, signed on Oct. 20, 1921, entered into force on April 6, 1922, for Denmark, Germany, Finland, France, Sweden and the United Kingdom, on May 11, 1922, for Italy and on June 29, 1922, for Poland.

The convention, based on a decision by the Council of the League of Nations, provided also that the Aalanders, who had in two plebiscites voted overwhelmingly in favour of Swedish sovereignty over the islands, should have far-reaching internal autonomy and be exempt from Finnish military service.

Soviet Treaties with Iran

1921 Soviet-Iranian Treaty. This treaty, signed between Iran and the Russian Socialist Federative Soviet Republic (RSFSR) on Feb. 26, 1921, consists of a preamble, 26 articles and an exchange of notes.

The provisions of the treaty included: Russian renunciation of all privileges which Iran had allowed Czarist Russia; the annulling of all treaties concerning Iran made by the former Russian regime with third powers; the opening of the Caspian Sea to Iran, in return for which Iran conceded fishing rights to the RSFSR; the restoration to validity of Iran's frontiers of 1881; and the cancellation of debts arising out of Czarist loans.

The most significant articles of the treaty were Articles 5 and 6. In Article 5 the two Governments agreed: (i) not to permit the creation or presence on their territory of any organization or group hostile to the RSFSR, Iran or their allies; (ii) not to permit any third party to import into, or convey through, the territory of either of the partners to the treaty any materials which could be used against the other partner; and (iii) to prevent, with all the means at their command, the presence of any military forces of a third power on their territory, in case the presence of such forces could be interpreted as a threat to the borders, the interests or the security of the other partner to the treaty.

Article 6 read as follows:

"If a third party should attempt to carry out a policy of usurpation by means of armed intervention in Iran, or if such power should desire to use Iran's territory as a base of operations against Russia, or if a foreign power should threaten the frontiers of Federal Russia (i.e. the RSFSR) or those of its allies, and if the Iranian Government should not be able to put a stop to such menace after having been called upon to do so by Russia, Russia shall have the right to advance her troops into the interior of Iran for the purpose of carrying out the military operations necessary for its defence."

In the exchange of notes Iran asked for clarification of Articles 5 and 6. The clarification given by the RSFSR read as follows:

"Articles 5 and 6 are intended to apply only to cases in which preparations have been made for a considerable armed attack upon Russia, or the Soviet Republics allied to her, by the partisans of the regime which has been overthrown (i.e., the Czarist regime), or by its supporters among the foreign powers which are in a position to assist the enemies of the Workers' and Peasants' Republics and at the same time to possess themselves, by force or by underhand methods, of part of Iran's territory."

1927 Amended Soviet-Iranian Treaty. This new treaty, signed on Oct. 1, 1927, embodied the clarification of Articles 5 and 6 of the 1921 treaty, and also included a new article providing for the neutrality of either party should the other be involved in conflict with one or several powers.

During Soviet-Iranian negotiations for a non-aggression treaty from Jan. 29 to Feb. 11, 1959, Iran requested the annulment of Articles 5 and 6 of the 1921 treaty, as being no longer applicable to the situation. The Iranian request was, however, refused by the USSR, and on this point—and others—the negotiations broke down.

On Nov. 5, 1979, however, the Government of the Islamic Republic of Iran announced its abrogation of the above Articles 5 and 6.

2. World War II: Treaties and Agreements on Territorial Changes, Frontiers and Other Matters arising out of the War

During and after World War II the Allied Powers, in a series of treaties and agreements, determined their proposed treatment of the countries of the Axis Powers after the conclusion of hostilities. The most important conferences, at which such agreements were reached, were the Yalta Conference and the Potsdam Conference of 1945. Also dealt with in this section are the Allied agreements regulating the post-war status of Germany and the post-1945 peace treaties between Allied Powers and Siam (Thailand), Bulgaria, Finland, Italy (including the later Italian-Yugoslav agreement on the status of Trieste), Hungary, Romania and Japan, as well as the 1955 Austrian State Treaty and the 1956 Franco-German Treaty on the Saar. (No peace treaty has been concluded between the World War II Allies and Germany.)

Inter-Allied Agreements on Shape of Post-War World

The Yalta Conference

At this conference, held in Yalta (Crimea) on Feb. 4-11, 1945, Churchill, Roosevelt and Stalin confirmed previous agreements on the occupation of Germany.

These agreements included acceptance of a proposal made by the European Advisory Commission of the Allied Powers at the Second Quebec Conference of September 1944; France, as a fourth occupying power, now associated herself with this proposal. It involved (*a*) Allied administration of Germany in British, French, Soviet and United States occupation zones; and (*b*) the control of Berlin by the four Allied Powers.

Further decisions reached at Yalta were:

(1) Britain and the USA would support membership in the United Nations General Assembly for the Soviet republics of the Ukraine and Byelorussia, in addition to the Soviet Union itself.

(2) Under the terms of a secret protocol, the Soviet Union would enter the war against Japan "within two or three months" after the surrender of Germany, and the Western Powers would in return (*a*) recognize the independence of Outer Mongolia and (*b*) agree to the transfer to the Soviet Union of Southern Sakhalin, adjacent islands, and the Kurile Islands, as well as to her recovery of certain rights in the Far East which Russia had lost in the war against Japan in 1904-05.

The Potsdam Conference

At the Potsdam Conference, held on July 17-Aug. 2, 1945, Clement Attlee (then British Prime Minister), Stalin and President Truman agreed inter alia on the following points:

(1) Germany was not to be partitioned, but to be treated as a single economic unit with certain central administrative departments though with a programme of decentralization to be carried out.

(2) Britain and the USA would support, at the eventual peace settlement, the Soviet annexation of the northern half of East Prussia (including Königsberg).

(3) "Pending the final delimitation of Poland's western frontier", the "former German territories" east of the Oder and Neisse Rivers and the former free city of Danzig were to be left under Polish administration and should not be considered as part of the Soviet zone of occupation in Germany.

(4) Peace treaties should be concluded with Bulgaria, Finland, Hungary, Italy and Romania.

(5) The remaining German population in Poland, Czechoslovakia and Hungary was to be transferred to Germany.

Decisions by the Allied Control Council

Allied policy on Germany was implemented by the Allied Control Council, consisting of the Supreme Commanders of the British, French, Soviet and US Armed Forces.

On June 5, 1945, the Allied Control Council declared that the four Allied Governments would "hereafter determine the boundaries of Germany or any part thereof and the status of Germany or of any area at present being part of Germany". It also established the occupation of Berlin by all four Powers and its government by an inter-Allied Kommandatura. (The Kommandatura was, however, reduced to its three Western members when the Soviet commandant withdrew from it on July 1, 1948, an event from which dates the division of the city into East Berlin and West Berlin.)

On March 1, 1947, the Allied Control Council decreed that "the Prussian State,

which from its early days has been a promoter of militarism and reaction in Germany, has de facto ceased to exist".

Establishment of Federal Republic of Germany

The Western Powers subsequently reached agreements which led to the establishment of the Federal Republic of Germany (often referred to as West Germany), without a peace settlement having been reached with Germany as a whole.

(1) A six-power conference agreed in London on June 2, 1948, on the structure of a German Federal Government for the British, French and US occupation zones; an Allied occupation statute; an economic merger of the French zone with the US and British zones (which had already been merged in a "bi-zone" on Jan. 1, 1947); and the establishment of an international coal and steel authority.

(2) The Paris Agreements of Oct. 23, 1954, gave full sovereign status to the Federal Republic of Germany as from May 5, 1955, and also gave it membership in the North Atlantic Treaty Organization and the Western European Union.

Peace Treaties between Allied Nations and Ex-Enemy Countries

Siam (Thailand)

The first peace treaty concluded by the Allied nations with an ex-enemy country was signed by Britain and India on the one hand and the Kingdom of Siam (now Thailand) on the other on Jan. 1, 1946.

The preamble stated inter alia that the British and Indian Governments had taken note of the fact that the Siamese Government had already repudiated the declaration of war against the British Empire made in 1942. The treaty nullified all Siamese acquisitions of British territories (in Malaya and Burma) made during the war; provided for Siamese collaboration in all international security arrangements approved by the United Nations, especially those relating to South-East Asia; and provided for the restoration of diplomatic, economic and commercial links between the parties. Siam also undertook not to construct a canal across the Kra Isthmus (linking the Indian Ocean and the Gulf of Siam) without British consent.

Countries in Europe

Peace treaties between the Allied and Associated Powers on the one hand and Bulgaria, Finland, Hungary, Italy and Romania were signed in Paris on Feb. 10,

1947. All these treaties contained provisions for reparations and imposed limitations on the armed forces of the countries concerned and in particular prohibited their possession or construction of atomic weapons. The five peace treaties came into force on Sept. 16, 1947, after the instruments of ratification had been deposited as required in the treaties.

BULGARIA

The Bulgarian peace treaty confirmed Bulgaria's frontiers as those of Jan. 1, 1941, i.e. as including the Southern Dobruja ceded by Romania in August 1940. It further stipulated inter alia: "Navigation on the Danube shall be free and open for the nationals, commercial vessels and goods of all states."

FINLAND

Under the Finnish peace treaty Finland confirmed the cession to the Soviet Union of the province of Petsamo (which meant that Finland no longer had direct access to the Arctic Ocean and the Soviet Union obtained a common frontier with Norway). The peace treaty also confirmed the frontier changes of the Moscow Peace Treaty of 1940, whereby the Soviet Union acquired the Karelian Isthmus, Viborg and other territories west of Lake Ladoga. Renouncing her right (under the terms of the 1940 treaty) of leasing the Hangö peninsula, the Soviet Union obtained a 50-year lease of the Porkkala-Udd area (S.W. of Helsinki) for the establishment of a Soviet naval base.

(The Porkkala base, however, was evacuated by the Soviet Union in 1955 after a 20-year extension of the Soviet-Finnish treaty of friendship and mutual assistance of 1948—see page 215.)

ITALY

The Italian peace treaty provided for the demarcation of Italy's frontiers with her neighbours, including the Free Territory of Trieste set up by the treaty, and involving cessions: (*a*) to France, of several areas in the Alps, among them the Little St Bernard Pass and the Mont Cenis plateau; (*b*) to Yugoslavia, of Zara and islands off the Dalmation coast; and (*c*) to Greece, of the Dodecanese Islands (in the Eastern Mediterranean). Italy also renounced all rights to Libya, Eritrea and Italian Somaliland, and recognized the independence of Albania and of Ethiopia.

South Tirol. The treaty also incorporated an agreement on South Tirol reached by the Austrian and Italian Governments on Sept. 5, 1946, providing full equality of rights with Italian-speaking inhabitants to German-speaking inhabitants of Bolzano Province and of bilingual townships in Trento Province.

A new treaty, giving extended rights to the German-speaking inhabitants of South Tirol, was concluded between Austria and Italy and initialled in Vienna on Dec. 2, 1969.

Status of Trieste. The status of the Free Territory of Trieste was ended under the terms of an agreement initialled in London on Oct. 5, 1954, whereby Italy provisionally obtained most of its northern part (known as Zone A) including the city and port of Trieste, and Yugoslavia its southern part (Zone B), together with about 5 square miles of Zone A. The agreement was implemented on Oct. 25-29, 1954.

The London agreement was, however, superseded by a treaty concluded by Italy and Yugoslavia in 1975 (known as the *Treaty of Osimo*), formally signed on Nov. 10, 1975, and duly ratified by the parliaments of both countries between Dec. 17, 1976, and March 1, 1977.

Under this treaty both Italy and Yugoslavia accepted the provisions of the London agreement as permanent, though with slight alterations to the frontier in favour of Italy, while guarantees were given relating to free access for shipping to Trieste and arrangements for free port facilities. National minorities were to be protected, with new citizenship regulations providing opportunities for members of such minorities to return to their respective country of origin and for citizenship to be regulated by Italian or Yugoslav law according to a person's place of residence at the time when the treaty came into force.

Under a simultaneous agreement co-operation was to be developed among the northern Adriatic ports, on the construction of natural gas terminals both in Italy and in Yugoslavia, and in industry and water resources management and transport, and a free industrial zone was to be set up on both sides of the frontier (this provision being subsequently approved by the European Communities).

HUNGARY

The Hungarian peace treaty re-established Hungary's frontiers as those of Jan. 1, 1938. This meant the reversion of Transylvania to Romania and of Eastern Slovakia to Czechoslovakia and confirmation of the transfer of Ruthenia to the Soviet Union—which had obtained this territory from Czechoslovakia under the terms of a treaty of June 29, 1945. Hungary also ceded several villages near Bratislava to Czechoslovakia. The treaty contained the same provisions for navigation on the Danube as the Bulgarian peace treaty.

An agreement between the USA and Hungary on the settlement of claims for war-damaged and nationalized American property in Hungary was signed on March 6, 1973.

ROMANIA

The Romanian peace treaty defined Romania's frontiers as those of Jan. 1, 1941 (i.e. including Transylvania) but with the cession of Bessarabia and the Bukovina to the Soviet Union and of the Southern Dobruja to Bulgaria. It also contained the clause on freedom of navigation on the Danube.

Peace Treaties of Japan

1951 Allied-Japan Peace Treaty. A peace treaty with Japan was signed in San Francisco on Sept. 8, 1951, by all Allied Powers represented at a 52-nation conference except Czechoslovakia, Poland and the Soviet Union. The conference was not attended by Burma, India and Yugoslavia.

The treaty came into force on April 28, 1952, after the instruments of ratification had been deposited in Washington by the USA and Japan and by nine out of 13 other countries specified in the treaty.

Under the terms of this treaty Japan recognized the independence of Korea; renounced all claims to Korea, Formosa (Taiwan) and the Pescadores, the Kurile Islands and South Sakhalin, and the Pacific Islands formerly mandated to Japan by the League of Nations. Japan also agreed to the proposal to place under the UN trusteeship system, with the USA as the sole administering authority, the Ryukyu Islands (south of 29° N.), the Bonin Islands, the Volcano Islands, Marcus Island and some smaller islands.

The treaty contained no specific definition of reparations to be made by Japan.

The Governments of both Communist China and Nationalist China took no part in the conclusion of the Japanese peace treaty.

1968 US-Japan Agreement. Under an agreement signed on April 5, 1968, by the USA and Japan, the Bonin and Volcano Islands, together with the Rosario, Parece and Marcus Islands, were returned to Japan.

The agreement also provided that the US-Japanese Security Treaty [see page 376] would apply to the islands after their return to Japan; that the USA would continue to use two radio stations on Iwo Jima (the largest of the Bonin Islands) and Marcus Island under a US-Japanese Status of Forces Agreement; but that all other installations and sites on the islands would be transferred to Japan.

Return of Ryukyu Islands. An agreement on the transfer of sovereignty over the Ryukyu Islands (including Okinawa) to Japan was signed on June 17, 1971, and after ratification of the agreement both in Japan and in the USA the reversion of the islands to Japanese jurisdiction took place on May 15, 1972.

The agreement accordingly amended the relevant article of the San Francisco Peace Treaty, but at the same time laid down that Japan would grant the United States, as from the date of entry into force of the agreement, the use of "facilities and areas" in the Ryukyu Islands in accordance with the 1960 Treaty of Mutual Co-operation and Security [see page 377]. These included the Kadena Air Force base on Okinawa, though the Japanese Government's approval was required for air or ground

military operations to be launched by the USA.

1978 China-Japan Peace Treaty. Following many years of negotiations a treaty of peace and friendship was signed in Peking (Beijing) on Aug. 17, 1978, between Japan and the People's Republic of China (which had taken no part in the conclusion of the peace treaty signed by Japan and the majority of the Allied Powers in 1951).

This treaty contains the following operative articles:

"**Art. 1.** (1) The contracting parties shall develop durable relations of peace and friendship between the two countries on the basis of the principles of mutual respect for sovereignty and territorial integrity, mutual non-aggression, non-interference in each other's internal affairs, equality and mutual benefit and peaceful coexistence.

"(2) In keeping with the foregoing principles and the principles of the United Nations Charter, the contracting parties affirm that in their mutual relations all disputes shall be settled by peaceful means without resorting to the use or threat of force.

"**Art. 2.** The contracting parties declare that neither of them should seek hegemony in the Asia-Pacific region or in any other region and that each is opposed to efforts by any other country or group of countries to establish such hegemony.

"**Art. 3.** The contracting parties shall, in a good-neighbourly and friendly spirit and in conformity with the principles of equality and mutual benefit and non-interference in each other's internal affairs, endeavour to further develop economic and cultural relations between the two countries and to promote exchanges between the peoples of the two countries.

"**Art. 4.** The present treaty shall not affect the position of either contracting party regarding its relations with third countries."

The treaty was concluded for a 10-year period and was to continue in force until terminated by one year's notice given by either party at any time after the initial 10-year period.

The treaty was ratified by the Standing Committee of the National People's Congress in Peking on Aug. 16, 1978, and by the Japanese Diet on Oct. 16-18, coming into force on Oct. 23, 1978 after instruments of ratification had been signed and exchanged in Tokyo.

The Soviet Union, which had concluded no peace treaty with Japan, repeatedly warned the Japanese Government that the Soviet side regarded the conclusion of such a treaty with China as a hostile act by Japan.

Other Agreements arising from World War II

The Austrian State Treaty

The Austrian State Treaty, which ended more than 10 years of Allied occupation

of Austria, preceded by seven years of German occupation, was signed at the Belvedere Palace in Vienna on May 15, 1955, by the Foreign Ministers and ambassadors

11

in Vienna of the four occupying powers (Soviet Union, Britain, USA and France) and by the Austrian Foreign Minister.

Its main operative clauses are as follows:

"**Art. 1. Re-establishment of Austria as a Free and Independent State.** The Allied and Associated Powers recognize that Austria is re-established as a sovereign, independent and democratic state.

"**Art. 2. Maintenance of Austria's Independence.** The Allied and Associated Powers declare that they will respect the independence and territorial integrity of Austria as established under the present treaty.

"**Art. 3. Recognition by Germany of Austrian Independence.** The Allied and Associated Powers will incorporate in the German peace treaty provisions for securing from Germany the recognition of Austria's sovereignty and independence and the renunciation by Germany of all territorial and political claims in respect of Austria and Austrian territory.

"**Art. 4. Prohibition of Anschluss.** (1) The Allied and Associated Powers declare that political or economic union between Austria and Germany is prohibited. Austria fully recognizes its responsibilities in this matter and shall not enter into political or economic union with Germany in any form whatsoever. . . .

"**Art. 5. Frontiers of Austria.** The frontiers of Austria shall be those existing on January 1, 1938. . . .

"**Art. 8. Democratic Institutions.** Austria shall have a democratic government based on elections by secret ballot and shall guarantee to all citizens free, equal and universal suffrage, as well as the right to be elected to public office without discrimination as to race, sex, language, religion or political opinion. . . .

"**Art. 13. Prohibition of Special Weapons.** (1) Austria shall not possess, construct, or experiment with (a) any atomic weapons, (b) any other major weapon adaptable now or in the future to mass destruction and defined as such by the appropriate organ of the United Nations, (c) any self-propelled or guided missiles or torpedoes, or apparatus connected with their discharge or control, (d) sea mines, (e), torpedoes capable of being manned, (f) submarines or other submersible craft, (g) motor torpedo-boats, (h) specialized types of assault craft, (i) guns with a range of more than 30 kilometres, (j) asphyxiating, vesicant or poisonous materials or biological substances in quantities greater than, or of types other than, are required for legitimate civil purposes. . . ."

Other articles deal with the rights of minority groups and the security of human rights. Most clauses, however, were of only transitional significance, dealing with matters immediately arising from the war.

Following the signature of the treaty, the Austrian Foreign Ministry published the text of a resolution on Austria's permanent neutrality, which was passed as a constitutional law by the *Nationalrat* (Austrian Lower House) on Oct. 26, 1955, and came into force on Nov. 5, 1955.

Its significant paragraphs were as follows:

(1) With the object of the lasting and perpetual maintenance of her independence from without and the inviolability of her territory, as well as in the interest of maintaining internal law and order, Austria declares of her own free will her perpetual neutrality, and is resolved to maintain and defend it with all means at her disposal.

(2) Austria, in order to secure these objectives, will join no military alliances and will not permit the establishment of military bases of foreign states on her territory.

The Franco-German Treaty on the Saar

The importance of the Saar region, the status of which was in dispute for decades, rests on its deposits of coal. After World War I the Saar came under the administration of the League of Nations. From 1920 to 1935 France possessed the rights to exploit the Saar coal fields, but in 1935, after a plebiscite, the region reverted to Germany. After World War II the Saar was first a *Land* within the French zone of Germany, and later, under a new Constitution ratified in November 1947, an autonomous state having an economic union with France. An agreement between France and the Federal Republic of Germany on the future status of the Saar, of October 1954, was rejected in a referendum a year later. A final treaty settling the future of the Saar region was signed by France and West Germany in Luxembourg on Oct. 27, 1956. The treaty provided for the political incorporation of the Saar into the Federal Republic of Germany on Jan. 1, 1957, and full economic re-integration with Germany by Dec. 31, 1959. Until that date the Franco-Saar customs union would remain in force and the Saar would retain French currency. For 25 years France would purchase from the Saar a total of 90,000,000 tons of coal; a special Franco-German organization would be set up to handle Saar coal supplies.

The Saar territory duly became part of the Federal Republic of Germany at midnight of Dec. 31, 1956. On June 25, 1959, the French and the German Federal Governments agreed that the Saar should be fully incorporated economically in the Federal Republic of Germany by July 6, 1959.

3. The United Nations

Seat: New York.
European Office: Geneva.

This section traces the origins of the United Nations and deals with the subsequent development of the organization from the signature of the UN Charter in June 1945 until the present day, with particular reference to the creation and role of the large number of specialized, associated and subsidiary bodies which form part of the UN organization as a whole. Also covered are the major UN declarations and conventions, while a table of membership of the UN and its related organizations is given on pages 50-54.

Historical Origins and Basic Principles

The United Nations came into being during World War II as a collaboration of the Allied nations against the Axis powers (Germany, Italy and Japan).

The Atlantic Charter

The first steps toward the working out of a programme of principles and policy—later to take shape as the Charter of the United Nations—were taken by President Roosevelt of the United States and the British Prime Minister, Winston Churchill, in August 1941. After a meeting between the two, on board ship in the Atlantic, a joint declaration of principles was issued on Aug. 14, 1941. This declaration, generally referred to as the *Atlantic Charter*, ran as follows:

"The President of the United States and the Prime Minister, Mr Churchill, representing HM Government in the United Kingdom, being met together, deem it right to make known certain common principles in the national policies of their respective countries on which they base their hopes for a better future for the world.

"(1) Their countries seek no aggrandisement, territorial or other.

"(2) They desire to see no territorial changes that do not accord with the freely expressed wishes of the peoples concerned.

"(3) They respect the right of all peoples to choose the form of government under which they will live; and they wish to see sovereign rights and self-government restored to those who have been forcibly deprived of them.

"(4) They will endeavour, with due respect for their existing obligations, to further enjoyment by all states, great or small, victor or vanquished, of access, on equal terms, to the trade and to the raw materials of the world which are needed for their economic prosperity.

"(5) They desire to bring about the fullest collaboration between all nations in the economic field, with the object of securing for all improved labour standards, economic advancement and social security.

"(6) After the final destruction of Nazi tyranny, they hope to see established a peace which will afford to all nations the means of dwelling in safety within their own boundaries, and which will afford assurance that all the men in all the lands may live out their lives in freedom from fear and want.

"(7) Such a peace should enable all men to traverse the high seas and oceans without hindrance.

"(8) They believe all of the nations of the world, for realistic as well as spiritual reasons, must come to the abandonment of the use of force. Since no future peace can be maintained if land, sea or air armaments continue to be employed by nations which threaten, or may threaten, aggression outside of their frontiers, they believe, pending the establishment of a wider and permanent system of general security, that the disarmament of such nations is essential. They will likewise aid and encourage all other practicable measures which will lighten for peace-loving peoples the crushing burden of armament."

The Atlantic Charter was referred to in a joint declaration of the 26 Allied nations at war with Germany, Italy and Japan, signed on Jan. 1, 1942. The declaration stated that the Governments of the Allies, "having subscribed to a common programme of purposes and principles embodied in the joint declaration . . . known as the Atlantic Charter, being convinced that complete victory over their enemies is essential to defend life, liberty, independence and religious freedom, and to preserve human rights and justice in their own lands as well as in other lands", pledged themselves to employ their full resources against the enemy and to make no separate armistice or peace.

Dumbarton Oaks Conference

A four-power conference was held at Dumbarton Oaks, near Washington, on Aug. 21-Oct. 7, 1944, to establish the framework of a post-war international security organization. The participants in the talks were the United States, Britain, the Soviet Union and China.

At the close of the conference it was stated that 90 per cent agreement had been reached by the four powers. The proposals contained in their draft for a post-war international security organization were largely embodied in the later Charter of the United Nations. They dealt with the maintenance of international peace and security and established most of the main organs of the United Nations, namely the General Assembly, the Security Council, the International Court of Justice and the Economic and Social Council.

The Yalta Conference

At the tripartite summit conference held at Yalta in the Crimea on Feb. 4-11, 1945 [see page 8], the participants—the United Kingdom, the United States and the Soviet Union—agreed, inter alia, that a conference of the United Nations should be called to meet at San Francisco on April 25, 1945. The question of voting procedure within the new organization, which had not been settled at Dumbarton Oaks, was resolved at the Yalta Conference.

The San Francisco Conference

The United Nations Conference on International Organization (UNCIO) was held at San Francisco from April 25 to June 25, 1945. It was sponsored by the United Kingdom, the USA, the Soviet Union and China. France, although she refused an invitation to become a sponsor, participated in all meetings of the sponsoring powers on a basis of full equality, forming one of the so-called "Big Five".

The three most controversial issues discussed at the conference were: (1) The question of the veto power of the "Big Five" and voting procedure in the Security Council; (2) the question of the integration of regional pacts and arrangements into the general framework of world security; (3) the question of trusteeship over dependent areas and backward peoples. All three questions were finally settled, although the solution of the first took several weeks.

The United Nations Charter

The Charter of the United Nations was signed on June 26, 1945, at the end of the San Francisco Conference. It entered into force on Oct. 24, 1945.

The contents of the Charter are described, with extracts, below.

Preamble

"We, the peoples of the United Nations,

"determined to save succeeding generations from the scourge of war, which twice in our lifetime has brought untold sorrow to mankind;

"to reaffirm faith in fundamental human rights, in the dignity and worth of the human person, and in the equal rights of men and women and of nations large and small;

"to establish conditions under which justice and respect for obligations arising from treaties and other sources of international law can be maintained;

"to promote social progress and better standards of life in larger freedom;

"to practise tolerance and live together in peace with one another as good neighbours;

"to unite our strength to maintain international peace and security;

"to ensure, by the acceptance of principles and the institution of methods, that armed force shall not be used, save in the common interest;

"to employ international machinery for the promotion of the economic and social advancement of all peoples;

"have resolved to combine our efforts to accomplish these aims, have agreed to the present Charter of the United Nations, and do hereby establish an international organization to be known as the United Nations.

Chapter 1

Purposes

"**Art. 1.** The purposes of the United Nations are:

"(1) To maintain international peace and security, and to that end: To take effective collective measures for the prevention and removal of threats to the peace and for the suppression of acts of aggression or other breaches of the peace, and to bring about by peaceful means, and in conformity with the principles of justice and international law, adjustment or settlement of international disputes or situations which might lead to a breach of the peace;

"(2) to develop friendly relations among nations based on respect for the principle of equal rights and self-determination of peoples, and to take other appropriate measures to strengthen universal peace;

"(3) to achieve international co-operation in solving international problems of an economic, social, cultural or humanitarian character, and in promoting and encouraging respect for human rights and for the fundamental freedoms for all without distinction of race, sex, language or religion; and

"(4) to be a centre for harmonizing the actions of nations in the attainment of these common ends.

Principles

"**Art. 2.** The organization and its members, in pursuit of the purposes stated in Art. 1, shall act in accordance with the following principles:

"(1) The organization is based on the principle of the sovereign equality of all its members.

"(2) All members shall fulfil in good faith the obligations assumed by them in accordance with the Charter.

"(3) All members shall settle their international disputes by peaceful means in such a manner that international peace, security and justice are not endangered.

"(4) All members shall refrain in their international relations from the threat or use of force against the territorial integrity or political independence of any member or state or in any other manner inconsistent with the purposes of the United Nations.

"(5) All members shall give the United Nations every assistance in any action it takes in accordance with the provisions of the Charter, and shall refrain from giving assistance to any state against which the United Nations is taking preventive or enforcement action.

"(6) The organization shall ensure that states not members act in accordance with these principles so far as may be necessary for the maintenance of international peace and security.

"(7) Nothing in the Charter shall authorize the United Nations to intervene in matters which are essentially within the domestic jurisdiction of any state, or shall require the members to submit such matters to settlement under the present Charter; but this principle shall not prejudice the application of enforcement measures under Chapter 7."

Chapter 2 deals with the conditions of membership and provides for the suspension or expulsion from the organization of erring members.

Chapter 3 enumerates the main organs and provides for universal eligibility to serve on them.

Chapter 4 gives details of the composition, functions and powers of, and procedure, in the General Assembly. Important provisions on voting are:

"**Art. 18.** Decisions of the General Assembly on important questions shall be made by a two-thirds majority of those present and voting. These questions shall include: Recommendations with respect to the maintenance of international peace and security; the election of non-permanent members of the Security Council; the election of members of the Economic and Social Council; the election of members of the United Nations which are to designate the members on the Trusteeship Council . . . ; the admission of new members to the United Nations; the expulsion of members; the suspension of the rights and privileges of members; questions relating to the operations of the trusteeship system; and budgetary questions. . . .

"**Art. 19.** A member in arrears in the payment of its financial contributions to the organization shall have no vote if the amount of arrears equals or exceeds the amount of the contributions due from it for the preceding two full years. The General Assembly may, nevertheless, permit such a member to vote if it is satisfied that the failure to pay is due to conditions beyond the member's control."

Chapter 5 gives details of the composition and responsibility of the Security Council and of its procedure. Amendments to the Charter, which came into force on Aug. 31, 1965, affected Articles 23 and 27 of this chapter, raising the membership of the Council from 11 to 15, and the number of affirmative votes to carry decisions from seven to nine.

Chapter 6
Pacific Settlement of Disputes

"**Art. 33.** (1) The parties to any dispute whose continuance is likely to endanger the maintenance of international peace and security shall, first of all, seek a solution by negotiation, inquiry, mediation, conciliation, arbitration, judicial settlement, resort to regional agencies or arrangements, or other peaceful means of their own choice.

"(2) The Security Council shall, when it deems necessary, call upon the parties to settle their dispute by such means.

"**Art. 34.** The Security Council may investigate any dispute, or any situation which might lead to international friction or give rise to a dispute, in order to determine whether its continuance is likely to endanger the maintenance of international peace and security.

"**Art. 35.** (1) Any member of the United Nations may bring any dispute or situation of the nature referred to in Art. 34 to the attention of the Security Council or the General Assembly.

"(2) A state which is not a member of the United Nations may bring to the attention of the Security Council or the General Assembly any dispute to which it is a party, if it accepts in advance, for the purposes of the dispute, the obligations of pacific settlement provided in the Charter. . . .

Chapter 7
Action with Respect to Threats to the Peace, Breaches of the Peace and Acts of Aggression

"**Art. 39.** The Security Council shall determine the existence of any threat to the peace, breach of the peace or act of aggression, and shall make recommendations, or decide what measures shall be taken in accordance with Art. 41 and 42, to maintain or restore international peace and security.

"**Art. 40.** In order to prevent an aggravation of the situation, the Security Council may, before making the recommendations or deciding upon the measures provided for in Art. 41, call upon the parties concerned to comply with such provisional measures as it deems necessary or desirable. Such provisional measures shall be without prejudice to the rights, claims or position of the parties concerned. The Security Council shall duly take account of failure to comply with such provisional measures.

"**Art. 41.** The Security Council may decide what measures not involving the use of armed force are to be employed to give effect to its decisions, and may call upon members of the United Nations to apply such measures. These may include complete or partial interruption of economic relations and of rail, sea, air, postal, telegraphic, radio and other means of communication, and the severance of diplomatic relations.

"**Art. 42.** Should the Security Council consider that measures provided for in Art. 41 would be inadequate, or have proved to be inadequate, it may take such action by air, sea or land forces as may be necessary to maintain or restore international peace and security. Such action may include demonstrations, blockade, and other operations by air, sea or land forces of members of the United Nations.

"**Art. 43.** (1) All members of the United Nations, in order to contribute to the maintenance of international peace and security, undertake to make available to the Security Council, on its call and in accordance with a special agreement or agreements, armed forces, assistance and facilities, including rights of passage, necessary for the purpose of maintaining international peace and security.

"(2) Such agreement or agreements shall govern the numbers and types of forces, their degree of readiness and general location, and the nature of the facilities and assistance to be provided.

"(3) The agreement or agreements shall be negotiated as soon as possible on the initiative of the Security Council. They shall be concluded between the Security Council and member states or between the Security Council and groups of member states, and shall be subject to ratification by the signatory states.

"**Art. 45.** In order to enable the United Nations to take urgent military measures, members shall hold immediately available national air force contingents for combined international enforcement action. The strength and degree of readiness of these contingents, and plans for their combined action, shall be determined, within the limits laid down in the special agreement or agreements referred to in Art. 43, by the Security Council with the assistance of the Military Staff Committee.

"**Art. 48.** (1) The action required to carry out the decisions of the Security Council for the maintenance of international peace and security shall be taken by all the members of the United Nations, or by some of them, as the Security Council may determine.

"(2) Such decisions shall be carried out by the members of the United Nations directly and through their action in the appropriate international agencies of which they are members.

"**Art. 50.** If preventive or enforcement measures against any state are taken by the Security Council, any other state, whether a member of the United Nations or not, which finds itself confronted with special economic problems arising from the carrying out of those measures, shall have the right to consult the Security Council with regard to a solution of those problems.

"**Art. 51.** Nothing in the present Charter shall impair the inherent right of individual or collective self-defence, if an armed attack occurs against a member of the organization, until the Security Council has taken the measures necessary to maintain international peace and security. Measures taken by members in the exercise of this right of self-defence shall be immediately reported to the Security Council and shall not in any way affect the authority and responsibility of the Security Council to take at any time such action as it may deem necessary in order to maintain or restore international peace and security.

Chapter 8
Regional Arrangements

"**Art. 52.** (1) Nothing in the present Charter precludes the existence of regional arrangements or agencies for dealing with such matters relating to the maintenance of international peace and security as are appropriate for regional action, provided that such arrangements or agencies and their activities are consistent with the purposes and principles of the organization.

"(2) The members of the United Nations entering into such arrangements or constituting such agencies shall make every effort to achieve peaceful settlement of local disputes through such regional arrangements or agencies before referring them to the Security Council.

"(3) The Security Council should encourage the development of peaceful settlement of local disputes through such regional arrangements or agencies either on the initiative of the states concerned or by reference from the Security Council.

"(4) This article in no way impairs the application of Arts. 34 and 35.

"**Art. 53.** (1) The Security Council shall, where appropriate, utilize such arrangements or agencies for enforcement action under its authority. But no enforcement action shall be taken under regional arrangements or by regional agencies without the authorization of the Security Council, with the exception of measures against any enemy state, as described below, or in regional arrangements directed against renewal of aggressive policy on the part of any such state, until such time as the organization may, on request of the governments concerned, be charged with the responsibility for preventing further aggression by such a state.

"(2) The term 'enemy state' applies to any state which during the Second World War has been an enemy of any signatory of the Charter.

Chapter 9
International Economic and Social Co-operation

"**Art. 55.** With a view to the creation of conditions of stability and well-being which are necessary for peaceful and friendly relations among nations, based on respect for the principle of equal rights and self-determination of peoples, the United Nations shall promote:

"(*a*) Higher standards of living, full employment and conditions of economic and social progress and development;

"(*b*) solutions of international economic, social, health and related problems and international cultural and educational co-operation; and

"(*c*) universal respect for, and observance of, human rights and fundamental freedoms for all without distinction as to race, sex, language or religion."

Chapter 10 gives details of the composition, functions and powers of, and procedure in the Economic and Social Council.

Chapter 11
Declaration Regarding Non-Self-Governing Territories

"**Art. 73.** Members of the United Nations which have or assume responsibilities for the administration of territories whose peoples have not yet attained a full measure of self-government recognize the principle that the interests of the inhabitants of these territories are paramount, and accept as a sacred trust the obligation to promote to the utmost the well-being of the inhabitants of these territories, and to this end:

"(*a*) To ensure, with due respect for the culture of the peoples concerned, their political, economic, social and educational advancement, their just treatment, and their protection against abuses;

"(*b*) to develop self-government, to take due account of the political aspirations of the peoples, and to assist them in the progressive development of their free political institutions, according to the particular circumstances of each territory and its peoples and their varying stages of advancement;

"(*c*) to further international peace and security;

"(*d*) to promote constructive measures of development, to encourage research, and to co-operate with one another and with appropriate international bodies with a view to the practical achievement of the social, economic and scientific purpose set forth in this paragraph; and

"(*e*) to transmit regularly to the Secretary-General for information purposes, subject to such limitations as security and constitutional considerations may require, statistical and other information of a technical nature relating to economic, social and educational conditions in the territories for which they are respectively responsible, other than those territories to which Chapters 12 and 13 apply.

Chapter 12
International Trusteeship System

"**Art. 75.** The United Nations shall establish under its authority an international trusteeship system for the administration and supervision of such territories as may be placed thereunder by subsequent individual agreements. These territories are hereafter referred to as 'trust territories'.

"**Art. 76.** The basic objectives of the trusteeship system shall be:

"(*a*) To further international peace and security;

"(*b*) to promote the political, economic, social and educational advancement of the inhabitants of the trust territories, and their progressive development towards self-government or independence as may be appropriate to the particular circumstances of each territory and its peoples and the freely expressed wishes of the peoples concerned, and as may be provided by the terms of each trusteeship agreement;

"(*c*) to encourage respect for human rights and for fundamental freedoms for all without distinction as to race, sex, language or religion, and to encourage recognition of the interdependence of the peoples of the world; and

"(*d*) to ensure equal treatment in social, economic and commercial matters for all members of the United Nations and their nationals, and also equal treatment for the latter in the administration of justice, without prejudice to the attainment of the foregoing objectives. . . .

"**Art. 77.** (1) The trusteeship system shall apply to such territories in the following categories as may be placed thereunder by means of trusteeship agreements:

"(*a*) Territories now held under mandate;

"(*b*) territories which may be detached from enemy states as a result of the Second World War; and

"(*c*) territories voluntarily placed under the system by states responsible for their administration.

"(2) It will be a matter for subsequent agreement as to which territories in the foregoing categories will be brought under the trusteeship system and upon what terms.

"**Art. 78.** The trusteeship system shall not apply to territories which have become members of the United Nations, relationship among which should be based on respect for the principle of sovereign equality.

"**Art. 79.** The terms of trusteeship for each territory to be placed under the trusteeship system, including any alteration or amendment, shall be agreed upon by the states directly concerned, including the mandatory power in the case of territories held under mandate by a member of the United Nations. . . ."

Chapter 13 deals with the composition, functions and powers of, and procedure in, the Trusteeship Council.

Chapter 14 deals with the International Court of Justice.

Chapter 15 deals with the Secretariat and includes details of the functions of the Secretary-General.

Chapter 16 contains miscellaneous provisions, including:

"**Art. 103.** In the event of a conflict between the obligations of the members of the United Nations under the Charter and any other international obligations to which they are subject, their obligations under the Charter shall prevail.

"**Art. 105.** (1) The organization shall enjoy in the territory of each of its members such privileges and immunities as are necessary for the fulfilment of its purposes.

"(2) Representatives of the members of the United Nations and officials of the organization shall similarly enjoy such privileges and immunities as are necessary for the independent exercise of their functions in connexion with the organization."

Chapter 17 provides for certain transitional security arrangements.

Chapter 18 gives the procedure for the adoption of amendments to the Charter and provides for the convening of a conference for the purpose of reviewing the Charter.

Chapter 19 contains provisions on the ratification and signature of the Charter.

The principles of the UN Charter incorporated those of the Kellogg Pact signed in Paris on Aug. 27, 1928 [see pages 3-4].

The Universal Declaration of Human Rights and the Covenants on Human Rights

The UN General Assembly on Dec. 10, 1948, adopted, by 48 votes to none (with eight abstentions by the Communist member states, South Africa and Saudi Arabia), the Universal Declaration of Human Rights, the first international Bill of Rights in human history.

The declaration is worded as follows:

Preamble

"Whereas recognition of the inherent dignity and of the equal and inalienable rights of all members of the human family is the foundation of freedom, justice and peace in the world;

"whereas disregard and contempt for human rights have resulted in barbarous acts which have outraged the conscience of mankind, and the advent of a world in which human beings shall enjoy freedom of speech and belief and freedom from fear and want has been proclaimed as the highest aspiration of the common people;

"whereas it is essential, if man is not to be compelled to have recourse, as a last resort, to rebellion against tyranny and oppression, that human rights should be protected by the rule of law;

"whereas it is essential to promote the development of friendly relations between nations;

"whereas the people of the United Nations have in the Charter reaffirmed their faith in fundamental human rights, in the dignity and worth of the human person and in the equal rights of men and women, and have determined to promote social progress and better standards of life in larger freedom;

"whereas member states have pledged themselves to achieve, in co-operation with the United Nations, the promotion of universal respect for and observance of human rights and fundamental freedoms;

"whereas a common understanding of these rights and freedoms is of the greatest importance for the full realization of this pledge;

"the General Assembly proclaims this Universal Declaration of Human Rights as a common standard of achievement for all peoples and nations, to the end that every individual and every organ of society, keeping this declaration constantly in mind, shall strive by teaching and education to promote respect for these rights and freedoms, and by progressive measures, national and international, to secure their universal and effective recognition and observance, both among the peoples of member states themselves and among the peoples of territories under their jurisdiction.

Articles

"**Art. 1.** All human beings are born free and equal in dignity and rights. They are endowed with reason and conscience, and should act towards one another in a spirit of brotherhood.

"**Art. 2.** Everyone is entitled to all the rights and freedoms set forth in this declaration, without distinction of any kind, such as race, colour, sex, language, religion, political or other opinion, national or social origin, property, birth or other status.

"Furthermore, no distinction shall be made on the basis of the political, jurisdictional or international status of the country or territory to which a person belongs, whether it be independent, trust, non-self-governing or under any other limitation of sovereignty.

"**Art. 3.** Everyone has the right to life, liberty and security of person.

"**Art. 4.** No one shall be held in slavery or servitude; slavery and the slave trade shall be prohibited in all their forms.

"**Art. 5.** No one shall be subjected to torture or to cruel, inhuman or degrading treatment or punishment.

"**Art. 6.** Everyone has the right to recognition everywhere as a person before the law.

"**Art. 7.** All are equal before the law and are entitled without any discrimination to equal protection of the law. All are entitled to equal protection against any discrimination in violation of this declaration and against any incitement to such discrimination.

"**Art. 8.** Everyone has the right to an effective remedy by the competent national tribunals for acts violating the fundamental rights granted him by the Constitution or by law.

"**Art. 9.** No one shall be subjected to arbitrary arrest, detention or exile.

"**Art. 10.** Everyone is entitled in full equality to a fair and public hearing by an independent and impartial tribunal, in the determination of his rights and obligations and of any criminal charge against him.

"**Art. 11.** (1) Everyone charged with a penal offence has the right to be presumed innocent until proved guilty according to law in a public trial at which he has had all the guarantees necessary for his defence.

"(2) No one shall be held guilty of any penal offence on account of any act or omission which did not constitute a penal offence, under national or international law, at the time when it was committed. Nor shall a heavier penalty be imposed than the one that was applicable at the time the penal offence was committed.

"**Art. 12.** No one shall be subjected to arbitrary interference with his privacy, family, home or correspondence, nor to attacks upon his honour and reputation. Everyone has the right to the protection of the law against such interference or attacks.

"**Art. 13.** (1) Everyone has the right to freedom of movement and residence within the borders of each state.

"(2) Everyone has the right to leave any country, including his own, and to return to his country.

"**Art. 14.** (1) Everyone has the right to seek and enjoy in other countries asylum from persecution.

"(2) This right may not be invoked in the case of prosecutions genuinely arising from non-political crimes or from acts contrary to the purposes and principles of the United Nations.

"**Art. 15.** (1) Everyone has the right to a nationality.

"(2) No one shall be arbitrarily deprived of his nationality nor denied the right to change his nationality.

"**Art. 16.** (1) Men and women of full age, without any limitation due to race, nationality or religion, have the right to marry and to found a family. They are entitled to equal rights as to marriage, during marriage, and at its dissolution.

"(2) Marriage shall be entered into only with the free and full consent of the intending spouses.

"(3) The family is the natural and fundamental group unit of society and is entitled to protection by society and the state.

"**Art. 17.** (1) Everyone has the right to own property alone as well as in association with others.

"(2) No one shall be arbitrarily deprived of his property.

"**Art. 18.** Everyone has the right to freedom of thought, conscience and religion. This right includes freedom to change his religion or belief, and freedom, either alone or in community with others, and in public or private, to manifest his religion or belief in teaching, practice, worship and observance.

"**Art. 19.** Everyone has the right to freedom of opinion and expression. This right includes freedom to hold opinions without interference and to seek, receive and impart information and ideas through any media and regardless of frontiers.

"**Art. 20.** (1) Everyone has the right to freedom of peaceful assembly and association.

"(2) No one may be compelled to belong to an association.

"**Art. 21.** (1) Everyone has the right to take part in the government of his country, directly or through freely chosen representatives.

"(2) Everyone has the right of equal access to public service in his country.

"(3) The will of the people shall be the basis of the authority of government; this will shall be expressed in periodic and genuine elections which shall be by universal and equal suffrage, and shall be held by secret vote or by equivalent free voting procedures.

"**Art. 22.** Everyone, as a member of society, has the right to social security and is entitled to the realization, through national effort and international co-operation and in accordance with the organization and resources of each state, of the economic, social and cultural rights indispensable for his dignity and the free development of his personality.

"**Art. 23.** (1) Everyone has the right to work, to free choice of employment, to just and favourable conditions of work and to protection against unemployment.

"(2) Everyone, without any discrimination, has the right to equal pay for equal work.

"(3) Everyone who works has the right to just and

favourable remuneration, ensuring for himself and his family an existence worthy of human dignity and supplemented, if necessary, by other means of social protection.

"(4) Everyone has the right to form and to join trade unions for the protection of his interests.

"**Art. 24.** Everyone has the right to rest and leisure, including reasonable limitation of working hours and periodic holidays with pay.

"**Art. 25.** (1) Everyone has the right to a standard of living adequate for the health and well-being of himself and his family, including food, clothing, housing, and medical care and necessary social services, and the right to security in the event of unemployment, sickness, disability, widowhood, old age or other lack of livelihood in circumstances beyond his control.

"(2) Motherhood and childhood are entitled to special care and assistance. All children, whether born in or out of wedlock, shall enjoy the same social protection.

"**Art. 26.** (1) Everyone has the right to education. Education shall be free, at least in the elementary and fundamental stages. Elementary education shall be compulsory. Technical and professional education shall be made generally available, and higher education shall be equally accessible to all on the basis of merit.

"(2) Education shall be directed to the full development of the human personality and to the strengthening of respect for human rights and fundamental freedoms. It shall promote understanding, tolerance and friendship among all nations, racial or religious groups, and shall further the activities of the United Nations for the maintenance of peace.

"(3) Parents have a prior right to choose the kind of education that shall be given to their children.

"**Art. 27.** (1) Everyone has the right freely to participate in the cultural life of the community, to enjoy the arts and to share in scientific advancement and its benefits.

"(2) Everyone has the right to the protection of the moral and material interests resulting from any scientific, literary or artistic production of which he is the author.

"**Art. 28.** Everyone is entitled to a social and international order in which the rights and freedoms set forth in this declaration can be fully realized.

"**Art. 29.** (1) Everyone has duties to the community in which alone the free and full development of his personality is possible.

"(2) In the exercise of his rights and freedoms, everyone shall be subject only to such limitations as are determined by law solely for the purpose of securing due recognition and respect for the rights and freedoms of others, and of meeting the just requirements of morality, public order and the general welfare in a democratic society.

"(3) These rights and freedoms may in no case be exercised contrary to the purposes and freedoms set forth herein.

"**Art. 30.** Nothing in this declaration may be interpreted as implying for any state, group or person any right to engage in any activity or to perform any act aimed at the destruction of any of the rights and freedoms set forth herein."

In implementation of the declaration, the UN General Assembly unanimously adopted, on Dec. 16, 1966, (*a*) an International Covenant on Economic, Social and Cultural Rights; (*b*) an International Covenant on Civil and Political Rights, and (*c*) an Optional Protocol to the latter.

The covenant under (*a*), consisting of 31 articles, recognizes, inter alia, the right to work, to social security, to adequate standards of living, to freedom from hunger, and to health and education. It provides that states parties to the covenant would report to the UN Economic and Social Council on the measures adopted and progress made towards the realization of these rights.

The covenant under (*b*), consisting of 53 articles, provides, inter alia, for the right to life, liberty, security and privacy; for the right to a fair trial and to freedom from arbitrary arrest; for freedom of thought, conscience and religion; and for freedom of association. Other articles provide for freedom of consent to marriage, the protection of children and the preservation of the cultural, religious and linguistic heritage of minorities. It is laid down that the implementation of this covenant will be supervised by a Human Rights Committee consisting of 18 persons elected by the states acceding to the covenant.

The optional protocol empowers the Human Rights Committee to receive and consider communications from individuals claiming to be victims of a violation by a state party to the covenant of any of the rights set forth in the covenant.

The covenant under (*b*) came into force on Jan. 3, 1976—three months after ratification by 35 governments; by Dec. 31, 1979, it had been acceded to by 58 countries (while those which had not signed it included the United States).

The covenant under (*a*) similarly came into force on March 23, 1976.

Organs of the United Nations

The General Assembly

The General Assembly, the main deliberative organ of the United Nations, is composed of delegations representing all the member countries of the United Nations. Each delegation comprises not more than five full representatives with their five deputies and any number of advisers and experts.

The General Assembly meets regularly once a year in ordinary session, but a special session may be convened at the request of the Security Council or of a majority of Assembly members.

The Assembly has power to make recommendations only, and not decisions binding on member states. Each member has one vote. Decisions on important questions are adopted by a two-thirds majority; other questions are decided by a simple majority.

The General Assembly is empowered to discuss and make recommendations on all questions which fall within the scope of the UN Charter. Under Article 12 of the Charter, however, "while the Security Council is exercising in respect of any dispute or situation the functions assigned to it in the present Charter, the General Assembly shall not make any recommendations with regard to that dispute or situation unless the Security Council so requests". On Nov. 3, 1950, the plenary session of the General Assembly adopted a plan of the US Government (the "United Action for Peace" Resolution), by which, at the request of any seven members of the Security Council, the General Assembly can be called in emergency session if the Security Council is prevented, through exercise of the veto, from taking action in any case "where there appears to be a threat to the peace, breach of the peace or act of aggression".

The General Assembly is led by a President, who is elected for each session, and a number of Vice-Presidents.

ASSEMBLY COMMITTEES

The seven main committees of the General Assembly, on which all UN members have the right of representation, are as follows:

(1) Political and Security Committee.
(2) Economic and Financial Committee.
(3) Social, Humanitarian and Cultural Committee.
(4) Decolonization Committee.
(5) Administrative and Budgetary Committee.
(6) Legal Committee.
(7) Special Political Committee (set up to aid the first Committee).

These committees consider questions referred to them by the General Assembly, and prepare draft resolutions for submission to the Assembly.

There are two procedural committees, the 25-man General (Steering) Committee and the nine-man Credentials Committee, and two principal standing committees, these being a 16-man Advisory Committee on Administrative and Budgetary Questions and an 18-man Committee on Contributions.

Under the American "United Action for Peace" Resolution of Nov. 3, 1950 [see above], two special committees were set up: a **Peace Observation Commission**, whose

14 members include the five permanent members of the Security Council; and a 14-member **Collective Measures Committee** to study "the measures which might be used and the resources, including armed forces, which are or might be made available to the United Nations in order to maintain international peace and security".

Another permanent subsidiary committee is the 25-member **International Law Commission**, which meets annually to discuss the development and codification of international law. The General Assembly also sets up ad hoc committees from time to time in accordance with the world situation.

Special Committee on Decolonization. In connexion with Trust Territories and colonial questions the UN General Assembly has set up a Special Committee on the situation with regard to the implementation of the declaration on the granting of independence to colonial countries and peoples (adopted by the UN General Assembly on Dec. 14, 1960, establishing the right of all peoples to self-determination and to "freely determine their political status"). This committee, formed in 1961 and for many years known as the "Committee of 24", at present has 25 members as follows: Afghanistan, Austria, Bulgaria, Chile, China, the Congo, Cuba, Czechoslovakia, Denmark, Ethiopia, Fiji, India, Indonesia, Iran, Iraq, the Ivory Coast, Mali, Sierra Leone, the Soviet Union, Syria, Tanzania, Trinidad and Tobago, Tunisia, Venezuela and Yugoslavia.

Council for Namibia. In the same connexion the UN Council for Namibia (originally the UN Council for South West Africa) was formed in 1967 for the purpose of taking over the administration of that territory from the Government of South Africa. The council has 31 members as follows: Algeria, Angola, Australia, Bangladesh, Belgium, Botswana, Bulgaria, Burundi, Cameroon, Chile, China, Colombia, Cyprus, Egypt, Finland, Guyana, Haiti, India, Indonesia, Liberia, Mexico, Nigeria, Pakistan, Poland, Romania, Senegal, the Soviet Union, Turkey, Venezuela, Yugoslavia and Zambia.

Other Bodies Responsible to the General Assembly

UNITED NATIONS CONFERENCE ON TRADE AND DEVELOPMENT (UNCTAD)

In December 1964 the General Assembly agreed to establish the UN Conference on Trade and Development, which had met in Geneva from March to June 1964, as one of its permanent organs. The principal function of the conference is to encourage international trade, particularly between countries at different levels of development and with different social and economic systems.

The conference, which has its headquarters in Geneva, is convened at intervals of not more than three years. Between sessions its work is carried out by the Trade and Development Board, which meets at least twice a year. Six main committees, on commodities, manufactures, invisibles and financing related to trade, shipping, transfer of technology, and economic co-operation among developing countries, implement the work of the Board.

The 77 developing countries represented at the 1964 Geneva meetings became known as the "Group of 77", and this group later expanded to 119 members.

At a meeting of ministers from 71 developing countries held in Algiers on Oct. 10-24, 1967, 63 of these ministers signed the "Algiers Charter of the Economic Rights of the Third World", which was to be presented to the developed nations. The Charter stated that between 1953 and 1966 the share of the developing countries in total world exports had fallen from 27 per cent to 19.3, and the purchasing power of their export earnings by one-tenth, while their debt service payments were equalling the entire amount of loans granted. The Charter therefore urged the implementation of a comprehensive programme of action.

(Later UNCTAD conferences are dealt with in Section 6 on International Economic Co-operation, page 83.)

UN DIRECTOR-GENERAL FOR DEVELOPMENT AND INTERNATIONAL ECONOMIC CO-OPERATION

A UN Director-General for Development and International Economic Co-operation (ranking immediately below the UN Secretary-General) was first appointed on March 14, 1978, in pursuance of a UN General Assembly resolution of Dec. 20, 1977.

His tasks were to ensure "the provision of effective leadership to the various components of the UN system in the field of development and international economic co-operation and . . . overall co-ordination within the system in order to ensure a multi-disciplinary approach to the problems of development on a system-wide basis", and also "within the United Nations, the coherence, co-ordination and efficient management of all activities in the economic and social fields financed by the regular budget or by extra-budgetary resources".

UNITED NATIONS RELIEF AND WORKS AGENCY FOR PALESTINE REFUGEES IN THE NEAR EAST (UNRWA)

The UN Relief and Works Agency, with headquarters in Vienna and Amman (Jordan), was founded in 1950 as a temporary body to bring immediate assistance to Palestinian Arab refugees and to help them become self-supporting. The organization is headed by a Commissioner-General assisted by a 10-member Advisory Commission.

Its mandate has repeatedly been renewed (most recently, on Dec. 13, 1977, until June 30, 1981), and its work has been extended to cover relief, health, education and welfare services to Palestinian refugees. As at June 30, 1979, there was a total of 1,803,564 refugees (in East Jordan, the Israeli-occupied West Bank, the Gaza Strip, Lebanon and Syria) registered with the Agency, whose budget for 1979 was $166,400,000.

The Security Council

The Security Council functions continuously, and its decisions are binding on all members of the United Nations. The Council is composed of 15 members, five of whom—China, France, the Soviet Union, the United Kingdom and the United States—are permanent. The remaining 10 members are elected by the General Assembly, normally to serve a term of two years. Each member state of the Council holds the Presidency for one month, the rotation following the English alphabetical order.

Each member has one vote. Decisions on important (non-procedural) questions must be carried by nine affirmative votes, but any one of the permanent members, exercising the right of veto, can prevent the adoption of a decision. Procedural matters may be decided by the affirmative votes of any nine members.

The Security Council has "primary responsibility for the maintenance of international peace and security", and to this end it acts for all UN members (Article 24 of the UN Charter). The tasks of the Security Council include the pacific settlement of international disputes (Articles 33-38), determination of the existence of any threat to the peace, breach of the peace or act of aggression, and, where necessary, the carrying out of preventive or enforcement measures of a political, economic or military nature through some or all UN members (Articles 39-45). Under Article 26 of the Charter the Security Council is also "responsible for formulating plans . . . for the establishment of a system for the regulation of armaments".

In all questions of a military nature the Council is aided by a Military Staff Committee, consisting of the Chiefs of Staff of the five permanent members of the Security Council.

Peace-Keeping Bodies Responsible to the Security Council

United Nations Truce Supervision Organization (UNTSO). Originally formed to maintain the 1949 Armistice Agreements between Israel on the one hand and the Arab nations of Egypt, Lebanon, Jordan and Syria on the other, the United Nations Truce Supervision Organization later had the task of supervising the ceasefire line established at the end of the six-day Arab-Israeli war of June 1967. In 1973 it was ordered to supervise a ceasefire in the Suez Canal area, and in July 1979 the UN Security Council charged it with monitoring compliance with the military provisions of the 1979 Egyptian-Israeli peace treaty and thus replacing a UN Emergency Force (UNEF) which had been established after the 1973 Arab-Israeli war. Its headquarters are in Jerusalem.

United Nations Military Observer Group for India and Pakistan (UNMOGIP). Established in 1949, UNMOGIP is responsible for supervising the Indian-Pakistani ceasefire line along the Kashmir border. The group consists of about 60 military observers and civilian specialists.

United Nations Command in Korea. The United Nations Command in Korea was set up in July 1950 to assist the Republic of Korea (South Korea) in defending itself against attack. The UN Force originally consisted of troops from 16 nations under the command of the United States. The force was later reduced to US troops only (about 30,000 men since mid-1977).

United Nations Peace-Keeping Force in Cyprus (UNFICYP). The UN Force in Cyprus was set up in March 1964, initially for three months, for the purpose of keeping the peace between the Greek and Turkish communities in Cyprus. Following the invasion of Cyprus by Turkish troops in July 1974 the UN Security Council authorized a strengthening of UNFICYP's forces and charged it with supervising a ceasefire between Turkish and Greek or Greek Cypriot forces and also with protecting Turkish enclaves after these were evacuated by Greek or Greek Cypriot troops. UNFICYP's mandate has since then been regularly renewed for a further six months each time.

United Nations Disengagement Observer Force (UNDOF). UNDOF was established on May 31, 1974, to secure the implementation of a disengagement agreement between Syrian and Israeli forces, and its mandate has repeatedly been extended for six months at a time.

United Nations Interim Force in Lebanon (UNIFIL). UNIFIL was set up by the UN Security Council in March 1978 "for the purpose of confirming the withdrawal of Israeli forces, restoring international peace and security and assisting the Government of Lebanon in ensuring the return of its effective authority in the area". In May 1978 the strength of UNIFIL was increased to 6,000 men, and its mandate has since then repeatedly been extended for six-monthly periods.

The Trusteeship Council

The task of the UN Trusteeship Council, with headquarters in New York, has been the supervision of the administration of UN Trust Territories, i.e. territories which had been dependencies of powers defeated in World War II and were subsequently placed under UN trusteeship with the object of leading these territories, through political, economic, social and educational development, to self-government and independence.

By the end of 1980 only one territory remained under UN trusteeship—the Trust Territory of the Pacific Islands (Micronesia), administered by the United States and placed, as a strategic area, under supervision by the Trusteeship Council under the authority of the UN Security Council. (Part of the territory, the Northern Marianas, became a commonwealth territory of the United States on Jan. 9, 1978.)

The members of the Trusteeship Council are the United States (as the administering country) and the four other permanent members of the UN Security Council.

The Economic and Social Council (ECOSOC)

The Economic and Social Council is responsible for co-ordinating the United Nations' policy in the economic, social, cultural and humanitarian fields.

Its functions are:

(1) To make studies of, and reports and recommendations on, world co-operation in these fields;
(2) to promote the observation and pursuit of human rights and fundamental freedoms for all;
(3) to convene international conferences;
(4) to consult with the Specialized Agencies (see below) and co-ordinate their activities;
(5) to consult with non-governmental organizations which are concerned with ECOSOC matters.

The UN General Assembly decided (i) on Dec. 17, 1963, to increase the membership of the Council from 18 to 27 (this decision coming into force on Aug. 31, 1965), and (ii) on Dec. 20, 1971, by 105 votes to 2 (France and Great Britain) and with 15 abstentions, to enlarge the Council from 27 to 54 members and to amend Article 61 of the Charter accordingly.

Under the second amendment, the General Assembly each year elects 18 members to the Council for a term of three years. Of the Council's 54 members, 14 were to be from African states; 11 from Asian states; 10 from Latin American states; 13 from Western European and other states; and six from socialist states of Eastern Europe.

Most of the work of ECOSOC is carried out through functional and regional commissions. The following are the functional commissions:

(1) Statistical Commission.
(2) Population Commission.
(3) Commission for Social Development.
(4) Commission on Human Rights.
(5) Commission on the Status of Women.
(6) Commission on Narcotic Drugs.

The regional commissions are the following:

(1) Economic Commission for Europe (ECE).
(2) Economic Commission for Asia and the Pacific (ESCAP).
(3) Economic Commission for Latin America (ECLA).
(4) Economic Commission for Africa (ECA).
(5) Economic Commission for Western Asia (ECWA), which was established on Jan. 1, 1974 (and does not include Israel).

ECOSOC also has the following committees and subsidiary bodies:

(1) Committee on Non-Governmental Organizations.
(2) Committee on Negotiations with Intergovernmental Organizations.
(3) Committee for Programme and Co-ordination (CPC).
(4) Committee for Development Planning.
(5) Committee on Natural Resources.
(6) Committee on Science and Technology for Development.
(7) Committee on Review and Appraisal.
(8) Committee on Crime Prevention and Control.
(9) Commission on Transnational Corporations.
(10) Commission on Human Settlements.

World Tourist Organization (WTO). Under a resolution adopted by the UN General Assembly on Dec. 19, 1977, the activities of the World Tourist Organization (WTO) were co-ordinated in ECOSOC. The WTO, founded in 1974 and with headquarters in Madrid, is an intergovernmental organization of 119 countries and 89 organizations.

ESCAP Prospecting Agreement. The UN Economic Commission for Asia and the Pacific (ESCAP)—until 1974 known as the Economic Commission for Asia and the Far East (ECAFE)—had in 1966 set up a committee for co-ordination of joint prospecting for mineral resources in Asian offshore areas, and at a meeting of this committee in Tokyo on Aug. 22, 1975, agreement was reached between Indonesia, Japan, the Republic of Korea, Malaysia, the Philippines, Singapore and Thailand on extending their offshore oil and mineral survey activities beyond the continental shelf.

Spain and ECLA. The UN Economic Commission for Latin America (ECLA) decided on April 27, 1979, to accept Spain as a full member.

Special Bodies functioning under the Authority of ECOSOC and the General Assembly

United Nations Development Programme (UNDP). The UN Development Programme was formed in November 1965 by the merger of the UN Special Fund and the Expanded Programme of Technical Assistance. Functioning under the joint authority of ECOSOC and the General Assembly, the UNDP supports pre-investment projects in developing countries. The fields of activity of the UNDP include development planning, agricultural and industrial productivity, education, health, and public and social services; the work is carried out through the various specialized agencies of the United Nations and also the UN Office of Technical Co-operation, three regional development banks, the Arab Fund for Economic and Social Development and the International Fund for Agricultural Development (IFAD).

The two organs of the UNDP are the Governing Council, whose 48 members include both developed and developing countries, and the Inter-Agency Consultative Board, composed of the UN Secretary-General and the Executive Heads of the UNDP's participating and executing agencies.

The UNDP also finances, and its Governing Council administers, a **United Nations Capital Development Fund** which was set up by the UN General Assembly in December 1966, became fully operational in 1974 and had, by 1978, resources exceeding the equivalent of $18,000,000 pledged by 68 countries.

In addition the UNDP Governing Council is the governing body of a **United Nations Fund for Population Activities** (UNFPA), set up in 1967 as the Trust Fund for Population Activities and constituted as a Fund of the UN General Assembly in 1972. It is headed by an Executive Director. Its function is to finance projects in the fields of basic population data, population dynamics and policy, family planning, and communication and education. A World Population Conference held in Bucharest in August 1974 adopted a plan of action which called, inter alia, for a reduction in birth rates by 1985 and the provision of family planning advice and services to all who wanted them.

United Nations High Commissioner for Refugees (UNHCR). The office of UN High Commissioner for Refugees was created in 1950. The High Commissioner is responsible to ECOSOC and the General Assembly for the "international protection" of refugees. His mandate does not, however, cover refugees who have the same rights and obligations as nationals of their country of residence, or who receive assistance from other UN agencies.

The activities of the High Commissioner include efforts to facilitate the naturalization of refugees and to improve their legal status; repatriation; local integration by helping refugees to become self-supporting; and resettlement through emigration. An important task of the UNHCR is to supervise the application of the 1951 Convention determining the status of refugees, this being the principal relevant legal document.

A *Convention on the Reduction of Statelessness*, signed in New York on Aug. 30, 1961 and May 31, 1962, provided for the acquisition of the nationality of the Contracting State by children born in its territory of stateless parents. By March 31, 1979, the convention had been ratified by 10 states.

The High Commissioner is elected by the General Assembly on the recommendation of the Secretary-General. He is assisted by a Deputy High Commissioner. A 40-member Executive Committee of the High Commissioner's Programme directs the policy of the programme at its twice-yearly meetings.

The High Commissioner's Office in Geneva has four divisions—external affairs, protection, assistance, and administration and management. There are 11 regional offices, 30 branch offices and 12 sub-offices, as well as a number of chargés de mission and honorary representatives or correspondents in 56 countries.

For the UNHCR general programmes for the year 1980 a sum of almost US $233,900,000 was approved by the Executive Committee in October 1979 (compared with an estimated requirement of $177,600,000 for 1979).

World Food Council (WFC). The WFC was set up under a resolution adopted by the UN General Assembly in December 1974 on a recommendation by a World Food Conference held in Rome in November 1974. The organization has its headquarters in Rome.

The WFC has 36 members (nine from Africa, eight from Asia, seven from Latin America, four from the socialist states in Eastern Europe and eight from West European and other countries).

The task of the WFC is to provide overall, integrated and continuing attention to the co-ordination of policies on food production, nutrition, food security, food trade and food aid as well as related matters among UN agencies.

At its third session, held in Manila in June 1977, the WFC adopted a 22-point "programme of action to eradicate malnutrition and hunger" which called for efforts to increase the growth of food production in 43 "food priority" countries from the existing 2.7 per cent to 4 per cent per annum. The programme estimated that the developing countries needed about $8,300 million in annual aid for agricultural development, and it called for the creation of an international emergency food reserve (IEFR) of 500,000 tonnes of grain (or the equivalent) by the end of 1977, and for the rapid conclusion of negotiations for an international grains arrangement and the attainment of a 10,000,000-tonne target for annual food aid to poor countries.

At its fifth session in Ottawa in September 1979 the WFC called for further replenishment of the IEFR, which then stood at 380,000 tonnes, and deplored the failure of the international community to "make the world's food system work for everyone".

The International Court of Justice

The principal judicial organ of the United Nations is the International Court of Justice, which sits at The Hague. It functions in accordance with a statute annexed to the Charter of the United Nations, and is permanently in session.

The 15 judges who constitute the Court are elected for nine years by both the General Assembly and the Security Council. Five new judges are elected every three years. In addition to possessing first-class legal qualifications the judges must be men of high moral character. No two judges may be of the same nationality, and the Court should include representatives of all the main legal systems of the world.

Functions and Powers. The International Court is not authorized to hear cases brought by individuals. Those states which may submit a dispute are all the members of the United Nations with the addition of Liechtenstein, San Marino and Switzerland.

The court has jurisdiction over all cases referred to it by the parties to its Statute, and also over matters specially provided for in the UN Charter and in treaties in force. In addition, 45 states which are parties to the Statute have voluntarily recognized the compulsory jurisdiction of the court in relation to states accepting the same obligation and over certain specified classes of international disputes.

Should a party to a case refuse to comply with the judgment of the court, the other party may have recourse to the Security Council, which may decide upon measures to give effect to the judgment.

The court may give advisory opinions on legal questions to the General Assembly, the Security Council and other organs of the United Nations if requested to do so.

The Secretariat and Secretary-General

The general administration of the United Nations is the responsibility of the Secretariat in New York, headed by the Secretary-General.

The Secretary-General is elected by the General Assembly, on the recommendation of the Security Council, for a period of five years and is re-eligible. The Secretary-General acts as the United Nations' chief administrative officer at all meetings of the General Assembly, the Security Council, the Economic and Social Council and the Trusteeship Council. Among his duties are the preparation of an annual report which he submits to the General Assembly, and general vigilance over the international scene, so that he may bring to the attention of the Security Council any situations which he considers to be a threat to international peace.

Offices of the Secretariat include one each for:

(1) Special Political Questions.
(2) Political and General Assembly Affairs.
(3) Economic and Social Matters.
(4) Legal Affairs.

There are also departments for:

(1) Political and Security Council Affairs.
(2) Political Affairs, Trusteeship and Decolonization.
(3) International Economic and Social Affairs.
(4) Technical Co-operation for Development.
(5) Administration and Management.
(6) Conference Services.
(7) Public Information.

Other bodies attached to the Secretariat are as follows:

(1) UN Centre on Transnational Corporations.
(2) Office of the UN Commissioner for Namibia.
(3) Secretariat of the Third UN Conference on the Law of the Sea.

EUROPEAN OFFICE OF THE UNITED NATIONS

The European Secretariat of the United Nations has its office at Geneva. It is headed by a Director-General and a Deputy Director, who are responsible to the Secretary-General in New York.

Other Bodies within the UN Framework

United Nations Children's Fund (UNICEF)

Headquarters: New York.

The United Nations Children's Fund is an operating agency of the United Nations, founded in December 1946 to aid mothers and children in need as a result of the devastation of war.

The work of UNICEF is carried out in conjunction with WHO, FAO, and UNESCO (see below under "Specialized Agencies"), and is now mainly directed towards aiding children and young people in developing countries through health, nutrition and social welfare projects.

The decision-making organ of UNICEF is its 30-member Executive Board, which meets annually. There is also a Secretariat, headed by an Executive Director.

United Nations Research Institute for Social Development (UNRISD)

Headquarters: Geneva.

UNRISD was established in 1964 as an autonomous UN body with the object of conducting research into problems and policy of social development and relationships between various types of social and economic development during different phases of economic growth, and of thus contributing to the work of other UN bodies and of national institutes. UNRISD's activities are supervised by a Board consisting of representatives of various UN bodies concerned with social and economic development.

United Nations Institute for Training and Research (UNITAR)

Headquarters: New York.

The United Nations Institute for Training and Research was inaugurated in March 1965. It was created, as an autonomous body within the framework of the United Nations, to train personnel—particularly from developing countries—for service with member governments and organizations of the United Nations. Another of UNITAR's functions is to study major questions relating to the promotion of economic and social development and the maintenance of international peace and security.

A Board of Trustees, whose members are appointed by the UN Secretary-General to sit for three years, directs the policy of the organization. Meetings of the Board take place once a year and are attended, where appropriate, by representatives of the specialized agencies. The direction and general administration of the Institute are the responsibility of an Executive Director.

United Nations Industrial Development Organization (UNIDO)

Headquarters: Vienna.

UNIDO was established in January 1967 as an organ of the UN General Assembly and subsequently operated principally as an executive agency of the UN Development Programme (UNDP), deriving its finance from that body and other sources within the UN system.

At its second session held in Lima (Peru) in March 1975 a recommendation was adopted to the effect that UNIDO should become a UN specialized agency, and this recommendation was endorsed at a special session of the UN General Assembly in September 1975. A conference of plenipotentiaries of 82 UN member countries held in Vienna from March 19 to April 8, 1979, adopted by consensus a Constitution and Final Act under which UNIDO would become a UN specialized agency subject to ratification by at least 80 participating states.

Under its new Constitution the objects of UNIDO would be (i) to encourage and extend, as appropriate, assistance to the developing countries for the develop-

ment, expansion and modernization of their industries; (ii) to assist the developing countries in the establishment and operation of industries, including agriculture-related as well as basic industries, to achieve the full utilization of locally available natural and human resources and contribute to self-reliance; (iii) to provide a forum and act as an instrument to serve the developing and industrialized countries in their contacts, consultations and negotiations; and (iv) to develop special measures designed to promote co-operation among developing countries and between the developed and developing states.

UNIDO's principal organs are, under the new constitution, the General Conference (generally meeting every two years); an Industrial Development Board consisting of 53 members (33 from developing countries, 15 from developed market-economy countries and five from countries with centrally-planned economies); and a Secretariat headed by a Director-General. UNIDO would continue to administer a UN Industrial Development Fund set up under a UN General Assembly resolution of Dec. 22, 1976.

United Nations Environment Programme (UNEP)

Headquarters: Nairobi.

The UN Environment Programme was set up under a resolution passed by the UN General Assembly on Dec. 15, 1972, by 116 votes to none with 10 abstentions in order to implement a recommendation made at a UN Conference on the Human Environment held in Stockholm on June 5-16, 1972.

Under the resolution the General Assembly established a 58-member Governing Council for Environmental Programmes elected for three years, with members selected as follows: 16 from African states, 13 from Asian states, 10 from Latin American states, 13 from West European and other states, and six from East European states (with one-third of the Council's membership being renewed every year).

The duties of the council were to include the promotion of international co-operation in the environmental field, the recommendation of appropriate policies, and the receiving and reviewing of reports by UNEP's Executive Director (elected for a four-year term) on the implementation of environmental programmes within the UN system.

The UN General Assembly also established UNEP's secretariat with headquarters at Nairobi (Kenya). Moreover, the Assembly set up a voluntary fund, effective Jan. 1, 1973, for financing inter alia regional and global monitoring, assessment and data-collecting systems—an "Earthwatch" to warn against impending crises—as proposed in an "Action Plan" of recommendations made by the Stockholm Conference.

United Nations Disaster Relief Office (UNDRO)

Headquarters: Geneva.

UNDRO was established in 1971 with the object of co-ordinating and mobilizing aid furnished by other bodies for international emergency relief to disaster-stricken areas and of promoting disaster preparedness and prevention. UNDRO is headed by a Disaster-Relief Co-ordinator who reports directly to the UN Secretary-General.

United Nations Universities

A UN University has been established in Tokyo under a UN General Assembly resolution (2951/XXVII) of Dec. 11, 1972, with the object of carrying out "action-orientated research into the pressing global problems of human survival, development and welfare that are the concern of the United Nations and its agencies, and . . . the post-graduate training of young scholars and research workers for the benefit of the world community".

A University for Peace, the establishment of which was approved by the UN General Assembly on Dec. 5, 1980 (in Resolution 35/55 adopted without a vote), was to be set up in Costa Rica under an international agreement and a charter as "a specialized international institution for post-graduate studies, research and dissemination of knowledge specifically aimed at training for peace within the system of the UN University".

Specialized Agencies, the IAEA and GATT

The United Nations specialized agencies are independent international organizations, which function in co-operation with the United Nations under agreements made with an ECOSOC Committee. They have responsibilities in a wide variety of fields. Membership of the specialized agencies is not restricted to the members of the United Nations (see table on pages 50-54).

1. International Labour Organization (ILO)

Headquarters: Geneva.

The International Labour Organization, which has existed since 1919, became the first specialized agency of the United Nations in 1946. Its main function is to promote international standards of acceptable labour conditions. It also provides technical assistance in such fields as productivity and management development, manpower organization, labour conditions, small-scale industries and handicrafts and social security.

The aims and purposes of the ILO were defined in the *Philadelphia Charter*, adopted on May 10, 1944, and reading as follows:

"The general Conference of the ILO, meeting in its 26th session in Philadelphia, hereby adopts the present declaration of the aims and purposes of the ILO and of the principles which should inspire the policy of its members.

"The Conference reaffirms the fundamental principles on which the organization is based and, in particular, that labour is not a commodity; that freedom of expression and association are essential to sustained progress; that poverty anywhere constitutes a danger to prosperity everywhere; and that accordingly the war against want, while it requires to be carried on with unrelenting vigour within each nation, equally requires continuous and concerted international effort in which the representatives of workers and employers, enjoying equal status with those of governments, join with them in free discussion and democratic decision with a view to the promotion of the common welfare.

"The Conference affirms that all human beings, irrespective of race, creed or sex, have the right to pursue both their material well-being and spiritual development in conditions of freedom and dignity, of economic security and equal opportunity, that the attainment of the conditions in which this shall be possible must constitute the central aim of national and international policy, and that all policies and measures, in particular those of an economic and financial character, must be judged in this light and accepted only in so far as they may be held to promote and not to hinder the achievement of this fundamental objective. The Conference declares that it is accordingly a responsibility of the ILO to examine all international economic and financial policies and measures in the light of this fundamental objective and that in discharging the tasks entrusted to it the ILO may consider all relevant economic and financial factors and include in its decisions and recommendations any provisions which it considers appropriate.

"Among the matters to which urgent attention should be given by the ILO, the Conference attaches special importance to the following: The maintenance of full employment and the raising of standards of living; the employment of workers in occupations in which they can have the satisfaction of giving the fullest measure of their skill and attainments and make their greatest contribution to the common well-being and, as a means to the attainment of this end, the provision under adequate guarantees for all concerned of facilities for training and the transfer of labour, including migration for employment and settlement; the application of policies in regard to wages, earnings, hours and other conditions of work calculated to ensure a just share of the fruits of progress to all, and the assurance of a minimum living wage to all in need of such protection; the effective recognition of the right of collective bargaining, the co-operation of management and labour in the continuous improvement of productive efficiency, and the collaboration of workers and employers in the initiation and application of social and economic measures; the extension to the whole population of social security measures providing a basic income in case of inability to work or to obtain work, and providing comprehensive medical care; the provision of adequate protection for the life and health of workers in all occupations; provision for child welfare and maternity protection, and the provision of adequate nutrition, housing and facilities for recreation and culture; the assurance of equality of educational and vocational opportunity.

"Confident that the fuller and broader utilization of the world's productive resources necessary for the achievement of the objectives set forth in this declaration can be secured by effective international and national action, including, for example, measures to avoid severe economic fluctuations, to maintain consumption at a high level, to ensure the productive investment of all savings, to promote the economic and social advancement of the less developed regions of the world, to assure greater stability in world prices of primary products, and to promote a high and steady volume of international trade, the Conference pledges the full co-operation of the ILO with such international bodies as may be entrusted with a share of the responsibility for this great task and for the promotion of the health, education and well-being of all peoples.

"The Conference affirms that the principles set forth in this declaration are fully applicable to all peoples everywhere and that, while the manner of their application must be determined with due regard to the stage of social and economic development reached by each people, their progressive application to peoples who are still dependent, as well as to those who have already achieved self-government, is a matter of concern to the whole civilized world."

The principal organ of the ILO is the **International Labour Conference**, which meets annually and is attended by delegations from the member nations. The delegations generally comprise two government delegates, one delegate representing employers and one representing workers. The other organs of the ILO are the **International Labour Office**, which is its secretariat, and the Governing Body, an executive council meeting at least three times a year. The 56-member Governing Body is formed by 28 representatives of governments, 14 representatives of employers, and 14 workers' representatives.

Two institutions founded by the ILO are the International Institute for Labour Studies, set up in March 1960 in Geneva as an advanced educational and research institute, and the International Centre for Advanced Technical and Vocational Training, established in March 1963 in Turin, Italy.

The ILO has approved some 150 conventions and more than 160 recommendations, forming an international labour code

intended to serve as a guideline for governments. Member countries are committed to conventions after ratification, and have to submit to the ILO periodical reports on their implementation.

The ILO has also inquired into alleged violations of human rights, e.g. in Chile, about which an ILO commission appointed in June 1974 reported in May 1975 (after a visit paid to Chile) that there was a lack of legal safeguards for trade union officials in that country, and in 1977-78 the ILO inquired into alleged violations of ILO conventions in the Soviet Union and Czechoslovakia.

The United States, on Nov. 5, 1975, gave the required two years' notice of termination of its ILO membership (after 41 years), stating that it objected to "the workers' and employers' groups in the ILO falling under the domination of governments", to the ILO's alleged failure to apply human rights universally, and to the "increasing politicization" of the ILO, i.e. its growing involvement "in political issues quite beyond its competence and mandate" (after the ILO had decided to allow certain liberation movements to address ILO conferences). A US resolution seeking to reform the ILO so as to exclude "political" matters from discussion without having first been "screened" was turned down by the International Labour Conference in June 1977, and the US withdrawal from the ILO became effective on Nov. 5, 1977. (The USA had met about one-quarter of the ILO's budget.) However, on Feb. 13, 1980, the US President announced that his country was rejoining the ILO, seeing that the latter had made efforts to "return to its original purposes".

China, on the other hand, had suspended its ILO membership on Nov. 8, 1977.

2. Food and Agriculture Organization (FAO)

Headquarters: Rome.

The Food and Agriculture Organization was formally set up at Quebec in October 1945. In FAO's constitution (accepted by over 20 countries by Aug. 30, 1945), the organization's aims were listed as follows:

"To raise levels of nutrition and standards of living among the peoples of the world; improve the efficiency of production and distribution of food and agricultural products; better the condition of the rural population; and thus contribute to an expanding world economy." To this end FAO would function principally as an advisory body, collecting, analysing and disseminating information on nutrition, food and agriculture, and promoting and recommending national and international action with respect to research, the improvement of education and administration relating to these subjects, the spread of public knowledge of nutritional and agricultural science and practice, the conservation of natural resources and the adoption of improved agricultural production methods, improved processing, marketing and distribution, and the provision of adequate agricultural credit. FAO was also to furnish technical assistance to governments when requested.

The supreme organ of FAO is the Conference of all the member nations, which sits every two years. Between sessions of the Conference the work of the organization is carried on by a 49-member Council, meetings of which are normally held twice a year and after each Conference session. There is also a Secretariat headed by a Director-General.

FAO has set up numerous commissions and councils with special functions in various areas for matters of agriculture, animal production and health, fisheries, food standards, forestry, horticulture, land and water use, locust control and plant protection.

An Office for Special Relief Operations (OSRO), first set up in 1973 to cope with the Sahel (West Africa) drought of that year, was in 1975 expanded in order to deal with such emergencies on a global scale.

A Technical Co-operation Programme (TCP) was launched in 1976 to enable FAO to meet emergencies created by natural disasters or project difficulties.

Under a major reform approved by the FAO Council in July 1976, substantial savings were made (on salaries, publications and meetings), the proceeds of which were used to set up a $18,500,000 technical co-operation fund to provide aid directly to developing countries for agricultural purposes.

A Global Information and Early Warning System to monitor world food supply and demand, with 42 governments participating in it, came into operation in 1977.

A World Conference on Agrarian Reform and Rural Development, convened by FAO and held in Rome on July 12-20, 1979, adopted a declaration of principles and recommended a programme of national and international action. It called on the international community to participate in the rural development policies defined by each country, with special attention to be given to priority for rural development, increased popular participation and recognition of the essential role of women in development.

Under a five-point plan for increased world food security, announced in March 1979 and approved by the FAO Conference in November of that year, FAO called on all countries to adopt national grain reserve policies, with targets of two months'

supply, and on exporting countries to hold additional cereal stocks against national shortages. It also proposed that guidelines for the release of reserve stocks, to be drawn up by a FAO Committee on World Food Security, should cover crop failures, natural disasters and the needs of poor countries for supplies at reasonable prices, and that the 10,000,000-tonne target for annual shipments by food donor countries (see under World Food Council, page 24) should be raised to 13,000,000 tonnes per annum by 1982 and to 16,000,000 tonnes per annum by 1985.

FAO's resources for the 1980-81 two-year period included a budget of $278,000,000 based on member states' assessed contributions (25 per cent from the United States and 30 per cent from Canada, the Federal Republic of Germany, Japan, Mexico and the United Kingdom together) as well as $178,000,000 in voluntary contributions by member states and $335,000,000 from the UN Development Programme.

World Food Programme. The World Food Programme (WFP), a joint UN-FAO enterprise established in 1963 to provide aid, in the form of food, to less developed countries, is headed by a Committee on Food Aid Policies and Programmes (CFAPP), appointed under a resolution of the UN General Assembly of Nov. 28, 1975, to replace an earlier Intergovernmental Committee of the WFP. The CFAPP consists of 15 members elected by ECOSOC and 15 others elected by FAO. The WFP's day-to-day activities are carried out by a Joint UN-FAO Administrative Unit headed by an Executive Director.

For the years 1977 and 1978 the UN General Assembly established (also on Nov. 28, 1975) a $750,000,000 target for voluntary contributions to the WFP, with "not less than one-third" being "in cash and/or services in the aggregate", and for 1979-80 this target was (on Dec. 15, 1977) set at $950,000,000.

3. United Nations Educational, Scientific, and Cultural Organization (UNESCO)

Headquarters: Paris.

UNESCO came into being in November 1945. The basic purpose of the organization is to promote international collaboration in the fields of education, science and culture, and through this, to foster and strengthen universal respect for the human rights and fundamental freedoms affirmed in the Charter of the United Nations.

Under UNESCO's Constitution, approved by representatives of 44 nations on Nov. 15, 1945, the main purposes of the organization were (i) to develop and maintain mutual understanding and appreciation of the life, culture, arts, humanities and sciences of the peoples of the world as a basis for effective international organization and world peace; (ii) to co-operate in extending and making available to all peoples for the service of common human needs the world's full body of knowledge and culture, and in assuring its contribution to economic stability, political security and general well-being.

To achieve these purposes UNESCO would (a) facilitate consultation among leaders in the educational and cultural life of all peace-loving countries; (b) assist the free flow of ideas and information among the peoples of the world through schools, universities, other educational and research institutions, libraries, publications, the press, radio, the cinema, international conferences and the exchange of students, teachers, etc., with special attention to exchange of information on major educational, cultural and scientific developments; (c) foster the growth within each country, and in its relations with other countries, of educational and cultural programmes supporting international peace and security; (d) develop and make available educational and cultural plans and materials for consideration and use by each country as it thinks fit; (e) conduct and encourage research and studies on educational and cultural problems related to the maintenance of peace and the advancement of human welfare; and (f) assist countries needing and requesting help in developing their educational and cultural activities.

The work of UNESCO includes the documentation of information of all kinds; the extension of free and compulsory education; the improvement of facilities for vocational and technical training and for higher education; the promotion of scientific research; the preservation of the world's cultural heritage in books, works of art, and historical and scientific monuments; and the improvement of all means of communication in order to encourage the free flow of ideas and knowledge.

The organs of UNESCO are a General Conference of the member nations, meeting every two years; a 45-member Executive Board which meets at least twice a year to prepare the organization's programme; and a Secretariat. National commissions and co-operating bodies within the member countries serve to co-ordinate the work of UNESCO with national efforts in the same fields.

UNESCO's member states are organized in five regional groups—for Europe, Africa, the Arab world, Asia and Latin America.

In 1963 UNESCO established in Paris an International Institute for Educational Planning (IIEP) to assist all UNESCO member states in planning their educational systems and obtaining competent experts in this field.

An International Bureau of Education (IBE), founded in 1925 and based in Geneva,

was incorporated in UNESCO in January 1969. Its Council is composed of representatives of 24 member states appointed by UNESCO's General Conference.

In 1978 UNESCO established in Paris an Intergovernmental Committee for Physical Education and Sport (ICPES), consisting of 30 representatives of UNESCO member states elected by the General Conference. The ICPES is to facilitate the adoption and implementation of an International Charter of Physical Education and Sport.

UNESCO CONVENTIONS AND DECLARATIONS

Conventions and declarations adopted by UNESCO's General Conference included the following:

Convention on the Preservation of the World's Cultural and Natural Heritage. This convention, adopted by a UNESCO General Conference on Nov. 16, 1972, by 75 votes to one (Thailand) with 17 abstentions, aimed at providing both emergency and long-term protection for monuments, monumental sculpture and painting, groups of buildings, archaeological sites, natural features and habitats of animals and plants of "outstanding universal value". States ratifying the convention would be required to take all necessary measures to protect their cultural and natural heritage; close international co-operation would be provided through an Intergovernmental Heritage Committee to ensure the protection of this heritage; and there would be an agency ready to provide immediate aid for the repair of monuments and sites damaged by catastrophes and to assist in preventive measures against latent dangers.

Signatory states were called upon to draw up an inventory of property belonging to their cultural and natural heritage, to be included in a "world heritage list" to be updated every two years. A second inventory "list of world heritage in danger" would include those monuments, buildings and sites for which major conservation operations were urgently needed. The convention also called for the establishment of a World Heritage Fund to be financed by compulsory and voluntary contributions by the states parties to the convention as well as by other states, international and other organizations or individuals.

The convention came into force on Dec. 17, 1975 (three months after ratification by 20 countries) and by Dec. 31, 1979, it was ratified by 49 countries (which did not include the Soviet Union, the United Kingdom and various other countries in Europe).

Declaration on Fundamental Principles for the Mass Media. The 20th session of UNESCO's General Conference adopted, in Paris on Nov. 22, 1978, by acclamation a "draft declaration on fundamental principles concerning the contribution of the mass media to strengthening peace and international understanding, the promotion of human rights, and to countering racialism, apartheid and incitement to war".

The declaration called for "a free flow and a wider and better balanced dissemination of information" to which the mass media had "a leading contribution to make". In particular, "access by the public to information should be guaranteed by the diversity of the sources and means of information available to it, thus enabling each individual to check the accuracy of facts and to appraise events objectively" and "it is important that the mass media be responsive to concerns of peoples and individuals, thus promoting the participation of the public in the elaboration of information" (Art. II (2)). The mass media should also give "expression to oppressed peoples who struggle against colonialism, neo-colonialism, foreign occupation and all forms of racial discrimination and oppression and who are unable to make their voices heard within their own territories" (Art. II (3)).

The declaration further stated that it was "necessary that states should facilitate the procurement, by the mass media in the developing countries, of adequate conditions and resources enabling them to gain strength and expand" and that "bilateral and multilateral exchanges of information among all states, and in particular between those which have different economic and social systems, be encouraged and developed" (Art. X).

4. World Health Organization (WHO)

Headquarters: Geneva.

The World Health Organization was established in April 1948. Its aim is to raise the standard of health of all peoples to the highest possible level through, inter alia, health education; the promotion of work to eradicate disease; the promotion of maternal and child health welfare; the fostering of mental health activities; and the improvement of environmental hygiene and sanitation. The WHO provides its members with both advisory services and technical assistance.

The constitution of the WHO, as proposed by ECOSOC and signed by 60 nations on July 22, 1946, defined the organization's functions as follows:

The WHO was to be "the directing and co-ordinating authority in all matters concerning international health" and in particular "(1) to assist governments in strengthening their national health services; (2) to furnish technical assistance and, in emergencies, give necessary aid at the request of governments; (3) to assist in developing an informed public opinion among all peoples in matters of health; (4) to stimulate and advance work to eradicate disease, particularly of an epidemic, endemic or social nature; (5) to promote research in the field of health; (6) to promote maternal and child health welfare; (7) to foster mental health activities necessary to improve and harmonize human relations; (8) to foster education through improved standards of teaching and training in the health, medical and related professions by means of fellowships, courses, study tours, etc.; (9) to study administrative and social techniques affecting sanitation and medical care from a curative and preventive point of view as regards both medical and hospital practice; (10) to develop central information services and the interchange of information with respect to health and medical care; (11) to promote, with the co-operation of other specialized agencies, the improvement of nutrition, working conditions, housing and other factors related to environmental hygiene and sanitation; (12) to establish an epidemiological and statistical service for the collection, analysis, interpretation and dissemina-

tion of information; (13) to establish and promote international standards with respect to pharmaceutical, biological and related products; (14) to standardize diagnostic procedure as desirable; (15) to establish and revise, as necessary, international nomenclature of diseases, causes of death and public health practice; (16) to promote conventions, regulations and agreements with respect to international health and sanitary matters; (17) to provide, on request of the United Nations, health services and facilities to special groups, including displaced persons and peoples of trust territories; (18) to establish and maintain effective collaboration with the United Nations and its affiliated organizations, with national health administrations and with other appropriate organizations". The WHO was also given authority to adopt regulations which would be binding on all member nations unless they notified the organization to the contrary.

The supreme organ of the WHO is the World Health Assembly, which meets annually to decide on a programme of world health. Other organs are the 31-man Executive Board which meets at least twice a year, and the Secretariat, headed by a Director-General.

An International Agency for Research on Cancer was established in Lyons (France) in 1965 as a self-governing body within the framework of the WHO.

The World Health Assembly decided in May 1976 that under "a new world health order" at least 60 per cent of the WHO's budget (of $146,184,000 for 1977) should be devoted to technical co-operation and services to the Third World.

In a report by the WHO's Director-General, approved by the World Health Assembly in May 1979, strategies were recommended to attain the goal of "health for all by the year 2000"; the report also endorsed the conclusions of an International Conference on Primary Health Care, held under the joint auspices of the WHO and the UN Children's Fund (UNICEF) in Alma Ata (Soviet Union) in September 1978, calling on governments to develop national strategies and action plans to implement primary health care and to end "the inadequate and inequitable distribution of health resources between and within countries".

On Oct. 26, 1979, the WHO's Director-General announced the eradication of smallpox throughout the world.

5. International Bank for Reconstruction and Development (IBRD, or World Bank)

Headquarters: Washington.

The International Bank for Reconstruction and Development, or World Bank as it is commonly designated, was set up in December 1945 to assist in the economic development of member nations by making loans to governments and private enterprises for productive purposes. The Bank's main objectives are to facilitate the investment of capital and to promote private foreign investment; to further the balanced growth of international trade; and to maintain equilibrium in the balance of payments of its members.

The Articles of Agreement of the IBRD of Dec. 27, 1945, read as follows:

"**Introductory Article.** The International Bank for Reconstruction and Development is established and shall operate in accordance with the following provisions:

"**Art. 1.** Purposes. The purposes of the Bank are:

"(i) To assist in the reconstruction and development of territories of members by facilitating the investment of capital for productive purposes, including the restoration of economies destroyed or disrupted by war, the reconversion of productive facilities to peacetime needs and the encouragement of the development of productive facilities and resources in less developed countries.

"(ii) To promote private foreign investment by means of guarantees or participations in loans and other investments made by private investors; and, when private capital is not available on reasonable terms, to supplement private investment by providing, on suitable conditions, finance for productive purposes out of its own capital, funds raised by it and its other resources.

"(iii) To promote the long-range balanced growth of international trade and the maintenance of equilibrium in balances of payments by encouraging international investment for the development of the productive resources of members, thereby assisting in raising productivity, the standard of living and conditions of labour in their territories.

"(iv) To arrange the loans made or guaranteed by it in relation to international loans through other channels so that the more useful and urgent projects, large and small alike, will be dealt with first.

"(v) To conduct its operations with due regard to the effect of international investment on business conditions in the territories of members and, in the immediate post-war years, to assist in bringing about a smooth transition from a wartime to a peacetime economy.

"The Bank shall be guided in all its decisions by the purposes set forth above."

The capital of the Bank is derived from the members' subscriptions, the amount of each subscription being based on the country's economic resources. The Bank acquires additional funds by borrowing in world capital markets, and by selling some of its loans to private investors.

The powers of the Bank are vested in the Board of Governors, on which each of the member nations is represented by one Governor. A body of 20 Executive Directors, to which the Board has delegated most of its power, meets monthly. The President of the Bank, who is also the Chairman of Executive Directors, is responsible for conducting the business of the Bank.

In 1955 the IBRD established an Eco-nomic Development Institute (EDI) for training government officials with responsibility for development programmes or projects.

The President of the IBRD is ex officio the non-voting chairman of the Administrative Council of an **International Centre for the Settlement of Investment Disputes** (ICSID), created in 1966 under a Convention on the Settlement of Investment Disputes between States and Nationals of Other States.

The IBRD is also chairman of a **Consultative Group for International Agricultural Research** (CGIAR), founded in 1971 under joint sponsorship with the Food and Agriculture Organization (FAO) and the UN Development Programme.

The total subscribed capital of the IBRD was, on June 30, 1980, $39,958,929,000, of which about 10 per cent had been paid in, while the Bank's outstanding debt was $29,668 million on that date.

On Jan. 14, 1980, it was announced that the Board of Governors had approved an increase equivalent to $40,000 million in the Bank's authorized capital (as recommended by the Board of Executive Directors on June 28, 1979), this representing roughly a doubling of the Bank's current authorized stock.

6. International Finance Corporation (IFC)

Headquarters: Washington.

The International Finance Corporation, an affiliate of the World Bank, came into being in July 1956.

Under its Charter the IFC was to encourage the growth of productive private enterprises, particularly in the less developed areas of the world, by investing in undertakings where sufficient private capital was not available on reasonable terms, by seeking to recruit private capital and to find experienced management, and by generally creating conditions which would stimulate investment. The IFC would be open to all members of the IBRD.

The IFC was to make its investments without governmental guarantee. It was authorized to make both fixed-interest loans and investments of other kinds, but not to invest in capital stock or to assume responsibility for managing the enterprises in which it invested. The IFC was also to serve as a clearing house to bring together investment opportunities, private capital and experienced management. It would seek to revolve its funds by selling its investments to private investors whenever it could appropriately do so on satisfactory terms. It was authorized to raise additional funds by selling its own obligations in the market.

The share of capital subscribed by the

IFC's members is supplemented by a loan provided by the World Bank.

The IFC is served by a President, an Executive Vice-President and three Vice-Presidents. Its Directors are drawn from the Executive Directors of the World Bank.

7. International Development Association (IDA)

Headquarters: Washington.

Like the IFC, the International Development Association is an affiliate of the World Bank. It was created in September 1960 and began operations in November 1960.

In the IDA's Charter the aims of the Association were defined as being "to promote economic development, increase productivity, and thus raise standards of living in the less-developed areas of the world included within the Association's membership, in particular by providing finance to meet their important developmental requirements on terms which are more flexible and bear less heavily on the balance of payments than those of conventional loans, thereby furthering the developmental objectives of the IBRD and supplementing its activities", and the IDA would finance any specific project which would make an important contribution to the development of the area or areas concerned, whether or not the project was revenue-producing or directly productive. In cases where a loan was made other than to a member government the IDA had discretion to decide whether or not a government guarantee was required.

The greater part of the Association's funds is derived from members' subscriptions, but supplementary resources include transfers from the World Bank. The IDA is operated concurrently with the World Bank by the same officers and staff.

The IDA's resources are periodically replenished by contributions from its affluent member countries. A fifth replenishment, agreed by 26 donor countries in March 1977 for the 1978-81 fiscal years, exceeded $7,637 million. As at June 30, 1979, the IDA's total resources amounted to $19,661 million in current US dollars. A sixth replenishment, agreed to by 33 countries and announced on Jan. 17, 1980, totalled $12,000 million and provided the IDA with commitment authority for the three years from July 1, 1980, to June 30, 1983.

8. International Monetary Fund (IMF)

Headquarters: Washington.

Established at the same time as the World Bank, the International Monetary Fund exists primarily to promote stability and international co-operation in the fields of trade and monetary exchange. Members may purchase foreign exchange from the Fund to make short-term or medium-term payments. Each member is assigned a quota which determines its subscription, its voting power, and the amount of foreign exchange which it may purchase. In addition to making available foreign exchange the Fund provides financial advice to its members on request.

The organs of the Fund are the Board of Governors, on which each member is represented by a Governor and an alternate, and a 21-member Board of Executive Directors.

The establishment of the IMF and the IBRD [see above] had been agreed upon at a conference held in Bretton Woods (New Hampshire) on July 1-22, 1944, and attended by representatives of 44 countries.

The Articles of Agreement of the IMF of Dec. 27, 1945, read as follows:

"**Introductory Article.** The International Monetary Fund is established and shall operate in accordance with the following provisions:

"**Art. 1.** Purposes. The purposes of the International Monetary Fund are:

"(i) To promote international monetary co-operation through a permanent institution which provides the machinery for consultation and collaboration on international monetary problems.

"(ii) To facilitate the expansion and balanced growth of international trade, and to contribute thereby to the promotion and maintenance of high levels of employment and real income and to the development of the productive resources of all members as primary objectives of economic policy.

"(iii) To promote exchange stability, to maintain orderly exchange arrangements among members, and to avoid competitive exchange depreciation.

"(iv) To assist in the establishment of a multilateral system of payments in respect of current transactions between members and in the elimination of foreign exchange restrictions which hamper the growth of world trade.

"(v) To give confidence to members by making the Fund's resources available to them under adequate safeguards, thus providing them with opportunity to correct maladjustments in their balance of payments without resorting to measures destructive of national or international prosperity.

"(vi) In accordance with the above, to shorten the duration and lessen the degree of disequilibrium in these international balances of payments of members.

"The Fund shall be guided in all its decisions by the purposes set forth in this article."

Under a **General Agreement to Borrow** (GAB), which was agreed to on Jan. 8, 1962, and came into force on Oct. 25, 1962, the "Group of Ten" major industrial countries outside the Communist world (the United States, the Federal Republic of Germany, the United Kingdom, France, Italy, Japan, Canada, the Netherlands, Belgium and Sweden) undertook to "stand ready to lend their currencies to the Fund up to specified amounts when the Fund and these countries consider that supplementary resources are needed to forestall or cope with an impairment of the international monetary system". The Group of Ten was joined by Switzerland, which is not a member of the IMF. The GAB was repeatedly renewed, most recently on Aug. 24, 1979, for a further five years with effect from Oct. 24, 1980.

The Fund's Articles of Agreement were amended in June 1968 so as to create a new facility of "special drawing rights" (SDRs), which came into force on July 28, 1969. The SDRs would be distributed among participating countries according to their Fund quotas and would entitle the countries concerned to make drawings of currency unconditionally to meet balance-of-payments difficulties. The SDRs would be additional to the Fund's normal stand-by and drawing arrangements, which would continue to be operated subject to certain conditions as before.

The IMF announced on July 28, 1972, the establishment of a Committee of the Board of Governors on Reform of the International Monetary System and Related Issues (the "Committee of Twenty"), representing both developed and developing countries. Its aim would be to "provide a forum in which momentum can be maintained at a high policy-making level for all aspects of reform of the international monetary system".

The Committee of Twenty was in June 1974 replaced by an Interim Committee of the Board of Governors, with advisory functions, pending the establishment of a Permanent and Representative Council with decision-making powers on the management and adaptation of the monetary system.

Subsequent to the amendment of the IMF's Articles of Agreement introducing the SDR, a second amendment, which came into force on April 1, 1978, inter alia enabled the IMF to use its holdings of each member country's currency in its operations and transactions and for promoting previously agreed objectives of reducing the role of gold in the international monetary system and making the SDR the principal reserve asset (with the official price of gold being abolished, a free market in gold being created and the IMF selling part of its gold holdings, the profits from such sales being used to set up a Trust Fund for poorer developing countries). Under this amendment the IMF would "exercise firm surveillance over the exchange rate policies" of its members and would "adopt specific principles for the guidance of all its members".

On March 31, 1978, it was decided that the "basket" of currencies, which formed the basis for calculating the value of the SDR, was to be revised every five years.

As at Jan. 1, 1980, the total of SDRs in existence was in excess of SDR 21,000 million.

IMF FINANCING FACILITIES

In January 1974 the IMF's Board of Governors decided to allow the Bank of International Settlements (BIS, see page 151) to hold IMF SDRs—which would enable IMF members holding SDRs to use them to obtain currency from the BIS, with the assurance that the BIS would use the same amount of SDRs within six months to obtain currency from the participants.

The nature and conditionality of the various financing facilities of the IMF are as follows:

Gold Tranche. Since July 1969, when the Articles of Agreement were amended [see above], gold tranche drawings (i.e. drawings in the first 25 per cent tranche, corresponding to the 25 per cent of quota which must be paid in gold rather than in the member's own currency) have been legally automatic.

First Credit Tranche. All requests for the use of the IMF's resources other than use of the gold tranche are examined by the Fund to determine whether the proposed use would be consistent with the provisions of the Articles of Agreement and with Fund policies. The criteria used by the Fund in determining whether assistance should be given are more liberal when the request is in the first credit tranche than when it is in higher credit tranches. For the first credit tranche, the member's programme is expected to show that it is making reasonable efforts to overcome its difficulties, but "performance criteria" are not set, and the member is not required to make drawings on an instalment basis.

Higher Credit Tranches. Requests for purchases in the higher credit tranches require substantial justification of the member's efforts to overcome its balance-of-payments difficulties, and under current practices purchases are normally made in instalments and under standby arrangements rather than outright. The programme presented for higher credit tranche assistance is usually comprehensive and in a quantified form, and the member's right to draw is made subject to the observance of certain key policy indicators or "performance criteria" described in the programme.

Extended Facility. This facility was set up in 1974 to provide medium-term assistance for up to three years to enable members to overcome structural balance-of-payments adjustments. A detailed statement of policies and measures for the first and subsequent 12-month periods is required, and resources are provided in the form of extended arrangements which include performance criteria and drawing in instalments.

Export Compensatory Facility. This facility, which was created in 1963 and expanded in 1966, is designed to compensate a member for a temporary shortfall in export earnings due to circumstances beyond its control. Use of the facility obliges a member to cooperate with the Fund in an effort to find appropriate solutions for balance-of-payments difficulties arising from the shortfall. The facility was further extended in December 1975.

Buffer Stock Financing Facility. Established in 1969, this facility is designed to assist members in financing contributions to buffer stocks in connexion with international commodity agreements. Members using it are obliged to co-operate with the Fund as under the compensatory facility.

Oil Facility. This facility was introduced in June 1974 and expanded in January 1975 to SDR 5,000 million, being designed to recycle surplus oil and other revenues by assisting members in balance-of-payments difficulties arising from the sharp increase in world oil prices of late 1973 and early 1974. Under the January 1975 arrangements, which also incorporated a special Subsidy Account from which most-seriously-affected (MSA) developing countries might obtain assistance with interest payable under the facility, access was subject to the Fund's assessment of the adequacy of the member's medium-term economic policies and the member's commitment to avoiding restrictive measures, as stipulated in the January 1974 Rome communiqué of the IMF. The final purchases under the 1975 oil facility were approved in March 1976, and the first payments under the Subsidy Account facility were made to 18 MSA countries on July 22, 1976 (SDR 13,800,000, representing a 5 per cent subsidy on qualifying drawings on the 1975 oil facility).

Witteveen Facility. A new "supplementary financing facility" (the "Witteveen facility") came into force on Feb. 23, 1979 (having been approved by the IMF's Executive Board on Aug. 29, 1977). This facility was designed to provide supplementary financing in conjunction with other IMF resources to members facing serious payment imbalances (large in relation to their IMF quota), in particular as a result of the rise of oil prices. The resources made available for this facility totalled SDR 7,754 million (including SDR 1,934 million from the Saudi Arabian Monetary Agency, SDR 1,550 million from the United States, SDR 1,050 from the Deutsche Bundesbank of the Federal Republic of Germany and SDR 900,000,000 from Japan).

9. International Civil Aviation Organization (ICAO)

Headquarters: Montreal.

The International Civil Aviation Organization formally came into being in April 1947, although the agreement for its creation had been concluded at a Chicago conference on civil aviation held on Nov. 1-Dec. 6, 1944.

The Chicago Convention on International Civil Aviation (of December 1944) contains the statutes of the ICAO as well as detailed provisions on the regulation of international civil aviation (with all aircraft involved to be registered by the ICAO). The latter's work covered mainly three areas—air navigation (in particular the safety and regularity of international flights, regulated by ICAO Standards and Recommended Practices adopted in 1949 as an amendment to the Chicago Convention), the economic

aspects of air transportation, and international air law.

The two organs of the ICAO are the Assembly of all the member nations, which meets every three years, and the Council, composed of representatives of the member nations elected by the Assembly, acting as executive organ and in session almost continuously. There are also an Air Navigation Commission, standing committees and regional offices.

A number of conventions have been adopted within the ICAO framework for dealing with specific problems.

A Warsaw *Convention on the Liability of Air Carriers for Damage* caused to Passengers and Cargo, agreed to in 1929, was repeatedly amended, in particular by the Hague Protocol of 1955, which doubled the maximum amount of compensation payable for such damage.

A 1952 Rome *Convention on Damage caused by Aircraft to Third Parties on the Surface*, which set limits on the operator's liability for such damage, replaced an earlier convention and protocol on this subject.

A *Convention on Aerial Collision*, drafted in March 1961, laid down limits for compensation payable for loss or damage caused by such collisions.

A *Convention on Offences and Certain Other Acts Committed on Board Aircraft*, opened for signature in Tokyo on Sept. 14, 1963, came into force on Dec. 4, 1969, after it had been ratified by 12 countries (including the USA, Denmark, Italy, Mexico, Norway, the Philippines, Portugal, Sweden and the United Kingdom). The convention laid down rules on jurisdiction over aircraft, also for extradition purposes, and defined the authority of the aircraft commander. All parties to the convention undertook to take all appropriate measures, in cases of hijacking, to restore control of the aircraft to its lawful commander.

A *Convention for the Suppression of Unlawful Seizure of Aircraft*, concluded by a Diplomatic Conference on Air Law under ICAO auspices in The Hague on Dec. 16, 1970, entered into force on Oct. 14, 1971, after it had been ratified by 10 countries (including Bulgaria, Hungary, Israel, Japan, Norway, Sweden, Switzerland and the USA). The convention defined unlawful seizure, or attempt at seizure, of civil aircraft as an offence and committed each contracting state to make the offence punishable by severe penalties. It also defined the jurisdiction of contracting states and laid down procedure against offenders, including their possible extradition to another contracting state. The convention further required offences to be reported to the ICAO; it enjoined the contracting states to submit any disputes to arbitration; and it authorized them to appeal, if necessary, to the International Court of Justice.

A *Convention for the Suppression of Unlawful Acts against the Safety of Civil Aviation* was adopted by a Diplomatic Conference on Air Law under ICAO auspices in Montreal on Sept. 23, 1971. The convention defined offences against the safety of civil aircraft and committed contracting states to make such offences punishable by severe penalties; to take all necessary measures to establish its jurisdiction; and to take offenders into custody. Other provisions of the convention were similar to those of the Convention for the Suppression of Unlawful Seizure of Aircraft [see above].

BILATERAL ANTI-HIJACKING AGREEMENTS

USA-Cuba. An agreement between the USA and Cuba on the prevention of aerial and maritime hijacking was signed on Feb. 15, 1973, and entered into force immediately. Its provisions included the following:

(1) Any person who hereafter seizes, removes, appropriates or diverts from its normal route or activities an aircraft or vessel registered under the laws of one of the parties and brings it to the territory of the other party shall be considered to have committed an offence and therefore shall either be returned to the party of registry of the aircraft or vessel, to be tried by the courts of that party in conformity with its laws, or be brought before the courts of the party whose territory he reached for trial in conformity with its laws for the offence punishable by the most severe penalty according to the circumstances and seriousness of the acts to which this article refers.

(2) Each party shall try with a view to severe punishment in accordance with its laws any person who, within its territory, hereafter conspires to promote, or promotes, or prepares, or directs, or forms part of an expedition which from its territory or any other place carries out acts of violence or depredation against aircraft or vessels of any kind or registration coming or going to the territory of the other party or who, within its territory, hereafter conspires to promote, or promotes, or prepares, or directs, or forms part of an expedition which from its territory or any other place carries out such acts or other similar unlawful acts in the territory of the other party.

Although Dr Castro (then Prime Minister of Cuba) announced in October 1976 that he would abrogate the agreement, its terms have largely continued to be observed by Cuba.

Canada-Cuba. A similar agreement between Canada and Cuba was signed simultaneously with the US-Cuban agreement. This contained undertakings by both governments to prosecute hijackers or to return them to the countries in which the hijackings had been committed.

Cuba-Mexico. An agreement on the prevention of aerial and maritime hijacking was signed by Cuba and Mexico on June 7, 1973. Under its terms the two parties undertook to try or to extradite hijackers other than those acting for political motives.

Cuba-Venezuela. An agreement on the prevention of aerial hijacking was signed by Cuba and Venezuela on July 6, 1973.

10. Universal Postal Union (UPU)

Headquarters: Berne.

The Universal Postal Union was established in Berne (Switzerland) in 1874, when the first International Postal Convention was signed, creating the General Union of Posts (which changed its name to UPU in 1878). In 1948 it became a UN specialized agency.

The convention was based on five principles:

(1) For the purposes of postal communication all member states formed a single territory. This means that in effect every member state has the full use of postal services throughout the world.

(2) Uniformity of postage rates and units of weight. After World War I this principle of a uniform rate was changed to that of a maximum and a minimum rate.

(3) Classification of mail matter into letters, postcards and "other matter", with detailed rules for their distinction.

(4) The making of definite payments by the country dispatching mail for the use of services of other countries—except the country of destination (it being assumed that the traffic in either direction is approximately equal).

(5) A universal system of registration and compensation.

The organs of the UPU are its Congress, a legislative body meeting every five years; a 40-member Executive Council elected by the Congress and meeting annually; a 35-member Consultative Council for Postal Studies (which in 1969 superseded a Consultative Committee for Postal Studies set up in 1957); and an International Bureau as the UPU's permanent administrative organ, headed by a Director-General.

Postal services other than letter mail are governed by eight special UPU agreements.

11. International Telecommunication Union (ITU)

Headquarters: Geneva.

The International Telecommunication Union originated in 1865 as the International Telegraph Union, and came into being under its present title in January 1934. The ITU became a UN specialized agency in November 1947. Its main functions are to promote international co-operation in telecommunications, and to encourage the development of radio, telegraph and telephone installations with their efficient operation at the lowest possible rates.

The supreme organ of the ITU is the Plenipotentiary Conference of all the members, which meets every five years. Other organs are the 36-member Administrative Council, which meets once a year, and the General Secretariat. Administrative Conferences are held from time to time in accordance with technical requirements.

Other bodies within the framework of the ITU are the International Frequency Registration Board (IFRB); the International Telegraph and Telephone Consultative Committee (CCITT); and the International Radio Consultative Committee (CCIR).

An *International Telecommunication*

Convention, as amended by a Final Protocol, Additional Protocols I to VI and an
Optional Additional Protocol adopted at a
Malaga-Torremolinos conference on Oct.
25, 1973, sets out the structure of the ITU,
the application of its provisions and regulations, relations with UN and other organizations and rules for telegraph and telephone
as well as for radio.

At a **World Administrative Radio Conference** held by the ITU in Geneva from
Sept. 24 to Dec. 6, 1979, agreements were
reached on the reallocation of radio frequencies between different types of usage
to take effect from Jan. 1, 1982.

12. World Meteorological Organization (WMO)

Headquarters: Geneva.

The World Meteorological Organization
became operative as a UN specialized
agency in April 1951, although the convention of the organization had been in effect
since March 1950.

The convention defined the purposes of the WMO
as being (i) to facilitate worldwide co-operation in
establishing networks of stations for meteorological
observations; (ii) to promote the rapid exchange of
weather information; (iii) to promote the standardization of meteorological observations and ensure the
uniform publication of statistics; (iv) to further the
application of meteorology to aviation, shipping,
agriculture and other activities; and (v) to encourage
research and training in meteorology, and to co-
ordinate the international aspects of such training.

The supreme organ of the WMO is the
World Meteorological Congress held every
four years and attended by representatives
of all the members of the organization. The
executive organ is the Executive Committee,
whose 29 members include the Presidents
of the six Regional Associations. The Executive Committee meets at least once a year.
There is also a Secretariat, which is
responsible for general administration. The
six Regional Associations are for Africa,
Asia, South America, North and Central
America, the South-West Pacific and
Europe.

The WMO implements a World Weather
Watch Programme and has set up a Global
Observing System (involving land stations,
aircraft, ships and satellites), a Global Data
Processing System and a Global Telecom-
munications System. Special programmes
of the WMO include a Tropical Cyclone
Programme, a Weather Modification Pro-
gramme, a Global Atmospheric Research
Programme, a Hydrology and Water Re-
sources Programme and a World Climate
Programme.

13. Inter-Governmental Maritime Consultative Organization (IMCO)

Headquarters: London.

The Inter-Governmental Maritime Consultative Organization was formally established as a UN specialized agency on Jan. 13,
1959, under a convention which was approved on March 6, 1948, at an international maritime conference (held in Geneva
and called by ECOSOC) and which came
into force on March 17, 1958 (following
ratification by the required number of 21
governments).

The 1948 convention laid down that IMCO was a
consultative and advisory body, whose functions were
(a) to provide machinery for inter-governmental
co-operation on regulations and practices affecting
shipping engaged in international trade, and to encourage the adoption of the highest practicable standards
of safety and efficient navigation; (b) to encourage
the removal of discriminatory action and unnecessary
governmental restrictions on international shipping,
though subsidies and other governmental assistance
for the development of national shipping and security
purposes would not constitute discrimination unless
based on measures (e.g., flag discrimination, arbitrary
port charges, etc.) designed to restrict the freedom of
shipping of all flags to take part in international
trade; (c) to consider unfair procedure by shipping
concerns which had proved incapable of settlement
through the normal processes of international shipping business; (d) to consider any matters connected
with shipping referred to it by any UN specialized
agency; (e) to provide for the exchange of information
among governments on matters under consideration
by the organization.

IMCO's organs are the Assembly, composed of representatives of all the member
states as well as various observers, and
meeting every two years, and a 16-member
Council, as the organization's governing
body, meeting about twice a year; the Council has established a Legal Committee, a
Facilitation Committee and a Committee
on Technical Co-operation (membership of
these committees being open to all IMCO
member states). There are also a Maritime
Safety Committee, meeting at least once a
year (and open to all IMCO members) and
a Maritime Environment Committee (set up
in 1973), as well as a Secretariat headed by
a Secretary-General.

IMCO is the depository for a number of
conventions on maritime practices and
safety at sea, not all of which have to date
entered into force.*

(1) An *International Convention on the Safety of
Life at Sea,* revising the 1948 convention which had
entered into force in 1952, was signed on July 17, 1960,
by 34 countries, six more signing during the following

---

* IMCO conventions relating to maritime pollution
are listed in Section 5, see pages 74-76.

month. The convention dealt with safety of navigation, provisions for nuclear ships and carriage of dangerous goods and came into force in 1965.

At the seventh meeting of the IMCO Assembly on Oct. 5-15, 1971, amendments were adopted to the convention, rendering mandatory the observance of traffic-routing schemes approved by IMCO, including a scheme for traffic separation in the Dover Strait.

(2) A 1965 *Convention on Facilitation of International Maritime Traffic* came into force in March 1967.

(3) A 1966 *International Convention on Load Lines* came into force in March 1967.

(4) A 1969 *International Convention on Tonnage Measurement of Ships* is due to enter into force on July 18, 1982.

(5) A *Convention relating to Civil Liability in the Field of Maritime Carriage of Nuclear Material,* adopted in December 1971, came into force on July 15, 1975 (90 days after the deposit of the fifth instrument of ratification, countries having ratified it being France, Spain, Denmark, Sweden and Norway). (By Dec. 31, 1979, it was also in force for the Federal Republic of Germany and the Yemen Arab Republic.)

(6) A 1972 *Convention on the International Regulations for the Prevention of Collisions at Sea* came into force in October 1978.

(7) A 1972 *International Convention for Safe Containers* came into force in September 1977.

(8) An *International Convention for the Safety of Life at Sea (Solas),* adopted at an IMCO conference which ended on Nov. 1, 1974, incorporated amendments to the 1960 International Convention on the Safety of Life at Sea [see above], repeatedly amended between 1966 and 1973. The revised convention contained new provisions on fire protection for passenger ships and tankers and on the carriage of grain in bulk. It came into force on May 25, 1980.

(9) A *Convention on an International Maritime Satellite Organization* (INMARSAT) was signed in London on Sept. 3, 1976, by representatives of 42 states. It provides for the use of satellites for maritime telecommunications, and it came into force in July 1979, when the organization was officially established in London.

14. World Intellectual Property Organization (WIPO)

Headquarters: Geneva.

This organization was established in 1970 under a convention adopted at a conference held in Stockholm from June 12 to July 14, 1967, by representatives of 132 countries (including the Soviet Union and other Communist states), and it became a UN specialized agency in December 1974.

WIPO's organs are (i) a General Assembly of representatives of all member states; (ii) a co-ordinating committee with consultative and executive functions; and (iii) a permanent secretariat designated as the International Bureau for Intellectual Property. WIPO's tasks include the centralization of the administration of intellectual property— i.e. industrial property (in inventions, trademarks and designs) and copyright—hitherto carried out by the United International

Bureaux for the Protection of Intellectual Property on behalf of the Union of Paris and the Union of the Berne Copyright Convention [see pages 4-5].

WIPO has since 1973 implemented a Permanent Programme for Development Co-operation related to Industrial Property and since 1976 a Permanent Programme for Development Co-operation related to Copyright and Neighbouring Rights. It has set up a WIPO Permanent Committee on Patent Information and an International Patent Documentation Centre (INPADOC, in Vienna).

It has operated the international registration of trademarks; the international deposit of designs; the international registration of the appellations of origin; and the recording of international applications for patents received under a *Patent Co-operation Treaty* which was signed in Washington on June 19, 1970, by representatives of 78 countries and which came into force on June 1, 1978. (Under this treaty an international patent application would be filed at a "receiving office" which would be either a national patent office or the European Patent Office in Munich—see page 4.) As at Dec. 31, 1979, the treaty was in force in 25 countries, including Austria, Brazil, Denmark, France, the Federal Republic of Germany, Japan, Luxembourg, the Netherlands, Norway, Romania, the Soviet Union, Sweden, Switzerland, the United Kingdom and the United States.

15. International Fund for Agricultural Development (IFAD)

Headquarters: Rome.

This fund held its constituent meeting on Dec. 13-16, 1977. It was established on a proposal made principally by member states of the Organization of Petroleum Exporting Countries (OPEC) at a World Food Conference in November 1974 and under an agreement which was reached at a Food and Agriculture Organization (FAO) conference held on June 10-13, 1976, and which came into force on Nov. 30, 1977. IFAD was recognized as a UN specialized agency in December 1977 and began its activities on Jan. 2, 1978, with a membership of 114 countries.

IFAD has a Governing Council on which each member state is represented by a Governor and an Alternative, and an Executive Board of 18 members and 18 alternatives elected by the Governing Council in which 600 votes are held by each of three groups of member states—*Group 1:* member states of the Organization for Economic Co-operation and Development (OECD); *Group*

2: OPEC member states; and *Group 3:* recipient developing countries. Within each group the votes are distributed as follows: Group 1—17.5 per cent divided equally among group members and 92.5 per cent divided on the basis of their financial contributions (giving the United States 179 votes, the Federal Republic of Germany and Japan 53 each, the Netherlands 45, and the United Kingdom and Canada 32 each); Group 2—25 per cent divided equally and 75 per cent on the basis of financial contributions; and Group 3—votes distributed equally among member countries. Each group is thus given one-third of the seats on the Board.

IFAD's objectives are to raise resources for concessional loans or grants for agricultural development projects, principally to the poorest countries with food deficits, in order to increase food production, to provide employment and additional income for poor and landless farmers and to reduce malnutrition. Grants are limited to 12.5 per cent of IFAD's resources committed during any financial year. In 1978 IFAD committed $120,000,000 to projects in 10 countries, and its investment target was $375,000,000 for 1979, and about $500,000,000 for 1980.

International Atomic Energy Agency (IAEA)

Headquarters: Vienna.

The International Atomic Energy Agency came officially into existence in July 1957. The Agency submits reports to the General Assembly, to ECOSOC, to the Security Council, and to other UN organs where appropriate, thus differing from the specialized agencies, which report only to ECOSOC.

Membership of the IAEA is open to all members of the United Nations and the specialized agencies.

The Agency's principal organs consist of a General Conference of all the member-nations, which meets annually; a 34-member Board of Governors (12 members being designated by the Board itself and 22 elected by the General Conference) meeting about four times a year and acting as the Agency's executive organ; and a Director-General, who heads a secretariat divided into departments for Technical Assistance and Publications, Technical Operations, Research and Isotopes, Safeguards and Inspection, and Administration. There is also a 15-man Scientific Advisory Committee of nuclear experts.

In its statute the IAEA was authorized:

(*a*) To encourage and assist research on and the development of atomic energy for peaceful uses throughout the world, and to act as an intermediary between members for the performance of services or the supply of materials, equipment or facilities;

(*b*) to make provision for the materials and services needed for the development of atomic energy for peaceful purposes, with due consideration for the needs of under-developed areas of the world;

(*c*) to foster the exchange of scientific and technical information on the peaceful uses of atomic energy;

(*d*) to encourage the exchange and training of scientists and experts;

(*e*) to establish and administer safeguards designed to ensure that special fissionable and other materials made available by the Agency should not be used in such a way as to further any military purpose;

(*f*) to acquire or establish any facilities, plant and equipment necessary for the execution of its authorized functions.

In carrying out these functions the Agency would:

(1) Conduct its activities in accordance with the purposes and principles of the United Nations to promote peace and international co-operation;

(2) establish control over the use of special fissionable materials received by the Agency to ensure that they would be used only for peaceful purposes;

(3) allocate its resources in such a manner as to secure efficient utilization and the greatest possible general benefit in all areas;

(4) submit reports on its activities annually to the UN General Assembly and, when appropriate, to the Security Council;

(5) submit reports to the Economic and Social Council and other UN organs on matters within their competence;

(6) assist members without any political, economic, military or other conditions incompatible with the provisions of the statute;

(7) show due respect for the sovereign rights of states. (Article 3.)

The IAEA has established a number of institutions: a laboratory for physics, chemistry and agriculture at Seibersdorf in Austria; a laboratory for medical physics and hydrology in Vienna; a laboratory in Monaco for the study of marine radio-activity and other forms of marine pollution; an International Centre for Theoretical Physics in Trieste; an International Nuclear Information System (INIS); and a Nuclear Data Section.

Safeguards agreements concluded by the IAEA (in addition to those under the 1968 Nuclear Non-Proliferation Treaty—see pages 57-60) include:

(*a*) One signed in Seoul on Oct. 31, 1975, entrusting the IAEA with control over nuclear equipment to be sold to the Republic of Korea by France and Canada so as to guarantee that this equipment would not be used for military purposes;

(*b*) one signed in Vienna on Sept. 6, 1976, with the United Kingdom and Euratom for the submission of UK non-military nuclear installations to IAEA supervision, this agreement coming into force on Aug. 14, 1978;

(*c*) one signed in Vienna on July 27, 1978, with France and Euratom (although France—not a signatory to the Nuclear Non-Proliferation Treaty—reserved the right to decide which of its installations would be open to inspection by the IAEA); and

(*d*) one with Cuba, signed on April 28, 1980.

Under an agreement signed in Vienna on Dec. 1, 1975, and coming into effect immediately, the IAEA and the Commission of the European Communities entered into close co-operation and regular consultation on matters of common interest.

In an exchange of letters with France (published in September 1979) Iraq undertook to provide the IAEA with design information of its nuclear facilities and to notify the IAEA of "any unexpected transfer into Iraq of nuclear material required to be subject to safeguards" if the shipment exceeded one effective kilo.

Trilateral agreements on the suspension of the application of safeguards and providing for the application of safeguards pursuant to the Non-Proliferation Treaty have been signed by the IAEA and the United States with the following countries:

(1) *Australia:* July 10, 1974, entry into force on the same day.

(2) *Austria:* Sept. 21, 1971; entry into force July 23, 1972.

(3) *Denmark:* March 1, 1972; entry into force on the same day.

(4) *Greece:* March 1, 1972; entry into force on the same day.

(5) *Iran:* June 19, 1973; entry into force May 15, 1974.

(6) *Norway:* Sept. 25, 1973; entry into force on the same day.

(7) *Philippines:* Feb. 21, 1973; entry into force Oct. 16, 1973.

(8) *Sweden:* April 14, 1975; entry into force May 6, 1975.

(9) *Thailand:* June 27, 1974; entry into force on the same day.

An agreement for co-operation in the civil uses of atomic energy between the IAEA and the United States was signed on May 11, 1959, and entered into force on Aug. 7, 1959.

General Agreement on Tariffs and Trade (GATT)

Headquarters: Geneva.

The General Agreement on Tariffs and Trade is a multilateral trade agreement concluded in October 1947 at a 23-nation UN Conference on Trade and Employment, held in Geneva from April 10 to Oct. 30, 1947. It co-operates with the United Nations at secretariat and intergovernmental levels but does not have the formal status of a UN specialized agency.

One of the main purposes of the 1947 conference was to draft a charter for a proposed International Trade Organization (ITO). The provisions of GATT were in-

tended to be superseded by the ITO Charter as soon as the latter should come into force. Although a final text of the ITO Charter was approved at the subsequent Havana Conference on Trade and Employment (Nov. 21, 1947-March 24, 1948), it has never been ratified. Thus, GATT—originally intended as an interim institution—has developed into a permanent international instrument for the regulation of world trading practices.

The aims of GATT are to raise standards of living, to ensure full employment, to develop resources, to expand the production and exchange of goods, and to promote economic development.

The GATT, published on Nov. 18, 1974, consisted of three parts. In the first part the principle of most-favoured-nation treatment (as set out in the ITO Charter) was specified as requiring that "with respect to customs duties and charges of any kind . . . any advantage, favour, privilege or immunity granted by any member to any product originating in or destined for any other country shall be accorded immediately and unconditionally to the like product originating in or destined for all other member countries respectively". In the second part rules were laid down inter alia for the equal treatment of imported and home-produced goods, the possible imposition of anti-dumping duties by importing countries, conditions for the imposition of import restrictions, the notification to other signatory countries of subsidies granted by any country, and non-discrimination by state enterprises. The third part allowed the formation of customs unions provided that no increase of duties was involved, and the modification of concessions by negotiation.

Tariff concessions negotiated at the same time were listed in 20 schedules to the Agreement.

In a fourth part of the Agreement, which was approved on Feb. 8, 1965, and came into force on June 27 of that year (for those contracting parties which had accepted it), rules were laid down for policies in relation to trade and economic development of developing countries with the object of promoting "rapid and sustained expansion" of these countries' export earnings and ensuring "stable, equitable and remunerative prices" for these exports. At the same time a Trade and Development Committee was established to administer the provisions of the fourth part of the Agreement and to make recommendations in connexion with them.

The members of GATT (contracting parties and other members) meet in session once a year. Matters arising between sessions are dealt with by a Council of Representatives, and there is also a Secretariat, headed by a Director-General and composed of trade specialists and administrative staff.

Conferences on the reduction and stabilization of tariffs are held at irregular intervals, as a result of which tariffs have been reduced on goods accounting for around half the world's trade.

An International Trade Centre, to provide information and advice to developing countries, was established in Geneva in May 1964.

The principal achievements of GATT include world-wide tariff reductions agreed upon:

(a) In the "Dillon Round" of 1960-62, under which many customs tariffs were reduced by an average of 20 per cent between the USA and the EEC, between the USA and Britain, between Britain and the EEC, and between the USA and other countries, with all bilateral concessions being granted to all other GATT member countries under the "most-favoured-nation" principle;

(b) in the "Kennedy Round" of 1963-67, in which the "linear approach" for tariff reductions "across the board", instead of item-by-item bargaining for different commodities, was applied for the first time; this approach eventually led to a reduction of tariffs for industrial goods, carried out in agreed stages, averaging over 30 per cent on trade between the participating countries, and reaching up to 50 per cent in many cases; and

(c) in the "Tokyo Round" of 1973-79, which resulted, in April 1979, in agreements with binding force as from Jan. 1, 1980, for those participants which had accepted them (while others might accept them until June 30, 1980); these agreements covered tariff reductions to be implemented generally in equal annual rate reductions between Jan. 1, 1980, and Jan. 1, 1987, in particular by the industrialized countries, and according to the GATT Secretariat the level of industrial tariffs was on average to be reduced by about one-third more, on which agreements were signed in Geneva on Dec. 17, 1979.

Major UN Conventions and Declarations

The UN General Assembly has adopted a number of conventions and declarations, among them those detailed below.

Convention on the Prevention and Punishment of the Crime of Genocide

This convention, adopted on Dec. 9, 1948, provided inter alia as follows:

"**Art. 1.** The Contracting Parties confirm that genocide, whether committed in time of peace or of war, is a crime under international law which they undertake to prevent and punish.

"**Art. 2.** Genocide means any of the following acts committed with intent to destroy, in whole or part, a national, ethnical, racial or religious group:

"(a) Killing members of the group;

"(b) causing serious bodily or mental harm to members of the group;

"(c) deliberately inflicting on the group conditions of life calculated to bring about its physical destruction in whole or part;

"(d) imposing measures intended to prevent births within the group;

"(e) forcibly transferring children of the group to another group.

"**Art. 3.** The following acts shall be punishable:

"(a) Genocide;

"(b) conspiracy to commit genocide;

"(c) direct and public incitement to commit genocide;

"(d) attempt to commit genocide;

"(e) complicity in genocide.

"**Art. 4.** Persons committing genocide or any of the other acts enumerated in Art. 3 shall be punished, whether they are constitutionally responsible rulers, public officials or private individuals.

"**Art. 5.** The Contracting Parties undertake to enact, in accordance with their respective constitutions, the necessary legislation to give effect to the provisions of the convention, and, in particular, to provide effective penalties for persons guilty of genocide or any of the other acts enumerated in Art. 3.

"**Art. 6.** Persons charged with genocide or any of the other acts enumerated in Art. 3 shall be tried by a competent tribunal of the state in the territory of which the act was committed, or by such international penal tribunal as may have jurisdiction with respect to such Contracting Parties as shall have accepted the jurisdiction of such tribunal.

"**Art. 7.** Genocide and the other acts enumerated in Art. 3 shall not be considered as political crimes for the purpose of extradition. The Contracting Parties pledge themselves in such cases to grant extradition in accordance with their laws and treaties in force.

"**Art. 8.** Any Contracting Party may call upon the competent organs of the United Nations to take such action under the UN Charter as they consider appropriate for the prevention and suppression of acts of genocide or any of the other acts enumerated in Art. 3.

"**Art. 9.** Disputes between the Contracting Parties relating to the interpretation, application, or fulfilment of the convention, including those relating to the responsibility of a state for genocide or any of the other acts enumerated in Art. 3, shall be submitted to the International Court of Justice at the request of any of the parties to the dispute."

The convention came into force on Jan. 12, 1951.

Supplementary Convention on the Abolition of Slavery, the Slave Trade, and Institutions and Practices Similar to Slavery

A United Nations convention on slavery, based on the 1951 report of a four-member committee appointed by the Secretary-General in 1949 at the request of the Economic and Social Council, was designed to supplement a League of Nations convention of 1926. (This convention on the abolition of slavery and the slave trade was amended in 1953 and was by Dec. 31, 1979, in force in 93 countries.) The Supplementary Convention on the Abolition of Slavery, the Slave Trade, and Institutions and Practices Similar to Slavery was adopted and opened for signature on Sept. 9, 1956, and has been in force since April 30, 1957. By the end of December 1979, 94 nations had ratified or acceded to it.

The UN convention differs from the earlier one in dealing with a number of institutions and practices similar to slavery in their effect. The institutions and practices outlawed by the 1956 convention are debt bondage, serfdom, marriage by payment or inheritance, and the exploitation of child labour.

The convention advocates the prescribing of minimum ages of marriage and the registration of marriages. It also provides for the punishment of persons participating in the slave trade and of persons guilty of enslaving another person or of inducing another person to give himself or a dependent into slavery. Provision is made for the co-operation of states parties to the convention to give effect to its provisions, and for the communication to the UN Secretary-General of laws, regulations and administrative measures enacted or put into effect to implement the provisions of the convention. The convention applies to all non-self-governing, trust, colonial and other non-metropolitan territories for the international relations of which any state party is responsible.

International Convention on the Elimination of All Forms of Racial Discrimination

On Dec. 21, 1965, the UN General Assembly adopted, by 106 votes to none (with Argentina abstaining) a 25-article convention on the elimination of all forms of racial discrimination. The convention entered into force on Jan. 4, 1969.

The convention defined (in Article 1) racial discrimination as "any distinction, exclusion, restriction, or preference based on race, colour, descent, or national or ethnic origin which has the purpose or effect of nullifying or impairing the recognition, enjoyment, or exercise, on an equal footing, of human rights and fundamental freedoms in the political, economic, social, cultural or any other field of public life".

In order to "eradicate all incitement to, or acts of, such discrimination" the states parties to the convention decided (in Article 4) to take the following measures:

(i) Declare as an offence punishable by law "all dissemination of ideas based on racial superiority or hatred, or incitement to racial discrimination, as well as all acts of violence or incitement to such acts against any group of persons of another colour or ethnic origin".

(ii) Declare illegal and prohibit "organizations, and also all propaganda activities, which promote and incite racial discrimination". Participation in such organizations and activities would constitute an offence punishable by law.

(iii) Not permit public authorities or public institutions, national or local, to promote or incite racial discrimination.

States parties to the convention were to guarantee (under Article 5) the following rights:

(i) The right to equal treatment before all organs administering justice.

(ii) The right to security of person and protection by the state against violence or bodily harm, "whether inflicted by government officials or by any individual, group, or institution".

(iii) Political rights, including the right to vote and to stand for election on the basis of universal and equal suffrage; to take part in the government and in the conduct of public affairs at any level; and to have equal access to the public service.

(iv) Other civil rights, including the right to freedom of movement and residence within the borders of the state; to leave the country and return thereto; to nationality; to marriage and choice of spouse; to own property; to inherit; to freedom of thought, conscience and religion; and to freedom of peaceful assembly and association.

(v) Economic, social and cultural rights, including the right to work; to free choice of employment; to just and favourable conditions of work; to protection against unemployment; to equal pay for equal work; to just and favourable remuneration; to form and join trade unions; to housing; to public health, medical care and social security; to education and training; and to equal participation in cultural activities.

(vi) The right of access to any place or service intended for use by the general public, e.g. transport, hotels, restaurants, cafés, theatres, parks.

The convention also provided (in Article 8) for the establishment of a committee on the elimination of racial discrimination "consisting of 18 experts of high moral standing and acknowledged impartiality" who would (as laid down in Article 9) consider reports submitted to the UN Secretary-General by states parties to the convention on measures which they had taken to give effect to the provisions of the convention. The Committee would have powers to deal with complaints by states parties to the convention and to appoint a conciliation commission to try to settle any disputes (Articles 12-13).

Convention on the Non-Applicability of Statutory Limitations to War Crimes and Crimes against Humanity

A *Convention on the Non-Applicability of Statutory Limitations to War Crimes and Crimes against Humanity*, drafted in the Third (Social, Humanitarian and Cultural) Committee of the UN General Assembly, was adopted by the Assembly on Nov. 26, 1968, by 58 votes to seven (Australia, El Salvador, Honduras, Portugal, South Africa, United Kingdom and United States), with 36 abstentions.

In its preamble, the convention affirmed "the principle that there is no period of limitation for war crimes and crimes against humanity", and in one of its articles the states parties to the convention undertook "to ensure that statutory or other limitations shall not apply to the prosecution and punishment" of such crimes.

The convention entered into force on Nov. 11, 1970, after ratification by 10 countries (all of them communist states).

Declaration of Principles of International Law concerning Friendly Relations and Co-operation among States

The General Assembly adopted without a vote, at its 25th regular session on Oct. 24, 1970, a *Declaration of Principles of International Law concerning Friendly Relations and Co-operation among States in Accordance with the Charter of the United Nations.*

In this declaration the Assembly solemnly proclaimed the following principles: (i) The principle that states shall refrain in their international relations from the threat or use of force against the territorial integrity or political independence of any state, or in any other manner inconsistent with the purposes of the United Nations; (ii) the principle that states shall settle their international disputes by peaceful means in such a manner that international peace and security and justice are not endangered; (iii) the principle concerning the duty not to intervene in matters within the domestic jurisdiction of any state, in accordance with the Charter; (iv) the duty of states to co-operate with one another in accordance with the Charter; (v) the principle of equal rights and self-determination of peoples; (vi) the principle of sovereign equality of states; and (vii) the principle that states shall fulfil in good faith the obligations assumed by them in accordance with the Charter (laying down also that where obligations arising out of international agreements are in conflict with the obligations of UN members under the UN Charter, the obligations under the Charter shall prevail).

It was also stated in the declaration that in their interpretation and application the above principles were interrelated and that each principle should be construed in the context of the other principles, and an appeal was made for strict observance of these "basic principles of international law".

Charter of Economic Rights and Duties of States

The UN General Assembly also adopted, on Dec. 12, 1974 (against the votes of Belgium, Britain, Denmark, the Federal Republic of Germany and the United States) a *Charter of the Economic Rights and Duties of States* (based on a proposal made by Mexico and approved by the UN Conference on Trade and Development—UNCTAD —in 1972).

This Charter read as follows:

Chapter I
Fundamentals of International Economic Relations
"Economic as well as political and other relations among states shall be governed, inter alia, by the following principles:
"(*a*) Sovereignty, territorial integrity and political independence of states;
"(*b*) sovereign equality of all states;
"(*c*) non-aggression;
"(*d*) non-intervention;
"(*e*) mutual and equitable benefit;
"(*f*) peaceful coexistence;
"(*g*) equal rights and self-determination of peoples;

"(*h*) peaceful settlement of disputes;
"(*i*) remedying of injustices which have been brought about by force and which deprive a nation of the natural means necessary for its normal development;
"(*j*) fulfilment in good faith of international obligations;
"(*k*) respect for human rights and fundamental freedoms;
"(*l*) no attempt to seek hegemony and spheres of influence;
"(*m*) promotion of international social justice;
"(*n*) international co-operation for development;
"(*o*) free access to and from the sea by land-locked countries within the framework of the above principles.

Chapter II
Economic Rights and Duties of States
"**Art. 1.** Every state has the sovereign and inalienable right to choose its economic system as well as its political, social and cultural systems in accordance with the will of its people, without outside interference, coercion or threat in any form whatsoever.

"**Art. 2.** (1) Every state has and shall freely exercise full permanent sovereignty, including possession, use and disposal, over all its wealth, natural resources and economic activities.

"(2) Each state has the right:
"(*a*) To regulate and exercise authority over foreign investment within its national jurisdiction in accordance with its laws and regulations and in conformity with its national objectives and priorities. No state shall be compelled to grant preferential treatment to foreign investment;

"(*b*) to regulate and supervise the activities of transnational corporations within its national jurisdiction and take measures to ensure that such activities comply with its laws, rules and regulations and conform with its economic and social policies. Transnational corporations shall not intervene in the internal affairs of a host state. Every state should, with full regard for its sovereign rights, co-operate with other states in the exercise of the right set forth in this subparagraph;

"(*c*) to nationalize, expropriate or transfer ownership of foreign property, in which case appropriate compensation should be paid by the state adopting such measures, taking into account its relevant laws and regulations and all circumstances that the state considers pertinent. In any case where the question of compensation gives rise to a controversy, it shall be settled under the domestic law of the nationalizing state and by its tribunals, unless it is freely and mutually agreed by all states concerned that other peaceful means be sought on the basis of the sovereign equality of states and in accordance with the principle of the choice of means.

"**Art. 3.** In the exploitation of natural resources shared by two or more countries, each state must co-operate on the basis of a system of information and prior consultations in order to achieve optimum use of such resources without causing damage to the legitimate interest of others.

"**Art. 4.** Every state has the right to engage in international trade and other forms of economic co-operation irrespective of any differences in political, economic and social systems. No state shall be subjected to discrimination of any kind based solely on such differences. In the pursuit of international trade and other forms of economic co-operation, every state is free to choose the forms of organization of its foreign economic relations and to enter into bilateral and multilateral arrangements consistent with its international obligations and with the needs of international economic co-operation.

"**Art. 5.** All states have the right to associate in organizations of primary commodity producers in order to develop their national economies to achieve stable financing for their development, and in pursuance of their aims assisting in the promotion of sustained growth of the world economy, in particular accelerating the development of developing countries. Correspondingly all states have the duty to respect that right by refraining from applying economic and political measures that would limit it.

"**Art. 6.** It is the duty of states to contribute to the development of international trade of goods particularly by means of arrangements and by the conclusion of long-term multilateral commodity agreements, where appropriate, and taking into account the interests of producers and consumers. All states share the responsibility to promote the regular flow and access of all commercial goods traded at stable, remunerative and equitable prices, thus contributing to the equitable development of the world economy, taking into account, in particular, the interests of developing countries.

"**Art. 7.** Every state has the primary responsibility to promote the economic, social and cultural development of its people. To this end, each state has the right and the responsibility to choose its means and goals of development, fully to mobilize and use its resources, to implement progressive economic and social reforms and to ensure the full participation of its people in the process and benefits of development. All states have the duty, individually and collectively, to co-operate in order to eliminate obstacles that hinder such mobilization and use.

"**Art. 8.** States should co-operate in facilitating more rational and equitable international economic relations and in encouraging structural changes in the context of a balanced world economy in harmony with the needs and interests of all countries, especially developing countries, and should take appropriate measures to this end.

"**Art. 9.** All states have the responsibility to co-operate in the economic, social, cultural, scientific and technological fields for the promotion of economic and social progress throughout the world, especially that of the developing countries.

"**Art. 10.** All states are judicially equal and, as equal members of the international community, have the right to participate fully and effectively in the international decision-making process in the solution of world economic, financial and monetary problems, inter alia, through the appropriate international organizations in accordance with their existing and evolving rules, and to share equitably in the benefits resulting therefrom.

"**Art. 11.** All states should co-operate to strengthen and continuously improve the efficiency of international organizations in implementing measures to stimulate the general economic progress of all countries, particularly of developing countries, and therefore should co-operate to adapt them, when appropriate, to the changing needs of international economic co-operation.

"**Art. 12.** (1) States have the right, in agreement with the parties concerned, to participate in sub-regional, regional and interregional co-operation in the pursuit of their economic and social development. All states engaged in such co-operation have the duty to ensure that the policies of those groupings to which they belong correspond to the provisions of the Charter and are outward-looking, consistent with their international obligations and with the needs of international economic co-operation, and have full regard for the legitimate interests of third countries, especially developing countries.

"(2) In the case of groupings to which the states concerned have transferred or may transfer certain competences as regards matters that come within the scope of this Charter, its provisions shall also apply to those groupings, in regard to such matters, consistent with the responsibilities of such states as members of such groupings. Those states shall co-operate in the observance by the groupings of the provisions of this Charter.

"**Art. 13.** (1) Every state has the right to benefit from the advances and developments in science and technology for the acceleration of its economic and social development.

"(2) All states should promote international scientific and technological co-operation and the transfer of technology with proper regard for all legitimate interests including, inter alia, the rights and duties of holders, suppliers and recipients of technology. In particular, all states should facilitate: the access of developing countries to the achievements of modern science and technology, the transfer of technology and the creation of indigenous technology for the benefit of the developing countries in forms and in accordance with procedures which are suited to their economies and their needs.

"(3) Accordingly, developed countries should co-operate with the developing countries in the establishment, strengthening and development of their scientific and technological infrastructures and their scientific research and technological activities so as to help to expand and transform the economies of developing countries.

"(4) All states should co-operate in exploring with a view to evolving further internationally accepted guidelines or regulations for the transfer of technology taking fully into account the interests of developing countries.

"**Art. 14.** Every state has the duty to co-operate in promoting a steady and increasing expansion and liberalization of world trade and an improvement in the welfare and living standards of all peoples, in particular those of developing countries. Accordingly, all states should co-operate, inter alia, towards the progressive dismantling of obstacles to trade and the improvement of the international framework for the conduct of world trade and, to those ends, co-ordinated efforts shall be made to solve in an equitable way the trade problems of all countries, taking into account the specific trade problems of the developing countries. In this connexion, states shall take measures aimed at securing additional benefits for the international trade of developing countries so as to achieve a substantial increase in their foreign exchange earnings, the diversification of their exports, the acceleration of the rate of growth of their trade, taking into account their development needs, an improvement in the possibilities for these countries to participate in the expansion of world trade and a balance more favourable to developing countries in the sharing of the advantages resulting from this expansion, through, in the largest possible measure, a substantial improvement in the conditions of access for the products of interest to the developing countries and, wherever appropriate, measures designed to attain stable, equitable and remunerative prices for primary products.

"**Art. 15.** All states have the duty to promote the achievement of general and complete disarmament under effective international control and to utilize the resources freed by effective disarmament measures for the economic and social development of countries, allocating a substantial portion of such resources as additional means for the development needs of developing countries.

"**Art. 16.** (1) It is the right and duty of all states, individually and collectively, to eliminate colonialism, apartheid, racial discrimination, neo-colonialism and all forms of foreign aggression, occupation and domination, and the economic and social consequences thereof, as a prerequisite for development. States which practise such coercive policies are economically responsible to the countries, territories and peoples affected for the restitution and full compensation for the exploitation and depletion of, and damages to, the natural and all other resources of those countries, territories and peoples. It is the duty of all states to extend assistance to them.

"(2) No state has the right to promote or encourage investments that may constitute an obstacle to the liberation of a territory occupied by force.

"**Art. 17.** International co-operation for development is the shared goal and common duty of all states. Every state should co-operate with the efforts of developing countries to accelerate their economic and social development by providing favourable external conditions and by extending active assistance to them, consistent with their development needs and objectives, with strict respect for the sovereign equality of states and free of any conditions derogating from their sovereignty.

"**Art. 18.** Developed countries should extend, improve and enlarge the system of generalized, non-reciprocal and non-discriminatory tariff preferences to the developing countries consistent with the relevant agreed conclusions and relevant decisions as adopted on this subject, in the framework of the competent international organizations. Developed countries should also give serious consideration to the adoption of other differential measures, in areas where this is feasible and appropriate and in ways which will provide special and more favourable treatment, in order to meet trade and development needs of the developing countries. In the conduct of international economic relations the developed countries should endeavour to avoid measures having a negative effect on the development of the national economies of the developing countries, as promoted by generalized tariff preferences and other generally agreed differential measures in their favour.

"**Art. 19.** With a view to accelerating the economic growth of developing countries and bridging the economic gap between developed and developing countries, developed countries should grant generalized preferential, non-reciprocal and non-discriminatory treatment to developing countries in those fields of international economic co-operation where it may be feasible.

"**Art. 20.** Developing countries should, in their efforts to increase their overall trade, give due attention to the possibility of expanding their trade with socialist countries, by granting to these countries conditions for trade not inferior to those granted normally to the developed market economy countries.

"**Art. 21.** Developing countries should endeavour to promote the expansion of their mutual trade and to this end may, in accordance with the existing and evolving provisions and procedures of international agreements where applicable, grant trade preferences to other developing countries without being obliged to extend such preferences to developed countries, provided these arrangements do not constitute an impediment to general trade liberalization and expansion.

"**Art. 22.** (1) All states should respond to the generally recognized or mutually agreed development needs and objectives of developing countries by promoting increased net flows of real resources to the developing countries from all sources, taking into account any obligations and commitments undertaken by the states concerned, in order to reinforce the efforts of developing countries to accelerate their economic and social development.

"(2) In this context, consistent with the aims and objectives mentioned above and taking into account any obligations and commitments undertaken in this regard, it should be their endeavour to increase the net amount of financial flows from official sources to developing countries and to improve the terms and conditions.

"(3) The flow of development assistance resources should include economic and technical assistance.

"**Art. 23.** To enhance the effective mobilization of their own resources, the developing countries should strengthen their economic co-operation and expand their mutual trade so as to accelerate their economic and social development. All countries, especially developed countries, individually as well as through the competent international organizations of which they are members, should provide appropriate and effective support and co-operation.

"**Art. 24.** All states have the duty to conduct their mutual economic relations in a manner which takes into account the interests of other countries. In particular, all states should avoid prejudicing the interests of developing countries.

"**Art. 25.** In furtherance of world economic development, the international community, especially its developed members, shall pay special attention to the particular needs and problems of the least developed among the developing countries, of land-locked developing countries and also island developing countries, with a view to helping them to overcome their particular difficulties and thus contribute to their economic and social development.

"**Art. 26.** All states have the duty to coexist in tolerance and live together in peace, irrespective of differences in political, economic, social and cultural systems, and to facilitate trade between states having different economic and social systems. International trade should be conducted without prejudice to generalized non-discriminatory and non-reciprocal preferences in favour of developing countries, on the basis of mutual advantage, equitable benefits and the exchange of most-favoured-nation treatment.

"**Art. 27.** (1) Every state has the right to fully enjoy the benefits of world invisible trade and to engage in the expansion of such trade.

"(2) World invisible trade, based on efficiency and mutual and equitable benefit, furthering the expansion of the world economy, is the common goal of all states. The role of developing countries in world invisible trade should be enhanced and strengthened consistent with the above objectives, particular attention being paid to the special needs of developing countries.

"(3) All states should co-operate with developing

countries in their endeavours to increase their capacity to earn foreign exchange from invisible transactions, in accordance with the potential and needs of each developing country, and consistent with the objectives mentioned above.

"**Art. 28.** All states have the duty to co-operate in achieving adjustments in the prices of exports of developing countries in relation to prices of their imports so as to promote just and equitable terms of trade for them, in a manner which is remunerative for producers and equitable for producers and consumers.

Chapter III
Common Responsibilities towards the International Community
"**Art. 29.** The seabed and ocean floor and the sub-soil thereof, beyond the limits of national jurisdiction, as well as the resources of the area, are the common heritage of mankind. On the basis of the principles adopted by the General Assembly in Resolution 2749 (XXV) of Dec. 17, 1970, all states shall ensure that the exploration of the area and exploitation of its resources are carried out exclusively for peaceful purposes and that the benefits derived therefrom are shared equitably by all states, taking into account the particular interests and needs of developing countries; an international regime applying to the area and its resources and including appropriate international machinery to give effect to its provisions shall be established by an international treaty of a universal character, generally agreed upon.

"**Art. 30.** The protection, preservation and the enhancement of the environment for the present and future generations is the responsibility of all states. All states shall endeavour to establish their own environment and developmental policies in conformity with such responsibility. The environmental policies of all states should enhance [and] not adversely affect the present and future development potential of developing countries. All states have the responsibility to ensure that activities within their jurisdiction or control do not cause damage to the environment of other states or of areas beyond the limits of national jurisdiction. All states should co-operate in evolving international norms and regulations in the fields of the environment.

Chapter IV
Final Provisions
"**Art. 31.** All states have the duty to contribute to the balanced expansion of the world economy, taking duly into account the close interrelationship between the well-being of the developed countries and the growth and development of the developing countries and that the prosperity of the international community as a whole depends upon the prosperity of its constituent parts.

"**Art. 32.** No state may use or encourage the use of economic, political or any other type of measures to coerce another state in order to obtain from it the subordination of the exercise of its sovereign rights.

"**Art. 33.** (1) Nothing in the present Charter shall be construed as impairing or derogating from the provisions of the Charter of the United Nations or actions taken in pursuance thereof.

(2) In their interpretation and application, the provisions of the present Charter are interrelated and each provision should be construed in the context of the other provisions.

"**Art. 34.** An item on the Charter of Economic

Rights and Duties of States shall be inscribed on the agenda of the General Assembly at its thirtieth session, and thereafter on the agenda of every fifth session. In this way a systematic and comprehensive consideration of the implementation of the Charter, covering both progress achieved and any improvements and additions which might become necessary, would be carried out and appropriate measures recommended. Such consideration should take into account the evolution of all the economic, social, legal and other factors related to the principles upon which the present Charter is based and on its purpose."

UN Definition of Aggression

A definition of aggression designed to command general acceptance by the international community was approved without a vote by the UN General Assembly on Dec. 14, 1974.

Such a definition had been unsuccessfully attempted on several previous occasions— at the 1815 Congress of Vienna, at the 1899 peace conference in The Hague, at the 1919 Versailles peace conference, and by the League of Nations between World Wars I and II—while at the 1945 San Francisco conference (which drafted the UN Charter) it was decided not to attempt to define aggression. The definition was approved without a vote on April 12, 1974, by a 35-member special commission which had been drafting it for the previous six years.

The text of the definition read as follows:

"**Art. 1.** Aggression is the use of armed force by a state against the sovereignty, territorial integrity or political independence of another state or in any other manner inconsistent with the Charter of the United Nations, as set out in this definition.

"*Explanatory Notes.* In this definition the term 'state'

"(*a*) is used without prejudice to questions of recognition or to whether a state is a member of the United Nations, and

"(*b*) includes the concept of a 'group of states' where appropriate.

"**Art. 2.** The first use of armed force by a state in contravention of the Charter shall constitute prima facie evidence of an act of aggression, although the Security Council may, in conformity with the Charter, conclude that a determination that an act of aggression has been committed would not be justified in the light of other relevant circumstances, including the fact that the acts concerned or their consequences are not of sufficient gravity.

"**Art. 3.** Any of the following acts, regardless of a declaration of war, shall, subject to and in accordance with the provisions of Article 2, qualify as an act of aggression:

"(*a*) The invasion or attack by the armed forces of a state of the territory of another state, or any military occupation, however temporary, resulting from such invasion or attack, or any annexation by the use of force of the territory of another state or part thereof;

"(*b*) bombardment by the armed forces of a state against the territory of another state or the use of any weapon by a state against the territory of another state;

"(*c*) the blockade of the ports or coasts of a state by the armed forces of another state;

"(*d*) an attack by the armed forces of a state on the land, sea or air forces, marine and air fleets of another state;

"(*e*) the use of armed forces of one state, which are within the territory of another state with the agreement of the receiving state, in contravention of the conditions provided for in the agreement or any extension of their presence in such territory beyond the termination of the agreement;

"(*f*) the action of a state in allowing its territory, which it has placed at the disposal of another state, to be used by that other state for perpetrating an act of aggression against a third state;

"(*g*) the sending by or on behalf of a state of armed bands, groups, irregulars or mercenaries, which carry out acts of armed force against another state of such gravity as to amount to the acts listed above, or its substantial involvement therein.

"**Art. 4.** The acts enumerated above are not exhaustive and the Security Council may determine that other acts constitute aggression under the provisions of the Charter.

"**Art. 5.** No consideration of whatever nature, whether political, economic, military or otherwise, may serve as a justification for aggression.

"A war of aggression is a crime against international peace. Aggression gives rise to international responsibility.

"No territorial acquisition or special advantage resulting from aggression are or shall be recognized as lawful.

"**Art. 6.** Nothing in this definition shall be construed as in any way enlarging or diminishing the scope of the Charter, including its provisions concerning cases in which the use of force is lawful.

"**Art. 7.** Nothing in this definition, and in particular Article 3, could in any way prejudice the right to self-determination, freedom and independence, as derived from the Charter, of peoples forcibly deprived of that right and referred to in the Declaration on Principles of International Law concerning Friendly Relations and Co-operation among States in accordance with the Charter of the United Nations, particularly peoples under colonial and racist regimes or other forms of alien domination; nor the right of these peoples to struggle to that end and to seek and receive support, in accordance with the principles of the Charter and in conformity with the above-mentioned declaration.

"**Art. 8.** In their interpretation and application the above provisions are inter-related and each provision should be construed in the context of the other provisions.''

Convention against the Taking of Hostages

An *International Convention against the Taking of Hostages* was adopted by consensus by the UN General Assembly on Dec. 17, 1979.

The convention contained a definition of the offence of hostage-taking; required states to make it a punishable offence; and gave procedures for extradition where relevant. In the last-named context it was stated (in Article 9) that states should not grant requests for

extradition if there were "substantial grounds for believing that the alleged offender would be punished on account of his race, religion, nationality, ethnic origin or political opinion" (this article being opposed by the Soviet Union).

The convention was to become effective after ratification by 22 states.

Conventions on the Status of Women

Political Rights of Women. A convention on the political rights of women, adopted by the UN General Assembly on March 31, 1953, came into force for the states parties to it on July 7, 1954, and by Dec. 31, 1979, it had been acceded to by a total of 87 states.

Nationality of Married Women. Based on the provisions of Art. 15 of the UN Declaration on Human Rights, an international convention on the nationality of married women was adopted by the UN General Assembly on Feb. 20, 1957, by 48 votes to two (Egypt and Syria) with 24 abstentions (including the United States). It laid down inter alia that neither the contracting nor the dissolution of a marriage between a national and an alien in the contracting states should automatically affect the nationality of the woman. By Dec. 31, 1979, the contracting states numbered 55 (though not including the United States).

Elimination of Discrimination against Women. The UN General Assembly on Nov. 7, 1967, adopted by 111 votes to nil, with 11 countries absent, a *Declaration on the Elimination of Discrimination against Women.*

The declaration proclaimed inter alia that women should have equal rights with men in the political sphere and in the field of civil law, in economic and social life and in education at all levels. It called for the abolition of all laws and customs which had the effect of discriminating against women and of all practices based on the idea of the inferiority of women; for the prohibition of child marriage and of betrothal of girls before puberty; and for measures to combat traffic in women and exploitation of prostitution. Among rights enumerated were those of a wife to retain her nationality if married to an alien; to have free choice of a husband; and to enjoy equality of treatment with men in respect of work of equal value.

Subsequently, a convention on the elimination of all forms of discrimination against women was adopted by the UN General Assembly on Dec. 18, 1979, by 130 votes to none with 10 abstentions (Bangladesh, Brazil, Comoros, Haiti, Mali, Mauritania, Mexico, Morocco, Saudi Arabia and Senegal). All states parties to the convention would commit themselves to measures to eliminate political, social, economic, legal and cultural discrimination against women.

After its entry into force a committee of members elected by the states parties would be set up to monitor progress in the implementation of the convention. It would come into force (for the states parties to it) following its ratification by the required minimum of 20 states.

Conventions on the Law of the Sea

A UN Conference on the Law of the Sea held in Geneva from Feb. 24 to April 28, 1958, adopted, after preparation by the International Law Commission, four conventions and a protocol on compulsory settlement of disputes, but reached no agreement on the maximum width of territorial waters and the maximum limits of exclusive fishing rights.

(a) The *Convention on the Territorial Sea and the Contiguous Zone* defined the "territorial sea"; laid down the right of "innocent passage" through the territorial sea; limited the "contiguous zone" of the high seas to an area up to 12 miles from the shore baselines; and authorized the coastal state to prevent infringements of its customs, fiscal, immigration or sanitary regulations committed within its territory or territorial sea and to punish such infringements.

(b) The *Convention on the High Seas* proclaimed the freedom of the high seas (including the freedom to fly over them) and the right of land-locked states to have free access to the sea; granted each state the right to determine conditions for the grant of its nationality to ships; gave immunity from the jurisdiction of any state other than the flag state to warships and other non-commercial government vessels on the high seas; and enjoined states to ensure safety at sea, to prevent slave trade and piracy and to prevent pollution of the sea.

(c) The *Convention on Fishing and Conservation of the Living Resources of the High Seas* provided inter alia for agreement on conservation measures and for arbitration procedure in the event of disputes.

(d) The *Convention on the Continental Shelf* gave coastal states exclusive rights to exploit universal and other non-living resources as well as "sedentary" living organisms (e.g. oysters) of the continental shelf, i.e. "the seabed and subsoil of the submarine areas adjacent to the coast, but outside the area of the territorial sea, up to the point where the waters above are 200 metres deep, or beyond that limit if the depth allows exploitation of natural resources". The boundary of the coastal shelf adjacent to any state lying opposite another state on the same shelf was to be determined by mutual agreement or, failing such agreement, would be the median line.

(e) The *Protocol on Settlement of Disputes* provided for compulsory jurisdiction of the International Court of Justice in disputes arising out of the interpretation or application of any Convention on the Law of the Sea (except as covered by the arbitration procedure under (c) above), as well as for arbitration or conciliation where both parties agreed to this procedure instead of resorting to the International Court of Justice.

A second UN Conference on the Law of the Sea, held in Geneva between March 17 and April 26, 1960, and dealing with the width of the territorial sea and the breadth of a "contiguous zone" in which coastal states would exercise exclusive fishing rights, failed to reach agreement on these subjects.

Sessions of a third UN Conference on the Law of the Sea were held in New York on Dec. 3-15, 1973, in Caracas from June 20 to Aug. 29, 1974, and in Geneva from March 7 to May 9, 1975, when provisional agreement was reached (i) on the establishment of an international seabed authority which would oversee the exploitation of ocean floor resources beyond national jurisdiction (i.e. in an area described as "the common heritage of mankind" in a "declaration on principles concerning the seabed, the ocean floor and the subsoil thereof" adopted by the UN General Assembly in 1970) and (ii) on a territorial limit of 12 nautical miles and a 200-mile economic zone in which coastal states would control both fisheries and mineral resources.

Further sessions of the third conference were held in New York from March 15 to May 7, 1976; from Aug. 2 to Sept. 17, 1976; and from May 23 to July 15, 1977 (whereafter an "informal composite negotiating text" was published, containing provisions for an international regime for the conduct of deep seabed mining—which were immediately rejected as "fundamentally unacceptable" by the United States); in Geneva from March 28 to May 19, 1978; in New York from Aug. 21 to Sept. 15, 1978; in Geneva from March 19 to April 27, 1979; in New York from July 19 to Aug. 24, 1979; in New York from Feb. 27 to April 3, 1980; and in Geneva from July 28 to Aug. 29, 1980.

Conventions on Diplomatic and Consular Relations

Vienna Convention on Diplomatic Relations. In terms of a resolution adopted by the UN General Assembly on Dec. 7, 1959, a conference was held in Vienna on April 2-14, 1961, leading to the approval of a convention on diplomatic relations, issued on April 18, 1961. The convention first came into force on April 24, 1964, and by Dec. 31, 1979, it was in force for 131 countries.

The convention contained definitions concerning the personnel and buildings of diplomatic missions, the tasks of such missions, procedures for their establishment, the rights and duties of their personnel, the right of the host country to declare any member of such a mission persona non grata without stating any reason, the conditions of immunity, and guaranteed uncontrolled communication for official purposes.

Vienna Convention on Consular Relations. A similar convention on consular relations was adopted at a Vienna conference on April 4, 1963; it first entered into force on March 19, 1967, and by Dec. 31, 1979, it was in force for 95 countries.

Law of Treaties Convention and Declarations

On the basis of 75 draft articles prepared by the International Law Commission, a UN convention on the law of treaties comprising 85 articles was approved by a UN conference on the law of treaties in Vienna on May 22, 1969, and was opened for signature on the following day.

The convention codified many fundamental principles of the customary international law of treaties concluded between states, including the universally-recognized principle of *pacta sunt servanda,* formulated as follows: "Every treaty in force is binding upon the parties to it and must be performed by them in good faith." (Article 26.)

The convention also laid down the pre-eminence of peremptory rules of international law (*jus cogens*) as follows: "A treaty is void if, at the time of its conclusion, it conflicts with a peremptory norm of general international law. For the purposes of the present convention, a peremptory norm of general international law is a norm accepted and recognized by the international community of states as a norm from which no derogation is permitted and which can be modified only by a subsequent norm of general international law having the same character." (Article 53.)

Procedures were provided for judicial settlement, arbitration and conciliation either by way of applica-tion to the International Court of Justice or by setting in motion the procedure specified in an annex. (Article 66.)

The convention was to enter into force on the 30th day after the deposition (with the UN Secretary-General) of the 35th ratification or accession document, while for countries ratifying it or acceding to it afterwards it would come into force on the 30th day after the deposition of their ratification or deposition document. (Article 84.)

The convention was adopted by 79 votes to one (France, which objected to Article 53) with 19 abstentions.

The conference also approved several declarations and resolutions, including a declaration on the prohibition of military, political or economic coercion in the conclusion of treaties in violation of the principles of the sovereign equality of states and freedom of consent.

A further UN conference held in Vienna in August 1978 approved a convention establishing international legal standards regulating the preservation in force or the termination of international treaties in the case of the formation of new states as a result of decolonization or of the unification or division of states, and also asserting the inviolability of existing frontiers.

Membership of the United Nations and Related Agencies

The table on the following pages lists the members of the United Nations, its specialized agencies and the International Atomic Energy Agency, and also the contracting parties to the General Agreement on Tariffs and Trade, as at Jan. 1, 1981. (☆ = member; ★ = associate member.)

The complete names of the organizations included in this table are:

UN	United Nations
ILO	International Labour Organization
FAO	Food and Agriculture Organization of the United Nations
UNESCO	United Nations Educational, Scientific and Cultural Organization
WHO	World Health Organization
IBRD	International Bank for Reconstruction and Development (World Bank)
IFC	International Finance Corporation
IDA	International Development Association
IMF	International Monetary Fund
ICAO	International Civil Aviation Organization
UPU	Universal Postal Union
ITU	International Telecommunication Union
WMO	World Meteorological Organization
IMCO	Inter-Governmental Maritime Consultative Organization
WIPO	World Intellectual Property Organization
IFAD	International Fund for Agricultural Development
IAEA	International Atomic Energy Agency
GATT	General Agreement on Tariffs and Trade

Countries which have not applied for UN membership are Andorra, Liechtenstein, Monaco, San Marino, Switzerland and the Vatican. Of these countries, Andorra is, in foreign relations, represented by France, and Liechtenstein by Switzerland.

Switzerland has refrained from applying for UN membership because it regards any sanctions imposed under Chapter VII of the UN Charter (such as were imposed against Rhodesia on Dec. 16, 1966) as being in conflict with its status of neutrality.

The question of UN membership of the People's Republic of China was the subject of a vote at almost every session of the UN General Assembly in the two decades after 1950. The United States announced on Jan. 21, 1951, that it recognized the Nationalist Chinese Government in Taiwan (Formosa) as the only legal representative of China, and until 1960 the USA succeeded in having discussion of the Chinese membership question deferred. From 1961 onwards the question of the admission of People's Republic was, at the instance of the United States, judged to be an "important" one to be decided upon only by a two-thirds majority in accordance with the UN Charter. It was not until 1970 that an Albanian move to give the People's Republic of China a seat in the United Nations obtained a simple majority in the General Assembly. On Oct. 15, 1971, however, the General Assembly adopted by 76 votes to 35, with 17 abstentions and three delegations absent, an Albanian resolution appointing the People's Republic of China to the Chinese seat in all its functions and to exclude the Taiwan Government, as having usurped these rights, from the organization. (The Government of Taiwan was thus the first to be expelled from the United Nations.) The People's Republic subsequently took its seat in all UN organs, including that of a permanent member of the Security Council, and in most of the specialized agencies, with the result that Taiwan is no longer represented in the UN system.

Both the Democratic People's Republic of Korea (North Korea) and the Republic of Korea (South Korea) first applied for UN membership in 1949, when the North Korean application was rejected by the UN Security Council and the South Korean application was vetoed by the Soviet Union, as were renewed applications by South Korea in 1955, 1957 and 1958. A Soviet proposal for the simultaneous admission to the United Nations of both Koreas was rejected by the Security Council in 1957 and 1958. On June 23, 1973, South Korea announced that it had abandoned its previous opposition to simultaneous entry of both Koreas, whereas North Korea proposed that the two states should enter the United Nations as a single confederal republic. On July 29, 1975, South Korea made a further application, which North Korea denounced as "aimed at perpetuating the division of the nation" and which failed to obtain the necessary nine votes to enable it to be placed on the Security Council's agenda (with the People's Republic of China, the Soviet Union, Byelorussia, Mauritania, Tanzania and Iraq opposing the proposal and Cameroon and Guyana abstaining from voting).

Country	UN	ILO	FAO	UNESCO	WHO	IBRD	IFC	IDA	IMF	ICAO	UPU	ITU	WMO	IMCO	WIPO	IFAD	IAEA	GATT
Afghanistan	☆	☆	☆	☆	☆	☆	☆	☆	☆	☆	☆	☆	☆	—	—	☆	☆	—
Albania	☆	—	☆	☆	☆	—	—	—	—	☆	☆	☆	—	—	—	—	☆	—
Algeria	☆	☆	☆	☆	☆	☆	—	☆	☆	☆	☆	☆	☆	☆	☆	☆	☆	—
Angola	☆	☆	☆	☆	☆	—	—	—	—	☆	☆	☆	☆	☆	—	☆	—	—
Argentina	☆	☆	☆	☆	☆	☆	☆	☆	☆	☆	☆	☆	☆	☆	☆	—	☆	☆
Australia	☆	☆	☆	☆	☆	☆	☆	☆	☆	☆	☆	☆	☆	☆	☆	☆	☆	☆
Austria	☆	☆	☆	☆	☆	☆	☆	☆	☆	☆	☆	☆	☆	☆	☆	☆	☆	☆
Bahamas	☆	☆	☆	—	☆	☆	—	—	☆	☆	☆	☆	☆	☆	—	—	—	—
Bahrain	☆	☆	☆	☆	☆	☆	—	—	☆	☆	☆	☆	—	☆	—	—	—	—
Bangladesh	☆	☆	☆	☆	☆	☆	☆	☆	☆	☆	☆	☆	☆	☆	—	☆	☆	☆
Barbados	☆	☆	☆	☆	☆	☆	—	—	☆	☆	☆	☆	☆	☆	☆	—	—	☆
Belgium	☆	☆	☆	☆	☆	☆	☆	☆	☆	☆	☆	☆	☆	☆	☆	☆	☆	☆
Benin	☆	☆	☆	☆	☆	☆	—	☆	☆	☆	☆	☆	☆	☆	☆	☆	—	☆
Bhutan	☆	—	—	—	—	—	—	—	—	—	☆	—	—	—	—	—	☆	—
Bolivia	☆	☆	☆	☆	☆	☆	☆	☆	☆	☆	☆	☆	☆	—	—	☆	☆	—
Botswana	☆	☆	☆	☆	☆	☆	☆	☆	☆	☆	☆	☆	☆	—	—	☆	—	—
Brazil	☆	☆	☆	☆	☆	☆	☆	☆	☆	☆	☆	☆	☆	☆	☆	☆	☆	☆
Bulgaria	☆	☆	☆	☆	☆	—	—	—	—	☆	☆	☆	☆	☆	☆	—	☆	—
Burma	☆	☆	☆	☆	☆	☆	☆	☆	☆	☆	☆	☆	☆	—	—	—	☆	☆
Burundi	☆	☆	☆	☆	☆	☆	☆	☆	☆	☆	☆	☆	☆	—	☆	☆	—	☆
Byelorussia	☆	☆	—	☆	☆	—	—	—	—	☆	☆	☆	—	☆	—	☆	—	☆
Cameroon	☆	☆	☆	☆	☆	☆	☆	☆	☆	☆	☆	☆	☆	☆	☆	☆	☆	☆
Canada	☆	☆	☆	☆	☆	☆	☆	☆	☆	☆	☆	☆	☆	☆	☆	☆	☆	☆
Cape Verde	☆	☆	☆	☆	☆	☆	—	☆	☆	☆	☆	☆	☆	☆	—	☆	—	—
Central African Republic	☆	☆	☆	☆	☆	☆	—	☆	☆	☆	☆	☆	☆	—	☆	☆	—	☆

50

Country	UN	ILO	FAO	UNESCO	WHO	IBRD	IFC	IDA	IMF	ICAO	UPU	ITU	WMO	IMCO	WIPO	IFAD	IAEA	GATT
Chad	☆	☆	☆	☆	☆	☆	—	☆	☆	☆	☆	☆	☆	—	☆	☆	—	☆
Chile	☆	☆	☆	☆	☆	☆	☆	☆	☆	☆	☆	☆	☆	☆	☆	☆	—	☆
China	☆	☆	☆	☆	☆	☆	☆	☆	☆	☆	☆	☆	☆	—	☆	—	—	—
Colombia	☆	☆	☆	☆	☆	☆	☆	☆	☆	☆	☆	☆	☆	☆	—	☆	☆	☆
Comoros	☆	☆	☆	☆	☆	—	☆	☆	—	☆	☆	☆	—	—	—	☆	—	—
Congo	☆	☆	☆	☆	☆	—	☆	☆	☆	☆	☆	☆	☆	☆	☆	☆	—	☆
Costa Rica	☆	☆	☆	☆	☆	☆	☆	☆	☆	☆	☆	☆	—	—	☆	☆	☆	—
Cuba	☆	☆	☆	☆	☆	—	—	—	—	☆	☆	☆	☆	☆	☆	☆	☆	☆
Cyprus	☆	☆	☆	☆	☆	☆	☆	☆	☆	☆	☆	☆	☆	☆	—	☆	☆	☆
Czechoslovakia	☆	☆	☆	☆	☆	—	—	—	—	☆	☆	☆	☆	☆	☆	—	☆	☆
Denmark	☆	☆	☆	☆	☆	☆	☆	☆	☆	☆	☆	☆	☆	☆	☆	☆	☆	☆
Djibouti	☆	☆	☆	—	☆	—	—	—	☆	☆	☆	☆	☆	☆	—	☆	—	—
Dominica	☆	—	☆	☆	☆	☆	☆	☆	☆	—	—	—	—	☆	—	☆	—	—
Dominican Republic	☆	☆	☆	☆	☆	☆	☆	☆	☆	☆	☆	☆	☆	☆	—	☆	☆	☆
Ecuador	☆	☆	☆	☆	☆	☆	☆	☆	☆	☆	☆	☆	☆	—	☆	☆	☆	—
Egypt	☆	☆	☆	☆	☆	☆	☆	☆	☆	☆	☆	☆	☆	☆	☆	☆	☆	☆
El Salvador	☆	☆	☆	☆	☆	☆	☆	☆	☆	☆	☆	☆	☆	—	☆	☆	☆	—
Equatorial Guinea	☆	—	—	☆	☆	☆	—	☆	☆	☆	☆	☆	—	☆	—	☆	—	—
Ethiopia	☆	☆	—	☆	☆	☆	☆	☆	☆	☆	☆	☆	☆	☆	—	☆	☆	—
Fiji	☆	☆	☆	—	☆	☆	☆	☆	☆	☆	☆	—	—	☆	☆	—	—	—
Finland	☆	☆	☆	☆	☆	☆	☆	☆	☆	☆	☆	☆	☆	☆	☆	☆	☆	☆
France	☆	☆	☆	☆	☆	☆	☆	☆	☆	☆	☆	☆	☆	☆	☆	☆	☆	☆
Gabon	☆	☆	☆	☆	☆	☆	☆	☆	☆	☆	☆	☆	☆	☆	☆	☆	☆	☆
The Gambia	☆	—	☆	☆	☆	☆	—	☆	☆	☆	☆	☆	☆	☆	—	☆	—	☆
German Democratic Republic	☆	☆	—	☆	☆	—	—	—	—	—	☆	☆	☆	☆	☆	—	☆	—
Germany, Federal Republic of	☆	☆	☆	☆	☆	☆	☆	☆	☆	☆	☆	☆	☆	☆	☆	☆	☆	☆
Ghana	☆	☆	☆	☆	☆	☆	☆	☆	☆	☆	☆	☆	☆	☆	☆	☆	☆	☆
Greece	☆	☆	☆	☆	☆	☆	☆	☆	☆	☆	☆	☆	☆	☆	☆	☆	☆	☆
Grenada	☆	☆	☆	☆	☆	☆	☆	☆	☆	—	☆	—	—	—	—	☆	—	—
Guatemala	☆	☆	☆	☆	☆	☆	☆	☆	☆	☆	☆	☆	—	—	☆	☆	☆	—
Guinea	☆	☆	☆	☆	☆	—	☆	☆	☆	☆	☆	☆	☆	—	☆	☆	—	—
Guinea-Bissau	☆	☆	☆	☆	☆	☆	☆	☆	☆	☆	☆	☆	☆	—	☆	—	—	—
Guyana	☆	☆	☆	☆	☆	☆	☆	☆	☆	☆	☆	☆	☆	☆	—	☆	—	☆
Haiti	☆	☆	☆	☆	☆	☆	☆	☆	☆	☆	☆	☆	☆	★	—	☆	☆	☆
Holy See	—	—	—	—	—	—	—	—	—	—	☆	☆	—	—	☆	—	☆	—
Honduras	☆	☆	☆	☆	☆	☆	☆	☆	☆	☆	☆	☆	☆	☆	—	☆	—	—
Hong Kong	—	—	—	—	—	—	—	—	—	—	—	—	☆	★	—	—	—	—
Hungary	☆	☆	☆	☆	☆	—	—	—	—	☆	☆	☆	☆	☆	—	☆	☆	☆
Iceland	☆	☆	☆	☆	☆	☆	☆	☆	☆	☆	☆	☆	☆	—	—	—	☆	☆
India	☆	☆	☆	☆	☆	☆	☆	☆	☆	☆	☆	☆	☆	☆	☆	☆	☆	☆

Country	UN	ILO	FAO	UNESCO	WHO	IBRD	IFC	IDA	IMF	ICAO	UPU	ITU	WMO	IMCO	WIPO	IFAD	IAEA	GATT
Indonesia	☆	☆	☆	☆	☆	☆	☆	☆	☆	☆	☆	☆	☆	☆	☆	☆	☆	☆
Iran	☆	☆	☆	☆	☆	☆	☆	☆	☆	☆	☆	☆	☆	—	☆	☆	☆	—
Iraq	☆	☆	☆	☆	☆	☆	☆	☆	☆	☆	☆	☆	☆	☆	☆	☆	☆	—
Ireland	☆	☆	☆	☆	☆	☆	☆	☆	☆	☆	☆	☆	☆	☆	☆	☆	☆	☆
Israel	☆	☆	☆	☆	☆	☆	☆	☆	☆	☆	☆	☆	☆	☆	☆	☆	☆	☆
Italy	☆	☆	☆	☆	☆	☆	☆	☆	☆	☆	☆	☆	☆	☆	☆	☆	☆	☆
Ivory Coast	☆	☆	☆	☆	☆	☆	☆	☆	☆	☆	☆	☆	☆	☆	☆	☆	☆	☆
Jamaica	☆	☆	☆	☆	☆	☆	—	☆	☆	☆	☆	☆	☆	☆	☆	☆	☆	☆
Japan	☆	☆	☆	☆	☆	☆	☆	☆	☆	☆	☆	☆	☆	☆	☆	☆	☆	☆
Jordan	☆	☆	☆	☆	☆	☆	☆	☆	☆	☆	☆	☆	☆	☆	☆	☆	☆	—
Kampuchea	☆	☆	☆	☆	☆	—	☆	☆	☆	☆	☆	☆	☆	—	—	—	☆	—
Kenya	☆	☆	☆	☆	☆	☆	☆	☆	☆	☆	☆	☆	☆	☆	☆	☆	☆	☆
Korea, Democratic People's Republic of	—	—	☆	☆	☆	—	—	—	—	☆	☆	☆	☆	—	☆	—	☆	—
Korea, Republic of	—	—	☆	☆	☆	☆	☆	☆	☆	☆	☆	☆	☆	☆	☆	☆	☆	☆
Kuwait	☆	☆	☆	☆	☆	☆	☆	☆	☆	☆	☆	☆	☆	☆	—	☆	☆	☆
Laos	☆	☆	☆	☆	☆	—	☆	☆	☆	☆	☆	☆	—	—	☆	—	—	—
Lebanon	☆	☆	☆	☆	☆	☆	☆	☆	☆	☆	☆	☆	☆	—	☆	—	☆	—
Lesotho	☆	☆	☆	☆	☆	☆	☆	☆	☆	☆	☆	☆	☆	—	☆	—	☆	—
Liberia	☆	☆	☆	☆	☆	☆	☆	☆	☆	☆	☆	☆	☆	—	☆	—	☆	—
Libya	☆	☆	☆	☆	☆	☆	☆	☆	☆	☆	☆	☆	☆	☆	☆	☆	☆	—
Liechtenstein	—	—	—	—	—	—	—	—	—	—	☆	☆	—	—	☆	—	☆	—
Luxembourg	☆	☆	☆	☆	☆	☆	☆	☆	☆	☆	☆	☆	☆	—	☆	☆	☆	☆
Madagascar	☆	☆	☆	☆	☆	☆	☆	☆	☆	☆	☆	☆	☆	—	☆	☆	☆	☆
Malawi	☆	☆	☆	☆	☆	☆	☆	☆	☆	☆	☆	☆	☆	—	☆	☆	—	☆
Malaysia	☆	☆	☆	☆	☆	☆	☆	☆	☆	☆	☆	☆	☆	—	—	—	☆	☆
Maldives	☆	—	☆	—	☆	—	☆	☆	☆	☆	☆	☆	☆	—	☆	—	—	—
Mali	☆	☆	☆	☆	☆	☆	☆	☆	☆	☆	☆	☆	☆	—	—	☆	☆	—
Malta	☆	☆	☆	☆	—	—	—	—	☆	☆	☆	☆	☆	☆	☆	—	—	☆
Mauritania	☆	☆	☆	☆	☆	☆	☆	☆	☆	☆	☆	☆	☆	☆	☆	☆	—	☆
Mauritius	☆	☆	☆	☆	☆	☆	☆	☆	☆	☆	☆	☆	☆	☆	☆	☆	☆	☆
Mexico	☆	☆	☆	☆	☆	☆	☆	☆	☆	☆	☆	☆	☆	☆	☆	☆	☆	☆
Monaco	—	—	—	☆	☆	—	—	—	—	—	☆	☆	—	—	☆	—	☆	—
Mongolia	☆	☆	☆	☆	☆	—	—	—	—	—	☆	☆	☆	—	☆	—	☆	—
Morocco	☆	☆	☆	☆	☆	☆	☆	☆	☆	☆	☆	☆	☆	☆	☆	☆	☆	—
Mozambique	☆	☆	☆	☆	☆	—	—	—	—	☆	☆	☆	☆	☆	—	☆	—	—
Namibia	—	☆	☆	☆	★	—	—	—	—	—	—	—	—	—	—	—	—	—
Nauru	—	—	—	—	—	—	—	—	—	☆	☆	☆	—	—	—	—	—	—
Nepal	☆	☆	☆	☆	☆	☆	☆	☆	☆	☆	☆	☆	☆	—	☆	—	☆	—
Netherlands	☆	☆	☆	☆	☆	☆	☆	☆	☆	☆	☆	☆	☆	☆	☆	☆	☆	☆
New Zealand	☆	☆	☆	☆	☆	☆	☆	☆	☆	☆	☆	☆	☆	☆	☆	—	☆	☆
Nicaragua	☆	☆	☆	☆	☆	☆	☆	☆	☆	☆	☆	☆	☆	☆	☆	—	☆	☆
Niger	☆	☆	☆	☆	☆	☆	—	☆	☆	☆	☆	☆	☆	—	☆	☆	☆	☆

Country	UN	ILO	FAO	UNESCO	WHO	IBRD	IFC	IDA	IMF	ICAO	UPU	ITU	WMO	IMCO	WIPO	IFAD	IAEA	GATT
Nigeria	☆	☆	☆	☆	☆	☆	☆	☆	☆	☆	☆	☆	☆	☆	—	☆	☆	☆
Norway	☆	☆	☆	☆	☆	☆	☆	☆	☆	☆	☆	☆	☆	☆	☆	☆	☆	☆
Oman	☆	—	☆	☆	☆	☆	☆	☆	☆	☆	☆	☆	☆	—	—	—	—	—
Pakistan	☆	☆	☆	☆	☆	☆	☆	☆	☆	☆	☆	☆	☆	☆	☆	☆	☆	☆
Panama	☆	☆	☆	☆	☆	☆	☆	☆	☆	☆	☆	☆	☆	☆	—	☆	☆	—
Papua New Guinea	☆	☆	☆	☆	☆	☆	☆	☆	☆	☆	☆	☆	☆	☆	—	☆	—	—
Paraguay	☆	☆	☆	☆	☆	☆	☆	☆	☆	☆	☆	☆	—	—	—	☆	☆	—
Peru	☆	☆	☆	☆	☆	☆	☆	☆	☆	☆	☆	☆	☆	☆	—	☆	☆	☆
Philippines	☆	☆	☆	☆	☆	☆	☆	☆	☆	☆	☆	☆	☆	☆	—	☆	☆	☆
Poland	☆	☆	☆	☆	☆	—	—	—	—	☆	☆	☆	☆	☆	☆	—	☆	☆
Portugal	☆	☆	☆	☆	☆	☆	☆	—	☆	☆	☆	☆	☆	☆	☆	☆	☆	☆
Qatar	☆	☆	☆	☆	☆	☆	—	—	☆	☆	☆	☆	☆	☆	☆	☆	☆	—
Romania	☆	☆	☆	☆	☆	☆	—	—	☆	☆	☆	☆	☆	☆	☆	☆	☆	☆
Rwanda	☆	☆	☆	☆	☆	☆	☆	☆	☆	☆	☆	☆	☆	—	—	☆	—	☆
St Lucia	☆	☆	☆	—	—	☆	—	—	☆	☆	—	—	—	☆	—	☆	—	—
St Vincent and the Grenadines	☆	—	—	—	—	—	—	—	☆	—	—	—	—	—	—	—	—	—
Samoa, Western	☆	—	☆	—	☆	☆	☆	☆	☆	—	—	—	—	—	—	☆	—	—
San Marino	—	—	—	☆	☆	—	—	—	—	—	☆	☆	—	—	—	—	—	—
São Tomé and Príncipe	☆	—	☆	☆	☆	☆	—	☆	☆	☆	☆	☆	☆	—	—	☆	—	—
Saudi Arabia	☆	☆	☆	☆	☆	☆	☆	☆	☆	☆	☆	☆	☆	☆	—	☆	☆	—
Senegal	☆	☆	☆	☆	☆	☆	☆	☆	☆	☆	☆	☆	☆	☆	☆	☆	☆	☆
Seychelles	☆	☆	☆	☆	☆	☆	—	—	☆	☆	☆	—	☆	☆	—	☆	—	—
Sierra Leone	☆	☆	☆	☆	☆	☆	☆	☆	☆	☆	☆	☆	☆	☆	—	☆	☆	☆
Singapore	☆	☆	—	☆	☆	☆	☆	—	☆	☆	☆	☆	☆	☆	—	—	☆	☆
Solomon Islands	☆	—	—	—	☆	—	—	—	☆	—	—	—	—	—	—	☆	—	—
Somalia	☆	☆	☆	☆	☆	☆	—	☆	☆	☆	☆	☆	☆	—	—	☆	—	—
South Africa	☆	—	—	—	☆	☆	☆	☆	☆	☆	—	☆	☆	—	☆	—	☆	☆
Spain	☆	☆	☆	☆	☆	☆	☆	☆	☆	☆	☆	☆	☆	☆	☆	☆	☆	☆
Sri Lanka	☆	☆	☆	☆	☆	☆	☆	☆	☆	☆	☆	☆	☆	☆	☆	☆	☆	☆
Sudan	☆	☆	☆	☆	☆	☆	☆	☆	☆	☆	☆	☆	☆	☆	☆	☆	☆	—
Suriname	☆	☆	☆	☆	☆	☆	—	—	☆	☆	☆	☆	☆	☆	☆	—	—	☆
Swaziland	☆	☆	☆	☆	☆	☆	☆	☆	☆	☆	☆	☆	—	—	—	☆	—	—
Sweden	☆	☆	☆	☆	☆	☆	☆	☆	☆	☆	☆	☆	☆	☆	☆	☆	☆	☆
Switzerland	—	☆	☆	☆	☆	—	—	—	—	☆	☆	☆	☆	☆	☆	☆	☆	☆
Syria	☆	☆	☆	☆	☆	☆	☆	☆	☆	☆	☆	☆	☆	☆	—	☆	☆	—
Tanzania	☆	☆	☆	☆	☆	☆	☆	☆	☆	☆	☆	☆	☆	☆	—	☆	☆	☆
Thailand	☆	☆	☆	☆	☆	☆	☆	☆	☆	☆	☆	☆	☆	☆	—	—	☆	—
Togo	☆	☆	☆	☆	☆	☆	☆	☆	☆	☆	☆	☆	☆	—	☆	☆	—	☆
Tonga	—	—	—	☆	☆	—	—	—	—	—	☆	☆	—	—	—	—	—	—
Trinidad and Tobago	☆	☆	☆	☆	☆	☆	☆	☆	☆	☆	☆	☆	☆	☆	—	—	—	☆

Country	UN	ILO	FAO	UNESCO	WHO	IBRD	IFC	IDA	IMF	ICAO	UPU	ITU	WMO	IMCO	WIPO	IFAD	IAEA	GATT
Tunisia	☆	☆	☆	☆	☆	☆	☆	☆	☆	☆	☆	☆	☆	☆	☆	☆	☆	—
Turkey	☆	☆	☆	☆	☆	☆	☆	☆	☆	☆	☆	☆	☆	☆	☆	☆	☆	☆
Uganda	☆	☆	☆	☆	☆	☆	☆	☆	☆	☆	☆	☆	—	☆	☆	☆	☆	☆
Ukraine	☆	☆	—	☆	☆	—	—	—	—	—	☆	☆	☆	—	☆	—	☆	—
USSR	☆	☆	—	☆	☆	—	—	—	—	☆	☆	☆	☆	☆	☆	—	☆	—
United Arab Emirates	☆	☆	☆	☆	☆	☆	☆	—	☆	☆	☆	☆	—	☆	☆	☆	☆	—
United Kingdom	☆	☆	☆	☆	☆	☆	☆	☆	☆	☆	☆	☆	☆	☆	☆	☆	☆	☆
United States	☆	☆	☆	☆	☆	☆	☆	☆	☆	☆	☆	☆	☆	☆	☆	☆	☆	☆
Upper Volta	☆	☆	☆	☆	☆	☆	☆	☆	☆	☆	☆	☆	—	☆	☆	—	—	☆
Uruguay	☆	☆	☆	☆	☆	☆	—	☆	☆	☆	☆	☆	☆	☆	☆	☆	☆	☆
Venezuela	☆	☆	☆	☆	☆	☆	☆	—	☆	☆	☆	☆	☆	☆	—	☆	☆	—
Vietnam	☆	☆	☆	☆	☆	☆	☆	☆	☆	☆	☆	☆	—	☆	☆	☆	☆	—
Yemen Arab Republic	☆	☆	☆	☆	☆	☆	☆	☆	☆	☆	☆	☆	☆	☆	☆	☆	—	—
Yemen, People's Democratic Republic of	☆	☆	☆	☆	☆	☆	—	☆	☆	☆	☆	☆	☆	—	☆	—	—	—
Yugoslavia	☆	☆	☆	☆	☆	☆	☆	☆	☆	☆	☆	☆	☆	☆	☆	☆	☆	☆
Zaïre	☆	☆	☆	☆	☆	☆	☆	☆	☆	☆	☆	☆	☆	☆	☆	☆	☆	☆
Zambia	☆	☆	☆	☆	☆	☆	☆	☆	☆	☆	☆	☆	—	☆	☆	☆	☆	—
Zimbabwe	☆	☆	—	☆	☆	☆	☆	☆	—	—	☆	—	☆	—	—	☆	—	☆
Totals	**154**	**144**	**147**	**151**[1]	**156**	**138**	**113**	**123**	**140**	**145**[2]	**157**[3]	**154**	**146**[4]	**118**	**88**	**134**	**110**	**86**

[1] UNESCO has one associate member—the British Eastern Caribbean Group.
[2] The USSR membership of the ICAO also covers Byelorussia and the Ukraine.
[3] Additional members of the UPU are the Netherlands Antilles and those overseas territories for whose international relations Britain is responsible.
[4] Additional members of the WMO are the British Caribbean Territories, French Polynesia, the Netherlands Antilles and New Caledonia.

4. Nuclear and Conventional Disarmament

This section deals with the major post-war initiatives and agreements on a multilateral level designed to promote both conventional and nuclear disarmament and safeguards, notably the 1963 nuclear test-ban treaty, the 1967 Tlatelolco treaty and the 1968 nuclear non-proliferation treaty.*

UN Disarmament Commissions and Committees

Since 1946 the United Nations has created a series of commissions and committees to consider the question of world disarmament.

The first of these, the **Atomic Energy Commission,** was approved by the General Assembly in January 1946. Its creation was followed, a year later, by the setting up of a **Commission for Conventional Armaments** under a resolution of the Security Council passed on Feb. 13, 1947. These two commissions were superseded by a new **Disarmament Commission** approved by a plenary session of the General Assembly in January 1952. Its 12 members were the 11 nations represented in the Security Council together with Canada.

In November 1957 the General Assembly approved the enlargement of the Disarmament Commission from 12 to 25 members, and a year later, in November 1958, the Commission was reconstituted to include all the members of the United Nations. It did not meet again after 1965.

A special session on disarmament of the UN General Assembly, held from May 23 to July 1, 1978, resolved, inter alia, to establish, as successor to the Disarmament Commission, "a Disarmament Commission composed of all states members of the United Nations" and added that it should be "a deliberative body, a subsidiary organ of the General Assembly, the function of which shall be to consider and make recommendations on various problems in the field of disarmament and to follow up the relevant decisions and recommendations of the special session devoted to disarmament".

Geneva Disarmament Committees

A 10-power **Disarmament Committee,** comprising five Eastern and five Western bloc nations, was set up in September 1959. The negotiations of this committee, which was not a UN organ, broke down in June 1960.

A joint resolution of the USA and the Soviet Union on the setting up of a new 18-nation **Disarmament Committee** was adopted by the General Assembly on Dec. 20, 1961. The committee, which was formed by five NATO countries (Britain, Canada, France, Italy and the USA), five Warsaw Pact countries (Bulgaria, Czechoslovakia, Poland, Romania and the Soviet Union) and eight uncommitted countries (Brazil, Burma, Ethiopia, India, Mexico, Nigeria, Egypt and Sweden), was in almost continuous session in Geneva. France, although a member of the committee, boycotted its work from its inception.

Following agreement between the United States and the Soviet Union, the Committee's membership was in 1969 enlarged from 18 to 26 by the addition of Japan, Mongolia, the Netherlands, Hungary, Argentina, Morocco, Pakistan and Yugoslavia, and its name was changed to the Conference of the Committee on Disarmament. As from March 1975 the conference was joined by five other countries—the German Democratic Republic, the Federal Republic of Germany, Iran, Peru and Zaïre.

In June-August 1975 the US and Soviet delegates at the conference reached "basic agreement" on a convention outlawing "weather warfare" by banning artificially induced changes in the elements and climate for the purpose of war and providing that signatories would not engage in "military or other hostile use of environmental techniques". [For convention to this effect see page 62 below.]

---

* Specifically East-West arms limitation and other agreements and negotiations are dealt with in Section 12, pages 221-57.

Creation of Committee on Disarmament, 1978-79. After agreement had been reached on June 28, 1978, at the special session of the UN General Assembly, by Britain, France, the Soviet Union and the United States on the creation of a new Committee on Disarmament, it was stated in the final document issued by the special session: "The Assembly attaches great importance to the participation of all the nuclear-weapon states in an appropriately constituted negotiating body, the Committee on Disarmament . . . [which] will be open to the nuclear-weapon states and 32 to 35 other states to be chosen in consultation with the President of the 32nd session of the Assembly; that the membership of the Committee on Disarmament will be reviewed at regular intervals; that [it] will be convened in Geneva not later than January 1979 . . . [and that] it will (i) conduct its work by consensus, (ii) adopt its own rules of procedure, (iii) request the (UN) Secretary-General . . . to appoint [its] secretary, (iv) rotate the chairmanship of the Committee among all its members on a monthly basis; and (v) adopt its own agenda."

The new Committee held its first formal session in January 1979 with the participation of France (which had boycotted the previous committee since 1962) and also of 35 non-nuclear-weapon states, namely Algeria, Argentina, Australia, Belgium, Brazil, Bulgaria, Burma, Canada, Cuba, Czechoslovakia, Egypt, Ethiopia, the German Democratic Republic, the Federal Republic of Germany, Hungary, India, Indonesia, Iran, Italy, Japan, Kenya, Mexico, Mongolia, Morocco, the Netherlands, Nigeria, Pakistan, Peru, Poland, Romania, Sri Lanka, Sweden, Venezuela, Yugoslavia and Zaïre. China took its seat on Feb. 5, 1980, with the result that all five nuclear-weapon states were represented on the Committee.

Nuclear Test-Ban Treaty

A treaty banning all nuclear tests except those held underground was signed in Moscow on Aug. 5, 1963, by the Soviet Union, the United Kingdom and the United States.

The operative articles of this treaty read as follows:

"**Art. 1.** (1) Each of the parties to this treaty undertakes to prohibit, to prevent and not to carry out any nuclear weapon test explosion, or any other nuclear explosion, at any place under its jurisdiction or control:

"(*a*) In the atmosphere; beyond its limits, including outer space; or under water, including territorial waters or high seas; or

"(*b*) in any other environment if such explosion causes radioactive debris to be present outside the territorial limits of the state under whose jurisdiction or control such explosion is conducted. It is understood

in this connexion that the provisions of this sub-paragraph are without prejudice to the conclusion of a treaty resulting in the permanent banning of all nuclear test explosions, including all such explosions underground, the conclusion of which, as the parties have stated in the preamble to this treaty, they seek to achieve.

"(2) Each of the parties to this treaty undertakes furthermore to refrain from causing, encouraging or in any way participating in the carrying out of any nuclear weapon test explosion, or any other nuclear explosion, anywhere, which would take place in any of the environments described, or have the effect referred to, in paragraph 1 of this article.

"**Art. 2.** (1) Any party may propose amendments to this treaty. The text of any proposed amendment shall be submitted to the depository governments, which shall circulate it to all parties to this treaty. Thereafter, if requested to do so by one-third or more of the parties, the depository governments shall convene a conference, to which they shall invite all the parties, to consider such amendment.

"(2) Any amendment to this treaty must be approved by a majority of the votes of all the parties to this treaty, including all of the original parties. The amendment shall enter into force for all parties upon the deposit of instruments of ratification by a majority of all the parties, including the instruments of ratification of all of the original parties.

"**Art. 3.** (1) This treaty shall be open to all states for signature. Any state which does not sign this treaty before its entry into force in accordance with paragraph 3 of this article may accede to it at any time.

"(2) This treaty shall be subject to ratification by signatory states. Instruments of ratification and instruments of accession shall be deposited with the governments of the original parties—the USSR, the United Kingdom and the United States—which are hereby designated the depository governments.

"(3) This treaty shall enter into force after its ratification by all the original parties and the deposit of their instruments of ratification.

"(4) For states whose instruments of ratification or accession are deposited subsequent to the entry into force of this treaty, it shall enter into force on the date of the deposit of their instruments of ratification or accession.

"(5) The depository governments shall promptly inform all signatory and acceding states of the date of each signature, the date of deposit of each instrument of ratification of and accession to this treaty, the date of its entry into force, and the date of receipt of any requests for conferences or other notices.

"(6) This treaty shall be registered by the depository governments pursuant to Article 102 of the Charter of the United Nations.

"**Art. 4.** This treaty shall be of unlimited duration. Each party shall, in exercising its national sovereignty, have the right to withdraw from the treaty if it decides that extraordinary events, related to the subject matter of this treaty, have jeopardized the supreme interest of its country. It shall give notice of such withdrawal to all other parties to the treaty three months in advance."

A joint statement issued by the three powers at the time of signature expressed the hope that other states would adhere to the treaty. From Aug. 8, 1963, the treaty was open for signature in all three capitals

(Washington, Moscow and London). By the date of the treaty's entry into force (Oct. 10, 1963) 105 nations had signed it, most of them in all three capitals. Of the states which refused to sign, the most important were the People's Republic of China and France; other governments which did not sign the treaty included those of Albania, Cambodia, Cuba, Guinea, North Korea and North Vietnam.

The Treaty of Tlatelolco

A Treaty for the Prohibition of Nuclear Weapons in Latin America was signed at Tlatelolco, Mexico, by representatives of 21 Latin American countries on Feb. 14, 1967.

Under Art. 1 of the treaty the contracting parties undertook "to use exclusively for peaceful purposes the nuclear material and facilities which are under their jurisdiction, and to prohibit and prevent in their respective territories (*a*) the testing, use, manufacture, production or acquisition . . . of any nuclear weapons, by the parties themselves, directly or indirectly, on behalf of anyone else or in any other way; and (*b*) the receipt, storage, installation, deployment and any form of possession of any nuclear weapon, directly or indirectly, by the parties themselves, by anyone on their behalf, or in any other way". The parties also undertook "to refrain from engaging in, encouraging or authorizing, directly or indirectly, or in any way participating in the testing, use, manufacture, production, possession or control of any nuclear weapon".

The zone of application of the treaty was precisely defined (in Art. 4) as part of the Western hemisphere south of 35°N except the continental part of the territory of the United States of America and its territorial waters.

Under the treaty the Agency for the Prohibition of Nuclear Weapons was to be set up with headquarters in Mexico City for the purpose of consultation and supervision of compliance with the obligations arising from the treaty (Art. 7). This agency was to have as its supreme organ a General Conference, which would hold general sessions every two years and special sessions as required (Art. 9), and which would elect a five-member Council, to function continuously (Art. 10).

Explosions of nuclear devices for peaceful purposes would be permitted, subject to prior notification of the International Nuclear Energy Agency (IAEA) (Art. 18).

Entry into force of the treaty was subject to the following requirements being met: (i) deposit of the instruments of ratification by all the sovereign states in the treaty's zone of application; (ii) signature and ratification of Additional Protocols I and II annexed to the treaty by the powers concerned; and (iii) conclusion of bilateral agreements with the IAEA on the application of safeguards on each country's nuclear activities.

Under *Additional Protocol I* Britain, France, the Netherlands and the United States undertook to apply the status of denuclearization to the territories for which they were internationally responsible and which were situated within the treaty zone.

Under *Additional Protocol II* the powers possessing nuclear weapons (the United States, the Soviet Union, Britain, France and the People's Republic of China) were requested to respect fully "the status of denuclearization of Latin America" and to undertake "not to use or threaten to use nuclear weapons" against the contracting parties of the treaty.

Additional Protocol I was quickly signed by Britain and the Netherlands, by the United States on May 26, 1977, and by France early in March 1979. Additional Protocol II was first signed by Britain and thereafter by the United States on May 12, 1971, by France on July 18, 1973, by China on Aug. 21, 1973, and by the Soviet Union on May 18, 1978. However, in the absence of signature and ratification by Cuba and Guyana the entry into force of the treaty remained in abeyance.

OPANAL. The agency provided for in Article 7 of the treaty—the Agency for the Prohibition of Nuclear Weapons in Latin America (*Organismo para la Proscripción de las Armas Nucleares en la América Latina,* OPANAL)—held its inaugural meeting on Sept. 2, 1969. In addition to administering the treaty, the functions of OPANAL included endeavours to provide protection against possible nuclear attacks and to strengthen the movement against the proliferation of nuclear weapons. The Agency's membership consisted of 22 states which had fully ratified the treaty.

Nuclear Non-Proliferation Treaty

The Treaty on the Non-Proliferation of Nuclear Weapons, adopted by the UN General Assembly on June 12, 1968, came into force on March 5, 1970, by which date a total of 47 countries had deposited instruments of ratification. The operative articles of the treaty (NPT) read as follows:

"**Art. 1.** Each nuclear-weapon state party to the treaty undertakes not to transfer to any recipient whatsoever nuclear weapons or other nuclear explosive devices or control over such weapons or explosive devices directly, or indirectly; and not in any way to assist, encourage, or induce any non-nuclear-weapon state to manufacture or otherwise acquire nuclear weapons or other nuclear explosive devices, or control over such weapons or explosive devices.

"**Art. 2.** Each non-nuclear-weapon state party to the treaty undertakes not to receive the transfer from any transferor whatsoever of nuclear weapons or other nuclear explosive devices or of control over such weapons or explosive devices directly, or indirectly; not to manufacture or otherwise acquire nuclear weapons or other nuclear explosive devices; and not to seek or receive any assistance in the manufacture of nuclear weapons or other nuclear explosive devices.

"**Art. 3.** (1) Each non-nuclear-weapon state party to the treaty undertakes to accept safeguards, as set forth in an agreement to be negotiated and concluded with the International Atomic Energy Agency in accordance with the Statute of the International Atomic Energy Agency and the Agency's safeguards system, for the exclusive purpose of verification of the fulfilment of its obligations assumed under this treaty with a view to preventing diversion of nuclear energy from peaceful uses to nuclear weapons or other nuclear explosive devices. Procedures for the safeguards required by this article shall be followed with respect to source or special fissionable material whether it is being produced, processed, or used in any principal nuclear facility or is outside any such facility. The safeguards required by this article shall be applied on all source or special fissionable material in all peaceful nuclear activities within the territory of such state, under its jurisdiction, or carried out under its control anywhere.

"(2) Each state party to the treaty undertakes not to provide: (*a*) source or special fissionable material, or (*b*) equipment or material especially designed or prepared for the processing, use, or production of special fissionable material, to any non-nuclear-weapon state for peaceful purposes, unless the source or special fissionable material shall be subject to the safeguards required by this article.

"(3) The safeguards required by this article shall be implemented in a manner designed to comply with Article 4 of this treaty, and to avoid hampering the economic or technological development of the parties or international co-operation in the field of peaceful nuclear activities, including the international exchange of nuclear material and equipment for the processing, use, or production of nuclear material for peaceful purposes in accordance with the provisions of this article and the principle of safeguarding set forth in the preamble.

"(4) Non-nuclear-weapon states party to the treaty shall conclude agreements with the International Atomic Energy Agency to meet the requirements of this article either individually or together with other states in accordance with the Statute of the International Atomic Energy Agency. Negotiation of such agreements shall commence within 180 days from the original entry into force of this treaty. For states depositing their instruments of ratification or accession after the 180-day period, negotiation of such agreements shall commence not later than the date of such deposit. Such agreements shall enter into force not later than eighteen months after the date of initiation of negotiations.

"**Art. 4.** (1) Nothing in this treaty shall be interpreted as affecting the inalienable right of all the parties to the treaty to develop research, production and use of nuclear energy for peaceful purposes without discrimination and in conformity with Articles 1 and 2 of this treaty.

"(2) All the parties to the treaty undertake to facilitate, and have the right to participate in, the fullest possible exchange of equipment, materials, and scientific and technological information for the peaceful uses of nuclear energy. Parties to the treaty in a position to do so shall also co-operate in contributing alone or together with other states or international organizations to the further development of the applications of nuclear energy for peaceful purposes, especially in the territories of non-nuclear-weapon states party to the treaty, with due consideration for the needs of the developing areas of the world.

"**Art. 5.** Each party to the treaty undertakes to take appropriate measures to ensure that, in accordance with this treaty, under appropriate international observation and through appropriate international procedures, potential benefits from any peaceful applications of nuclear explosions will be made available to non-nuclear-weapon states party to the treaty on a non-discriminatory basis and that the charge to such parties for the explosive devices used will be as low as possible and exclude any charge for research and development. Non-nuclear-weapon states party to the treaty shall be able to obtain such benefits, pursuant to a special international agreement or agreements, through an appropriate international body with adequate representation of non-nuclear-weapon states. Negotiations on this subject shall commence as soon as possible after the treaty enters into force. Non-nuclear-weapon states party to the treaty so desiring may also obtain such benefits pursuant to bilateral agreements.

"**Art. 6.** Each of the parties to the treaty undertakes to pursue negotiations in good faith on effective measures relating to cessation of the nuclear arms race at an early date and to nuclear disarmament, and on a treaty on general and complete disarmament under strict and effective international control.

"**Art. 7.** Nothing in this treaty affects the right of any group of states to conclude regional treaties in order to assure the total absence of nuclear weapons in their respective territories.

"**Art. 8.** (1) Any party to the treaty may propose amendments to this treaty. The text of any proposed amendment shall be submitted to the depositary governments which shall circulate it to all parties to the treaty. Thereupon, if requested to do so by one-third or more of the parties to the treaty, the depositary governments shall convene a conference, to which they shall invite all the parties to the treaty, to consider such an amendment.

"(2) Any amendment to this treaty must be approved by a majority of the votes of all the parties to the treaty, including the votes of all nuclear-weapon states party to the treaty and all other parties which, on the date the amendment is circulated, are members of the Board of Governors of the International Atomic Energy Agency. The amendment shall enter into force for each party that deposits its instrument of ratification of the amendment upon the deposit of such instruments of ratification by a majority of all the parties, including the instruments of ratification of all nuclear-weapon states party to the treaty and all other parties which, on the date the amendment is circulated, are members of the Board of Governors of the International Atomic Energy Agency. Thereafter, it shall enter into force for any other party upon the deposit of its instrument of ratification of the amendment.

"(3) Five years after the entry into force of this treaty, a conference of parties to the treaty shall be held in Geneva, Switzerland, in order to review the operation of this treaty with a view to assuring that the purposes of the preamble and the provisions of the treaty are being realized. At intervals of five years thereafter, a majority of the parties to the treaty may obtain, by submitting a proposal to this effect to the depositary governments, the convening of further conferences with the same objective of reviewing the operation of the treaty.

"**Art. 9.** (1) This treaty shall be open to all states for signature. Any state which does not sign the treaty before its entry into force in accordance with paragraph 3 of this article may accede to it at any time.

"(2) This treaty shall be subject to ratification by signatory states. Instruments of ratification and instruments of accession shall be deposited with the Governments of the Union of Soviet Socialist Republics, the United Kingdom of Great Britain and Northern Ireland and the United States of America, which are hereby designated the depositary governments.

"(3) This treaty shall enter into force after its ratification by the states, the governments of which are designated depositaries of the treaty, and forty other states signatory to this treaty and the deposit of their instruments of ratification. For the purposes of this treaty, a nuclear-weapon state is one which has manufactured and exploded a nuclear weapon or other nuclear explosive device prior to Jan. 1, 1967.

"(4) For states whose instruments of ratification or accession are deposited subsequent to the entry into force of this treaty, it shall enter into force on the date of the deposit of their instruments of ratification or accession.

"(5) The depositary governments shall promptly inform all signatory and acceding states of the date of each signature, the date of deposit of each instrument of ratification or of accession, the date of the entry into force of this treaty, and the date of receipt of any requests for convening a conference or other notices.

"(6) This treaty shall be registered by the depositary governments pursuant to Article 102 of the Charter of the United Nations.

"**Art. 10.** (1) Each party shall in exercising its national sovereignty have the right to withdraw from the treaty if it decides that extraordinary events, related to the subject-matter of this treaty, have jeopardized the supreme interests of its country. It shall give notice of such withdrawal to all other parties to the treaty and to the United Nations Security Council three months in advance. Such notice shall include a statement of the extraordinary events it regards as having jeopardized its supreme interests.

"(2) Twenty-five years after the entry into force of the treaty, a conference shall be convened to decide whether the treaty shall continue in force indefinitely, or shall be extended for an additional fixed period or periods. This decision shall be taken by a majority of the parties to the treaty. . . ."

STATES PARTIES TO NPT

The treaty was signed on July 1, 1968, by the Soviet Union, the United Kingdom and the United States, 56 other countries signing on the same day.

As of Sept. 1, 1980, a total of 115 states were parties to the treaty. Of these states, 78 non-nuclear-weapon states had negotiated safeguards agreements with the International Atomic Energy Agency (IAEA), and 69 of these agreements were in force, while another nine such agreements, approved by the IAEA Board of Governors, were awaiting entry into force.

In the following list states marked * do not have safeguards agreements in force; states marked † have safeguards agreements approved and awaiting entry into force; and dates given in parentheses indicate the time by which safeguards agreements should have entered or should enter into force.

Afghanistan
Australia
Austria
Bahamas* (10.1.75)
Bangladesh* (27.3.81)
Barbados
Belgium
Benin* (30.4.74)
Bolivia† (5.3.72)
Botswana* (5.3.72)
Bulgaria
Burundi* (19.9.72)
Cameroon* (5.3.72)
Canada
Cape Verde
Central African Republic* (25.4.72)
Chad* (10.9.72)
Congo* (23.4.80)
Costa Rica
Cyprus
Czechoslovakia
Denmark
Dominican Republic
Ecuador
El Salvador
Ethiopia
Fiji
Finland
Gabon† (7.8.75)
The Gambia
German Democratic Republic
Federal Republic of Germany
Ghana
Greece
Grenada* (19.2.76)
Guatemala† (22.3.72)
Guinea-Bissau* (20.2.78)
Haiti† (2.6.72)
Holy See
Honduras
Hungary
Iceland
Indonesia* (12.1.81)
Iran
Iraq
Ireland
Italy
Ivory Coast* (6.9.74)
Jamaica
Japan
Jordan
Democratic Kampuchea* (2.12.73)
Kenya* (5.3.72)
Republic of Korea
Laos* (5.3.72)
Lebanon
Lesotho

Liberia* (5.3.72)
Libya* (26.11.76)
Liechtenstein
Luxembourg
Madagascar
Malaysia
Maldives
Mali* (5.3.72)
Malta* (5.3.72)
Mauritius
Mexico
Mongolia
Morocco
Nepal
Netherlands
New Zealand
Nicaragua
Nigeria* (5.3.72)
Norway
Panama* (13.7.78)
Paraguay
Peru
Philippines
Poland
Portugal
Romania
Rwanda* (20.11.76)
St Lucia
San Marino† (5.3.72)
Senegal† (17.6.72)
Sierra Leone† (26.8.76)
Singapore
Somalia* (5.3.72)
Soviet Union
Sri Lanka* (5.9.80)
Sudan
Suriname
Swaziland
Sweden
Switzerland
Syria* (5.3.72)
Taiwan* (5.3.72)
Thailand
Togo* (5.3.72)
Tonga† (7.1.73)
Tunisia* (5.3.72)
Turkey
Tuvalu* (19.7.80)
United Kingdom
United States
Upper Volta* (5.3.72)
Uruguay
Venezuela† (26.3.77)
Vietnam
Western Samoa
People's Democratic Republic of Yemen* (1.12.80)
Yugoslavia
Zaïre

Countries which had not signed the treaty by the end of 1980 included France (which had, however, indicated that it would abide by the treaty's principles), Argentina, Brazil, China, Cuba, Israel and South Africa.

Following the signature of the treaty by five member states of the European Communities—Belgium, West Germany, Italy,

Luxembourg and the Netherlands—the European Commission began negotiations with the IAEA on an inspection agreement as stipulated in Article 3, with the objective of reaching agreement on how the Euratom control system, as previously applied, could be adapted and verified by the Agency in accordance with the treaty requirements. The Council of Ministers on Sept. 25, 1972, approved the text of the agreement, which was signed on April 5, 1973.

NPT REVIEW CONFERENCES

First Review Conference. A first review conference (as provided for in Article 8 of the treaty) was held in Geneva on May 5-30, 1975.

Of the non-signatory countries, 10—including Argentina, Brazil, Chile, Israel, Pakistan, Saudi Arabia and Spain—were then considered to have the capability of becoming nuclear-weapon states within the next two years. Of the above seven, only Argentina, Brazil and Israel were represented at the conference as observers, as were also Algeria, Cuba, South Africa, the Arab League and the Agency for the Prohibition of Nuclear Weapons in Latin America (OPANAL). Of the existing nuclear-weapon states, China, France and India (which had conducted its first nuclear test explosion on May 18, 1974) were not represented at the conference. (Among potential nuclear-weapon states, Canada, Iran and Sweden have specifically decided to forgo the production or acquisition of nuclear arms.)

The conference adopted by consensus a declaration calling inter alia for (*a*) International Atomic Energy Agency safeguards against the diversion of fissionable materials imported for peaceful purposes; (*b*) efficient protection against accidents and theft of nuclear materials during their use, storage and transport; (*c*) accelerated negotiations between the Soviet Union and the United States for the conclusion of a further strategic arms limitation agreement [for the first such agreement, see page 239]; (*d*) the seeking of a complete ban on nuclear-weapon tests and, pending such a ban, the restriction of underground tests to a minimum; and (*e*) the creation of internationally-recognized zones free from nuclear weapons, and set up on the initiative and with the approval of the states directly interested in the zone concerned and with the co-operation of the nuclear-weapon powers.

Second Review Conference. A second review conference was held in Geneva from Aug. 11 to Sept. 7, 1980. At this conference the Director-General of the IAEA stated that there were 50,000 nuclear weapons on earth with a total explosive capacity a million times that of the bomb dropped on Hiroshima (Japan) in 1945. He also said that 95 per cent of the nuclear plants in all the non-nuclear-weapon countries—whether parties to the NPT or not—were under IEAE

safeguards, and that 69 of the NPT parties had IEAE safeguards in force. The conference, however, did not issue a final document, mainly because of disagreements between the nuclear-weapon powers and the non-nuclear-weapon states.

Delegates of the latter accused the Soviet Union, the United Kingdom and the United States of failure to fulfil their treaty obligations to reduce nuclear arsenals and to ban nuclear tests, and also of protecting their own nuclear monopoly by restricting the supply of peaceful nuclear technology to non-nuclear-weapon countries; these delegates unsuccessfully called for (i) the immediate cessation of all nuclear tests (of which 53 had been carried out in 1979); (ii) negotiation of a comprehensive test-ban treaty to be carried out within the Geneva Committee on Disarmament, rather than by the Soviet Union, the United Kingdom and the United States (as currently); (iii) a commitment by the USA and the USSR to honour the strategic arms limitation treaty (SALT II—see page 246) pending its ratification by the US Senate; (iv) a demand for an end to nuclear co-operation with Israel and South Africa.

The conference was nevertheless reported to have made progress towards agreements on an international plutonium-storage system, incentives for other non-nuclear-weapon states to adhere to the NPT, and drafting measures to protect fissionable materials in transit. It was also said that the participants' support for non-proliferation remained undiminished and that they had agreed to tighten safeguards against the abuse of exported nuclear technology while ensuring that it was shared for peaceful purposes.

Nuclear Suppliers' Group

In an exchange of letters on Jan. 27, 1976, agreement was reached on the establishment of a Nuclear Suppliers' Group by seven countries—Canada, France, the Federal Republic of Germany, Japan, the Soviet Union, the United Kingdom and the United States—with the object of harmonizing their export policy in regard to nuclear materials (fuels, reactors and enrichment or retreatment plants). (The group is also known as the London Club.)

The agreement embodied the principles (i) that the seven countries agreed to consult each other on any negotiations for foreign sales of fuels and materials and to adopt the same rules of conduct to avoid competition and (ii) that control by the International Atomic Energy Agency (IAEA) would be extended from fuel to nuclear materials in order to avoid that a country buying a nuclear reactor or plant would later be able to reproduce them on its own or even to re-export them.

The Nuclear Suppliers' Group was in June 1976 enlarged by the accession of the German Democratic Republic, Italy, the Netherlands and Sweden, and subsequently by that of Belgium, Czechoslovakia and Poland, and on April 20, 1977, by that of Switzerland.

At a meeting of the group held in London on April 28-29, 1977, the United States was reported to have informed the other members of the group that it intended to prevent (or severely limit) the spread of nuclear weapons to some 12 to 15 countries said to be capable of producing them and having political reasons for doing so. According to the (US) Ford Foundation these nuclear "threshold countries" were (i) five "insecure states"—Israel, the Republic of Korea, South Africa, Taiwan and Yugoslavia; (ii) four "status-seeking states"—Brazil, India, Iran and Spain; and (iii) four "traditional rivals" of some of the above countries—Argentina, Egypt, the Democratic People's Republic of Korea and Pakistan.

A set of rules for the export of nuclear equipment and fuel, adopted by the group in London on Sept. 21, 1977, was published by the US State Department on Jan. 11, 1978.

Under these rules countries purchasing such equipment and fuel would have to give formal assurances not to use the material or facilities for producing a nuclear explosive device for either military or peaceful purposes; they must accept international inspection by the IAEA; they must give adequate guarantees for the effective physical protection of imported materials and equipment against theft and sabotage; these guidelines would apply also to exports of such material or equipment to a third country, with prior permission of the original exporting country being required for the export of sensitive items; and in the event of a clear or suspected violation of these rules the supplying countries would consult together to decide on any possible sanctions to be taken. (It was said that these rules would not be applied retroactively to transactions already concluded.)

Treaty on Control of Arms on the Seabed

A Treaty on the Prohibition of the Emplacement of Nuclear Weapons and Other Weapons of Mass Destruction on the Seabed and the Ocean Floor and in the Subsoil thereof, which had been submitted to the UN General Assembly by the Conference of the Committee on Disarmament, was signed on Feb. 11, 1971, by the Soviet Union, the United Kingdom and the United States. By the time of its entry into force on May 18, 1972, a total of 34 countries had deposited instruments of ratification, while another five had signed the treaty but not yet ratified it.

The parties to the treaty undertook not to place on the seabed "any nuclear weapons or any other types of weapons of mass destruction as well as structures, launching installations, or any other facilities specifically designed for storing, testing, or using such weapons".

Convention on the Prohibition and Destruction of Bacteriological Weapons

The UN General Assembly adopted on Dec. 16, 1971, by 110 votes to none, with one abstention, a resolution commending for signature a draft *Convention on the Prohibition of the Development, Production and Stockpiling of Bacteriological (Biological) and Toxin Weapons and on their Destruction*, which had been submitted to it by the Conference of the Committee on Disarmament.

The convention provided inter alia:

Art. 1. Each state party to this convention undertakes never in any circumstances to develop, produce, stockpile or otherwise acquire or retain:

(*a*) Microbial or other biological agents or toxins, whatever their origin or method of production, of types and in quantities that have no justification for prophylactic, protective or other peaceful purposes;

(*b*) weapons, equipment or means of delivery designed to use such agents or toxins for hostile purposes or in armed conflict.

Art. 2. Each state party to this convention undertakes to destroy, or to divert to peaceful purposes, as soon as possible but not later than nine months after the entry into force of the convention, all agents, toxins, weapons, equipment, and means of delivery specified in Article 1 . . . , which are in its possession or under its jurisdiction or control. In implementing the provisions of this article all necessary precautions shall be observed to protect populations and the environment.

Art. 8. Nothing in this convention shall be interpreted as in any way limiting or detracting from the obligations assumed by any state under the Protocol . . . signed at Geneva on June 17, 1925 [see page 3].

The convention was signed on April 10, 1972, by the Soviet Union, the United Kingdom and the United States, about 70 other countries signing on the same day. It came into force on March 26, 1975, when instruments of ratification were deposited by the Soviet Union, the United Kingdom, and the United States (as the three depository governments), a total of 37 of the more than 100 signatories having ratified it.

UN Resolutions on Zones of Peace or Nuclear-Weapon-Free Zones

In a declaration adopted by the UN General Assembly on Dec. 16, 1971, by 61 votes to none with 55 abstentions, the Indian Ocean, together with the airspace above it and the ocean floor below it, was "designated for all time as a zone of peace", from which the great powers were asked to eliminate "all bases, military installations, logistical supply facilities, disposition of nuclear weapons and weapons of mass destruction".

A further resolution, urging all states to accept the above resolution, was adopted by the UN General Assembly on Dec. 6, 1973, by 95 votes to none with 35 abstentions (including four of the five permanent members of the UN Security Council—France, the Soviet Union, the United Kingdom and the United States).

On Dec. 11, 1975, the UN General Assembly adopted by 110 votes to none with 20 abstentions a resolution endorsing the idea of establishing a nuclear-weapon-free zone in the South Pacific.

Later UN General Assembly resolutions (adopted without negative votes on Dec. 12, 1977) called for nuclear-weapon-free zones in Africa, the Middle East and South Asia.

Convention on the Prohibition of Military or Any Other Hostile Use of Environmental Modification Techniques

This convention was adopted by the UN General Assembly on Dec. 10, 1976, by 96 votes to eight with 30 abstentions (being approved by all nuclear powers except France, which abstained, and China, which took no part in the vote). Provisions contained in this convention included the following:

"**Art. I.** (1) Each state party to this Convention undertakes not to engage in military or any other hostile use of environmental modification techniques having widespread, long-lasting or severe effects as the means of destruction, damage or injury to any other state party.

"(2) Each state party to this Convention undertakes not to assist, encourage or induce any other state, group of states or international organization to engage in activities contrary to the provisions of paragraph 1 of this article.

"**Art. II.** As used in Article I, the term 'environmental modification techniques' refers to any technique for changing—through the deliberate manipulation of natural processes—the dynamics, composition or structure of the earth, including its biota, lithosphere, hydrosphere and atmosphere, or of outer space.

"**Art. III.** (1) The provisions of this Convention shall not hinder the use of environmental modification techniques for peaceful purposes and shall be without prejudice to generally recognized principles and applicable rules of international law concerning such use. . . ."

The convention was to be of unlimited duration, but its operation was to be reviewed by a conference of the states parties to the convention to be convened five years after its entry into force—which would take place upon the deposit of instruments of ratification by 20 governments.

The convention came into force on Oct. 5, 1978, the 20 countries which had ratified it by then comprising mainly communist states but also Cyprus, Denmark, Sri Lanka, Tunisia, Finland, Britain, Ghana and Spain.

Declaration on the Preparation of Societies for Life in Peace

This declaration, approved by the UN General Assembly on Dec. 15, 1978, by 138 votes to none (with Israel and the United States abstaining and China not voting), contained the following paragraphs:

"(1) Every nation and every human being, regardless of race, conscience, language or sex, has the inherent right to life in peace. Respect for that right, as well as for the other human rights, is in the common interest of all mankind and an indispensable condition of advancement of all nations, large and small, in all fields.

"(2) A war of aggression, its planning, preparation or initiation are crimes against peace and are prohibited by international law.

"(3) In accordance with the purposes and principles of the United Nations, states have the duty to refrain from propaganda for wars of aggression.

"(4) Every state, acting in the spirit of friendship and good-neighbourly relations, has the duty to promote all-round, mutually advantageous and equitable political, economic, social and cultural co-operation with other states, notwithstanding their socio-economic systems, with a view to securing their common existence and co-operation in peace, in conditions of mutual understanding and of respect for the identity and diversity of all peoples, and the duty to take up actions conducive to the furtherance of the ideals of peace, humanism and freedom.

"(5) Every state has the duty to respect the right of all peoples to self-determination, independence, equality, sovereignty, the territorial integrity of states and the inviolability of their frontiers, including the right to determine the road of their development, without interference or intervention in their internal affairs. . . .

"(7) Every state has the duty to discourage all manifestations and practices of colonialism, as well as racism, racial discrimination and apartheid, as contrary to the right of peoples to self-determination and to other human rights and fundamental freedoms."

Convention on the Protection of Nuclear Material

A *Convention on the Physical Protection of Nuclear Material,* drawn up under the auspices of the International Atomic Energy Agency, was opened for signature on March 3, 1980, and was to enter into force 30 days after ratification, acceptance or approval by 21 states.

The convention is designed to achieve international co-operation in order "to avert the potential dangers posed by the unlawful taking and use of nuclear material", to make it possible to ensure the prevention, detection and punishment of such offences, "to facilitate the safe transfer of nuclear material" and to protect it "in domestic use, storage and transport" (while stressing the need for "stringent physical protection" for nuclear material used for military purposes). Under the convention the unlawful taking and use of nuclear material as well as attempts at such action, or to use force or other forms of intimidation in this connexion or to use nuclear material "to cause death or injury to persons or substantial property damage" are made punishable and extraditable offences. In two annexes to the convention detailed levels of protection are given for three different categories of nuclear materials.

The implementation of the convention was to be reviewed five years after its entry into force. It also provided for an optional procedure for the settlement of disputes concerning the interpretation or application of the convention.

5. Agreements on Scientific, Space and Environmental Co-operation

The following section covers (i) the major international and multilateral agreements entered into by governments in the field of scientific co-operation; (ii) international co-operation and agreements on matters of space research and utilization; (iii) major international declarations, conventions and conferences on environmental problems; (iv) organizations for the preservation of the living resources of the sea; and (v) international fisheries organizations for the regulation of fisheries in various regions of the world's oceans and seas.

Agreements in the Field of Scientific Co-operation

Antarctic Treaty

On Dec. 1, 1959, a 30-year treaty was signed in Washington at the end of a 12-nation conference on peaceful international scientific co-operation in Antarctica. The 12 original signatories were Argentina, Australia, Belgium, Britain, Chile, France, Japan, New Zealand, Norway, South Africa, the Soviet Union and the United States, who have subsequently been joined by Brazil, Czechoslovakia, Denmark, the German Democratic Republic, the Federal Republic of Germany, the Netherlands, Poland (as a consultative member) and Romania. The treaty came into force on June 23, 1961.

The main provisions of the treaty are summarized below:

Art. 1. Antarctica shall be used for peaceful purposes only. The contracting parties are forbidden to establish military bases in the area, to carry out military manoeuvres, or to test any kind of weapons.

Art. 2. Freedom of scientific investigation and co-operation towards that end should be maintained.

Art. 3. Scientific information and personnel should be exchanged by the contracting parties.

Art. 4. Nothing contained in the treaty may be interpreted as a renunciation, denial or support of a claim to territorial sovereignty in Antarctica. No new claim to territorial sovereignty may be asserted while the treaty is in force.

Art. 5. Any nuclear explosions in Antarctica and the disposal there of radioactive waste shall be prohibited.

Art. 6. The provisions of the treaty apply to the land area south of 60 degrees South latitude.

Art. 7. Each contracting party has the right to send observers to carry out inspections in Antarctica. Notification must be given of all expeditions and stations in Antarctica.

Art. 8. Observers and scientific personnel in Antarctica are subject to the jurisdiction of their own country.

Art. 9. The contracting parties shall meet at suitable intervals to consult together on measures for the furtherance of the principles and objectives of the treaty.

Later Agreements. In February 1972 the treaty's original signatories concluded an agreement on the protection of seals in the Antarctic, including those in the open sea and on floating ice, and this agreement came into force on March 11, 1978.

At a consultative meeting of the treaty signatories held in Washington from Sept. 17 to Oct. 5, 1979, it was agreed (i) to maintain voluntary restraint in the exploration and exploitation of Antarctic minerals (notably oil and gas), (ii) to move towards adoption of a draft convention for the regulation of fishing, and (iii) to co-operate in telecommunications, the development of guidelines for tourism and the study of the impact of various measures on the environment.

Living Resources Convention. A convention on the conservation of Antarctic living resources, in particular krill (a protein-rich crustacean), was signed at a meeting held in Canberra (Australia) on May 7-20, 1980, by 15 countries and by observers (including the European Community). Agreement on the convention had been reached by the 12 original signatories of the Antarctic Treaty and also by Poland, the German Democratic Republic and the Federal Republic of Germany. Under the convention an international commission was to be established in Hobart (Tasmania) to supervise the preservation of marine life, to study the foodchain of Antarctic fish and bird life and to recommend measures to protect the species.

International Hydrographic Organization

Headquarters: Monaco.

Members: Argentina, Australia, Brazil, Canada, Chile, Cuba, Denmark, the Dominican Republic, Ecuador, Egypt, Finland, France, the German Democratic Republic, the Federal Republic of Germany, Greece, Guatemala, Iceland, India, Indonesia, Iran, Italy, Japan, the Republic of Korea, Malaysia, Monaco, the Netherlands, New Zealand, Nigeria, Norway, Pakistan, the Philippines, Poland, Portugal, Singapore, South Africa, the Soviet Union, Spain, Sweden, Syria, Taiwan, Thailand, Turkey, Venezuela, the United Kingdom, the United States, Yugoslavia and Zaïre.

The main purpose of this organization, which was founded in 1921, is to make international navigation safer and easier by coordinating and expanding hydrographic work and giving relevant assistance to developing countries.

International Phase of Ocean Drilling

A deep-sea drilling project carried out by the United States for the previous seven years to obtain samples of the earth's crust from below the ocean floor was late in 1975 succeeded by a new programme known as the International Phase of Ocean Drilling, with a three-year budget of $50,000,000, to which Japan, the Soviet Union and the United Kingdom had each agreed to contribute $1,000,000 a year, with other contributions being expected from France and the Federal Republic of Germany.

Uranium Institute

The Uranium Institute was set up in London in June 1975 by uranium producers from Australia, Canada, France, South Africa and the United Kingdom, representing about 60 per cent of the non-communist world's uranium production (the bulk of the remainder being that of US companies).

The main object of the Institute is to promote development in the use of uranium in order to safeguard energy supplies.

International Nuclear Fuel Cycle Evaluation Programme

Under an international nuclear fuel cycle evaluation (INFCE) programme, first proposed at the economic summit meeting held in London in May 1977 [see page 86], a first meeting was held in Washington on Oct. 19-21, 1977, being attended by representatives of 40 countries and of four international organizations.

The meeting agreed to conduct an international nuclear fuel cycle evaluation to explore the best means of advancing the objective of making nuclear energy for peaceful purposes widely available in order to meet the world's energy needs—although without participants being committed to the INFCE's results.

The work of the programme, carried out by eight working groups over a two-year period and with the eventual participation of 66 countries and six international organizations, was completed at a conference held in Vienna on Feb. 25-27, 1980.

The 66 countries which took part in the programme were: Albania, Algeria, Argentina, Australia, Austria, Belgium, Brazil, Bulgaria, Canada, Chile, Colombia, Cuba, Cyprus, Czechoslovakia, Denmark, Ecuador, Egypt, Finland, France, the German Democratic Republic, the Federal Republic of Germany, Greece, Guatemala, India, Indonesia, Iran, Iraq, Ireland, Israel, Italy, Japan, the Republic of Korea, Liberia, Libya, Liechtenstein, Mexico, Morocco, the Netherlands, New Zealand, Niger, Nigeria, Norway, Pakistan, Panama, Paraguay, Peru, the Philippines, Poland, Portugal, Qatar, Romania, Saudi Arabia, Senegal, South Africa, the Soviet Union, Spain, Sweden, Switzerland, Thailand, Tunisia, Turkey, the United Kingdom, the United States, Venezuela, Yugoslavia and Zaïre.

The six international organizations involved were: the Commission of the European Community, the International Atomic Energy Agency (IAEA), the International Energy Agency (IEA), the Nuclear Energy Agency (NEA) of the OECD, the Agency for the Prohibition of Nuclear Weapons in Latin America (OPANAL) and the United Nations.

In its final report the conference strongly endorsed the development and use of fast-breeder reactors (i.e. plutonium-based energy systems which effectively reduce the net usage of uranium required)—contrary to an earlier US intention to reduce the possibility of nuclear weapons proliferation by gaining international support for a ban on the reprocessing and recycling of plutonium (which can be used for the production of nuclear weapons) for use in fast breeders. The conference, however, also produced a consensus that the IAEA should be responsible for supervising the storage of plutonium not needed for an individual country's research and fast-breeder requirements. The conference expressed the belief that the construction of fast breeders by West European countries, the United States and Japan would be technically feasible by the year 2000 and that this would lead to "nuclear power deployment for all practical purposes free from uranium-supply constraints".

The conference adopted two outlines for the growth of nuclear power outside the

Communist bloc. It also concluded that effective safeguards already existed for the prevention of any misuse of peaceful nuclear technology, including fast breeders, for military ends. Furthermore, the conference declared inter alia that effective measures should be taken to meet the specific needs of developing countries as regards access to nuclear energy capability for peaceful purposes.

Co-operation in Space Research and Utilization

Agreements on Satellite Communications Systems

A **European Conference on Satellite Communication** (CETS) was established in 1963 by member governments of the European Conference of Postal and Telecommunications Administrations (CEPT) as a medium of consultation on global telecommunications.

The main objectives of the CETS were achieved by the conclusion of two agreements on the establishment of an international communications satellite system, signed in Washington on Aug. 20, 1964, by the United States, Britain and nine other countries. The first, an intergovernmental agreement, outlined the general organizational principles of the system, while the second agreement, concluded between the "designated communications entities of each country" (e.g. the US Communications Satellite Corporation) dealt with the commercial, financial and technical operations, and provided for the setting up of a management committee.

The provisions of the intergovernmental treaty included the following:

(1) The design, development, construction and establishment of satellites, and the ground installations for their control, would be a co-operative international enterprise. The telecommunications ground stations would be owned by the countries or groups of countries in which they were located.

(2) The US Communications Satellite Corporation (COMSAT) would be responsible for the management of the satellite system, and would bear the greatest part of the cost.

(3) Part ownership of the system would be open to any member of the International Telecommunication Union [see page 36].

A supplementary agreement on arbitration was concluded in Washington on June 4, 1965.

The International Telecommunications Satellite Consortium set up under these agreements became, on Feb. 12, 1973, the **International Telecommunications Satellite Organization** (Intelsat) which had, by the end of 1980, 105 member states.

By 1980 Intelsat had 10 intercontinental communications satellites in orbit, and a further satellite, Intelsat V, launched in December 1980, was capable of providing 12,000 telephone channels and two television channels simultaneously (i.e. it had twice the capacity of any of its predecessors).

An agreement on the establishment of an international space communications organization to be known as **Intersputnik** was signed in Moscow on Nov. 15, 1971, by Bulgaria, Cuba, Czechoslovakia, the German Democratic Republic, Hungary, Mongolia, Poland, Romania and the Soviet Union. Intersputnik would be open to accession by all countries and would co-ordinate its activities with the International Telecommunication Union and with the other organizations concerned with the use of communications satellites.

Outer Space Treaty

It was announced at the United Nations on Dec. 8, 1966, that agreement had been reached on the first international treaty governing space exploration. The treaty, officially designated the *Treaty on the Principles of the Activity of States in the Exploration and Use of Outer Space Including the Moon and Other Celestial Bodies,* was unanimously approved by the UN General Assembly on Dec. 19, 1966. It was signed by the United States, the Soviet Union, and the United Kingdom in their respective capitals on Jan. 27, 1967, and by the date of its entry into force (Oct. 10, 1967), it had been signed in Washington, London or Moscow by a total of 93 nations.

The operative articles of the treaty read as follows:

"**Art. 1.** The exploration and use of outer space, including the moon and other celestial bodies, shall be carried out for the benefit and in the interests of all countries, irrespective of their degree of economic or scientific development, and shall be the province of all mankind.

"Outer space, including the moon and other celestial bodies, shall be free for exploration and use by all states without discrimination of any kind, on a basis of equality and in accordance with international law, and there shall be free access to all areas of celestial bodies.

"There shall be freedom of scientific investigation in outer space, including the moon and other celestial bodies, and states shall facilitate and encourage international co-operation in such investigation.

"**Art. 2.** Outer space, including the moon and other celestial bodies, is not subject to national appropriation by claim of sovereignty, by means of use or occupation or by any other means.

"**Art. 3.** States parties to the treaty shall carry on

activities in the exploration and use of outer space, including the moon and other celestial bodies, in accordance with international law, including the Charter of the United Nations, in the interest of maintaining international peace and security and promoting international co-operation and understanding.

"**Art. 4.** States parties to the treaty undertake not to place in orbit around the earth any objects carrying nuclear weapons or any other kinds of weapons of mass destruction, install such weapons on celestial bodies, or station such weapons in outer space in any other manner.

"The moon and other celestial bodies shall be used by all states parties to the treaty exclusively for peaceful purposes. The establishment of military bases, installations and fortifications, the testing of any type of weapons, and the conduct of military manoeuvres on celestial bodies shall be forbidden. The use of military personnel for scientific research or for any other peaceful purposes shall not be prohibited. The use of any equipment or facility necessary for peaceful exploration of the moon and other celestial bodies shall also not be prohibited.

"**Art. 5.** States parties to the treaty shall regard astronauts as envoys of mankind in outer space and shall render to them all possible assistance in the event of accident, distress or emergency landing on the territory of another state party or on the high seas. When astronauts make such a landing, they shall be safely and promptly returned to the state of registry of their space vehicle.

"In carrying on activities in outer space and on celestial bodies, the astronauts of one state party shall render all possible assistance to the astronauts of other states parties.

"States parties to the treaty shall immediately inform the other states parties to the treaty or the Secretary-General of the United Nations of any phenomena they discover in outer space, including the moon and other celestial bodies, which could constitute a danger to the life or health of astronauts.

"**Art. 6.** States parties to the treaty shall bear international responsibility for national activities in outer space, including the moon and other celestial bodies, whether such activities are carried on by governmental agencies or by non-governmental entities, and for assuring that national activities are carried out in conformity with the provisions set forth in the present treaty.

"The activities of non-governmental entities in outer space, including the moon and other celestial bodies, shall require authorization and continuing supervision by the state concerned. When activities are carried on in outer space, including the moon and other celestial bodies, by an international organization, responsibility for compliance with this treaty shall be borne both by the international organization and by the states parties to the treaty participating in such organization.

"**Art. 7.** Each state party to the treaty that launches or procures the launching of an object into outer space, including the moon and other celestial bodies, and each state party from whose territory or facility an object is launched, is internationally liable for damage to another state party to the treaty or to its natural or juridical persons by such object or its component parts on the earth, in airspace, or in outer space, including the moon and other celestial bodies.

"**Art. 8.** A state party to the treaty on whose registry an object launched into outer space is carried shall retain jurisdiction and control over such object, and over any personnel thereof, while in outer space or

on a celestial body. Ownership of objects launched into outer space, including objects landed or constructed on a celestial body, and of their component parts, is not affected by their presence in outer space, including the body, or by their return to the earth. Such objects or component parts found beyond the limits of the state party to the treaty on whose registry they are carried shall be returned to that state, which shall, upon request, furnish identifying data prior to their return.

"**Art. 9.** In the exploration and use of outer space, including the moon and other celestial bodies, states parties to the treaty shall be guided by the principle of co-operation and mutual assistance and shall conduct all their activities in outer space, including the moon and other celestial bodies, with due regard to the corresponding interests of all other states parties to the treaty.

"States parties to the treaty shall pursue studies of outer space, including the moon and other celestial bodies, and conduct exploration of them so as to avoid their harmful contamination and also adverse changes in the environment of the earth resulting from the introduction of extra-terrestrial matter, and, where necessary, shall adopt appropriate measures for this purpose.

"If a state party to the treaty has reason to believe that an activity or experiment planned by it or its nationals in outer space, including the moon and other celestial bodies, would cause potentially harmful interference with activities of other states parties in the peaceful exploration and use of outer space, including the moon and other celestial bodies, it shall undertake appropriate international consultations before proceeding with any such activity or experiment.

"A state party to the treaty which has reason to believe that an activity or experiment planned by another state party in outer space, including the moon and other celestial bodies, would cause potentially harmful interference with activities in the peaceful exploration and use of outer space, including the moon and other celestial bodies, may request consultation concerning the activity or experiment.

"**Art. 10.** In order to promote international co-operation in the exploration and use of outer space, including the moon and other celestial bodies, in conformity with the purposes of this treaty, the states parties to the treaty shall consider on a basis of equality any requests by other states parties to the treaty to be afforded an opportunity to observe the flight of space objects launched by those states. The nature of such an opportunity for observation and the conditions under which it could be afforded shall be determined by agreement between the states concerned.

"**Art. 11.** In order to promote international co-operation in the peaceful exploration and use of outer space, states parties to the treaty conducting activities in outer space, including the moon and other celestial bodies, agree to inform the Secretary-General of the United Nations as well as the public and the international scientific community, to the greatest extent feasible and practicable, of the nature, conduct, locations and results of such activities. On receiving the said information, the UN Secretary-General should be prepared to disseminate it immediately and effectively.

"**Art. 12.** All stations, installations, equipment and space vehicles on the moon and other celestial bodies shall be open to representatives of other states parties to the treaty, on a basis of reciprocity. Such representatives shall give reasonable advance notice of a projected visit, in order that appropriate consultations may be held and that maximum precautions may be taken to assure safety and to avoid interference with normal operations in the facility to be visited.

"**Art. 13.** The provisions of this treaty shall apply to the activities of states parties to the treaty in the exploration and use of outer space, including the moon and other celestial bodies, whether such activities are carried on by a single state party to the treaty or jointly with other states, including cases where they are carried on within the framework of international inter-governmental organizations.

"Any practical questions arising in connexion with activities carried on by international inter-governmental organizations in the exploration and use of outer space, including the moon and other celestial bodies, shall be resolved by the states parties to the treaty either with the appropriate international organization or with one or more state members of that international organization, which are parties to this treaty.

"**Art. 14.** (1) This treaty shall be open to all states for signature. Any state which does not sign this treaty before its entry into force in accordance with Paragraph 3 of this article may accede to it at any time.

"(2) This treaty shall be subject to ratification by signatory states. Instruments of ratification and of accession shall be deposited with the Governments of the Union of Soviet Socialist Republics, the United Kingdom of Great Britain and Northern Ireland and the United States of America, which are hereby designated the depositary governments.

"(3) This treaty shall enter into force upon the deposit of instruments of ratification by five governments, including the governments designated as depositary governments.

"(4) For states whose instruments of ratification or accession are deposited subsequent to the entry into force of this treaty, it shall enter into force on the date of the deposit of their instruments of ratification or accession.

"(5) The depositary governments shall promptly inform all signatory and acceding states of the date of each signature, the date of deposit of each instrument of ratification of and accession to this treaty, the date of its entry into force, and other notices.

"(6) This treaty shall be registered by the depositary governments pursuant to Article 102 of the UN Charter.

"**Art. 15.** Any state party to the treaty may propose amendments to this treaty. Amendments shall enter into force for each state party to the treaty accepting the amendments upon their acceptance by a majority of the states parties to the treaty, and thereafter for each remaining state party to the treaty on the date of acceptance by it.

"**Art. 16.** Any state party to the treaty may give notice of its withdrawal from the treaty one year after its entry into force by written notification to the depositary governments. Such withdrawal shall take effect one year from the date of receipt of this notification."

A UN Committee on the Peaceful Uses of Outer Space, set up by the General Assembly in 1959, was, by a resolution passed by the Assembly on Dec. 20, 1977, enlarged from 37 to 47 members.

A further UN conference on the exploration and peaceful uses of outer space has been scheduled to be held in Vienna in August 1982.

Agreement on Rescue and Return of Astronauts

An *Agreement on the Rescue of Astronauts, the Return of Astronauts and the Return of Objects Launched into Outer Space* was approved by the UN General Assembly on Dec. 19, 1967, by 115 votes to none, with no abstentions.

Under this agreement, which had been worked out by the United States and the Soviet Union in co-operation with the Committee on Outer Space of the UN General Assembly, signatories were bound to render "all possible assistance to astronauts in the event of accident, distress, emergency or unintended landing". The agreement also provided for safe and prompt return of astronauts and space objects, and reimbursement of expenses to the launching state, as well as for notification of unplanned landings by space travellers or spacecraft.

The agreement entered into force on Dec. 3, 1968, after ratification by Britain, the Soviet Union and the United States.

Convention of International Liability

The UN General Assembly approved on Nov. 29, 1971, by 93 votes to none with four abstentions (Canada, Iran, Japan and Sweden) a *Convention on International Liability for Damage Caused by Space Objects*. The convention was signed in London, Moscow and Washington on March 29, 1972, and by Dec. 31, 1979, it was in force for 55 countries.

Convention on Registration of Objects launched into Outer Space

On Nov. 12, 1974, the UN General Assembly unanimously approved a *Convention on Registration of Objects launched into Outer Space* (which in effect was an extension of the provisions of the Treaty on Principles governing the Activities of States in the Exploration and Use of Outer Space—see above).

The convention required each launching state to keep a registry showing details of any space object launched into earth orbit or beyond and this information to be furnished to the UN Secretary-General for entry in a register to be kept by him and offering "full and open access" to its information. The convention was to enter into force for those states which had ratified it upon the deposit of the fifth instrument of ratification with the UN Secretary-General and for other states on the date of the deposit of their instrument of ratification or accession. The convention was subject to review 10 years after its entry into force, or after five years upon request by one-third of the states parties to it.

The convention came into force in 1976 after being ratified by the United States, Bulgaria, Canada, France and Sweden (with 22 other countries having signed but not ratified it).

Agreement on Monitoring of the Stratosphere

An agreement between France, the United Kingdom and the United States regarding monitoring of the stratosphere was signed in Paris on May 5, 1976.

Agreement governing the Activities of States on the Moon and Other Celestial Bodies

This agreement was adopted without a vote by the UN General Assembly on Dec. 5, 1979. Its operative articles read as follows:

"**Art. 1.** (1) The provisions of this agreement relating to the moon shall also apply to other celestial bodies within the solar system, other than the earth, except in so far as specific legal norms enter into force with respect to any of these celestial bodies.

"(2) For the purposes of this agreement reference to the moon shall include orbits around or other trajectories to or around it.

"(3) This agreement does not apply to extraterrestrial materials which reach the surface of the earth by natural means.

"**Art. 2.** All activities on the moon, including its exploration and use, shall be carried out in accordance with international law, in particular the Charter of the United Nations, and taking into account the Declaration on Principles of International Law concerning Friendly Relations and Co-operation among States in accordance with the Charter of the United Nations, adopted by the General Assembly on Oct. 24, 1970, in the interests of maintaining international peace and security and promoting international co-operation and mutual understanding, and with due regard to the corresponding interests of all other states parties. [For the 1970 Declaration on Principles of International Law, see page 43.]

"**Art. 3.** (1) The moon shall be used by all states parties exclusively for peaceful purposes.

"(2) Any threat or use of force or any other hostile act or threat of hostile act on the moon is prohibited. It is likewise prohibited to use the moon in order to commit any such act or to engage in any such threat in relation to the earth, the moon, spacecraft, the personnel of spacecraft or man-made space objects.

"(3) States parties shall not place in orbit around or other trajectory to or around the moon objects carrying nuclear weapons or any other kinds of weapons of mass destruction or place or use such weapons on or in the moon.

"(4) The establishment of military bases, installations and fortifications, the testing of any type of weapons and the conduct of military manoeuvres on the moon shall be forbidden. The use of military personnel for scientific research or for any other peaceful purposes shall not be prohibited. The use of any equipment or facility necessary for peaceful exploration and use of the moon shall also not be prohibited.

"**Art. 4.** (1) The exploration and use of the moon shall be the province of all mankind and shall be carried out for the benefit and in the interests of all countries, irrespective of their degree of economic or scientific development. Due regard shall be paid to the interests of present and future generations as well as to the need to promote higher standards of living and conditions of economic and social progress and development in accordance with the Charter of the United Nations.

"(2) States parties shall be guided by the principle of co-operation and mutual assistance in all their activities concerning the exploration and use of the moon. International co-operation in pursuance of this agreement should be as wide as possible and may take place on a multilateral basis, on a bilateral basis or through international intergovernmental organizations.

"**Art. 5.** (1) States parties shall inform the Secretary-General of the United Nations as well as the public and the international scientific community, to the greatest extent feasible and practicable, of their activities concerned with the exploration and use of the moon. Information on the time, purposes, locations, orbital parameters and duration shall be given in respect of each mission to the moon as soon as possible after launching, while information on the results of each mission, including scientific results, shall be furnished upon completion of the mission. In the case of a mission lasting more than 60 days, information on conduct of the mission, including any scientific results, shall be given periodically at 30-day intervals. For missions lasting more than six months, only significant additions to such information need be reported thereafter.

"(2) If a state party becomes aware that another state party plans to operate simultaneously in the same area of or in the same orbit around or trajectory to or around the moon, it shall promptly inform the other state of the timing of and plans for its own operations.

"(3) In carrying out activities under this agreement, states parties shall promptly inform the Secretary-General, as well as the public and the international scientific community, of any phenomena they discover in outer space, including the moon, which could endanger human life or health, as well as of any indication of organic life.

"**Art. 6.** (1) There shall be freedom of scientific investigation on the moon by all states parties without discrimination of any kind, on the basis of equality and in accordance with international law.

"(2) In carrying out scientific investigations and in furtherance of the provisions of this agreement, the states parties shall have the right to collect on and remove from the moon samples of its mineral and other substances. Such samples shall remain at the disposal of those states parties which caused them to be collected and may be used by them for scientific purposes. States parties shall have regard to the desirability of making a portion of such samples available to other interested states parties and the international scientific community for scientific investigation. States parties may in the course of scientific investigations also use mineral and other substances of the moon in quantities appropriate for the support of their missions.

"(3) States parties agree on the desirability of exchanging scientific and other personnel on expeditions to or installations on the moon to the greatest extent feasible and practicable.

"**Art. 7.** (1) In exploring and using the moon, states parties shall take measures to prevent the disruption of the existing balance of its environment whether by introducing adverse changes in that environment, by its harmful contamination through the introduction of extra-environmental matter or otherwise. States parties shall also take measures to avoid harmfully affecting the environment of the earth through the introduction of extraterrestrial matter or otherwise.

"(2) States parties shall inform the Secretary-General of the United Nations of the measures being adopted by them in accordance with Paragraph 1 of this article and shall also, to the maximum extent feasible, notify him in advance of all placements by them of radioactive materials on the moon and of the purposes of such placements.

"(3) States parties shall report to other states parties and to the Secretary-General concerning areas of the moon having special scientific interest in order that, without prejudice to the rights of other states parties, consideration may be given to the designation of such areas as international scientific preserves for which special protective arrangements are to be agreed upon in consultation with the competent bodies of the United Nations.

"**Art. 8.** (1) States parties may pursue their activities in the exploration and use of the moon anywhere on or below its surface, subject to the provisions of this agreement.

"(2) For these purposes states parties may, in particular:

"(*a*) Land their space objects on the moon and launch them from the moon;

"(*b*) place their personnel, space vehicles, equipment, facilities, stations and installations anywhere on or below the surface of the moon.

"Personnel, space vehicles, equipment, facilities, stations and installations may move or be moved freely over or below the surface of the moon.

"(3) Activities of states parties in accordance with Paragraphs 1 and 2 of this article shall not interfere with the activities of other states parties on the moon. Where such interference may occur, the states parties concerned shall undertake consultations in accordance with Article 15, Paragraphs 2 and 3 of this agreement.

"**Art. 9.** (1) States parties may establish manned and unmanned stations on the moon. A state party establishing a station shall use only that area which is required for the needs of the station and shall immediately inform the Secretary-General of the United Nations of the location and purposes of that station. Subsequently, at annual intervals that state shall likewise inform the Secretary-General whether the station continues in use and whether its purposes have changed.

"(2) Stations shall be installed in such a manner that they do not impede the free access to all areas of the moon by personnel, vehicles and equipment of other states parties conducting activities on the moon in accordance with the provisions of this agreement or of Article 1 of the Treaty on Principles governing the Activities of States in the Exploration and Use of Outer Space, including the Moon and Other Celestial Bodies.

"**Art. 10.** (1) States parties shall adopt all practicable measures to safeguard the life and health of persons on the moon. For this purpose they shall regard any person on the moon as an astronaut within the meaning of Article V of the Treaty on Principles governing the Activities of States in the Exploration and Use of Outer Space, including the Moon and Other Celestial Bodies and as part of the personnel of a spacecraft within the meaning of the Agreement of the Rescue of Astronauts, the Return of Astronauts and the Return of Objects launched into Outer Space.

"(2) States parties shall offer shelter in their stations, installations, vehicles and other facilities to persons in distress on the moon.

"**Art. 11.** (1) The moon and its natural resources are the common heritage of mankind, which finds its expression in the provisions of this agreement, in particular in Paragraph 5 of this article.

"(2) The moon is not subject to national appropriation by any claim of sovereignty, by means of use or occupation, or by any other means.

"(3) Neither the surface nor the subsurface of the moon, nor any part thereof or natural resources in place, shall become property of any state, international intergovernmental or non-governmental organization, national organization or non-governmental entity or of any natural person. The placement of personnel, space vehicles, equipment, facilities, stations and installations on or below the surface of the moon, including structures connected with its surface or subsurface, shall not create a right of ownership over the surface or the subsurface of the moon or any areas thereof. The foregoing provisions are without prejudice to the international regime referred to in Paragraph 5 of this article.

"(4) States parties have the right to exploration and use of the moon without discrimination of any kind, on the basis of equality and in accordance with international law and the provisions of this agreement.

"(5) States parties to this agreement hereby undertake to establish an international regime, including appropriate procedures, to govern the exploitation of the natural resources of the moon as such exploitation is about to become feasible. This provision shall be implemented in accordance with Article 18 of this agreement.

"(6) In order to facilitate the establishment of the international regime referred to in Paragraph 5 of this article, states parties shall inform the Secretary-General of the United Nations as well as the public and the international scientific community, to the greatest extent feasible and practicable, of any natural resources they may discover on the moon.

"(7) The main purposes of the international regime to be established shall include:

"(*a*) The orderly and safe development of the natural resources of the moon;

"(*b*) the rational management of those resources;

"(*c*) the expansion of opportunities in the use of those resources;

"(*d*) an equitable sharing by all states parties in the benefits derived from those resources, whereby the interests and needs of the developing countries, as well as the efforts of those countries which have contributed either directly or indirectly to the exploration of the moon, shall be given special consideration.

"(8) All the activities with respect to the natural resources of the moon shall be carried out in a manner compatible with the purposes specified in Paragraph 7 of this article and the provisions of Article 6, Paragraph 2, of this agreement.

"**Art. 12.** (1) States parties shall retain jurisdiction and control over their personnel, space vehicles, equipment, facilities, stations and installations on the moon. The ownership of space vehicles, equipment, facilities, stations and installations shall not be affected by their presence on the moon.

"(2) Vehicles, installations and equipment or their component parts found in places other than their intended location shall be dealt with in accordance with Article 5 of the Agreement on the Rescue of Astronauts, the Return of Astronauts and the Return of Objects launched into Outer Space.

"(3) In the event of an emergency involving a threat to human life, states parties may use the equipment, vehicles, installations, facilities or supplies of other states parties on the moon. Prompt notification of such use shall be made to the Secretary-General of the United Nations or the state party concerned.

"**Art. 13.** A state party which learns of the crash-landing, forced landing or other unintended landing on the moon of a space object, or its component parts, that were not launched by it, shall promptly inform the launching state party and the Secretary-General of the United Nations.

"**Art. 14.** (1) States parties to this agreement shall bear international responsibility for national activities on the moon, whether such activities are carried out by governmental agencies or by non-governmental entities, and for assuring that national activities are carried out in conformity with the provisions set forth in this agreement. States parties shall ensure that non-governmental entities under this jurisdiction shall engage in activities on the moon only under the authority and continuing supervision of the appropriate state party.

"(2) States parties recognize that detailed arrangements concerning liability for damage caused on the moon, in addition to the provisions of the Treaty on Principles governing the Activities of States in the Exploration and Use of Outer Space, including the Moon and Other Celestial Bodies, and the Convention on International Liability for Damage caused by Space Objects, may become necessary as a result of more extensive activities on the moon. Any such arrangements shall be elaborated in accordance with the procedure provided for in Article 18 of this agreement.

"**Art. 15.** (1) Each state party may assure itself that the activities of other states parties in the exploration and use of the moon are compatible with the provisions of this agreement. To this end, all space vehicles, equipment, facilities, stations and installations on the moon shall be open to other states parties. Such states parties shall give reasonable advance notice of a projected visit, in order that appropriate consultations may be held and that maximum precautions may be taken to assure safety and to avoid interference with normal operations in the facility to be visited. In pursuance of this article, any state party may act on its own behalf or with the full or partial assistance of any other state party or through appropriate international procedures within the framework of the United Nations and in accordance with the Charter.

"(2) A state party which has reason to believe that another state party is not fulfilling the obligations incumbent upon it pursuant to this agreement or that another state party is interfering with the rights which the former state has under this agreement may request consultations with that state party. A state party receiving such a request shall enter into such consultations without delay. Any other state party which requests to do so shall be entitled to take part in the consultations. Each state party participating in such consultations shall seek a mutually acceptable resolution of any controversy and shall bear in mind the rights and interests of all states parties. The Secretary-General of the United Nations shall be informed of the results of the consultations and shall transmit the information received to all states parties concerned.

"(3) If the consultations do not lead to a mutually acceptable settlement which has due regard for the rights and interests of all states parties, the parties concerned shall take all measures to settle the dispute by other peaceful means of their choice appropriate to the circumstances and the nature of the dispute. If difficulties arise in connexion with the opening of consultations or if consultations do not lead to a mutually acceptable settlement, any state party may seek the assistance of the Secretary-General, without seeking the consent of any other state party concerned, in order to resolve the controversy. A state party which does not maintain diplomatic relations with another state party concerned shall participate in such consultations, at its choice, either itself or through another state party or the Secretary-General as intermediary.

"**Art. 16.** With the exception of Articles 17 to 21, references in this agreement to states shall be deemed to apply to any international intergovernmental organization which conducts space activities if the organization declares its acceptance of the rights and obligations provided for in this agreement and if a majority of the states members of the organization are states parties to this agreement and to the Treaty on Principles governing the Activities of States in the Exploration and Use of Outer Space, including the Moon and Other Celestial Bodies. States members of any such organization which are states parties to this agreement shall take all appropriate steps to ensure that the organization makes a declaration in accordance with the provisions of this article.

"**Art. 17.** Any state party to this agreement may propose amendments to the agreement. Amendments shall enter into force for each state party to the agreement accepting the amendments upon their acceptance by a majority of the states parties to the agreement and thereafter for each remaining state party to the agreement on the date of acceptance by it.

"**Art. 18.** Ten years after the entry into force of this agreement, the question of the review of the agreement shall be included in the provisional agenda of the General Assembly of the United Nations in order to consider, in the light of past application of the agreement, whether it requires revision. However, at any time after the agreement has been in force for five years, the Secretary-General of the United Nations, as depository, shall, at the request of one-third of the states parties to the agreement and with the concurrence of the majority of the states parties, convene a conference of the states parties to review this agreement. A review conference shall also consider the question of the implementation of the provisions of Article 11, Paragraph 5, on the basis of the principle referred to in Paragraph 1 of that article and taking into account in particular any relevant technological developments.

"**Art. 19.** (1) This agreement shall be open for signature by all states at United Nations Headquarters in New York.

"(2) This agreement shall be subject to ratification by signatory states. Any state which does not sign this agreement before its entry into force in accordance with Paragraph 3 of this article may accede to it at any time. Instruments of ratification or accession shall be deposited with the Secretary-General of the United Nations.

"(3) This agreement shall enter into force on the 30th day following the date of deposit of the fifth instrument of ratification.

"(4) For each state depositing its instrument of ratification or accession after the entry into force of this agreement, it shall enter into force on the 30th day following the date of deposit of any such instrument.

"(5) The Secretary-General shall promptly inform all signatory and acceding states of the date of each signature, the date of deposit of each instrument of ratification or accession to this agreement, the date of its entry into force and other notices.

"**Art. 20.** Any state party to this agreement may give notice of its withdrawal from the agreement one year after its entry into force by written notification to the Secretary-General of the United Nations. Such withdrawal shall take effect one year from the date of receipt of this notification. . . .''

European Space Agency

The European Space Agency (ESA) was established on May 30, 1975, under an agreement signed in Brussels on July 31, 1973, at a meeting of the European Space Conference—set up on Dec. 13, 1966, and consisting of representatives of the European Launcher Development Organization (ELDO), the European Space Research Organization (ESRO) and the European Conference on Satellite Communications (CETS).

ELDO had been formed under a convention which was signed on April 12, 1962 (by Australia, Belgium, France, the Federal Republic of Germany, Italy, the Netherlands and the United Kingdom). The object of ELDO was to develop a European earth-satellite launcher in preparation for the possible use of satellites for various purposes. ELDO's original programme (ELDO-A) covered the development and construction of a three-stage satellite-launching vehicle, with the work being distributed among the ELDO member countries and firings to be made at Woomera (Australia). In 1966 this programme was modified in order to enable a synchronous telecommunications satellite to be placed in orbit; the modified programme—ELDO-PAS—required two additional stages and an equatorial launching site.

In July 1966 it was decided to apply a new scale of contributions to the implementation of the ELDO-PAS programme, with an overall cost ceiling of about $330,000,000 to be divided between the United Kingdom (27 per cent), the Federal Republic of Germany (27 per cent), France (25 per cent), Italy (12 per cent) and Belgium and the Netherlands (4½ per cent each) and to use Kourou (French Guiana) as an operational equatorial launching site. The British Government, however, announced on April 16, 1968, that it would make no further contributions after 1971 because the costs were prohibitive and the potential applications of the programme were "both limited and speculative". In fact, ELDO launcher firings made at Woomera in 1967-70 were failures, and one made at Kourou in November 1971 also failed. The United Kingdom withdrew from ELDO with effect from Jan. 1, 1973, and all further work on ELDO programmes was discontinued in April 1973.

ESRO was set up under a convention which was signed on June 14, 1962, by representatives of 12 countries (Austria, Belgium, Denmark, France, the Federal Republic of Germany, Italy, the Netherlands, Norway, Spain, Sweden, Switzerland and the United Kingdom) and entered into force on March 21, 1964. ESRO's first work programme for an eight-year period included the firing of fully instrumental vertical sounding-rockets, the launching of satellites (at first in near-earth orbits and later in eccentric orbits), of fully instrumental space probes or large satellites, and eventually of several large astronomical satellites. Some 300 research rockets were fired (from Sardinia) from July 1964 onwards. An ESRO spacecraft was first successfully launched on May 17, 1968. Between 1968 and 1972 ESRO conducted a series of satellite launchings using US rocket vehicles fired in the United States.

Under ESRO, installations were established as follows:

(1) A Space Technology Centre (ESTEC) at Noordwijk (Netherlands), responsible for technical research connected with ESRO's launching programme;

(2) a Space Research Laboratory (ESLAB) at Noordwijk, to co-ordinate the various projects;

(3) a Data Centre (ESDAC) at Darmstadt (Federal Republic of Germany);

(4) a Sounding-Rocket Launching Range (ESRANGE) at Kiruna in Arctic Sweden, operational from 1966 onwards;

(5) a Space Research Institute (ESRIN) at Frascati (Italy) for theoretical research on the physical and chemical phenomena of space;

(6) a Tracking and Telemetry Network (ESTRACK) to track and communicate with satellites, with four stations—at Fairbanks (Alaska), Ny-Alesund (Svalbard), Port Stanley (Falkland Islands) and Redu (Belgium).

For the Svalbard station ESRO concluded two agreements in September 1965: (i) with the Norwegian Government on the construction and conditions of operation of the station; and (ii) with the Norwegian Technical and Scientific Research Council on the operation of the station; both agreements were conditional upon restricting the station's activities to purely scientific and peaceful ends.

The CETS was established in 1963 by member governments of the European Conference of Postal and Telecommunications Administrations (CEPT, which had been formed in 1959 to harmonize and improve technical services among these administrations and which had been joined by 26 European countries—all except those of the Soviet bloc, Albania and Andorra). The main task of the CETS was achieved with the conclusion of the Intelsat agreements of August 1964 [see above].

The 10 countries signing the convention on the establishment of the ESA were Belgium, Denmark, France, the Federal Republic of Germany, Italy, the Netherlands, Spain, Sweden, Switzerland and the United Kingdom. Ireland signed the agreement on Dec. 30, 1975; Austria, Canada and Norway attended the first ministerial-level meeting of the ESA's council in Paris on Feb. 14-15, 1977, as observers; Austria became an associate member of the ESA on Oct. 17, 1979, as did Norway on April 2, 1981; and the Irish Republic became its 11th full member on Dec. 10, 1980. The ESA convention entered into force on Oct. 30, 1980.

The ESA was not to be involved in the International Telecommunications Satellite Organization (Intelsat) or the UK Skynet defence satellite system, but it took up three projects, namely (i) a French proposal for developing the L3-S (Ariane) satellite launcher; (ii) a 10 per cent share in the US post-Apollo space shuttle programme, for which a European space laboratory was to be created; and (iii) the development of a satellite for marine communications. The first European-built satellites under ESA auspices were put into orbit in August 1975 and April 1977 by US Delta rockets under co-operation agreements with the (US) National Astronautics and Space Administration.

Agreements signed between the ESA and France on May 5, 1976, provided that (i) the space station at Kourou was made available for unrestricted use by the ESA and each of its member states, with administrative control of Kourou being transferred to the ESA from the French *Centre national d'études spatiales* (CNES) and (ii) the ESA and its member states were given full access to the L3-S rocket launcher being developed at the site.

The launching of the first European telecommunications satellite (Orbital Test Satellite, OTS) from Cape Canaveral (USA) on Sept. 13, 1977, was a failure, but a second OTS, successfully launched on May 11, 1978, was on May 24 of that year placed in geostationary orbit 36,000 kilometres above the earth and by Oct. 17, 1978, completed its first tests transmitting television programmes beyond continental Europe. [See also below under European Telecommunications Satellite Organization—Eutelsat.]

A first meteorological satellite was, under an ESA programme, launched into orbit from Cape Canaveral on Nov. 22, 1977, and inter alia carried out two research projects for the World Meteorological Organization (WMO).

The ESA also co-operated in the launching, in the United States in October 1977 and January 1978, of two International Sun-Earth Explorer Satellites. Europe's first geostationary scientific satellite, Geos-2, was launched by a Delta rocket on July 14, 1978, with a scientific payload supplied by 11 research institutes in eight of the ESA member countries.

European Telecommunications Satellite Organization (Eutelsat)

The establishment of this organization was agreed in May 1977 by more than 20 European countries, including the full members of the ESA, with the object of providing a regional satellite system for telephone and broadcasting links between the members of the CEPT [see above]. Eutelsat subsequently planned an operational satellite network which in the 1980s would be able to handle two television channels and 5,000 telephone calls simultaneously.

Bilateral US-Soviet Space Co-operation

Bilateral co-operation in space matters between the United States and the Soviet Union was first implemented by the link-up in space of a (US) *Apollo* and a (Soviet) *Soyuz* spacecraft on July 17, 1975, as provided for under plans agreed upon in May 1972. This was followed by a meeting of US and Soviet officials in October 1976 to discuss the possible establishment of a network of satellites to search for stranded ships and downed aircraft and to measure air pollution.

An agreement on co-operation between the two states in the exploration and use of outer space for peaceful purposes, signed in Geneva on May 18, 1977, contained the following operative articles:

"**Art. 1.** The parties will continue to develop co-operation in such fields of space science and applications as space meteorology; study of the natural environment; exploration of near-Earth space, the Moon and the planets; space biology and medicine; satellite search and rescue systems; and, in particular, will co-operate to take all appropriate measures to encourage and achieve the fulfilment of the Summary of Results of Discussion on Space Co-operation between the Academy of Sciences of the USSR and the US National Aeronautics and Space Administration [NASA], dated Jan. 21, 1971, periodically renewed.

"**Art. 2.** The parties will carry out such co-operation through their appropriate national agencies by means of mutual exchanges of scientific information and delegations, and meetings of scientists and specialists of both countries, and also in such other ways as may be mutually agreed. Joint working groups may be created for the development and implementation of appropriate programmes of co-operation.

"**Art. 3.** The parties will take all necessary measures for the further development of co-operation in the area of manned space flight for scientific and practical objectives, including the use in joint flights of compatible docking and rendezvous systems derived from those developed during the experimental flight of *Soyuz* and *Apollo* spacecraft in July 1975. Joint work in this direction will be carried out in accordance with the Agreement between the Academy of Sciences of the USSR and the US National Aeronautics and Space Administration on Co-operation in the Area of Manned Space Flight dated May 11, 1977.

"**Art. 4.** The parties will encourage international efforts to resolve problems of international law in the exploration and use of outer space for peaceful purposes with the aim of strengthening the legal order in space and further developing international space law and will co-operate in this field.

"**Art. 5.** The parties may by mutual agreement determine other areas of co-operation in the exploration and use of outer space for peaceful purposes.

"**Art. 6.** This agreement shall enter into force on May 24, 1977, and shall remain in force for five years. It may be modified or extended by mutual agreement of the parties. . . .''

This agreement replaced one signed in 1972 (during a visit to Moscow by President Nixon—see page 239).

There followed a further agreement, concluded in November 1977, on discussion of the operation of an international space station in the 1980s, and the inauguration on Jan. 16, 1978, of a two-channel system of direct space communication between Washington and Moscow.

Both parties have concluded agreements on co-operation in space research with a number of other countries.

Declarations and Conventions on Environmental Problems

Declarations issued under Council of Europe Auspices

(1) A *Declaration on the Management of the Natural Environment of Europe* was adopted on Feb. 12, 1970, by a European Conservation Conference convened in Strasbourg by the Council of Europe and attended by the Council's 17 members as well as by representatives of 10 other countries (Canada, Czechoslovakia, Finland, Israel, Liechtenstein, Portugal, Romania, Spain, the United States and Yugoslavia).

The declaration laid down guidelines for the "rational use and management of the environment"; for the harmonization of legislation for safeguarding the environment; and for co-operation between public authorities, industry and conservationists.

(2) A *Declaration on the Problem of Sea Pollution* was issued by the Consultative Assembly of the Council of Europe on Sept. 24, 1970, calling on member governments to "take forthwith drastic measures" to end pollution of the sea which threatened "directly the very life of the sea and . . . put in question the survival of humanity as a whole".

Conventions administered by the Oslo Commission

Conventions and an agreement administered by the Oslo Commission, set up in London under the first convention listed below, are as follows:

(1) A *Convention against Marine Pollution,* designed to prevent sea pollution by the dumping of waste from ships and aircraft, was signed in Oslo on Feb. 15, 1972, by Belgium, Denmark, Finland, France, the Federal Republic of Germany, Iceland, the Netherlands, Norway, Portugal, Spain, Sweden and the United Kingdom.

The area covered by the convention comprised the high seas and territorial waters of the north-east Atlantic and part of the Arctic area, its western boundary being the longitude of Greenland and its southern boundary the latitude of the Straits of Gibraltar.

This convention came into effect on April 7, 1974, after the required ratification by seven of its 12 signatories, i.e. by Denmark, France, Iceland, Norway, Portugal, Spain and Sweden.

(2) A *Convention for the Prevention of Marine Pollution from Land-based Sources* was signed in Paris on June 4, 1974, by Belgium, Denmark, France, the Federal Republic of Germany, Iceland, Ireland, Luxembourg, the Netherlands, Norway, Portugal,

Spain, Sweden and the United Kingdom, as well as by the European Communities. It entered into force on May 6, 1978.

(3) An *Agreement for Co-operation in Dealing with Pollution of the North Sea by Oil* was concluded in Bonn on June 9, 1969, by representatives of Belgium, Denmark, France, the Federal Republic of Germany, Norway, Sweden and the United Kingdom on June 9, 1969. It required the signatory governments to request ships and aircraft to report major oil slicks; to circulate reports on the presence, extent and movements of slicks; and on request to use their best endeavours to assist other countries in disposing of oil threatening their coasts. The agreement also established zones of responsibility for each country in the North Sea area.

The agreement entered into force on Aug. 9, 1969, in all signatory states except Norway, where it came into force on Nov. 28, 1970, and it was acceded to by the Netherlands on March 8, 1974.

Conventions on Protection of Wildlife

(1) A *Convention on Wetlands of International Importance, especially as Wildfowl Habitat,* was adopted at a conference at Ramsar (Iran) on Feb. 2, 1971.

(2) A *Convention on International Trade in Endangered Species of Wild Fauna and Flora* was signed in Washington on March 3, 1973.

(3) A *Convention on the Conservation of Migratory Species of Wild Animals* was opened for signature until June 22, 1980.

IMCO Conventions on Marine Pollution

A number of conventions have been concluded under the auspices of the Intergovernmental Maritime Consultative Organization (IMCO) [see page 37] with the object of preventing pollution of the sea and of dealing with such pollution.

(1) An *International Convention for the Prevention of Pollution of the Sea by Oil,* agreed on May 12, 1954, and banning the discharging into the sea of crude oil, fuel oil, diesel oil and lubricating oil within specified zones, came into force for tankers on July 26, 1958, and for dry cargo ships on July 26, 1961. Amendments to this convention were signed in 1962, 1969, and 1971.

(2) An *International Convention Relating to Intervention on the High Seas in Cases of Oil Pollution Casualties* was adopted at

the end of a conference held by IMCO from Nov. 10 to 29, 1969. The convention dealt with the right of a coastal state to protect its own interests when a casualty occurred on the high seas which might damage those interests. This convention entered into force on May 6, 1975.

(3) At the same conference, an *International Convention on Civil Liability for Oil Pollution Damage* was adopted, providing that the owner of a ship from which polluting oil escaped would be held liable for any pollution damage caused. This convention entered into force on June 19, 1975.

At a complementary conference held on Nov. 29-Dec. 18, 1971, another agreement resulted, known as the *Convention on the Establishment of an International Fund for Compensation for Oil Pollution Damage,* which came into force on Oct. 16, 1978. The fund was designed to offer compensation in cases of large-scale pollution where the terms of provisions for civil liability were inadequate to cover the damage incurred. It was also complementary to the *Tanker Owners' Voluntary Agreement concerning Liability for Oil Pollution* (Tovalop), which came into effect on Oct. 6, 1969, and was repeatedly amended and renewed, most recently on June 1, 1979, for a period of two years (with further renewals to be considered annually thereafter).

(4) A *Convention on the Prevention of Marine Pollution by Dumping* was adopted at an intergovernmental conference held in London on Oct. 30-Nov. 13, 1972, and attended by representatives of 81 Governments and observers from 12 other countries. The Soviet Union participated, but the People's Republic of China was absent.

The main aim of the convention is to prevent indiscriminate disposal at sea of waste chemicals and minerals, on the understanding that the sea's capacity to assimilate waste and to regenerate natural resources is not unlimited. The dumping of certain categories of waste will be prohibited or subject to permit.

At the close of the conference the convention had been initialled by 57 countries. It came into force on Aug. 30, 1975, after ratification by the required seven of the 12 signatories, i.e. by Denmark, France, Iceland, Norway, Portugal, Spain and Sweden. By Dec. 31, 1979, it was in force in 42 countries.

(5) A *Convention for the Prevention of Pollution from Ships* was adopted at a conference held in London from Oct. 8 to Nov. 2, 1973, and attended by delegates from 79 countries and numerous international organizations.

The convention contained provisions aimed at eliminating pollution of the sea by both oil and other noxious substances which might be discharged operationally, and at minimizing the amount of oil which would be released accidentally in collisions or strandings by ships of any type whatsoever, including also fixed or floating platforms. The convention did not, however, deal with dumping—which was covered by the convention listed in item (4) above—nor with the release of harmful substances directly arising from the exploration, exploitation and associated offshore processing of seabed mineral resources. The convention incorporated certain amendments made earlier to the convention described in Section 1 above. It also laid down that the Mediterranean, the Black Sea, the Baltic Sea, the Red Sea and the Gulf area (including the Sea of Oman) were designated as special areas in which oil discharge was completely prohibited (except by very small ships). Moreover, the convention contained special requirements for the control of pollution by over 400 different noxious substances and for sewage and garbage disposal.

The convention was to enter into force 12 months after ratification by 15 states representing at least 50 per cent of the world's merchant shipping; when in force it was to supersede the convention which came into force in 1958-61—see item (1) above; and would form part of the Law of the Sea under negotiation within the framework of the United Nations.

(6) A Protocol extending the provisions of the 1969 convention—dealt with in item (2) above—to cover noxious substances other than oil was adopted at the same conference; it was to enable states to take preventive action outside their territorial waters when faced with massive pollution or the threat of it.

Other Agreements by Coastal States

In addition to the conventions agreed upon under the auspices of IMCO, a number of multilateral or bilateral conventions and agreements were concluded by coastal states in various areas of the globe.

English Channel. The British Government announced on Aug. 9, 1972, that it had made agreements with France and Belgium on co-operation in the surveillance of oil slicks in the Channel area.

Baltic Sea. Ministers in charge of environmental affairs from seven countries bordering the Baltic Sea—Denmark, Finland, the German Democratic Republic, the Federal Republic of Germany, Poland, the Soviet Union and Sweden—signed, in Helsinki on March 22, 1974, a convention on the protection of the marine environment of the Baltic Sea and the prevention of pollution of the sea.

The signatory countries undertook to prevent the spread of "hazardous substances" (including mercury and cadmium) in the Baltic; to prohibit the release of oil and liquid chemicals from ships, and also the dumping of refuse; to establish close co-operation

75

between the competent national organizations; and to set up, in Helsinki, a permanent commission to supervise the implementation of the convention, which came into force on May 3, 1980. Immediately afterwards, the newly established Baltic Marine Environment Protection Commission issued its first recommendations for further measures against pollution.

In April 1974 Denmark and Sweden signed a bilateral convention on the protection of the Öresund (linking the Baltic with the North Sea), involving the construction by 1979 of a purification plant to reduce pollution by industrial and organic waste.

Mediterranean Sea. An action plan for the protection of the Mediterranean Sea was agreed upon at a conference of representatives of 16 Mediterranean coastal states (i.e. all except Albania and Cyprus), of three observer countries (Britain, the Soviet Union and the United States) and of several international organizations, held in Barcelona from Jan. 28 to Feb. 4, 1975, under the auspices of UNEP.

The plan provided for "integrated planning of the development and management of the resources of the Mediterranean basin"; "co-ordinated pollution monitoring and research" in the Mediterranean; the drafting of a "framework convention and related protocols with their technical annexes for the protection of the Mediterranean environment"; and "institutional and financial procedures" to be followed in respect of the plan.

At a further conference of the 16 coastal states, held in Barcelona on Feb. 2-16, 1976, under UNEP auspices, a treaty and two protocols were signed by 12 of these states.

The treaty laid down that its signatories should take all necessary measures to prevent pollution of the sea by dumping from ships and aircraft, by exploitation of the continental shelf and the seabed, or by sources of pollution on land such as rivers or sewage effluent. The first protocol banned the dumping at sea of toxic substances from ships and aircraft and contained a "black list" of prohibited substances and a restricted list of substances for which a special permit was required. The second protocol provided for co-ordinated action in the event of oil spills and for the establishment of regional headquarters to direct such operations.

Such headquarters were opened in Malta on Dec. 11, 1976, and the treaty and protocols entered into force on Feb. 12, 1978.

A "blue plan", designed to cover the period up to the end of the century and to harmonize activities in order to ensure continuous economic and social development of the ecological environment of the whole Mediterranean region was unanimously adopted at a meeting in Split (Yugoslavia) from Jan. 31 to Feb. 4, 1977, by representatives of 15 nations (i.e. all coastal countries except Albania, Lebanon and Syria).

A protocol on the protection of the Mediterranean against pollution from land-based sources was signed at a conference organized by UNEP and held in Athens on May 12-17, 1980. An annex to the convention listed prohibited substances (as laid down in the first protocol to the Barcelona treaty —see above) to be eliminated progressively from wastes and also specified common guidelines, criteria or standards for implementing the protocol.

All Mediterranean coastal states except Albania had in February 1979 agreed to take over the burden of financing the Mediterranean action plan, with UNEP aid to cease by 1981. In May 1980 it was announced that the headquarters of the secretariat for the Mediterranean action plan would be transferred from Geneva to Barcelona.

Persian Gulf. A conference held in Kuwait on April 15-25, 1978, by representatives of eight states bordering the Persian Gulf— Bahrain, Iran, Iraq, Kuwait, Qatar, Saudi Arabia and the United Arab Emirates—under UNEP auspices approved a framework convention, a protocol and an action plan.

In the convention the signatory states undertook to "prevent, abate and combat pollution . . . caused by intentional or accidental discharge from ships . . . , by dumping of waste and other matter from ships and aircraft, . . . by discharges from land reaching the sea, whether water-borne or directly from the coast, including outfalls and pipelines" or "resulting from land reclamation and associated suction dredging and coastal dredging".

The protocol called upon the signatories to "co-operate in protection of the coastline" from "the threats and effects of pollution due to the presence of oil or other harmful substances . . . resulting from marine emergencies".

The action plan stressed the need for applied research and development, for contingency planning for accidents and for the establishment of a permanent pollution monitoring system.

River Pollution

In Western Europe commissions have been set up by riparian states of the Rhine, the Moselle and the Saar to prevent pollution of these rivers.

Rhine. The **International Commission for the Protection of the Rhine against Pollution** was established on July 1, 1950, and on April 29, 1963, its members, the Governments of France, the Federal Republic of Germany, Luxembourg, the Netherlands and Switzerland, signed a convention. The Commission is responsible for all necessary research on the nature, quantity and origin of pollution of the Rhine, and its technical secretariat works out proposals for the protection of the river's waters. In May 1976 the Commission agreed on a long-term plan involving the underground storage of salt from potash mines in Alsace (previously discharged into the Rhine) and also decided to take precautions against thermal pollution of the Rhine by nuclear power stations.

Moselle. The **International Commission for the Protection of the Moselle against Pollution** was established on Dec. 21, 1961, by France, the Federal Republic of Germany and Luxembourg with the object of recommending to member governments measures to protect the river against further pollution (including the inspection of sewage farms).

Saar. The **International Commission for the Protection of the Saar** against pollution, established by France and the Federal Republic of Germany, holds meetings simultaneously with those of the Commission for the Protection of the Moselle.

Air Pollution

A *Convention and Resolution on Long-Range Transboundary Air Pollution* was adopted, under the auspices of the (UN) Economic Commission for Europe, in Geneva on Nov. 13, 1979, by the United States, Canada and all European states except Albania, Cyprus and Malta. It obliged signatory states to "develop without undue delay policies and strategies which shall serve as a means of combating the discharge of air pollutants" and to engage in full exchange of information on environment protection technology.

Environmental Conferences

1972 Stockholm Conference. The Stockholm Conference on the Human Environment held on June 5-16, 1972, and which had recommended the establishment of the UN Environment Programme [see page 26], also issued a *Declaration on the Human Environment* enumerating 26 principles (of which the first 25 were approved by acclamation and the 26th by a separate vote, against opposition by China).

The 26 principles were as follows:

(1) "Man has the fundamental right to freedom, equality and adequate conditions of life, in an environment of a quality which permits a life of dignity and well-being, and bears a solemn responsibility to protect and improve the environment for present and future generations. In this respect, policies promoting or perpetuating apartheid, racial segregation, discrimination, colonial and other forms of oppression and foreign domination stand condemned and must be eliminated.

(2) "The natural resources of the earth including the air, water, land, flora and fauna, and especially representative samples of natural ecosystems, must be safeguarded for the benefit of present and future genera-

tions through careful planning or management as appropriate.

(3) "The capacity of the earth to produce vital renewable resources must be maintained and wherever practicable restored or improved.

(4) "Man has a special responsibility to safeguard and wisely manage the heritage of wildlife and its habitat which are now gravely imperilled by a combination of adverse factors. Nature conservation including wildlife must therefore receive importance in planning for economic development.

(5) "The non-renewable resources of the earth must be employed in such a way as to guard against the danger of their future exhaustion and to ensure that benefits from such employment are shared by all mankind.

(6) "The discharge of toxic substances or of other substances and the release of heat, in such quantities or concentrations as to exceed the capacity of the environment to render them harmless, must be halted in order to ensure that serious or irreversible damage is not inflicted upon ecosystems. The just struggle of the peoples of all countries against pollution should be supported.

(7) "States shall take all possible steps to prevent pollution of the seas by substances that are liable to create hazards to human health, to harm living resources and marine life, to damage amenities or to interfere with other legitimate uses of the sea.

(8) "Economic and social development is essential for ensuring a favourable living and working environment for man and for creating conditions on earth that are necessary for the improvement of the quality of life.

(9) "Environmental deficiencies generated by the conditions of under-development and natural disasters pose grave problems and can best be remedied by accelerated development through the transfer of substantial quantities of financial and technological assistance as a supplement to the domestic effort of the developing countries and such timely assistance as may be required.

(10) "For the developing countries, stability of prices and adequate earnings for primary commodities and raw material are essential to environmental management since economic factors as well as ecological processes must be taken into account.

(11) "The environmental policies of all states should enhance, not adversely affect, the present or future development potential of developing countries, nor should they hamper the attainment of better living conditions for all, and appropriate steps should be taken by states and international organizations with a view to reaching agreement on meeting the possible national and international economic consequences resulting from the application of environmental measures.

(12) "Resources should be made available to preserve and improve the environment, taking into account the circumstances and particular requirements of developing countries and any costs which may emanate from their incorporating environmental safeguards into their development planning and the need for making available to them, upon their request, additional international technical and financial assistance for this purpose.

(13) "In order to achieve a more rational management of resources and thus to improve the environment, states should adopt an integrated and co-ordinated approach to their development planning so as to ensure that development is compatible with the need to protect and improve the human environment for the benefit of their population.

(14) "Rational planning constitutes an essential tool for reconciling any conflict between the needs of development and the need to protect and improve the environment.

(15) "Planning must be applied to human settlements and urbanization with a view to avoiding adverse effects on the environment and obtaining maximum social, economic and environmental benefits for all. In this respect projects which are designed for colonialist and racist domination must be abandoned.

(16) "Demographic policies, which are without prejudice to basic human rights and which are deemed appropriate by governments concerned, should be applied in those regions where the rate of population growth or excessive population concentrations are likely to have adverse effects on the environment or development, or where low population density may prevent improvement of the human environment and impede development.

(17) "Appropriate national institutions must be entrusted with the task of planning, managing or controlling the environmental resources of states with the view to enhancing environmental quality.

(18) "Science and technology, as part of their contribution to economic and social development, must be applied to the identification, avoidance and control of environmental risks and the solution of environmental problems and for the common good of mankind.

(19) "Education in environmental matters, for the younger generation as well as adults, giving due consideration to the underprivileged, is essential in order to broaden the basis for an enlightened opinion and responsible conduct by individuals, enterprises and communities in protecting and improving the environment in its full human dimension. It is also essential that mass media of communications avoid contributing to the deterioration of the environment, but, on the contrary, disseminate information of an educational nature on the need to enable man to develop in every respect.

(20) "Scientific research and development in the context of environmental problems, both national and multinational, must be promoted in all countries, especially the developing countries. In this connexion, the free flow of up-to-date scientific information and transfer of experience must be supported and assisted, to facilitate the solution of environmental problems; environmental technologies should be made available to developing countries on terms which would encourage their wide dissemination without constituting an economic burden on the developing countries.

(21) "States have, in accordance with the Charter of the United Nations and the principles of international law, the sovereign right to exploit their own resources pursuant to their own environmental policies, and the responsibility to ensure that activities within their jurisdiction or control do not cause damage to the environment of other states or of areas beyond the limits of national jurisdiction.

(22) "States shall co-operate to develop further the international law regarding liability and compensation for the victims of pollution and other environmental damage caused by activities within the jurisdiction or control of such states to areas beyond their jurisdiction.

(23) "Without prejudice to such criteria as may be agreed upon by the international community, or to the standards which will have to be determined nationally, it will be essential in all cases to consider the systems of values prevailing in each country, and the extent of

the applicability of standards which are valid for the most advanced countries but which may be inappropriate and of unwarranted social cost for the developing countries.

(24) "International matters concerning the protection and improvement of the environment should be handled in a co-operative spirit by all countries, big or small, on an equal footing. Co-operation through multilateral or bilateral arrangements or other appropriate means is essential to effectively control, prevent, reduce and eliminate adverse environmental effects resulting from activities conducted in all spheres, in such a way that due account is taken of the sovereignty and interest of all states.

(25) "States shall ensure that international organizations play a co-ordinated, efficient and dynamic role for the protection and improvement of the environment.

(26) "Man and his environment must be spared the effects of nuclear weapons and all other means of mass destruction. States must strive to reach prompt agreement, in the relevant international organs, on the elimination and complete destruction of such weapons."

1976 UN Habitat Conference. A UN Conference on Human Settlements (Habitat) was held in Vancouver (Canada) from May 31 to June 11, 1976.

The Conference adopted a *Vancouver Declaration of Human Settlements* by 89 votes to 15 (of the member states of the European Communities, Australia, Canada, Israel, New Zealand, Norway and the United States) with 10 abstentions.

The declaration embodied a number of principles listed by a preparatory committee as the main objectives of human settlement policies and strategies, as follows:

(1) The rapid and continuous improvement in the quality of life of all people, beginning with the satisfaction of the basic needs and without discrimination of any kind.

(2) According of priority to the needs of the least advantaged people.

(3) Protection of the environmental resources upon which life itself depends.

(4) Reduction of disparities between rural and urban areas, between regions and within the urban areas themselves.

(5) Preservation of diversities reflected in cultural and aesthetic values.

(6) Effective use of all human resources, skilled and unskilled.

(7) Full participation of people in making and implementing decisions affecting their lives.

The conference reinforced these principles by declaring:

"Land, because of its unique nature and the crucial role it plays in human settlement, cannot be treated as an ordinary asset, controlled by individuals and subject to the pressures and inefficiencies of the market. Private land ownership also is a principal instrument of accumulation and concentration of wealth and therefore contributes to social injustice. If unchecked it may become a major obstacle in the planning and implementation of development schemes."

On water the conference recommended the launching of an international programme for the supply of drinking water to the entire population of the world, if possible by 1999.

On urban growth the conference's final recommendation reflected a move away from total urban renewal to small-scale development retaining much of the traditional architecture.

The declaration contained no decisions on new institutional arrangements within the United Nations.

1977 UN Water Conference. A UN Water Conference was held at Mar del Plata (Argentina) on March 14-25, 1977, after being prepared by a 54-member UN Committee on Natural Resources set up in 1970.

The conference made numerous recommendations, including (i) an action plan on community water supply and waste disposal, calling on national governments "to provide all people with water of safe quality and adequate quality and basic sanitary facilities by 1990, according priority to the poor and less privileged", with activities to be focussed on an "International Drinking Water Supply and Sanitation Decade" during 1980-90; (ii) an action programme for agricultural water use (consuming more than 80 per cent of all water used by man), aimed at improving and extending irrigation and rain-fed agriculture and protecting agricultural land from flooding and waterlogging; (iii) conservation and rational exploitation of fisheries; and (iv) the development of economic measures of re-using and recycling water, and economic incentives to use water efficiently and to treat wastes at their source. The conference also called, inter alia, for a national water policy to be formulated by each country and for the strengthening of international water law.

1977 UN Desertification Conference. A UN Desertification Conference was held in Nairobi from Aug. 29 to Sept. 9, 1977, under UNEP auspices. The conference unanimously adopted a plan of action containing 26 specific recommendations designed to halt the spread of deserts by the year 2000.

Corrective measures proposed were the efficient planning, development and management of water resources, the improvement of degraded rangelands and the introduction of suitable systems of rangeland, livestock and wildlife management; soil conservation and improvement; prevention or control of waterlogging, salinization or alkalinization of irrigated lands; improved irrigation and drainage systems; and improvement of the social and economic conditions of people dependent on irrigation culture—which would include "maintenance of an adequate rural labour force, sedentarization of nomads and resettlement of those migrating from rural to urban areas" as well as "an adequate level of primary health care services, including family planning where necessary".

With regard to energy, the plan recommended that the use of conventional energy sources based on vegetation (e.g. firewood and charcoal burning) should be controlled and improved, and it called for research to be "vigorously pursued on the use of alternative or unconventional energy sources in the drylands that will yield simple, inexpensive, useful and socially acceptable devices to serve the needs of the dryland people".

Among recommendations for international action and co-operation, the first was to enlist the aid of UN organizations, and another was that countries of a region should co-operate in the sound and judicious management of shared water resources as a means of effectively combating desertification.

Immediate initial actions proposed at national level were the setting-up of governmental authorities to combat desertification, the preparation of national plans of action, and the preparation of requests for international support for specific activities. At the regional level such actions included in particular the implementation of transnational regional projects (such as studies on the major regional aquifers—or underground water-bearing strata—of North-East Africa and the Arabian peninsula, a proposed "green belt" in North Africa, and the transnational development of grazing resources in the Sudano-Sahel regions).

Organizations for the Preservation of the Living Resources of the Sea

International Whaling Commission (IWC)

Headquarters: Cambridge, England.

Members: Argentina, Australia, Brazil, Canada, Chile, Denmark, France, Iceland, Japan, the Republic of Korea, Mexico, the Netherlands, New Zealand, Norway, Oman, Peru, Seychelles, South Africa, the Soviet Union, Spain, Sweden, Switzerland, the United Kingdom and the United States.

An international agreement on the protection of whales had first been signed in London on June 8, 1937, by representatives of nine Governments (Argentina, Australia, Germany, the Irish Free State, New Zealand, Norway, South Africa, the United Kingdom and the United States). The agreement provided for a nine-month close season for ships attached to floating factories, for the absolute protection of certain species and classes of whales and a six-month close season for whaling at land stations. The agreement was amended by a protocol adopted at a conference in London in November 1945, which inter alia required contracting governments to supply an International Bureau of Whaling Statistics with weekly data of blue whale units caught by each factory ship.

The IWC was set up under an *International Convention for the Regulation of Whaling* signed in Washington on Dec. 2, 1946. Measures prescribed in a schedule to the convention have been reviewed and revised as necessary; they provide inter alia for the complete protection of certain species of whales; the designation of specified ocean areas as sanctuaries; and the fixing of maximum catches, open and closed seasons and areas for whaling. In 1972 the IWC gave complete protection to five species and imposed quotas on individual species in the major whaling grounds. In August of that year Japan, Norway and the Soviet Union agreed on quotas for whales caught in the Antarctic.

Since 1974 whale stocks have been classified into three categories—initial management stocks (allowed to be reduced in a controlled manner), sustained management stocks (maintained at optimum levels as determined) and protection stocks (which are below the maximum sustainable yield and are therefore fully protected).

In July 1979 the Commission decided to ban factory-ship whaling for 10 years (except for minke whales) and to impose a complete ban on all whaling in the Indian Ocean. The meeting also determined quotas for certain species of whales in other seas. (By 1980 only 10 of the member countries—Brazil, Chile, Denmark, Iceland, Japan, Korea, Norway, Peru, the Soviet Union and Spain —were still conducting whaling operations, the others having never done so or having ceased to do so. Among non-members of the IWC, China and Portugal are still engaged in commercial whaling.)

Bilateral agreements on observer schemes were concluded between Japan and the Soviet Union for pelagic whaling in the northern Pacific and in the southern hemisphere (the latter signed on Oct. 22, 1979, to be in effect until Aug. 31, 1980). The two countries also signed an agreement on minke whaling in the southern hemisphere on Nov. 29, 1979 (to be in force until the end of the 1979-80 whaling season).

North Pacific Fur Seal Commission

Headquarters: Washington, D.C.

Members: Canada, Japan, the Soviet Union and the United States.

This commission was established in 1958 to implement an Interim Convention on the Conservation of North Pacific Fur Seals, which was signed by the four member governments in Washington on Feb. 9, 1957, and which entered into force on Oct. 14, 1957. The object of the convention was to achieve "maximum sustainable productivity of the fur seal resources of the North Pacific Ocean with due regard to the productivity of other living marine resources of the area". It was repeatedly amended and extended, most recently on May 7, 1976, for a period of four years from Oct. 12, 1976, and a further four-year extension was planned.

International Fisheries Organizations and Arrangements

Inter-American Tropical Tuna Commission (IATTC)

Headquarters: La Jolla (California, USA).

Members (1980): Canada, France, Japan, Nicaragua, Panama and the United States.

The IATTC was established under a convention which was signed by the United States and Costa Rica on May 31, 1949, and came into force on March 3, 1950. The object of the IATTC is to facilitate maintaining maximum sustainable catches of tuna in the eastern tropical Pacific Ocean.

International Baltic Sea Fishery Commission

Headquarters: Warsaw.

Members: Denmark, Finland, the German Democratic Republic, the Federal Republic of Germany, Poland, the Soviet Union and Sweden.

This Commission was set up under a convention on fishing and the preservation of living resources in the Baltic Sea and the Danish Straits, signed in Gdansk (Poland) on Sept. 13, 1973, by the seven member states. The Commission has inter alia laid down fishing quotas for the Baltic coastal states. However, since 1977 new arrangements have been made for the division of fishing rights in the Baltic Sea [see below].

International Commission for the Conservation of Atlantic Tunas (ICCAT)

Headquarters: Madrid.

Members: Angola, Benin, Brazil, Canada, Cape Verde, Cuba, France, Gabon, Ghana, Ivory Coast, Japan, Republic of Korea, Morocco, Portugal, Senegal, South Africa, Soviet Union, Spain and the United States.

The ICCAT was set up under an *International Convention for the Conservation of Atlantic Tunas* approved at a conference of 17 countries in Rio de Janeiro on May 2-14, 1966. It has a standing committee on research and statistics; has inter alia laid down maximum sizes for yellowfin and a maximum catch for bluefin tunas; and has organized an International Skipjack Year Programme for 1979-83 for research on the skipjack tuna (believed to be the most abundant of the commercial tuna species).

International Commission for the Southeast Atlantic Fisheries (ICSEAF)

Headquarters: Madrid.

Members: Angola, Bulgaria, Cuba, France, the German Democratic Republic, the Federal Republic of Germany, Iraq, Israel, Italy, Japan, Poland, Portugal, Romania, South Africa, the Soviet Union and Spain.

A conference on the living resources of the South-East Atlantic, called by the (UN) Food and Agriculture Organization and held in Rome on Oct. 14-23, 1969, with the participation of Belgium, Cuba, France, the Federal Republic of Germany, Italy, Japan, the Republic of Korea, Panama, Portugal, South Africa, Spain and Togo, adopted a convention setting up the ICSEAF. In it the convention area was defined as the ocean area bordered by the coast of Africa and lying between the latitudes of 6°S and 50°S and the longitudes of 20°W and 40°E. The objects of the ICSEAF were to study the living resources in the area and to make recommendations for the regulation of catches, which would, under specified conditions, be binding on the contracting parties. The convention came into force on Oct. 24, 1971.

The ICSEAF has repeatedly imposed quotas for catches, among them one (laid down in December 1976) for an annual quota of 700,000 tons of whitefish (hake) in South Africa's 200-mile economic zone (including 149,000 tons for South Africa itself).

International Council for the Exploration of the Sea (ICES)

Headquarters: Copenhagen.

Members: Belgium, Canada, Denmark, Finland, France, the German Democratic Republic, the Federal Republic of Germany, Iceland, Ireland, the Netherlands, Norway, Poland, Portugal, the Soviet Union, Spain, Sweden, the United Kingdom and the United States.

Established in 1902 under an agreement between Denmark, Finland, Germany, the Netherlands, Norway, Sweden, Russia and the United Kingdom, the ICES was under a 1964 convention mainly concerned with the North Atlantic Ocean. It has acted as a scientific advisory body to the North-East Atlantic Fisheries Commission and the International Baltic Sea Fishery Commission, and its numerous committees include an advisory committee on marine pollution.

International North Pacific Fisheries Commission

Headquarters: Vancouver, B.C.

Members: Canada, Japan and the United States.

The Commission was established under an *International Convention for the High Seas Fisheries* in the North Pacific concluded on May 9, 1952, and in force from June 12, 1953. The convention was amended on April 25, 1978, by a protocol signed by Canada, Japan and the United States to cover the new fishing management rights of Canada and the United States in their respective 200-mile economic zones, and also to provide for promotion and co-ordination of research activities. Agreement was also reached on the regulation of salmon fishing in the North Pacific (east of 175°W and with limited Japanese fishing between 175°W and 170°E, including parts of the Bering Sea and areas north and south of the Aleutian Islands) and on the demarcation of off-limit areas in international waters outside the US 200-mile zone.

International Pacific Salmon Fisheries Commission

Headquarters: New Westminster, B.C. (Canada).

Members: Canada and the United States.

This Commission was established under a *Sockeye Salmon Convention* concluded between the United States and Canada in 1973, and designed to protect, preserve and extend the sockeye fisheries of the Fraser River system (in British Columbia, Canada).

North-East Atlantic Fisheries Commission (NEAFC)

Headquarters: London.

Members: Bulgaria, Cuba, Denmark (for the Faroe Islands), Finland, the German Democratic Republic, Ireland, Poland, Portugal, the Soviet Union and Spain.

The NEAFC was established under a North-East Atlantic Fisheries Convention which was signed on Jan. 24, 1959, by representatives of Belgium, Denmark, France, the Federal Republic of Germany, Iceland, Ireland, the Netherlands, Norway, Poland, Portugal, the Soviet Union, Spain, Sweden and the United Kingdom, and which came into force on June 27, 1963. The convention applied to parts of the Atlantic and Arctic Oceans north of 36°N and between the longitudes of 42°W and 51°E (excluding the Mediterranean and Baltic Seas) and also part of the Atlantic Ocean north of 59°N and between 44°W and 42°W. The commission's tasks were to consider measures required for the conservation of fish stocks and to make relevant recommendations which would be binding on the contracting states.

Northwest Atlantic Fisheries Organization (NAFO)

Headquarters: Dartmouth, Nova Scotia (Canada).

Members: Bulgaria, Canada, Cuba, Denmark (for the Faroe Islands), the European Economic Community, the German Democratic Republic, Iceland, Japan, Norway, Poland, Portugal, Romania and the Soviet Union.

The NAFO, which replaced an earlier International Commission for the North-west Atlantic Fisheries established in 1950 to explore, protect and conserve fish stocks in the area, was set up under a Convention on Future Multilateral Co-operation in the Northwest Atlantic Fisheries of Oct. 24, 1978, which was, by January 1980, ratified or approved by all the current members of the Commission (but not by the United States, which had been a member of the previous Commission). In the convention it was noted that the coastal states involved had extended their jurisdiction over the living resources of their adjacent waters to 200 nautical miles, and the convention defined the "convention area" as the waters of the North-West Atlantic off the coasts of the United States, Canada and Greenland and bordered in the south by the 35°N parallel and in the east by the 42°W meridian (with an adjustment south of Greenland). The convention applied to all fishery resources in the area except salmon, tunas and marlins (nor to whales or sedentary species on the continental shelf).

Baltic Sea Fisheries Arrangements

Sweden decided (as announced on Aug. 11, 1977) to extend its fishing limits in the Baltic Sea and the Skagerrak (but not in the Kattegat, between Sweden and Denmark) with effect from Jan. 1, 1978, with special arrangements to be concluded with the Baltic countries. Later in 1977 Sweden signed fisheries agreements with the German Democratic Republic and with the Soviet Union (the latter on Dec. 25, 1977, allowing Soviet fishermen to catch quotas of herring, sprats and cod within the Swedish zone, i.e. up to the median line, but with a disputed area around the island of Gotland remaining subject to further negotiations). On June 22, 1978, Sweden also concluded a treaty with the German Democratic Republic on the delimitation of the continental shelves and fishing zones on the basis of the median line in the Baltic sea. (With effect from July 1, 1979, Sweden's territorial waters limit was extended from four to 12 miles.)

Poland extended its fishing zone (as approved by the *Sejm* on Dec. 17, 1977) from 35 to 85 miles off the coast with effect from Jan. 1, 1978.

The Soviet Union, on April 1, 1978, extended its fishing zone in the Baltic to 200 miles, or the median line where applicable.

The Federal Republic of Germany announced on June 12, 1978, that as from June 15, 1978, it would extend its own fishing zone in the Baltic (which would, however, not extend far beyond the 12-mile territorial limit).

6. International Economic Co-operation

The need for international economic co-operation, including that of arresting and eventually reversing the widening gap between the economies of the developed and those of the developing countries, has been the subject of declarations and resolutions adopted by the UN General Assembly and also of consultations leading to agreements between groups of nations as well as between individual governments. Within the developed world, co-operation on international economic questions has been pursued not only within established institutions but also at a series of summit conferences of the major non-communist industrialized states beginning in 1975. Also covered in this section are the Conference on International Economic Co-operation (the "North-South dialogue"), the Independent Commission on International Development Issues (the "Brandt Commission"), recent sessions of the UN Conference on Trade and Development (UNCTAD) on international economic co-operation and the Customs Co-operation Council (CCC).

Special UN General Assembly Sessions

April-May 1974. A special session of the UN General Assembly on the problem of raw materials and development was held in New York from April 9 to May 2, 1974, and ended with the adoption of a Declaration on the Establishment of a New International Economic Order and of a Programme of Action to carry it out.

The Declaration read as follows:

"We, the members of the United Nations;

"Having convened a special session of the General Assembly to study for the first time the problems of raw materials and development, devoted to the consideration of the most important economic problems facing the world community;

"Bearing in mind the spirit, purposes and principles of the Charter of the United Nations to promote the economic advancement and social progress of all peoples;

"Solemnly proclaim our united determination to work urgently for the Establishment of a New International Economic Order based on equity, sovereign equality, interdependence, common interest and co-operation among all states, irrespective of their economic and social systems, which shall correct inequalities and redress existing injustices, make it possible to eliminate the widening gap between the developed and the developing countries, and ensure steadily accelerating economic and social development in peace and justice for present and future generations.

"The greatest and most significant achievement during the last decades has been the independence from colonial and alien domination of a large number of peoples and nations which has enabled them to become members of the community of free peoples. Technological progress has also been made in all spheres of economic activities in the last three decades, thus providing a solid potential for improving the well-being of all peoples. However, the remaining vestiges of alien and colonial domination, foreign occupation, racial discrimination, apartheid and neo-colonialism in all its forms continue to be among the greatest obstacles to the full emancipation and progress of the developing countries and all the peoples involved. The benefits of technological progress are not shared equitably by all members of the international community. The developing countries, which constitute 70 per cent of the world population, account for only 30 per cent of the world's income. It has proved impossible to achieve an even and balanced development of the international community under the existing international economic order. The gap between the developed and the developing countries continues to widen in a system which was established at a time when most of the developing countries did not even exist as independent states and which perpetuates inequality.

"The present international economic order is in direct conflict with current developments in international political and economic relations. Since 1970 the world economy has experienced a series of grave crises which have had severe repercussions, especially on the developing countries because of their generally greater vulnerability to external economic impulses. The developing world has become a powerful factor that makes its influence felt in all fields of international activity. These irreversible changes in the relationship of forces in the world necessitate the active, full and equal participation of the developing countries in the formulation and application of all decisions that concern the international community.

"All these changes have thrust into prominence the reality of interdependence of all the members of the world community. Current events have brought into sharp focus the realization that the interests of the developed countries and the interests of the developing countries can no longer be isolated from each other; that there is close inter-relationship between the prosperity of the developed countries and the growth and development of the developing countries; and that the prosperity of the international community as a whole depends upon the prosperity of its constituent parts.

"International co-operation for development is the shared goal and common duty of all countries. Thus the political, economic and social well-being of present and future generations depends more than ever on co-operation between all members of the international community on the basis of sovereign equality and the removal of the disequilibrium that exists between them.

"The new international economic order should be founded on full respect for the following principles:

"(a) Sovereign equality of states, self-determination of all peoples, inadmissibility of the acquisition of territories by force, territorial integrity and non-interference in the internal affairs of other states;

"(b) broadest co-operation of all the member states of the international community, based on equity, whereby the prevailing disparities in the world may be banished and prosperity secured for all;

"(c) full and effective participation on the basis of equality of all countries in the solving of world economic problems in the common interest of all countries, bearing in mind the necessity to ensure the accelerated development of all the developing countries, while devoting particular attention to the adoption of special measures in favour of the least developed, land-locked and island developing countries, as well as those developing countries most seriously affected by economic crises and natural calamities, without losing sight of the interests of other developing countries;

"(d) every country has the right to adopt the economic and social system that it deems to be the most appropriate for its own development and not to be subjected to discrimination of any kind as a result;

"(e) full permanent sovereignty of every state over its natural resources and all economic activities. In order to safeguard these resources each state is entitled to exercise effective control over them and their exploitation with means suitable to its own situation, including the right to nationalization or transfer of ownership to its nationals, this right being an expression of the full permanent sovereignty of the state. No state may be subjected to economic, political or any other type of coercion to prevent the free and full exercise of this inalienable right;

"(f) all states, territories and peoples under foreign occupation, alien and colonial domination or apartheid have the right to restitution and full compensation for the exploitation and depletion of, and damages to, the natural and all other resources of those states, territories and peoples;

"(g) regulation and supervision of the activities of transnational corporations by taking measures in the interest of the national economies of the countries where such transnational corporations operate on the basis of the full sovereignty of those countries;

"(h) right of the developing countries and the peoples of territories under colonial and racial domination and foreign occupation to achieve their liberation and to regain effective control over their natural resources and economic activities;

"(i) extending of assistance to developing countries, peoples and territories under colonial and alien domination, foreign occupation, racial discrimination or apartheid or which are subjected to economic, political or any other type of measures to coerce them in order to obtain from them the subordination of the exercise of their sovereign rights and to secure from them advantages of any kind, and to neo-colonialism in all its forms, and which have established or are endeavouring to establish effective control over their natural resources and economic activities that have been or are still under foreign control;

"(j) just and equitable relationship between the prices of raw materials, primary products, manufactured and semi-manufactured goods exported by developing countries, and the prices of raw materials, primary commodities, manufactures, capital goods and equipment imported by them with the aim of bringing about sustained improvement in their unsatisfactory terms of trade and the expansion of the world economy;

"(k) extension of active assistance to developing countries by the whole international community, free of any political or military conditions;

"(l) ensuring that one of the main aims of the reformed international monetary system shall be the promotion of the development of the developing countries and the adequate flow of real resources to them;

"(m) improving the competitiveness of natural materials facing competition from synthetic substitutes;

"(n) preferential and non-reciprocal treatment for developing countries, wherever feasible, in all fields of international economic co-operation;

"(o) securing favourable conditions for the transfer of financial resources to developing countries;

"(p) to give the developing countries access to the achievements of modern science and technology, to promote the transfer of technology and the creation of indigenous technology for the benefit of the developing countries in forms and in accordance with procedures which are suited to their economies;

"(q) necessity for all states to put an end to the waste of natural resources, including food products;

"(r) the need for developing countries to concentrate all their resources for the cause of development;

"(s) strengthening through individual and collective actions of mutual economic, trade, financial and technical co-operation among the developing countries, mainly on a preferential basis;

"(t) facilitating the role which producers' associations may play, within the framework of international co-operation, and in pursuance of their aims, inter alia, assisting in promotion of sustained growth of the world economy and accelerating development of developing countries.

"The unanimous adoption of the International Development Strategy for the Second Development Decade [i.e. the years 1971-80] was an important step in the promotion of international economic co-operation on a just and equitable basis. The accelerated implementation of obligations and commitments assumed by the international community within the framework of the Strategy, particularly those concerning imperative development needs of developing countries, would contribute significantly to the fulfilment of the aims and objectives of the present Declaration.

"The United Nations as a universal organization should be capable of dealing with problems of international economic co-operation in a comprehensive manner and ensuring equally the interests of all countries. It must have an even greater role in the establishment of a new international economic order. The Charter of Economic Rights and Duties of States [see pages

43-46], for the preparation of which this Declaration will provide an additional source of inspiration, will constitute a significant contribution in this respect. All the states members of the UN are therefore called upon to exert maximum efforts with a view to securing the implementation of this Declaration, which is one of the principal guarantees for the creation of better conditions for all peoples to reach a life worthy of human dignity.

"This Declaration on the Establishment of a New International Economic Order shall be one of the most important bases of economic relations between all peoples and all nations."

The Programme of Action contained, inter alia, a 12-month emergency aid programme for those poor countries which were most severely affected by the sharply increased prices of essential imports such as foodstuffs, fertilizers, oil and capital goods. In addition it called for the establishment of a special fund under UN auspices to provide emergency relief and assistance as from Jan. 1, 1975, and for 12 special aid measures for the neediest countries, including "soft" loans and debt renegotiation.

September 1975. A special session of the UN General Assembly, devoted to development and international co-operation, was held on Sept. 1-16, 1975, in order to deal with the possible implementation of the decisions taken at the Assembly's 1974 special session [see above].

The session unanimously adopted a lengthy resolution containing proposals for taking numerous measures in the fields of international trade; the transfer of real resources for financing the development of developing countries and international monetary reform; the use of science and technology for development; industrialization; an increase in food production in developing countries; and co-operation among these countries.

The proposals included in particular the creation of an Ad Hoc Committee on the Restructuring of the Economic and Social Sectors of the UN System, which would be a committee of the whole of the General Assembly open to participation of all states.

Summits of Major Non-Communist Industrialized States

The original proposal which led to a series of summit conferences of the major non-communist industrialized states was made by President Giscard d'Estaing of France in July 1975, when he proposed that a conference of the "Group of Five" (the United States, Japan, West Germany, France and the United Kingdom) and possibly other industrialized countries should be held to discuss international monetary problems arising from the massive increase in world

oil prices dating from 1973-74. The first such conference, attended by the "Group of Five" and Italy, was held in France in November 1975 and further conferences took place in succeeding years as described below. Canada took part from the second such summit in 1976 and the European Community was represented as such from the third in 1977. The agendas of this series of conferences have steadily been expanded to cover broader aspects of international economic co-operation and also pressing political questions affecting the international situation.

Rambouillet Summit. The first of this series of summits, involving the heads of government of six major non-communist economic powers (the United States, Japan, the Federal Republic of Germany, France, the United Kingdom and Italy), was held at Rambouillet (near Paris) on Nov. 15-17, 1975. Agreement was reached by the participants on the world economic situation, as expressed in a joint declaration.

After affirming their determination to play their full parts and to strengthen their "efforts for closer international co-operation and constructive dialogue with all countries" and "to overcome high unemployment, continuing inflation and serious energy problems" by means of "growth that is steady and lasting", the six leaders continued: "Growth and price stability will be fostered by maintenance of an open trading system. . . . There is a responsibility on all countries, especially those with strong balance-of-payments positions and on those with current deficits, to pursue policies which will permit the expansion of world trade to their mutual advantage. . . . Multilateral trade negotiations (within the framework of the General Agreement on Trade and Tariffs—GATT) should be accelerated . . . ; they would aim at substantial tariff cuts, even eliminating tariffs in some areas, at significantly expanding agricultural trade and at reducing non-tariff measures. They should aim at achieving the maximum possible level of trade liberalization therefrom. We propose as our goal the completion of the negotiations in 1977. We look to an orderly and fruitful increase in our economic relations with socialist countries as an important element in progress on détente, and on world economic growth. . . .

"A co-operative relationship and improved understanding between the developing nations and the industrial world is fundamental to the prosperity of each. . . . Early practical action is needed to assist the developing countries. . . . We will play our part, through the International Monetary Fund and other appropriate international fora, in making urgent improvements in international arrangements for the stabilization of the export earnings of developing countries and in measures to assist them in financing their deficits. In this context, priority should be given to the poorest developing countries."

The participants of the meeting also agreed that they would continue to co-operate in order to reduce their dependence on imported energy, and they added: "Through these measures, as well as through international co-operation between producer and consumer countries responding to long-term interests of both, we shall spare no effort in order to ensure more balanced conditions and a harmonious and steady development in the world energy market.''

Puerto Rico Summit. A further meeting of the six heads of government of the countries represented at Rambouillet in November 1975 and also that of Canada took place in Puerto Rico on June 27-28, 1976.

This meeting adopted a declaration in which it was noted that economic recovery was "well under way". At the same time it was stated that what was needed was "to manage effectively a transition to expansion which will be sustainable, which will reduce the high level of unemployment which persists in many countries and will not jeopardize our common aim of avoiding a new wave of inflation". The meeting welcomed "the steady growth in East-West trade" and stated: "Our efforts for international economic co-operation must be considered as complementary to the policies of the developing countries themselves to achieve sustainable growth and rising standards of living". The declaration continued: "We attach the greatest importance to the dialogue between the developed and developing nations in the expectation that it will achieve concrete results in areas of mutual interest. And we reaffirm our countries' determination to participate in this process in the competent bodies, with a political will to succeed, looking towards negotiations in appropriate cases."

London Summit. A third economic summit conference was held in London on May 7-8, 1977, by the heads of government of the seven major non-communist states. Under a compromise agreement the President of the European Commission was enabled to participate in the deliberations on the second day of the conference (although the European Community had not as such been represented at the previous two conferences).

The conference resulted in the publication of a communiqué and an accompanying appendix in which it was stated that the heads of government had entered into seven main undertakings—to create more jobs; to maintain economic growth; to improve international financial resources; to expand opportunities for trade; to bring the Conference on International Economic Co-operation (CIEC) to a successful conclusion; and to initiate a special study on the supply of nuclear equipment to non-nuclear countries.

Bonn Summit. The fourth economic summit conference of the above seven powers was held in Bonn on July 16-17, 1978, with the European Community being represented "for discussion of matters within the Community's competence" by the President of the European Commission and the President-in-office of the Community's Council of Ministers.

The proceedings of the conference were described in a declaration issued afterwards, listing in particular specific measures which each of the participating countries had taken or was taking to ensure non-inflationary

economic growth; reaffirming the leaders' commitment to reduce their countries' dependence on imported oil and emphasizing the need to reverse "the slippage in the execution of nuclear power programmes"; reaffirming their determination to expand international trade; and stating their undertaking to provide an increased flow of financial assistance and other resources to the developing countries.

In a separate statement the participants in the conference stated their intention to intensify their joint efforts to combat international terrorism through action in cases of hijackings of aircraft.

Tokyo Summit. The fifth economic summit conference of the seven powers was held in Tokyo on June 28-29, 1979, with the European Community being represented by the Presidents of the European Council and of the European Commission.

The conference was mainly concerned with energy policy, and in their final declaration the participants deplored "the very serious economic and social consequences" of the latest oil price increases agreed upon by the Organization of Petroleum Exporting Countries (OPEC); expressed their readiness to discuss with oil-exporting countries "how to define supply and demand prospects on the world oil market"; and give details of agreement on a common strategy to reduce oil consumption and to hasten the development of alternative energy sources, stemming largely from proposals earlier agreed upon by the European Community.

Venice Summit. The sixth summit conference was held in Venice (Italy) on June 22-23, 1980, again with the participation of the seven major non-communist industrial powers and the European Community.

A declaration issued by the heads of government again stressed the adverse effects of further oil price rises, particularly on developing countries, and expressed the belief "that these consequences are increasingly coming to be appreciated by some of the oil-exporting countries". Reiterating that the reduction of inflation "is our immediate top priority", the declaration said that the existing link between economic growth and oil consumption must be broken in the 1980s, to which end certain oil consumption and conservation targets were laid down and a commitment entered into to develop other energy sources such as coal and nuclear power. The declaration also dealt with relations with developing countries, international monetary problems and trade, it being stressed under this last heading that the participating countries would "resist pressures for protectionist actions, which can only be self-defeating and aggravate inflation".

On political aspects of the international situation, the Venice summit (i) condemned as "unacceptable" the Soviet military intervention in Afghanistan dating from late December 1979; (ii) expressed deep concern "at the plight of the ever-increasing number of refugees throughout the world"; (iii) emphasized that "hijacking remains a threat to international civil aviation" and looked forward to "continuing co-operation with all other governments to combat this threat; and (iv) condemned "the taking of hostages and the seizure of diplomatic and consular premises and personnel in contravention of the basic norms of international law and practice".

Conference on International Economic Co-operation (CIEC)

In October 1974 President Giscard d'Estaing of France proposed, in the context of the transformed international economic situation created by the massive rise in world oil prices from late 1973, that a tripartite conference of industrialized, oil-producing and other developing countries should be held to work out an agreement on oil prices and international inflation. The developing countries subsequently pressed for a broadening of the conference's agenda to encompass other raw materials, development and international financial questions, with the result that a first preparatory meeting held in Paris in April 1975 ended in failure. However, after the industrialized countries had made progress within the framework of the International Energy Agency [see page 163] towards co-ordinating their energy supply policies, agreement was reached in mid-1975 to expand the scope of the Paris conference as requested by the developing countries. Accordingly, a second preparatory meeting held in Paris in October 1975 reached broad agreement on the agenda and purposes of a fullscale ministerial conference.

First CIEC Conference. A ministerial level Conference on International Economic Co-operation (CIEC)—also referred to as the "North–South dialogue"—duly took place in Paris on Dec. 16-19, 1975, under the co-chairmanship of Canada and Venezuela; 19 of the 27 seats were occupied by oil-exporting and other developing countries and the remaining eight by industrialized nations (including the European Economic Community as a single participant). The principal outcome of the conference was an agreement to establish four expert-level commissions—on energy, raw materials, development and financial questions—which were instructed to draw up concrete proposals for a further ministerial conference.

The 19 oil-producing and other developing countries participating in CIEC were: Algeria, Argentina, Brazil, Cameroon, Egypt, India, Indonesia, Iran, Iraq, Jamaica, Mexico, Nigeria, Pakistan, Peru, Saudi Arabia, Venezuela, Yugoslavia, Zaïre and Zambia.

The eight industrialized participants were: Australia, Canada, European Economic Community, Japan, Spain, Sweden, Switzerland and the United States.

Second CIEC Conference. A second and final CIEC ministerial session took place in Paris from May 30 to June 2, 1977, with the same participants as at the Paris session of December 1975.

This session reached agreement on (i) increased aid from the industrialized to the developing countries and (ii) the eventual establishment of a common fund to support commodity prices, but not on other items of its agenda, notably future formal consultations on energy questions and on the rescheduling of developing countries' debts.

On aid to developing countries it was agreed, inter alia, that provision should be made "by developed countries of $1,000 million in a special action programme for individual low-income countries facing general problems of transfer of resources", and that assistance should be given to "infrastructure development in developing countries with particular reference to Africa". The establishment of "a common (commodity) fund with purposes, objectives and other constituent elements" was to be further negotiated in the UN Conference on Trade and Development (UNCTAD) [see below].

Later Developments. Although the CIEC initiative itself ended with the mid-1977 conference in Paris, the state of the "North–South dialogue" was further discussed at an informal meeting held in Jamaica on Dec. 28-29, 1978, by the heads of government of Australia, Canada, the Federal Republic of Germany and Norway on the one hand and of Jamaica, Nigeria and Venezuela on the other.

The participants agreed on the need of "speedy conclusion of negotiations on the common fund" and on the desirability of inviting the Soviet Union, China and other communist countries to participate in the common fund and other aspects of the North–South dialogue. Other points of agreement included the recognition that measures to curb population growth and to modernize agriculture in developing countries were important aspects of future progress towards a new international economic order.

Subsequently the focus of the North–South dialogue was provided by the recommendations of the Brandt Commission published in February 1980 [see below].

Independent Commission on International Development Issues (ICIDI)

As proposed in January 1977 by the then President of the World Bank (Mr Robert McNamara) as a measure to "enable the international community to break out of the current impasse" in the North–South dialogue, an Independent Commission on International Development Issues (ICIDI) was set up in November 1977 by Herr Willy Brandt (former Chancellor of the Federal Republic of Germany) with the object of "identifying those ways of restructuring international economic relations which would command the widest possible support''.

The Commission, under the chairmanship of Herr Brandt, comprised 17 other members drawn from both developed and developing countries, as well as an honorary treasurer, an executive secretary-general and a director of its secretariat, established in Geneva. The Commission held eight sessions in various parts of the world, and its report was published in February 1980.

Passages from the Commission's summary of recommendations are quoted below.

The Poorest Countries. "An action programme must be launched comprising emergency and longer-term measures, to assist the poverty belts of Africa and Asia and particularly the least developed countries. Measures would include large regional projects of water and soil management; the provision of health care and the eradication of such diseases as river-blindness, malaria, sleeping sickness and bilharzia; afforestation projects; solar energy development; mineral and petroleum exploration; and support for industrialization, transport and other infrastructural investment.

"Such a programme would require additional financial assistance of at least $4,000 million per year for the next two decades, at grant or special concessional terms, assured over long periods and available in flexibly usable forms. New machinery is required on a regional basis to co-ordinate funding and to prepare plans in co-operation with lending and borrowing countries. Greater technical assistance should be provided to assist such countries with the preparation of programmes and projects.

Hunger and Food. "There must be an end to mass hunger and malnutrition. The capacity of food-importing developing countries, particularly the low-income countries, to meet their food requirements should be expanded and their mounting food import bill reduced through their own efforts and through expanded financial flows for agricultural development. Special attention should be given to irrigation, agricultural research, storage and increased use of fertilizer and other inputs, and to fisheries development.

"Agrarian reform is of great importance in many countries both to increase agricultural productivity and to put higher incomes into the hands of the poor.

"International food security should be assured through the early establishment of an International Grains Arrangement, larger international emergency reserves, and the establishment of a food financing facility.

"Food aid should be increased and linked to employment promotion and agricultural programmes and projects without weakening incentives to food production.

"Liberalization of trade in food and other agricultural products within and between North and South would contribute to the stabilization of food supplies.

"Support for international agricultural research institutions should be expanded with greater emphasis given to regional co-operation.

Population: Growth, Movement and the Environment. "In view of the vicious circle between poverty and high birth rates, the rapid population growth in developing countries gives added urgency to the need to fight hunger, disease, malnutrition and illiteracy.

"We also believe that development policies should include national population programmes aiming at a satisfactory balance between population and resources and making family planning freely available. International assistance and support of population programmes must be increased to meet the unmet needs for such aid.

"The many migrant workers in the world should be assured fair treatment, and the interests of their home countries and the countries of immigration must be better reconciled. Governments should seek bilateral and multilateral co-operation to harmonize their policies of emigration and immigration, to protect the rights of migrant workers, to make remittances more stable and to mitigate the hardships of unanticipated return migration.

"The rights of refugees to asylum and legal protection should be strengthened. We also believe that commitments to international co-operation in the resettlement of refugees in the future will be necessary to protect countries of first asylum from unfair burdens. . . .

"Ocean resources outside the 'exclusive economic zones' of 200 miles should be developed under international rules in the balanced interests of the whole world community.

Disarmament and Development. "The mutual distrust which stimulates the arms race between East and West calls for continuing the process of détente through agreements on confidence-building measures. All sides should be prepared for negotiations (including those on the regional level) to get the arms race under control at a time before new weapons systems have been established.

"The world needs a more comprehensive understanding of security which would be less restricted to the purely military aspects.

"Every effort must be made to secure international agreements preventing the proliferation of nuclear weapons.

"A globally respected peace-keeping mechanism should be built up, strengthening the role of the United Nations (UN). In securing the integrity of states such peace-keeping machinery might free resources for development through a sharing of military expenditures, a reduction in areas of conflict and of the arms race which they imply.

"Military expenditure and arms exports might be one element entering into a new principle for international taxation for development purposes. A tax on arms trade should be at a higher rate than that on other trade.

"Increased efforts should be made to reach agreements on the disclosure of arms exports and exports of arms-producing facilities. The international community should become more seriously concerned about the consequences of arms transfers or of exports of arms-producing facilities and reach agreement to restrain such deliveries to areas of conflict or tension.

"More research is necessary on the means of converting arms production to civilian production which could make use of the highly skilled scientific and technical manpower currently employed in arms industries.

The Task of the South. "In countries where essential reforms have not yet taken place, redistribution of productive resources and incomes is necessary. A broader package of policy improvements would include expansion of social services to the poor, agrarian reform, increased development expenditures in rural areas, stimulation of small-scale enterprises and better tax administration. Such measures are important both for satisfying elementary needs and for increasing productivity, particularly in rural areas.

"The full potential of the informal sector to contribute to economic development requires the provision of increased resources in the form of easier access to credit, and expanded training and extension services.

"The strengthening of indigenous technological capacity often requires a more scientific bias in education, the encouragement of a domestic engineering industry, increased emphasis on intermediate technology and the sharing of experience.

"Improved economic management and the increased mobilization of domestic resources are essential to the promotion of development. In many countries there is scope for improvements in such fields as taxation policies, public administration and the operation of the pricing system.

"Wider participation in the development process should be encouraged; measures to achieve this could include decentralized governmental administrative systems and support for relevant voluntary organizations.

"Regional and sub-regional integration, or other forms of close co-operation, still offer a viable strategy for accelerated economic development and structural transformation among developing countries, especially the smaller ones. It supports industrialization and trade expansion and provides opportunities for multi-country ventures.

"Developing countries should take steps to expand preferential trade schemes among themselves. This could be encouraged by such measures as the untying of aid.

"Developing countries should give special attention to the establishment and extension of payments and credit arrangements among themselves to facilitate trade and to ease balance of payments problems.

"The emergence of capital-surplus developing countries provides special scope for the establishment of projects on the basis of tripartite arrangements involving developing countries alone or in partnership with industrialized countries. Such arrangements should be supported by both developed and developing countries. Tripartite projects (including, when appropriate, industrialized countries) should be encouraged by nations with complementary resources such as capital and technology.

"Developing countries should consider what forms of mutual assistance organization might help them to participate more effectively in negotiations and in the work of international organizations and to promote economic co-operation among themselves.

Commodity Trade and Development. "The commodity sector of developing countries should contribute more to economic development through the greater participation of these countries in the processing, marketing and distribution of their commodities. Action for the stabilization of commodity prices at remunerative levels should be undertaken as a matter of urgency.

"Measures to facilitate the participation of developing countries in processing and marketing should include the removal of tariff and other trade barriers against developing countries' processed products, the establishment of fair and equitable international transport rates, the abolition of restrictive business practices, and improved financial arrangements for facilitating processing and marketing.

"Adequate resources should be provided to enable the Common Fund [part of the Integrated Commodity Programme then under negotiation in the United Nations Conference on Trade and Development (UNCTAD)—see page 92] to encourage and finance effective international commodity agreements (ICAs) which would stabilize prices at remunerative levels; to finance national stocking outside ICAs; and to facilitate the carrying out of 'second window' activities such as storage, processing, marketing, productivity improvement and diversification.

"Greater efforts should be made to bring to a rapid and successful conclusion negotiations on individual commodity agreements wherever these are feasible.

"Compensatory financing facilities should be expanded and improved to provide more adequately for shortfalls in real commodity export earnings.

"The mutual interest of producing and consuming countries in the development of mineral resources requires the creation of new financial arrangements leading to more equitable and stable mineral development agreements, greater assurance of world mineral supplies and increased developing country participation in their resource development. A new financing facility, whose primary function will be to provide concessional finance for mineral exploration, should be established on the basis of a global responsibility for investment in mineral development.

Energy. "An orderly transition is required from high dependence on increasingly scarce non-renewable energy sources.

"Immediate steps towards an international strategy on energy should be taken as part of the emergency programme recommended in the final chapter of the report."

(These recommendations were that (i) all oil-exporting countries should assure levels of production and not reduce supplies arbitrarily or suddenly, with special arrangements being made to ensure supplies to developing countries; (ii) all major energy-consuming countries should agree on targets to hold down their consumption of oil and other energy; (iii) oil prices should be agreed in such a way as to avoid sudden major increases; and (iv) there should be major investment in oil and natural gas development in third-world countries and also in available alternative energy sources and in research and development in new types of energy use.)

"A global energy research centre should be created under UN auspices to co-ordinate information and projections and to support research on new energy resources.

Industrialization and World Trade. "The industrialization of developing countries, as a means of their overall development efforts, will provide increasing opportunities for world trade and need not conflict with long-term interests of developed countries. It should be facilitated as a matter of international policy.

"Protectionism threatens the future of the world economy and is inimical to the long-term interests of developing and developed countries alike. Protectionism by industrialized countries against the exports of developing countries should be rolled back; this should be facilitated by improved institutional machinery and new trading rules and principles.

"Adjustment to new patterns of world industrial production should be accepted as a necessary and desirable process. Industrialized countries should vigorously pursue positive and time-bound adjustment programmes developed through international consultation and subject to international surveillance.

"Safeguard measures must be internationally negotiated and should be taken only on the basis of established need. They should be non-discriminatory, of limited duration and subject to international surveillance.

"The generalized system of preferences (GSP—see page 91) should be eased in respect of its rules of origin, its exceptions and its limits. It should be extended beyond its present expiration and not be liable to unilateral termination.

"Financial support and technical assistance should be given to the poorer countries to facilitate their establishment of improved commercial infrastructure and their participation in international trade negotiations.

"Fair labour standards should be internationally agreed in order to prevent unfair competition and to facilitate trade liberalization.

"An international trade organization incorporating both the General Agreement on Tariffs and Trade (GATT) and UNCTAD is the objective towards which the international community should work. Meanwhile, there is need for improvement in existing arrangements including wider development of trade co-operation in such matters as the establishment and administration of rules, principles and codes covering restrictive business practices and technology transfer.

Transnational Corporations, Investment and the Sharing of Technology. "Effective national laws and international codes of conduct are needed to govern the sharing of technology, to control restrictive business practices, and to provide a framework for the activities of transnational corporations.

"The investment regime we propose would include (i) reciprocal obligations on the part of host and home countries covering foreign investment, transfer of technology, and repatriation of profits, royalties and dividends, (ii) legislation, co-ordinated in home and host countries, to regulate transitional corporation activities in matters such as ethical behaviour, disclosure of information, restrictive business practices and labour standards, (iii) intergovernmental co-operation in regard to tax policies and the monitoring of transfer pricing, and (iv) harmonization of fiscal and other incentives among host developing countries.

"In addition to improved access to international development finance, the bargaining capacity of developing countries, particularly of the smaller and least developed countries, vis-à-vis the transnational corporations should be strengthened with the technical assistance now increasingly available from the UN and other agencies.

"Permanent sovereignty over natural resources is the right of all countries. It is necessary, however, that nationalization be accompanied by appropriate and effective compensation, under internationally comparable principles which should be embodied in national laws. Increasing use should also be made of international mechanisms for settling disputes.

"Greater international, regional and national efforts are needed to support the development of technology in developing countries and the transfer of appropriate technology to them at reasonable cost.

"There should be increased efforts in both rich and poor countries to develop appropriate technology in the light of changing constraints regarding energy and ecology; the flow of information about such technology should be improved. The international aid agencies should change those of their practices which restrict the recipients' freedom to choose technology, and

should make more use of local capacities in preparing projects.

The World Monetary Order. "The reform of the international monetary system should be urgently undertaken by all interested parties building on the large measure of consensus which emerged in the Committee of Twenty [the Committee of the Board of Governors of the International Monetary Fund—IMF—on Reform of the International Monetary System and Related Issues, which held its final meeting in June 1974—see page 34], and taking account of current difficulties and dangers. Reform involves improvements in the exchange rate regime, the reserve system, the balance of payments adjustment process, and the overall management of the system which should permit the participation of the whole international community.

"Mechanisms should be agreed for creating and distributing an international currency to be used for clearing and settling outstanding balances between central banks. Such a currency would replace the use of national currencies as international reserves. It could take the form of an improved special drawing right (SDR), and could be facilitated by an appropriately designed 'substitution account'.

"New SDRs should be created to the extent called for by the need for non-inflationary increases in world liquidity. The distribution of such unconditional liquidity should favour the developing countries who presently bear high adjustment burdens. Such a distribution, often referred to as an SDR link, would also assist the adjustment process of the international monetary system.

"There should be agreement on an adjustment process which will not increase contractionist pressures in the world economy. The adjustment process of developing countries should be placed in the context of maintaining long-term economic and social development. The IMF should avoid inappropriate or excessive regulation of their economies, and should not impose highly deflationary measures as standard adjustment policy. It should also improve and greatly extend the scope of its compensatory financing facility, for example by relaxing quota limits, measuring shortfalls in real terms and making repayment terms more flexible. Surplus countries should accept greater responsibility for payments adjustments, and IMF measures to encourage this should be considered.

"Increased stability of international exchange rates, particularly among key currencies, should be sought through domestic discipline and co-ordination of appropriate national policies.

"The participation of developing countries in the staffing, management and decision-making of the IMF should be enlarged.

"In furthering the demonetization of gold, the bulk of the IMF gold stock should, after the completion of the present sales arrangements, be used as collateral against which the IMF can borrow from the market for onward lending particularly to middle-income developing countries. Staggered sales should also be undertaken and accruing profits of such sales should be used as interest subsidy on loans to low-income developing countries.

A New Approach to Development Finance. "There must be a substantial increase in the transfer of resources to developing countries in order to finance (i) projects and programmes to alleviate poverty and to expand food production, especially in the least developed countries, (ii) exploration and development of energy and mineral resources, and (iii) stabilization of the prices and earnings of commodity exports and expanded domestic processing of commodities.

"The flow of official development finance should be enlarged by (i) an international system of universal revenue mobilization, based on a sliding scale related to national income, in which East European and developing countries (except the poorest countries) would participate, (ii) the adoption of timetables to increase official development assistance (ODA) from industrialized countries to the level of 0.7 per cent of gross national product (GNP) by 1985, and to 1 per cent before the end of the century, and (iii) introduction of automatic revenue transfers through international levies on some of the following: international trade, arms production or exports; international travel; the global commons, especially seabed minerals.

"Lending through international financial institutions should be improved through (i) effective utilization of the increased borrowing capacity of the World Bank resulting from the recent decision to double its capital to $80,000 million [see page 32], (ii) doubling the borrowing-to-capital ratio of the World Bank from its present gearing of 1:1 to 2:1, and similar action by regional development banks, (iii) abstaining from the imposition of political conditions on the operations of multilateral financial institutions, (iv) channelling an increasing share of development finance through regional institutions, (v) a substantial increase in programme lending, (vi) the use of IMF gold reserves either for further sales, whose profits would subsidize interest on development lending, or as collateral to borrow for on-lending to developing countries, and (vii) giving borrowing countries a greater role in decision-making and management.

"Resource transfers should be made more predictable by long-term commitments to provide ODA, increasing use of automatically mobilized revenues, and the lengthening of the International Development Association (IDA) replenishment period.

"Consideration should be given to the creation of a new international financial institution—a World Development Fund—with universal membership, and in which decision-making is more evenly shared between lenders and borrowers, to supplement existing institutions and diversify lending policies and practices. The World Development Fund would seek to satisfy the unmet needs in the financing structure, in particular that of programme lending. Ultimately, it could serve as a channel for such resources as may be raised on a universal and automatic basis.

"There is need for major additional multilateral finance to support mineral and energy exploration and development in developing countries. Some of this will come from existing institutions, but we believe there is a case for a new facility for this purpose.

"The flow of lending from commercial banks and other private financial bodies to developing countries must be strengthened. Middle-income countries need special measures to lengthen the maturity of their debt structures and poorer developing countries should be enabled to borrow more easily in the market. The World Bank and other international financial institutions should assist this process by co-financing, by the provision of guarantees, and by using concessional funds to improve lending terms and reduce interest rates.

"Measures should be adopted to facilitate the placing of bonds by developing countries in international markets. These should include the removal of restric-

tions and the provision of guarantees and adequate arrangements for the assessment of risks.

International Organizations and Negotiations. "Policies, agreements and institutions in the field of international economic, financial and monetary co-operation should be guided by the principle of universality.

"The UN system, which faces ever-expanding tasks, needs to be strengthened and made more efficient. This calls for more co-ordination of budgets, programmes and personnel policies, to avoid duplication of tasks and wasteful overlapping.

"The performance of the various multilateral organizations in the field of international development should be regularly monitored by a high-level advisory body.

"There needs to be a review of the present system of negotiations to see whether more flexible, expeditious and result-oriented procedures can be introduced without detracting from co-operation within established groups.

"Increased attention should be paid to educating public opinion and the younger generation about the importance of international co-operation.

"The occasional use of limited summit meetings should be considered to advance the cause of consensus and change."

Sessions of UN Conference on Trade and Development

The problems of international economic co-operation were dealt with at successive sessions of the UN Conference on Trade and Development (UNCTAD).

Second UNCTAD Session. At the second UNCTAD session, held in New Delhi from Feb. 1 to March 29, 1968, the demands of the developing countries for increased aid were supported by the Communist countries (with the Soviet Minister for Foreign Trade calling on the capitalist countries and the international lending institutions to provide more aid as "compensation for damage caused by colonial domination and neo-colonialist policies"). Representatives of the United States and Britain, on the other hand, stressed the difficulties of further increasing their countries' large aid commitments in times of balance-of-payments crises.

Among the numerous resolutions adopted by the conference was one setting a new target for transfers from developed to developing countries at 1 per cent of the gross national product (as against the previously agreed target of 1 per cent of the national income). Newly elected members of UNCTAD's Trade and Development Board comprised representatives of 22 African and Asian countries, 18 developed market-economy countries, nine Latin American nations, and six from socialist countries.

The UNCTAD Trade and Development Board adopted, on Oct. 31, 1971, a system of preferential tariffs for imports from developing countries by developed industrialized countries on the basis of a concept of "generalized tariff preferences" discussed at UNCTAD sessions since 1964 and finally agreed to by a special UNCTAD committee on preferences on Oct. 11, 1970. The agreement was first put into effect by the European Economic Community on July 1, 1971, and by most major industrialized countries on Jan. 1, 1972.

Third UNCTAD Session. At the third UNCTAD session, held in Santiago (Chile) between April 13 and May 21, 1972, some 40 resolutions were adopted, including:

(1) One urging "the widest possible participation of developed and developing countries" in "a more satisfactory system of monetary co-operation", with strong representation of the developing countries in a proposed "Committee of Twenty" to advise the International Monetary Fund (IMF) on a reform of the international monetary system;

(2) one asking for relief, both by donor-countries and by the IMF, for developing countries, which had suffered adverse effects from currency realignments;

(3) one containing recommendations for special treatment of 25 countries regarded as the "least developed" of the "Third World", i.e. mainly those with a per capita gross domestic product of $100 or less; and

(4) others containing suggestions on improvements to existing aid systems and on setting up a special UNCTAD body to investigate the effects of debt-service payments on economic growth in developing countries.

Fourth UNCTAD Session. At the fourth UNCTAD session, held in Nairobi on May 5-31, 1976, a report drawn up by the organization's secretariat described the situation of the developing countries as follows:

In the 20 years ending in 1972 the average per capita income of developing countries had risen from $125 to $300, while that of developed market-economy countries had grown from $2,000 to $4,000; the latter countries, with 20 per cent of the world's population, enjoyed about two-thirds of the world's income, whereas the poorest countries with 30 per cent of the world's population had only 3 per cent of world income.

The real value of official development assistance from the developed market-economy countries—in terms of purchasing power—had declined by about 3 per cent over the past 10 years. The indebtedness of developing countries had risen from $9,000 million at the end of 1956 to $19,000 million (for the non-oil-exporting developing countries) at the end of 1973, and their overall payments deficit had increased from $12,000 million in 1973 to $45,000 million in 1975.

Among resolutions adopted by the session was one on "a programme of global action to improve market structures in international trade in commodities of interest to developing countries".

This "integrated programme" was to achieve "stable conditions in commodity trade" at levels which would "(a) be remunerative and just to producers and equitable to consumers; (b) take account of world inflation and changes in the world economic and monetary situations; and (c) promote equilibrium between supply and demand within expanding commodity trade". The programme was also to improve and sustain real

income of developing countries through increased export earnings, improved market access, diversified production and expanded processing of primary products in developing countries, and it would seek to improve the competitiveness of natural products competing with synthetics and substitutes, and to increase developing countries' earnings from marketing, distribution and transport of their products. The programme was to cover "bananas, bauxite, cocoa, coffee, copper, cotton and cotton yarns, hard fibres and products, iron, jute and products, manganese, meat, phosphates, rubber, sugar, tea, tropical timber, tin and vegetable oils (including olive oil and oil-seeds)—as proposed by the 'Group of 77' [see page 394]—it being understood that other products could be included".

The programme also provided for steps to be taken towards the negotiation of the common fund to support market prices of raw materials [see page 87].

With reference to co-operation among developing countries, the conference declared the commitment of "both the developed market-economy countries and the socialist countries of Eastern Europe" to "abstain from adopting any kind of measure which could adversely affect the decisions of the developing countries in favour of the strengthening of their economic co-operation and the diversification of their production structures". Socialist countries of Eastern Europe were asked to provide "technical assistance for setting up state export and import enterprises and to promote links . . . between the transferable rouble system of the International Bank for Co-operation (set up by the Council for Mutual Economic Assistance, CMEA) and regional payments arrangements of developing countries", and also "effectively and substantially to increase economic and technical assistance to developing countries" and to ensure that the flow of mutual trade should not necessarily and always be conducted on the basis of equivalent volumes of exports and imports.

In a resolution adopted by 84 votes to none with 16 abstentions, it was recommended that action should be taken to achieve "a reorientation in the activities of transnational corporations towards more complete manufacture in developing countries" and towards further processing of raw materials, and that there should be increased participation by national enterprises of developing countries in the activities of transnational corporations, with rules to be developed to control practices of transnational corporations likely to have adverse effects on developing countries' trade in manufactures.

Fifth UNCTAD Session. The fifth UNCTAD session was held in Manila from May 7 to June 3, 1979.

A UN negotiating conference on the proposed common fund had in March 1979 agreed that the fund should have an initial capital of $750,000,000, of which $400,000,000 would be for the "first window" ($150,000,000 contributed in cash by governments, a further $150,000,000 available in case of need, and $100,000,000 in callable capital for use by fund managers as security for raising loans on the open market).

Each commodity agreement linked to the fund would raise one-third of its own requirements for buffer stock operations and would be able to draw a further two-thirds in credits from the fund. A minimum contribution to the fund of $1,000,000 per member country was agreed. Of the $150,000,000 thus raised, $80,000,000 would go to the "first window", with the balance contributed by country groups in a fixed ratio (68 per cent coming from the industrialized countries). The "second window" of $350,000,000 would be funded, in addition to the $70,000,000 from the minimum contributions, by voluntary contributions.

The negotiating conference had also agreed on a voting system, which inter alia provided that the "Group of 77" developing countries would hold 47 per cent of the votes, the industrialized countries 42 per cent, the East European socialist countries 8 per cent and China 3 per cent.

The UNCTAD session itself called for intensified efforts to draft articles of agreement for the common fund and urged governments to announce contributions to the "second window" (with the result that by the end of the session 13 countries had specifically pledged voluntary contributions totalling some $87,000,000).

The session also proposed the establishment of a framework for studies and consultations on expanding the integrated commodity programme agreed upon in Nairobi in 1976 [see above] to cover not only price regulation but also processing, marketing and distribution.

With regard to the target of 0.7 per cent of gross national product (GNP) to be devoted to official development assistance by developed countries, the session recommended that, in order to reach this target, the aid budgets should be increased annually by a fixed percentage (in real terms) and that 1 per cent of the annual growth in the GNP of the developed countries should be earmarked for aid.

The session also launched an action programme for "least developed countries" (as defined by the UN General Assembly), as well as special measures to aid landlocked and island developing countries, which would include: (i) "greatly expanded assistance" in 1979-81 and (ii) a concerted strategy embracing structural change, social needs, transformational investment and emergency support in the forthcoming decade.

The world's "least developed countries" (LDC, i.e.

those with an average GNP of less than $280 per annum per head of the population) were listed by the United Nations on Oct. 7, 1977, as comprising the following 28: Afghanistan, Bangladesh, Benin, Bhutan, Botswana, Burundi, the Central African Republic, Chad, Ethiopia, The Gambia, Guinea, Haiti, Laos, Lesotho, Malawi, Maldives, Mali, Nepal, Niger, Rwanda, Somalia, the Sudan, Tanzania, Uganda, Upper Volta, Western Samoa, North Yemen and South Yemen. The names of the Comoros and the Cape Verde Islands were added on Dec. 13, 1977, while the fifth UNCTAD session voted for the inclusion of Djibouti and Tonga.

The following 45 countries were in March 1978 listed as the "most seriously affected" (MSA) by increases in prices of essential imports: Afghanistan, Bangladesh, Benin, Burma, Burundi, Cambodia, Cameroon, the Cape Verde Islands, the Central African Republic, Chad, Egypt, El Salvador, Ethiopia, The Gambia, Ghana, Guatemala, Guinea, Guinea-Bissau, Guyana, Haiti, Honduras, India, the Ivory Coast, Kenya, Laos, Lesotho, Madagascar, Mali, Mauritania, Mozambique, Nepal, Niger, Pakistan, Rwanda, Senegal, Sierra Leone, Somalia, Sri Lanka, the Sudan, Tanzania, Uganda, Upper Volta, Western Samoa, North Yemen and South Yemen.

UNCTAD Common Fund. Articles of agreement for the proposed common fund for commodity stabilization were adopted at a negotiating conference in Geneva on June 27, 1980, and were opened for signature and ratification on Sept. 1, 1980. They would, however, not come into force until ratified by at least 90 states contributing at least two-thirds of the total of $470,000,000 to be directly contributed to the fund, a further condition for the articles' entry into force, relating to the minimum voluntary contribution to the fund's "second window" [see above], having already been met.

Customs Co-operation Council (CCC)

Headquarters: Brussels.

Members (in June 1977): Algeria, Argentina, Australia, Austria, Bahamas, Belgium, Bulgaria, Burundi, Cameroon, Canada, Chile, Congo, Cyprus, Czechoslovakia, Denmark, Egypt, Ethiopia, Finland, France, Gabon, the Federal Republic of Germany, Ghana, Greece, Guyana, Haiti, Hungary, Iceland, India, Indonesia, Iran, Ireland, Israel, Italy, Ivory Coast, Jamaica, Japan, Jordan, Kenya, the Republic of Korea, Lebanon, Liberia, Luxembourg, Madagascar, Malawi, Malaysia, Malta, Mauritius, Morocco, Netherlands, New Zealand, Nigeria, Norway, Pakistan, Paraguay, Peru, Poland, Portugal, Romania, Rwanda, Saudi Arabia, Senegal, Sierra Leone, Singapore, South Africa, Spain, Sri Lanka, Sudan, Sweden, Switzerland, Syria, Tanzania, Thailand, Trinidad and Tobago, Tunisia, Turkey, Uganda, the United Kingdom, the United States, Upper Volta, Yugoslavia and Zaïre (81 countries in all).

The CCC was established on Dec. 15, 1950, under a convention signed by 13 governments, which at the same time also signed conventions on customs nomenclature and customs valuation.

The object of the CCC is to create harmony and uniformity in customs systems, to circulate information on customs regulations and procedures, and to supervise and take conciliatory action in regard to the uniform application of customs conventions prepared by it.

7. Commodity and Raw Material Producers' Organizations and Agreements

This section covers the organizations of producers of commodities and raw materials which have been set up by a number of governments for various products as well as the international agreements which have been concluded in this field.

Bananas

The **Union of Banana Exporting Countries** (Unión de Países Exportadores de Banano, UPEB), with headquarters at Panama, was formally established on Sept. 18, 1974, under an agreement concluded in April 1974 by representatives of Colombia, Costa Rica, Ecuador, Guatemala, Honduras, Nicaragua and Panama. The UPEB was, however, not joined by Ecuador (the world's major banana producers) or Nicaragua, whereas the Dominican Republic became a member in 1975.

On March 5, 1977, the member states of the UPEB signed a charter establishing a multinational banana corporation known as **Comercializador Multinacional de Banano** (Comunbana) for the promotion of banana sales, especially in Eastern Europe and the Arab countries.

Bauxite

The **International Bauxite Association** (IBA), with headquarters in Kingston (Jamaica), was set up at a meeting held in Conakry (Guinea) on Feb. 28-March 8, 1974, by representatives of Australia, Guinea, Guyana, Jamaica, Sierra Leone, Suriname and Yugoslavia (these seven countries then producing about 63 per cent of the world's bauxite).

Under its charter drafted in 1974, the IBA's aim was to "promote the orderly and rational development of the bauxite industry" and "to secure fair and reasonable profits for member countries in the processing and marketing of bauxite, bearing in mind the interests of the consumer countries". The charter called for bauxite-producing countries to process their bauxite so as to become producers of aluminium and thus to increase their income, and it also stated that multinational companies should not be allowed to operate to the detriment of any one country and that member governments should "secure the maximum national ownership of their natural resources".

The IBA's ministerial council held its first annual meeting in Georgetown (Guyana) in November 1974, and by November 1975 the organization's membership had been increased to 11 countries by the accession of the Dominican Republic, Ghana, Haiti and Indonesia (while Greece, India and Trinidad and Tobago were subsequently admitted as observers).

At its fourth annual meeting, held in Kingston in December 1977, the IBA's ministerial council decided to approve an agreed minimum price of $24 per tonne c.i.f. for base-grade bauxite ore exported to the North American market in 1978 (while no announcement was made on any other bauxite pricing).

Cocoa

An *International Cocoa Agreement* was, after 16 years of negotiations, concluded in Geneva on Oct. 21, 1972. This three-year agreement, the main features of which were an export quota system for producing countries, a fixed price range for cocoa and a buffer stock to support the agreed prices, also provided for the establishment of an International Cocoa Council to supervise its implementation. Following signature by countries representing some 70 per cent of cocoa consumption, the agreement came into provisional effect on June 30 and was formally implemented on Oct. 31, 1973. (Its main provisions, however, remained inoperative as during 1973 the world market price of cocoa rose to twice the maximum envisaged in the agreement.)

The 1972 agreement also led to the formation, in 1973, of the **International Cocoa Organization** (ICCO), with headquarters in London, which at a meeting held in Geneva from Sept. 22 to Oct. 20, 1975, negotiated a new agreement laying down new arrangements for a scale of maximum and minimum prices, an export quota system, a mechanism for adjusting quotas and the buffer stock. This agreement, however, was opposed by the United States (the largest cocoa importer), but it came into force provisionally on Oct. 1, 1976. By 1977 the ICCO had a membership of 18 exporting and 27 importing countries.

A new *International Cocoa Agreement*, concluded on Nov. 19, 1980, by delegates from 63 out of 67 countries represented at a UN cocoa conference in Geneva, set minimum and maximum prices (at $1.00 and $1.60 respectively per lb. payable to the producer) with buffer stock operations to stabilize prices within this range. The agreement, to become operative after ratification by countries accounting for 80 per cent of total cocoa exports, was not accepted by Gabon, the Ivory Coast, Togo and the United States.

A **Cocoa Producers' Alliance** (COPAL) had earlier been formed in May 1962 as a forum for discussion of cocoa producers' problems and had eventually been joined by eight states (Brazil, Cameroon, Ecuador, Gabon, Ghana, the Ivory Coast, Nigeria and Togo). In 1977 the COPAL member states agreed that the minimum and maximum prices laid down in the 1975 agreement of the ICCO should be increased.

Coconuts

The **Asian Coconut Community** was formed on Oct. 16, 1968, under the sponsorship of the (UN) Economic Commission for Asia and the Far East (ECAFE) and with headquarters at Jakarta, by Ceylon (Sri Lanka), India, Indonesia, Malaysia, the Philippines, Singapore and Thailand. It was later joined by Papua New Guinea and Western Samoa and was in December 1975 renamed the **Asian and South Pacific Coconut Council,** of which the Solomon Islands and the (US) Trust Territory of the Pacific Islands became associate members.

The Council's objectives are to promote and co-ordinate the coconut industry's activities by improving production, processing, marketing and research.

Coffee

The **International Coffee Organization** (ICO), with headquarters in London, was set up at a conference of coffee-producing countries in Rio de Janeiro in January 1958; by the end of 1980 it had a total membership of 69 (including 44 exporting and 24 importing countries, as well as the European Economic Community). It concluded a number of *International Coffee Agreements* (annually between 1958 and 1962, and for five-year periods from Dec. 27, 1963, and from Dec. 30, 1968). The ICO fixed export quotas, agreed on an "indicator price range" and took other measures to bring supply and demand more into line with one another. The 1968 agreement was approved by 41 coffee-exporting and 20 coffee-importing countries, but it lapsed on Sept. 30, 1973.

It was eventually replaced by a new agreement of Jan. 31, 1976, which became fully effective on Aug. 1, 1977, and which was to remain in force for six years (although it was subject to renegotiation after three years). It provided for the continuation of the **International Coffee Council** first set up under the 1962 agreement, but its export quotas were unrealistic in view of the world coffee shortage which set in during the early 1970s. This agreement was adhered to by 44 exporting countries or territories (representing over 99 per cent of world coffee exports) and 24 importing countries (accounting for about 88 per cent of world imports).

Following the lapse of the 1968 *International Coffee Agreement* in 1973, two smaller organizations were set up by coffee-producing countries, viz.

(1) **Café Mundial,** a London-based producers' marketing organization formed by Brazil, Colombia and the Ivory Coast (the world's largest coffee producers) in August 1973; and

(2) **Cafés Suaves Centrales,** set up in March 1975 by Costa Rica, El Salvador, Mexico and Venezuela with the object of protecting coffee prices.

Three other regional coffee organizations (whose members are also members of the ICO) are:

(1) The **Inter-African Coffee Organization** (IACO), with headquarters in Abidjan (Ivory Coast), founded in 1960 to study common problems and to ensure the smooth disposal of production and the optimum level of selling prices, with its members being 19 coffee-producing countries in Africa (Angola, Benin, Burundi, Cameroon, the Central African Republic, the Congo, Ethiopia, Gabon, the Ivory Coast, Kenya, Liberia, Madagascar, Nigeria, Rwanda, Sierra Leone, Tanzania, Togo, Uganda and Zaïre).

(2) The **African and Malagasy Coffee Organization** (OAMCAF), with headquarters in Paris, with eight member-countries —Benin, Cameroon, the Central African Republic, the Congo, Gabon, the Ivory Coast, Madagascar and Togo.

96

(3) The **Pan-American Coffee Bureau,** with headquarters in New York, formed in 1937 to study coffee problems of common interest to Latin American countries; to promote the consumption of coffee in the United States and Canada; and to promote international co-operation in dealing with coffee problems (its membership consisting of 12 South and Central American governments).

Copper

The **Intergovernmental Council of Copper Exporting Countries** (Conseil Intergouvernemental des Pays Exportateurs du Cuivre—CIPEC), with headquarters at Neuilly-sur-Seine (France), was established in May 1967 with the object of co-ordinating research and information policies among its member countries, namely Chile, Indonesia, Peru, Zaïre and Zambia (in addition to which Australia, Mauritania, Papua New Guinea and Yugoslavia have been admitted as associate members).

To counter a fall in world copper prices CIPEC reduced its member states' copper exports by 10 per cent in November 1974, by another 5 per cent in February 1975 and by a further 5 per cent in April 1975. As these measures proved inadequate to sustain prices, a conference held in March 1976 by CIPEC member states and copper-consuming countries (under UNCTAD auspices) decided to establish a permanent international consultative body on copper, but no agreement has yet been reached on this issue. The position of the CIPEC member countries is weakened by the fact that the United States is not only the world's largest consumer of copper but also its biggest producer (followed by the Soviet Union).

Cotton

The **International Cotton Advisory Committee** (ICAC) was established as a cotton producers' association in Washington in 1939 and was opened in 1945 to all nations "interested in the production, export and import of cotton". With a membership of 48 countries, it collects and disseminates statistics on developments in the world's cotton situation and suggests to its member states suitable measures for the joint maintenance and development of a sound cotton economy in the world.

The **International Institute for Cotton** (IIC), set up in Brussels in 1966 and with 11 member countries (Brazil, Greece, India, Iran, the Ivory Coast, Mexico, Nigeria, Spain, Tanzania, Uganda and the United States), conducts research in the utilization of and markets for cotton, promotes sales and constitutes a link between exporting countries and the principal importing countries. The IIC has a technical research centre in Manchester (United Kingdom) and an office in Washington (D.C.).

Groundnuts

The **African Groundnut Council,** with its head office in Lagos (Nigeria) and a sales promotion office in Geneva, was set up in June 1964, its members being The Gambia, Mali, Niger, Nigeria, Senegal and the Sudan. Its objects are to ensure remunerative prices for groundnuts and their by-products, and the promotion of groundnut consumption and also of solidarity among member states.

Iron Ore

The **Association of Iron-Ore Exporting Countries** (AIOEC) formally came into being on Oct. 12, 1975, under an agreement signed at a meeting held in Geneva on April 2-3, 1975, by ministers from Algeria, Australia, Brazil, Chile, India, Mauritania, Peru, Sierra Leone, Sweden, Tunisia and Venezuela (while other countries represented at the meeting but not signatories to the agreement were Canada, Liberia and the Philippines). The agreement was, however, not ratified by Brazil, Peru, Sierra Leone, Sweden and Tunisia, which therefore did not become members of the AIOEC.

The Association was to play merely a consultative role without powers for concerted governmental action by its member countries, and its aims were to ensure the orderly and healthy growth of the export trade in iron ore, to secure fair and remunerative returns from its exploration, processing and marketing, and to promote close co-operation among member countries.

Lead and Zinc

The **International Lead and Zinc Study Group** (superseding an earlier Lead and Zinc Study Committee set up in 1958) was established in 1959 with headquarters in London and held its first meeting in Geneva in 1960.

It has a standing committee serving as a forum for consultation between producing and consuming countries (inter alia on world trade), and it also has an economic and a statistical committee. The Group has 31 member governments, namely Algeria, Australia, Austria, Belgium, Bulgaria, Canada, Czechoslovakia, Denmark, Finland, France, the Federal Republic of Germany, Hungary, India, Ireland, Italy, Japan, Mexico, Morocco, the Netherlands, Norway, Peru, Poland, South Africa, the Soviet Union, Spain, Sweden, Tunisia, the United Kingdom, the United States, Yugoslavia and Zambia.

Olive Oil

The **International Olive Oil Council** (IOOC) was set up in Madrid under an international agreement concluded in 1958 (and amended in 1963, 1967, 1969 and 1973) with the object of promoting international co-operation in dealing with olive oil problems; preventing unfair competition in the world's olive oil trade; taking and applying measures to extend the production, consumption and sale of olive oil; and preventing disruption caused by fluctuations in supply. The IOOC has 12 mainly producing and 12 mainly exporting member countries (including Algeria, Chile, the Dominican Republic, Egypt, Greece, Israel, Lebanon, Libya, Morocco, Panama, Portugal, Spain, Tunisia, Turkey and Yugoslavia), with the European Communities being also a member and 20 other countries having attended IOOC seminars as observers.

A new international olive oil agreement was concluded at a meeting held in Geneva in March-April 1979 by representatives of 33 countries and entered into force on Jan. 1, 1980.

Pepper

The **Pepper Community** came into being early in 1972 after an agreement had been signed by India, Indonesia and Malaysia during the 27th session of the ECAFE on April 21, 1971. The objects of the Community were to co-ordinate action among pepper-producing countries in regard to standard, supplies and marketing of pepper.

Petroleum

Organization of Petroleum Exporting Countries. The Organization of Petroleum Exporting Countries (OPEC) was set up, as announced on Sept. 24, 1960, as a result of a conference of representatives from Iraq, Iran, Kuwait, Saudi Arabia and Venezuela held in Baghdad on Sept. 10-14 of that year, with the above five countries as its initial members. Qatar became a member in January 1961, Indonesia and Libya joined it in June 1962, Abu Dhabi in November 1967, Algeria in July 1969, Ecuador in December 1973 and Gabon (which had become an associate member in December 1973) in June 1975. The membership of Abu Dhabi was transferred to the United Arab Emirates (UAE) in January 1974.

The member countries of OPEC, which established its headquarters in Vienna, supply about 85 per cent of the world's oil exports outside the Soviet bloc, but do not include the world's two largest single oil-producing countries—the Soviet Union and the United States.

OPEC's supreme authority is its Conference which is responsible for formulating the organization's general policy. OPEC's management is directed by a Board of Governors consisting of one Governor from each member country and meeting at least twice a year. OPEC also has an economic commission which is to assist the organization in promoting stability in international oil prices at an equitable level.

OPEC's main object was to increase the share of revenue accruing to its members. An agreement concluded in Tehran on Feb. 14, 1971, by Abu Dhabi, Iran, Kuwait and Saudi Arabia with 23 international oil companies provided for security of supply and stability in financial arrangements for the five-year period from 1971 to 1975.

Agreements subsequently concluded were (i) the Geneva agreement of Jan. 20, 1972, providing for an immediate rise of 8.49 per cent in the posted price of crude oil at the Persian Gulf and at Eastern Mediterranean terminals and for further adjustments until 1975, based on an index measuring significant changes in the exchange rate of the US dollar, and (ii) the Geneva agreement of June 2, 1973, when eight of OPEC's 11 member states raised posted prices of crude oil by an aggregate of 11.9 per cent and a new mechanism was provided to make monthly adjustments in prices in future.

Following a 10 per cent devaluation of the US dollar in February 1973, further negotiations between OPEC and oil companies broke down and on Oct. 17, 1973, the Gulf states unilaterally declared 70 per cent increases in posted prices (from $3.01 to $5.11 per barrel). At a further conference held in Tehran on Dec. 22-23, 1973, OPEC increased the posted price by almost 130 per cent (from $5.11 to $11.56 per barrel) from Jan. 1, 1974. At an extraordinary OPEC conference in Geneva in January 1974 prices were held at the current level, which was eventually maintained for the remainder of 1974.

At a meeting in Quito (Ecuador) in June 1974 royalties charged on oil companies were increased from 12.5 to 14.1 per cent by all OPEC member states except Saudi Arabia. Further royalty and tax increases were decided at a Vienna meeting in September 1974 (raising royalties on equity crude oil to 16.67 per cent and taxes to 65.65 per cent, again except in Saudi Arabia).

At a first summit conference, held by the heads of state of eight of OPEC's 13 member countries in Algiers on March 4-6, 1975, a "solemn declaration" was issued on OPEC's role in the world economic crisis.

In their declaration the heads of state attributed "the present world economic crisis" to "profound inequalities in the economic and social progress among countries" which had their "decisive causes" in "longstanding and persistent ills which have been allowed to accumulate over the years, such as the general tendency of the developed countries to consume excessively and to waste scarce resources", as well as "inappropriate and shortsighted policies". They therefore rejected any allegation that the price of petroleum was responsible for the existing instability of the world economy and claimed that oil was "the cheapest source of energy available". They reaffirmed the solidarity of OPEC and pointed out that the OPEC member countries had "contributed through multilateral and bilateral channels to the development efforts and balance of payments adjustments of other developing countries as well as industrialized nations". They emphasized that the developed countries "must contribute to the progress and development of the developing countries through concrete action".

At a ministerial meeting held in Vienna in September 1975 OPEC oil prices were raised by a further 10 per cent until June 1976. A meeting of OPEC member countries' Ministers of Finance in Vienna on Nov. 17-18, 1975, agreed to recommend to their governments the establishment of a new facility for providing additional financial support to developing countries. (According to an UNCTAD report of Nov. 25, 1975, the OPEC member countries' contribution to official development aid for the Third World had risen from 10 per cent in 1973 to almost 23 per cent in 1974.) In January 1976 the OPEC Finance Ministers signed an agreement establishing a joint "Special Fund" to "provide interest-free long-term loans to developing countries", with an initial one-year commitment of $800,000,000 to be made to the fund, of which one-half was to be used for agricultural development provided that developed countries also made substantial aid pledges for this purpose. The Special Fund came into operation in August 1976. An agreement signed in New York on Sept. 30, 1977, provided for disbursement of up to $20,000,000 from this fund for projects administered by the UN Development Programme.

On prices no unanimous decision was made at an OPEC ministerial conference held in Bali (Indonesia) in May 1976, but Saudi Arabia's prices remained unchanged. At a further such conference, held at Doha (Qatar) on Dec. 15-17, 1976, price increases amounting to about 10.3 per cent on Jan. 1, 1977, and a further 4.7 per cent on July 1, 1977, were made by 11 OPEC member states, but these proposals were not accepted by Saudi Arabia, with the result that the new prices in force from Jan. 1, 1977, were increased by varying percentages (ranging from 3 to 11.5 per cent). In *The Times* of Nov. 30, 1976, it was calculated that the "real" price of OPEC oil had risen by 385 per cent since 1972.

A more or less uniform price level was restored at an OPEC ministerial conference held at Saltsjøbaden (Sweden) in July 1977, when Saudi Arabia and the UAE agreed to raise their prices by 5 per cent and the other member states waived price increases which they had proposed earlier. A second 1977 conference, held in Caracas in December,

failed to reach any agreement on prices. An informal ministerial meeting held at At Ta'if (Saudi Arabia) on May 6-7, 1978, concentrated on long-term policies and appointed a committee to study them. At a formal conference held in Geneva on June 17-19, 1978, it was generally accepted that market conditions precluded any rise in the basic "marker" price from the current level of $12.70 per barrel (in force for 11 countries since Jan. 1, 1977, and for Saudi Arabia and the UAE since July 1, 1977) and that, on Saudi Arabia's insistence, the pricing in US dollars should be retained (contrary to a proposal made at a conference in Gabon in June 1974 to quote prices in Special Drawing Rights—SDRs—of the International Monetary Fund).

However, at an OPEC conference held in Abu Dhabi on Dec. 16-17, 1978, it was decided, in view of the "high rate of inflation and dollar depreciation over the last two years", to increase the price of oil by 10 per cent on average over the year 1979 (by means of quarterly adjustments). This decision was changed at an extraordinary session of the OPEC Conference in Geneva on March 26-27, 1979, when the 1979 adjustments were brought forward to April 1 of that year and each OPEC member country was allowed to add to its price market premia deemed justifiable. The average official price for OPEC crude oil thereupon rose to $17.28 per barrel in May 1979, while the unofficial "spot" price reached up to $40.

Even higher minimum prices were agreed at OPEC meetings during 1980. A meeting in Algiers on June 9-10, 1980, decided, against the votes of Saudi Arabia and the United Arab Emirates, to set the theoretical base and ceiling prices at $32 and $37 per barrel respectively. At a conference held in Bali (Indonesia) on Dec. 15-16, 1980, it was decided to fix the official price of the marker crude oil at $32 per barrel, with a ceiling of $36 per barrel for deemed marker crude and a maximum price for OPEC crudes of $41 per barrel.

Organization of Arab Petroleum Exporting Countries. The Organization of Arab Petroleum Exporting Countries (OAPEC) was set up under an agreement signed in Beirut on Jan. 9, 1968, by its initial members—Kuwait, Libya and Saudi Arabia—which were joined in May 1970 by Abu Dhabi, Algeria, Bahrain, Dubai and Qatar, and in March 1972 by Egypt, Iraq and Syria. Dubai withdrew in December 1972; Abu Dhabi was replaced by the United Arab Emirates (UAE) in June 1974; and Egypt's membership was suspended in March 1979 as a result of a decision by an Arab ministerial meeting held in Baghdad in the wake of the Egyptian-Israeli peace treaty signed in March 1979.

OAPEC, with headquarters in Kuwait, was to represent the special interests of Arab petroleum exporting countries while respecting the charter of OPEC. The organization's supreme authority is its Council, normally composed of the member countries' Ministers of Petroleum and meeting at least twice a year.

The possible use of petroleum as a political weapon to force the United States (as the largest importer) to apply an "impartial" policy on the Arab-Israeli conflict was first discussed at a meeting of the Foreign Ministers of the 10 OAPEC member countries on Sept. 4, 1973. On Oct. 17 of that year OAPEC's member states decided to reduce their production by at least 5 per cent progressively each month until Israel had withdrawn its forces completely from Arab territories occupied in the 1967 war and the legal rights of Palestinians had been restored. In addition OAPEC member states imposed total embargoes on oil shipments to the United States and also to the Netherlands. On Nov. 4-5, 1973, it was decided to increase the overall production cutback from Sept. 1, 1973, to 25 per cent, but by the end of 1973 this decision was reversed, and (following a disengagement agreement concluded between Egypt and Israel in January 1974) the embargo against the United States was lifted in March 1974, and that against the Netherlands in July 1974.

At a meeting of ministers from OAPEC member countries and a special commission of the Organization of African Unity held in Cairo on Jan. 22-23, 1974, the OAPEC ministers agreed to accelerate the establishment of an Arab bank for the economic development of Africa (as decided at an Algiers Arab summit meeting) with an increased capital of $500,000,000, and to recommend the creation of a $200,000,000 fund for the granting of credits to African countries (at no or purely nominal interest) for the purchase of Arab oil.

Between 1973 and 1977 OAPEC established the following subsidiary organizations:

(1) The **Arab Maritime Petroleum Transport Company** with a subscribed capital of $500,000,000, formed in 1973 and based in Kuwait, which had by early 1975 ordered six supertankers for delivery by 1978.

(2) The **Arab Petroleum Investment Company** with an initial capital of about $1,100,000,000, to assist the development of oil industry projects in Arab countries, as decided on July 10, 1974.

(3) The **Arab Shipbuilding and Repair Yard Company** with a subscribed capital of $340,000,000, formed in Bahrain in December 1974; it opened a drydock in Bahrain in December 1977.

(4) The **Arab Petroleum Services Company** with an authorized capital of $350,000,000 and with specialized subsidiaries to provide technical services to Arab state companies, established in Tripoli (Libya) in January 1977.

Rubber

The **Association of Natural Rubber Producing Countries** (ANRPC), with headquarters in Kuala Lumpur (Malaysia), was formed in October 1970 as a result of a meeting organized in October 1967 by rubber producing countries. In 1978 its members were India, Indonesia, Malaysia, Papua New Guinea, Singapore, Sri Lanka and Thailand. The objects of the ANRPC were to achieve co-operation among its member states as well as fair and stable prices.

At a meeting of the ANRCP in Kuala Lumpur in May 1975 it was agreed in principle to introduce a buffer-stock system and a "supply rationalization scheme" and also to limit member countries' combined exports.

At a further ANRPC meeting (in Jakarta) an *International Rubber Agreement on Price Stabilization* was signed on Nov. 30, 1976, by ministers from Indonesia, Malaysia, Singapore, Sri Lanka and Thailand, establishing an international council to stabilize rubber prices by stockpiling and production controls. This International Natural Rubber Council was to operate the agreement and to determine the proportion of buffer-stock resources to be contributed in rubber and cash by each member state and the price levels governing buffer-stock intervention in the market to limit price fluctuations.

A new *International Natural Rubber Agreement* (INRA) reached under UNCTAD auspices on Oct. 6, 1979, included provisions for price stabilization (between minimum and maximum indicative prices set at 150 and 270 Malaysian/Singapore cents per kilogramme) with semi-automatic procedures for the periodic revision of the agreed price range every 30 months. The sole mechanism for price stabilization was the operation of buffer stocks of 500,000 tonnes in all, the creation of which would begin only after the agreement had definitely entered into force. The **International Natural Rubber Council** (INRC), with headquarters at Kuala Lumpur, was to administer the agreement.

The INRA entered provisionally into force on Oct. 24, 1980, after being ratified by countries accounting for 65 per cent of the world's natural rubber production and consumption respectively, and its definitive entry into force would take place only after ratification by countries accounting for 80 per cent of world production and consumption respectively.

Sugar

The **International Sugar Organization,** with headquarters in London and a membership of 40 exporting and 16 importing countries, was set up under a 1968 *International Sugar Agreement* (ISA), negotiated under UNCTAD auspices, covering fixed prices and export quotas and in force from 1969 to 1973.

This ISA was superseded by a new agreement which was in force from 1974 to 1976 but contained no economic provisions. A new ISA negotiated in 1977 by a UN Sugar Conference came into force provisionally on Jan. 1, 1978 (as the first international commodity agreement negotiated since the fourth UNCTAD session had adopted an "integrated programme for commodities" —see page 92).

The objectives of this ISA, as defined in its Article 1, included the raising of "the level of international trade in sugar, particularly to increase the export earnings of the developing exporting countries"; the achievement of "stable conditions in the international trade in sugar"; provision of "adequate supplies of sugar to meet the requirements of importing countries at fair and reasonable prices"; and "adequate participation in, and growing access to, the markets of the developed countries for sugar from the developing countries". The extensive provisions of the ISA were to be administered by an **International Sugar Council** (ISC). Among arrangements excluded from the ISA's provisions were those for exports of sugar to the European Economic Community (under the 1975 Lomé Convention or under agreements with other states).

Inter alia the ISA laid down "basic export tonnages" (i.e. quotas) totalling 15,905,000 tonnes for 29 major sugar-exporting countries (subject to revision and renegotiation) and also of 70,000 tonnes for each of 22 smaller exporting countries. In addition the ISA contained provisions for a price stabilization mechanism. By Jan. 1, 1978, the ISA had been approved by 25 exporting countries or territories (Argentina, Australia, Barbados, Belize, Brazil, Costa Rica, Cuba, El Salvador, Fiji, Guatemala, Honduras, Hungary, India, Jamaica, Madagascar, Mauritius, Nicaragua, Panama, St Kitts-Nevis-Anguilla, South Africa, Swaziland, Thailand, Trinidad and Tobago, and Venezuela) and also by eight importing countries (including Canada, Japan, the Soviet Union and the United States).

The **Group of Latin American and Caribbean Sugar Exporting Countries** (GEPLACEA), with headquarters in Mexico City, was formed in March 1976. Its objects were to serve as a forum for consultation on the production and sale of sugar; to take up agreed positions at international meetings on sugar; to exchange scientific and technical knowledge; to co-ordinate the various branches of sugar processing; and to achieve fair and remunerative prices. Its membership comprises 22 Latin American and Caribbean countries.

Tea

The **International Tea Committee** (ITC), with headquarters in London, was created in 1933 under an *International Tea Agreement* (ITA) signed by representatives of the tea industries in India, Ceylon and the Netherlands East Indies.

The last ITA was signed on May 8, 1950, between India, Pakistan, Ceylon (Sri Lanka) and Indonesia; it expired on March 31, 1955, and has not been renewed. The ITC's current duties are confined to supplying statistical and other information. Its members are Bangladesh, India, Indonesia, Kenya, Malawi, Mozambique, Sri Lanka, Tanzania and Uganda.

Textiles

The **Multi-Fibre Arrangement** (MFA), concluded in Geneva on Dec. 30, 1973, by representatives of some 50 countries meeting under the auspices of the General Agreement on Tariffs and Trade (GATT), laid down, for a four-year period, rules for international trade in textile products of wool, cotton and man-made fibres.

This arrangement came into force on Jan. 1, 1974, and provided for the establishment of a permanent **Textiles Surveillance Body** (superseding an earlier arrangement on world trade in cotton textiles agreed upon in February 1962). The basic objects of the arrangement were (i) to expand the trade through progressive liberalization of world trade in textile products while ensuring the orderly and equitable development of the trade and avoidance of disruptive effects in both importing and exporting countries, and (ii) "to further the economic and social development of developing countries and secure substantial increases in their export earnings from textile products and to provide scope for a greater share for them in world trade in these products". The operation of the arrangement was to be reviewed by a Textile Committee of representatives of all participating countries.

The arrangement was signed by the European Communities and 41 governments of countries other than the former's members. It was endorsed by the GATT Council on Jan. 28, 1974, and on Dec. 14, 1977, was extended unchanged for a further four years from Jan. 1, 1978.

Bilateral textile agreements were concluded in 1978-79 by the European Economic Community with a total of 27 low-price textile exporting countries—four from the Eastern bloc in Europe (Bulgaria, Hungary, Poland and Romania), Yugoslavia, Egypt, eight countries in Latin America and 13 in Asia (including China—in July 1979). An agreement with Malta was concluded later.

101

Timber

The **Inter-African Organization for Forestry Economy and Marketing of Timber,** with headquarters at Libreville (Gabon), was established under a decision taken at a meeting held on May 26, 1975, by ministers from 11 African states—Cameroon, the Central African Republic, the Congo, Equatorial Guinea, the Ivory Coast, Gabon, Ghana, Liberia, Madagascar, Tanzania and Zaïre. The object of the organization was to secure easier access to markets for timber producers, to stabilize prices and to take "a unified stand towards carriers so as to ensure acceptable prices for transport services".

The **South-East Asia Lumber Producers' Association** (SEALPA) was set up in December 1974 by Indonesia, Malaysia and the Philippines with the object of collecting economic and marketing data from timber-using countries as a guideline for the formulation of joint sales and production measures, maintaining a minimum fair price level and protecting the economic interests of the member countries. For the year 1975 SEALPA imposed export quotas for logs.

Tin

The **International Tin Council** (ITC), established in 1956 with headquarters in London, and with 28 member governments, operates the *International Tin Agreement* (ITA).

The first ITA, drawn up in 1953, had come into force on July 1, 1956; it had established a 25,000-ton buffer stock and fixed floor and ceiling prices per long ton. Similar second, third and fourth agreements were in force between 1962 and 1976. During a period of generally low prices the ITC imposed, in 1968, quotas on exports by the then six producer countries, but in December 1969 the ITC lifted export controls.

Under a fifth ITA, reached in June 1975 and in force provisionally from July 1, 1976, and definitively from June 14, 1977, the buffer stock was increased to 30,000 tons. Among the general objectives of the fifth ITA were "to provide for adjustment be-

tween world production and consumption of tin", "to prevent excessive fluctuations in the price of tin and in export earnings from it"; "to increase the export earnings from tin, especially those of the developing producing countries"; and "to improve further the expansion in the use of tin and the indigenous processing of tin, especially in the developing producing countries". Producer countries which approved the fifth ITA were Australia, Bolivia, Indonesia, Malaysia, Thailand and Zaïre (but not Burma and China), and consumer countries which did so included the member states of the European Communities, Canada, Japan, the United States and also the Communist countries of Europe (except the German Democratic Republic).

Wheat

The **International Wheat Council** was established on July 1, 1949, with headquarters in London and a membership of nine wheat exporting countries and 40 importing countries—the exporting countries being Argentina, Australia, Canada, Greece, Kenya, Spain, Sweden, the Soviet Union and the United States (with the European Economic Community being both an exporter and an importer). The Council has been responsible for the administration of the *Wheat Trade Convention* of 1971 which was part of an *International Wheat Agreement* concluded on Feb. 20, 1971, and in force from July 1 of that year. The agreement covered arrangements for consultation and exchange of information but contained no provisions for price control mechanisms. It was repeatedly extended, most recently in March 1977 until June 30, 1981.

Wine

The **International Wine and Vine Office** (Office International de la Vigne et du Vin) with headquarters in Paris was set up in 1924, mainly to study all problems connected with the vine and its products, to promote contacts among researchers and to establish international research programmes. It has 30 member countries.

8. West European Groupings, Treaties and Agreements

West European groupings, treaties and agreements covered in this section comprise (i) the major international organizations set up in the aftermath of World War II, (ii) the European Communities, (iii) the European Free Trade Association, (iv) West European co-operation in other important spheres and (v) major bilateral treaties and agreements in force.

Post-War Co-operation in Western Europe

Western European Union (WEU)

Headquarters: London.

Members: Belgium, France, the Federal Republic of Germany, Italy, Luxembourg, the Netherlands and the United Kingdom.

The basis of this alliance was laid in a Treaty of Dunkirk, an Anglo-French treaty of alliance signed on March 4, 1947, when the two signatories agreed to give mutual support to each other in the event of renewed German aggression and to take common action should either party be prejudiced by any failure of Germany to fulfil its economic obligations.

A Brussels Treaty, signed on March 17, 1948, by representatives of Belgium, France, Luxembourg, the Netherlands and the United Kingdom, implemented proposals for a Western European Union made earlier by the UK Foreign Secretary (Ernest Bevin). This treaty, concluded for a period of 50 years, had among its aims the strengthening of economic, social and cultural ties between the signatories, the co-ordination of efforts to create a firm basis for European economic recovery, and mutual assistance in maintaining international peace and security. Article 4 of the treaty provided for mutual automatic military assistance in the event of an armed attack in Europe, and Article 7 created a Consultative Council to discuss matters covered by the treaty.

Following a breakdown of discussions on the creation of a European Defence Council, the Brussels Treaty was amended and expanded by the Paris Agreements which were concluded at a nine-power conference held in London from Sept. 28 to Oct. 3, 1954, and signed in Paris on Oct. 23, 1954, by representatives of Belgium, Canada, France, the Federal Republic of Germany, Italy, Luxembourg, the Netherlands, the United Kingdom and the United States, and which came into force on May 5, 1955. The expanded Brussels Treaty Organization was renamed the Western European Union (WEU).

Those documents of the Paris Agreements which are relevant to the formation of the WEU comprise four protocols and a resolution on the production and standardization of armaments.

Protocol I amended the Brussels Treaty of 1948 to permit the entry of the Federal Republic of Germany and Italy into the Treaty Organization. The system of mutual automatic assistance in case of attack was extended to the two new entrants. The Consultative Council set up under the original treaty was given powers of decision and renamed the Council of Western European Union.

Protocol II laid down the maximum strength of land and air forces to be maintained in Europe at the disposal of the Supreme Allied Commander of NATO by each of the member countries of the WEU in peacetime. The contribution of naval forces to NATO by each of the WEU countries would be determined annually. Regular inspections would be held by the Supreme Allied Commander, Europe, to ensure that the limits were observed. A special article recapitulated an undertaking by Britain not to withdraw or diminish her forces in Europe against the wishes of the majority of her partners. In 1957 Britain was given permission, by the WEU Council, to withdraw some of her forces from the Federal Republic of Germany.

Protocol III embodied resolutions on the control of armaments on the European mainland. The Federal Republic of Germany was forbidden to manufacture atomic, biological or chemical weapons, and stocks of such weapons in other countries of continental Europe were to be strictly controlled. In addition, Germany undertook not to manufacture long-range and guided missiles, influence mines, warships and strategic bombers unless the competent NATO Supreme Commander should recommend any change in the ruling.

Protocol IV set up an Agency for the Control of Armaments and defined its functions, these being mainly to enforce the provisions of Protocol III.

Organization of Western European Union

Council

- at ministerial level: consisting of Foreign Ministers of the seven member states, with rotating chairmanship.
- at ambassadorial level: consisting of ambassadors of member states and a high UK official. In permanent session. Decisions taken unanimously, with certain exceptions.

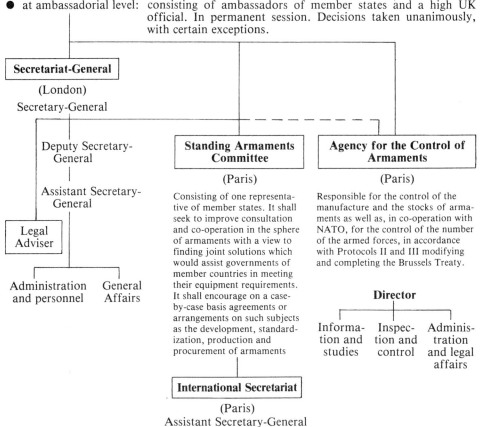

Secretariat-General

(London)
Secretary-General

Deputy Secretary-General

Assistant Secretary-General

Legal Adviser

Administration and personnel   General Affairs

Standing Armaments Committee

(Paris)

Consisting of one representative of member states. It shall seek to improve consultation and co-operation in the sphere of armaments with a view to finding joint solutions which would assist governments of member countries in meeting their equipment requirements. It shall encourage on a case-by-case basis agreements or arrangements on such subjects as the development, standardization, production and procurement of armaments

Agency for the Control of Armaments

(Paris)

Responsible for the control of the manufacture and the stocks of armaments as well as, in co-operation with NATO, for the control of the number of the armed forces, in accordance with Protocols II and III modifying and completing the Brussels Treaty.

Director

Information and studies   Inspection and control   Administration and legal affairs

International Secretariat

(Paris)
Assistant Secretary-General

Assembly

Consisting of representatives of Western European Union member states in the Consultative Assembly of the Council of Europe. Ordinary meetings twice a year, usually in Paris. Total membership 89: United Kingdom, France, Federal Republic of Germany and Italy each 18, Belgium and the Netherlands each seven, Luxembourg three members.

The Bureau   **The Presidential Committee**

Permanent Committees

Defence questions and armaments   General affairs (Political Committee)   Budgetary affairs and administration   Scientific technological and aerospace   Rules of procedures and privileges   Relations with Parliaments

Office of the Clerk

The Clerk
The Clerk Assistant
Committee Services

LATER DECISIONS OF THE WEU

The most important decisions taken at subsequent meetings of the WEU have concerned amendments to Protocol III of the revised Brussels Treaty.

The first such decision was taken at a meeting of the Permanent Council on April 23, 1958, when West Germany's request to manufacture short-range, anti-tank, guided missiles with only conventional warheads was approved.

On Oct. 21, 1959, the Council of the WEU removed the restriction on the construction of ground-to-air and air-to-air anti-aircraft missiles by Germany.

Between May 1961 and October 1963, the WEU approved a number of revisions to the permitted limits on West German naval construction. On May 24, 1961, the Council of the WEU raised the tonnage limit for eight West German destroyers to 6,000 tons (double the existing general limit), and permitted the Federal Republic of Germany to build fleet auxiliary vessels of up to 6,000 tons and to manufacture influence mines for port protection.

On Oct. 19, 1962, the WEU announced its agreement to increase from 350 to 450 tons the limit for West German submarines "to fulfil NATO requirements". A year later, on Oct. 9, 1963, the WEU Permanent Council agreed to raise the tonnage limit for West German submarines from 450 to 1,000 tons, and to allow six submarines of the latter size to be built in the Federal Republic of Germany.

These limits were subsequently further relaxed under a series of amendments, so that by 1980 the permitted limits were (i) 3,000 tons for combat vessels except eight destroyers of up to 6,000 tons and one training ship of up to 5,000 tons; (ii) 6,000 tons for permanent auxiliary vessels and (iii) 1,800 tons for submarines.

On July 21, 1980, the Council of the WEU unanimously agreed to a proposal (approved by the WEU Parliamentary Assembly on June 2 by 55 votes to six) to remove with immediate effect all restrictions on the permitted size of West German warships.

TEMPORARY FRENCH WITHDRAWAL FROM MINISTERIAL COUNCIL

France withdrew from meetings of the WEU Ministerial Council on Feb. 19, 1969, and did not return to them until June 5, 1970.

France's withdrawal followed (i) discussions by the Council on Oct. 21-22, 1968, and Feb. 6-7, 1969, of the "Harmel Plan" —a proposal made by Pierre Harmel, the Belgian Foreign Minister, for co-operation between the European Community and Britain in the fields of foreign, defence, technological and monetary policy, and (ii) a meeting held by the WEU Permanent Council, against France's wishes and without her participation, for discussions on the Middle East situation.

OTHER WEU ACTIVITIES

Since the entry of the United Kingdom into the European Communities in 1973 the WEU has concentrated its activities on deliberations concerning political questions, including East-West relations, the changes brought about by the institution of democratic regimes in Greece, Portugal and Spain and the Arab-Israeli conflict.

Council of Europe

Headquarters: Strasbourg.

Members: Austria, Belgium, Cyprus, Denmark, France, the Federal Republic of Germany, Greece, Iceland, Ireland, Italy, Liechtenstein, Luxembourg, Malta, Netherlands, Norway, Portugal, Spain, Sweden, Switzerland, Turkey and the United Kingdom.

The Council of Europe was established under its Statute, signed on May 5, 1949, by the Foreign Ministers of 10 European states—Belgium, Denmark, France, Ireland, Italy, Luxembourg, the Netherlands, Norway, Sweden and the United Kingdom —and effective from Aug. 3, 1949. The Council was subsequently joined by Greece and Turkey (August 1949), Iceland (March 1950), the Federal Republic of Germany (May 1951), Austria (April 1956), Cyprus (April 1961), Switzerland (May 1963), Malta (January 1965), Portugal (September 1976), Spain (November 1977) and Liechtenstein (November 1978), bringing the Council's total membership to 21.

Greece was not a member of the Council between December 1969 and November 1974, having withdrawn from membership after the Council had, on Sept. 26, 1967, released a report describing the regime set up in Greece on April 21, 1967, as "undemocratic, illiberal, authoritarian and repressive", and being readmitted after the restitution of parliamentary democracy in Greece in 1974.

The principal clauses of the Statute of the Council of Europe are given below:

Chapter I: Aim of the Council of Europe

"**Art. 1.** (*a*) The aim of the Council of Europe is to achieve a greater unity between its members for the purpose of safeguarding and realizing the ideals and principles which are their common heritage and facilitating their economic and social progress.

"(*b*) This aim shall be pursued through the organs of the Council by discussion of questions of common concern and by agreements and common action in economic, social, cultural, scientific, legal and administrative matters.

"(*c*) Participation in the Council of Europe shall not affect the collaboration of its members in the work of the United Nations and of other international organizations or unions to which they are parties.

"(*d*) Matters relating to national defence do not fall within the scope of the Council of Europe.

Chapter II: Membership

"**Art. 2.** The members of the Council of Europe are the parties to this statute.

"**Art. 3.** Every member of the Council of Europe must accept the principles of the rule of law and of the enjoyment by all persons within its jurisdiction of human rights and fundamental freedoms, and collaborate sincerely and effectively in the realization of the aim of the Council as specified in Chapter I.

"**Art. 4.** Any European state, which is deemed to be able and willing to fulfil the provisions of Art. 3, may be invited to become a member of the Council of Europe by the Committee of Ministers. Any state so invited shall become a member on the deposit on its

behalf with the Secretary-General of an instrument of accession to the present statute." (By a later revision of this article the Council's Consultative Assembly must be consulted before the issue of an invitation to join the Council.)

Other articles of the statute deal with the functions and activities of the various organs of the Council, with matters of finance, and with the privileges and immunities to be enjoyed by representatives of members of the Council of Europe in the territories of members of the Council.

ORGANS OF THE COUNCIL OF EUROPE

(1) The Committee of Ministers. The Committee of Ministers, consisting of the 21 Foreign Ministers of the member states, meets in Strasbourg twice a year. Its work programme is based on a medium-term (five-year) plan revised every two years according to political developments and re-

Map 1 Member states of Council of Europe

sults achieved. The Committee decides on recommendations submitted to it by the Parliamentary Assembly and on proposals made by committees of government experts, and its decisions may take the form of resolutions recommending common measures to governments, or of conventions or agreements binding on the states which ratify them. The Committee's decisions are taken by a simple or a two-thirds majority while unanimity is required for major issues.

The Committee's work programme is implemented by 11 (permanent) steering committees, five ad hoc committees of experts (set up for the duration of a specific activity) and 88 committees of experts (dissolved upon completion of their work).

The Foreign Ministers' Deputies, being the permanent representatives of their governments to the Council of Europe, meet every fortnight.

(2) The Parliamentary Assembly. This consultative Assembly consists of 170 representatives (and an equal number of substitutes) appointed by the national parliaments as follows: 18 each from France, the Federal Republic of Germany, Italy and the United Kingdom; 12 each from Spain and Turkey; seven each from Belgium, Greece, the Netherlands and Portugal; six each from Austria, Sweden and Switzerland; five each from Denmark and Norway; four from Ireland; three each from Cyprus, Iceland, Luxembourg and Malta; and two from Liechtenstein. The representatives have formed six multinational groups—Socialists, Christian Democrats, Independents (Conservatives), a Joint Group of Democrats (of the French *Rassemblement pour la république,* the Spanish Democratic Centre Union and the Portuguese Social Democrats), Liberals and Communists.

The Assembly holds three public sessions a year (from one week to 10 days each) in Strasbourg, with Israel being admitted as an observer. The Assembly's President is elected for one year but may be re-elected and normally remains in office for three years.

The Assembly has a Standing Committee consisting of the Assembly's President, its Vice-Presidents, the chairman of the specialized committees and a number of parliamentarians per member state. It meets at least three times a year and is empowered to adopt recommendations and resolutions.

There are 12 specialized committees consisting of members of the Assembly for various fields as follows: Political affairs; economic affairs and development; social and health questions; legal affairs; culture and education; science and technology; regional planning and local authorities; agriculture; relations with European non-member countries; the budget and the inter-governmental work programme; migration, refugees and demography; and parliamentary and public relations.

(3) The Conference of Local and Regional Authorities. This Conference (which has no equivalent in any other European inter-governmental organization) is composed of 170 representatives (and an equal number of substitutes) appointed directly or elected by local and regional authorities in the Council of Europe's 21 member states. The Conference meets annually, has consultative powers and provides liaison between the Council of Europe and the European Communities.

(4) Conferences of Specialist Ministers. Such conferences are organized periodically to analyse major problems in the fields of justice, education, family affairs, regional planning, the environment, labour, culture, sport, local government and social security, and projects suitable for inclusion in the Council of Europe's work programme are communicated to the Committee of Ministers.

(5) Specific Bodies. Certain sections of the Council's work programme are assigned to the following specific bodies: The European Commission of Human Rights; the European Court of Human Rights; the European Youth Centre; and the European Youth Foundation.

(6) The Secretariat. The Council of Europe's permanent international secretariat, located in Strasbourg, provides services to the organization's ministerial, governmental and parliamentary committees. Its 800 members are required to undertake (i) not to be influenced by national considerations and (ii) not to accept instructions from any government.

The Secretary-General, Deputy Secretary-General and Clerk of the Parliamentary Assembly are elected for five years by the Assembly from a list of candidates proposed by the Committee of Ministers. The Secretariat has eight directorates, in addition to the Office of the Clerk of the Parliamentary Assembly.

(7) Committees of Experts. Among the Council's committees of experts are (i) the European Committee on Legal Co-operation (CDCJ), which drafts conventions and recommendations on questions relating to civil, commercial, administrative and international law and encourages consultation in the preparatory stages of legislation, and (ii) the European Committee on Crime Problems (CDPC) with competence in penal law, criminology and penology, and assisted by a Criminological Scientific Council of seven distinguished criminologists.

The Council for Cultural Co-operation (CCC) (on which all member states and also Finland and the Holy See are represented) implements the Council of Europe's educational and cultural programme and is assisted by a Standing Conference on University Problems (CC-PU) dealing with all matters concerning tertiary education.

The Committee for the Development of Sport (with the same membership as the CCC) was formed in 1977 and implements a European Sport for All Charter drawn up in 1975 by European ministers responsible for sport.

(8) **The European Resettlement Fund.** This Fund was set up in 1956 under an agreement by eight of the Council of Europe's member states with a subscribed capital of $7,000,000. By 1979 the Fund had 18 member states (Belgium, Cyprus, Denmark, France, the Federal Republic of Germany, Greece, the Holy See, Iceland, Italy, Liechtenstein, Luxembourg, Malta, the Netherlands, Norway, Portugal, Sweden, Switzerland and Turkey). By the end of 1979 the Fund had made loans of over 25,000 million French francs (about £300,000,000) for programmes designed to create opportunities for employment of refugees and surplus population and for resettlement overseas.

CONVENTIONS AND AGREEMENTS
Human Rights

The *European Convention for the Protection of Human Rights and Fundamental Freedoms,* signed in Rome on Nov. 4, 1950, and in force since Sept. 3, 1953, differs from the United Nations' Declaration on Human Rights of 1948 [see page 17] in that it sets up machinery for the examination of complaints of any violation of human rights and fundamental freedoms on the part of signatories to the convention. These decision-taking bodies are the European Commission of Human Rights and the European Court of Human Rights.

All member-countries of the Council of Europe have signed and ratified the convention and are thus bound by its provisions.

The principal provisions relating to specific human rights are given below:

Art. 2. (1) Everyone's right to life shall be protected by law. No one shall be deprived of his life intentionally save in the execution of a sentence of a court following his conviction of a crime for which this penalty is provided by law. . . .

Art. 3. No one shall be subjected to torture or to inhuman or degrading treatment or punishment.

Art. 4. (1) No one shall be held in slavery or servitude.

(2) No one shall be required to perform forced or compulsory labour.

Art. 5. (1) Everyone has the right to liberty and security of person. . . .

Art. 6. (1) In the determination of his civil rights and obligations, or of any criminal charge against him, everyone is entitled to a fair and public hearing within a reasonable time by an independent and impartial tribunal established by law. . . .

Art. 7. (1) No one shall be held guilty of any criminal offence on account of any act or omission which did not constitute a criminal offence under national or international law at the time when it was committed. Nor shall a heavier penalty be imposed than the one that was applicable at the time the criminal offence was committed. . . .

Art. 8. (1) Everyone has the right to respect for his private and family life, his home and his correspondence. . . .

Art. 9. (1) Everyone has the right to freedom of thought, conscience and religion. . . .

Art. 10. (1) Everyone has the right to freedom of expression. . . .

Art. 11. (1) Everyone has the right to freedom of peaceful assembly and to freedom of association with others. . . .

Art. 12. Men and women of marriageable age have the right to marry and to found a family. . . .

Art. 14. The enjoyment of the rights and freedoms set forth in this convention shall be secured without discrimination on any ground such as sex, race, colour, language, religion, political or other opinion, national or social origin, association with a national minority, property, birth or other status. . . .

The *Fourth Protocol* to the convention, which came into force on May 2, 1968, provides for freedom from imprisonment for inability to fulfil a contractual obligation; freedom of movement and residence; freedom from exile; and a guarantee against the collective expulsion of exiles.

The **European Commission of Human Rights** is composed of a number of representatives equal to that of the High Contracting Parties to the convention. It is competent to receive petitions from governments or individuals claiming violation of the provisions of the convention. Before the Commission could begin to exercise its powers, which it did on July 5, 1955, its competence to receive individual petitions had to be recognized by a minimum of six signatory countries.

After it has examined a petition and tried to bring about a settlement, the commission submits a report to the Committee of Ministers of the Council of Europe, which then decides, by a majority of two-thirds of its members, whether there has been a violation of the convention. In some cases, however, the matter is referred to the Court of Human Rights.

The **European Court of Human Rights**

consists of a number of judges equal to that of the members of the Council of Europe. Under Article 56 of the convention, the Court of Human Rights could come into being only when eight of the High Contracting Parties had declared acceptance of the Court's compulsory jurisdiction. The Icelandic and Austrian declarations of acceptance on Sept. 3, 1958, brought the total of acceptances up to the required number.

The Court functions through a chamber composed of seven judges. Only the Commission of Human Rights and the governments of the High Contracting Parties to the convention may bring a case before the Court, and then only after the Commission has acknowledged the failure of efforts to reach a friendly settlement. The judgment of the Court is final.

The original provisions of the convention dealing with the Commission and Court of Human Rights have been amended by the *Second* and *Third Protocols,* which came into force on Nov. 21, 1970. The *Second Protocol* gives the Court of Human Rights advisory powers in legal matters concerning the convention, while the *Third Protocol* amends the original convention to accelerate and simplify procedure before the Commission of Human Rights.

Peaceful Settlement of Disputes

The *European Convention for the Peaceful Settlement of Disputes* was signed in Strasbourg on April 29, 1957, and came into force on April 30, 1958, for those countries which had ratified it.

Under this convention the signatories agreed to submit to the International Court of Justice all international legal disputes which might arise between them. For other disputes the convention provided for the establishment of a five-member Conciliation Commission whenever requested by a party to a dispute, and also for an Arbitral Tribunal for such disputes as remained unresolved within one month after the end of the conciliation procedure.

(In an agreement concluded between Austria and Italy on July 17, 1971, the provisions of the convention were made retroactive to before the date of its entry into force for these two countries.)

The European Social Charter

In order to provide protection for social rights, as the Convention for Human Rights protects civil and political rights, the *European Social Charter* was drawn up by a Social Committee of experts in collaboration with the International Labour Office, the Parliamentary Assembly of the Council of Europe, and employers and trade union organizations. After approval by the Committee of Ministers, the charter was signed on Oct. 18, 1961, and came into effect on Feb. 26, 1965.

In Part I of the charter, the signatory governments "accept as the aim of their policy, to be pursued by all appropriate means, both national and international in character, the attainment of conditions in which the following rights and principles may be effectively realized:

"(1) Everyone shall have the opportunity to earn his living in an occupation freely entered upon.

"(2) All workers have the right to just conditions of work.

"(3) All workers have the right to safe and healthy working conditions.

"(4) All workers have the right to a fair remuneration sufficient for a decent standard of living for themselves and their families.

"(5) All workers and employers have the right to freedom of association in national or international organizations for the protection of their economic and social interests.

"(6) All workers and employers have the right to bargain collectively.

"(7) Children and young persons have the right to a special protection against the physical and moral hazards to which they are exposed.

"(8) Employed women, in case of maternity, and other employed women as appropriate, have the right to a special protection in their work.

"(9) Everyone has the right to appropriate facilities for vocational guidance with a view to helping him choose an occupation suited to his personal aptitude and interests.

"(10) Everyone has the right to appropriate facilities for vocational training.

"(11) Everyone has the right to benefit from any measures enabling him to enjoy the highest possible standard of health attainable.

"(12) All workers and their dependants have the right to social security.

"(13) Anyone without adequate resources has the right to social and medical assistance.

"(14) Everyone has the right to benefit from social and welfare services.

"(15) Disabled persons have the right to vocational training, rehabilitation and resettlement, whatever the origin and nature of their disability.

"(16) The family as a fundamental unit of society has the right to appropriate social, legal and economic protection to ensure its full development.

"(17) Mothers and children, irrespective of marital status and family relations, have the right to appropriate social and economic protection.

"(18) The nationals of any one of the Contracting Parties have the right to engage in any gainful occupation in the territory of any one of the others on a footing of equality with the nationals of the latter, subject to restrictions based on cogent economic or social reasons.

"(19) Migrant workers who are nationals of a Contracting Party and their families have the right to protection and assistance in the territory of any other Contracting Party."

Parts II and III of the charter, comprising 38 articles, lay down procedures for the application of the above principles, and include provisions for (i) derogations in time of war or emergency; (ii) the partial or complete application of the charter by a signatory government to non-metropolitan territories for whose international relations it is responsible; and (iii) the granting to refugees of "treatment as favourable as possible". Acceptance of Part I of the charter (the statement of aims) and of a specified minimum of individual articles was laid down as a requirement for ratification by a signatory government.

Suppression of Terrorism

A *European Convention on the Suppression of Terrorism* was adopted by the Council's Committee of Ministers at deputy level on Nov. 10, 1976 (with Ireland abstaining from voting on it).

The aim of the convention was to facilitate the extradition and prosecution of perpetrators of terrorist acts even though such acts might be politically motivated and therefore be excluded from extradition arrangements.

The provisions of the convention are as follows:

Art. 1 stated: "For the purposes of extradition between contracting states none of the following offences shall be regarded as a political offence or as an offence connected with a political offence or as an offence inspired by political motives.

"(*a*) An offence within the scope of the Convention for the Suppression of Unlawful Seizure of Aircraft, signed at The Hague on Dec. 16, 1970 [see page 35];

"(*b*) an offence within the scope of the Convention for the Suppression of Unlawful Acts against the Safety of Civil Aviation, signed at Montreal on Sept. 23, 1971 [ibid.];

"(*c*) a serious offence involving an attack against the life, physical integrity or liberty of internationally protected persons, including diplomatic agents;

"(*d*) an offence involving kidnapping, the taking of a hostage or serious unlawful detention;

"(*e*) an offence involving the use of a bomb, grenade, rocket, automatic firearm or letter or petrol bomb if this use endangers persons;

"(*f*) an attempt to commit any of the foregoing offences or participation as an accomplice of a person who commits or attempts to commit such an offence."

Art. 2 specified that in addition to the offences listed in Article 1, contracting states might also "decide not to regard as a political offence . . . a serious offence involving an act of violence . . . against life, physical integrity or liberty of a person" or one which "created a collective danger for persons". The same option would apply also to "an attempt to commit any of the foregoing offences or participation as an accomplice of a person who commits or attempts to commit such an offence".

Art. 3 stated: "The provisions of all extradition treaties and arrangements applicable between contracting states . . . are modified . . . to the extent that they are incompatible with this convention."

Art. 4 provided that any of the offences mentioned in Articles 1 and 2 which were not listed as extraditable offences in existing extradition arrangements between contracting states "shall be deemed to be included as such therein".

Art. 5 stated: "Nothing in this convention shall be interpreted as imposing an obligation to extradite if the requested state has substantial grounds for believing that the request for extradition for an offence men-

tioned in Article 1 or 2 has been made for the purpose of prosecuting or punishing a person on account of his race, religion, nationality or political opinion, or that the person's position may be prejudiced for any of these reasons."

Art. 6 committed a contracting state to taking "such measures as may be necessary to establish its jurisdiction over an offence mentioned in Article 1 in the case where the suspected offender is present in its territory and it does not extradite him after receiving a request for extradition from a contracting state whose jurisdiction is based on a rule of jurisdiction existing equally in the law of the requested state".

The article also specified that the convention "does not exclude any criminal jurisdiction exercised in accordance with national law".

Art. 7 stated: "A contracting state in whose territory a person suspected to have committed an offence mentioned in Article 1 is found and which has received a request for extradition under the conditions mentioned in Article 6 . . . shall, if it does not extradite that person, submit the case, without exception whatsoever and without undue delay, to its competent authorities for the purpose of prosecution. Those authorities shall take their decision in the same manner as in the case of any offence of a serious nature under the law of that state."

Art. 8 provided: "(1) Contracting states shall afford one another the widest measure of mutual assistance in criminal matters in connexion with proceedings brought in respect of the offences mentioned in Articles 1 or 2. The law of the requested state concerning the mutual assistance in criminal matters shall apply in all cases. Nevertheless this assistance may not be refused on the sole ground that it concerns a political offence or an offence connected with a political offence or an offence inspired by political motives."

Similarly to Article 5, the article also specified that a requested state would be under no obligation to provide such mutual assistance if it had grounds for believing that it might lead to prosecution or punishment on account of a person's race, religion, nationality or political opinion, or that the person's position might be prejudiced for any of these reasons.

Article 8 also stated that all existing mutual assistance treaties and arrangements between contracting states "are modified . . . to the extent that they are incompatible with this convention".

Art. 9 specified that the Council of Europe's European Committee on Crime Problems "shall be kept informed regarding the application of this convention" and "shall do whatever is needful to facilitate a friendly settlement of any difficulty which may arise out of its execution".

Art. 10 stipulated: "(1) Any dispute between contracting states concerning the interpretation or application of this convention which has not been settled in the framework of Article 9 . . . shall, at the request of any party to the dispute, be referred to arbitration. Each party shall nominate an arbitrator and the two arbitrators shall nominate a referee. If any party has not nominated its arbitrator within the three months following the request for arbitration, he shall be nominated at the request of the other party by the President of the European Court of Human Rights. If the latter should be a national of one of the parties to the dispute, this duty shall be carried out by the Vice-President of the court or, if the Vice-President is a national of one of the parties to the dispute, by the most senior judge of the court not being a national of one of the parties to the dispute. The same procedure shall be observed if the arbitrators cannot agree on the choice of referee.

"(2) The arbitration tribunal shall lay down its own procedure. Its decisions shall be taken by majority vote. Its award shall be final."

Art. 11 stated that the convention was open to signature by the member states of the Council of Europe and subject to ratification, acceptance or approval —instruments in respect of the latter procedure to be deposited with the Secretary-General of the Council of Europe; (ii) that it would enter into force three months after the date of the deposit of the third instrument of ratification, acceptance or approval; and (iii) that in respect of a signatory state ratifying, accepting or approving subsequently, the convention would come into force three months after the deposit of appropriate instruments.

Art. 12 stipulated (i) that at ratification contracting states could "specify the territory or territories to which this convention shall apply"; and (ii) that either at ratification or at any later date a contracting state could by means of a declaration "extend this convention to any other territory or territories specified in the declaration and for whose international relations it is responsible or on whose behalf it is authorized to give undertakings".

Art. 13 stated: "(1) Any state may at the time of signature or when depositing its instrument of ratification, acceptance or approval, declare that it reserves the right to refuse extradition in respect of any offence mentioned in Article 1 which it considers to be a political offence, an offence connected with a political offence or an offence inspired by political motives, provided that it undertakes to take into due consideration, when evaluating the character of the offence, any particularly serious aspects of the offence, including:

"(*a*) That it created a collective danger to the life, physical integrity or liberty of persons; or

"(*b*) that it affected persons foreign to the motives behind it; or

"(*c*) that cruel or vicious means have been used in the commission of the offence.

"(2) Any state which has made a reservation in accordance with the foregoing paragraph may wholly or partly withdraw it. Such withdrawal shall be effected by means of a declaration addressed to the Secretary-General of the Council of Europe which shall become effective as from the date of its receipt.

"(3) A state which has made a reservation in accordance with paragraph 1 of this article may not claim the application of Article 1 by any other state; it may, however, if its reservation is partial or conditional, claim the application of that article in so far as it has itself accepted it."

Art. 14 provided that any contracting state could denounce the convention by means of a written notification addressed to the Secretary-General of the Council of Europe and that any such denunciation would take effect immediately or at such later date as might be specified in the notice.

Art. 15 stated that the convention "ceases to have effect in respect of any contracting state which withdraws from or ceases to be a member of the Council of Europe".

Art. 16 laid down that the Secretary-General of the Council of Europe should notify member states of all signatures, ratifications, entries into force, declarations, etc., as provided for under the terms of the convention.

Following ratification by Austria (in August 1977), Sweden (in September 1977) and the Federal Republic of Germany (in January 1978), the convention came into force on Aug. 4, 1978. It was later also ratified by Denmark (on Sept. 28, 1978), the United Kingdom (on Oct. 25, 1978), Cyprus (on May 27, 1979) and Liechtenstein (on Sept. 14, 1979), entering into force for these countries on the dates shown.

Other Conventions and Agreements in Force

Social Matters

	Date of Entry into Force
Interim Agreements on Social Security	July 1, 1954
Convention and Protocol on Social and Medical Assistance	July 1, 1954
European Code of Social Security, and Protocol thereto	March 17, 1968
Convention on the Adoption of Children	April 26, 1968
Agreement on "au pair" Placement	May 30, 1971
Convention on Social Security and Supplementary Agreement for the Application of the European Convention on Social Security	March 1, 1977
Convention on the Social Protection of Farmers	June 17, 1977
Convention on the Legal Status of Children born out of Wedlock	Aug. 11, 1978

Public Health

Agreement on Exchange of War Cripples for Medical Treatment	Jan. 1, 1956
Agreement on Exchange of Therapeutic Substances of Human Origin (Creation of European "Blood Bank")	Jan. 1, 1959
Agreement on Duty-free Importation of Medical, Surgical and Laboratory Equipment	July 29, 1960
Agreement for Mutual Assistance in Special Medical Treatment and Climatic Facilities.	June 15, 1962
Agreement for Exchange of Blood Grouping Reagents.	Oct. 14, 1962

Public Health—*cont.*

Agreement on the Issue to Civil and Military War Disabled of International Vouchers for the Repair of Prosthetic and Orthopaedic Appliances..   Dec. 27, 1963

Agreement on the Instruction and Education of Nurses   Aug. 7, 1969

Agreement on the Restriction of the Use of Certain Detergents in Washing and Cleaning Products   Feb. 16, 1971

Convention on the Elaboration of a European Pharmacopoeia   May 5, 1974

Agreement on the Transfer of Corpses   Nov. 11, 1975

Agreement on the Exchange of Tissue-Typing Reagents   April 23, 1977

Cultural Matters

Convention on Equivalence of Diplomas for Admission to Universities   April 20, 1954

European Cultural Convention (designed "to foster among the nationals of all members . . . the study of the languages, history and civilization of the others and of the civilization which is common to them all")   May 5, 1955

Convention on Equivalence of Periods of University Studies ..   Sept. 18, 1957

Convention on Academic Recognition of University Qualifications ..   Nov. 27, 1961

Convention on the Protection of the Archaeological Heritage   Nov. 20, 1970

Agreement on continued Payment of Scholarships to Students studying abroad   Oct. 2, 1971

Patents

Convention relating to Formalities required for Patent Applications..   June 1, 1955

Convention on International Classification of Patents ..   Aug. 1, 1955

Television and Broadcasting

Agreement on Programme Exchanges by Means of Television Films..   July 1, 1961

Agreements for Protection of Television Broadcasts   July 1, 1961

Agreement for the Prevention of Broadcasts transmitted from Stations outside National Territories   Oct. 19, 1967

International Law

Convention on Information on Foreign Law   Dec. 17, 1969

Convention on State Immunity   June 11, 1976

Penal Law

Convention on Extradition..   April 18, 1960

Convention on Mutual Assistance in Criminal Matters   June 12, 1962

Convention on the Punishment of Road Traffic Offences   Aug. 18, 1972

Convention on the International Validity of Criminal Judgments ..   July 26, 1974

Convention on the Supervision of conditionally sentenced or conditionally released Offenders ..   Aug. 22, 1975

Convention on the Transfer of Proceedings in Criminal Matters   March 30, 1978

Other Legal Matters

Agreement relating to Application of the European Convention on International Commercial Arbitration ..   Jan. 25, 1965

Convention on Establishment (laying down common rules for the treatment of nationals of member states on an equal footing when residing in each other's countries)   Feb. 23, 1965

Convention on Liability of Hotel-keepers for Property of their Guests   Feb. 15, 1967

Convention on the Reduction of Cases of Multiple Nationality and on Military Obligations in Cases of Multiple Nationality   March 28, 1968

Convention on Compulsory Insurance against Civil Liability in respect of Motor Vehicles   Sept. 22, 1969

Convention for the Protection of Animals during International Transport..   Feb. 20, 1971

Convention on the Establishment of a Scheme of Registration of Wills   March 20, 1976

Agreement on the Transmission of Applications for Legal Aid   Feb. 28, 1977

Convention for the Protection of Animals kept for Farming Purposes   Sept. 10, 1978

Other Legal Matters—*cont.*

Convention relating to Stops on Bearer Securities in International
Circulation. . . . . Feb. 11, 1979

Movement of Persons

Agreement on Regulations governing Movement of Persons between
States . . . . Jan. 1, 1958
Agreement on Abolition of Visas for Refugees . . . . Sept. 3, 1960
Agreement on Travel by Young Persons on Collective Passports . . Jan. 1, 1962

The conventions and agreements reflect a general European consensus and may be signed and applied by governments in their territories. It is rare for a convention to be ratified by all the Council's member states, but almost all of them are open to non-member states and thus allow for international co-operation beyond Europe (e.g. under the Convention on the Suppression of Terrorism).

Nordic Council

Headquarters: Stockholm.

Members: Denmark, Finland, Iceland, Norway and Sweden.

The Nordic Council was formally inaugurated in Copenhagen on Feb. 13, 1953, by Denmark, Iceland, Norway and Sweden, with Finland becoming a member in 1955. The establishment of such a Council had first been advocated by a Danish Foreign Minister in 1939 and had been recommended by the Nordic Interparliamentary Union in 1951. This recommendation was approved by the Foreign Ministers of Denmark, Norway and Sweden and the Icelandic Minister in Copenhagen on March 16, 1952.

The constitution and functions of the Nordic Council, as then agreed, were as follows:

Membership. The four participating countries would be represented by 16 members from each of the Danish, Norwegian and Swedish Parliaments and five from the Icelandic *Althing*. The Prime Ministers and Foreign Ministers of the member countries, as well as other ministers, would also be able to attend all meetings but would have no voting power. It was provided that Finland could enter the Council whenever she wished [which she in fact did on Oct. 28, 1955].

Functions. In its relations with the Parliaments of the participating countries, the functions of the Nordic Council would be purely advisory, and would be aimed at "stimulating initiative and shaping opinion", though its decisions would have no binding character. It would, however, develop the existing co-operation between the Scandinavian countries; would aim at co-ordinating their legislation wherever desirable; would, as far as possible, try to bring about uniformity in administrative practice as far as the status of their citizens was concerned; would deal with all such questions where there was a possibility of co-ordinated action; would submit suitable proposals to the governments concerned; and would stimulate joint initiative. The sover-

eignty of the participating countries would not be affected.

Meetings. The Nordic Council would meet at least once a year in ordinary session. It would set up permanent secretariats in each capital which would carry out joint investigations on behalf of the Council and function as information centres.

AGREEMENTS AND CONVENTIONS

At its first meeting on Feb. 20-21, 1953, the Council set up committees to deal with economic, cultural, social and legal matters, and a further one to deal with questions of communications. Recommendations of the committees adopted by the Council included the relaxation and eventual abolition of all passport and currency controls for inter-Scandinavian travel by nationals of the Council's member countries, and increased economic, social, cultural and postal co-operation.

On May 22, 1954, representatives of the Council's four member countries signed an agreement creating a single labour market, to come into force on July 1, 1954. They also concluded an agreement exempting Danish, Finnish, Norwegian and Swedish nationals from the need to carry a passport when entering any of the four countries or to obtain residential permits for stays longer than three months (as required hitherto).

A *Convention on Social Security,* adopted in 1955, provided for co-operation in social and health policy, the text being amended in 1975 so as to establish new rights concerning sickness, pregnancy and birth.

Under a convention concluded on July 12, 1957, all identity controls at frontiers between member states were lifted, including that over foreigners who had entered one member country and wished to proceed to another. The provisions concerning foreigners were, however, modified as from Aug. 26, 1979, under an agreement enabling each member country to reserve the right to restore regular and permanent control of foreigners' movements (as had been desired by Sweden in order to stem clandestine immigration via Denmark).

At a meeting held in Helsinki on March 23, 1962, the Council's five member nations initialled a *Treaty of Nordic Co-operation,* also known as the *Helsinki Convention,* covering the principal subjects of Nordic co-operation since 1953. The main provisions of the treaty (which was amended on Feb. 13, 1971, and on March 11, 1974) were as follows:

Cultural Co-operation. Uniformity of vocational training, mutual recognition of the validity of academic degrees and other examinations throughout the area, and joint planning of educational and research centres.

Juridical Co-operation. Mutual law enforcement, making judgments given by courts in one country enforceable also in the others, and co-operation in jurisprudence.

Social Co-operation. Co-operation of labour exchanges throughout the area; unification of vocational guidance; co-ordination of measures to protect workers; and social benefits and welfare measures in each member country to be the same for citizens of the other countries as for its own citizens—the aim of all these measures being the continuation of the existing single labour market.

Economic Co-operation. Mutual consultation on economic policy, with emphasis on the possibility of parallel measures; co-ordination of production and investment, and promotion of direct arrangements between private enterprises in two or more of the Nordic countries; maximum possible freedom of capital investment in the Nordic area; mutual consultation on questions of international trade policy; joint development measures for regions belonging to two or more member countries, if economically desirable; co-operation in trying to find joint solutions on payments and foreign exchange questions; co-ordination of customs legislation; simplification of customs rules to facilitate mutual commercial exchanges; maximum facilities for border traffic; collaboration in projects to assist underdeveloped countries; and co-ordination of statistics.

Communications. Co-operation in the construction of communications, and joint measures relating to safety of road traffic.

A Nordic agreement relating to the administration of joint assistance projects in

Map 2   Benelux Economic Union and Nordic Council

developing countries was signed on July 18, 1968, with a supplementary protocol being signed on Dec. 3, 1971, and a protocol on the accession of Iceland on May 25, 1973.

Harmonization of Nordic Law. The Nordic Council has achieved almost perfect harmonization in certain areas of the law (especially in civil and family law, in mercantile law and in copyright, patents, trade marks and industrial designs) and in the common principles of basic legal rules.

A Nordic Transport Agreement of 1974 provided for both collaboration and division of labour with the object of achieving increased efficiency in transport and communications.

In October 1975 agreement was reached on voting rights, and in 1976 all Nordic citizens who had been resident in Finland and Sweden for the preceding three years obtained the right to vote in local elections.

A convention on the protection of the environment came into force on Oct. 5, 1976.

NORDIC COUNCIL'S STRUCTURE

Following the conclusion of a *Treaty of Cultural Co-operation* between the Council's five member states in 1971, and revisions carried out in 1972 and 1974 of the 1962 Treaty of Co-operation, the structure of Nordic Council organizations is as follows:

Plenary Assembly. The Nordic Council's Plenary Assembly contains (i) 78 members elected annually from the parliaments of each of the five member countries (18 each from Denmark, Finland, Norway and Sweden and six from Iceland, with the Danish members including one each from the Faroes and Greenland) and (ii) appointed non-voting representatives of the five member governments and the executive bodies of the Faroe and (Finnish) Aaland islands. The Assembly has purely consultative functions, and its recommendations are sent to the Council of Ministers [see below]. It has five standing committees (on economic, cultural, legal, social and environmental, and communications affairs) and two special committees (for information and the budget).

Presidium. The Presidium, appointed by the Plenary Assembly from among its elected members and consisting of a President and four Vice-Presidents (these five representing respectively the five member countries), is in charge of the Council's work between Assembly sessions. The Presidium has its own secretariat in Stockholm, which is responsible for relations with the Council of Ministers.

Council of Ministers. This Council, based in Oslo, was established under an agreement (amending the 1962 Treaty of Nordic Co-operation) which was signed in Copenhagen on Feb. 13, 1971, and entered into force on July 1, 1971. It holds meetings which are attended by ministers responsible for the subjects under discussion. It can only act with the formal approval of the member governments; its decisions have to be unanimous and are binding except in cases where ratification in each Parliament is required. It has its own secretariat (in Oslo). The Council's meetings are prepared by committees of deputies and of senior officials.

Secretariat for Nordic Cultural Co-operation. This separate secretariat for Nordic cultural co-operation is based in Copenhagen.

INSTITUTIONS

The numerous institutions set up under Nordic Council auspices include the following:

The **Nordic Institute for Theoretical Atomic Physics** (NORDITA), established in Copenhagen as a result of a Nordic Council decision taken in February 1957 to promote scientific research, co-operation in theoretical atomic physics and advanced training for physicists from the Council's five member states.

The **Nordic Investment Bank,** set up under an agreement signed by the Council of Ministers on Dec. 4, 1975, with an initial capital equivalent to SDRs 400,000,000 (with Sweden contributing 45 per cent, Denmark 22 per cent, Finland and Norway 16 per cent each and Iceland 1 per cent), and with headquarters in Helsinki, where the bank was inaugurated on June 9, 1976.

Benelux Economic Union

Headquarters: Brussels.

Members: Belgium, Luxembourg and the Netherlands.

The Benelux Economic Union Treaty, establishing an Economic Union between Belgium, the Netherlands and Luxembourg, was signed on Feb. 3, 1958, at The Hague and came into effect on Nov. 1, 1960.

The purposes of the Economic Union were defined as the free mutual movement of persons, goods, services and capital; the co-ordination of national economic policies; and the pursuance of a common trade policy towards third countries.

(A *Belgian-Luxembourg economic and monetary convention*, under which the currency of Luxembourg was linked with that of Belgium, had been signed in 1921 and was extended for 10 years in 1971 and again in 1981.)

History. On Sept. 5, 1944, the Governments of Belgium, Luxembourg and the Netherlands—then in exile in London—signed a treaty establishing Benelux. It was not until Jan. 1, 1948, however, that the London agreement, involving measures to introduce a common customs tariff vis-à-vis third countries and to abolish import duties in mutual trade relations, could come into force. The organs provided for in the London agreement—a Customs Regulation Council, a Trade Treaties Council and an Economic Union Council—were set up at the same time.

At a ministerial conference in Luxembourg in October 1949 the three countries concluded the so-called Pre-Union Treaty, as an introductory stage to a fully-fledged economic union. Under this treaty, the exchange of goods between the three countries was made progressively free from quantitative restrictions, except for a special arrangement for agricultural products, and the three countries undertook not to change this liberalization of their mutual trade except by common agreement.

A period of instability for Benelux in the early 1950s was followed on July 24, 1953, by a protocol which laid down that the member countries would in future co-ordinate their economic and social policies. A further protocol was signed on Dec. 9, 1953, under which the three countries started concluding joint trade agreements with third countries.

Further steps in the extension of economic co-operation between the Benelux countries included (a) the treaty of July 8, 1954, which largely liberalized the mutual exchange of capital; (b) a protocol signed on May 3, 1955, on the progressive harmonization of their agricultural policies within a seven-year period; and (c) the setting-up of a common labour market under interim regulations in April 1957, as a transitional stage in the implementation of a Labour Treaty which had been signed on June 7, 1955.

An agreement of Nov. 5, 1955, provided for the establishment of an Interparliamentary Benelux Advisory Council [see below].

The Economic Union Treaty was formally initialled on Sept. 17, 1957, by the Foreign Ministers of Belgium, the Netherlands and Luxembourg, and submitted to the Benelux Interparliamentary Advisory Council which approved it in November 1957. On July 1, 1960, shortly before the treaty came into force, passport controls were abolished for nationals of the Benelux countries travelling between those countries. Foreigners travelling across the inner frontiers of the three countries could also, from that date, obtain a Benelux visa.

From Nov. 1, 1960, all remaining customs duties within the Benelux frontiers were abolished, and from Jan. 1, 1961, all trade agreements with third countries were to be concluded by Benelux as an entity. It was established that, by November 1965, all remaining obstacles to the free flow of goods among the three countries should be eliminated.

Following the "floating" of most of the world's major currencies in 1971, the three Benelux members decided on Aug. 21, 1971, to form a single monetary block whose currency exchange rates would not diverge by more than 1½ per cent in either direction. This arrangement, however, was terminated on March 15, 1976.

BENELUX TREATY

The principal provisions of the treaty are summarized below:

Free Movement of Persons. The nationals of the three member countries will be free to move within the whole territory of the Economic Union, and the nationals of each member country will enjoy in the other two countries the same treatment as is accorded to the nationals of those countries.

Free Exchange of Goods, Capital and Services. Trade between the three countries will be free from all import duties, taxes or levies, as well as from any import or export restrictions of a quantitative, qualitative or currency nature; capital movements from one country to the other will also be free; the exchange of services will be subject to the same principles as merchandise trade.

Co-ordination of Economic, Financial and Social Policies. The three governments will jointly consult on their national economic policies with a view to creating the necessary conditions for the economic integration of their countries.

Co-ordinated and Joint Action towards Third Countries. In addition to co-ordinating their internal economic policies, member countries will also consult each other to determine the Union's attitude at meetings of international bodies and in matters relating to regional economic integration, or in relation to matters with third countries, insofar as these matters affect the aims of the Union. There will also be common policy to cover trade and payments with third countries.

The two principal provisions of Part IV laid down (1) that the scope of the treaty would be limited to the territories of the member countries in Europe, although the interests of Belgian and Dutch overseas territories could be safeguarded in trade agreements concluded with third countries; (2) that the treaty would be concluded for a period of 50 years, but could be tacitly extended by further 10-year terms unless any of the parties wished to terminate it by giving advance notice of one year.

INSTITUTIONS

The institutions of the Benelux Economic Union are as follows:

The Committee of Ministers. This committee, consisting of nine members (three from each member country), is the directing body of the Union, being charged with the implementation of the treaty and the taking of the necessary measures to that end. Decisions must be taken by unanimous vote and be binding on the three governments. The committee also gives directives to the bodies operating under it, and maintains contact with the Consultative Interparliamentary Council.

Interparliamentary Council. Consisting of 21 members each from Belgium and the Netherlands and seven from Luxembourg, the Consultative Interparliamentary Council (first established on Nov. 5, 1955) advises on questions of closer economic, political, cultural and legal co-operation between the three countries.

Council of the Economic Union. This body, which functions under the Committee of Ministers as a co-ordinator of the other institutions, consists of three chairmen appointed by each of the member governments, and of representatives of the committees similarly designated by member governments.

Committees and Special Committees. There are eight committees: on foreign economic relations; on monetary and financial questions; on industry and commerce; on agriculture, foods and fisheries; on customs duties and taxes; on transport; on social questions; and on the movement and establishment of persons.

There are also special committees for co-ordination statistics; comparing the budgets of public and semi-public institutions; public tenders; public health; the "trading middle class" (i.e. small and medium businesses); movement of persons (control of external frontiers); territorial planning; tourism; administrative and judicial co-operation; and the environment.

All these committees are empowered to make proposals to the directing organs of the Union; they also possess executive and supervisory powers regarding the administration of decrees by the member governments.

Secretariat-General. Established at Brussels, it is directed by a Netherlander, its organization and powers agreeing broadly with those of the Secretariat-General already existing under the Customs Agreement of 1944. To the budget of the Secretariat-General, Belgium and the Netherlands each contribute 48.5 per cent and Luxembourg 3 per cent.

Joint Services. The Committee of Ministers is empowered to institute joint services if a need for these should arise. Those set up by 1978 were (i) a Benelux Office for trade marks and brands and (ii) a Joint Service for the registration of medicaments.

Court of Arbitration. The original Board of Arbitrators set up to discuss disputes over the application of the treaty has been superseded by a Court of Arbitration. A convention concerning the establishment of such a court was adopted during a meeting of the Interparliamentary Council at The Hague on Feb. 22, 1964. Composed of three judges from each of the Benelux countries, the court supervises the execution of the Benelux Agreements.

Court of Justice. A Benelux Court of Justice, founded in 1974, consists of senior judges of the three member countries and has power to make binding decisions on the interpretation of common legal rules when requested by a national court, and serves in a consultative capacity when requested by a member government.

Economic and Social Consultative Council. This body (whose members are appointed by the three governments) gives advice—at the request of the Committee of Ministers or on its own initiative—on matters directly related to the operation of the Union. It has 27 members and 27 deputy members from economic and social organizations, with each of the three member countries supplying one-third of these members.

The European Communities

The Three Communities

Headquarters: Brussels.

Members: Belgium, Denmark*, France, Federal Republic of Germany, Greece†, Italy, Ireland*, Luxembourg, the Netherlands and the United Kingdom* (* with effect from Jan. 1, 1973; † with effect from Jan. 1, 1981).

The three European Communities—European Coal and Steel Community (ECSC), European Economic Community (EEC), and European Atomic Energy Community (Euratom)—were formed under separate treaties and, until July 1967, were directed by separate organs, while sharing a common European Parliament and Court of Justice. A treaty providing for the merger of the High Authority of the ECSC, the Commission of the EEC, and the Commission of Euratom, and the merger of the Councils of Ministers of all three, was signed on April 8, 1965, the mergers coming into effect on July 1, 1967.

European Coal and Steel Community (ECSC)

The European Coal and Steel Community was set up under a 50-year treaty, providing for the institution of a common market by the abolition of import and export duties, subsidies and other restrictive practices on the movement of coal and steel between the participating countries. The Community is financed by a levy of 0.25 per cent on the value of production.

Creation of the ECSC. On May 9, 1950,

the French Foreign Minister, Robert Schuman, issued a declaration approved by the French Cabinet, proposing the creation of a single authority to control the production of coal and steel in France and the Federal Republic of Germany. The organization would be open for membership to other European countries and would be associated with the United Nations. This plan, known as the "Schuman Plan", represented the first step toward a federation of Europe, since it proposed that individual nations should entrust part of their sovereignty to a supra-national authority. It was felt that economic co-operation in Europe, particularly between France and Germany, which had long been traditional enemies, would form a firm basis for later political federation.

A six-nation conference for the pooling of the coal and steel resources of Western Europe under a supra-national authority, as put forward in the Schuman Plan, was held in Paris on June 20-27, 1950, and attended by delegations from France, the Federal Republic of Germany, Italy, Belgium, Luxembourg, and the Netherlands (the "Six"). Negotiations on the drafting of a treaty for the proposed Community continued throughout the following nine months, culminating in the signing in Paris, on April 18, 1951, of a Joint Declaration formally setting up the European Coal and Steel Community. The treaty entered into force on July 25, 1952, and the High Authority (created as the principal organ of the Community) began operations on Aug. 10, 1952.

Britain was an associate member of the ECSC until Dec. 31, 1972, whereupon it became a full member on its accession to the Communities on Jan. 1, 1973.

ECSC TREATY

The character, aims and functions of the ECSC are contained in Articles 1-6 of the treaty.

Art. 1. By the present treaty the High Contracting Parties institute among themselves a European Coal and Steel Community, based on a common market, common objectives and common institutions.

Art. 2. The mission of the European Coal and Steel Community is to contribute to economic expansion, the development of employment, and the improvement of the standard of living in the participating countries through the institution, in harmony with the general economy of the member states, of a common market as defined in Art. 4.

The Community must progressively establish con-

ditions which will in themselves assure the most rational distribution of production at the highest possible level of productivity, while safeguarding the continuity of employment and avoiding the creation of fundamental and persistent disturbances in the economies of the member states.

Art. 3. Within the framework of their respective powers and responsibilities, the institutions of the Community should: (*a*) See that the common market is regularly supplied, taking account of the needs of third countries; (*b*) assure to all consumers in comparable positions within the common market equal access to the sources of production; (*c*) seek the establishment of the lowest prices which are possible without requiring any corresponding rise either in the prices charged by the same enterprises in other transactions or in the price-level as a whole in another period, while at the same time permitting necessary amortization and providing normal possibilities of remuneration for capital invested; (*d*) see that conditions are maintained which will encourage enterprises to expand and improve their ability to produce and to promote a policy

A = Albania
B = Belgium
L = Luxembourg
N = Netherlands
S = Switzerland

= European Community members

= EFTA members

= EFTA associate member

Map 3 European Communities and European Free Trade Association (EFTA)

of rational development of natural resources, avoiding inconsiderate exhaustion of such resources; (e) promote the improvement of the living and working conditions of the labour force in each of the industries under its jurisdiction so as to make possible the equalization of such conditions in an upward direction; (f) further the development of international trade and see that equitable limits are observed in prices charged on external markets; (g) promote the regular expansion and the modernization of production, as well as the improvement of its quality, under conditions which preclude any protection against competing industries, except where justified by illegitimate action on the part of such industries or in their favour.

Art. 4. The following were recognized to be incompatible with the common market for coal and steel, and were therefore "abolished and prohibited" within the Community: (a) Import and export duties, or charges with an equivalent effect, and quantitative restrictions on the movement of coal and steel; (b) measures or practices discriminating among producers, buyers or consumers, specifically as concerned prices, delivery terms and transportation rates, as well as measures or practices which hampered the buyer in the free choice of his supplier; (c) subsidies or state assistance, or special charges imposed by the state, in any form whatsoever; (d) restrictive practices tending towards the division of markets or the exploitation of the consumer.

Art. 5. The Community would accomplish its mission with "limited direct intervention", and to this end it would: "Enlighten and facilitate the action of the interested parties" by collecting information, organizing consultations and defining general objectives; place financial means at the disposal of enterprises for their investments and participate in the expenses of readaptation; assure the establishment, maintenance and observance of normal conditions of competition, and take direct action with respect to production and the operation of the market only when circumstances made it absolutely necessary; publish the justifications for its action and take the necessary measures to ensure observance of the rules set forth in the treaty. The institutions of the Community should carry out these activities with "as little administrative machinery as possible" and in close co-operation with the interested parties.

Art. 6 provided that the Community should have "juridical personality" and that it should enjoy, in its international relationships, "the juridical capacity necessary to the exercise of its functions and the attainment of its ends".

Arts. 7-45 are concerned with the institutions of the Community—the High Authority, the Assembly, the Council and the Court—the functions of which have since been taken over by the European Commission, the European Parliament, the joint Council of Ministers, and the European Court of Justice respectively.

Arts. 46-75 contain the technical details for the realization of the objectives of the treaty. The remaining provisions are concerned, inter alia, with such general matters as the privileges and immunity of the Community in the territory of member states, settlements of disputes and relations with other international organizations.

Among the documents accompanying the treaty was a *Convention on Transitional Provisions,* setting forth the measures necessary for the creation of the common market. These covered a five-year period from the creation of the common market for coal.

DEVELOPMENTS

ECSC Common Market. The common market between the six original member countries of the ECSC was opened for coal, iron ore and scrap on Feb. 10, 1953; for steel on May 1, 1953; and for special steels on Aug. 1, 1954. The market came into full operation on Feb. 10, 1958, when the five-year transitional period of its formation came to an end. By this time all barriers to trade in coal and steel—such as customs duties, currency restrictions and quantitative restrictions—had been abolished, all subsidies had been eliminated and discriminatory practices abolished, and a harmonized external tariff for the whole Community had been introduced.

Trade and Production. In the initial period after the formation of the ECSC the production of all commodities covered by the ECSC treaty (coal, coke, iron ore, pig iron, crude steel and finished rolled products) rose considerably, as also did the volume of trade among Community countries and between Community countries and other countries. Since 1957, however, the coal industry has declined, although steel production continued to rise until 1974.

In view of the ensuing recession in steel production, measures were taken from December 1976 onwards, under a common steel policy drawn up in that year by Henri Simonet (then Belgian Foreign Minister and member of the European Commission with responsibility for the steel industry) to control prices and set limits on the production of steel, and in May 1977 compulsory licensing was introduced for steel imports from third countries. Efforts were also made to rationalize the steel industry.

Labour Aid. The Community plays an active part in overcoming the social problems within its sphere of activity. It has evolved adaptation schemes to protect workers against the risk of unemployment, these being particularly applicable to workers in the coal industry; has carried out programmes of house-building to accommodate workers; has developed vocational training and research in industrial health and medicine; and has made loans for industrial development in certain areas.

European Economic Community (EEC)

The Foreign Ministers of the six ECSC nations met at Messina (Italy) on June 2-4, 1955, to discuss certain proposals for further European economic integration which had been put forward by the three Benelux countries on May 20, 1955.

The Benelux proposals called for (a) the establishment of a "common organization" to study development plans for a European network of roads, canals and railways, and for the co-ordination of civil aviation policies; (b) the study of methods of co-ordinating power policy in Europe; (c) the creation of a "common authority" for the development of atomic energy for peaceful purposes, with the pooling of investment funds, technical knowledge and research facilities; and (d) the progressive integration of the national economies of the six member countries and the harmonization of economic, financial and social policies. To implement this programme the Benelux governments proposed that a conference should be called to work out (a) a treaty on the pooling of transport, power and atomic energy; (b) a treaty on general economic integration; and (c) a treaty defining the European institutions necessary to carry out the programme.

At the end of their meeting the Foreign Ministers adopted the "Messina Resolution", which included a plan for the creation of "a common European market free from all customs barriers and quantitative restrictions", to be realized by stages. The six ministers also envisaged the creation of a joint organization having "the responsibility and the facilities" for ensuring the development of atomic energy for peaceful purposes. An Intergovernmental Committee was set up to study the problems raised and to prepare draft treaties.

The final drafts of the treaties establishing the EEC and Euratom were completed by the Intergovernmental Committee on March 9, 1957, and were signed in Rome by Belgium, France, the Federal Republic of Germany, Italy, Luxembourg and the Netherlands on March 25, 1957. Both came into force on Jan. 1, 1958.

EEC TREATY

The main provisions of the treaty setting up the European Economic Community (the Treaty of Rome) are summarized below.

Aims

In the preamble to the treaty, the six signatory countries declared their intention of establishing "the foundations of an enduring and closer union between European peoples" by gradually removing the economic effects of their political frontiers. A common market and a common external tariff (customs union) would be established for all goods; common policies would be devised for agriculture, transport, labour mobility and important sectors of the economy; common institutions would be set up for economic development; and the overseas territories and possessions of member states would be associated with the new Community for an experimental five-year period. All these measures would have one "essential aim"—the steady improvement in the conditions of life and work of the peoples of the member countries.

The tasks of the Community were defined in Article 1 of the treaty as the achievement of a harmonious development of the economy within the whole Community, a continuous and balanced economic expansion, increased economic stability, a more rapid improvement in living-standards, and closer relations between the member countries.

Progressive Implementation of Common Market— Procedure during Transitional Period

One of the principal characteristics of the process of creating a common market would be its irrevocable character—i.e. once the process had been set in motion, the ultimate aim would have to be achieved. This constituted an important safeguard for the member countries inasmuch as their sacrifices in adjusting themselves to the new conditions would not be in vain, and would not involve a risk of a complete standstill and a subsequent return to the previous status after a number of years. The change from one stage to the next would thus in principle take place automatically.

The common market would be progressively established in three stages within a transitional period of 12 years, which might be extended to 15 years. Within the basic 12-year period there would be three stages, each lasting in principle four years. However, if at the end of the first four years the Council of Ministers and the Commission were not unanimously agreed that the objectives of that stage had been essentially accomplished, the stage would automatically be extended for one year. At the end of the fifth year there would be another one-year extension on the same condition, whilst at the end of the sixth year (when the decision of the Council of Ministers would no longer require unanimity but would be taken by a weighted majority) a further extension could be granted only if a request by a member state for such an extension was recognized as justified by an ad hoc arbitration tribunal of three members appointed by the Council of Ministers.

The second and third stages could either be prolonged or shortened by unanimous decision of the Council of Ministers, subject to the maximum limit of 15 years for the whole transitional period.

Removal of Tariffs and Quantitative Restrictions—Development of Agriculture

The European Economic Community would be based on a customs union covering the whole trade of member countries and entailing (a) a prohibition on imposing import or export duties or similar levies between member countries; (b) the introduction of a common tariff on imports from non-Community countries; (c) the abolition of all quantitative import and export restrictions and other similar measures between member countries. The free exchange of goods within the Community would apply not only to goods produced in the member countries but also to those which had been imported by a member country from outside the Community, and on which customs duties had been paid on entry. The only exception from the application of the common customs tariff vis-à-vis non-Community countries would be in the case of goods landed in a free trade zone where each member country could apply its own customs tariff.

Internal Tariffs. Tariff restrictions on trade between member countries would have to be abolished entirely by the end of the transitional period at the latest.

All export duties and similar levies on goods destined for other Community countries would be abolished not later than the end of the first stage.

External Tariffs. A common tariff on imports from non-Community countries would be established in full not later than the end of the transitional period.

Quantitative Restrictions. All quantitative restrictions on trade within the Community would be progressively eliminated by a series of quota increases. Thus, one year after the coming into force of the treaty, the member states would convert all their existing bilateral import quotas into global quotas in favour of all other member countries, without any discrimination between them. All these global import quotas would then be increased annually by at least 20 per cent as regards their overall value, and by at least 10 per cent as regards each individual product; bigger increases would be made in the case of quotas amounting initially to less than 3 per cent of the domestic output of a given product.

Agriculture. Agricultural products would be included in the common market, although a special regime would apply in view of the different social structure of agriculture in the various member countries, which made it impossible to introduce a completely liberalized market.

A common agricultural policy would be implemented in the course of the transitional period, aiming at increased agricultural productivity, safeguarding an adequate standard of living for the agricultural population, stabilization of agricultural markets, an assurance of adequate supplies and fair prices for consumers.

A joint organization of agricultural markets would be created, but, because of the diversity of market conditions for individual products, this development would not take place under prearranged rules but through decisions of the organs of the Community, varying from case to case.

Freedom of Movement for Labour, Services and Capital—Joint Transport Policy

Labour, Settlement, Services and Capital. The free circulation of labour, services and capital, as well as the right to settle, work and trade anywhere in the Community, would be fully established by the end of the transitional period.

All restrictions on the right to settle freely in any member country, or the right of nationals of any member country to set up agencies, branches or subsidiary companies in the territory of another, would be gradually removed during the transitional period.

All restrictions on the offering of services by insurance companies, banks, finance houses, the wholesale and retail trade, and by members of the professions would be gradually removed within the Community during the transitional period.

Existing restrictions on the movement of capital between the Community countries would be progressively removed. As far as was necessary for the proper working of the common market, restrictions on current payments relating to the movement of capital (e.g. interest, dividends, rents, premiums) would be completely abolished not later than the end of the first stage of the transitional period.

Transport. The Council of Ministers would establish a joint transport policy and common rules for international transport within or through the Community, covering rail, road and inland water transport.

Common Policies

To ensure free and equal competition within the Community, common rules and policies would be introduced in the member countries as summarized below.

Common Rules. Any agreement or association preventing, restraining or distorting competition within the Community would be forbidden—e.g. agreements or associations directly or indirectly fixing prices; regulating or controlling production, investment or technical development; sharing markets; requiring the acceptance of additional goods besides those needed by the customer; or providing for discriminatory conditions of supply.

Dumping practices by any member country within the common market would be prohibited.

Unless otherwise provided by the treaty, state subsidies (of whatever kind) which distorted or threatened to distort competition would be prohibited.

Economic Policy. Member countries would harmonize their general economic, foreign exchange and foreign trade policies.

The general economic policies of member countries would be regarded as a matter of joint interest, and the countries concerned would consult each other as well as the Commission on the measures which should be taken to meet changing circumstances.

A common external trade policy would be established by the end of the transitional period.

The common external trade policy after the end of the transitional period would cover the application of a common customs tariff; the joint conclusion of trade and customs agreements; the unification of trade liberalization measures; the working-out of common export policies; and the joint application of protective measures, e.g. against dumping or subsidies by non-Community countries.

Social Policy. The EEC Commission would promote the co-ordination of the social policies of member countries, with particular reference to employment, labour legislation, conditions of work, vocational training, social security, prevention of industrial accidents and occupational diseases, health protection, trade union rights, and collective bargaining between employers and employed.

Provisions for Association and Future Membership

The overseas territories of Belgium, France, Italy and the Netherlands would be associated with the Community. A special convention annexed to the treaty laid down the details of this association for the initial five-year period.

Any other European country could apply for membership in the Community; the terms of its admission, and any consequential amendments of the treaty which might become necessary, would be agreed between the original member countries and the applicant country.

Agreements might also be concluded with another country or group of countries for their association with the Community, based on certain mutual rights and obligations, joint action and special procedures. Similar agreements of association might be entered into with international organizations.

The treaty was concluded for an unlimited period.

European Atomic Energy Community (EAEC or Euratom)

As described in the section above on the European Economic Community, the European Atomic Energy Community came into being under the March 1957 Rome Treaty which entered into force on Jan. 1, 1958.

EURATOM TREATY

The aims of the Community were defined in the preamble as the raising of living standards in the member countries and the promotion of trade with non-Community countries. The tasks of Euratom were defined in Article 1 of the treaty as the creation, within a short period, of the technical and industrial conditions necessary to utilize nuclear discoveries, and especially to produce nuclear energy on a large scale. This result would be achieved by joint measures of the member countries and through the activities of the institutions of the Community.

The main functions of Euratom, as laid down in the treaty, can be summarized as follows:

(1) The promotion, facilitation, and co-ordination of research in member countries, and the execution of a research programme of its own; (2) the dissemination of information on atomic energy, and the acquisition of information on all patents, patent applications and working models of inventions which would be useful to the Community; (3) the establishment of a code of basic standards governing personal safety against dangers resulting from ionizing radiation; (4) the promotion of a planned development of investments by public and private undertakings in the nuclear energy fields; and (5) the formation of Community undertakings for the development of nuclear industry within Euratom.

Other significant provisions of the treaty are as follows:

Supplies. A joint policy would be pursued with regard to the supply of ores, raw materials and special fissile matter on the basis of the principle of equal access to resources. For this purpose the Commission would set up a Commercial Agency which would be a corporate body, vested with financial independence and able to conduct its affairs according to business rules, but controlled by the Commission. The Agency (the majority of whose capital would have to be owned by the Community and the member countries) would possess (i) an option to purchase any of the materials in question produced in member states; and (ii) the exclusive right to conclude contracts for the purchase or sale of such materials outside the Community.

The Commission would be entitled to make recommendations regarding prospecting and the exploitation of mines, and might participate financially in such activities. Member states would be required to send the Commission annual reports on prospecting, reserves and mining investments.

Security. The Commission would be required to ensure (i) that ores, raw materials and special fissile matter were not diverted from their intended use as declared by their consumers; and (ii) that arrangements for their supply, and any special control measures accepted by the Community in an agreement with a non-Community state or international organization were observed.

To this end, the Commission would:

(a) Request declarations from all the undertakings concerned describing the basic technical characteristics of their equipment;

(b) request statements of all transactions in order to facilitate accounting of ores, raw materials and special fissile matter;

(c) insist, if necessary, on all surplus special fissile matter temporarily not in use being placed in deposit;

(d) arrange for its inspectors to carry out checks and, where necessary, impose sanctions ranging from a warning to the complete withdrawal of raw materials or special fissile matter.

Ownership of Special Fissile Matter. All special fissile matter would be the property of the Community. Member states, undertakings or individuals, however, would be entitled to the widest possible utilization and consumption of the special fissile matter which had legitimately come into their possession.

Common Market in Nuclear Materials. A common market in nuclear materials would be set up, involving the following obligations on member countries:

(a) To introduce, one year after the coming into force of the treaty, a common customs tariff for nuclear minerals, materials and products imported from non-Community countries;

(b) to repeal between each other, after the same one-year period, all import and export duties and taxes on such minerals, materials and products (the non-European territories of member states being entitled, however, to continue to levy duties and taxes of a purely fiscal character);

(c) to apply the procedure laid down in the Common Market Treaty for the gradual abolition of internal tariffs and quantitative import restrictions between member countries, and for the introduction of a uniform customs tariff, to all other products which might be used in the nuclear industry;

(d) to admit nationals of the other member countries, without discrimination, to all posts and occupations requiring qualifications in the nuclear sphere, as well as to participation in the construction of nuclear undertakings;

(e) to set up an insurance scheme covering risks arising from the use of atomic energy;

(f) to facilitate the transfer between member countries of capital needed for nuclear projects, and to permit the transfer to other member countries of payments in connexion with nuclear transactions and employment in nuclear industries or research.

Implementation of the Treaty

Nuclear Research. A Joint Research Centre, set up under the Euratom Treaty, includes four important establishments for nuclear research. These are:

(1) The Nuclear Research Centre at Ispra (Italy), transferred by Italy to Euratom under an agreement signed on July 22, 1959;

(2) the Central Nuclear Measurements Bureau at Geel (Belgium);

(3) the Transuranium Elements Institute at Karlsruhe (Federal Republic of Germany); and

(4) the General Purpose Centre at Petten (Netherlands).

Euratom has signed several hundred research contracts with public and private undertakings in the member countries of the Community. Under these contracts the Community contributes both finance and personnel. One of the most important such agreements is with the Belgian Nuclear Study Centre at Mol, whose high-neutron-flux reactor (BR-2) for the testing of materials is jointly operated by the Centre and by Euratom, the latter bearing two-thirds of the running costs. Other fields of research covered by such agreements include fast-breeder and high temperature gas reactors, nuclear ship propulsion and the uses of nuclear energy in agriculture and medicine.

Part of Euratom's research programme is carried out in conjunction with that of the broader Nuclear Energy Agency of the OECD [see pages 161-62]. The Community also co-operates with the International Atomic Energy Agency of the United Nations.

Information on the various research projects with which Euratom is concerned is disseminated through an atomic information and documentation centre.

Following the completion of a second five-year research programme in December 1967, the member states failed to agree on a further multi-annual programme, and research continued at a reduced level by means of a series of five interim annual programmes until the end of 1972. During this period the emphasis in Euratom research shifted from participation in the development of future generations of nuclear power reactors to more basic studies in the nuclear field and also to work in other scientific sectors.

Promotion of the Atomic Energy Industry. Euratom has adopted a number of measures by which it promotes the development of the peaceful uses of atomic energy in Europe. These include:

(1) The creation of the common market for nuclear materials and equipment (in operation since Jan. 1, 1959);

(2) the introduction of the freedom of movement within the Community for technical workers in the atomic energy industry;

(3) the preparation of an insurance convention under which the Community as a whole will have third-party coverage for damages arising out of the atomic energy industry;

(4) financial assistance for power reactor projects in return for access to all planning, constructional and operational information; and

(5) the creation of a special bureau (Eurisotop) to provide information on the use of radio isotopes in industry.

Under a **Joint European Torus** (JET), a thermonuclear fusion programme designed to lead to the provision of virtually unlimited supplies of cheap and "clean" energy by the end of the 20th century, a first prototype reactor was to be built at Culham (near Oxford, England), as decided by the Council of Ministers on Oct. 25, 1977.

Supplies, Health and Security. A Supply Agency, as provided for in the treaty, came into operation on June 1, 1960. This agency, which is a commercially-operating independent department attached to the Commission, has an option to purchase any ores, raw materials and special fissile matter produced in the member countries, and has the exclusive right to conclude contracts for the purchase or sale of such materials outside the Community.

To protect workers in the atomic energy industry, and also the rest of the population, Euratom has drawn up a code of basic health standards (February 1959). The code, which has been made binding on the governments concerned, has been incorporated in the national legislation of each of the member countries of the Community. The regulations, whose coverage includes X-ray installations and the use of radioactive materials in the manufacture of household goods and cosmetics, represented the first attempt anywhere to set up a comprehensive legal system to cover radiation health risks.

A security control system to supervise the proper use of ores, raw materials and special fissile materials, as provided for in the treaty, has been set up by the Commission. The control system is binding on the member governments. (*Note:* Euratom has no control over nuclear materials or installations intended for military purposes.)

AGREEMENTS INVOLVING EURATOM MEMBERS

On April 5, 1973, Belgium, the Federal Republic of Germany, Italy, Luxembourg and the Netherlands signed an agreement in Brussels enabling the International Atomic Energy Agency (IAEA) to verify the safeguard system of Euratom as a precondition of their signing the Nuclear Non-Proliferation Treaty.

An agreement signed in Vienna on Sept. 6, 1976, by Euratom, the IAEA and the United Kingdom provided for the submission of UK non-military nuclear installations to international safeguards under IAEA supervision; the agreement entered into force on Aug. 14, 1978.

An agreement which was concluded by Euratom, the IAEA and seven member countries of the European Communities—Belgium, Denmark, the Federal Republic of Germany, Italy, Luxembourg and the Netherlands—and came into force in February 1977 provided for the application of IAEA and Euratom safeguards to the nuclear installations of these countries "with a view to preventing diversion of nuclear energy from peaceful uses to nuclear weapons or other explosive devices".

Under an agreement signed in Vienna on July 27, 1978, between Euratom, the IAEA and France (which is not a signatory of the Nuclear Non-Proliferation Treaty), certain French non-military nuclear installations were to be submitted to international safeguards under IAEA supervision (although France retained the effective right to decide which installations would be open to such inspection).

AGREEMENTS WITH NON-MEMBERS

Agreements made by Euratom with non-member countries concerning the peaceful uses of atomic energy are as follows:

Euratom—USA. The United States has concluded agreements with Euratom as follows:

(1) Agreement relating to co-operation for peaceful applications of atomic energy; May 29 and June 19, 1958; entry into force Aug. 27, 1958.

(2) Agreement for co-operation concerning peaceful uses of atomic energy: Nov. 8, 1958; entry into force Feb. 18, 1959; extended and amended May 21-22, 1962. (Under this agreement the USA promised technical and financial help in the construction and running of from six to eight power-producing reactors with a total capacity of 1,000,000 kilowatts, and provision was made for collaboration of the USA and Euratom in a 10-year nuclear research and development programme.)

(3) Additional agreement for co-operation concerning peaceful uses of atomic energy: June 11, 1960; entry into force July 25, 1960; extended and amended May 21-22, 1962; Aug. 22 and 27, 1963; and Sept. 20, 1972.

(4) Arrangement in the field of nuclear safety research: March 19, 1979.

Euratom—Britain. An agreement on collaboration in developing nuclear energy for peaceful purposes was signed by Euratom and Britain in February 1959. Under it a standing committee for co-operation was set up. Aspects of nuclear research in which the two parties have co-operated include (i) the study of controlled thermo-nuclear reactions for peaceful purposes; (ii) fast-breeder reactor techniques; and (iii) advanced gas-cooler reactor systems.

The original 10-year agreement was extended for another two years on Feb. 4, 1969.

Euratom—Canada. Two agreements with Canada were signed on Oct. 5, 1959. An outline agreement concluded with the Canadian Government laid down the conditions under which Canada and Euratom would exchange nuclear data, materials, and equipment between individuals and corporations. The second agreement, a technical agreement between Euratom and Atomic Energy of Canada Ltd., provided for a joint research and development programme in the use of reactors powered by uranium fuel moderated by heavy water.

Under an agreement of Jan. 16, 1978, new safeguards arrangements were established for the supply of nuclear material and equipment by Canada to the member states of the European Communities (which had been suspended by Canada since Jan. 1, 1977).

Euratom—Brazil. A 20-year agreement for co-operation between Euratom and Brazil in the peaceful uses of atomic energy was signed on June 9, 1961. The agreement covered exchange of information on research and development; means of health protection; installations and equipment; utilization of minerals, raw materials, special fissile matter, and nuclear fuels and radio-isotopes; exchange of personnel; and the granting of patent licences.

Euratom—Argentina. A similar agreement to that between Euratom and Brazil was concluded between Euratom and Argentina on Sept. 4, 1962.

Euratom—CMEA. An agreement approved by the International Atomic Energy Agency (IAEA) at its 19th annual conference in Vienna on Sept. 22-26, 1975, provided for co-operation between Euratom and the Council for Mutual Economic Assistance (CMEA) in the peaceful use of nuclear energy, consultation on matters of mutual interest, joint participation in meetings, exchange of information and permanent contact between the two organizations' secretaries.

Common Organs of the European Communities

European Council. The European Council consists of the heads of government of the member states who, accompanied by their Foreign Ministers, generally meet three times a year in order "gradually to adopt common positions and co-ordinate their diplomatic action in all areas of international affairs which affect the interests of the European Community"—as decided at a conference held in Paris on Dec. 9-10, 1974, by the heads of government of the then nine member states.

At this conference it was also decided to set up an administrative secretariat of the Council, and it was stated that the heads of government considered it "necessary to renounce the practice which consists of making agreement on all questions conditional on the unanimous consent of the member states". Although the European Council possesses no legal standing under the Community treaties, it has nevertheless become the forum where the major strategic decisions affecting the development of the Community are taken.

Conferences of the heads of state or government of the member countries, first of the European Economic Community (EEC) and later of the European Communities, had earlier been held on various occasions to discuss not only future Community policies but also the international economic situation. Such conferences were held:

(1) In Paris on Feb. 10-11, 1961, when the participants expressed their wish to seek agreements aimed at maintaining and developing exchanges with other countries, "in particular with Great Britain".

(2) In Bonn on July 18, 1961, when the leaders of the six EEC member states decided to hold regular meetings, inter alia, in order to "further the political unification of Europe and thus to strengthen the Atlantic Alliance".

(3) In Rome on May 29-30, 1967, when it was decided to merge the executives of the EEC, the European Coal and Steel Community (ECSC) and the European Atomic Energy Community (Euratom) in one Commission on July 1, 1967.

(4) In The Hague on Dec. 1-2, 1969, when it was stated in a communiqué that the entry of other countries of Europe into the Communities "would undoubtedly help the Communities to grow to dimensions more in conformity with the present state of world economy and technology"; it was also agreed that "a plan in stages should be worked out . . . with a view to the creation of an economic and monetary union".

(5) In Paris on Oct. 19-20, 1972, attended by the French President and heads of government of eight other countries—including also three "applicant" countries—Denmark, Ireland and the United Kingdom —as well as a delegation of the European Communities, and issuing a lengthy communiqué reaffirming the Communities' objectives and stating in particular (i) that the leaders would establish the Community's position in world affairs as "a distinct entity determined to promote a better international equilibrium"; (ii) that as "the driving force of the European construction" the member states affirmed "their intention to transform before the end of the present decade the whole complex of their relations into a European union"; (iii) that they reaffirmed "the determination

of the member states of the enlarged European Communities irreversibly to achieve the economic and monetary union" previously agreed upon in March 1971 and March 1972, for which they laid down a timetable and decided on the use of a European monetary unit of account and on "fixed but adjustable parity" and the general convertibility of member countries' currencies [see page 140].

(6) In Copenhagen on Dec. 14-15, 1973, after which the participants issued a general communiqué, a statement on the energy crisis and a declaration on European identity.

In the communiqué they stated inter alia that they had decided to meet more frequently; that "the growing unity of the Nine" [member countries] would "strengthen the West as a whole and . . . be beneficial for the relationship between Europe and the United States"; and that they had agreed on the establishment of a regional development fund on Jan. 1, 1974.

The statement on the energy crisis envisaged inter alia a comprehensive Community programme on alternative sources of energy (including "a European capacity for enrichment of uranium"), and it "confirmed the importance of entering into negotiations with oil-producing countries on comprehensive arrangements comprising co-operation on a wide scale for the economic and industrial development of these countries, industrial investment, and stable energy supplies to the member countries at reasonable prices".

In the declaration on European identity the heads of state or government described as "fundamental elements of the European identity" "the principles of representative democracy, of the rule of law, of social justice—the ultimate goal of economic progress—and of respect for human rights".

Following the 1974 conference in Paris, the European Council held further conferences as follows:

(1) In Dublin on March 10-11, 1975, when decisions taken included approval of a budgetary correction mechanism to be applied when a member country was "a disproportionate contributor" to the Communities' budget and also in economic difficulties.

(2) In Brussels on July 16-17, 1975, when it was stated that the Community was "prepared to initiate discussions on closer economic and financial co-operation with Portugal" (which was, in October 1975, granted emergency aid by the Communities of up to 150,000,000 units of account).

(3) In Rome on Dec. 1-2, 1975, when it was, inter alia, decided that direct elections to the European Parliament would take place in May or June 1978.

(4) In Luxembourg on April 1-2, 1976.

(5) In Brussels on July 12-13, when the number and distribution of seats in the European Parliament were agreed upon.

(6) In The Hague on Nov. 29-30, 1976.

(7) In Rome on March 25-26, 1977.

(8) In London on June 29-30, 1977. While the London conference and its two predecessors dealt mainly with economic problems, the Council reiterated, at the London conference, its principles for the achievement of a lasting settlement of the Arab-Israeli conflict based on "the inadmissibility of the acquisition of territory by force, the need for Israel to end the territorial occupation which it has maintained since the conflict of 1967, respect for the sovereignty, territorial integrity and independence of every state in the area and their legal right to live in peace within secure and recognized boundaries, and recognition that in the

establishment of a lasting peace account must be taken of the legitimate rights of the Palestinians''.

(9) In Brussels on Dec. 5-6, 1977, when the Council approved in principle (i) the creation of a new Community facility of 1,000 million European units of account (EUA), to be managed by the European Investment Bank, and (ii) the establishment of a European Foundation to promote understanding and human contacts among the peoples of the Community (as proposed in a report on the overall concept of European union prepared by Léo Tindemans, then Belgian Prime Minister, and published in January 1976).

(10) In Copenhagen on April 7-8, 1978, when it was agreed that the elections to the European Parliament should take place on June 7-10, 1979 (and not in May or June 1978, as previously intended).

(11) In Bremen (Federal Republic of Germany) on July 6-7, 1978, when it was agreed in principle to create a system of closer monetary co-operation leading to a "zone of monetary stability in Europe" and the introduction of the European currency unit (ECU) as the Community's monetary unit within a European monetary system (EMS) [see also page 141].

(12) In Brussels on Dec. 4-5, 1978, when it was resolved to set up the EMS as from Jan. 1, 1979 (with Belgium, Denmark, France, the Federal Republic of Germany, Luxembourg and the Netherlands committing themselves to full participation from the outset and Ireland and Italy deciding in December 1978 to join the EMS but the United Kingdom remaining outside). The implementation of the EMS was, however, deferred after France had decided in December 1978 to block it pending the resolution of a dispute over common agricultural policy prices.

(13) In Paris on March 12-13, 1979, when, after the dispute with France had been resolved, it was decided to implement the EMS from March 13, 1979 (without UK participation), and also to reduce the Community's oil consumption in 1979 to about 500,000,000 tonnes (or about 25,000,000 tonnes less than originally estimated).

(14) In Strasbourg on June 21-22, 1979, when the Council considered a British request to bring about a reduction in the net UK contribution to the Communities' budget.

(15) In Dublin on Nov. 29-30, 1979, when no agreement was reached on the question of the UK contribution to the Communities' budget, mainly because the proposals made contained no guarantees beyond 1980.

(16) In Luxembourg on April 27-28, 1980, when the heads of government (i) stated in a declaration on the international situation that in view of recent events (in Afghanistan, Iran and the Middle East) unity among the Communities' member states was needed more than ever; (ii) reiterated that the problem of Afghanistan should be solved by that country's return to the position of a neutral and non-aligned state; (iii) expressed satisfaction at the stability of the European Monetary System (EMS) during its first year of operation, but (iv) reached no agreement on various items, including fisheries, agriculture and the UK budget contribution.

(17) In Venice on June 12-13, 1980, when agreement was reached on the UK contribution question on the basis of a formula agreed upon by the Communities' Council of (Foreign) Ministers in Brussels on May 29-30, 1980, whereby the UK contribution for 1980-81 was reduced by a total of 2,585 million European units of account (EUA) or then about £1,577 million, while measures were proposed to prevent "the recurrence of unacceptable situations" for member states in later years.

(18) In Luxembourg on Dec. 1-2, 1980, when the heads of government came to the conclusion that the prospects for the European economy had "never required more vigilant attention", especially to the problems of unemployment and of continued payment imbalances.

The Council of Ministers. The common Council of Ministers, with headquarters in Brussels, fulfils the same functions as did the separate organs of the three Communities, and exercises its rights and obligations under the same conditions as provided for in the treaties for each Community.

Each member state is represented by a member of its government, usually the Minister of Foreign Affairs, Finance, Agriculture or Economics, according to the subject to be discussed, and more than one minister from a member state may attend.

The basic function of the Council of Ministers is to co-ordinate the economic policies of the member countries within the framework of the three treaties for the Communities, and to make decisions for the implementation of the treaties.

Most decisions of the Council are taken by a simple majority vote, but in certain cases the treaties require a unanimous vote or a qualified majority. For a qualified majority the votes are as follows: France, Italy, the Federal Republic of Germany and the United Kingdom have 10 votes each; Belgium, Greece and the Netherlands have five votes each; Denmark and Ireland three each; and Luxembourg two.

Where the treaties require a previous proposal of the Commission [see below], at least 45 out of the 63 votes are needed to carry a decision, but in all other cases the votes must include a favourable vote by at least six of the member countries. On Jan. 29, 1966, the Council resolved that, in deciding on issues "very important to one or more member countries", the members of the Council would "try within a reasonable time to reach solutions which can be adopted by all members of the Council while respecting their mutual interests and those of the Community"—so that in effect the Council has generally taken decisions by unanimity and not by a majority vote.

The Council is authorized to request the Commission to examine proposals which may be submitted to it, and to make studies towards the achievement of the common objectives.

The European Commission. The European Commission, based in Brussels, exercises its rights and obligations under the same conditions as provided for in the treaties of the Communities for their individual organs.

The membership of the Commission was in May 1970 reduced from 14 to nine—two each from France, the Federal Republic of Germany and Italy, and one each from Belgium, Luxembourg, and the Netherlands—but was increased to 13 on Jan. 1, 1973, when Britain (two members), Denmark (one) and Ireland (one) joined the Communities, and to 14 following the admission of Greece on Jan. 1, 1981. The members are appointed for a renewable four-year term by the governments of the member states, but they are independent and neither solicit nor accept instructions from their governments. Each member is responsible for a particular sphere of economic activity.

The President and the five Vice-Presidents of the Commission are appointed for renewable two-year terms of office.

Decisions of the Commission are taken by simple majority vote. The work of the Communities is directed by the Commission through four variously binding types of decision: (a) Regulations, which are compulsory and directly applicable in any member state; (b) directives, under which member states are obliged to achieve a particular result but are free to choose their own ways and means; (c) decisions, which are obligatory on the parties concerned; and (d) recommendations and opinions, which have no binding force.

The functions of the Commission are to supervise the application of the treaties and of measures adopted within their framework; to make proposals to the Council which the latter cannot amend except by unanimous vote; to formulate opinions and recommendations on matters within the scope of the treaties; to take decisions for which it has authority; and to publish an annual general report.

The Commission's administration comprises a secretariat, a legal service, a statistical office, an administration of the customs union, an environment and consumer protection service and 19 specialized directorates.

The European Parliament. The European Parliamentary Assembly, usually known as the European Parliament, had, as agreed upon by the heads of government of the member countries of the European Community in July 1976, a total of 410 members (81 each from France, the Federal Republic of Germany, Italy and the United Kingdom; 25 from the Netherlands; 24 from Belgium; 16 from Denmark; 15 from Ireland; and six from Luxembourg) chosen by direct elections in the various member states, with each country making its own decisions on constituencies, voting and the qualifications of election candidates—in particular whether they had to be, or might or might not be, members of national legislatures. As from Jan. 1, 1981, Greece was allotted 24 seats in the European Parliament [see below], which was thus enlarged to 434 members.

The first elections of the 410 members took place on June 7 and 10, 1979, when over 110,000,000 voters, or an average 60 per cent of the electorate, cast their votes. In the new Parliament, in which the members sit in political (not national) groups, the seats were eventually distributed as follows: Socialists 113, European People's Party (Christian Democrats) 107, European Democrats (Conservatives) 64, Communists and Allies 44, Liberal and Democratic Group 40, European Progressive Democrats 22, Technical Co-ordination Group for the Defence of the Interests of Independent Groups and Members 11, non-affiliated nine.

The new Parliament, which has its seat in Luxembourg but also holds sessions in Strasbourg, has 16 committees and five sub-committees, which sometimes meet in Brussels as well as in Strasbourg and Luxembourg.

The European Parliament has no executive powers. Its function is to supervise the work of the executive organs of the three Communities and to guide it by means of resolutions and expressions of opinion. Its members are entitled to request information on all aspects of the Communities' work from the Commission and the Council of Ministers. The latter decided in October 1973 that relations between itself and Parliament should be improved, in particular by granting Parliament the right to debate Community trade agreements with third countries after their signature but before ratification.

As from the end of 1974 the powers of Parliament in respect of the budget were expanded, and Parliament was given the right to reject a draft budget in its entirety, while a conciliation committee (as a joint Parliament-Council of Ministers consultative body) was created in February 1975. The Parliament also has powers to enforce, by a two-thirds majority, the resignation of the Commission.

The Court of Justice. The task of the Court of Justice, based in Luxembourg, is to safeguard the law in the interpretation and application of the treaties under which the Communities have been set up.

The Court is composed of a President of the Court, a First Advocate-General and three Chambers consisting each of a President and two judges, in addition to whom there are three advocates-general. The members of the Court are appointed by the Communities' member governments for renewable six-year terms, and the President of the Court is appointed for a renewable three-year term by the judges from among themselves. A partial renewal of the Court takes place every three years.

The jurisdiction of the Court covers the settlement of all disputes within the Communities. The Court is the final arbiter on the legality of decisions—other than recommendations or opinions—of the executive. It hears appeals on the part of the executive or of a member state on grounds of incompetence, violation of essential rules of procedure, infringement of the treaties or of any rule implementing them, or an abuse of power. Any person or legal entity may, under the same terms, appeal against a decision which affects him.

Other matters which come under the jurisdiction of the Court include compensation for damage, and disputes between the Communities and their employees.

The Court of Auditors. The Court of Auditors, consisting of one member from each of the nine member countries appointed for six years by the Council of Ministers, was set up under the second Budget Treaty which came into force on June 1, 1977. It replaced an Audit Board established in 1974, as decided at the December 1973 summit conference in Copenhagen, and the auditor of the ECSC. Its functions are to examine not only the revenue and expenditure of the Community and of any body created by it but also those of the European Development Fund. It has to co-operate with national audit bodies which supervise the national authorities responsible for enforcing Community law.

Economic and Social Committee. This committee assists the Council of Ministers and the Commission in an advisory capacity. It is composed of 156 members (24 each from France, the Federal Republic of Germany, Italy and the United Kingdom), 12 each from Belgium, Greece and the Netherlands, nine each from Denmark and Ireland and six from Luxembourg) appointed for four-year renewable terms by the Council of Ministers. One-third of its members represent employers, one-third employees and one-third the general economic interest.

Consultative Committee of the ECSC. The European Coal and Steel Community's Consultative Committee has a minimum membership of 60 and a maximum membership of 81. Its members, who are appointed by the Council of Ministers for a two-year term, include producers, workers, dealers and consumers.

Under the terms of the ECSC treaty the advice of the Consultative Committee must be sought by the Commission in certain cases before a decision can be reached. It may also be consulted on any other relevant matter.

Institutions of the European Communities

European Investment Bank. The European Investment Bank (EIB) was set up under the Treaty of Rome as an independent legal unity. Its members are the governments of the 10 member countries of the European Communities and its headquarters are in Luxembourg.

The functions of the bank are to promote a common investment policy within the Communities and thus to contribute to the smooth functioning of the common market. The EIB grants, on a non-profit basis, loans or guarantees for (i) projects in underdeveloped regions; (ii) the modernization, reorganization or extension of already established enterprises; and (iii) new enterprises of joint interest to several member countries because the size or special character of these enterprises makes it difficult for a single member country to finance them. The EIB is also authorized to grant loans to non-member countries in Europe and to countries and territories with association or co-operation agreements with the European Communities.

The powers of the EIB are vested in a Board of Governors, usually consisting of the Finance Ministers of the member countries. Its executive organ is a Board of Directors comprising 19 members and 11 alternate members, with France, Germany, Italy and the United Kingdom each nominating three members and two alternate members, the three Benelux countries each one member and jointly one alternate member, Denmark, Greece and Ireland each one member and jointly one alternate member, and the European Commission one of each. There is also a Management Committee consisting of a President and four Vice-Presidents.

Following the accession of Greece as from Jan. 1, 1981, the subscribed capital of the EIB totalled 7,200 million EUA, of which France, Germany and the United Kingdom had each subscribed 1,575 million EUA, Italy 1,260 million EUA, Belgium and the Netherlands 414,750,000 EUA each, Denmark 210,000,000 EUA, Greece 112,500,000 EUA, Ireland 52,500,000 EUA and Luxembourg 10,500,000 EUA. By the end of 1980 the total of loans granted by the EIB since its inception was about 17,000 million EUA.

European Social Fund. The European Social Fund was created under the Treaty of Rome to facilitate employment and the mobility of labour within the Community. By improving oppportunities of employment the Social Fund helps to raise the standard of living in the common market countries.

At the request of a member state the Fund pays 50 per cent of the cost incurred by that country or any of its public bodies in (i) retraining or granting resettlement allowances to workers who have become unemployed as a result of common market activities, and (ii) granting aid to workers temporarily forced to work for a short time or suspended as a result of changes in production in the undertaking employing them, so that these workers may maintain their standard of living pending the restoration of their full employment.

The Fund is administered by the Commission assisted by a committee consisting of representatives of member governments, trade unions and employers' associations.

The Council of Ministers on Nov. 26, 1970, approved proposals for changing the Social Fund into a "dynamic instrument" of a common employment policy. The major change under the new reforms was to enable an increasing proportion of the Fund's budget to help workers directly affected, or likely to be affected, by the execution of Community policies.

The Council decided on the same date to establish a Standing Committee on Employment to provide a forum for co-operation between the Council, the Commission, employers and unions. The Committee held its first meeting in Brussels on March 18, 1971.

On Dec. 20, 1977, the Council of (Foreign) Ministers adopted regulations revising the rules of the European Social Fund with effect from Jan. 1, 1978, "to make utilization of the fund's resources more effective and better co-ordinated with the Community's other structure-oriented financial instruments, to increase the rate of the fund's intervention to help projects in backward or declining regions, to increase aid for the vocational training of women and to widen the fund's field of activity".

European Regional Development Fund. The ERDF, as endorsed by the heads of state or government of the nine member states in December 1974, was inaugurated as from Jan. 1, 1975, with the aim of providing funds for the development of less-favoured regions within the Community. It had total resources of 1,300 million u.a. (then about US$1,600 million) for the three years from 1975 to 1977, and 1,850 million for the period 1978-80. By the end of 1980 the Fund had made payments totalling 2,058 million EUA.

With the accession of Greece to full Community membership as from Jan. 1, 1981, member states' percentage quotas of ERDF disbursement were fixed as follows: Italy 35.49 per cent, UK 23.80 per cent, France 13.64 per cent, Greece 13.00 per cent, Ireland 5.94 per cent, Federal Republic of Germany 4.65 per cent, Netherlands 1.24 per cent, Belgium 1.11 per cent, Denmark 1.06 per cent and Luxembourg 0.07 per cent.

Other Funds. The *European Agricultural Guidance and Guarantee Fund* (EAGGF, or FEOGA) was set up in 1962 to finance the Community's common agricultural policy [see also pages 133-35]. By means of variable import levies it keeps the prices of imports at a threshold level, while the prices of domestic products are supported by the authorities committed to buy at an official intervention price; the Fund also makes grants towards the structural reform of agriculture.

The *European Monetary Co-operation Fund* (FECOM) was set up in 1973 in the context of moves towards monetary union, its task including the management of the "snake" (i.e. the joint float within permitted fluctuation margins of member countries' currencies) and also of the settlement of debts and credits among member countries and of short-term credits granted by central banks to a member state in temporary balance of payments difficulties. Under the new European Monetary System introduced in 1979 it was envisaged that FECOM would eventually be replaced by a fully-fledged European Monetary Fund [see pages 140-41].

The *European Development Fund* (EDF) is designed mainly to increase production and modernize infrastructures and services in the developing countries by means of the disbursement of aid for specific projects. Such aid is granted mainly to those developing countries associated with the Community under the Lomé Convention [see pages 141-43], but increasing amounts are also allocated to non-associated developing countries, notably those of the Indian subcontinent.

Enlargement of the Community

At the end of protracted negotiations on the enlargement of the European Community—which in the case of Britain had been conducted over a period of more than 10 years—a *Treaty of Accession to the European Communities* (the *Treaty of Brussels*) was signed in Brussels on Jan. 22, 1972, by the Prime Ministers of Britain, Denmark, the Republic of Ireland and Norway. As described below, Norway subsequently decided against accession.

The three principal documents making up the treaty were:

(*a*) The "Treaty concerning the accession of the Kingdom of Denmark, Ireland, the Kingdom of Norway and the United Kingdom of Great Britain and Northern Ireland to the European Economic Community and the European Atomic Energy Community".

(*b*) The "Decision of the Council of the European Communities of Jan. 22, 1972, concerning the accession of the Kingdom of Denmark, Ireland, the Kingdom of Norway and the United Kingdom of Great Britain and Northern Ireland to the European Coal and Steel Community".

(*c*) The "Act concerning the conditions of accession and the adjustments to the treaties", covering under a number of heads the negotiations between Britain, Ireland, Denmark and Norway with the Six over the previous 18 months. Unlike (*a*) and (*b*), which were relatively short documents, (*c*) was an Act of great complexity and detail, embodying 161 articles and with numerous annexes.

As regards (*a*) and (*b*), a separate procedure was required for accession to the European Economic Community and Euratom on the one hand, and to the European Coal and Steel Community on the other, because of legal differences between the original treaties—the Treaties of Rome and the Treaty of Paris respectively.

The treaty on accession contained the following provisions:

Art. 1. (1) The Kingdom of Denmark, Ireland, the Kingdom of Norway and the United Kingdom of Great Britain and Northern Ireland hereby become members of the European Economic Community and of the European Atomic Energy Community and parties to the treaties establishing these Communities as amended or supplemented.

(2) The conditions of admission and the adjustments to the treaties establishing the European Economic Community and the European Atomic Energy Community necessitated thereby are set out in the Act annexed to this treaty. The provisions of that Act concerning the European Economic Community and the European Atomic Energy Community shall form an integral part of this treaty.

(3) The provisions concerning the rights and obligations of the member states and the powers and jurisdiction of the institutions of the Communities as set out in the treaties referred to in Paragraph 1 shall apply in respect of this treaty.

Art. 2. This treaty will be ratified by the high contracting parties in accordance with their respective constitutional requirements. The instruments of ratification will be deposited with the Government of the Italian Republic by Dec. 31, 1972, at the latest.

This treaty will enter into force on Jan. 1, 1973, provided that all the instruments of ratification have been deposited before that date and that all the instruments of accession to the European Coal and Steel Community are deposited on that date.

If, however, the states referred to in Article 1(1) have not all deposited their instruments of ratification and accession in due time, the treaty shall enter into force for those states which have deposited their instruments. . . .

The Decision of the Council contained provisions as follows:

Art. 1. (1) The Kingdom of Denmark, Ireland, the Kingdom of Norway and the United Kingdom of Great Britain and Northern Ireland may become members of the European Coal and Steel Community by acceding, under the conditions laid down in this Decision, to the treaty establishing that Community, as amended or supplemented.

(2) The conditions of accession and the adjustments to the treaty establishing the European Coal and Steel Community necessitated thereby are set out in the Act annexed to this Decision. The provisions of that Act concerning the European Coal and Steel Community shall form an integral part of this Decision.

(3) The provisions concerning the rights and obligations of the member states and the powers and jurisdiction of the institutions of the Community as set out in the treaty referred to in Paragraph 1 shall apply in respect of this Decision.

Art. 2. The instruments of accession of the Kingdom of Denmark, Ireland, the Kingdom of Norway and the United Kingdom of Great Britain and Northern Ireland to the European Coal and Steel Community will be deposited with the Government of the French Republic on Jan. 1, 1973.

Accession will take effect on Jan. 1, 1973, provided that all the instruments of accession have been deposited on that date and that all the instruments of ratification of the treaty concerning Accession to the European Economic Community and the European Atomic Energy Community have been deposited before that date.

If, however, the states referred to in the first paragraph of this article have not all deposited their instruments of accession and ratification in due time, accession shall take effect for the other acceding states. . . .

The 161 articles of the Act specified the transitional arrangements agreed upon in the negotiations leading to the conclusion of the treaty. During a transitional period of five years the new member countries undertook:

(*a*) To reduce customs barriers and nontariff obstacles for industrial products between them and the old members of the Community in five phases at 20 per cent per annum;

(*b*) to adopt the Community's common external tariff at the end of the five-year period by adjustment in four phases of 40 per cent on Jan. 1, 1974, and 20 per cent on Jan. 1 of the three succeeding years.

In regard to agriculture the new member countries adopted the Community system of support under the common agricultural policy, with adjustments to full Community price levels in six steps over the five-year transitional period.

Approval of Enlargement in Britain, Denmark and Ireland. In *Britain,* the European Communities Bill, providing for the United Kingdom's entry into the European Economic Community, was given a second reading in the House of Commons on Feb. 17, 1972, by 309 votes (304 Conservatives and five Liberals) to 301 (279 Labour members, 15 Conservatives, six independents, and one Liberal), with eight abstentions and three members absent. The Bill passed its third reading in the House of Commons on July 13, 1972, by 301 votes (296 Conservatives and five Liberals) to 284 (264 Labour members, 16 Conservatives, and four independents), with four Conservatives and 13 Labour members abstaining. In the House of Lords the Bill was approved by far larger majorities—189 votes to 19 at its second reading on July 26, and 161 votes to 21 at its third reading on Sept. 20. The Bill became law on Oct. 17, 1972.

In *Denmark,* ratification of the Treaty of Accession was approved by Parliament on Sept. 8, 1972, by 272 votes to 95, with one blank vote. Denmark's entry into the Community was also approved in a referendum on Oct. 3 by 1,958,115 votes (63.3 per cent of the votes cast) to 1,135,691 (36.7 per cent), with 11,907 blank and 7,409 other invalid papers, in a 90.1 per cent poll. Royal Assent was given to the ratification on Oct. 11, 1972.

In the *Republic of Ireland,* the necessary amendment to the Constitution, enabling the Republic to become a member of the European Communities, was approved by the *Dail* (Lower House of Parliament) on Jan. 26, and by the Senate on March 8, 1972. As required by the Constitution, the proposal to amend it was submitted to a popular referendum on May 10, 1972, with the result that 1,041,880 voters (83 per cent of those voting) voted for the amendment, and 211,888 (17 per cent) against it, in a 71 per cent poll—so that those in favour constituted over 58 per cent of the electorate, and those against about 12 per cent. The Bill was signed by President de Valera on June 8, 1972.

Rejection in Norway. In Norway the decision to join the European Communities was, under the Norwegian Constitution, subject to a three-quarters' majority in the *Storting* (Parliament) being in favour; the Government, which did not command a parliamentary majority, did not expect to gain the required support in Parliament and decided to seek the people's approval of entry in a referendum (which is not provided for in the Norwegian Constitution), in the expectation that a popular majority in favour of entry would enable it subsequently to obtain the necessary parliamentary majority. In the event, the referendum held on Sept. 24-25, 1972, resulted in 1,099,389 votes (53.5 per cent of the poll) being cast against entry and 956,043 (or 46.5 per cent) in favour, in a 77.6 per cent poll.

The Norwegian Government consequently informed the representatives of the Euro-

pean Communities' member countries in Brussels on Sept. 26 that Norway was withdrawing its participation in the consultative negotiating committees, and it was officially announced on the same day that the Government had decided not to submit a proposal for membership of the European Communities to the *Storting.*

Norway's failure to ratify the Treaty of Accession necessitated a number of amendments to the treaty and its attendant documents, and these amendments were subsequently made, including the deletion of special protocols previously agreed upon with the Norwegian Government, and the reduction in the number of judges at the Court of Justice to nine (instead of the 11 previously envisaged).

Approval of Ratification by the Six. In France, ratification of the Treaty of Accession by the French President was approved in a referendum held throughout metropolitan France and the French overseas departments and territories on April 23, 1972, the official result being as follows:

	Actual figure	*Percentage of electorate*	*Percentage of valid votes*
"Yes" votes	10,847,554	36.37	68.31
"No" votes	5,030,934	16.87	31.68
Blank or spoilt papers	2,086,119	6.99	—
Abstentions	11,855,857	39.75	—

Ratification of the treaty was approved in Belgium by the Senate on June 30, 1972, and by the Chamber of Deputies on Dec. 8; in Western Germany by the *Bundestag* on June 21 and by the *Bundesrat* on July 7; in Italy by the Chamber of Deputies on Dec. 5 and by the Senate on Dec. 19; in Luxembourg by the Parliament on Dec. 20; and in the Netherlands by the Second Chamber of the States-General on Sept. 14 and by the First Chamber on Nov. 14.

Accession of Britain, Denmark and Ireland. Britain, Denmark and the Republic of Ireland became members of the European Communities on Jan. 1, 1973, in accordance with the provisions of the Treaty of Accession. The transitional period for the three acceding members ended on June 30, 1977.

The Danish Treaty of Accession to the European Communities extended also to Greenland but not to the Faroe Islands for which a special status was provided, with the effect that the Faroes participated in the Communities' free trade arrangements only with a status similar to that of the EFTA member countries, and they were therefore not bound by any other common policy arrangements, including those on fisheries.

UK Renegotiation and Referendum. The British (Labour) Government officially demanded, on April 1, 1974, a renegotiation of the terms of UK membership of the Communities on a number of grounds, including the proposed economic and monetary union to be achieved by 1980 (which the British Government described as "over-ambitious"); the European Union into which the relations of member states were to be transformed by 1980 (which was said to be "not desired . . . by the British people"); the common agricultural policy (which was said "not to take sufficient account of the differing interests and circumstances of member countries" and to confer "privileges on some and unfair burdens on others"); trade with Commonwealth and developing countries, the conditions of which should be improved; and the Communities' budget, to which Britain was making an excessive contribution.

However, on March 18, 1975, the British Government announced that it had decided to recommend to the British people to vote for continued UK membership of the European Communities in a referendum fixed for June 5, 1975, on the grounds that the UK Government had secured a satisfactory result in the response to its renegotiation demands.

These results included revisions in the common agricultural policy; the introduction of a corrective mechanism to deal with unfair contributions to the Communities' budget; the tacit abandonment of achieving economic and monetary union (EMU) by 1980; changes in regional, industrial and fiscal policies; agreements on Commonwealth sugar and New Zealand dairy products; the benefits accruing to developing countries under the Lomé Convention; and avoidance of uniformity in the application of value-added tax.

The referendum of June 5, 1975, resulted in 17,378,581 votes (or 67.2 per cent of the total votes cast) in favour of Britain's continued membership of the European Communities, and 8,470,073 votes (32.8 per cent) against it in a poll of about 64 per cent.

Accession of Greece. Under a treaty of accession signed in Athens on May 28, 1979, Greece—which had formally applied for Community membership on June 12, 1975 —became the 10th member of the European Communities on Jan. 1, 1981, following ratification of the treaty by all 10 countries concerned.

The treaty provided for a five-year transitional period for Greek adaptation to Community membership, with a seven-year period for the abolition of tariffs in a small number of agricultural products (in particular tomatoes and peaches) and for free movement of labour (although preference would be given, during the transitional period, to Greek workers where it was found necessary to recruit workers from outside the Communities, and Greek workers already legally employed in Community member states would be able progressively to bring in their families).

Greece would appoint a member to the Communities' Council of Ministers and another to the European Commission; it would have 24 seats in the European Parliament; there would be 12 Greek members in the Communities' Economic and Social Committee; and Greece would appoint a representative to the Board of Governors of the European Investment Bank.

A 1962 agreement providing for Greece's associate membership of the EEC had been virtually suspended in 1967 (following the military coup in Greece during April of that year) but had been reactivated in December 1974 after the new Greek Government had stated that it wished to transform its existing association into full membership in the very near future. Under a protocol to the association agreement, Greece had on Feb. 27, 1977, been granted loans and aid of 280,000,000 EUA up to Oct. 31, 1981.

Portuguese and Spanish Applications. Applications for full membership of the European Communities were also made by Portugal on March 28, 1975, and by Spain on July 28 of that year.

Progress of the EEC

Progressive Implementation of the Common Market. The progressive implementation of the common market in three four-year stages, as envisaged in the Treaty of Rome, proceeded without prolonging any of the stages as provided for in the treaty. The most critical changeover was that from the first to the second stage which took place on Jan. 14, 1962. On this date, after a series of 45 meetings, the Council of Ministers finally reached unanimous agreement on a common policy for agriculture, without which the French Government had refused to agree to the move into the second stage of the common market's transitional period.

During the first stage of the treaty a unanimous decision of the Council of Ministers was required for the settlement of most issues, only a limited number of questions being decided by a qualified majority vote. The application of a qualified majority vote was extended in the second stage, when the unanimous vote was retained only on important questions of economic union and common policies.

The third stage of implementation of the treaty, which began on Jan. 1, 1966, saw yet a further extension of the application of the qualified majority vote, the unanimous vote being retained only for a relatively small number of important decisions. It continued to be true, however, that in practice no major issues were decided without the unanimous agreement of member states.

Acceleration of Economic Integration. From the middle of 1959 economic and political conditions within the Community improved to such an extent that adherence to the programme of economic integration laid down in the Treaty of Rome was no longer necessary. On May 12, 1960, the Council of Ministers therefore agreed on a plan to speed up implementation of the treaty from Jan. 1, 1961.

In connexion with its decision of May 12, 1960, to accelerate the reduction of customs duties between member countries and the adjustment of their duty rates to a common external tariff [see above], the Council of Ministers issued on the same date a "declaration of intention" to carry out such an acceleration also in all other spheres of economic integration, especially in the implementation of social measures, notably vocational training of employees, their freedom to accept employment anywhere, the application of social security schemes, and equal pay for men and women.

Customs duties within the European Economic Community were reduced on Jan. 1, 1962, by a further 10 per cent, making a total of 40 per cent for industrial products, 35 per cent for non-liberalized agricultural products, and 30 per cent for agricultural products liberalized since the formation of the Community. The 40 per cent reduction had been made in four stages of 10 per cent each on Jan. 1, 1959; July 1, 1960; Jan. 1, 1961; and Jan. 1, 1962. The reduction of duty for each industrial product by a minimum of 25 per cent, which was the target under the Treaty of Rome in the first stage of the transitional period up to Jan. 1, 1962, had therefore been substantially exceeded.

The European Economic Community took its first step towards a common external tariff policy on Dec. 31, 1960, i.e. the alignment of individual national tariffs with the proposed common tariff. The Treaty of Rome originally set the date for this at Dec. 31, 1961 (the end of the first transitional period), but the Council of Ministers decided on May 12, 1960, to bring it forward by one year, i.e. to Dec. 31, 1960. The treaty specified that where individual duties were higher or lower than the common tariff rate by not more than 15 per cent, the common tariff rate was to be introduced at the first stage of alignment; in other cases the individual rates were to be increased or de-

creased towards the level of the common tariff by 30 per cent of the difference between the common tariff rate and the individual national rate. For the first move on Dec. 31, 1960, which applied only to industrial products while agricultural commodities were expressly excluded, the Community modified the basis of calculation by requiring the alignment to be carried out towards the rates shown in the common tariff nationally reduced by 20 per cent. The downward alignment of national rates on the common tariff, as calculated on this basis, was subject to the proviso that the resultant rate must not be less than that shown in the common tariff before the national 20 per cent reduction.

At its meeting of May 15, 1962, the Council of Ministers decided also to bring forward the second stage of adjustment between national tariffs and the common external tariff, this time by 18 months, i.e. from Dec. 31, 1965 (the end of the second stage), to July 1, 1963. From the latter date, therefore, a second 30 per cent alignment would come into force, reducing the difference between national tariffs and the common external tariff by 60 per cent.

Further Tariff Reductions. Customs duties on industrial and agricultural goods were reduced by 10 per cent on July 1, 1963, Jan. 1, 1965, and Jan. 1, 1966. By the last-named date there had been a total reduction of 80 per cent on industrial goods, 65 per cent on non-liberalized agricultural goods, and 60 per cent on agricultural goods liberalized since the establishment of the Community. A further lowering of customs duties in the industrial sector took place on July 1, 1967, when duties were reduced by another 5 per cent, bringing the total reduction up to 85 per cent. The final abolition of these duties came into force on July 1, 1968, thereby completing the customs union in the industrial sector.

Formation of Common Agricultural Policy. The principal cause of disagreement within the EEC has been agricultural policy.

In 1960 the EEC Commission proposed the formation of a common agricultural policy based on common prices, a single fund for price supports, and joint import levies. It was not until Jan. 14, 1962, however, that an agreement for the first stage of a common agricultural policy for the EEC was adopted by the Council of Ministers.

Policy Objectives. The main objectives of the common policy for agriculture were outlined as follows:

(a) To balance supply and demand within the Community and externally by influencing supply by such measures as more regional specialization, stockpiling and structural reforms, and increasing demand by improving the quality of products.

(*b*) To provide farmers with a fair income by structural and regional improvements, the consolidation of holdings, electricity supplies, better transport and farming methods, information services and education.

(*c*) To stabilize the market by protecting farmers from speculative price fluctuations while not insulating them from the influence of long-term movements in world markets.

(*d*) To ensure equitable supplies to consumers by enabling the processing industries to find external outlets at reasonable or competitive prices, and by preventing prices from being fixed on the basis of marginal production costs.

Products. The regulations adopted by the Ministers applied to grain, pigmeat, eggs, poultry, fruit and vegetables, and wine. Fundamental decisions were also taken on the remaining major farm products (rice, beef and veal, dairy produce and sugar) and a time-table was set for the publication of the full regulations on all these items in 1962. The products covered constituted over 46 per cent of the total inter-Community trade in farm produce.

Transition Period. A seven-year transition period pending the full implementation of the common policy was fixed from July 1, 1962, to Dec. 31, 1969, but a decision to shorten this period to six years could be taken in the third year.

Other clauses of the agreement provided for common quality standards, harmonization of prices and a system of levies. The agreement also provided for the setting up of five management committees for grain, pigmeat, eggs and poultry, fruit and vegetables, and wine respectively.

The common agricultural policy would be financed by a European Agricultural Guidance and Guarantee Fund (EAGGF or FEOGA) consisting, for the first three years, of financial contributions by the member states. As soon as a common market system for agricultural products came into force the Community expenditure would be directly financed by receipts from levies on imports from non-member countries.

The common marketing organizations for grain, pigmeat, eggs and poultry, fruit and vegetables, and wine came into operation on July 30, 1962. Agreement on other agricultural marketing organizations was reached on Dec. 23, 1963.

An important agreement on cereal prices was reached by the Council of Ministers on Dec. 15, 1964. The ministers agreed on the settling of common prices for cereals, to be effective from July 1, 1967, and they also agreed to establish a common fund to help in harmonizing agriculture throughout the Community. The agreement was based on a set of proposals presented by the Commission to the Council of Ministers in November 1963. This plan set target prices for the whole Community for all cereals, and provided for compensation from the EEC

budget for farmers who would thereby suffer loss of income.

The 1964-66 Crisis. On Dec. 15, 1964, the Council of Ministers asked the EEC Commission for proposals, to be presented before April 1, 1965, on how the common agricultural policy should be financed for the period 1965-70.

The Commission accordingly submitted its proposals to the Council on April 1, 1965. These covered not only the renewal of levies on agricultural goods but also proposed that both these levies and industrial import duties should be paid into the EEC fund. As these receipts represented enormous amounts and constituted the EEC's financial resources, the Commission proposed that the European Parliament should be strengthened by being given powers to determine the Community's revenue, and that it should also receive wider powers over the Community's budget.

The Commission's scheme was considered by the Council of Ministers at a meeting in Brussels which opened on June 28, 1965, under the chairmanship of M. Couve de Murville, the French Foreign Minister, who immediately rejected the Commission's proposals, maintaining that political conditions had been imposed by the Commission which were totally unacceptable to France, and that the sole question to be settled was the renewal of levies after the expiration of the existing agricultural finance regulations on June 30, 1965.

Following the breakdown on July 2, 1965, of talks between the Foreign Ministers of the Six, the French Government announced on July 5, that it was withdrawing its representatives from a number of the Commission's working committees. France also boycotted the next meeting of the Council of Ministers on July 26-27, 1965, and did not in fact meet again with the other five EEC member states until January 1966. The main issues on which France felt unable to co-operate with her fellow-members of the EEC were (i) the granting to the Commission of significant supra-national authority, in particular of a budget of its own, financed from agricultural levies and customs duties, and (ii) the application of majority decisions, to which France could not agree on matters of importance.

These questions were discussed at the two Council meetings held in Luxembourg on Jan. 17-18 and Jan. 28-29, 1966. On the question of the powers of the Commission, the Council adopted a number of points for improving its relations with the Commission. These included the following:

(1) The Commission should consult the member governments at the appropriate level before submitting

proposals for Community action of particular importance to the Council.

(2) Commission proposals should not be made known to the European Parliament or the public before their submission to the Council.

(3) The executive powers granted to the Commission in any policy field should be precisely formulated, leaving no room for its discretion.

(4) The Council should exercise a closer control over the Commission's budget.

The question of majority decisions was solved as follows:

(1) When issues very important to one or more member countries were at stake, the members of the Council would try, within a reasonable time, to reach solutions which could be adopted by all members of the Council, while respecting their mutual interests, and those of the Community, in accordance with Article 2 of the Treaty. (This article aimed at approximating the economic policies of EEC members to create a common market.)

(2) The French delegation considered that, when very important issues were at stake, discussion must be continued until unanimous agreement was reached.

(3) The six delegations noted that there was a divergence of views on what should be done in the event of a failure to reach complete agreement.

(4) They considered that this divergence did not prevent the Community's work being resumed in accordance with normal procedure.

On Feb. 2, 1966, the Commission issued a communiqué stating that the Community would resume its normal activities.

1966 Agreement on Agricultural Policy. Following the French delegation's return to the conference table, the Foreign Ministers decided in Luxembourg on Jan. 31, 1966, to proceed with all speed in an effort to reach agreement on the common agricultural policy and the industrial customs union, including the completion of a common external tariff. Accordingly, at their meeting on May 11 the ministers agreed on details of the Farm Fund and set July 1, 1968, as the target date for the coming into force of complete common markets for both industrial and agricultural goods. Finally, following a further series of meetings which opened on July 21 and lasted four days and two nights, full agreement was reached on the outstanding agricultural questions and also on the common external tariff for industrial goods.

Between 1966 and 1970 agreement was reached on common organization of markets in most agricultural sectors and also with respect to fisheries.

Financing of Agricultural Fund. After lengthy discussions, agreement was reached on financing the EAGGF. For the two years 1965-66 and 1966-67 the cost of the common agricultural policy would be met entirely by percentage contributions from the member countries to the Fund. From July 1, 1967 onwards, 90 per cent of the levies on imports of foodstuffs would be handed over by the member governments to the European Fund. This would, in fact, cover some 45 per cent of the Fund's expenditure, and the remainder of the cost would be paid from the national exchequers of the member countries in agreed proportions.

Agreement was also reached by the Council of Ministers on Feb. 5-7, 1970, on a regulation for financing the common agricultural policy as from Jan. 1, 1971, provided the preconditions for the coming into force of the arrangements replacing the contributions by member countries to the Community by the Community's own revenues had been met by that date. When the regulations became effective, the Guarantee Section of the Agricultural Fund took over complete financing responsibility from the national governments.

Adoption of Common Agricultural Policy by Acceding Members. The common agricultural policy was officially adopted by Britain, Ireland and Denmark on Feb. 1, 1973. The adoption followed a compromise agreement reached a few days earlier on prices for cereals, pigmeat, poultry and eggs, and sugar. In this context Britain agreed, in view of the de facto devaluation of sterling against the Community's unit of account, to a new (reduced) reference rate for the purposes of the agricultural policy (involving a devaluation of sterling by 9.2 per cent since June 1972, when sterling had been allowed to float).

Developments in Other Fields

LABOUR QUESTIONS

On July 20, 1960, the EEC Commission sent a formal recommendation to member states on the fulfilment of the principle of equal pay for men and women in return for equal work. The Council approved the reduction of the maximum differences to 15 per cent by June 30, 1962, and to 10 per cent by June 30, 1963, with their complete elimination by Dec. 31, 1964.

The first regulations on the free movement of workers within the Community came into force on Sept. 1, 1961. These were superseded by new regulations effective from May 4, 1964. The principal changes were as follows:

Abandonment of Priority for Home Labour Market. The new regulations provided, in principle, for equal right of access to employment throughout the Community territory for all wage-earners, and particularly seasonal and frontier workers, who had previously not been covered by any regulation regarding free movement.

To prevent the balance of the labour market from being upset in certain regions, or the aggravation of crises in certain occupations, a member state, if it should consider such action necessary, might provisionally maintain or reinstate priority for the home labour market with specific limits (i.e. lay down that any available vacancies on the national labour market should be filled within three weeks by the domestic administration from its own nationals, but that after this period offers of employment should be transmitted to the other Community countries). A member state must inform the Commission of its decision, giving its reasons for taking such action.

Prolongation of Employment Rights. The period of "assimilation" of foreign workers in the country of employment (making them eligible for any employment within the Community) was reduced from four to two years. A foreign worker who had been in regular employment for two years and who subsequently returned to his country of origin would retain for two years afterwards the rights acquired under the provision for prolongation of employment.

Eligibility of Workers for Election to Representative Bodies in Places of Employment. Hitherto, foreign workers had enjoyed the right to vote for but not the right to election to representative bodies in the firm in which they were working. Under the new regulations foreign workers could be elected to these bodies provided they satisfied the same conditions as national workers and had worked for the firm for three years.

Admission of Foreign Workers' Families. The earlier regulations allowed the worker the right to be accompanied or joined by his wife and children under the age of 21. Under the new regulations this right was extended to all dependent relatives and any other relative living in the worker's home. Admission of a worker's family would continue to depend on whether he could house them in a manner regarded as normal for local workers in the area where he was employed.

FREEDOM OF ESTABLISHMENT AND FREEDOM TO SUPPLY SERVICES

A programme of gradually abolishing restrictions on setting up businesses and supplying services was adopted by the Council of Ministers on Oct. 25, 1961.

The programme envisaged the abolition of discriminations based on nationality, hitherto restricting access to numerous activities as follows:

(1) By Dec. 31, 1963, for the textile, footwear, paper, basic chemicals and metalworking industries, and for the wholesale trade, banking and dealings in property;

(2) by Dec. 31, 1965, for retail distribution, department stores and the food industry;

(3) by Dec. 31, 1967, for pharmacies (chemists), veterinary surgeons, insurance agents and transport;

(4) by Dec. 31, 1969, for education, film production and publicity material.

Certain general principles on freedom of establishment and freedom to supply services were approved by the Council of Ministers at its meeting in November 1963. They included the following:

(1) Self-employed people who wished to establish themselves or supply services in another member country had the right to membership in Chambers of Commerce and professional associations in that country, and would be eligible to hold office in these organizations provided that such officers would not exercise public authority.

(2) Where specific qualifications were required for certain occupations, the host country would only be able to require that the applicant had passed a supplementary examination if the practice of a profession was subject to special conditions.

(3) Persons who supplied services would have the right to be accompanied by members of their staff in the country in which the service was performed.

FREEDOM OF MOVEMENT FOR CAPITAL

On May 12, 1960, the Council of Ministers approved a directive on freedom of movement for capital, which entered into force on June 27, 1960.

It established:

(1) Unconditional freedom of capital movements connected with the freeing of trade in goods, of services, and of the movement of persons, and also with the free exercise of the right to establishment;

(2) unconditional and irreversible freedom for sale and purchase of stocks and shares quoted in the Community stock markets;

(3) conditional freedom with regard to the issuing and placing of stocks and shares on capital markets, and for the purchase of unquoted stocks and shares. Any Community country might, however, maintain or reimpose existing restrictions if their abolition was likely to hinder the achievement of its economic policy objectives.

The Federal Republic of Germany, Belgium and Luxembourg were not required to take any further liberalization measures in this respect since their foreign currency legislation already went beyond the obligations imposed by the Community directive.

COMMON TRANSPORT POLICY

On Feb. 27, 1962, the Council of Ministers asked the Commission to present detailed proposals for a common transport policy for roads, railway and inland waterways. The programme, which was submitted on June 1, 1962, was based on the principles of equality of treatment; financial independence; freedom of action for transport enterprises; free choice by the user of the means of transport; and co-ordination of investment.

An actual common transport policy was not agreed upon by the Council of Ministers until June 22, 1965. The Community transport system was intended to regulate competition in all sectors by the progressive introduction of fixed-rate limits in two separate stages.

During the first stage—1966 to 1969—only commercial transport between member countries would be subject to EEC regulations. Upper and lower tariff limits would be published for certain classes of road and rail traffic, though contracts could be made outside these rates under certain circumstances provided the details were published. Non-binding reference limits would be fixed for water transport, but contracts made outside these limits would also be published.

In the second stage—1969 to 1972—the

reference limit system would be extended to certain categories of national and international traffic of heavy goods (the Council had still to decide on a definition) and also on other forms of national transport. By 1970, therefore, almost all road transportation and a significant part of rail goods traffic in the common market would be covered by a strict system of rate control, while a more flexible system would apply to all waterborne traffic and the remaining section of railway traffic, though probably to only a small part of road haulage.

The Ministers also agreed that during the two stages of the programme the harmonization of national regulations affecting their transport sectors should be achieved and an attempt made to reach a common position on competition questions, including subsidies for national railways.

COMPETITION POLICY

Following a decision of the Council of Ministers on Dec. 19, 1961, to adopt a common anti-trust policy, detailed regulations on monopolistic practices were approved by the Council on Feb. 6, 1962.

The regulations (1) reaffirmed Articles 85-86 of the Treaty of Rome, which places a general ban on agreements, decisions, and concerted practices of an anti-competitive character; (2) required all such agreements, decisions, and practices already in force to be registered with the Commission by Nov. 1, 1962, if they had been made or agreed between more than two participants, and by Feb. 1, 1963, if between two participants; (3) laid down that all agreements etc. entered into after the coming into force of the regulations must be notified to the Commission; (4) exempted, however, from the stipulations under (2) and (3) certain types of agreements, decisions and concerted practices; (5) gave the Commission power with regard to provision of information, control, and, in the cases where the rules were not observed, the imposition of penalties and fines.

It was stated that the rules would apply in principle also to transport, though they might be modified by the common transport policy; that they would apply to agriculture only in so far as they did not affect the aims of the common agricultural policy; and that they applied to oil but not to coal, for which the European Coal and Steel Community was responsible.

On March 14, 1967, the EEC Commission adopted a regulation on block exemption for some 30,000 exclusive dealing agreements between manufacturers and distributors, which had been notified to the Commission in accordance with the regulations of Feb. 6, 1962. Under each of these agreements, which was between a manufacturer and a dealer, the dealer could acquire a sole right of re-sale of products in a specific area of the Community. The new regulation came into force on May 1, 1967.

The achievement of the customs union in July 1968 was followed by rapid development of competition policy with the aim of maintaining the free trade facilitated by the removal of tariff barriers. The application of the relevant articles of the Treaty of Rome and of the 1962 regulations was carried out by means of further block exemptions for certain business agreements and also by means of a series of test cases, designed to identify restrictive business practices which the Commission judged to be in contravention of the Community rules.

On July 29, 1968, the Commission published a list of forms of co-operation between small and medium-sized companies which it actively encouraged, and illustrated its intentions by a number of individual decisions with respect to certain forms of agreement. In parallel with this action the Commission also took a number of decisions forbidding various forms of cartels and in July 1969 for the first time imposed fines against members of two cartels.

The decisions to impose fines and, in one of the two cases, to act against companies based outside the Community, were upheld by the Court of Justice in July 1970 and in July 1972. On Dec. 16, 1972, the Commission announced that it had imposed fines totalling 9,000,000 units of account on members of a sugar cartel, the heaviest penalty thus far inflicted to enforce competition policy.

The first interpretation of Community competition policy with regard to Article 86 (dealing with abuse of a dominant position) was made with a decision against the West German performing rights society on June 2, 1971, and was followed by a further decision against an American metal container company on Dec. 13, 1971. The latter decision was the first in which the Commission had attempted to define Article 86 of the Rome Treaty as an instrument for controlling economic concentrations.

COMMON TURNOVER TAX SYSTEM

On Feb. 9, 1967, the Council of Ministers adopted two directives on the harmonization of the turnover tax system in member countries, to be completed by Jan. 1, 1970. The system adopted by the Six was the "value-added" system (VAT), by which only the value added to a product at different stages of production is liable to taxation, as opposed to the "cascade" system, by which the whole value of the product at different stages of production is taxed.

The system was adopted by three member countries—France, West Germany and the Netherlands—before the deadline; by Luxembourg on Jan. 1, 1970; by Belgium on Jan. 1, 1971; and by Italy on Jan. 1,

1973. VAT had already been in force in Denmark since 1967; was introduced in Ireland on Nov. 1, 1972; and came into force in Britain on April 1, 1973.

COMMON COMMERCIAL POLICY

The European Communities' common commercial policy came into force on Jan. 1, 1970, i.e. at the end of the 15-year transitional period as laid down in the Treaty of Rome.

However, the Council of Ministers decided on Oct. 17, 1969, that member countries would be allowed to conclude bilateral trade agreements with other countries for a three-year period from Jan. 1, 1970, provided such agreements had received prior authorization from the Council, which would have to approve the agreement before signature. [This ruling enabled EEC member states to conclude individual agreements with member states of the Council for Mutual Economic Assistance (CMEA or Comecon), which had declined to negotiate with the EEC as one unit.] After Jan. 1, 1973, all trade negotiations with non-EEC countries had to be conducted by the Commission of the EEC as a whole.

GENERALIZED SYSTEM OF PREFERENCES

The Council of Ministers decided on March 30, 1971, to introduce as from July 1, 1971, a generalized system of preferences (GSP) in favour of manufactured and semi-manufactured goods exported to the EEC by developing countries, involving the abolition of duties on such exports as well as on certain processed agricultural products—within certain limits.

These limits included the imposition of "ceilings" on imports of manufactures from developing countries and the limitation of preferences for the most competitive of the developing countries so as to reserve a substantial quota for the less developed ones.

On Dec. 16, 1980, the Council of Ministers adopted an outline GSP scheme for the five-year period 1981-85 within the context of a commitment to apply such arrangements at least until 1990.

MONETARY AGREEMENTS

The European Commission on Feb. 12, 1969, sent to EEC member governments a proposal—the so-called "Barre plan" (named after the Commission's Vice-President, M. Raymond Barre)—for co-ordination of economic policies and monetary co-operation.

Under this plan, each member country undertook to place part of its reserves at the disposal of the others, and in the event of difficulties any member might call on its partners for assistance within a ceiling to be fixed subsequently. Joint consultations would then be held with a view to re-establishing equilibrium. If no agreement could be reached, the receiving country's indebtedness should not exceed three months, but if agreement was reached the credits might be renewed or converted into medium-term assistance, all such arrangements having to be accompanied by increased co-ordination of economic policies.

The Council of Ministers approved the plan on March 4, 1969, with the proviso that the arrangements should be between the various central banks rather than between the governments.

COMMUNITY BUDGET

Following a conference of the member countries' heads of state or government at The Hague on Dec. 1-5, 1969, the Council of Ministers reached agreement on Dec. 22, 1969, on the Communities' budget as follows:

From Jan. 1, 1971, all receipts from levies would be allocated to the Communities, and there would be a similar gradual allocation of the receipts from customs duties from the same date. Any deficit during an interim period would be covered by national contributions according to an agreed scale, and after the interim period these contributions would be replaced by receipts corresponding to a uniform rate of the harmonized value-added tax (VAT).

As from the adoption of the 1975 budget the European Parliament would have powers to amend, by a majority vote of its members, any draft budget submitted by the Council of Ministers, although any amendment of the VAT rate would have to remain within the limit set by the Council's decree introducing this tax. Any amendments made by the European Parliament might be altered by the Council by a qualified majority vote; any such alterations by the Council could be changed by the European Parliament by a decision of a majority of its membership and subject to three-fifths of the votes cast being in favour; the Parliament would thus adopt the budget in its final form, but if Parliament failed to reach a decision within a fixed period, the budget would stand as drawn up by the Council.

Procedures for the European Parliament's control of the budget were approved by the Council on April 22, 1970.

The 1979 budget of the Communities was the first to be financed by "own resources" accruing from the Community system of VAT, applied from Jan. 1, 1979, by six of the member states (Belgium, Denmark, France, Italy, the Netherlands and the United Kingdom), while the three other member states (the Federal Republic of Germany, Ireland and Luxembourg) paid financial contributions based on their gross national product. However, these three subsequently also applied the VAT-based system, the Federal Republic of Germany from Jan. 1, 1980.

After a protracted dispute in 1979 and early 1980 over the UK Government's demand for a reduction in its net contribution to the Community budget, the Council of Ministers on May 29-30, 1980, reached agreement on a formula under which (i) the United Kingdom would obtain a rebate of about two-thirds of the Commission's estimate of its net contribution of some £2,380 million overall for the two years 1980 and 1981, (ii) the United Kingdom would bear only a portion of any net UK contribution in excess of the Commission's estimates for 1980 and 1981, and (iii) similar arrangements would apply in 1982 if no restructuring of the Community budget had been agreed in the intervening period, the Commission being instructed to put forward detailed proposals in the latter respect.

Under this agreement, the United Kingdom would receive substantial rebates of original payments on the basis of (i) a revision of the budgetary correcting mechanism set up in 1976 in an earlier attempt to solve Britain's difficulties and (ii) special supplementary measures under which Community funds would be available to support certain categories of UK public expenditure programmes.

Moves towards European Union

Political Union. After the Hague conference of EEC heads of state and government of December 1969 [see page 125] had agreed to an examination of "the best way of achieving progress in the matter of political unification", a group of Foreign Ministry officials under the chairmanship of Vicomte Etienne Davignon (Belgium) subsequently prepared two reports, the final version of the second report being adopted by the EEC Foreign Ministers on Oct. 27, 1970.

Listing the objects of a united Europe, the Davignon Report stated that it should be "based on a common heritage of respect for the liberty and rights of man and bring together democratic states with freely elected parliaments".

Proposals made in the report were inter alia that Foreign Ministers should meet at least once every six months; conferences of heads of state or government should be held when deemed desirable; and "in the event of a serious crisis or special urgency" there should be extraordinary consultation between the member states' governments. The ministerial meetings should be prepared by a Political Committee, and the Council's President-in-office should, once a year, provide the European Parliament with a progress report on the work done in this field.

At the summit conference of heads of government or of state of the Nine held in Paris in October 1972, a communiqué was issued setting out the future policies of the enlarged Community. Member countries agreed as follows:

(1) To create before Dec. 31, 1973, a Regional Development Fund;

(2) to draw up by Jan. 1, 1974, action programmes in the fields of social policy, industrial, scientific and technological policy and environmental policy;

(3) to define guidelines for external relations with developing countries and with Eastern Europe. In this field the Community also attached major importance to the multilateral negotiations in the context of GATT in which it would participate.

(4) With regard to foreign policy, Foreign Ministers would in future meet four times a year instead of twice as hitherto, and would prepare a second stage report on political integration by June 30, 1973.

(5) Support would be given to measures aimed at clarifying relationships between Community institutions and member states, and practical steps towards this end would be taken before June 30, 1973.

The meeting requested the institutions of the Community to draw up a report by the end of 1975 on the incorporation before the end of the decade of "the whole complex of the relations of member states into a European union". However, although by the end of 1980 member states had made some progress towards co-ordinating their foreign policies and also towards greater economic and monetary union [see below], the original aim of a full-scale European union had by the mid-1970s ceased to be regarded as a realistic goal for the foreseeable future. In a further report on European union published in January 1976, the then Belgian Prime Minister, M. Léo Tindemans, "deliberately refused" to draw up a draft constitution for a future union since it was "difficult to lay down at this stage the date of completion of the European union". Instead, the report set out "the objective and methods whereby Europe can be invested with a new vitality and current obstacles can be overcome", stressing in particular the role of a directly-elected European Parliament.

Economic and Monetary Union. With a view to achieving complete economic and monetary union of the EEC member countries by December 1980, the Council endorsed in February 1971 plans for the first of three stages for this scheme. The details were contained in the so-called Werner

Report, drawn up by a working party under the chairmanship of M. Pierre Werner, the Luxembourg Prime Minister and Minister of Finance.

The final part of this report, completed on Oct. 8, 1970, restated the objectives of economic and monetary union as affirmed by the Hague conference of EEC heads of state and government in December 1969 [see page 125].

The report made it clear that the proposed union would mean that the principal decisions of economic policy would be taken at Community level, and that the necessary powers would therefore be transferred from the national plane to the Community plane, which would entail the progressive development of political co-operation. In the long run, the report said, this development was bound to lead to political union.

The proposed monetary union would imply, the report continued, "the total and irreversible convertibility of currencies, the elimination of margins of fluctuation in rates of exchange, the irrevocable fixing of parity ratios and the total liberation of movements of capital".

The Community's centre of decision would be politically responsible to a European Parliament.

The report also laid down procedures for the first stage of this programme, covering three years as from Jan. 1, 1971.

After adopting the above plan on Feb. 9, 1971, the Council defined its objectives in a resolution, approved on March 22, 1971, and including the following details:

At the end of the three-stage, 10-year plan, the Community would be:

(1) "An area within which persons, goods, services and capital can circulate freely . . . without leading to structural and regional disequilibrium . . .";

(2) "an individual monetary unit within the international system, . . . comprising a Community organization of the central banks"; and

(3) in possession of institutions empowered to ensure the management of economic and monetary union "subject to the deliberations and control" of the European Parliament.

The resolution also laid down what measures would have to be taken within the first three-year stage. These included the establishment of Community rules determining the uniform assessment of the value-added tax; harmonization in the application, assessment and collection of excise duties; and harmonization of other taxes. It was also stressed that "the Community must progressively adopt common positions in monetary relations with third countries and international organizations".

Another decision by the Council involved approval for a four-year scheme (later renewable every five years) for providing medium-term financial aid for member countries which might be in, or threatened by, balance-of-payments difficulties—this decision being an implementation of the "Barre plan" of 1969 [see above].

At their meeting on Feb. 8-9, 1971, the EEC Ministers of Foreign Affairs and Finance agreed, at a request by the Federal Republic of Germany, to an "escape clause", under which, if progress in the harmonization of the economic policies of the member countries was in the view of one or more members insufficient and further negotiations to reach an agreed solution of the outstanding problems remained unsuccessful, it would become possible for dissatisfied members to demand, by Dec. 31, 1975, the termination of the various measures of monetary co-operation although it was agreed, on French insistence, that the decision not to widen the fluctuation margins between Community currencies could not be revoked.

Joint Currency Float. The Council of Ministers on March 21, 1972, formally approved an agreement in principle on the implementation of the 1971 resolution on economic and monetary union [see above]. The main element of the agreement was that by July 1, 1972, at the latest, the maximum margin of fluctuation between the currencies of any two member states would be fixed at 2.25 per cent, while the longer-term aim was the complete elimination of any fluctuation margin.

This joint currency float—also known as "the snake in the tunnel" or the "snake" —was implemented by the then six member countries of the European Communities as from April 24, 1972, by Denmark and Ireland from May 1, 1972, and by Norway from May 23, 1972.

The "snake", however, did not operate without disturbances. The United Kingdom and Ireland devalued their currencies in the second half of June 1972, when the Danish currency was allowed to float within margins of 4½ per cent; Denmark, however, rejoined the "snake" on Oct. 10 of that year. France temporarily withdrew from the "snake" from Jan. 19, 1974, until July 10, 1975, and it again withdrew on March 15, 1976. Italy effectively left the "snake" on Jan. 22, 1973, by introducing a two-tier exchange rate. Norway finally left the "snake" on Dec. 12, 1978 (leaving only the three Benelux countries, Denmark and the Federal Republic of Germany within the "snake").

The Swiss National Bank was from December 1975 included in the consultation mechanism linking the central banks of the "snake" countries.

European Monetary System. With effect from March 13, 1979, a European Monetary System (EMS) entered into operation on the basis of new central rates fixed on the previous day for each of the then nine member countries' currencies against the European currency unit (ECU), with fluctuation limits of plus or minus 2.25 per cent (6 per cent for the Italian lira). The United Kingdom decided not to participate in the exchange-rate mechanism, although it became associated with other aspects of the EMS.

The new exchange rates remained in force until Sept. 24, 1979, when the West German mark was revalued by 5 per cent against the Danish currency and by 2 per cent against the currencies of the other EMS participants. The ECU was from the outset of the EMS defined as identical with the European unit of account (EUA).

Further Activities, 1973-80

Environmental Action Programme. A two-year programme of environmental action, adopted by the Council of Ministers on July 20, 1973, was aimed at the harmonization of national programmes on the basis of a common long-term plan. The programme laid down certain principles, among them that "the cost of preventing and abolishing nuisances (caused by pollution) must be borne by the polluter" and that the interests of the developing countries must be taken into account, with any adverse consequences of measures taken on their economic development being reduced as far as possible.

Social Action Programme. A three-year social action programme, approved by the Council of Ministers on Dec. 11, 1973, and coming into force on Jan. 1, 1964, was aimed inter alia at "appropriate consultation between member states on their employment policies" and "better co-operation by national employment services"; an "action programme for migrant workers"; a "common vocational training policy"; "equality between men and women" in employment, vocational training and advancement, working conditions and pay; consultation on social protection policies; an initial action programme on health and safety at work and the health of workers; and also "specific measures to combat poverty". Also within the context of this programme, a series of directives were adopted in the late 1970s providing for freedom of movement and practice throughout the Community of certain professions, including doctors (June 1975), lawyers (March 1977), dentists (June 1978) and veterinary surgeons (December 1978).

Industrial Action Programme. On Dec. 17, 1973, the Council of Ministers adopted proposals relating to an "initial action programme" on industrial policy with a view to initiating a uniform industrial base in the EEC's member countries, with the abolition of technical, fiscal and legal barriers between undertakings in the various member states.

Scientific and Technological Programme. On Jan. 16, 1974, the Council of Ministers adopted proposals for an action programme on scientific and technological policy involving (i) the creation of a Committee for Scientific and Technical Research (CREST) for co-ordinating national policies not subject to military or industrial secrecy; (ii) the promotion of basic research through participation in a proposed European Science Foundation; and (iii) research projects in various fields, including the development of the European Communities over the next 30 years (a "Europe plus 30" project). (CREST held its first meeting in Brussels on Feb. 18-19, 1974.)

The Lomé Conventions

First Convention. A five-year convention establishing an overall trading and economic co-operation relationship between the EEC and 46 developing African, Caribbean and Pacific (ACP) countries was signed in Lomé (Togo) on Feb. 28, 1975, and came into full force on April 1, 1976, following ratification by all signatory states.

The original ACP countries were (i) 17 mainly French-speaking African states (Benin—then Dahomey, Burundi, Cameroon, the Central African Republic, Chad, the Congo, Gabon, the Ivory Coast, Mali, Mauritania, Niger, Rwanda, Senegal, Somalia, Togo, Upper Volta and Zaïre), Madagascar and Mauritius, which had earlier been associated with the EEC—all except Mauritius under a First Yaoundé Convention of July 20, 1963, and all 19 under a second Yaoundé Convention of July 29, 1969, which expired on Jan. 31, 1975, but was extended to July 31, 1975; (ii) the then members of the East African Community (Kenya, Tanzania and Uganda), which had been associated with the EEC under an Arusha agreement of July 26, 1968, and later under the Arusha Convention running parallel with the second Yaoundé Convention; (iii) other Commonwealth states in Africa (Botswana, The Gambia, Ghana, Lesotho, Malawi, Nigeria, Sierra Leone, Swaziland and Zambia), in the Caribbean (the Bahamas, Barbados, Grenada, Guyana, Jamaica and Trinidad and Tobago) and in the Pacific (Fiji, Tonga and Western Samoa); and (iv) other African states (Equatorial

Guinea, Ethiopia, Guinea, Guinea-Bissau, Liberia and the Sudan).

The Lomé Convention's main provisions covered (i) the granting by the Community of duty-free access on a non-reciprocal basis to all industrial and to 96 per cent of agricultural imports from ACP countries; (ii) the creation of an export stabilization scheme ("Stabex") guaranteeing the ACP countries a certain level of income on exports of their primary products; (iii) increased development aid for the ACP countries from Community sources; (iv) increased industrial co-operation between the Community's member states and the ACP countries; and (v) the creation of three new bodies to provide the institutional framework for the operation of the agreement—a Council of Ministers (comprising members of the Community's Council of Ministers, of the European Commission and of each of the ACP states' governments), a committee of ambassadors and a Consultative Assembly comprising members of the European Par-

liament and representatives designated by the ACP states, to meet once a year, inter alia to discuss a report by the Council of Ministers.

The convention also contained special arrangements, among them one for continued imports into the Community of up to 1,400,000 tonnes of cane sugar annually from ACP countries, mainly from Commonwealth producers for the UK market.

In addition the convention provided for the accession of any other state of comparable economic structure and production, subject to agreement by the Community's nine member states and the ACP countries themselves.

Total Community aid for the ACP countries during the five-year period was to amount to 3,390 million u.a. (then about $4,270 million, compared with about $918,000,000 under the second Yaoundé Convention), of which 3,000 million u.a. was to be made available through a new European Development Fund (2,100 million

Map 4 African and Middle East states linked with European Community

of it in grants) and the remainder through the European Investment Bank in the form of ordinary loans. The resources of the European Development Fund were to be financed, at 3,150 million u.a., outside the normal Community budget by contributions from member states in fixed proportions.

The constituent session of the Consultative Assembly, comprising 184 members (two from each of the ACP states and an equal number of members of the European Parliament) was held in Luxembourg on June 1-3, 1976, and the inaugural meeting of the ACP-EEC Council of Ministers in Brussels on July 14-15 of that year, when approval was given to the accession to the Convention of six newly-independent countries (the Cape Verde Islands, the Comoro Islands, Papua New Guinea, São Tomé and Príncipe, Seychelles and Suriname).

The Communities' Council of Ministers had earlier, on June 29, 1976, decided that the Lomé Convention would also apply to the overseas territories still dependent on EEC member states and had allocated a further 160,000,000 u.a. for financial and technical assistance for these dependencies.

These territories comprised (i) Netherlands and French dependencies already associated with the European Communities under the Treaty of Rome and (ii) certain other territories whose eventual association with the Communities was provided for by the UK Treaty of Accession. Of these territories, Djibouti, the Solomon Islands, Tuvalu, Dominica, St Lucia, Kiribati (the Gilbert Islands) and St Vincent subsequently became independent states, and as such full partners in the EEC-ACP association agreement in 1978-80.

An application for ACP membership by Zimbabwe, the former Rhodesia, on April 18, 1980 (the date when it achieved independence), was granted by the EEC-ACP Council of Ministers meeting in Nairobi on May 8-9, 1980 (while Mozambique, Zimbabwe's neighbour, and also Angola had refused to enter into an association with the European Communities). Zimbabwe's accession raised the number of ACP states to 60. On Oct. 7, 1980, the Council of Ministers welcomed a formal application for membership by Vanuatu, which was to become the 61st ACP member state.

Second Convention. The 1975 convention, which expired on March 1, 1980, was renewed under a second Lomé Convention, which was signed on Oct. 31, 1979, and entered fully into force on Jan. 1, 1981.

Under this second convention the duty-free arrangements for the bulk of ACP agricultural exports into the European Community were retained, while these concessions were extended to a number of products, mainly coming under the Community's common agricultural policy; existing preferential arrangements for beef and veal were extended; the "Stabex" scheme was expanded to cover a total of 44 products or by-products in order to afford more balanced protection for different countries' exports; and a special fund of 280,000,000 EUA (£174,000,000) was to protect the producers of minerals (copper and cobalt, phosphates, bauxite and aluminium, manganese, tin, iron ore and iron pyrites) against falls in export earnings or other untoward events.

The principal objects of the second convention were to improve and increase industrial development in the ACP countries, in particular in the production of manufactured goods, with technical and financial assistance being given to small and medium enterprises, and to develop new sources of energy, with investment through the European Investment Bank or by private capital. For agriculture, for which 40 per cent of the European Development fund had been allocated under the first Lomé Convention, a new Technical Centre for Agricultural and Rural Co-operation was to be established.

The funds available under the second convention were to be raised to a grand total of 5,607 million EUA (excluding food aid and joint financing given to ACP countries outside the convention).

Other Association Agreements

Turkey. An agreement on Turkey's associate membership in the EEC was signed in Ankara on Sept. 12, 1963, and entered into force on Dec. 1, 1964.

This agreement provided for Turkey's becoming a full member of the EEC when her economic progress should permit this.

The objective of the agreement—the continuous strengthening of the economic and commercial relations between Turkey and the EEC—would be attained by stages.

(1) During a five-year preparatory stage Turkey, with the assistance of the EEC, would continue her efforts to strengthen her economic and commercial position. The assistance would take the form of (i) tariff quotas, to be gradually increased, allowing Turkey to sell specified amounts of tobacco, raisins, dried figs and hazelnuts in the common market; and (ii) loans for economic development granted through the European Investment Bank.

(2) The second or transitional stage, lasting a maximum of 12 years, would see the gradual establishment of a customs union between Turkey and the EEC. Although the details would depend on the situation at the end of the initial phase of the agreement, a framework for the trade and economic arrangements in the second stage was laid down. Under the arrangements, which would cover all trade, Turkey would be expected to adopt the common customs tariff, and to bring her economic policy with regard to free movement of persons, transport policy and rules of competition into line with that of the EEC.

(3) The third or definitive stage would be based on a full customs union, including a common external tariff.

The application of the agreement is supervised by a Council of the Association, the members of which are drawn from the Council of Ministers, the Commission, the governments of the EEC member states and the Turkish Government.

The main developments under the Agreement of Association between the EEC and Turkey took the form of quota increases for Turkish tobacco, raisins, dried figs and hazelnuts as provided for in the initial stage of the agreement. The largest such increases were agreed upon by the Council of the Association on Nov. 23, 1966.

By Dec. 31, 1965, Turkey had received loans amounting to more than $50,000,000 from the European Investment Bank, the money being devoted mainly to infrastructure projects.

A supplementary protocol agreed on July 22, 1970, and signed on Nov. 23, 1971, regulated the transition from the preparatory to the second (transitional) stage. Under an interim agreement, pending ratification of the above protocol, but in any case valid only until Sept. 30, 1972, Turkish industrial goods (except petroleum products and certain textile goods) were able to enter EEC countries without tariff or quantitative restrictions from Sept. 1, 1971, and about 90 per cent of Turkey's agricultural exports were granted preferential treatment. In return Turkey would start to apply tariff reductions for industrial goods from the EEC.

An annex to the protocol provided for loans of $220,000,000 over five years and a 10-year schedule as from 1976 for the free movement and social rights of Turkish workers employed in the EEC. The provisions concerning free movement of labour were not, however, implemented by the Community side.

Under a new agreement signed on July 1, 1980, Turkey's associate membership of the EEC was renewed, with EEC tariffs on Turkish agricultural exports being gradually lowered from 1981 onwards and to be eliminated by 1987, while Turkish workers legally employed in EEC member countries gained full social security benefits. EEC aid to Turkey amounted to $840,000,000—including $455,000,000 in 40-year loans at 1 per cent interest; $70,000,000 in direct loans; and $315,000,000 in loans by the European Investment Bank at market rates of interest.

Malta. An association agreement between Malta and the EEC was approved by the EEC Council of Ministers on Nov. 26, 1970, and signed on Dec. 5. It came into force on April 1, 1971, and was aimed at the completion of a customs union by 1981 in two five-year stages.

During the first stage the EEC would grant Malta a 70 per cent reduction in customs duties on industrial products, except petroleum and some textiles which would remain subject to quotas. Malta would reduce its import duties on EEC products by 15 per cent on April 1, 1971; 10 per cent at the start of the third year of the agreement; and another 10 per cent at the start of the fifth year. In the second stage Malta would reduce these duties by at least a further 35 per cent.

On March 4, 1976, this agreement was extended until June 30, 1977; it was adapted to UK, Danish and Irish membership of the European Communities; and provision was made for Community financial aid to Malta of 26,000,000 EUA over a five-year period. On June 29, 1977, agreement was reached on extending the existing association provisions until Dec. 31, 1980, further extensions being envisaged of this first stage of association pending agreement on the content of and transition to the second stage.

Cyprus. An association agreement between Cyprus and the European Economic Community was signed on Dec. 19, 1972, providing for reciprocal tariff reductions on industrial and agricultural products during the course of a first stage ending on June 30, 1977.

For industrial products the EEC agreed to make an immediate 70 per cent reduction in tariffs, while Cyprus undertook to reduce its tariffs by 35 per cent in three steps over a four-year period. In the agricultural sector EEC tariffs would be cut by 40 per cent with regard to citrus fruits, while carobs would enter the EEC duty-free. In addition, special arrangements were made for continuing Cypriot exports of sherry to the United Kingdom and Ireland for a two-year period and within quota limitations.

On June 22, 1977, the existing association arrangements with Cyprus were extended until Dec. 31, 1979, and provision was made for Community financial aid to Cyprus of 30,000,000 EUA over a five-year period. The arrangements were further extended on an annual basis pending agreement on the content of and transition to the second stage of association.

Trade and Co-operation Agreements

Various agreements have been signed between the EEC and countries outside the Community, as follows:

Iran. A three-year agreement between

144

the EEC and Iran, signed on Oct. 14, 1963, and in force since Dec. 1, 1963, provided inter alia for temporary reductions in the EEC's common external tariff for products of special importance to Iran's economy (such as carpets, dried grapes and apricots) and fixed a tariff quota for raisins imported by the EEC from Iran (at 15 per cent of such imports from non-member and non-associated countries). The agreement was amended in 1967 and extended for a further three years from Dec. 1, 1970, but it was allowed to expire on Nov. 30, 1973, because of the changed economic situation of Iran.

Israel. A trade agreement between the EEC and Israel, signed on June 4, 1964, was in force from July 1, 1964, for a three-year period with a possible extension. No formal extension was approved, although certain special trade arrangements between Israel and the EEC were continued.

A new trade agreement, for five years, signed on June 29, 1970, provided for mutual tariff reductions as from Oct. 1, 1970.

These agreements included provisions for a 40 per cent reduction in the EEC tariff for citrus and other fruit from Israel, and an immediate 30 per cent reduction on a wide range of industrial products, with further 5 per cent annual reductions so as to reach a total of 50 per cent by Jan. 1, 1974. These measures were expected to benefit about 55 per cent of Israel's industrial exports to the EEC, and about 80 per cent of her agricultural exports. Israel granted tariff preferences ranging from 5 to 30 per cent by 1974 for about half of her industrial and agricultural imports from the EEC subject to duties.

A new agreement was concluded on Jan. 23, 1975, and came into force on July 1, 1975, for the progressive dismantling of all tariff and quota barriers on industrial goods for all Community imports from Israel by July 1, 1977; for 60 per cent of Israeli imports from the Community by Jan. 1, 1980; and for the remaining 40 per cent by Jan. 1, 1985; the Community would make substantial tariff cuts on about 85 per cent of Israel's agricultural exports; and Israeli tariffs on industrial goods from the Community would be abolished not later than Jan. 1, 1989. This agreement was effectively converted into a full-scale economic co-operation agreement on Feb. 8, 1977, with Israel to receive Community loans and grants of 30,000,000 u.a. up to Oct. 31, 1981.

Arab Countries. An agreement on trade and technical co-operation between the Community and its member countries on the one hand and Lebanon on the other was signed on May 21, 1965. The agree-

ment was valid for a period of three years and was renewed several times, pending the conclusion of a more comprehensive preferential trade agreement.

Between the EEC and the ECSC on the one hand and seven Arab countries on the other, free trade and co-operation agreements were signed as follows: (i) with Tunisia on April 25, 1976; (ii) with Algeria on April 26, 1976; (iii) with Morocco on April 27, 1976 (all three with effect from July 1, 1976); (iv) with Egypt, Jordan and Syria on Jan. 18, 1977; and (v) with Lebanon on May 3, 1977 (these four with effect from July 1, 1977).

All these agreements were of indefinite duration except for their financial co-operation provisions which were to extend to Oct. 31, 1981, and which involved loans and grants channelled through the European Investment Bank of 95,000,000 units of account (u.a.) for Tunisia, 114,000,000 u.a. for Algeria, 130,000,000 u.a. for Morocco, 170,000,000 u.a. for Egypt, 40,000,000 u.a. for Jordan, 60,000,000 u.a. for Syria and 30,000,000 u.a. for Lebanon. (The agreements with Tunisia and Morocco replaced earlier association agreements which had been in force since Sept. 1, 1969, and extended pending completion of the new agreements.)

Yugoslavia. A trade agreement with Yugoslavia, signed on March 19, 1970, and in force from May 1, 1970, provided for most favoured-nation treatment between the two sides; an acceleration of the import duty concessions proposed under the Kennedy Round; concessions for Yugoslav beef exports; and the establishment of a mixed commission to carry out the agreement. It was replaced by a new agreement for five years, signed in Brussels on June 26, to come into effect on Sept. 1, 1973.

A new preferential trade and co-operation agreement between the EEC and Yugoslavia, signed on April 2, 1980, provided, in the industrial sector, for unrestricted duty-free access to the European Community for five years for the majority of Yugoslav products except for (i) 29 industrial products on which duty would be payable when agreed import quotas had been reached; (ii) certain non-ferrous alloys and metals of which agreed import quotas would be subject to a progressive reduction of Community duties from 40 per cent on July 1, 1980, to 100 per cent on Jan. 1, 1984; and (iii) textile products on which quotas had been agreed under the international Multifibre Arrangement. In the agricultural sector Yugoslavia was granted tariff concessions on a range of special products.

Under this agreement Yugoslavia would continue to benefit from the Community's generalized system of preferences for developing countries and would in turn accord the Community most-favoured-nation status (subject to any measures deemed necessary for Yugoslavia's industrial and economic development). Among the provisions for co-operation was one designed to enable Yugoslav workers in the Community to enjoy the same conditions of work and social security benefits as Community countries' nationals. A joint co-operation council was to be established, and over a five-year period loans totalling 200,000,000 EUA would be available to Yugoslavia from the EIB.

Spain. A trade agreement with Spain, signed on June 29, 1970, and in force from Oct. 1, 1970, envisaged preferential arrangements which would within a reasonable time lead to a customs union. The agreement covered about 95 per cent of the EEC's industrial imports from Spain subject to tariffs, and 62 per cent of agricultural imports, as well as about 61 per cent of Spanish imports from the EEC. For most industrial goods from Spain the tariff reductions would be 30 per cent initially; 50 per cent from Jan. 1, 1972; 60 per cent from Jan. 1, 1973; and 70 per cent from Jan. 1, 1974. (This agreement was extended in full to the United Kingdom on Jan. 1, 1978.)

Argentina. The first trade agreement of the EEC with a Latin American country was that with Argentina, signed in Brussels on Nov. 8, 1971, for a three-year period from Jan. 1, 1972.

This non-preferential agreement, providing for mutual most-favoured-nation treatment, afforded Argentina tariff advantages for frozen beef exports to the EEC; it also provided for duty-free imports of Argentine industrial and processed farm goods within the EEC's "generalized preferences" scheme for developing nations, which came into effect from July 1, 1971 [see above]. The agreement was implemented by a joint commission set up between Argentina and the EEC and charged with examining possible further tariff concessions.

This agreement was repeatedly renewed, most recently with effect from Dec. 31, 1978, but was allowed to lapse by the Argentinian Government at the end of 1980.

Uruguay. A three-year non-preferential trade agreement with Uruguay was signed in Luxembourg on April 25, 1973. It provided for an effective increase of Uruguayan beef and veal imports by up to 30 per cent and a suspension, as far as possible, of import levies in Uruguayan refrigerated beef products. This agreement, in force since Aug. 1, 1974, is automatically extended from year to year unless denounced by either party three months before the expiry date.

Brazil. A trade agreement with Brazil, signed on Dec. 19, 1973, and in force from Aug. 1, 1974, provided for (i) increased EEC imports of Brazilian beef and veal; (ii) facilitation of Brazilian exports to the EEC of cocoa butter and soluble coffee; (iii) agricultural and commercial co-operation; (iv) the easing of shipment conditions

for EEC exports to Brazil; and (v) the creation of a joint committee for the development of economic co-operation.

This agreement was replaced by a five-year non-preferential trade and economic co-operation agreement between the EEC and Brazil, signed on Sept. 18, 1980, and providing for the development and diversification of exchanges between the two sides, the intensification of industrial relations between them and an increase in EEC investment in Brazil.

Mexico. A five-year non-preferential commercial co-operation agreement between the EEC and Mexico, renewable by tacit approval, was signed in Brussels on July 15, 1975. It provided inter alia for the mutual granting of most-favoured-nation status and for the establishment of a joint committee to supervise the functioning of the agreement and to improve it.

India. A trade agreement with India (the first between the EEC and a Commonwealth member state and an Asian developing country), signed in Brussels on Dec. 17, 1973, covering a five-year period from April 1, 1974 and renewable by tacit consent, provided for (i) the mutual granting of most-favoured-nation status; (ii) consolidation of certain tariff suspensions operated by the EEC on Indian goods; (iii) possible amendments to the system of generalized preferences as it affected India; and (iv) the creation of a joint commission for economic and commercial co-operation. Commodity agreements in operation are one for handicraft products (from Jan. 1, 1973), and one for cane sugar (for five years from July 18, 1975).

Sri Lanka, Pakistan and Bangladesh. Comprehensive five-year commercial co-operation agreements were signed between the EEC and (i) Sri Lanka on July 22, 1975, effective Dec. 1, 1975; (ii) Pakistan on June 1, 1976, effective July 1, 1976; and (iii) Bangladesh on Oct. 19, 1976, effective Dec. 1, 1976.

These agreements were closely modelled on that between the EEC and India. In a Declaration of Intent annexed to the British Treaty of Accession to the European Communities it had been stated that a solution would be sought to the problems arising for Asian Commonwealth countries from Britain's entry into the EEC, and limited commodity agreements had been operated by the EEC with the above three countries since 1973-74, especially for textiles and jute.

Canada. A framework agreement for non-preferential commercial and economic co-operation between the European Communities and Canada was signed in Ottawa on July 6, 1976, and it came into force on Oct. 1 of that year for an indefinite period (although either side was empowered to terminate it after five years, subject to one year's notice). In this agreement the two sides confirmed their wish to accord each other most-favoured-nation treatment on an equal and reciprocal basis, and they agreed that economic co-operation should be promoted inter alia by joint ventures and increased two-way investment; that there should be joint co-operation by the private sectors in third countries; and that a joint co-operation committee should be set up and meet at least once a year.

China. A five-year preferential trade agreement, which was signed on April 3, 1978, and came into force on June 1 of that year, provided for most-favoured-nation treatment between China and the EEC, for trading at "market-related prices" and for the establishment of a joint committee to ensure the satisfactory working of the agreement. A reduction of EEC tariffs on 20 items was approved by the Council of Ministers on Sept. 19, 1978. A preliminary agreement of July 17, 1979, effectively allowed China to double its textile exports to the EEC from 21,000 to 41,000 tonnes a year.

Association of South East Asian Nations (ASEAN). A framework non-preferential five-year agreement on co-operation between the EEC and the five member states of the ASEAN (Indonesia, Malaysia, the Philippines, Singapore and Thailand), signed in Kuala Lumpur on March 7, 1980, provided for (i) the mutual granting of most-favoured-nation status; (ii) commercial co-operation involving the removal of trade barriers, improved access to each other's markets and promotion and consultation in trade matters; (iii) economic co-operation in all fields deemed suitable by the two parties in order to create closer industrial and technological links between private enterprises; (iv) development co-operation; and (v) the establishment of a joint co-operation committee.

Romania. Between the EEC and Romania a five-year non-preferential trade agreement and an agreement of unlimited duration for the establishment of a joint committee were signed on July 28, 1980, and entered into force on Jan. 1, 1981. The industrial trade agreement—the first to be concluded between the EEC and a full member of the CMEA—covered about two-thirds of current exchanges between the two sides.

EFTA Member Countries. A special relations agreement signed on May 14, 1973,

provided for both the EEC and Norway to establish all tariffs on industrial goods in five successive reductions of 20 per cent each between July 1, 1973, and July 1, 1977, and for concessions to Norway in respect of fish, a number of sensitive products and semi-manufactured agricultural products. A separate agreement signed at the same time provided for free trade for ECSC products by July 1, 1977.

A special relations agreement between Finland (an associate member of EFTA) on the one hand and the EEC and the ECSC on the other, signed on Oct. 5, 1973, was ratified by the Finnish Diet on Nov. 16, 1973, and entered into force on Jan. 1, 1974. It provided for free trade in industrial goods within four years, with a longer transition period for certain sensitive products.

Under trade agreements concluded by the EEC with Austria, Iceland, Portugal, Sweden and Switzerland duty-free trade in most industrial goods was also reached by July 1, 1977.

Relations with the CMEA

Until 1972 the Soviet Union, as the principal partner in the Council for Mutual Economic Assistance (CMEA, or Comecon) evinced hostility to the European Communities, but on March 20 of that year Leonid Brezhnev (the General Secretary of the Communist Party of the Soviet Union) recognized the Communities' existence and stated that Soviet relations with their member states would depend on the extent to which they recognized "the realities obtaining in the socialist part of Europe" and particularly the interests of the member countries of the CMEA.

Several CMEA member countries had earlier concluded limited technical agreements with the Communities, mainly concerning their agricultural exports (thus Poland in 1965 and Bulgaria, Hungary and Romania in 1969). In 1973 EEC member countries accounted for 25 per cent of the CMEA's external trade (although the Communities' trade with the CMEA countries was only 4 per cent of its total).

Protracted negotiations begun in February 1975 on the drafting of a framework agreement on co-operation between the EEC and the CMEA were broken off by the EEC at the end of March 1980 because no agreement was in sight on certain points considered fundamental by the EEC.

Whereas the CMEA desired a global agreement to cover also economic and trade co-operation, the EEC insisted that it should be free to negotiate trade agreements with individual CMEA member countries because, in the opinion of the EEC, the CMEA had no organizational powers comparable to those held by the EEC over its members. The EEC had accepted (in

November 1979) that such individual agreements should include most-favoured-nation treatment. The CMEA, however, had asked for the collective application of this treatment to the CMEA as a whole and had proposed the creation of a joint commission which would supervise economic and trade relations between the two sides and their members—but this proposal was not accepted by the EEC.

European Free Trade Association (EFTA)

Headquarters: Geneva.

Members: Austria, Iceland, Norway, Portugal, Sweden, Switzerland.

Associate Member: Finland.

The European Free Trade Association (EFTA)—an organization comprising Austria, Iceland, Norway, Portugal, Sweden and Switzerland, and until Dec. 31, 1972, Britain and Denmark—formally came into being on May 3, 1960, following the ratification of the Treaty of Stockholm (signed between Dec. 29, 1959, and Jan. 4, 1960). This treaty established the Association and laid down its aims, functions, procedure and organization.

History

The first definite moves toward the creation of a European free trade area, comprising the then six EEC member countries and the 11 other members of the OEEC (Organization for European Economic Co-operation, see page 156), were made at ministerial meetings of the OEEC on Feb. 13, March 8, and Oct. 17, 1957. At the last-mentioned meeting a resolution was unanimously passed expressing the Council's "determination to secure the establishment of a European free trade area which would comprise all member countries of the Organization (i.e. the OEEC); which would associate, on a multilateral basis, the European Economic Community with the other member countries; and which, taking fully into consideration the objectives of the European Economic Community, would in practice take effect parallel with the Treaty of Rome."

Discussions were continued throughout the next year, but little progress was made because of the French Government's opposition to some aspects of the free trade area as proposed in a working paper then being considered. A complete breakdown in negotiations finally took place at a session of the Inter-Governmental Committee of the OEEC on Nov. 13-14, 1958, when the French Minister of Information stated that the French Cabinet saw no possibility of establishing a free trade area on the lines proposed, since there were no provisions for a common external tariff nor for harmonization of social and economic systems.

With the imminent threat of an economic rift between the EEC members of the OEEC and the 11 other member countries, a conference of senior trade officials of the so-called "Outer Seven" countries (Austria, Britain, Denmark, Norway, Portugal, Sweden and Switzerland) was held on Dec. 1-2, 1958, at Geneva.

A statement was issued after the meeting by the chairman of the conference, Dr. Schaffner (of the Swiss Ministry of Economics), which (i) expressed the identity of views of the Governments represented on both the short-term and long-term objectives of the free trade area negotiations with the six EEC countries; and (ii) reaffirmed their intention to pursue their efforts to find a satisfactory formula of multilateral association between the Six and the other members of the OEEC.

A further meeting of experts of the "Outer Seven" countries was held on March 17-18, 1959, at Saltsjøbaden, Sweden. The delegates decided that the Hallstein Report—a memorandum of the EEC Commission on possible measures to overcome the crisis between the two economic groups in Europe —did not constitute a satisfactory basis for negotiations with the European Community countries. It was decided that investigations into the possibilities of stimulating trade between the "Outer Seven" countries, by the gradual removal of tariffs and quantitative import restrictions, should be opened.

These investigations led to a meeting of experts of the "Outer Seven" countries to draw up a plan for a "trading association". The draft plan was examined by ministers at a meeting in Stockholm on July 20-21, 1959, and it was finally announced that the ministers would recommend to their governments "that a European Free Trade Association among the seven countries should be established".

The EFTA Convention

The *Convention of the European Free Trade Association* was drafted between Oct. 8 and Nov. 5, 1959, and initialled at a ministerial meeting in Stockholm on Nov. 20, 1959. On Dec. 12, 1959, the seven EFTA states decided on the establishment of a permanent Secretariat which, it was subsequently announced, would have its headquarters in Geneva.

Art. 2 of the Convention of the European Free Trade Association described the Association's objectives as (a) "to promote within the area of the association and within each member state a sustained expansion of economic activity, full employment, increased productivity and the rational use of resources, financial stability, and a continuous improvement in living standards"; (b) to secure that trade between member states took place in conditions of fair competition; (c) to avoid significant disparity in the supply of raw materials; and (d) to contribute to the harmonious development and expansion of world trade.

Art. 3 laid down that as from the dates shown below no member state might apply an import duty on any product at a level exceeding the percentage of the basic duty as applied by that country on Jan. 1, 1961 —or March 1, 1960, in the case of Denmark —as follows:

	Percentage of basic duty
July 1, 1960	80 per cent
Jan. 1, 1962	70 per cent
July 1, 1963	60 per cent
Jan. 1, 1965	50 per cent
Jan. 1, 1966	40 per cent
Jan. 1, 1967	30 per cent
Jan. 1, 1968	20 per cent
Jan. 1, 1969	10 per cent

All import duties were to be eliminated by Jan. 1, 1970.

Each member state declared its willingness to apply import duties at lower levels if it considered that its economic and financial position and the position of the sector concerned so permitted.

The actual rate of tariff reduction is shown in the following table:

	Percentage of basic duty
Jan. 1, 1960	80 per cent
Jan. 1, 1961	70 per cent
March 1-Sept. 1, 1962..	60 per cent
Oct. 31-Dec. 31,1962	50 per cent
Dec. 31, 1963	40 per cent
Jan. 1, 1965	30 per cent
Dec. 31, 1965	20 per cent
Jan. 1, 1967	0 per cent

The first decision to accelerate tariff reductions was made at a meeting of the Ministerial Council in Geneva on Feb. 14-16, 1961. At the Council's meeting in Lisbon on May 9-11, 1963, it was decided that the tariff reduction should be complete by Dec. 31, 1966. Almost all remaining tariffs and quotas on trade in industrial goods between the seven EFTA countries were in fact abolished with effect from Dec. 31, 1966, with only a few exceptions under special arrangements.

Art. 4. Goods would qualify for area tariff treatment if (a) they had been wholly produced within the area of the associa-

tion, or (b) they had been produced by certain processes within the area of the association (the "process rule"), or (c) not more than 50 per cent of their value consisted of non-area materials (the "percentage rule"). Provision was made for certain materials of which there were large imports from outside the area (i.e. basic materials) to be treated as if they had originated from within the area.

The main provisions of the remainder of the convention are summarized below:

Safeguards. Member countries will be free to take action which they consider necessary for the protection of their essential security interests and, consistently with their other international obligations, their balance of payments. In certain circumstances a member state may also take special safeguarding action where the application of the convention leads to serious difficulties in a particular sector of industry.

Competition. The convention contains provisions to ensure that the benefits which are expected from the removal of tariffs and quotas are not nullified through the use of other measures by governments, public undertakings or private industries. These include provisions about subsidies, restrictive business practices and discriminatory restrictions against nationals of member states wishing to establish businesses anywhere in the area.

Agriculture and Fish. Special arrangements have been made for agricultural goods and fish and other marine products. The objective is to facilitate reasonable reciprocity to those member states whose economies depend to a great extent on agricultural or fish exports. Arrangements have also been concluded between several member countries in respect of trade in agricultural goods.

The Council. The convention establishes a Council charged with the general oversight of the application of the convention and with the task of considering what further action should be taken to promote the objectives of the Association and to facilitate close association with other countries or groups of countries. The Council is empowered to establish relationships with other international organizations. Each member state has one vote on the Council. Decisions and recommendations are to be made by unanimous vote where new obligations are involved. On a wide range of issues, and particularly in dealing with any complaints which may be made by member states, decisions will be by majority vote.

Consultation and Complaints. The procedure for consultation and complaints is an important part of the convention, and a member country may refer to the Council any case in which it considers that a benefit conferred upon it by the convention or an objective of the Association is being or may be frustrated. Member states intend to pursue economic and financial policies in a manner which will promote the objectives of the Association, and to exchange views about them from time to time.

Extension. The Council is empowered to make arrangements for the accession of other countries, and member states may propose the extension of the convention to cover non-European territories for which they are responsible.

After the Danish Government had proposed, in December 1967, that the convention should be made applicable to the Faroe Islands, this territory was included in the EFTA area as from Jan. 1, 1968.

Annex on Portugal. Special arrangements concerning Portugal were contained in Annex G of the Convention. By these arrangements Portugal was permitted to apply a slower rate of import duty reduction than other EFTA members. The planned reduction of the percentage of the basic duty was to 50 per cent by 1970. An accelerated rate of duty reduction was provided for in the case of exporting industries.

Organs of EFTA

In addition to the Council, which consists of delegations led by ministers and which normally meets twice a year, there are standing committees for customs, trade, the budget, economic development and economic problems. There are also (i) a consultative committee consisting of employers' representatives, trade union leaders and other individuals and (ii) a committee of members of parliament of the EFTA member countries. EFTA's secretariat is headed by a Secretary-General assisted by a Deputy Secretary-General.

Agreements and Activities

Industrial Development Fund. The Council of EFTA approved, on April 7, 1976, the statutes of a $100,000,000 Industrial Development Fund (based in Geneva) to help develop Portuguese industry over a five-year period (with Sweden and Switzerland contributing 30 and 25 per cent respectively).

Finnish Association with EFTA. Under an agreement signed in Helsinki on March 27, 1961, Finland became associated with EFTA. The agreement, which entered into force on June 26, 1961, contained special provisions in favour of Finland in order to prevent conflict with the provisions of her existing trade treaty with the Soviet Union. A Finland-EFTA Joint Council was subsequently established with powers to take unanimous decisions on a wide range of issues, including tariffs.

Yugoslav Observers. It was announced on Dec. 11, 1967, that it had been agreed that Yugoslavia could send observers to EFTA technical meetings, including those on double taxation, patents, and probably customs.

On June 20, 1978, it was decided to replace an existing working group established between EFTA and Yugoslavia by a full joint committee to promote intensified economic co-operation between the two sides.

Iceland's Accession. Iceland became a full member of EFTA, and also a party to the Finland-EFTA agreement, on March 1, 1970.

Iceland's protective import duties on EFTA industrial products were reduced immediately by 30 per cent, with seven further annual reductions by 10 per cent to follow from Jan. 1, 1974, so that all such tariffs would be abolished by Jan. 1, 1980.

Special Relations Agreements. Following the withdrawal of Britain and Denmark from EFTA on Jan. 31, 1972, Special Relations Agreements entered into force between four of the seven remaining members or associates of EFTA—Austria, Portugal, Sweden and Switzerland—on the one hand and the EEC on the other, thus inaugurating a programme of tariff reductions and other measures which would lead to a free trade area embracing the 13 countries involved.

The agreements, concluded in Brussels on July 22, 1972, provided for the gradual achievement of free trade in industrial goods between the six original members of the EEC and Ireland on the one hand and each of the six EFTA countries which had not applied for full EEC membership on the other, while at the same time preserving the existing free trade among all countries which were members of EFTA at the time of signature of the agreements, including Britain, Norway and Denmark. The agreements differed fundamentally from the terms reached for full membership with the other three EFTA countries and Ireland in that the six countries would have no power of decision in Community affairs, and they would not take part in any institutions except in a joint executive committee which would meet twice a year to manage the free trade arrangements.

The free trade area was further extended when (i) the Finnish Government had signed the terms of a Special Relations Agreement initialled in July 1972 but not formally signed by the end of that year; (ii) a similar agreement had been negotiated by Norway with the Communities, following the Norwegian decision not to become a full member [see page 131]; and (iii) the Icelandic Parliament had approved the agreement signed in July 1972 with the Communities.

Vienna Declaration. At a meeting held in Vienna on May 13, 1977, the Council adopted a declaration in which it was stated inter alia: "The EFTA governments recognize that their economies react with particular sensitivity to problems in the world economy. The share of external trade in their economies is considerable; while representing only 1 per cent of world population the EFTA countries together account for 7 per cent of total world trade." The declaration welcomed the achievement, on July 1, 1977, of a free trade system for industrial products between the 16 countries of EFTA and the European Communities, constituting a market of 300,000,000 people; it stressed, however, that it was "important to ensure that the advantages deriving from free trade are not jeopardized as a result of diverging economic developments and policies" and that it was desirable to "develop the existing co-operation within EFTA and . . . between EFTA countries and the European Communities".

EFTA and Spain. A multilateral free trade agreement between Spain and the seven EFTA member states (including Finland, an associated member) was initialled in Geneva on Dec. 7, 1978, and signed on June 26, 1979. It provided mainly for the application of the same rules for industrial trade as existed between Spain and the European Communities, and also for any future concessions on industrial products made by Spain to the European Communities to apply similarly to EFTA member countries.

Bilateral agreements with Spain were reached at the same time by Austria, Finland, Norway, Sweden and Switzerland to facilitate trade in agricultural products.

All these agreements came into force on May 1, 1980.

European Co-operation in Other Spheres

Bank for International Settlements (BIS)

Headquarters: Basle (Switzerland).

The BIS was established in 1930 with the object of promoting co-operation among European central banks, providing additional facilities for international financial operations and acting as trustees or agents in connexion with international financial settlements entrusted to it.

The BIS has a Board of Directors composed of the governors or presidents of the central banks of Belgium, France, the Federal Republic of Germany, Italy, the Netherlands, Sweden, Switzerland and the United Kingdom and five other members nominated by some of these governors.

Intergovernmental Committee for European Migration (ICEM)

Headquarters: Geneva.

Members: Argentina, Austria, Belgium, Bolivia, Brazil, Chile, Colombia, Costa Rica, Cyprus, Denmark, the Dominican Republic, Ecuador, El Salvador, the Federal Republic of Germany, Greece, Honduras, Israel, Italy, Luxembourg, Malta, the Netherlands, Nicaragua, Norway, Panama, Paraguay, Peru, Portugal, South Africa, Spain, Switzerland, the United States, Uruguay and Venezuela.

The ICEM was established as a Provisional Intergovernmental Committee for the Movement of Migrants from Europe by representatives of 16 governments attending an international migration conference in Brussels in 1951. The ICEM adopted its present name on Nov. 15, 1952. Its objects have been to effect the movement of refugees to countries offering final settlement

and also to promote social and economic advancement of Latin American countries through selective migration. Between 1952 and 1978 it moved over 2,000,000 migrants overseas. It has a Council, which determines policy, and an Executive Committee assisted by sub-committees on the budget and finance and on co-ordination of transport.

European Conference of Ministers of Transport (ECMT)

Headquarters: Paris.

Members: Austria, Belgium, Denmark, Finland, France, the Federal Republic of Germany, Greece, Ireland, Italy, Luxembourg, the Netherlands, Norway, Portugal, Spain, Sweden, Switzerland, Turkey, the United Kingdom and Yugoslavia.

Associate Members: Australia, Canada, Japan and the USA.

The ECMT was set up at a conference of Transport Ministers from a number of European countries, held in Brussels between Oct. 12 and 17, 1953. The aim of the organization is to achieve the best use and most economical development of the means of transport for inter-European communications. It has adopted a general transport policy, based on common principles, in the fields of railways, roads, inland waterways, forecasting of transport demand, co-operation between surface and air transport, and research in transport economics.

Organs. The organs of the ECMT are:

(1) A Council of Ministers, composed of the Ministers of Transport of the member countries, meeting twice a year.

(2) A Committee of Deputies, composed of officials of the member countries acting as the ministers' depu-

ties. The committee, which meets six times a year, prepares—with the assistance of a number of specialized subsidiary bodies—the material to be discussed at meetings of the Council of Ministers.

(3) A Secretariat, which is responsible for the everyday administration of the Conference.

Although it is an autonomous institution, the ECMT works in close co-operation with other international organizations, in particular with the OECD, the Council of Europe and the United Nations Economic Commission for Europe (ECE).

Establishment of EUROFIMA. At a conference held on Oct. 18-20 the ECMT established a company (EUROFIMA) for the financing of railway rolling stock with the participation of the national railway administrations of Austria, Belgium, Denmark, France, the Federal Republic of Germany, Greece, Italy, Luxembourg, the Netherlands, Norway, Portugal, Spain, Sweden, Switzerland, Turkey and Yugoslavia.

European Organization for Nuclear Research (CERN)

Headquarters: Geneva.

Members: Austria, Belgium, Denmark, France, the Federal Republic of Germany, Greece, Italy, the Netherlands, Norway, Sweden, Switzerland and the United Kingdom.

Observers: Poland, Turkey and Yugoslavia.

History. On May 8, 1952, a European Council for Nuclear Research was set up under the auspices of UNESCO, as a result of an agreement signed by Denmark, France, West Germany, Greece, Italy, the Netherlands, Sweden, Switzerland and Yugoslavia on Feb. 15, 1952. Norway and Belgium later adhered to the agreement.

At a meeting on June 21, 1952, the Council decided to build a nuclear research institute which would house two of the world's largest particle accelerators—a proton-cyclotron and a synchro-cyclotron. The project would be a co-operative venture. On Oct. 6, 1962, the Council decided that the European Nuclear Research Laboratory should be sited at Geneva.

The preparation of a convention transforming the European Council for Nuclear Research into a full international organization took place at meetings of the Council in January, March and June 1953. The Convention of the European Organization for Nuclear Research (Conseil Européen pour la Recherche Nucléaire, or CERN) was signed in Paris on July 1, 1953, by representatives of Belgium, Britain, Denmark, France, the Federal Republic of Germany,

Greece, Italy, the Netherlands, Norway, Sweden, Switzerland and Yugoslavia. It entered into force on Sept. 29, 1954.

The Convention. The functions of the organization are defined in the basic programme outlined in the convention.

These are "the construction and operation of an international laboratory for research on high energy particles, including work in the field of cosmic rays" and "organizing and sponsoring international co-operation in nuclear research, including co-operation outside the laboratory". Specifically, mention is made of co-operative work in nuclear physics and cosmic rays, the promotion of contacts between and interchange of scientists, the dissemination of information, the provision of advanced training for research workers, and collaboration with national research institutes. The work is carried out on a purely theoretical basis and solely for non-military purposes, and its results are published for general distribution.

Provision is made for the entry into the organization of other states by the unanimous vote of the existing member states.

The funds to finance the organization are provided by the member states on a relative scale based on their average net national incomes.

The Organs. The governing body of CERN is the Council, on which each member state is represented by two delegates. The Council meets at least once a year to determine policy, approve plans and adopt the budget. The Council is assisted by a Scientific Policy Committee, a Finance Committee and a European Committee for Future Accelerators.

Developments. The construction programme undertaken by CERN was completed in 1961, the foundation-stone for the laboratory at Meyrin near Geneva having been laid on June 10, 1955. The installations include a 600 million electron volt synchro-cyclotron, which entered into operation on Aug. 17, 1957, and a 30,000 million electron volt proton-synchrotron, brought into operation in November 1959. These two machines form the basis of CERN's experimental research programme, which is primarily concerned with high-energy particles. The experiments are conducted by mixed teams of scientists from the member countries of the organization.

The organization's Council decided on Feb. 19, 1971, that a 300,000 million electron volt particle accelerator (proton-synchrotron) for high-energy nuclear physics should be built on a site adjacent to CERN's existing installations at Meyrin.

Under an agreement of October 1965 the area of the CERN laboratory was extended across the Swiss border into France.

On June 16, 1960, it was announced that an agreement had been made with the USSR for the exchange of scientists from CERN with scientists from the Nuclear Research Centre at Dubna near Moscow.

In 1963 Yugoslavia withdrew from membership of CERN, but remained associated with the organization as an observer. Poland and Turkey also became observers in 1963. Spain withdrew from membership on Dec. 31, 1968.

By 1979 the major experimental facilities of CERN were a synchro-cyclotron (of 600 MeV), a proton-synchrotron (of 25-28 GeV), intersecting storage rings (ISR) and a super proton-synchrotron (of 400 GeV).

CERN has a special arrangement for collaboration with the USSR State Committee for the Utilization of Atomic Energy at Serpukhov (south of Moscow).

European Organization for the Safety of Air Navigation (EUROCONTROL)

Headquarters: Brussels.

Members: Belgium, France, the Federal Republic of Germany, Ireland, Luxembourg, the Netherlands and the United Kingdom.

The Aviation Ministers of the then six member countries of the European Economic Community approved, at a meeting in Rome on June 9-10, 1960, a draft convention and protocol for a unified air traffic control system for Western Europe. The convention was signed in Brussels on Dec. 13, 1960, by the above six countries and the United Kingdom, and EUROCONTROL was established in 1963.

It is headed by a permanent commission consisting of the ministers responsible for civil and military aviation in each of the member states, and its budget makes provision, inter alia, for the joint financing of the operating costs of traffic control services for the upper airspace of the Benelux countries and the Federal Republic of Germany.

Group for Co-operation in Scientific and Technical Research

A Group for European Co-operation in the Field of Scientific and Technical Research (COST Group) formed by 19 European countries held a conference in Brussels on Nov. 22-23, 1971, when co-operation agreements were concluded between various groups of countries.

These agreements covered (i) the creation of a European data processing network; (ii) a research programme on telecommunications aerials; (iii) joint action on material for gas turbines and sea-water desalination plants with respect to metallurgical research; (iv) three programmes on technical aspects of air, water and waste pollution; and (v) agreement in principle on a European computer programme information centre and on a European centre for medium-term weather forecasting.

The last-named centre was established under a convention signed on Oct. 23, 1973, by its members—Austria, Belgium, Denmark, Finland, France, the Federal Republic of Germany, Greece, Italy, the Netherlands, Portugal, Spain, Sweden, Switzerland and Yugoslavia.

Co-operation among Balkan States

A meeting on co-operation among Balkan states, held in Athens on Jan. 26-Feb. 5, 1976, was attended by representatives of the Governments of Bulgaria, Greece, Romania, Turkey and Yugoslavia (at the Greek Prime Minister's invitation, which was declined by Albania).

In a joint communiqué issued on Feb. 5 the participants emphasized their spirit of good-neighbourliness, co-operation and mutual understanding and listed proposals for co-operation to be submitted to their respective governments—on the understanding that all proposals would have to be approved unanimously before being adopted at a further conference, and that multinational co-operation would in no way affect any intended bilateral co-operation among Balkan states. (In July 1975 Bulgaria had given Greece a formal assurance on the inviolability of the Greek-Bulgarian frontier in the event of an armed conflict between Greece and Turkey.)

Alps-Adria Regional Economic Grouping

Under a protocol signed in Venice on Nov. 20, 1978, by representatives of nine border regions of Austria, the Federal Republic of Germany, Italy and Yugoslavia, an Alps-Adria Regional Economic Grouping was formed with the object of increasing regional trade and scientific co-operation and promoting integration of various economic sectors. The regions involved were Veneto and Friuli-Venezia Giulia (in Italy), Carinthia, Styria and Upper Austria (in Austria), Croatia and Slovenia (in Yugoslavia) and also, as observers, Salzburg (in Austria) and Bavaria (in the Federal Republic of Germany).

Major Bilateral Treaties and Agreements in Western Europe

Belgium and Federal Republic of Germany. A treaty dealing with the ratification of the two countries' common border and other questions concerning mutual relations was signed on Sept. 24, 1956, and came into force on Aug. 28, 1958, and the border was demarcated under a protocol of Sept. 6, 1960.

An agreement on mutual secrecy in regard to defence-related inventions and technical knowledge was signed on Feb. 1, 1963, and came into force on March 1 of that year.

Belgium and the Netherlands. A treaty on the formation of a Netherlands language union was signed in Brussels on Sept. 9, 1980, by the Governments of Belgium and of the Netherlands.

The union was to achieve integration between the Netherlands and the Netherlands-speaking community in Belgium in the field of the Netherlands language (in Belgium also referred to as Flemish) and literature and to provide a legal framework for establishing uniformity in the use of the language. The union's policy was to be formulated and implemented by a ministerial committee consisting of at least two Belgian and two Netherlands ministers with responsibility for education and culture. This committee would seek the advice of a Council of the Netherlands Language and Literature composed of 45 experts from the Netherlands and the Netherlands-speaking community in Belgium. The treaty also provided for the establishment of an interparliamentary commission which would deliberate on all matters concerning the union and would advise the ministerial committee. The preparation and implementation of the union's policy would be carried out by a general secretariat.

The treaty was subject to ratification by the Netherlands Parliament and the Netherlands-language Cultural Council in Belgium.

Denmark and Federal Republic of Germany. A treaty on the delimitation of the North Sea continental shelf near the coast was signed on June 9, 1965, and came into force on May 27, 1966. A further treaty on the delimitation of the continental shelf below the North Sea was signed on Jan. 28, 1971, and came into force on Dec. 7, 1972.

Denmark and Switzerland. A treaty of friendship, establishment and commerce was signed on Feb. 10, 1875.

Finland and Federal Republic of Germany. A joint declaration on the normalization of relations between the two countries, signed in Bonn on Sept. 19, 1974, covered the mutual renunciation of the use of force and a West German agreement to respect Finland's policy of neutrality, and it also settled part of financial and legal questions outstanding since the end of World War II (Finland having requested compensation for damage caused by German troops in 1944-45).

France and Federal Republic of Germany. An agreement on mutual secrecy in the treatment of defence-related inventions and technical experience was signed and came into force on Sept. 28, 1961.

A treaty of co-operation signed on Jan. 22, 1963, providing for the co-ordination of the policies of the two countries in foreign affairs, defence, information and cultural affairs, entered into force on July 2, 1963.

The principal provisions are summarized below.

There would be regular meetings of the heads of state, Foreign and Defence Ministers, and Chiefs of Staff of the two countries. An inter-ministerial commission would be set up in each country to supervise questions of co-operation. Under the programme of co-operation set forth in the treaty, the two governments undertook to "consult each other before taking any decision on all major questions of foreign policy".

In the sphere of defence the treaty provided for the setting up of Franco-German operational research institutes, for the exchange of personnel between the two armed forces, and for the organization of joint activities in the field of armaments.

The cultural programme outlined in the treaty included: The extension of reciprocal language-teaching; the adoption of arrangements for equivalent values of periods of education, examinations, degrees and diplomas; and an increase in co-operation in scientific research.

Except for the clauses concerning defence, the treaty also applies to West Berlin.

An agreement signed on Feb. 2, 1971, empowered West German legal authorities to bring to trial alleged Nazi war criminals already convicted in absentia by French courts, this agreement being finally ratified by the German Federal Parliament on Feb. 21, 1975.

An agreement signed in Bonn on May 18, 1976, by the French Atomic Energy Commission and two West German companies provided for co-operation in the development, production and sale of fast-breeder nuclear reactors.

France and Spain. A five-year military co-operation agreement was signed in Madrid on June 22, 1970, and was automatically renewable for two years unless six months' notice was given by either side. It provided for close co-operation in defence and armaments, involving joint defence exercises, exchanges of personnel and units, and collaboration in respect of equipment, "including missiles, munitions and spare parts".

Two agreements on the delimitation of the continental shelf and territorial waters in the Bay of Biscay, signed on Jan. 29, 1974, provided inter alia for the designation of a special zone, about 50 kilometres square (some 200 kilometres off the north coast of Spain), where the two countries would co-operate in the exploitation of hydrocarbon reserves.

France and Switzerland. A co-operation agreement on the use of atomic energy for peaceful purposes was signed on May 14, 1970.

Greece and Federal Republic of Germany. An agreement on economic co-operation was signed on Nov. 27, 1958, and an agreement on scientific and technical co-operation on Nov. 30, 1958, when it also came into force.

Greece and Italy. An agreement on the delimitation of the two countries' common border on the continental shelf was signed in Athens on May 24, 1977. This agreement laid down that the border was to be based on the median line between the two countries' coasts, with the proviso that in the area of the Ionian Islands equidistance was to be measured from the western end of the shelf of these islands. (Italy had not signed the 1958 Convention on the Continental Shelf—see page 48.)

Italy and Federal Republic of Germany. A treaty of friendship, commerce and navigation of Nov. 21, 1957, came into force on Nov. 19, 1961.

An agreement on mutual secrecy in the treatment of defence-related inventions and technical experience, signed on Jan. 27, 1960, came into force on March 28, 1972.

Malta and Italy. Under an agreement initialled on Sept. 15, 1980, (i) the Government of Malta formally declared its neutrality and undertook not to allow foreign forces or military bases on its territory and to make its shipbuilding yards available neither to the US nor to the Soviet Navy; (ii) Italy called on all countries to respect Malta's neutrality and undertook to enter into immediate consultations in the event of this neutrality being threatened or violated, and to afford Malta military assistance if this was considered necessary "by the Italian side also"; and (iii) Italy pro-

mised to provide Malta, during the first few years of its neutrality, with direct economic aid, credit facilities and technical co-operation.

Netherlands and Federal Republic of Germany. A treaty on the lateral delimitation of the continental shelf near the coast, concluded on Dec. 1, 1964, came into force on Aug. 27, 1965, and a treaty on the delimitation of the continental shelf below the North Sea, signed on Jan. 28, 1971, came into force on Dec. 7, 1972.

Netherlands and Switzerland. A treaty of friendship, establishment and commerce was signed on Aug. 19, 1875.

Spain and Federal Republic of Germany. An agreement on economic co-operation was signed and came into force on May 9, 1961. A framework agreement on co-operation in scientific research and technological development came into force on March 10, 1971. An agreement on co-operation in the field of solar energy and an agreement on co-operation in the peaceful use of nuclear energy, signed on Dec. 5, 1978, came into force on Dec. 13, 1978. An agreement on scientific and technical co-operation in agricultural research was signed and came into force on Oct. 22, 1979.

Spain and Portugal. A 10-year treaty of friendship and co-operation (superseding an Iberian Pact signed on March 17, 1939, by Portugal and Spain and due to expire in 1980) was signed in Madrid on Nov. 22, 1977. It was approved by the Spanish *Cortes* (Parliament) on March 9 and by the Portuguese Legislative Assembly on April 18, 1978, and was ratified on May 5, 1978 (during a visit to Portugal by the King of Spain).

The treaty provided for the establishment of a Hispano-Portuguese council under the chairmanship of the two countries' Foreign Ministers; mutual preferential trade arrangements; co-ordination of economic policies; and the development of border areas. Both countries undertook not to interfere in each other's internal affairs and to extend to each other military and economic co-operation (with the resumption of joint military exercises, which had been suspended since 1974).

Turkey and Switzerland. A treaty of friendship between the two countries was signed on Sept. 19, 1925.

9. Organization for Economic Co-operation and Development (OECD)

This section covers the history, aims, structure and activities of the OECD, together with the autonomous and semi-autonomous bodies related to it, notably the International Energy Agency.

History, Aims, Structure and Activities of OECD

Headquarters: Paris.

Members: Australia, Austria, Belgium, Canada, Denmark, Finland, France, Federal Republic of Germany, Greece, Iceland, Ireland, Italy, Japan, Luxembourg, the Netherlands, New Zealand, Norway, Portugal, Spain, Sweden, Switzerland, Turkey, United Kingdom and United States.

Special Status: Yugoslavia.

The OEEC

The basis of European economic co-operation after World War II was the so-called Marshall Plan, a programme of American economic aid to Europe, first put forward by the US Secretary of State, George C. Marshall, in a speech at Harvard on June 5, 1947. In this speech Marshall called on the European nations themselves to unite in planning their economic rehabilitation and in forming a joint programme of reconstruction.

On July 5, 1947, Britain and France invited 22 European nations to send delegations to a European Economic Conference, where a programme of the resources and needs of Europe would be drawn up. This conference, when it opened on July 12, 1947, was attended by Britain, France and 14 of the countries invited, viz. Austria, Belgium, Denmark, Greece, Iceland, Ireland, Italy, Luxembourg, the Netherlands, Norway, Portugal, Sweden, Switzerland and Turkey. The conference approved the creation of a Committee of Economic Co-operation, on which all 16 nations would be represented, to draw up a report for the US Government on European availabilities and requirements on the basis of information freely supplied by the participating countries.

The report of the Committee of Economic Co-operation, which was signed in Paris on Sept. 22, 1947, contained an outline of the European Recovery Programme, a four-year programme of reconstruction which was to form the basis of the Marshall Plan (1948-51). The report also contained the suggestion that a permanent organization of the 16 nations participating in the European Recovery Programme (ERP) should be set up.

At a further conference of the 16 nations, held in Paris on March 15-16, 1948, a working party was set up to draft a convention for European economic co-operation. Under this convention, signed on April 16, 1948, by representatives of the 16 ERP countries and also by military representatives for the Anglo-American and French zones of Germany, the Organization for European Economic Co-operation (OEEC) was established.

The membership of the OEEC eventually reached 18 with the accession of the Federal Republic of Germany in October 1949, and of Spain in July 1959. In addition the USA and Canada participated in the work of the OEEC as associate members; Yugoslavia took a full part in certain OEEC activities; and Finland sent observers to certain of the organization's committees.

The OECD

A Special Economic Committee, comprising representatives from Belgium, Canada, Denmark, France, the Federal Republic of Germany, Greece, Italy, the Netherlands, Portugal, Sweden, Switzerland, the United Kingdom and the USA, and also from the Commission of the European Economic Community (EEC), met in

Paris on Jan. 12-13, 1960. At this meeting it was decided, inter alia, that a new improved organization for economic co-operation should be formed. As a preliminary measure, a four-man group—the "Group of Four on Economic Organization"—was appointed to study the matter and make recommendations.

The group published its report on April 20, 1960. The report said that economic co-operation between Western Europe and North America since the end of the Second World War, especially through the OEEC, had achieved "extraordinary progress"; that this co-operation should be continued and extended; that the targets envisaged in the Marshall Plan had been reached but that new problems "no less pressing" had arisen; and that the richer nations had a responsibility toward the poorer countries.

The report recommended that an Organization for Economic Co-operation and Development, in which Canada and the USA would participate as full members, should be established with the aim of promoting "within the framework of free political institutions" policies designed (i) to facilitate the attainment of the highest sustainable economic growth, while maintaining financial stability and high levels of employment, and thus to contribute to the development of the world economy and the promotion of world trade on a multilateral and non-discriminatory basis; and (ii) to contribute to sound economic growth in areas in the process of economic development, both in member countries and elsewhere, by appropriate means, including the encouragement of the flow of development capital to those areas.

Map 5 European members of Organization for Economic Co-operation and Development (OECD)

Representatives of the 18 members of the OEEC and of the USA, Canada and the Commission of the EEC met in Paris on May 24-25, 1960, and again on July 22-23, 1960, to discuss a draft convention for the proposed OECD. At the second meeting the broad outlines of the draft convention were agreed upon, and a preparatory committee was then charged with completing the final draft. This meeting also approved the setting up of a trade committee within the OECD, its functions being defined as the confrontation of general trade policies and practices; the examination of specific trade problems affecting members; and the examination of other short-term and long-term trade problems.

OECD CONVENTION

The final draft of the Convention of the Organization for Economic Co-operation and Development was signed on Dec. 14, 1960, by the 18 full members of the OEEC and by Canada and the USA. It entered into force on Sept. 30, 1961.

The preamble and a summary of the principal articles of the convention are given below:

"**Preamble.** Considering that economic strength and prosperity are essential for the attainment of the purposes of the United Nations, the preservation of individual liberty and the increase of general well-being;

"believing that they can further these aims most effectively by strengthening the tradition of co-operation which has evolved among them;

"recognizing that the economic recovery and progress of Europe, to which their participation in the OEEC has made a major contribution, have opened new perspectives for strengthening that tradition and applying it to new tasks and broader objectives;

"convinced that broader co-operation will make a vital contribution to peaceful and harmonious relations among the peoples of the world;

"recognizing the increasing interdependence of their economies;

"determined by consultation and co-operation to use more effectively their capacities and potentialities so as to promote the highest sustainable growth of their economies and improve the economic and social well-being of their peoples;

"believing that the economically more advanced nations should co-operate in assisting to the best of their ability the countries in process of economic development;

"recognizing that the further expansion of world trade is one of the most important factors favouring the economic development of countries and the improvement of international economic relations; and

"determined to pursue these purposes in a manner consistent with their obligations in other international organizations or institutions in which they participate or under agreements to which they are a party;

"the signatories of the convention agree on the following provisions for the reconstitution of the Organization for European Economic Co-operation as the Organization for Economic Co-operation and Development:—

"**Art. 1.** The aims of the OECD shall be to promote policies designed:

"(a) To achieve the highest sustainable economic growth and employment and a rising standard of living in member countries, while maintaining financial stability, and thus to contribute to the development of the world economy;

"(b) to contribute to sound economic expansion in member as well as non-member countries in the process of economic development; and

"(c) to contribute to the expansion of world trade on a multilateral, non-discriminatory basis, in accordance with international obligations.

"**Art. 2.** In pursuit of these aims, the members agree that they will, both individually and jointly,

"(a) promote the efficient use of their economic resources;

"(b) in the scientific and technological field, promote the development of their resources, encourage research, and promote vocational training;

"(c) pursue policies designed to achieve economic growth and internal and external financial stability and to avoid developments which might endanger their economies or those of other countries;

"(d) pursue their efforts to reduce or abolish obstacles to the exchange of goods and services and current payments, and maintain and extend the liberalization of capital movements; and

"(e) contribute to the economic development of both member and non-member countries in the process of economic development by appropriate means and in particular by the flow of capital to those countries, having regard to the importance to their economies of receiving technical assistance and of securing expanding export markets.

"**Art. 3.** The members therefore agreed that they would

"(a) keep each other informed and furnish the Organization with the information necessary for the accomplishment of its tasks;

"(b) consult together on a continuing basis, carry out studies, and participate in agreed projects; and

"(c) co-operate closely, and where appropriate take co-ordinated action. . . ."

Art. 5. In order to achieve its aims, the OECD might:

"(a) take decisions which, except as otherwise provided, shall be binding on all the members;

"(b) make recommendations to members; and

"(c) enter into agreements with members, non-member states and international organizations."

Art. 6. Unless the organization otherwise agrees unanimously for special cases, decisions shall be taken and recommendations shall be made by mutual agreement of all the members.

Each member shall have one vote. If a member abstains from voting on a decision or recommendation, such abstention shall not invalidate the decision or recommendation, which shall be applicable to the other members but not to the abstaining member.

No decision shall be binding on any member until it has complied with the requirements of its own constitutional procedures. The other members may agree that such a decision shall apply provisionally to them.

Arts. 7-9. A council composed of all the members should be set up as the executive body of the organization and might meet in sessions of Ministers or of Permanent Representatives. It would designate each year a Chairman to preside at its ministerial sessions, and two Vice-Chairmen, and might establish an Executive Committee and "such subsidiary bodies as required for the achievement of the aims of the Organization". A Chairman could be re-elected only for two consecutive terms.

Arts. 10-11. A Secretary-General responsible to the Council would be appointed by it for a term of five years, and would be assisted by one or more Deputy or Assistant Secretaries-General appointed by the Council on his recommendation. He would serve as Chairman of the Council meeting at sessions of Permanent Representatives; would assist the Council in all appropriate ways; might submit proposals to the Council or to any other body of the organization; and would appoint the staff required in accordance with organizational plans approved by the Council. Staff regulations would be subject to Council approval.

Having regard to the international character of the organization, the Secretary-General, the Deputy or Assistant Secretaries-General and the staff shall neither seek nor receive instructions from any of the members or from any government or authority external to the organization.

Art. 12. Upon such terms and conditions as the Council may determine, the organization may (*a*) address communications to non-member states or organizations; (*b*) establish and maintain relations with non-member states or organizations; and (*c*) invite non-member governments or organizations to participate in activities of the organization.

Art. 13 and Supplementary Protocol No. 1 provided that representation in the OECD of the European Communities established by the Treaty of Paris of April 18, 1951, and the Treaty of Rome of March 25, 1957, should be determined in accordance with the institutional provisions of those Treaties, and that the Commissions of the EEC and of the European Atomic Energy Community (Euratom), as well as the High Authority of the European Coal and Steel Community, should take part in the work of the OECD.

Art. 15. When this convention comes into force, the reconstitution of the OEEC shall take effect, and its aims, organs, powers and name shall thereupon be as provided herein. The legal personality possessed by the OEEC shall continue in the organization, but decisions, recommendations and resolutions of the OEEC shall require approval of the Council to be effective after the coming into effect of this convention.

Art. 19 and Supplementary Protocol No. 2 set out the legal capacity of the organization and the privileges, exemptions and immunities of the organization, its officials and representatives.

In addition to the two Supplementary Protocols [see above], a protocol was signed dealing with the revision of the Convention for European Economic Co-operation of April 16, 1948.

Under this protocol, the members of the OEEC, "desirous that the aims, organs, and powers of the OEEC be re-defined and that the Governments of Canada and the USA be members of that organization as reconstituted", agreed (*a*) that the convention should be revised and replaced by the Convention on the OECD; (*b*) that the Protocol should come into force together with the Convention on the OECD, and that the Convention for European Economic Co-operation should cease to have effect as regards any signatory of the Protocol when the Convention on the OECD came into force.

Japan became a full member of the OECD on April 28, 1964; Finland on Jan. 28, 1969; Australia on June 7, 1971; and New Zealand on May 29, 1973, bringing the membership to 24.

Yugoslavia has the status of a full member in the following fields of activity: Comparison of economic policies; science and technology; agriculture and fisheries; technical assistance; and productivity. In all other fields it has observer status.

OECD STRUCTURE

The supreme body of the OECD is its Council, composed of one representative for each member country. The Council meets either at permanent representative level (about once a week) under the chairmanship of the Secretary-General, or at ministerial level (usually once a year) under the chairmanship of a minister elected annually. Decisions and recommendations are adopted by mutual agreement of all members of the Council.

The Council is assisted by an Executive Committee composed of 14 members of the Council designated annually by the latter. The major part of the OECD's work is, however, prepared and carried out by numerous specialized committees and working parties, of which there exist more than 200. The principal committees are those for:

Economic Policy
Economic and Development Review
Development Assistance (DAC)
Trade
Invisible Transactions
Financial Markets
Fiscal Affairs
Restrictive Business Practices
Consumer Policy
Tourism
Maritime Transport
International Investment and Multinational
   Enterprises
Energy Policy
Industry
Steel
Scientific and Technological Policy
Education
Manpower and Social Affairs
Environment
Agriculture
Fisheries

There is also a High-Level Group on Commodities.

An International Secretariat, headed by the Secretary-General of the OECD, services the Council, the committees and other bodies. There are two Deputy Secretaries-General, a co-ordinator of energy policies (who is the Executive Director of the International Energy Agency—see below), an economic adviser and two special counsellors to the Secretary-General.

The Secretariat comprises an economics and statistic department and directorates for agriculture; data processing and statistical services; development co-operation; the environment; financial and fiscal affairs; science, technology and industry; social affairs, manpower and education; trade; and the executive; as well as an information service and a technical co-operation service.

OECD ACTIVITIES

Co-operation with Other Organizations. Among intergovernmental organizations, the Commission of the European Communities generally takes part in the work of the OECD (under Supplementary Protocol No. 1 signed at the same time as the OECD Convention); the European Free Trade Association (EFTA) may send representatives to OECD meetings; and most of the UN specialized agencies have official relations with the OECD, as have the European Conference of Ministers of Transport (ECMT), the Organization of American States (OAS), the Intergovernmental Committee for European Migration (ICEM) and the Customs Co-operation Council.

The OECD Council also decided on March 13, 1962, that international non-governmental organizations deemed to be widely representative in general economic matters or in a specific economy sector might be granted consultative status enabling them to discuss subjects of common interest with a liaison committee under the chairmanship of the OECD Secretary-General and to be consulted in a particular field by the relevant OECD committee or its officers.

Financial Support Fund. Under a formal agreement signed in Paris on April 9, 1975, by ministers and representatives of all full member countries of the OECD except Turkey (which signed the agreement in May of that year) and previously approved by the "Group of Ten" (leading member countries of the International Monetary Fund), a two-year Financial Support ("safety net") Fund of $25,000 million, open to all OECD member countries, was set up to enable these countries to finance their external deficits. The agreement fixed quotas according to the member countries' gross national product and foreign trade (and ranging from 27.8 per cent of the total for the United States to 2.3 per cent for Australia and New Zealand). The fund would grant loans for a period not exceeding seven years under strict conditions of approval by member countries other than the prospective borrowing country. The fund was intended to be used only as a last resort in a "severe balance of payments crisis".

Economic Outlook. One of the OECD's important activities has been the publication of a bi-annual Economic Outlook, which surveys economic performance in the OECD member countries and makes forecasts on the rates of growth of their gross national product, of consumer price inflation, of wages and of unemployment, and on their balances of current accounts, trends in investment and fiscal and monetary policies of OECD member governments. In these reports the OECD also makes recommendations for dealing with unemployment, inflation and declining real income per head of the population.

Guidelines and Declarations. The OECD has also issued guidelines on various matters from time to time.

In June 1976 all its member governments except that of Turkey adopted a set of guidelines for multinational enterprises (as part of a package of measures aimed at improving the international investment climate).

In May 1980 the OECD adopted a set of guidelines designed to control the testing and marketing of new chemicals, enabling member governments to work to common standards in developing chemicals which would be universally acceptable on both health and environmental grounds.

In June 1980 the OECD issued a declaration on trade policies, emphasizing the need to strengthen trade with developing countries and to pursue, during the 1980s, policies which contribute to their economic prosperity. The declaration stressed the crucial importance of export earnings for developing countries and the favourable effect of high growth in those countries on the world economy, and it contained commitments by the OECD member countries to maintain and improve the open and multilateral trading system; to strengthen the role of the General Agreement on Trade and Tariffs (GATT); to avoid restrictive trade measures which could have an adverse effect on inflation, productivity and growth; and to avoid policies leading to a distortion of export competition, in particular in the field of export financing.

Development Assistance Committee. Of the OECD's committees, the Development Assistance Committee (DAC) has 18 members (the Governments of Australia, Austria, Belgium, Canada, Denmark, Finland, France, the Federal Republic of Germany, Italy, Japan, the Netherlands, New Zealand, Norway, Sweden, Switzerland, the United Kingdom and the United States, and the Commission of the European Communities).

The Special Economic Committee which

met in Paris on Jan. 12-13, 1960 [see also page 156], had adopted a resolution on the formation of a Development Assistance Group to co-ordinate aid to under-developed countries.

The founder-members of the group were Belgium, Canada, France, the Federal Republic of Germany, Italy, Japan, Portugal, the United Kingdom, the USA, and the EEC Commission. The Netherlands joined later in 1960.

In a communiqué of Dec. 14, 1960, it was stated that, on the inception of the OECD, the Development Assistance Group would be constituted as an organ of the OECD to be known as the Development Assistance Committee (DAC).

The main objectives of the DAC are to examine ways of increasing the volume of development assistance; to assess the indebtedness of the less-developed countries and the appropriate terms of assistance; and to co-ordinate assistance efforts, both capital and technical.

The DAC works primarily through the Annual Aid Review, a systematic and detailed examination of each member country's programme of aid, taking in the volume, financial terms, geographical distribution, purposes and techniques of the assistance. Meetings of the DAC are also held to discuss specific subjects connected with development aid.

According to provisional figures (published on June 19, 1980) of the volume of official development aid (ODA) from the DAC member countries to developing countries in 1979 the total of net ODA disbursements was US$22,300 million (as against $20,000 million in 1978), representing 0.34 per cent of members' gross national product (against 0.35 per cent in 1978) and constituting an increase in real terms (after taking account of increased prices) of about 2.4 per cent. Of the 17 member countries of the DAC, Denmark, the Netherlands, Norway and Sweden exceeded the target of 0.7 per cent of their gross national products, whereas the contributions of Austria, Finland, Italy, Japan, New Zealand, Switzerland and the United States were only about 0.2 per cent of their gross national products and the remaining six member countries had an average of about 0.5 per cent. At the same time the debt of the developing countries to DAC member countries was estimated at $62,800 million (against $49,200 million in 1978).

Autonomous and Semi-Autonomous Bodies of the OECD

OECD Nuclear Energy Agency (NEA)

Headquarters: Paris.

Members: All full members of the OECD except New Zealand.

The NEA was set up as the European Nuclear Energy Agency (ENEA) with effect from Feb. 1, 1958, after its statutes had been adopted by the OEEC on Dec. 20, 1957, and it was taken over by the OECD on the latter's foundation in September 1961. The ENEA changed its name to NEA in May 1972.

The NEA is governed by a Steering Committee consisting of a chairman and two vice-chairmen, and it has a Secretariat headed by a Director-General and a Deputy Director-General. It also has a number of committees, in particular for: Technical and economic studies on nuclear energy development and the fuel cycle; safety of nuclear installations; radiation protection and public health; radioactive waste management; nuclear data; and reactor physics. It also has a Group of Governmental Experts on third-party liability in the field of nuclear energy and a co-ordinating group on gas-cooled fast reactor development.

The main purpose of the NEA is to promote international co-operation within the OECD area for the development and application of nuclear power for peaceful purposes through international research and development projects and exchange of scientific and technical experience and information. The NEA also maintains a continual survey, with the co-operation of other organizations, notably the International Atomic Energy Agency (IAEA), of world uranium resources, production and demand, and of economic and technical aspects of the nuclear fuel cycle. An expanding part of the NEA's work is devoted to safety and regulatory aspects of nuclear energy, including the development of uniform standards governing safety and health protection, and a uniform legislative regime for nuclear liability and insurance.

The NEA has been involved in the following joint projects:

Eurochemic. The European Company for Chemical Processing of Irradiated Fuels (Eurochemic) was formed as an international shareholding company in 1959, with the Governments of Austria, Belgium, Denmark, the Federal Republic of Germany, the Netherlands, Norway, Switzerland and Turkey, and the atomic energy authorities of France, Italy, Portugal, Spain and Sweden becoming shareholders. The company's plant for treating irradiated fuel, located at Mol (Belgium), was completed in July 1966 but ceased operations in 1974, whereafter a programme was developed for the solidification, conditioning and storage of radioactive waste. Under a 1978 convention the company's installations were to be progressively transferred to the Belgian Government.

The Halden Reactor. The Experimental Boiling Heavy Water Reactor at Halden in southern Norway was built by the Norwegian *Institutt for Atomenergi*. It became a joint undertaking under the ENEA in June 1958, and a research and development programme was initiated in July 1958. This programme, completed early in 1964, was succeeded by a further programme of specialized research and development work, scheduled for completion at the end of 1969; extensions of the programme provided for its further continuation, and under an extension of the original agreement the project was to be continued until 1981.

Participants in the programme have been atomic energy institutions or authorities in Britain, Denmark, Finland, Italy, Japan, the Netherlands, Norway and Sweden; the Swiss Government; and a West German industrial group working in agreement with the Federal Ministry of Scientific Research. The Austrian Atomic Energy Study Company and the US Atomic Energy Commission have participated as associate members.

Other Projects. An International Project on Food Irradiation was established in Karlsruhe (Federal Republic of Germany) in 1971 to carry out testing of irradiated food items and to conduct a systematic review of all available data from national institutions. It is jointly sponsored by the NEA, the IAEA and the Food and Agriculture Organization (FAO), with 24 countries participating in its programme.

An NEA Data Bank, set up in 1978 at Saclay (France), replaced an earlier Computer Programme Library (at the Euratom Joint Research Establishment at Ispra, Italy) and a Neutron Data Compilation Centre (at Saclay). It enables the 17 participating countries to share computer programmes used in reactor calculations and also nuclear data applications; it is one of a worldwide network of four nuclear data centres.

Conventions. A convention on security control was signed by the OEEC Council on Dec. 20, 1957.

The basic rules of this security control closely follow those defined in the statute of the International Atomic Energy Agency and the Euratom Treaty. They provide for an examination of all plants subject to con-trol; a system of quantitative control for nuclear fuel; on-the-spot supervision by international inspectors; and, in cases of non-observance, the possibility of imposing penalties by a majority vote. Provision was made for an international tribunal to settle certain disputes to which the exercise of control might give rise.

An important convention providing for uniform rules on third-party liability in the field of nuclear energy was signed in Paris on July 29, 1960, and came into force on April 1, 1968.

The convention is designed to ensure that the effects of a nuclear incident do not stop at political or geographical boundaries, and that claimants may proceed with their claims against any reactor operator in any of the signatory countries. The liability of reactor operators for any damage caused by the escape of radioactive material from nuclear installations is absolute in the sense that there is liability without any need to prove fault or blame on the part of the reactor owner; liability will cover all incidents occurring both in connexion with the installations and in the course of transport of radioactive substances.

A supplementary convention was signed in Brussels in January 1963, extending the maximum limit of compensation.

OECD Development Centre

Headquarters: Paris.

Members: All full OECD members except New Zealand.

The Development Centre was established by a decision of the OECD Council in 1962 with the object of bringing together the knowledge and experience available in member countries of both economic development and the formulation and execution of general policies of economic aid, and of placing such knowledge and experience at the disposal of developing countries as adapted to their needs. Although an integral part of the OECD, the Development Centre enjoys autonomy and thus has scientific independence. Its activities include research on basic development problems, such as employment, technology and industrialization, social development and demography. The centre co-operates with the OECD and with other international organizations dealing with development matters.

Centre for Educational Research and Innovation (CERI)

Members: All full OECD member countries and Yugoslavia.

CERI was established in 1968 with the objects of promoting and assisting the development of research activities in the field of education, and of carrying out advanced experiments designed to test innovations in education and to stimulate research and development.

International Energy Agency (IEA)

Headquarters: Paris.

Members: Australia, Austria, Belgium, Canada, Denmark, the Federal Republic of Germany, Greece, Ireland, Italy, Japan, Luxembourg, the Netherlands, New Zealand, Norway, Portugal, Spain, Sweden, Switzerland, Turkey, the United Kingdom and the United States. The Commission of the European Communities is also represented on the IEA's Governing Board.

The IEA was set up by the Council of the OECD in November 1974 under an agreement approved by 16 oil-consuming countries (Austria, Belgium, Canada, Denmark, the Federal Republic of Germany, Ireland, Italy, Japan, Luxembourg, the Netherlands, Spain, Sweden, Switzerland, Turkey, the United Kingdom and the United States), with Finland, France and Greece abstaining from voting on the Council's decision and Norway taking no part in the agreement.

The agreement, concluded for 10 years but subject to a general review after five years, provided inter alia for an oil-sharing scheme coming automatically into operation in the event of a shortfall of 7 per cent or more affecting any or all of the participating countries. In the event of overall supplies of oil falling short by 12 per cent, each country would have to curb demand by 10 per cent even if not directly affected. The agreement also provided for weighted majority decisions on over 20 subjects relating inter alia to stock-piling, oil-sharing and conservation, under a complex voting system which gave each member a vote approximately in proportion to its oil consumption in 1973 and under which a total of 148 votes was distributed as follows: United States 51, Japan 18, Federal Republic of Germany 11, United Kingdom and Italy 9 each, Canada 8, Belgium, the Netherlands, Spain and Sweden 5 each, Austria, Denmark, Switzerland and Turkey 4 each and Ireland and Luxembourg 3 each. The automatic activation of the oil-sharing scheme could be prevented by 89 (or 60 per cent) of the 148 votes or by the votes of at least 12 countries. The participating countries were also to maintain contingency oil stocks equal to at least 60 days' consumption initially (90 days at a date to be agreed later) and would, if the oil-sharing scheme came into operation, have to make specific cutbacks in consumption and to use existing stocks on an agreed basis.

The IEA has a Governing Board assisted by four standing groups (on energy questions, long-term co-operation, the oil market and relations with producer and other consumer countries).

At a meeting of the IEA's Governing Board in Paris on March 1-2, 1979, it was decided that IEA member countries would reduce their oil consumption by about 2,000,000 barrels per day or 5 per cent.

The Agency was subsequently joined by New Zealand and Norway, and with the admission of Portugal on April 23, 1980, all the full members of the OECD with the exception of Finland, France and Iceland were also members of the IEA.

10. North Atlantic Treaty Organization (NATO)

This section covers the origins, formation, aims and structure of NATO. It also traces the development and activities of the organization since 1949 and surveys the principal multilateral and bilateral agreements concluded by member states within the NATO framework.

Origins, Formation, Aims and Structure of NATO

Headquarters: Brussels.

Members: Belgium, Canada, Denmark, France, the Federal Republic of Germany, Greece, Iceland, Italy, Luxembourg, the Netherlands, Norway, Portugal, Turkey, the United Kingdom and the United States.

The North Atlantic Treaty was signed on April 4, 1949, to provide for the collective defence and security of the Western world through an international organization.

Origins

The necessity for the creation of a defence alliance of Western Powers became apparent soon after the end of World War II. The tension which had arisen between the Allied Nations of Western Europe and the Soviet bloc came to a head in 1948 with the Communist coup d'état in Czechoslovakia and the Soviet blockade of Berlin.

In addition, the authority of the United Nations, as guardian of world peace and security, had shown itself to be severely restricted by the use of the veto in the Security Council, which precluded the settlement of many important questions.

In the years immediately following the war the Soviet Union formed a close network of military alliances in Eastern Europe. In answer to this Belgium, Britain, France, Luxembourg and the Netherlands created their own defence system in the Western Union, based on the Brussels Treaty of March 17, 1948 [see page 103]. It was, however, apparent that, without the participation of the United States, such an alliance would in no way counterbalance the defence system of Eastern Europe.

The Vandenberg Resolution. The principles upon which the USA would be willing to join a defensive alliance of Western nations were set out in a resolution introduced in the US Senate Foreign Relations Committee by Senator Vandenberg, the Republican Party's foreign affairs specialist, and approved on May 19, 1948. The resolution committed the United States, in principle, to military assistance to regional alliances and other collective arrangements entered into within the framework of the United Nations. It was stressed, however, that the USA would not enter into any "automatic commitments"; that any action associating the USA with defence pacts such as the Western Union would require congressional approval; and that any regional defence arrangements must provide for the "continuous and effective self-help" of the countries concerned before the question of US participation could be considered.

A report commending the policy outlined in the Vandenberg Resolution was formally adopted by the Senate Foreign Relations Committee on May 27, 1948, and approved by the full Senate on June 11.

The report declared that "certainty in advance concerning the intentions of the USA should constitute a vital factor in deterring aggression", and stressed that regional alliances or other "collective arrangements" should be promised the "association and help" of the USA, subject to final approval by Congress, if they guaranteed among themselves "continuous and effective self-help and mutual aid". Senator Vandenberg, speaking on the necessity for a plain declaration by the USA that aggression would mean war, declared: "The experience of World War I and World War II suggests that the best deterrent to aggression is the certainty that immediate and effective counter-measures will be taken against those who violate the peace. The principle of individual and collective self-defence is fundamental to the independence and integrity of the members of the United Nations. This is recognized in Art. 51 [of the UN Charter]. By reaffirming now its allegiance to this principle, the USA would take an important step in the direction of removing any dangerous uncertainties that might mislead potential aggressors. Such a reaffirmation is directed against no one and threatens no one. It is directed solely against aggression.''

The report pointed out that peace-loving people everywhere were ''concerned over the present inability of the United Nations to assure international peace'' and were troubled by the excessive use of the veto and the failure of arms control, and went on: ''The present sense of insecurity in many parts of the world retards and hampers the efforts which the USA is making to promote international economic recovery. It is clear that the security aspects of world economic recovery cannot be ignored. The people of the world look to the USA, as the strongest free nation, for leadership in making the United Nations an effective instrument for peace and security.''

The North Atlantic Treaty

On the basis of the Vandenberg Resolution negotiations were opened in July 1948 between the members of the Western Union on the one hand and the USA and Canada on the other. Further exploratory talks on the proposed North Atlantic Alliance were held in December 1948 and January 1949, but it was only after several weeks of discussions that, in March 1949, the final draft treaty was agreed upon by the USA, Canada, Belgium, Britain, France, Luxembourg, the Netherlands and Norway (which had taken part in the later stages of the negotiations). The treaty was signed on April 4, 1949, by the eight nations listed above and by Denmark, Iceland, Italy and Portugal, which had received invitations to join the pact.

Later adherents to the North Atlantic Treaty were Greece and Turkey (Feb. 18, 1952), and the Federal Republic of Germany (May 5, 1955).

THE TREATY

The text of the North Atlantic Treaty,

Map 6   North Atlantic Treaty Organization (NATO) and the Warsaw Treaty Organization

which entered into force on Aug. 24, 1949, is given below:

"**Preamble.** The parties to this treaty reaffirm their faith in the purposes and principles of the UN Charter and their desire to live in peace with all peoples and all governments.

"They are determined to safeguard the freedom, common heritage and civilization of their peoples, founded on the principles of democracy, individual liberty and the rule of law.

"They seek to promote stability and well-being in the North Atlantic area.

"They are resolved to unite their efforts for collective defence for the preservation of peace and security.

"They therefore agree to this North Atlantic treaty.

"**Art. 1.** The parties undertake, as set forth in the UN Charter, to settle any international dispute in which they may be involved by peaceful means in such a manner that international peace and security and justice are not endangered, and to refrain in their international relations from the threat or use of force in any manner inconsistent with the purposes of the United Nations.

"**Art. 2.** The parties will contribute towards the further development of peaceful and friendly international relations by strengthening their free institutions, by bringing about a better understanding of the principles upon which these institutions are founded, and by promoting conditions of stability and well-being. They will seek to eliminate conflict in their international economic policies and will encourage economic collaboration between any or all of them.

"**Art. 3.** In order more effectively to achieve the objectives of this treaty, the parties, separately and jointly, by means of continuous and effective self-help and mutual aid, will maintain and develop their individual and collective capacity to resist armed attack.

"**Art. 4.** The parties will consult together whenever, in the opinion of any of them, the territorial integrity, political independence or security of any of the parties is threatened.

"**Art. 5.** The parties agree that an armed attack against one or more of them in Europe or North America shall be considered an attack against them all, and consequently agree that, if such an armed attack occurs, each of them, in exercise of the right of individual or collective self-defence recognized by Art. 51 of the UN Charter, will assist the party or parties so attacked by taking forthwith, individually and in concert with the other parties, such action as it deems necessary, including the use of armed force, to restore and maintain the security of the North Atlantic area. Any such armed attack, and all measures taken as a result thereof, shall immediately be reported to the Security Council. Such measures shall be terminated when the Security Council has taken the measures necessary to restore and maintain international peace and security.

"**Art. 6.** For the purpose of Art. 5 an armed attack on one or more of the parties is deemed to include an armed attack on the territory of any of the parties in Europe or North America, on the Algerian Departments of France, on the occupation forces of any party in Europe, on the islands under the jurisdiction of any party in the North Atlantic area north of the Tropic of Cancer, or on the vessels or aircraft in this area of any of the parties."

[To provide for the accession to NATO of Greece and Turkey, Article 6 was reworded in a protocol to the treaty (signed on Oct. 22, 1951) as follows:

"For the purpose of Art. 5 an armed attack on one or more of the parties is deemed to include an armed attack—(i) on the territory of any of the parties in Europe or North America, on the Algerian Departments of France, on the territory of Turkey, or on the islands under the jurisdiction of any of the parties in the North Atlantic area north of the Tropic of Cancer; (ii) on the forces, vessels, or aircraft of any of the parties, when in or over these territories or any other area in Europe in which occupation forces of any of the parties were stationed on the date when the treaty entered into force, or the Mediterranean Sea, or the North Atlantic area north of the Tropic of Cancer."

In January 1963 the clauses of this article referring to the Algerian Departments of France were recognized by the North Atlantic Council as having become inapplicable since July 3, 1962 (the date of Algerian independence).]

"**Art. 7.** This treaty does not affect, and shall not be interpreted as affecting, in any way the rights and obligations under the Charter of the parties which are members of the United Nations, or the primary responsibility of the Security Council for the maintenance of international peace and security.

"**Art. 8.** Each party declares that none of the international engagements now in force between it and any other of the parties or any third state is in conflict with the provisions of this treaty, and undertakes not to enter into any international engagement in conflict with this treaty.

"**Art. 9.** The parties hereby establish a Council, on which each of them shall be represented, to consider matters concerning the implementation of this treaty. The Council shall be so organized so as to be able to meet promptly at any time. It shall set up such subsidiary bodies as may be necessary; in particular, it shall establish immediately a Defence Committee, which shall recommend measures for the implementation of Arts. 3 and 5.

"**Art. 10.** The parties may, by unanimous agreement, invite any other European state in a position to further the principles of the treaty, and to contribute to the security of the North Atlantic area, to accede to this treaty. Any state so invited may become a party to the treaty by depositing its instrument of accession with the US Government.

"**Art. 11.** This treaty shall be ratified and its provisions carried out by the parties in accordance with their respective constitutional processes. The instruments of ratification shall be deposited as soon as possible with the US Government, which will notify all the other signatories of each deposit. The treaty shall enter into force between the states which have ratified it as soon as the ratifications of the majority of the signatories, including those of Belgium, Canada, France, Luxembourg, the Netherlands, the United Kingdom and the United States, have been deposited, and shall come into effect with respect to other states on the date of deposit of their ratifications.

"**Art. 12.** After the treaty has been in force for 10 years, or at any time thereafter, the parties shall, if any of them so requests, consult together for the purpose of reviewing the treaty, having regard for the factors then affecting peace and security in the North Atlantic area, including the development of universal as well as regional arrangements under the UN Charter for the maintenance of international peace and security.

"**Art. 13.** After the treaty has been in force for 20 years, any party may cease to be a party one year after notice of denunciation has been given to the US Government, which will inform the governments of the other parties of the deposit of each notice of denunciation.

"**Art. 14.** This treaty, of which the English and French texts are equally authentic, shall be deposited in the archives of the US Government. Duly certified copies will be transmitted by that government to the governments of the other signatories."

In an official NATO analysis of the treaty it is pointed out that the treaty is of unlimited duration, and in connexion with Art. 6 (as amended) it is stated: "The definition of the military area in which the treaty is applicable in no way implies that political events occurring outside it cannot be the subject of consultations within the Council, for it is the overall international situation which is liable to affect the preservation of peace and security in the area in question, and it is to consideration of this situation that the Council must, and indeed does, devote its attention as a matter of course."

Accession of West Germany. A Protocol to the North Atlantic Treaty on the Accession of the Federal Republic of Germany formed one of the Paris Agreements of Oct. 23, 1954. The document was signed by the 14 North Atlantic Treaty countries. A Resolution of Association, welcoming and recapitulating a Declaration made by the Federal Republic of Germany and a Joint Declaration issued by the United States, British and French Governments at the London Nine-Power Conference of Sept. 28-Oct. 3, 1954, was signed at the same time [see also Western European Union, pages 103-05]. The German declaration ran as follows:

"The Federal Republic of Germany has agreed to conduct its policy in accordance with the principles of the United Nations Charter.

"Upon her accession to the North Atlantic Treaty and the Brussels Treaty, the Federal Republic of Germany declares that she will refrain from any action inconsistent with the strictly defensive character of the two treaties. In particular, the Federal Republic of Germany undertakes never to have recourse to force to achieve the reunification of Germany or the modification of the present boundaries of the Federal Republic of Germany, and to resolve by peaceful means any disputes which may arise between the Federal Republic and other states."

In the tripartite Joint Declaration the three governments, after stating their resolution to devote their efforts to the strengthening of peace in accordance with the UN Charter, declare that:

(1) They consider the Government of the Federal Republic as the only German Government freely and legitimately constituted, and therefore entitled to speak for Germany as the representative of the German people in international affairs.

(2) In their relations with the Federal Republic they will follow the principles set out in Article 2 of the UN Charter.

(3) A peace settlement for the whole of Germany, freely negotiated between Germany and her former enemies, which should lay the foundation of a lasting peace, remains an essential aim of their policy. The final determination of the boundaries of Germany must await such a settlement.

(4) The achievement through peaceful means of a fully free and unified Germany remains a fundamental goal of their policy.

(5) The security and welfare of Berlin and the maintenance of the position of the three powers there are regarded by the three powers as essential elements of the peace of the free world in the present international situation. Accordingly they will maintain armed forces within the territory of Berlin as long as their responsibilities require it. They therefore reaffirm that they will treat any attack against Berlin from any quarter as an attack upon their forces and themselves.

(6) They will regard as a threat to their own peace and safety any recourse to force which, in violation of the principles of the UN Charter, threatens the integrity and unity of the Atlantic Alliance or its defensive purposes. In the event of any such action the three governments will consider the offending government as having forfeited its rights to any guarantee and any military assistance provided for in the North Atlantic Treaty and its protocols. They will act in accordance with Article 4 of the North Atlantic Treaty with a view to taking other measures which may be appropriate.

The provision in Paragraph (1) above must be considered as superseded by the 1972 Basic Treaty between the Federal Republic of Germany and the German Democratic Republic (see Section 12 on East-West Treaties).

North Atlantic Council

The supreme authority of the Atlantic Alliance is the North Atlantic Council, a political assembly composed of representatives of the governments of the 15 member countries. The Council meets at the level of ministers or of permanent representatives.

Ministerial meetings, which are generally held twice a year, are attended by Ministers for Foreign Affairs, Defence or Economic Affairs from each of the member countries. The agenda of each meeting determines which ministers should attend. Member countries are occasionally represented by their heads of state.

The Council functions continuously at the level of permanent representatives who are of ambassadorial rank and who lead national delegations accredited to NATO. The permanent representatives meet at least once a week.

The Chairman of the Council, at both ministerial and permanent representatives' level, is the Secretary General of NATO. The presidency, held by the Foreign Minister of each member country in turn, rotates annually.

Council Committees. Much of the work of the North Atlantic Council is carried out through permanent and temporary committees, which give advice and make recommendations on technical matters.

The principal committees are those for:

Political Affairs
Nuclear Defence Affairs
Economic Affairs
Defence Review
Armaments
Science
Infrastructure
Senior Civil Emergency Planning
Information and Cultural Relations
Challenges of Modern Society
Civilian Budget
Military Budget
European Airspace Co-ordination
NATO Pipelines

The **Nuclear Defence Affairs Committee** (NDAC), established in 1966, is composed of Defence Ministers of all NATO member countries except France, Iceland and Luxembourg. A Nuclear Planning Group (also set up in 1966) consists of seven or eight members of the NDAC with periodical changes in composition. It meets regularly at the level of permanent representatives and twice a year at that of Defence Ministers.

The Council has a number of civilian agencies under its authority, as follows:

(1) **Central Europe Pipeline System** (CEPS), established in 1957 for the operation and maintenance of an integrated military pipeline network and located at Versailles (France).

(2) **NATO Hawk Production and Logistics Organization** (NHPLO), established in 1959 to supervise the multinational production of the Hawk surface-to-air missile system in Europe and located at Rueil-Malmaison (France).

(3) **NATO Maintenance and Supply Organization** (NAMSO), established in 1958 for the supply of spare parts and logistic support for certain jointly-used weapon systems or equipment and located in Luxembourg.

(4) **NATO Multi-Role Combat Aircraft Development and Production Management Organization** (NAMMO), established in 1969 as an intergovernmental body supported by the Federal Republic of Germany, Italy and the United Kingdom, and located in Munich (Germany).

(5) **NATO Integrated Communications System Organization** (NICSO), established in 1971 to supervise the planning and management of NATO's Integrated Communi-

cations System (NICS), including the NATO Satellite Communications System, and located in Brussels.

Defence Planning Committee (DPC)

NATO's military policy is discussed in its Defence Planning Committee (DPC) composed of representatives of the member countries taking part in NATO's integrated defence system. Whether at ministerial or at permanent representative level, the PDC meets (like the Council) under the chairmanship of the Secretary General.

The DPC works with the Council's committees and also other committees such as that on NATO's integrated Air Defence System. An Executive Working Group (EWG) is responsible to the DPC for the principal aspects of defence and the overall conduct of the long-term defence programme.

Since 1966 there have been a **Nuclear Defence Affairs Committee** (NDAC) and a **Nuclear Planning Group** (NPG) whose members are chosen from the NDAC. The Secretary General is chairman of both these bodies.

The Secretary General's international staff comprises the Office of the Secretary General; the Office of the Executive Secretary; five major divisions (for political affairs; defence planning and policy; defence support; infrastructure, logistics and Council operations; and scientific and environmental affairs); the Office of Management; and the Financial Controller.

Military Committee

NATO's highest military authority is its Military Committee composed of the chiefs-of-staff of all member countries except France and Iceland (of which the latter has no military forces); it normally meets three times a year. It elects a permanent chairman for a period of two or three years; he represents the Military Committee on the Council.

The Military Committee has a number of military agencies under its authority, as follows:

(1) **Allied Communications Security Agency** (ACSA), located in Brussels.

(2) **Allied Long Lines Agency** (ALLA), created in 1951 to formulate policies and plans for NATO's long lines requirements, and located in Brussels.

(3) **Allied Naval Communications Agency** (ANCA), established in 1951 and located in London.

(4) **Allied Radio Frequency Agency** (ARFA), formed in 1951, providing inter alia engineering assistance to all nations and NATO commands in the selection of

suitable radio frequencies, and located in Brussels.

(5) **Allied Tactical Communications Agency** (ATCA), established in 1972, inter alia effecting liaison with ANCA for joint operations involving naval forces, and located in Brussels.

(6) **Allied Tactical Data Systems Interoperability Agency** (ATADSIA), inaugurated in 1979 to plan, develop and maintain common procedural standards for automated tactical data systems for NATO's command and control systems, and located in Brussels.

(7) **Advisory Group for Aerospace Research and Development** (AGARD), created in 1952 and located in Neuilly-sur-Seine (France).

(8) **Military Agency for Standardization** (MAS), set up in 1951 to enable NATO forces to operate together in the most effective manner, and located in Brussels.

(9) **NATO Defence College** (NADEFCOL), founded in 1951 for the training of civilian and military officials for key posts in NATO or in national ministries and located in Rome.

(10) **NATO Electronic Warfare Advisory Committee** (NEWAC), formed in 1956 and located in Brussels.

(11) **SACLANT Anti-Submarine Warfare Research Centre** (SACLANTCEN), created in 1962 for research in submarine detection and oceanographic problems, and located at La Spezia (Italy).

(12) **SHAPE Technical Centre** (STC), created in 1960 to provide scientific and technical advice to the Supreme Allied Commander Europe (to whom it is responsible) and located in The Hague.

Eurogroup

The Eurogroup, formed in 1968, is an informal group of Defence Ministers open to all European NATO member countries and currently consisting of the Defence Ministers of Belgium, Denmark, the Federal Republic of Germany, Greece, Italy, Luxembourg, the Netherlands, Norway, Portugal, Turkey and the United Kingdom.

Its object is to make the European contribution to the common defence strong and cohesive and also to encourage and support the continuing (and vital) presence in Europe of Canadian and US forces. In 1970 it launched a **European Defence Improvement Programme** (EDIP) extending over five years and involving a cost exceeding $1,000 million, this being supplementary to existing national plans; the programme was designed to procure extra aircraft (both combat and transport) and additional funds for the NATO integrated communications system and the building of some 1,600 hardened aircraft shelters.

North Atlantic Assembly

A North Atlantic Assembly (created in 1955 as the NATO Parliamentarians' Conference, which assumed its present name in 1966) is an informal assembly of 172 members delegated by the NATO member countries' parliaments (with each country's representation being weighted according to its population and thus ranging from 36 from the United States to three each from Iceland and Luxembourg). The purpose of the Assembly is to promote the aims of the North Atlantic Treaty and to encourage solidarity and co-operation in national parliaments. It meets once a year; it has five committees and an International Secretariat; and it is based in Brussels.

Development and Activities of NATO

1949-1955

The first phase of NATO's existence, roughly covering the period from its inception to the mid-1950s, saw the evolution of the organization's complex military and civilian structure.

The first meeting of the NATO Council, set up under Article 9 of the North Atlantic Treaty, was held on Sept. 17, 1949. The Council, which consisted of the Foreign Ministers of the member countries, decided to set up a Defence Committee. This Committee, to be composed of the Ministers of Defence of the NATO countries, was to have the initial function of drawing up unified defence plans for the North Atlantic area. Other bodies formed at this meeting were the Military Committee, composed of high military representatives of each member country, to advise on military matters; a Standing Group, comprising one representative each of Britain, France and the USA, to provide military information and guidance; and five Regional Planning Groups to prepare plans for the defence of each region (Northern Europe, Western Europe, Southern Europe, the Western Hemisphere and the North Atlantic).

At its second session, held on Nov. 18, 1949, the Council created a Defence Financial and Economic Committee and a Defence Production Board. The function of the latter was to promote the co-ordinated production, standardization and further technical development of armaments.

NATO's Military Structure

Military Committee
(*Chairman:* NATO Secretary General)

International Military Staff

Major Commands

Canada-US Regional Planning Group

Allied Command Atlantic (ACLANT) Norfolk, Virginia (USA)
Commander: Supreme Allied Commander Atlantic (SACLANT)

- Western Atlantic, Norfolk (USA)
  - Submarine Force Western Atlantic Area Command
  - Ocean Sub-Area Command
  - Canadian Atlantic Sub-Area Command
  - Bermuda Command
  - Azores Command
  - Greenland Command
- Eastern Atlantic, Northwood (UK)
  - Commander Maritime Air Eastern Atlantic Area
  - Commander Northern Sub-Area
  - Commander Maritime Air Northern Sub-Area
  - Commander Central Sub-Area
  - Commander Maritime Air Central Sub-Area
  - Commander Submarine Force Eastern Atlantic Area
  - Island Commanders of Iceland and the Faroes
- Striking Fleet, Afloat
  - Commander Carrier Striking Force
  - Commanders Carrier Striking Groups I and II
- Submarines, Norfolk (USA)
- Iberian Atlantic (IBERLANT), Lisbon (Portugal)
  - Island Command of Madeira
- Standing Naval Force Atlantic (STANAVFORLANT), Afloat

Allied Command Europe (ACE) Supreme Headquarters Allied Powers Europe (SHAPE), Mons (Belgium)
Commander: Supreme Allied Commander Europe (SACEUR)

- Northern Europe, Kolsaas (Norway)
  - Allied Forces North Norway
  - Allied Forces South Norway
  - Allied Forces Baltic Approaches
- Central Europe, Brunssum (Netherlands)
  - Northern Army Group
  - Central Army Group
  - Allied Air Forces Central Europe
  - 2nd Allied Tactical Air Force
  - 4th Allied Tactical Air Force
- Southern Europe, Naples (Italy)
  - Allied Land Forces Southern Europe
  - Allied Land Forces South-Eastern Europe
  - Allied Air Forces Southern Europe
  - Allied Naval Forces Southern Europe
  - Naval Striking and Support Forces Southern Europe
- UK Air Forces, High Wycombe (UK)
- Allied Command Mobile Force, Seckenheim (Germany)

Allied Command Channel (ACCHAN) Northwood (UK)
Commander: Supreme Allied Commander-in-Chief, Channel Command (CINCHAN)

- Nore Channel, Rosyth (UK)
- Plymouth Channel, Plymouth (UK)
- Benelux Channel, Walcheren (Netherlands)
- Allied Maritime Air Force Channel Command (COMMAIRCHAN), Northwood (UK)
- Standing Naval Force Channel (Mine Counter Measures) (STANAVFORCHAN), Afloat

Two important organizational decisions were made at the fourth session of the Council (the second at ministerial level), held on May 15-18, 1950. It was decided to form a Permanent Council of Deputies to the Foreign Ministers and to create a North Atlantic Planning Board for Ocean Shipping.

In December 1950, after a meeting of the Foreign and Defence Ministers of the 12 NATO countries, it was announced that arrangements had been completed for an integrated defence force under centralized control and command, to which all the participating governments would contribute contingents. The Supreme Headquarters Allied Powers in Europe (SHAPE) was set up in Paris in 1951.

In May 1951 a reorganization of the North Atlantic Council was announced. The Defence Committee and the Defence Financial and Economic Committee [see above] ceased to exist as separate organs, but were incorporated in the North Atlantic Council, which thus became the sole ministerial body of NATO. Henceforth the Ministerial Council might be formed by Foreign, Defence or Finance Ministers according to the agenda of the meeting. The functions of the Council of Deputies were defined as being to co-ordinate and guide all other permanent organs of NATO and to exchange views on political matters within the scope of the treaty. A new body set up at this time was the Financial and Economic Board to make recommendations on financial and economic matters.

At a meeting of the North Atlantic Council in September 1951 it was agreed, inter alia, to support the entry into NATO of Greece and Turkey. A Temporary Committee of the Council (TCC) was set up to study the problems of reconciling the requirements for the fulfilment of a militarily acceptable defence plan with the realistic politico-economic capabilities of the member countries. The final report of the TCC was adopted by the Council at its session in February 1952, after which the Committee was wound up. On the basis of the report the Council agreed on a "definite programme of measures to increase defensive strength in following years". Organizational changes agreed upon were the creation of the post of Secretary General to head a unified international Secretariat, and the formation of a North Atlantic Council in permanent session through the appointment of permanent representatives. The Council would assume the functions hitherto performed by the Council of Deputies, the Defence Production Board and the Financial and Economic Board.

Early 1952 also saw the formation of the other two main NATO military commands: the Atlantic Ocean Command, headed by the Supreme Allied Commander Atlantic (SACLANT), and the Channel Command, headed by the Allied Commander-in-Chief Channel (CINCHAN).

In the same year the North Atlantic Council agreed upon close association with the proposed European Defence Community (EDC) of Belgium, France, the Federal Republic of Germany, Italy, Luxembourg and the Netherlands. After the French rejection of the EDC treaty in August 1954, however, the integration of the Federal Republic of Germany into a defence system of the West had to be reconsidered. The results of these considerations, carried out at the nine-power London conference of September 1954, were embodied in the Paris Agreements which included the protocol on the entry of Western Germany into NATO [see page 103].

1956-1965

In the decade from 1955 to 1965 the actual structure of NATO underwent relatively little alteration, the main developments within the organization being an increase in its political role, and the improvement and adaptation of its defensive system.

Political Development. At a North Atlantic Council meeting in May 1956 it was decided, inter alia, to set up a committee of three ministers (known as the "three wise men") to examine "ways and means to improve and extend NATO co-operation in non-military fields and develop greater unity within the Atlantic community". The report of this committee, which was adopted by the Council on Dec. 13, 1956, recommended full and timely consultation between NATO member governments on issues of common concern. The following points were given as a guideline to such consultation:

(1) Members should inform the Council of any development which significantly affected the Alliance. They should do this not merely as a formality but as a preliminary to effective political consultation.

(2) Both individual member governments and the Secretary General should have the right to raise for discussion in the Council any subject which was of common NATO interest, and not of a purely domestic character.

(3) A member government should not, without adequate advance consultation, adopt firm policies or make major political announcements on matters which significantly affected the alliance or any of its members, unless circumstances made such prior consultation obviously and demonstrably impossible.

(4) In developing their national policies, members should take into consideration the interests and views of other governments—particularly those most directly

concerned—as expressed in NATO consultation, even where no community of view or consensus of opinion had been reached in the Council.

(5) Where consensus had been reached, it should be reflected in the formation of national policies. When for national reasons the consensus was not followed, the government concerned should offer an explanation to the Council. It was even more important that, where an agreed and formal recommendation had emerged from the Council's discussions, governments should give it full weight in any national actions or policies related to the subject of that recommendation.

(6) To strengthen the process of consultation it was recommended that at each spring meeting the Foreign Ministers should make an appraisal of the political progress of the Alliance and consider the lines along which it should advance.

(7) To prepare for this discussion, the Secretary General should submit an annual report analysing the major political problems of the Alliance; reviewing the extent to which member governments had consulted and co-operated in such problems; and indicating the problems and the possible developments which might require consultation, so that difficulties might be resolved and positive and constructive initiatives taken.

(8) To assist the permanent representatives (of member countries) and the Secretary General in discharging their responsibilities for political consultation, a committee of political advisers from each delegation should be constituted under the Council, aided when necessary by specialists.

Settlement of Members' Disputes. It was further recommended that NATO members should submit any dispute between them which had not proved capable of direct settlement to "good offices" procedures under NATO before restoring to any other international agency. Exceptions to this procedure would be legal questions which could be dealt with more appropriately by a judicial tribunal, or economic questions which could more appropriately be dealt with in the specialized economic organizations.

All member countries, as well as the Secretary General, had the right and the duty to bring to the Council's attention matters which in their opinion might threaten the solidarity or effectiveness of the Alliance. The Secretary General should be empowered to offer his good offices informally to the parties to a dispute and, with their consent, "to initiate or facilitate procedures of inquiry, mediation, conciliation or arbitration". For this purpose, he should be able to use the assistance of not more than three permanent representatives chosen by him in each instance.

While approving the report, the United States informed the North Atlantic Council that it could not subject its policies or actions throughout the world to prior consultation within NATO.

The NATO Political Committee was formed in January 1957, meeting once a week to discuss questions of political interest to the members of the Atlantic Alliance.

At the ministerial meeting of the North Atlantic Council held in December 1959 in Paris, proposals were adopted for long-term planning, to cover the following ten years, on the objectives of the Alliance in the political, military, scientific and econ-

omic fields and in regard to arms control.

An "Atlantic Convention", attended by 98 delegates (private citizens appointed by their governments) of all NATO member countries, was held in Paris between Jan. 8 and Jan. 20, 1962, to make recommendations for the further political development of the Atlantic Community. The convention finally adopted the *Declaration of Paris,* calling for "the creation of a true Atlantic Community within the next decade". The declaration included recommendations for the creation of new political, judicial and cultural organs; for the harmonization of political, military and economic policy on matters affecting the Atlantic Community as a whole; and for closer economic co-operation with developing countries. The declaration was endorsed by the Parliamentarians' Conference in November 1962, but its proposals have not been adopted by the North Atlantic Council.

Military and Defence Developments. From Dec. 16 to 19, 1957, the heads of government of the NATO countries met in conference in Paris. Their most important decision was to establish stocks of nuclear warheads in the treaty area, and to place intermediate-range ballistic missiles (IRBMs) at the disposal of the Supreme Allied Commander Europe (SACEUR). They also decided to set up the Science Committee composed of qualified representatives of each NATO country, and to appoint a scientist of outstanding qualifications as science adviser to the Secretary General of NATO.

In December 1957 the United States stated its willingness to participate in a NATO atomic stockpile, and also to make available to other NATO members intermediate-range ballistic missiles for deployment according to the plans of SACEUR. Each country concerned would have to make a separate agreement with the United States with respect to material, training of personnel and other necessary arrangements. Agreements on co-operation in the field of atomic weapons were signed by the USA with Canada, France, the Federal Republic of Germany, Greece, the Netherlands, Turkey and the United Kingdom in May 1959. A similar agreement was signed with Italy in December 1960.

On March 2, 1960, it was announced by SACEUR that a multi-national Allied task force, to be equipped with both conventional and atomic weapons, would be established. The constituent units would be brought together occasionally for joint training, but would generally remain with their national formations. The multi-national task force came officially into existence in July 1961, when it comprised five reinforced infantry battalions.

Meanwhile, the new Anti-Submarine Warfare Research Centre at La Spezia, Italy, had been formally inaugurated in May 1959. This was completely reorganized to receive full NATO support as an international military organization in January 1963.

Nuclear Force for NATO. At a Ministerial Council meeting held in Athens in May 1962, the United States made two important announcements on defence matters: (i) That it would not remove or diminish its nuclear stockpiles in Europe without prior consultation; and (iii) that five Polaris submarines would be immediately committed to NATO (these had already been promised in December 1960). At this meeting the Council decided to set up a special committee of all member countries "to receive and exchange information about NATO's nuclear defences".

In December 1962 President Kennedy of the United States and the British Prime Minister, Harold Macmillan, met at Nassau (Bahamas), where they signed an agreement on US provision of Polaris missiles to Britain. In a joint statement issued at the time the two leaders put forward a suggestion for a NATO multilateral nuclear force, which would initially consist of some part of the force already in existence. "This would include allocations from US strategic forces, from UK Bomber Command and from tactical nuclear forces now held in Europe. Such forces would be assigned as part of a NATO nuclear force and targeted in accordance with NATO plans."

At the Ministerial Council meeting in Ottawa in May 1963 it was decided to set up such a multinational nuclear force by reorganizing the nuclear forces already assigned to SACEUR. The principal steps approved by the Council were: (1) The assignment of the British V-bomber force and three US Polaris submarines to SACEUR; (2) the appointment by SACEUR of a Deputy responsible to him for nuclear affairs; (3) arrangements for broader participation by NATO officers in nuclear activities in Allied Command, Europe, and in co-ordination of operational planning; and (4) fuller information to national authorities. The Ministerial Council also directed the Council in Permanent Session to undertake studies towards a satisfactory balance between nuclear and conventional forces.

At the Kennedy-Macmillan meeting at Nassau in December 1962 [cf. above] the US President put forward a plan for the formation of a mixed-manned seaborne nuclear force to be assigned to NATO and to which non-nuclear powers could contribute. Discussions on the technical details of such a force were opened in October 1963 and continued throughout 1964. In addition, the United States made available a destroyer for an experiment in mixed manning which began in May 1964. No agreement on the mixed-manned nuclear force (MLF) has, however, been concluded, as the new British Labour Government opposed the idea of a mixed-manned nuclear surface fleet. Britain proposed, as an alternative, an Atlantic Nuclear Force (ANF) comprising the British V-bomber force; a British fleet of Polaris submarines; at least an equal number of US Polaris submarines; and some kind of mixed-manned or jointly-owned element in which the non-nuclear powers could participate.

An agreement concluded between all 15 NATO member states on co-operation in the field of nuclear information was signed on June 18, 1964, and came into force on March 12, 1965.

New Committees. It was announced on Aug. 25, 1964, that a NATO Defence Research Directors' Committee had been set up with the aim of attempting to "establish a more direct relevance between science and the military needs" of the organization. It would supplement the work of the NATO Science Committee (established in 1957, see above), which devoted most of its activities to civilian science.

At a NATO Defence Ministers' meeting in Paris on May 31-June 1, 1965, the US Defence Secretary Robert McNamara proposed the creation of a "select committee" of a few member countries to study ways of extending nuclear planning and consultation within the alliance. This proposal led, in November 1965, to the creation of a ten-member "special committee" of Defence Ministers, i.e. the Defence Ministers of all NATO countries except France, Luxembourg, Norway, Portugal and Iceland (which has none). The committee set up three working groups to deal with Communications, Data Exchange, and Nuclear Planning.

1966-1967

The years 1966-67 saw the withdrawal of France from the military side of NATO, and the subsequent removal of all NATO installations from French soil.

French Withdrawal from NATO. French opposition to the integrated military organization was already of several years' standing, the French President, General de Gaulle, having repeatedly affirmed since 1959 that, although she was in favour of the Atlantic Alliance, France could no longer support an integrated defence system which deprived her of sovereignty over her own military forces.

In March 1959 the French Mediterranean Fleet was withdrawn from the integrated command, and French naval units were withdrawn from the Atlantic and Channel Commands from Jan. 1, 1964. In April 1964 the French Government gave formal notification of the withdrawal of all French naval officers serving in NATO naval command posts or on NATO naval staffs.

In February and March 1966 the French Government made it clear that France intended to withdraw completely from the integrated organization, while remaining a member of the Atlantic Alliance. She was, however, ready to conclude arrangements for liaison between French and NATO forces, and also to retain French forces in the Federal Republic of Germany under new terms.

On March 29, 1966, the French Government, in an aide-mémoire to the other NATO members, set a timetable for France's withdrawal. The withdrawal of French forces in West Germany from NATO command, and of French personnel from Allied commands and staffs, was timed for July 1, 1966; the removal of SHAPE, the Allied Forces Central Europe (AFCENT) command and the NATO Defence College from French territory was to be carried out by April 1, 1967; and the withdrawal of most US and Canadian military installations was also to be completed by April 1, 1967. This timetable was, in fact, adhered to.

On Sept. 7, 1966, France stated her intention of stopping her financial contributions to the military budget from Jan. 1, 1967, but expressed a wish to continue participation in the NATO Air Defence Ground Environment System, or NADGE, an automatic air defence system due for completion in 1971; in SHAPE's technical research centre at The Hague; in the anti-submarine warfare centre at La Spezia; and in the management organization of the Hawk missile (produced by a consortium of five European NATO countries). At the end of September France withdrew from the NATO Military Committee.

Removal of NATO Institutions from French Territory. (1) The new headquarters of SHAPE, near Mons in southern Belgium, were officially opened by the Supreme Allied Commander Europe on March 31, 1967.
(2) The headquarters of Allied Forces Central Europe (AFCENT) were removed from Fontainebleau to Brunssum, a site in the Netherlands province of Limburg, at the beginning of April 1967.
(3) Formerly located at the Ecole Militaire in Paris, the NATO Defence College opened its first session in the Palazzo Fondiaria, on the outskirts of Rome, on Jan. 18, 1967.
(4) In October 1966 it was decided to move the headquarters of the NATO Council from Paris to Brussels.

Reorganization of Military Structure. The Standing Group, which was formed in 1949, was abolished on July 1, 1966, as a result of France's withdrawal from NATO's military organization [see above]. It was replaced by a temporary international staff.

The removal of the Military Committee from Washington to Brussels was authorized in November 1966.

The Allied Land Forces Central Europe (LANDCENT) and Allied Air Forces Central Europe (AIRCENT) lost their individual identity to be merged with AFCENT from Nov. 15, 1966.

Changes in the naval organization which were made in 1966-67 were as follows:
(1) In January 1966 the Commander-in-Chief Eastern Atlantic assumed the additional NATO post of Commander-in-Chief Channel.
(2) On Feb. 22, 1967, a new Command, the Iberian Command Atlantic (IBERLANT), was inaugurated. IBERLANT, based in Lisbon, is attached to Allied Command Atlantic.
(3) Another new Command, Naval Command South (NAVSOUTH), was inaugurated on June 5, 1967. This Command, responsible to the Commander-in-Chief Allied Forces Southern Europe, replaced the Commander-in-Chief Allied Forces Mediterranean.

The 1967 Harmel Report. In a Report on the Future Tasks of the Alliance, prepared on an initiative by the Belgian Minister of Defence (then Pierre Harmel), and approved by the Council's ministerial meeting in Brussels on Dec. 12-13, 1967, it was stated inter alia:

"(4) Since the North Atlantic Treaty was signed in 1949 the international situation has changed significantly and the political tasks of the Alliance have assumed a new dimension. Amongst other developments, the Alliance has played a major part in stopping communist expansion in Europe; the USSR has become one of the two world super-powers but the communist world is no longer monolithic; the Soviet doctrine of 'peaceful coexistence' has changed the nature of the confrontation with the West but not the basic problems. Although the disparity between the power of the United States and that of the European states remains, Europe has recovered and is on its way towards unity. The process of decolonization has transformed European relations with the rest of the world; at the same time, major problems have arisen in the relations between developed and developing countries.

"(5) The Atlantic Alliance has two main functions. Its first function is to maintain adequate military strength and political solidarity to deter aggression and other forms of pressure and to defend the territory of member countries if aggression should occur. Since its inception, the Alliance has successfully fulfilled this task. But the possibility of a crisis cannot be excluded as long as the central political issues in Europe, first and foremost the German question, remain unsolved. Moreover, the situation of instability and uncertainty still precludes a balanced reduction of military forces. Under these conditions, the Allies will maintain as necessary a suitable military capability to assure the balance of forces, thereby creating a climate of stability, security and confidence.

"In this climate the Alliance can carry out its second function, to pursue the search for progress towards a more stable relationship in which the underlying political issues can be solved. Military security and a policy of détente are not contradictory but complementary. Collective defence is a stabilizing factor in world politics. It is the necessary condition for effective policies directed towards a greater relaxation of tensions. The way to peace and stability in Europe rests in particular on the use of the Alliance constructively in the interest of détente. The participation of the USSR and the USA will be necessary to achieve a settlement of the political problems in Europe.

"(6) From the beginning the Atlantic Alliance has been a co-operative grouping of states sharing the same ideals and with a high degree of common interest. Their cohesion and solidarity provide an element of stability within the Atlantic area.

"(7) As sovereign states the Allies are not obliged to subordinate their policies to collective decision. The Alliance affords an effective forum and clearing-house for the exchange of information and views; thus, each of the Allies can decide his policy in the light of close knowledge of each other's problems and objectives. To this end the practice of frank and timely consultations needs to be deepened and improved. Each ally should play its full part in promoting an improvement in relations with the Soviet Union and the countries of Eastern Europe, bearing in mind that the pursuit of détente must not be allowed to split the Alliance. The chances of success will clearly be greatest if the Allies remain on parallel courses, especially in matters of close concern to them all; their actions will thus be all the more effective.

"(8) No peaceful order in Europe is possible without a major effort by all concerned. The evolution of Soviet and East European policies gives ground for hope that those governments may eventually come to recognize the advantages to them of collaborating in working towards a peaceful settlement. But no final and stable settlement in Europe is possible without a solution of the German question, which lies at the heart of present tensions in Europe. Any such settlement must end the unnatural barriers between Eastern and Western Europe, which are most clearly and cruelly manifested in the division of Germany.

"(9) Accordingly the Allies are resolved to direct their energies to this purpose by realistic measures designed to further a détente in East-West relations. The relaxation of tensions is not the final goal but is part of a long-term process to promote better relations and to foster a European settlement. The ultimate political purpose of the Alliance is to achieve a just and lasting peaceful order in Europe accompanied by appropriate security guarantees.

"(10) Currently, the development of contacts between the countries of Western and Eastern Europe is now mainly on a bilateral basis. Certain subjects, of course, require by their very nature a multilateral solution.

"(11) The problem of German reunification and its relationship to a European settlement has normally been dealt with in exchanges between the Soviet Union and the three Western powers having special responsibilities in this field. In the preparation of such exchanges the Federal Republic of Germany has regularly joined the three Western powers in order to reach a common position. The other Allies will continue to have their views considered in timely discussions among the Allies about Western policy on this subject, without in any way impairing the special responsibilities in question.

"(12) The Allies will examine and review suitable policies designed to achieve a just and stable order in Europe, to overcome the division of Germany, and to foster European security. This will be part of a process of active and constant preparation for the time when fruitful discussions of these complex questions may be possible bilaterally or multilaterally between Eastern and Western nations.

"(13) The Allies are studying disarmament and practical arms control measures, including the possibility of balanced force reductions. These studies will be intensified. Their active pursuit reflects the will of the Allies to work for an effective détente with the East.

"(14) The Allies will examine with particular attention the defence problems of the exposed areas, e.g. the south-eastern flank. In this respect the current situation in the Mediterranean presents special problems, bearing in mind that the current crisis in the Middle East falls within the responsibilities of the United Nations.

"(15) The North Atlantic Treaty area cannot be treated in isolation from the rest of the world. Crises and conflicts arising outside the area may impair its security either directly or by affecting the global balance. Allied countries contribute individually within the United Nations and other international organizations to the maintenance of international peace and security and to the solution of important international problems. In accordance with established usage the Allies, or such of them as wish to do so, will also continue to consult on such problems without commitment and as the case may demand. . . .''

1968-1971

In 1968-71 the NATO Council's decisions were designed to counteract growing Soviet power both on the continent of Europe and in the Mediterranean, and any proposals for a reduction of armed forces were treated with reserve.

The NATO Nuclear Planning Group declared on April 19, 1968, that the deployment of an anti-ballistic missile system in Europe was not justified at that time, although developments in that field should be kept under constant review.

On June 25, 1968, the Council issued a *Declaration on Mutual and Balanced Force*

Reductions (MBFR), in which its Ministers affirmed that "the overall military capability of NATO should not be reduced except as part of a pattern of mutual force reductions balanced in scope and timing". At the same time they agreed that "it was desirable that a process leading to mutual force reductions should be initiated". (For MBFR talks, see page 182 below.)

The Ministers also decided that, in view of the recent expansion of Soviet activity in the Mediterranean, measures should be taken to enhance the effectiveness and co-ordination of allied surveillance in that area.

The Brussels Council meeting of Nov. 15-16, 1968, was strongly influenced by the Soviet invasion of Czechoslovakia on Aug. 20-21, 1968.

The Ministers' communiqué stated inter alia: "World opinion has been profoundly shocked by this armed intervention carried out against the wishes of the Government and people of Czechoslovakia. . . . The contention of the Soviet leadership that there exists a right of intervention in the affairs of other states deemed to be within a so-called 'Socialist Commonwealth' runs counter to the basic principles of the UN Charter [and] is dangerous to European security. . . . Applied to Germany [these] policies . . . would be contrary to the four-power agreements relating to Germany as a whole." In this context the Ministers reaffirmed "the determination of the Alliance to persevere in its efforts to contribute to a peaceful solution of the German question based on the free decision of the German people and on the interests of European security", and they reiterated their governments' non-recognition of the German Democratic Republic.

In response to the Soviet action, the Ministers declared:

"The quality, effectiveness and deployment of NATO's forces will be improved in terms of both manpower and equipment in order to provide a better capability for defence as far forward as possible. The quality of reserve forces will also be improved and their ability to mobilize rapidly will be increased.

"Renewed attention will be directed to the provision of reinforcements for the flanks and the strengthening of local forces there.

"The conventional capability of NATO's tactical air forces will be increased. Certain additional national units will be committed to the major NATO Commanders. Specific measures have been approved within these categories of action for improving the conventional capability of NATO's forces."

They added: "Prospects for mutual balanced force reductions have suffered a severe setback."

At a meeting of the Defence Planning Committee on Nov. 14, 1968, increased military contributions by member governments were announced by Defence Ministers of most member countries.

The Canadian Government, on the other hand, decided in April 1969 to reduce the size of Canadian forces in Europe.

The Defence Planning Committee approved on Dec. 3, 1969, provisional political guidelines for the initial defensive use of tactical nuclear weapons, as drawn up by the Nuclear Planning Group in November. The group had also completed a review of procedures for consultation on the possible use of nuclear weapons in defence of NATO.

On May 27, 1970, the Council issued a further *Declaration on Mutual and Balanced Force Reductions*, calling for exploratory talks by interested states and stating inter alia that any reduction agreed upon should include "stationed and indigenous forces and their weapons systems in the area concerned", with "adequate verification and controls".

A European Defence Improvement Programme was announced in Brussels on Dec. 1, 1970, after a meeting of Defence Ministers of the European NATO member countries except France, Iceland and Portugal. Based on the assumption that US forces in Europe would be maintained "at substantially current levels", the programme comprised a "special European scheme" involving a contribution of about $420,000,000 towards the acceleration and extension of (i) the NATO Integrated Communications System (NICS) and (ii) aircraft survival measures to improve the ability of NATO Air Forces to survive enemy strikes on their bases.

At its meeting on Dec. 3-4, 1970, the Council discussed in detail a comprehensive study "AD-70" setting out the problems for allied defence in the 1970s, with NATO's approach to security continuing to be "based on the twin concepts of defence and détente", and with the "special military and political role of US forces in Europe as an irreplaceable contribution to the common defence".

The Defence Planning Committee, in a communiqué issued on May 28, 1971, stated inter alia that, in view of "the continuing increase in real terms in the allocation of resources to military and military-related programmes by the Soviet Union and other Warsaw Pact countries", and "in order to continue providing modern and sufficient nuclear and conventional forces and to improve the situation in the important areas highlighted in the AD-70 Study, some overall increase in defence outlay was needed". The Committee had therefore given the NATO Military Authorities the necessary guidance for the planning period 1973-78.

Command Changes. A Standing Naval Force Atlantic (STANAVFORLANT), consisting of destroyers and frigates, under the overall command of SACLANT and responsible, when in European waters, to

CINCHAN and C.-in-C. Eastern Atlantic, was established at Portland (UK) on Jan, 13, 1968.

A new command called Maritime Air Forces Mediterranean (MARAIRMED), subordinated to Allied Naval Forces Southern Europe (NAVSOUTH), was inaugurated in Naples on Nov. 21, 1968.

The Council's Defence Planning Committee decided on May 28, 1969, that NATO's Military Authorities should establish a naval on-call force for the Mediterranean, the concept of which had been approved by the Council on Jan. 16, 1969.

It was announced at NATO headquarters in Brussels on Aug. 20, 1971, that in accordance with the wishes of the Government of Malta and also with long-term planning aims agreed upon in 1965, the headquarters of Allied Naval Forces, Southern Europe, should be moved from Malta to Naples.

NATO Air Defence System. A programming and training centre forming part of a computerized underground control point for NATO's air defence system, was opened at Glons (Belgium) on April 9, 1968, for eventual incorporation in NADGE.

NATO Communications Satellite. The first NATO communications satellite, *NATO-1,* was launched from Cape Kennedy (USA) on March 20, 1970; it was to link NATO headquarters in Brussels, national capitals, and NATO land and sea commands.

Committee on Challenges of Modern Society. The Council decided on Nov. 6, 1969, upon a proposal made by President Nixon on April 10, to establish a Committee on the Challenges of Modern Society (CCMS) to consider problems of the human environment, and at its first meeting on Dec. 8-10, 1969, the new committee recommended pilot studies to be carried out on road safety, disaster relief, air and water pollution, and problems of individual and group motivations in a modern industrial society, as well as of the transmission of scientific knowledge to the decision-making sectors of government.

1972-1978

At a meeting of the North Atlantic Council on Dec. 7-8, 1972, the Defence Planning Committee noted with concern the growing military capability of the Soviet Union and her allies, which it described as "greatly in excess of that required for purely defensive purposes", and endorsed the principle that "the overall military capability of NATO should not be reduced except as part of a pattern of mutual force reductions, balanced in scope and timing". The committee adopted a five-year NATO Force Plan for 1973-77 in the light of each nation's force commitment for 1973.

The Eurogroup Ministers met on Dec. 5, 1972. They reviewed the European Defence Improvement Programme [see page 169] and noted with satisfaction that its implementation was well under way.

The Committee on the Challenges of Modern Society met on Nov. 14-15, 1972. It endorsed a new project on urban transportation and sponsored the signing of a memorandum on the development of "clean" automobile engines by France, the Federal Republic of Germany, Italy, the United Kingdom and the USA.

A Standing Naval Force Channel (STANAVFORCHAN) was commissioned on May 11, 1973, to be under the operational command of the Commander-in-Chief, Channel Command.

A ministerial meeting of the Defence Planning Committee was held in Brussels on June 7, 1973, during which the committee reviewed the capabilities of NATO in the light of a further report on the Allied Defence Problems in the 1970s (*AD-70*). The report summarized progress in the preceding two years in improving NATO's effectiveness in each region, and also identified areas requiring further improvement. The committee undertook to concentrate on these areas and to allocate more resources for the modernization and re-equipment of NATO forces. An increased need was recognized to improve co-operation in logistics and in the research, development and production of armaments.

Following a meeting of the Nuclear Planning Group in The Hague on Nov. 6-7, 1973, the ministers stated in a communiqué inter alia: "Ministers emphasized the important bearing which the strength and readiness of NATO's conventional forces, particularly those located in Europe, have upon NATO's overall deterrent posture. The ministers also discussed a report by the NATO military authorities describing the operational concepts and doctrine that currently govern their military planning, and which reflect the NATO strategy of flexibility in response."

At a Ministerial Council meeting in Brussels on Dec. 10-11, 1973, ministers noted progress by the CCMS, in particular in the fields of the development of supplemental energy resources through the use of solar and geothermal energy and of the disposal of hazardous wastes and toxic industrial effluents.

Ottawa Declaration. At the Council's ministerial meeting in Ottawa on June 18-19,

1974, ministers adopted, on the occasion of the 25th anniversary of the establishment of the Alliance, an "Ottawa Declaration" reaffirming the aims and ideals of the North Atlantic Treaty.

In the declaration it was noted in particular: "The members of the Alliance . . . realize that the circumstances affecting their common defence have profoundly changed in the last 10 years. The strategic relationship between the United States and the Soviet Union has reached a point of near equilibrium. Consequently, although all the countries of the Alliance remain vulnerable to attack, the nature of the danger to which they are exposed has changed. . . . The European members, who provide three-quarters of the conventional strength of the Alliance in Europe, and two of whom possess nuclear forces capable of playing a deterrent role of their own contributing to the overall strengthening of the deterrence of the Alliance, undertake to make the necessary contribution to maintain the common defence at a level capable of deterring and if necessary repelling all actions directed against the independence and territorial integrity of the members of the Alliance.

"The United States, for its part, reaffirms its determination not to accept any situation which would expose the Allies to external political or military pressure likely to deprive them of their freedom and states its resolve, together with its allies, to maintain forces in Europe at the level required to sustain the credibility of the strategy of deterrence and to maintain the capacity to defend the North Atlantic area should deterrence fail. . . .

"All members of the Alliance agree that the continued presence of Canadian and substantial US forces in Europe plays an irreplaceable role in the defence of North America as well as of Europe. Similarly, the substantial forces of the European allies serve to defend Europe and North America as well. It is also recognized that the further progress towards unity, which the member states of the European Community are determined to make, should in due course have a beneficial effect on the contribution to the common defence of the Alliance of those of them who belong to it. . . ."

Withdrawal of Greek Forces. As a result of the occupation of about one-third of the territory of Cyprus by Turkish troops on Aug. 14, 1974, the Government of Greece decided to withdraw its armed forces from NATO and to remain a member of NATO "only in connexion with its political aspects" on the ground of NATO's "inability to prevent Turkey from creating a state of conflict between two allies".

The US Congress, on Dec. 10, 1974, passed legislation which in effect suspended US military aid to Turkey pending "substantial progress" towards a negotiated settlement of the Cyprus problem, and on Dec. 30 of that year the US President signed foreign aid legislation further suspending US military assistance as well as arms deliveries to Turkey with effect from Feb. 5, 1975. (See also US-Turkish bilateral agreements, page 186.)

Greece, however, did not return to parti-cipation in NATO's military activities until October 1980 [see page 182].

Strengthening of NATO Forces. At a meeting of NATO's Nuclear Planning Group in London on Nov. 17-18, 1976, ministers inter alia discussed "the need to maintain an adequate defence and deterrent capability in the light of recent developments and deployments over the full spectrum of Soviet forces"; drew attention to "interdependencies between developments in the threat, new weapons technologies and arms control measures"; "stressed the importance of maintaining the essential linkage between the three elements of the NATO triad—strategic nuclear, theatre nuclear and conventional forces—and especially the importance of strong conventional forces"; and discussed "improvements in the effectiveness of NATO's theatre nuclear force posture considered necessary to support the Alliance's strategy of flexibility in response".

At a meeting of the Defence Planning Committee on Dec. 7-8, 1976, ministers approved a NATO force plan for the period 1977-81 involving in particular the procurement or development of additional modern aircraft by Canada, the United Kingdom and the United States and the restructuring of US and German forces.

Arrangements for the purchase of new aircraft by four other NATO member countries had in April-June 1976 resulted in firm orders for a total of 306 US F-16 fighter aircraft (72 for Norway, 84 for the Netherlands, 48 for Denmark and 102 for Belgium) to replace the ageing US F-104G Starfighter aircraft in use since the early 1960s.

Under a memorandum of understanding signed on July 29, 1976, by the Governments of the Federal Republic of Germany, Italy and the United Kingdom, a full production programme was launched for 809 multirole combat aircraft (MRCA) known as the Tornado (385 for the UK Royal Air Force, 324 for the West German Air Force and Navy and 100 for the Italian Air Force), production contracts being signed on behalf of the three Governments by NATO's MRCA Development and Production Management Organization (NAMMO).

At a Ministerial Council meeting held in London on May 10-11, 1977, and attended by the Presidents of the United States and of Portugal and the heads of government of 11 other member governments (with France and Iceland being represented by their respective Foreign Ministers), the "essential purpose" of NATO was strongly reaffirmed as follows:

"The essential purpose of the Alliance is to safeguard the independence and security of its members, enabling them to promote the values of democracy and respect for human rights, individual freedom, justice and social progress, and to make possible the creation of a lasting structure of peace. The Allies are firmly resolved to maintain and enhance the effectiveness of the Alliance and the ties which unite them.''

The leaders also reaffirmed ''their support for an equitable world system in which all countries, developing as well as developed, will see their best interests served and which can sustain the economic progress of all''. They expressed their intention of mobilizing their efforts towards the attainment of that objective in the appropriate form, and they invited the Warsaw Pact countries to do the same.

At a Defence Planning Committee meeting in Brussels on May 17-18, 1977, approval was given to ministerial guidance on the development of force proposals for 1979-84 ''designed to correct current deficiencies'' in NATO defence.

This guidance was summarized as follows:

''**NATO Objectives.** The overall strategic concept of NATO is to preserve peace and to provide for the security of the North Atlantic Treaty area primarily by a credible deterrence effected by confronting any possible threatened or actual aggression with adequate NATO forces, within the concept of forward defence and flexibility in response.

''**Recent Developments in the Threat.** The Warsaw pact forces are increasingly offensive in posture and capable of projecting Soviet power on a global scale. Soviet nuclear forces continue to improve with the appearance of new nuclear missile systems equipped with multiple warheads, including the expected deployment of the SS-20 mobile intermediate range system capable of striking targets in the whole of Europe and beyond. It is in the conventional field, however, where the growth of the Warsaw Pact capability has been most pronounced. In particular, the Warsaw Pact ground forces have the capability to stage a major offensive in Europe without reinforcement. The improved offensive and deep penetration capabilities of the Warsaw Pact tactical air forces now permit the Warsaw Pact to conduct the initial stages of an air attack to a greater extent than hitherto with in-place forces. The capabilities of the Soviet Union to exercise sea power all around the world have been enhanced by the introduction of new and improved ships, submarines and aircraft.

''The steady growth in military power is backed in the Soviet Union by an allocation of resources for defence estimated at between 11 per cent and 13 per cent of gross national product (nearly three times the NATO average) and by an annual increase in real terms in defence expenditure of about 5 per cent. The heavy investment by the Soviet Union in military research and development has begun to erode the qualitative advantage in military equipment long employed by NATO.

''**Implications for NATO.** The Allies are undertaking significant equipment replacement and modernization programmes. However, many deficiencies remain in NATO forces, and the disparity in conventional military capabilities between NATO and the Warsaw Pact continues to widen. This adverse trend points to certain areas of critical importance that should be taken into account in both national and NATO planning.

''**NATO Strategy and Crisis Management.** NATO's strategic concept for deterrence and forward defence remains valid. However, if NATO is to retain the ability to carry out this strategy and to avoid the need to use nuclear weapons at an early stage of a conflict, a balanced force improvement programme should be carried out with emphasis placed on conventional force improvements. While NATO should be capable of dealing with the entire spectrum of possible Warsaw Pact aggressions, particular attention should be paid to NATO's ability to respond to an attack by ready forces after very little warning. For deterrence as well as defence, NATO governments need to be able to take prompt political decisions in times of tension, so that NATO can deploy its forces in a timely and orderly fashion.

''**NATO Forces.** The enhanced ability of the Warsaw Pact to launch an attack at short notice places additional emphasis on NATO's need for adequate, fully trained and exercised in-place forces. Reserve forces should be capable of being deployed rapidly as organized, equipped and sufficiently trained units. Systems for rapid call-up should be maintained and exercised. Reinforcement and augmentation forces should reach an area of potential conflict before an aggression takes place or, if warning time is very short, early enough to affect the initial course of hostilities. Special emphasis should be placed on prestocking, on the timely provision of sea and airlift capabilities and an adequate reception facilities. All the forces committed to NATO should be brought up to standards established by the major NATO commanders as soon as possible.

''**Defence against Armour.** Although the Alliance has improved its anti-armour capabilities, a gap persists between these capabilities and the threat posed by the Warsaw Pact's armoured forces, and more anti-armour weapons should be acquired.

''**Maritime.** If the Alliance is to maintain the ability to cope with the emerging threat at sea, and to protect the sea lanes for the timely reinforcement and resupply of Europe, it is imperative that the rate of improvement of NATO's maritime forces be increased.

''**Air Defence.** The increasing offensive capability of Warsaw Pact air forces emphasizes the need to improve NATO's air defences over land and at sea. To enhance the survivability of NATO forces, the Alliance's integrated air defence system needs to be expanded and modernized.

''**Regional Aspects.** The defence of the North Atlantic area is indivisible. On the flanks an adequate allocation of forces and a balanced military effort must be assured; continued efforts must be made to strengthen local mobilization capabilities, advance the arrival times of external reinforcements and improve reception and other logistic arrangements. For some countries assistance from external sources is required as well as the need for improved reinforcement capabilities.

''**New Technology.** Efficient application of modern technology, while not offering any inexpensive solutions, can provide opportunities, if applied through co-operative and timely efforts, for substantial improvement to the deterrent and defence caabilities of the Alliance.

''**Alliance Co-operation.** NATO resources can be employed to best effect if, in the development of national plans and programmes, greater account is taken of the collective needs of the Alliance, recognizing that the prerogatives of sovereign governments and national systems of finance are bound to place limits on the pace and degree to which integration can be achieved. Some progress has been made but there is still much room for a better allocation of defence resources, especially through greater Alliance co-operation. This process would be greatly facilitated by the establishment of a more comprehensive framework for defence planning incorporating a longer-term approach. Only thus would it be possible to establish in a timely and orderly way the necessary requirements, set the priorities, reconcile demands on resources for co-operative efforts with those required for national efforts, and identify areas for co-operation.

"**Armaments Planning.** The trend for the cost of equipment to increase disproportionately in relation to most other defence costs has continued. In many cases the cost of major defence projects is beyond the capability of most member nations to finance alone. The cost of equipment is also of major importance for potential buyers among Allies because of the budgetary impact on their defence planning. Interested countries should therefore be involved in relevant projects as early as possible. Separate research, development and production of different weapon systems for similar roles has led to problems of non-standardization and the lack of interoperability between forces and equipment of member nations.

"On-going studies should therefore be pursued with a view to harmonizing national defence equipment planning procedures and developing NATO long-term armaments planning. The aim of these efforts should be standardization and, where this is not possible, full interoperability. In pursuing these objectives a better balance in the traffic in the 'two-way street' between Europe and North America in weapons and equipment procurement will be necessary.

"**Impact on NATO Planning.** In developing more rational procedures for NATO's long-term planning for defence, the Alliance must seek to harmonize planning mechanisms for the various co-operative and supporting programmes, and to dovetail the results of this effort with the present NATO force planning procedures into a comprehensive approach for Alliance defence planning. The need for early identification of the resource implications for major co-operative projects will be of special importance. The activities of regional groups, such as the Eurogroup, will have an important contribution to make in this context.

"**Resources for Defence.** Against the background of adverse trends in the NATO-Warsaw Pact military balance and in order to avoid a continued deterioration in the relative force capabilities, an annual increase in real terms in defence budgets should be aimed at by all member countries. This annual increase should be in the region of 3 per cent, recognizing that for some individual countries economic circumstances will affect what can be achieved; present force contributions may justify a higher level of increase. Specific target figures for each country will need to be determined in the normal course of the defence planning review. Nations should provide full compensation for the inflationary impact of rising pay and price levels to ensure that planned real increases are achieved. It is, moreover, imperative that nations increase the cost effectiveness of their defence expenditures, in particular the percentage of such expenditure devoted to major equip-

ment, but without detriment to combat readiness. The effective use of resources will depend to a large extent on progress in Alliance co-operation.

"**Priorities.** Priority should be given to those capabilities which contribute directly to deterrence and to NATO's ability to withstand the initial phases of attack and, in particular, to measures which will enhance readiness and reinforcement capabilities and promote a collective approach to equipping, supporting and training Alliance forces."

At a meeting in Brussels on Dec. 8-9, 1977, the Ministerial Council approved a NATO force plan for the period up to 1982.

The Defence Planning Committee, at a meeting in Brussels on May 18-19, 1978, adopted a long-term defence programme and endorsed new force goals for 1979-84 to cover the whole spectrum of NATO's forces. The main elements of the long-term defence programme were summarized under the headings of readiness, reinforcement, reserve mobilization, maritime posture, air defence, communication, command and control, electronic warfare, consumer logistics, rationalization and theatre nuclear modernization.

1977-78 US Decisions on Nuclear Weapons. In July 1977 President Carter announced the following modifications in the context of the US defence programme: (i) The cancellation of plans for a strategic B-1 intercontinental bomber (to replace the B-52 in use since the mid-1950s) with a top speed of 1,350 miles per hour (Mach 2.1) and capable of flying at the speed of sound at very low altitudes (and thus difficult to detect by radar); (ii) the continued development of the advanced Cruise missile, a small jet-propelled missile with a "terrain contour matching" (Tercon) guidance system enabling it to fly at very low altitudes at subsonic speeds and with projected ranges of some 300 miles in the tactical (conventional) role and 2,000 miles in the strategic (nuclear) role (different versions being either sea-launched or air-launched); and (iii) the allocation of funds for the development of "neutron" warheads, an "enhanced radiation" weapon or thermonuclear fusion device with a nuclear fission detonator (in effect a small hydrogen bomb triggered by a smaller atomic bomb) which, because of its "limited collateral damage", would be especially effective against tanks and armoured personnel carriers in areas where other nuclear explosives would cause much damage to "friendly" forces, civilians and buildings.

On April 7, 1978, however, President Carter announced that he had decided to defer the production of the enhanced radiation weapon (i.e. the neutron bomb); that the ultimate decision on the "incorporation of enhanced radiation features into our modernized battlefield" would be made later; and that it would be "influenced by the degree to which the Soviet Union shows restraint in its conventional and nuclear arms programmes and force deployments affecting the security of the United States and Western Europe". (The Supreme Commander of NATO forces in Europe had, however, said on March 21, 1978, that "from the purely military point of view" the neutron bomb was "a most desirable modernization step to be undertaken by the Alliance".)

In April 1978 President Carter was reported to have suggested, during a visit to Warsaw on Dec. 30, 1977, that the United States might be prepared to enter into an agreement with the Soviet Union which would prevent the European NATO member countries from obtaining the Cruise missile.

However, on Oct. 18, 1978, the US Government announced that the President had endorsed the production of tactical nuclear warheads for the Lance missile and an eight-inch artillery weapons system adaptable for use as enhanced radiation weapons (neutron bombs).

1978-1980

At a meeting in Washington on May 30-31, 1978, the NATO Ministerial Council inter alia welcomed a US intention to preposition heavy equipment for three additional US divisions in the central region of Allied Command Europe by 1982.

At a Defence Planning Committee meeting in Brussels on Dec. 5-6, 1978, ministers again expressed their concern at the military strength of the Warsaw Pact countries and in particular the introduction of the SS-20 mobile intermediate-range ballistic missile with multiple warheads and the Backfire (Tupolev V-G) bomber systems capable of striking targets in the whole of Europe and beyond, also from locations far in the interior of the Soviet Union. The ministers inter alia approved the programme for a NATO airborne early warning and control system (AWACS) and the NATO force plan for 1979-83. (The AWACS was to consist of 16 to 18 modified Boeing 707 aircraft, renamed E3A, equipped with radar and computers capable of monitoring military activities up to 300 or 400 miles inside Eastern Europe, and stationed in West Germany from early in 1982.)

At a further Defence Planning Committee meeting in Brussels on May 15-16, 1979, ministers again expressed concern at recent developments in the Warsaw Pact countries' military capabilities, stating: "Specifically, the SS-20 missile introduces a new dimension of threat in the theatre nuclear field. For the first time a weapon on the continental scale can reach all the territories of Western Europe with multiple warheads from mobile launchers based in the Soviet Union. . . . Ministers also noted improvements in new Soviet intercontinental and submarine-launched ballistic missiles, all with multiple independently targetable, re-entry vehicles (MIRVs), which have enhanced substantially the Soviet strategic capability."

In December 1979 NATO Foreign and Defence Ministers (i) decided to install new long-range theatre nuclear weapons (Pershing II launchers and ground-launched Cruise missiles) in Western Europe; (ii) called for negotiations between the United States and the Soviet Union on reducing the numbers of such weapons on both sides; and (iii) made new proposals on mutually and balanced force reductions (MBFR) in Central Europe.

In particular the ministers decided on Dec. 12 to deploy in Europe 108 Pershing II launchers (replacing existing Pershing I-A launchers) and 464 ground-launched Cruise missiles (GLCM), all with single warheads. At the same time 1,000 US warheads were to be withdrawn from Europe as soon as possible and the above 572 long-range theatre nuclear force (LRTNF) warheads would be accommodated within the reduced level. (All 108 Pershing II launchers were to be deployed in the Federal Republic of Germany, and of the Cruise missiles 160 were to be placed in the United Kingdom, 112 in Germany, 96 in Italy and 48 each in Belgium and the Netherlands.)

A special consultative group on arms control, the establishment of which had been announced at the same meeting, stated after its first session on Jan. 25, 1980, that NATO was still firmly committed to the parallel approach of modernizing its LRTNF in Europe while seeking agreement with the Soviet Union on limiting the number of such weapons on either side.

The Defence Planning Committee, meeting on Dec. 11-12, 1979, adopted a NATO force plan for 1980-84, and at a meeting in Brussels on May 13-14, 1980, it endorsed NATO force goals for the 1981-86 period.

At a meeting of the (Foreign Ministers') Council in Ankara on June 25-26, 1980, the ministers condemned as "unacceptable" the Soviet armed intervention in Afghanistan ("a traditionally neutral and non-aligned country of the Third World") and reaffirmed a UN General Assembly resolution calling for the "immediate, unconditional and total withdrawal of foreign troops from Afghanistan". They declared inter alia: "It is vital that the Soviet Union should be left in no doubt as to the extremely grave view which the Allies take of this situation which jeopardizes world peace." Of the Soviet activities in the field of LRTNF systems the ministers noted that, in addition to the existing force of 450 SS-4 and SS-5 medium and inter-mediate-range ballistic missiles, the Soviet Union had "deployed approximately 450 warheads on 150 SS-20 launchers" (i.e. new intermediate or limited range missiles), and that the USSR was in the process of deploying for its SS-20 force alone more warheads than were planned for the entire modernization programme agreed to in December 1979 (whereas deployments in Allied countries would not begin until late in 1983).

A meeting of the Nuclear Planning Group held on Nov. 13-14, 1980, discussed inter alia a new US "countervailing strategy" which had been set out in a Presidential Directive (which became known in August 1980) requiring US nuclear forces to be able to undertake precise, limited nuclear strikes against military facilities in the Soviet Union rather than concentrating their efforts on destroying Soviet cities as in the past.

A meeting of the Defence Planning Committee on Dec. 9-10, 1980, adopted the NATO force plan for 1981-85.

In the communiqué issued at the end of the North Atlantic Council's meeting on Dec. 11-12, 1980, it was stated inter alia that the Soviet Union's bases for mobile intermediate-range ballistic missiles (SS-20) already identified would alone support more warheads than were planned under NATO's entire modernization programme, and that the withdrawal of 1,000 nuclear warheads as an integral part of this modernization had been completed.

Reintegration of Greece. The Government of Greece announced on Oct. 20, 1980, that it had decided to rejoin the military organization of NATO (which it had left in 1974—see above), and this decision was approved by the Greek Parliament on Oct. 24 by 182 votes to 20 after 85 deputies (including 94 of the Panhellenic Socialist Movement—PASOK) had left the Chamber before the vote and while three others were absent.

Inter-Allied Committee for East-West Trade

An Inter-Allied Co-ordinating Committee for East-West Trade (COCOM), consisting of all NATO member countries except Iceland and of Japan, was set up following a resolution adopted by the UN General Assembly on May 18, 1951 (by 48 votes to none with eight abstentions), recommending an embargo on the shipment to areas under the control of the Governments of the People's Republic of China and of North Korea of "arms, ammunition and implements of war, atomic energy materials, petroleum and items useful in the production of implements of war" (this recommendation following the condemnation of China as an aggressor, because of its military intervention in Korea, by the UN General Assembly on Jan. 31, 1951).

The original embargo agreed upon by COCOM against the countries of the Soviet bloc, China, North Korea and North Vietnam was, with effect from Aug. 15, 1958, reduced to a prohibition of the shipment to these countries of "strictly strategic goods" (although the United States maintained a complete embargo on all US trade with China, North Korea and North Vietnam). In 1965 COCOM agreed on procedures whereby East European countries could purchase from a COCOM member country a nuclear reactor for the production of electric power, one of the conditions for such a purchase being that the buyer would have to agree to observe the safeguard system of the International Atomic Energy Agency [see page 39].

Vienna Talks on Mutual and Balanced Force Reductions in Central Europe

Talks between representatives of NATO and Warsaw Pact countries with troops in Central Europe on mutual and balanced force reductions (MBFR) in that area—which had first been suggested in the North Atlantic Council's MBFR Declaration of June 25, 1968 [see page 175]—were conducted in Vienna from 1973 onwards.

At the first such talks, held on Oct. 30-31, 1973, policy statements made by the two sides revealed, according to a NATO spokesman, the following divergencies: (1) Whereas NATO wanted to start with US and Soviet force reductions, the Warsaw Pact powers were pressing for cuts affecting both national and other troops; (2) NATO wished to limit reductions to ground forces, while the Warsaw Pact powers aimed to reduce both ground and air forces; (3) while the Warsaw Pact powers wanted to reduce nuclear arms, NATO preferred to concentrate on conventional armaments; and (4) NATO insisted that the Warsaw Pact powers should make the biggest cuts because of their superiority in manpower and armaments, while these powers challenged this concept.

During the following years the talks continued without leading to agreement.

On July 17, 1975, a NATO spokesman defined the object of the talks as "the achievement of approximate parity between the two sides in ground forces in Central Europe in the form of a common ceiling on ground force manpower plus reductions of Soviet tanks", whereas the Warsaw Pact side wanted force reductions to apply also to air forces and nuclear-equipped units.

On Dec. 16, 1975, the US representative submitted a proposal for the withdrawal of 1,000 tactical nuclear warheads (out of NATO's total of 7,000) and of 29,000 US troops, against a reduction of Soviet troops by 68,000 men and 1,700 tanks (out of 15,000), to achieve a "common ceiling" of about 700,000 men on either side. The Warsaw Pact side, however, continued to insist on "an equal percentage reduction of ground and air forces"—a proposal which had been criticized by NATO because it failed to state any figures on which these percentages should be calculated.

At the ministerial meeting of the North Atlantic Council held on Dec. 13-14, 1979, new proposals were made, envisaging a two-phase reduction in NATO and Warsaw Pact forces levels, under which about 13,000 US and 30,000 Soviet troops were to be withdrawn from Central Europe, with the aim of achieving "a common collective ceiling in ground force manpower for each side at approximately 900,000". Although these proposals were subsequently discussed in Vienna, the North Atlantic Council's ministerial meeting held in Brussels on Dec. 11-12, 1980, found that the Eastern countries had "regrettably still not provided the information necessary to reach agreement on the size of the forces of the Soviet Union in Central Europe which is an essential prerequisite to a Phase 1 agreement", and that they had not responded adequately to Western proposals concerning associated measures designed to ensure verification of force reductions and limitation and to enhance stability.

Survey of Agreements Basic to the NATO Structure

NORTH ATLANTIC TREATY AND SUBSEQUENT ACCESSIONS

(1) North Atlantic Treaty between Belgium, Canada, Denmark, France, Iceland, Italy, Luxembourg, the Netherlands, Norway, Portugal, the United Kingdom and the USA, signed on April 4, 1949 (for text see page 166).

(2) Protocol to the North Atlantic Treaty on the accession of Greece and Turkey, signed on Oct. 22, 1951.

(3) Protocol to the North Atlantic Treaty on the accession of the Federal Republic of Germany, signed on Oct. 23, 1954.

(4) Resolution of the North Atlantic Council on Implementation of Section IV of the Final Act of the London Conference, signed on Oct. 23, 1954. This document, one of the Paris Agreements, provided for the placing of the armed forces of the NATO countries stationed on the continent of Europe under the authority of the Supreme Allied Commander Europe (SACEUR); the location and integration of the forces; closer co-ordination of logistics; the right of inspection of forces in Europe by SACEUR; and the indefinite duration of the North Atlantic Treaty.

(5) Resolution of Association with the Tripartite Declaration of Oct. 3, 1954, signed on Oct. 23, 1954 [see page 167].

AGREEMENTS OF THE STATUS OF NATO

(1) Agreements on the Status of the North Atlantic Treaty Organization, National Representatives, and the International Staff, signed on Sept. 20, 1951.

(2) Agreements between the USA and the North Atlantic Treaty Organization, pursuant to Article 19 of the Agreement on the Status of the North Atlantic Treaty Organization, signed: (i) on Sept. 29, 1951; (ii) on July 23, 1958.

AGREEMENTS ON THE STATUS OF FORCES

(1) Agreement between member states of the North Atlantic Treaty on the Status of their Forces, signed on June 19, 1951.

(2) Agreement between the USA and Canada relating to the application of the NATO Status of Forces Agreement to the US forces in Canada, signed on April 28 and 30, 1952, in effect since Sept. 27, 1953.

(3) Agreements concluded between the USA and Turkey relating to implementation of the NATO Status of Forces Agreement, signed: (i) on June 23, 1954; (ii) on July 21, 1955.

(4) Agreement on the status of NATO forces stationed in Germany, signed on Aug. 3, 1959 (in effect for Germany since July 1, 1963).

AGREEMENTS ON THE STATUS OF INTERNATIONAL MILITARY HEADQUARTERS

(1) Agreement concerning the employment by the International Military Headquarters of US nationals, signed on Feb. 25, 1953.

(2) Agreement concluded by the United States regarding the headquarters of the Supreme Allied Commander Atlantic, signed on Oct. 22, 1954 (operative since April 10, 1954).

(3) Agreement between the Government

of the Turkish Republic and the Supreme Allied Commander Europe, signed on Feb. 22, 1956.

(4) Agreement between the Government of the Italian Republic and SACEUR regarding special conditions of establishment and operation on Italian territory of International Military Headquarters which are or might be located there, signed on July 26, 1961.

(5) Agreement between the Government of the Kingdom of the Netherlands and SACEUR regarding special conditions of establishment and operation on Dutch territory of International Military Headquarters, signed on May 25, 1964.

AGREEMENTS SIGNED IN THE FRAMEWORK OF NATO

(1) Agreement between the 15 member countries for co-operation regarding atomic information, signed on June 18, 1964 (approved by the North Atlantic Council on April 13, 1955).

(2) Agreement concluded by the 15 member countries for the mutual safeguarding of secrecy of inventions relating to defence, for which applications for patents have been made, signed on Sept. 21, 1960.

Military Assistance Agreements concluded by the USA with NATO Partners

On Oct. 6, 1949, the US President signed the Mutual Defence Assistance Act of 1949 providing for military aid from the USA to the signatory governments of the North Atlantic Treaty. An amended form of this Act, known as the Mutual Security Act, was passed in 1951.

Bilateral agreements between the USA and NATO member countries, within the framework of the Mutual Security Act of 1951, can be broadly classified into the following categories: Mutual defence agreements including military aid; agreements relating to the assurances required under the Mutual Security Act; facilities assistance agreements; offshore procurements agreements; agreements for the return of military equipment; agreements allowing members of the Land, Naval and Air Force Missions to act as a military Advisory Group, and agreements relating to military missions; mutual security military sales agreements; and weapons production agreements.

Agreements Relating to Defence concluded between NATO Countries

The NATO defence system has been strengthened by the many agreements con-cluded between the various NATO countries. US defence agreements with NATO countries may be found in the chapter "Defence Treaties of the USA", pages 307ff.

Agreements among the other NATO countries are given below.

AGREEMENTS CONCLUDED BY BRITAIN

The United Kingdom has concluded agreements within the NATO framework with:

(1) *Belgium and Canada:* on transit and stationing in Belgium of Canadian forces, signed on March 30, 1953; in force from July 29, 1953.

(2) *Belgium:* on the establishment of a military base at Campine, Nov. 12, 1952.

(3) *Denmark:* relating to the Agreement on the Status of Forces of June 19, 1951 [see page 183], Oct. 8, 1956.

(4) *France:* an agreement in principle, concluded in Paris on Oct. 6, 1976, on the exchange of information on the world naval situation, including the size and movements of third-country navies.

(5) *Federal Republic of Germany:* (i) on British bases in the German Federal Republic, Sept. 9, 1952; Oct. 15 and 18, 1954; May 22 and 31, 1957; (ii) relating to the Convention on Foreign Forces stationed in Germany [see below], April 11, 1957; and (iii) on the maintenance cost of British forces stationed in Germany, June 7, 1957; Oct. 3, 1958; April 28, 1967. Under an agreement signed on Oct. 18, 1977, the Federal Republic was to pay no further support costs for British troops in Germany after 1980.

(6) *The Netherlands:* relating to the Convention on Foreign Forces stationed in Germany [see below], June 11 and 13, 1956. Extension signed on June 7, 1957.

(7) *Turkey:* on the sale of destroyers to Turkey, Aug. 16, 1957. Amended on Jan. 12, 1959.

AGREEMENTS CONCLUDED BY CANADA

Canada has concluded agreements within the NATO framework with:

(1) *Belgium and Britain* (see above under "Agreements concluded by Britain").

(2) *Denmark:* on aircrew training for NATO, April 17, 1957. Renewed on March 25, 1960; extended on June 30, 1964.

(3) *France:* (i) pursuant to the Convention on Foreign Forces stationed in Germany: April 19, 1955; Jan. 26, 1956; and (ii) on the exchange of defence-science information, May 25, 1962.

(4) *Federal Republic of Germany:* on the training of German aircrews in Canada, Sept. 17 and Dec. 10, 1956.

(5) *Greece:* on the exchange of defence-science information, July 17 and 18, 1962.

(6) *The Netherlands:* on the extension of the NATO aircrew training programme, April 12 and 13, 1957.

(7) *Norway:* (i) on the transfer of three *Prestonian* class frigates to Norway, July 1, 1958; (ii) on the continuation of Canada's NATO air training programme, June 30, 1964; and (iii) on the exchange of information on defence, May 24, 1960.

AGREEMENTS CONCLUDED BY FRANCE

France has concluded agreements within the NATO framework with:

(1) *Belgium and Luxembourg:* on co-operation between the three countries for internal defence, July 25, 1959.

(2) *Canada* [see above].

(3) *Federal Republic of Germany:* (i) on logistics and training of German forces, Oct. 25, 1960; and (ii) on co-operation in the field of political, defence, information, cultural and scientific matters, Jan. 22, 1963 [see page 154].

(4) *Portugal:* on the setting up, by France, of a tracking station for ballistic missiles in the Azores, April 9, 1964.

AGREEMENTS CONCLUDED BY THE FEDERAL REPUBLIC OF GERMANY

The Federal Republic of Germany has concluded agreements within the NATO framework as follows:

(1) *Convention on Relations between the Three Powers* (the USA, Britain and France) and the Federal Republic of Germany and related conventions, signed on May 26, 1952. Amended by the Paris Agreements of Oct. 23, 1954.

[For bilateral agreements pursuant to these conventions see above under "Agreements concluded by Britain" and "Agreements concluded by Canada".]

(2) *Agreements with the Netherlands* on (i) cost of maintenance of Dutch forces in the Federal Republic, July 10, 1957; (ii) reparations for damage caused by Dutch military units stationed in Germany, Jan. 29, 1957.

(3) *Agreement with Norway* on the delivery of armaments spare parts, Oct. 30, 1957.

(4) *Agreement with Britain* on the development and production of a howitzer, Aug. 9, 1968.

(5) *Agreement with Portugal* on West German use of Beja air base, announced on Dec. 27, 1968. An earlier agreement on training and storage facilities for West German forces in Portugal had been concluded on June 12, 1964.

AGREEMENTS CONCLUDED BY BELGIUM

Belgium has concluded agreements within the NATO framework with:

(1) *Luxembourg and France* (see above under "Agreements concluded by France").

(2) *Luxembourg:* on an alarm network, Feb. 19 and 21, 1955.

Important Agreements related to Military Bases and Nuclear Weapons

The more significant defence agreements between NATO partners are described below.

USA-Britain. During 1948 the USA and Britain concluded an agreement on the use of air bases in Eastern England by the US Strategic Air Command. Details of this agreement were, however, not made public. In 1952, after a meeting in Washington between President Truman and the British Prime Minister, Winston Churchill, it was stated that "the use of these bases in an emergency would be a matter for joint decision by HM Government and the US Government in the light of the circumstances prevailing at the time".

An agreement relating to the supply by the USA to Britain of intermediate-range ballistic missiles was signed on Feb. 22, 1958. In the agreement it was stressed that the arrangements were made "in consonance with the North Atlantic Treaty and in pursuance of the Mutual Defence Assistance Agreement of Jan. 27, 1950". Although ownership of the missiles would eventually pass to Britain, all nuclear warheads would remain "in full US ownership, custody and control". The decision to launch the missiles would be a matter for joint decision by the two Governments.

In 1960 the USA and Britain concluded an informal agreement under which the British Government agreed to provide facilities for US Polaris nuclear submarines at a floating-base in Holy Loch on the Clyde (Scotland).

On Dec. 21, 1962, a joint communiqué was issued by President Kennedy and the British Prime Minister, Harold Macmillan, after their meeting at Nassau where, inter alia, the question of nuclear missiles was discussed. The communiqué announced that the US Government would make available to Britain, "on a continuing basis", Polaris missiles without warheads; that Britain would provide the necessary submarines; and that these forces, together with at least equal US forces, would be made available for inclusion in a NATO multilateral nuclear force. An agreement on the terms of sale by the United States of up to 100 Polaris missiles in Britain was signed on April 6, 1963. The Polaris agreement superseded an earlier agreement, concluded during 1960, for the development of the Skybolt missile by the US Government for the joint use of the US and British air forces.

USA-Canada. On Aug. 16, 1963, it was announced that Canada and the United States had reached agreement on "the conditions under which nuclear warheads will be made available for Canadian forces engaged in North American defence and assigned to NATO". The terms of the agreement were not made public, but it was stated that stockpiles of nuclear warheads would be stored at Canadian bases under Canadian command and control, but would remain under US custody. The warheads could only be used operationally with the joint authorization of the US and Canadian Governments.

Before the conclusion of this agreement the storage of US nuclear warheads on Canadian territory had been the subject of political controversy in Canada.

USA-Italy. On March 30, 1959, it was announced that an agreement between the USA and Italy had been signed in Rome, under which the Italian armed forces would be equipped with American intermediate-range ballistic missiles (IRBMs). Italian personnel would receive training in the use of the missiles, but the nuclear warheads would remain under US control. It was stressed that any decision to use the missiles and warheads would need the approval of both the Italian Government and SHAPE.

USA-Turkey. A similar agreement on the supply of IRBMs to Turkey came into force on Oct. 29, 1959. Other agreements concluded with Turkey were as follows:

(1) Agreement relating to the implementation of the NATO agreement on status of forces of June 19, 1951: June 23, 1954.

(2) Agreement of co-operation: March 5, 1959.

(3) Agreement relating to the introduction of modern weapons into NATO defence forces in Turkey. Exchanges of notes Sept. 18 and Oct. 28, 1959; entry into force Oct. 28, 1959.

(4) Agreement for the establishment of a facility for repairing and rebuilding M-12 range finders in Turkey: Nov. 30, 1959.

(5) Agreement on a weapons production programme: March 2, 1960.

Under an agreement between the United States and Turkey, signed in Ankara on July 3, 1969, and replacing over 50 earlier agreements concluded since 1959, Turkey's absolute sovereignty over all military installations in Turkey was emphasized; the agreement also laid down that Turkey would not lease or rent territory to the USA or exclude Turkish personnel from bases, and that Turkey would, within the general framework of NATO defence policies, have co-determination with the USA on the number of US troops and their weapons and equipment to be stationed in Turkey.

In 1974, however, the US Government suspended military aid to Turkey and imposed an arms embargo against that country [see page 178]. After an attempt to reverse this decision had failed in the US House of Representatives on July 24, 1975, the Turkish Government declared on the following day that the 1960 joint US-Turkish defence co-operation agreement and other agreements connected with it had lost their validity, and that the activities of all joint US-Turkish defence installations in Turkey would be suspended and the installations placed under full Turkish control. (This did not apply to the Incirlik joint defence installation, which would be reserved for its NATO task alone.)

The US arms embargo was, however, lifted under legislation signed by President Carter on Sept. 26, 1978, but this legislation did not authorize the resumption of military aid to Turkey. On Oct. 9, 1978, the Turkish Government reopened four of the 26 US military bases closed down in July 1975, these four being three intelligence gathering stations and a navigational base.

During the 1979 US-Soviet negotiations on a second strategic arms limitation treaty (SALT II—see pages 246-52) the Turkish Government took the view that this was a bilateral agreement which did not directly involve NATO and in which Turkey wished to remain neutral.

A US House of Representatives-Senate conference committee agreed on Sept. 26, 1979, to include in the 1980 US foreign aid authorization bill a total of $450,000,000 of economic and military aid for Turkey, of which $252,000,000 would constitute military aid—

(i) a long-term low-interest loan of $50,000,000 to Turkey for the purchase of US military equipment; (ii) $200,000,000 in other military loans; and (iii) $2,000,000 for the training in Turkey and in the United States of Turkish military officers. (At the same time a long-term low-interest loan of $42,000,000 was to be made available to Greece for military expenditure.)

A new five-year defence and economic co-operation agreement, renewable annually, was concluded in Ankara on March 29, 1980.

The agreement laid down that defence co-operation between the two countries would be limited to the obligations arising from the North Atlantic Treaty, and that a total of 12 military bases in Turkey, including the four reopened by Turkey on Oct. 9, 1978 [see above], were to be used again by the United States (although only within the framework of NATO and each being under the command of a Turkish officer).

Three supplementary agreements were concluded at the same time for (i) mutually agreed US financial and technical assistance to Turkey; (ii) enhanced co-operation in the production of defence material and a listing of Turkish projects under consideration; and (iii) US participation in joint defence measures in specified Turkish armed forces installations (with 13 implementing agreements concerning the technical arrangements in each installation). [See also page 316.]

USA-Portugal. An agreement between the USA and Portugal was signed on Sept. 6, 1951, defining the facilities in the Azores granted by Portugal to the USA for the purposes of the common defence. Under the agreement these facilities were integrated into the NATO framework. The agreement was extended on Nov. 15, 1957, until the end of 1962, and was again provisionally extended on Jan. 4, 1963.

The lease of a US air base in the Azores under the US-Portuguese agreement of Jan. 5, 1951, was on Nov. 15, 1957, extended to Dec. 31, 1962, and on Jan. 4, 1963, until a new lease was agreed. A new agreement was subsequently signed in Brussels on Dec. 9, 1971, granting the USA the continued use until Feb. 4, 1974, of air and naval bases on the island of Terceira, in the Azores, in return for economic assistance to Portugal by the USA.

Under a further agreement signed on June 18, 1979, the USA was allowed continued use of the strategic Lajes base on Terceira until February 1983 in return for US economic and military aid to Portugal worth $140,000,000 (including $60,000,000 for the modernization of Portugal's Air Force and for other military purposes).

USA-Greece. An agreement giving American forces the use of air and naval bases in Greece, and authorizing the USA to develop Greek roads and railways for military purposes under the NATO defence pact, was signed on Oct. 12, 1953. This agreement was partially abrogated by the agreement on the status of US forces in Greece of Sept. 7, 1956.

Under a new defence co-operation agreement between the USA and Greece, initialled on July 28, 1977, the operation of US military bases in Greece was to be limited to those which (in the Greek Prime Minister's words) "served Greek national defence needs", i.e. a naval-air base (in Crete), monitoring and communications bases (also in Crete and near Athens) and an air base at Athens, with these four bases being Greek installations under Greek command and with up to 50 per cent Greek personnel; the USA would not be permitted to store nuclear weapons at these bases or use them for war purposes without the express consent of the Greek Government. The agreement, however, remained unsigned owing to Greek objections to massive US aid granted to Turkey which the Greek Government regarded, by 1980, as upsetting the Greek-Turkish military balance.

USA-Iceland. A new agreement between the USA and Iceland on the presence of US defence forces in Iceland was announced on Dec. 6, 1956. Under the agreement an Iceland Defence Standing Group was set up to consult on the defence needs of Iceland and NATO in general, and to prepare for the training of Icelandic personnel to man the US bases. In 1960 the US forces in Iceland were reduced to leave only Air Force and Navy personnel at the air base and the radar installations.

Britain-France. An Anglo-French military air transit agreement was signed on April 19, 1948. It governed flights by military aircraft over both countries and their servicing at British and French airfields.

Rocket Training Centre in Crete. On June 11, 1964, eight NATO countries—Belgium, Denmark, France, the Federal Republic of Germany, Greece, the Netherlands, Norway, and the USA—signed an agreement on the building of a rocket training centre in Crete, to be completed in 1965. Turkey, which had wished the centre to be built on Turkish territory, refused to sign the agreement.

The centre, including a guided-missile firing range at Akrotiri, was completed and taken over by NATO on May 17, 1968.

11. The Communist World

Aspects of international co-operation involving the states of the communist world dealt with in this section include (i) the early international organizations of Communist parties, the more recent international conferences of such parties and the development of serious divisions within the world communist movement, (ii) the Warsaw Treaty Organization, (iii) the Council for Mutual Economic Assistance, (iv) the major bilateral treaties between Communist states and (v) certain major bilateral treaties concluded with non-Communist countries by the Soviet Union and China.

International Communist Organizations and Contacts

The Comintern (1919-1943)

The Comintern, the Third (Communist) International, was founded in 1919 by Lenin in Moscow. The First International had been founded in 1864 by Karl Marx and Friedrich Engels, but broke up in 1874 on account of internal dissensions. The Second International was formed in 1889, but collapsed on the outbreak of war in 1914. The Comintern served as a roof organization of the Communist parties of the world, the individual national Communist parties being in effect sections of the world revolutionary Communist party.

On June 8, 1943, the Presidium of the Executive Committee of the Communist International met to dissolve the Comintern formally with the approval of the majority of world Communist parties and without any of the existing sections of the Communist International having raised any objections to the dissolution.

The proposal for the dissolution of the Comintern, as put before the Executive Committee at a meeting on May 15, 1943, was worded as follows:

"(1) The Communist International, as the directing centre of the international working-class movement, is to be dissolved.

"(2) The sections of the Communist International are to be freed from the obligations of their rules and regulations and from the decisions of the congress of the Communist International.

"(3) The Presidium calls on all supporters of the Communist International to concentrate their energies on whole-hearted support for and active participation in the war of liberation waged by the peoples and states of the anti-Hitlerite coalition for the speediest defeat of the deadly enemy of the working-class—German fascism and its associates and vassals."

The Cominform (1947-1956)

On Oct. 5, 1947, it was announced that the Communist parties of Bulgaria, Czechoslovakia, France, Hungary, Italy, Poland, Romania, the Soviet Union and Yugoslavia had decided to set up a Communist Information Bureau (the Cominform), with its headquarters in Belgrade. Its purpose was stated to be to "organize the exchange of experience" and "where necessary to co-ordinate the activities of the Communist parties on the basis of mutual agreement".

On June 28, 1948, it was disclosed that Yugoslavia had been expelled from the Cominform on grounds, inter alia, of deviation from Marxism-Leninism, of nationalism and of hostility towards the Soviet Union.

The official announcement of the dissolution of the Cominform appeared on April 18, 1956, signed by the eight national communist parties which then formed the membership of the organization. It was stated that the eight had unanimously agreed that the Cominform had "exhausted its function".

International Communist Conferences of 1957 and 1960

Since the dissolution of the Cominform in 1956 there has been no co-ordinating body for the Communist parties in various countries. Conferences held in 1957 and 1960 failed to preserve the unity of the communist movement.

THE 1957 CONFERENCE

This conference, which was held in

Moscow on Nov. 14-16, 1957, issued the *Moscow Declaration* approved by 12 parties:—The Communist parties of the USSR, China, Bulgaria and Czechoslovakia, the Polish United Workers' Party, the Hungarian Socialist Workers' Party, the Romanian Workers' Party, the Socialist Unity Party in East Germany, the Albanian Party of Labour, the (North) Korean Party of Labour, the Working People's Party of (North) Vietnam and the Mongolian People's Revolutionary Party.

This declaration, drawn up without the participation of the League of Communists of Yugoslavia, was expressly rejected by the latter on Dec. 7, 1957.

The declaration consisted of four sections:

(1) Denunciation of "Imperialism". This section described the USA as "the centre of world reaction"; accused "American, British, French and other imperialists and their stooges" of waging wars in various parts of the world; blamed the "aggressive imperialist forces" for their "flat refusal" to reduce armaments or prohibit nuclear weapons; attacked NATO, SEATO and "West German militarism and revanchism"; and asserted that "the cause of peace is upheld by . . . the invincible camp of socialist countries headed by the Soviet Union". It added that other "powerful peace forces" were "the peace-loving countries of Asia and Africa taking an anti-imperialist stand"; the "international working class and above all its vanguard, the Communist Party"; the "liberation movement of the peoples of colonies and semi-colonies"; the "peoples of the European countries which have proclaimed neutrality"; and "the peoples of Latin America". This section also affirmed that the 12 Communist parties signing the declaration adhered to the "Leninist principles of peaceful coexistence . . . which . . . coincide with the Five Principles put forward jointly by China and India and with the programme adopted at the Bandung conference of Afro-Asian countries" [see page 387].

(2) Co-operation between Communist Countries. The declaration described the principles, upon which collaboration among the Communist states should be constructed, in these terms:

"The socialist countries base their relations on principles of complete equality, respect for territorial integrity, state independence and sovereignty, and non-interference in one another's affairs. These are vital principles. However, they do not exhaust the essence of the relations among them. Fraternal mutual aid is part and parcel of these relations. . . . The socialist states also advocate all-round expansion of economic and cultural relations with all other countries, provided they desire it, on a basis of equality, mutual benefit and non-interference in internal affairs. . . ."

(3) "Revisionism" and "Sectarianism". In this section the "international phenomena" of "revisionism", "sectarianism" and "dogmatism" were attacked, and it was claimed that Marxism-Leninism, "deriving from historical materialism", was a "world outlook reflecting the universal law of development of nature, society and human thinking" and was "valid for the past, present and future".

The declaration continued: "In condemning dogmatism, the Communist parties believe that the main danger at present is revisionism—in other words, right-wing opportunism as a manifestation of bourgeois ideology paralysing the revolutionary energy of the working-class and demanding the preservation or restoration of capitalism. However, dogmatism and sectarianism can also be the main danger at different phases of development in one party or another. It is for each Communist party to decide what danger threatens it more at a given time. . . . Modern revisionism seeks to smear the teaching of Marxism-Leninism, declares that it is 'out-moded', and alleges that it has lost its significance for social progress. . . . The revisionists deny the historical necessity for a proletarian revolution and the dictatorship of the proletariat during the period of transition from capitalism to socialism; reject the principles of proletarianism; and call for the rejection of the Leninist principles of party organization and democratic centralism. Above all, they call for the transformation of the Communist party from a militant revolutionary party into some kind of debating society. . . ."

(4) Relations with Non-Communist Parties. A section on this theme was worded as follows:

". . . The working class and its vanguard—the Marxist-Leninist party—seek to achieve the socialist revolution by peaceful means. . . . In a number of capitalist countries the working-class today has the opportunity—given a united working-class and people's front, or other workable forms of political co-operation between the different parties and organizations—to unite a majority of the people, win power without civil war, and ensure the transfer of the basic means of production to the hands of the people . . . [The] . . . working-class . . . can secure a firm majority in parliament, transform parliament from an instrument serving the class interests of the bourgeoisie into an instrument serving the working people, launch a non-parliamentary mass struggle, smash the resistance of the reactionary forces, and create the necessary conditions for the peaceful realization of the socialist revolution. . . .

"In the event of the ruling classes resorting to violence against the people, the possibility of non-peaceful transition to socialism should be borne in mind. Leninism teaches, and experience confirms, that the ruling classes never relinquish power voluntarily. In this case the degree of bitterness and the forms of the class struggle will depend not so much on the proletariat as on the resistance put up by the reactionary circles. . . . The possibility of one or another way to socialism depends on the concrete conditions in each country. . . .

"In the struggle for winning power and building socialism, the Communist parties seek co-operation with the socialist parties. Although right-wing socialist party leaders are doing their best to hamper this co-operation, there are increasing opportunities for co-operation between communists and socialists on many issues. The ideological differences between the Communist and socialist parties should not keep them from establishing unity of action on the many pressing issues that confront the working-class movement. . . ."

THE 1960 CONFERENCE

This, the largest conference since the seventh world congress of the Communist International held in 1935, took place in Moscow in November 1960, and was attended by delegations of 81 countries, excluding Yugoslavia, whose League of Communists had not been invited. The conference was not attended by Chairman Mao Tse-tung (Mao Zedong) of the Chinese Communist Party, nor by Palmiro Togliatti, then general secretary of the Italian Communist Party—although both these parties were represented by delegations.

The 1960 conference was faced with the possibility of a split in the international communist movement as a result of the controversy between the Soviet and Chinese parties on questions of theory and policy. The main issues of this controversy may be summarized as follows:

(1) The Soviet party upheld the view, put forward by Nikita Khrushchev (then First Secretary of the party's Central Committee) at its 20th congress in 1956, that Lenin's theory of the inevitability of war under capitalism was no longer valid because of the growing strength of the socialist bloc, the neutral policy pursued by many former colonial countries, and the strength of "anti-war" movements in capitalist countries. Chinese spokesmen, on the other hand, maintained that it was a "naive illusion" to think that war could be avoided before capitalism had been abolished.

(2) The Soviet party emphasized that nuclear war would prove equally disastrous to all concerned, and used this argument in favour of peaceful coexistence between countries with different social systems. The Chinese Communists, however, maintained that China could survive a nuclear war and that a third world war would result in further victories for communism.

(3) The Chinese Communists rejected the policy of peaceful coexistence as involving a rejection of the class struggle and an attitude of "peace at any price".

(4) The Chinese Communists also rejected as "very wrong" the view that nationalist movements in colonial and underdeveloped countries might possibly endanger world peace and should therefore not necessarily be supported by the Soviet Union and international communism.

(5) Soviet theoreticians contended that in underdeveloped countries communists should ally themselves with the "bourgeoisie" in the struggle for national independence, which would prepare the way for the transition to socialism. The Chinese Communists, however, declared in August 1960: "If we view the movement led by the bourgeoisie in colonial countries as the mainstream of the national liberation movement and give full support to it, while ignoring, or expressing contempt for, the anti-imperialist struggle waged by the revolutionary masses, it will in fact mean the adoption of bourgeois viewpoints."

(6) The Chinese Communists did not accept the Soviet view, then expressed by N. Khrushchev, that in certain countries it was possible for Communist parties to attain power by parliamentary means without violent revolution.

(7) Against the accepted Marxist theory that intensive industrialization was an essential prerequisite for the transition from socialism to full communism, the Chinese Communists contended that agricultural expansion was "the one essential base".

(8) The Chinese party continued to uphold the assertion of the 1957 Moscow declaration [see above] that "revisionism" was "the main danger" to the international communist movement and rejected the Soviet

party's relaxation (since 1959) of its campaign against the "revisionism" of the Yugoslav Communists.

The declaration of the Moscow conference published on Dec. 5, 1960, reflected the Soviet view, although with some concessions made in its wording to the Chinese position. It contained the following significant passages:

War and Peace. "The aggressive nature of imperialism has not changed, but real forces have appeared that are capable of foiling its plans of aggression. War is not fatally inevitable. . . . World war can be prevented by the joint efforts of the world socialist camp, the international working class, the national liberation movement, all the countries opposing war, and all peace-loving forces. . . . The policy of peaceful coexistence is also favoured by a definite section of the bourgeoisie of the developed capitalist countries, which takes a sober view of the relationship of forces and of the dire consequences of a modern war. . . . But should the imperialist maniacs start war, the peoples will sweep capitalism out of existence and bury it. . . .

"The near future will bring the forces of peace and socialism new successes. The USSR will become the leading industrial power of the world. China will become a mighty industrial state. The socialist system will be turning out more than half the world's industrial product. The peace zone will expand. . . . In these conditions a real possibility will have arisen of excluding world war from the life of society even before socialism achieves complete victory on earth, with capitalism still existing in a part of the world. . . .

"Peaceful coexistence of countries with different social systems does not mean conciliation of the socialist and bourgeois ideologies. On the contrary, it implies intensification of the struggle of the working class, of all the Communist parties, for the triumph of socialist ideas. But ideological and political disputes between states must not be settled through war. . . .' "

Colonial and Under-developed Countries. "Communists have always recognized the progressive, revolutionary significance of national liberation wars. . . . The peoples of the colonial countries win their independence both through armed struggle and by nonmilitary methods, depending on the specific conditions in the country concerned. . . .

"The urgent tasks of national rebirth facing the countries that have shaken off the colonial yoke cannot be effectively accomplished unless a determined struggle is waged against imperialism and the remnants of feudalism by all the patriotic forces of the nation, united in a single national democratic front. . . . The alliance of the working class and the peasantry is the most important force in winning and defending national independence, accomplishing far-reaching democratic transformations, and ensuring social progress. . . . The extent to which the national bourgeoisie participates in the liberation struggle depends to no small degree upon its strength and stability. . . . In present conditions the national bourgeoisie of the colonial and dependent countries unconnected with imperialist circles is objectively interested in the accomplishment of the principal tasks of the anti-imperialist, antifeudal revolution, and therefore retains the capacity of participating in the revolutionary struggle against imperialism and feudalism. In that sense it is progressive. But it is unstable, and is inclined to compromise with imperialism and feudalism. . . .

"The socialist countries are true and sincere friends

of the peoples fighting for liberation and of those who have thrown off the imperialist yoke. While rejecting on principle any interference in the internal affairs of young national states, they consider it their internationalist duty to help the peoples in strengthening their independence. . . .''

Moving on to another major area of international communist policy, the declaration also called for joint action on a national and international scale between Communist and social democratic parties in support of complete disarmament under international control, the abolition of military bases on foreign soil, assistance to the nationalist movements in colonial and dependent countries, and the improvement of living standards.

Forms of Transition to Socialism. ''The imperialist reactionaries'', the declaration continued, ''intimidate the masses by alleging that the communists need wars between states to overthrow the capitalist system and establish a socialist system. The Communist parties emphatically reject this slander. The fact that both World Wars, which were started by the imperialists, ended in socialist revolutions by no means implies that the way to social revolution is necessarily through world war. . . . The choice of its social system is the inalienable right of the people of each country. Socialist revolution is not an item of export, and cannot be imposed from without. . . .

''Today in a number of capitalist countries the working class, headed by its vanguard, has the opportunity . . . to unite a majority of the people, win state power without civil war, and ensure the transfer of the basic means of production to the hands of the people. . . . The working class can defeat the reactionary anti-popular forces, secure a firm majority in parliament . . . and create the necessary conditions for peaceful realization of the socialist revolution. . . . In the event of the exploiting classes resorting to violence against the people, the possibility of non-peaceful transition to socialism should be borne in mind. . . . The actual possibility of the one or the other way of transition to socialism in each individual country depends on the concrete historical conditions.''

Revisionism and Dogmatism. After condemning ''the personality cult, which shackles creative thought and initiative'', the declaration denounced ''the Yugoslav variety of international opportunism'' and asserted that ''further exposure of the leaders of the Yugoslav revisionists, and active struggle to safeguard the communist and working-class movement from the anti-Leninist ideas of the Yugoslav revisionists, remains an essential task of the Marxist-Leninist parties''. It repeated the formula of the 1957 declaration that ''revisionism . . . remains the main danger'' but that ''dogmatism and sectarianism in theory and practice can also become the main danger at some stage of development of individual parties'', and called for ''a determined struggle'' against both. In conclusion, the declaration referred to the Soviet party as ''the universally recognized vanguard of the world communist movement'', and described the decisions of its 20th congress as initiating ''a new stage in the world communist movement''.

Intensification of the Sino-Soviet Dispute

During 1961 China concluded agreements with Albania providing for increased trade between the two countries and including a declaration on the two Governments' ''complete agreement on ideological questions''. During the same year Albania's relations with the Soviet Union began to deteriorate, and at the 22nd congress of the Soviet Communist Party on Oct. 17-31, 1961, Khrushchev openly broke with Albania, alleging that its leaders had ''begun to depart from the common agreed line of the communist movement of the whole world on major issues'' and were ''using the same methods as were current in our country at the time of the personality cult'' (i.e. under Stalin).

The break between the USSR and China was widened at this congress, with Chou En-lai (Zhou Enlai, the Chinese Foreign Minister) leaving Moscow before the end of the conference after blaming the Soviet party for ''laying bare a dispute between fraternal parties or fraternal countries, openly in the face of the enemy''—which, he said, was ''not a serious Marxist-Leninist attitude''.

The congress was followed by the breaking-off of diplomatic relations between the USSR and Albania and open expression of support for Albania by the Chinese Communist Party in December 1961.

During the years 1962-64 the Sino-Soviet conflict intensified. The Chinese Government disapproved of N. Khrushchev's approaches to Yugoslavia in May 1962; of his compromise with the USA over the Cuban issue in October 1962; and of Soviet military aid given to India in the Sino-Indian War of October-November 1962.

On June 14, 1963, the Chinese party approved a letter to the Soviet party, in which it put forward ''25 points'' for discussion at talks to be held in Moscow. These points included:

(3) ''If the general line of the international communist movement is one-sidedly reduced to 'peaceful coexistence', 'peaceful competition' and 'peaceful transition', this is to violate the revolutionary principles of the 1957 declaration and the 1960 statement. . . .

(4) ''The fundamental contradictions in the contemporary world . . . are: The contradiction between the socialist camp and the imperialist camp; the contradiction between the proletariat and the bourgeoisie in the capitalist countries; the contradiction between the oppressed nations and imperialism; and the contradictions among imperialist countries and among monopoly capitalist groups. . . .

(5) ''The following erroneous views should be repudiated . . . : (a) The view which blots out the class content of the contradiction between the socialist and imperialist camps . . . ; (b) the view which recognizes only the contradiction between the socialist and imperialist camps . . . ; (c) the view which maintains . . . that the contradiction between the proletariat and the bourgeoisie can be resolved without a proletarian

revolution in each country and that the contradiction between the oppressed nations and imperialism can be resolved without revolution . . . ; (*d*) the view which denies that the development of the inherent contradictions in the contemporary capitalist world inevitably leads to a new situation in which the imperialist countries are locked in an intense struggle, and asserts that the contradictions among the imperialist countries can be reconciled or even eliminated by 'international agreements among the big monopolies'; and (*e*) the view which maintains that the contradiction between the two world systems of socialism and capitalism will automatically disappear in the course of 'economic competition', . . . and that a 'world without wars', a new world of 'all-round co-operation', will appear. . . .

(9) "The oppressed nations and peoples of Asia, Africa and Latin America are faced with the urgent task of fighting imperialism and its lackeys. . . . In these areas extremely broad sections of the population refuse to be slaves of imperialism. They include not only the workers, peasants, intellectuals and petty bourgeoisie, but also the patriotic national bourgeoisie and even certain kings, princes and aristocrats. . . . The proletariat and its party must . . . organize a broad united front against imperialism. . . . The proletarian party should maintain its ideological, political and organizational independence and insist on the leadership of the revolution. The proletarian party and the revolutionary people must learn to master all forms of struggle, including armed struggle. . . . The policy of the proletarian party should be . . . to unite with the bourgeoisie, in so far as they tend to be progressive, anti-imperialist and anti-feudal, but to struggle against their reactionary tendencies to compromise and collaborate with imperialism and the forces of feudalism. . . .

(10) "In the imperialist and capitalist countries the proletarian revolution and the dictatorship of the proletariat are essential. . . . It is wrong to refuse to use parliamentary and other legal forms of struggle when they can and should be used. However, if a Marxist-Leninist party falls into legalism or parliamentary cretinism, confining the struggle within the limits permitted by the bourgeoisie, this will inevitably lead to renouncing the proletarian revolution and the dictatorship of the proletariat.

(11) "Marx and Lenin did raise the possibility that revolutions may develop peacefully. But, as Lenin pointed out, the peaceful development of revolution is an opportunity 'very seldom to be met with in the history of revolution'. As a matter of fact, there is no historical precedent for peaceful transition from capitalism to socialism. . . . The proletarian party must never base its thinking, its policies for revolution and its entire work on the assumption that the imperialists and reactionaries will accept peaceful transformation. . . .

(14) ". . . Certain persons now actually hold that is is possible to bring about 'a world without weapons, without armed forces, and without wars' through 'general and complete disarmament' while the system of imperialism and of the exploitation of man by man still exists. This is sheer illusion. . . .

(15) "The emergence of nuclear weapons does not and cannot resolve the fundamental contradictions in the contemporary world, does not and cannot alter the law of class struggle, and does not and cannot change the nature of imperialism and reaction. It cannot, therefore, be said that with the emergence of nuclear weapons the possibility and the necessity of social and national revolutions have disappeared, or that the basic

principles of Marxism-Leninism, and especially the theories of proletarian revolution and the dictatorship of the proletariat . . . have become out-moded. . . .

(21) "Relations between socialist countries, whether large or small, and whether more developed or less developed economically, must be based on the principles of complete equality. . . .

(22) "If the principle of independence and equality is accepted in relations among fraternal parties, then it is impermissible for any party to place itself above others, to interfere in their internal affairs and to adopt patriarchal ways in relations with them. . . ."

The central committee of the Soviet party answered the above "25 points" on July 14, 1963.

In their reply the Soviet party blamed the Chinese for having themselves caused the deterioration in relations and described their views as "erroneous". In particular, the Soviet party claimed that the Chinese "obviously underestimated the whole danger of nuclear war", and also the importance of "the struggle for disarmament". The Soviet party emphasized that "the nuclear bomb does not distinguish between the imperialists and working people" and that it would not be possible, as suggested by Mao Tse-tung, "to build a bright future on the ruins of a destroyed imperialism".

The Soviet party also accused the Chinese leaders of "organizing and supporting various anti-party groups of renegades", including dissident communist groups in various countries, and of having "pushed the Albanian leaders on to the road of open struggle against the Soviet Union".

Following bitter polemics in the press of the two countries, the Chinese party rejected on May 7, 1964, a Soviet proposal for a world conference to be held in the autumn of 1964 to end the dispute.

After N. Khrushchev's removal from office on Oct. 14, 1964, the dispute was aggravated by disagreements on communist policy on Vietnam during 1965. The Chinese party refused to attend a meeting of Communist parties in Moscow in March 1965 and also to send a delegation to the 23rd Soviet party congress in March-April 1966.

During the period of the "Great Proletarian Cultural Revolution" in China the conflict was further intensified, and on Dec. 13, 1966, the Soviet party for the first time condemned the policy of "Mao Tse-tung and his group", whose actions, it said, had "nothing in common with Marxism-Leninism" and "objectively" assisted imperialism. Further fierce criticism of Mao Tse-tung and his policies followed in the Soviet press from February 1967 onwards.

The Soviet invasion of Czechoslovakia on Aug. 20-21, 1968, was condemned by Chou En-lai on Aug. 23 as "the most barefaced and typical specimen of fascist power politics played by the Soviet revisionist clique against its so-called allies"—a clique which had, he claimed, "degenerated into a gang of social-imperialists and socialfascists''. At the same time Chinese statements strongly denounced the Dubcek regime in Czechoslovakia for its ''revisionism'' and its failure to organize armed resistance to the invasion.

The ''Brezhnev Doctrine''

Leonid Brezhnev, the General Secretary of the Soviet Communist Party, in an address to a Polish United Workers' Party congress in Warsaw on Nov. 12, 1968, put forward the doctrine of ''limited sovereignty'' in an attempt to justify the Soviet intervention in Czechoslovakia earlier that year. L. Brezhnev declared inter alia:

''When internal and external forces that are hostile to socialism try to turn the development of some socialist country towards the restoration of a capitalist regime, when socialism in that country and the socialist community as a whole are threatened, it becomes not only a problem of the country concerned, but a common problem and concern of all socialist countries. Naturally, an action such as military assistance to a fraternal country designed to avert the threat to the social system is an extraordinary step, dictated by necessity.'' Such a step, he added, ''may be taken only in case of direct actions of the enemies of socialism within a country and outside it, actions threatening the common interests of the socialist camp''.

In China, Marshal Lin Piao (Lin Biao, then party vice-chairman) commented on the theory on April 1, 1969, in his report to the ninth congress of the Chinese Communist Party, and prophesied that the Soviet Government would be overthrown by its own people.

''Since Brezhnev came to power,'' he said, ''. . . the Soviet revisionist renegade clique has been practising social-imperialism and social-fascism more frantically than ever. Internally, it has intensified its suppression of the Soviet people and speeded up the all-round restoration of capitalism. Externally, it has stepped up its collusion with US imperialism and its suppression of the revolutionary struggles of the people of various countries, intensified its control over and its exploitation of various East European countries and the People's Republic of Mongolia, and intensified its threat of aggression against China. . . .

''In order to justify its aggression and plunder, the Soviet revisionist renegade clique trumpets the so-called theory of 'limited sovereignty', the theory of 'international dictatorship' and the theory of 'socialist community'. What does all this stuff mean? It means that your sovereignty is 'limited', while his is unlimited. . . . We firmly believe that the proletariat and the broad masses of the people in the Soviet Union, with their glorious revolutionary tradition, will surely rise and overthrow this clique consisting of a handful of renegades.''

In another passage of his report, in which he reaffirmed the party's views on the inevitability of war, Marshal Lin Piao opposed the ''social-imperialist'' countries (i.e. the USSR) to the socialist countries (i.e.

China and Albania), and suggested that a conflict existed in the former between the proletariat and the ''bourgeoisie'', implying that the USSR had ceased to be a socialist country.

L. Brezhnev, however, denied during a visit to Yugoslavia on Sept. 22, 1971, that the so-called ''doctrine of limited sovereignty'' existed. The story of this ''doctrine'', he said, had been circulated by forces intent upon ''driving a wedge between Yugoslavia and the USSR'', and it was not worth wasting time on denying ''these slanderous inventions''.

The Sino-Soviet dispute was further aggravated by Chinese claims on Soviet territory, arising out of the fact that large areas formerly under Chinese suzerainty had been annexed by Czarist Russia between 1858 and 1881.

These areas included over 75,000 square miles north and west of Lake Balkhash, ceded to Russia in 1864 and 1881; 230,000 square miles of territory north of the river Amur, acquired by Russia under the Treaty of Aigun (1858); and 150,000 square miles east of the Ussuri river, incorporated into the Russian Empire under the Treaty of Peking (1860).

China regarded these treaties as being two of nine ''unequal treaties'' which were forced upon the Chinese Empire between 1842 and 1901. These also included the 1881 Treaty of St Petersburg confirming Russia's annexations of 1864; the 1895 Treaty of Shimonoseki, under which Japan obtained control of Taiwan (Formosa) and the Pescadores; and an 1898 Convention on the expansion of the territory of Hong Kong.

In addition, the Soviet Union and China disagreed on the exact demarcation of their common frontier, and boundary negotiations were intermittently conducted by the two Governments from 1964 onwards without reaching final conclusions.

Meanwhile armed clashes had taken place along the border between March and August 1969, and the press and radio on both sides continued their polemics from time to time.

Despite their dispute, negotiations between the two Governments led to (a) an agreement concluded on Aug. 8, 1969, on navigation on the Amur and Ussuri rivers, and (b) a trade and payments agreement concluded on Nov. 22, 1970.

The 1969 Conference

A further conference of Communist parties in Moscow on June 5-17, 1969, with 66 of the 75 parties taking part, approved a document entitled ''Tasks at the present stage of the struggle against imperialism and united action of the Communist and Workers' parties and all anti-imperialist forces''.

Parties not taking part in this conference included those of Albania, Iceland, the Netherlands and Yugoslavia.

L. Brezhnev declared on June 7: "We cannot afford to ignore the divergences existing in the communist movement today". In particular, he attacked the Chinese Communist Party for classifying as "revisionists" the "overwhelming majority of the socialist countries and Communist parties" and for organizing "subversive splinter groups" against these parties. He also accused Maoism of calling for war, instead of for a struggle against war, and of directing its spearhead of foreign policy chiefly "against the Soviet Union and the other socialist countries".

During the conference the Soviet intervention in Czechoslovakia in August 1968 was criticized by representatives of the British, Italian, Spanish and Swedish Communist parties.

The document finally approved by the conference (a) reaffirmed the communist movement's support for the policy of peaceful coexistence of states with different social systems, which did "not contradict the right of any oppressed people to fight for its liberation" (in which context the document called for "all-round support for the heroic Vietnamese people . . . in order to compel US imperialism to withdraw its interventionist troops from Vietnam"); (b) expressed the view that the Communist countries made their "primary contribution to the struggle against capitalism" by their economic development, though it emphasized that this did not mean abandonment of support for revolutionary movements; (c) accepted the possibility of a peaceful transition to socialism in certain countries, while accepting the use of force as inevitable in others; and (d) asserted that there was "no leading centre of the international communist movement" (thus in effect repudiating the 1960 Moscow conference statement that the Soviet party was "the universally recognized vanguard of the world communist movement").

Soviet-Yugoslav Reconciliation

A normalization of relations between the Soviet Union and Yugoslavia—which had been expelled from the Cominform in 1948 [see above]—was effected by a visit to Yugoslavia in May 1955 by a delegation led by Nikita Khrushchev. In a joint Belgrade declaration signed on June 2, 1955, the two sides expressed "their determination to develop their future relations in the spirit of friendly co-operation". This reconciliation was further strengthened by a visit to Moscow by President Tito in June 1956,

after N. Khrushchev had included a friendly reference to the Yugoslav leader in his denunciation of the Stalin regime at the 20th congress of the Communist Party of the Soviet Union (CPSU) in February 1956.

An agreement on increased co-operation between the Soviet Union and Yugoslavia in the use of atomic energy for peaceful purposes was signed in Belgrade on Jan. 10, 1963, and trade and co-operation agreements were signed in 1964 and 1965.

However, the 1968 Soviet action in Czechoslovakia was strongly condemned by President Tito, his Government and the League of Communists of Yugoslavia on April 21 of that year as constituting a violation of the sovereignty of an independent socialist state, and in October 1968 President Tito repudiated L. Brezhnev's "limited sovereignty" doctrine.

Three years later, after an "unofficial friendly visit" to Yugoslavia by L. Brezhnev on Sept. 22-25, 1971, Soviet-Yugoslav relations were again placed on a basis of "equality and mutual respect" as well as "non-interference in internal affairs", as expressed in the Belgrade declaration of 1955 and also a declaration signed in Moscow by the two leaders in June 1956. This reconciliation was confirmed during a visit to Moscow by President Tito on July 5-10, 1972.

Conferences of European Communist Parties, 1974-80

The 1974 Conference. A conference of 20 West European Communist parties, held in Brussels on Jan. 26-28, 1974, adopted a political declaration on future policy strategy, in particular with reference to the European Community.

Parties represented at the conference were those of Austria, Belgium, Denmark, Finland, France, the Federal Republic of Germany, Greece, Ireland, Italy, Luxembourg, Portugal, San Marino, Spain, Turkey and the United Kingdom, as well as the Socialist Unity Party of West Berlin, the Cyprus Progressive Party of Working People, the Communist Left Party of Sweden and the Swiss Party of Labour (while the Netherlands Communist Party was represented as an observer and the Norwegian Communist Party did not send a delegate).

In the declaration the parties noted that the Communist parties of the six original member states of the European Communities were "fighting against its monopolistic orientation and also for its democratization", whereas the parties of the three new member countries of the Communities (Denmark, Ireland and the United Kingdom) were "campaigning for complete withdrawal" and those of non-member or associated states "against attempts to include their countries in the sphere of influence of the monopolies which dominate the Communities''. Nevertheless the parties reaffirmed that "a joint response to the policy of monopolistic economic integration" was "possible and necessary", and that they intended "to campaign together to secure acceptance, in the light of the problems which confront the peoples of Western Europe as a whole, of solutions which correspond to the interests of all these peoples, as well as for European co-operation which is genuinely democratic, responding to the interests of each of their countries and of all". All participating parties expressed their total opposition to European Communities membership or association for the "fascist regimes" of Europe and condemned any attempt to establish a European Defence Community. The declaration also called for a "broad alliance of all workers' and democratic forces" and for efforts by the parties to seek "convergencies and joint actions and initiatives" with socialist, social-democratic and Christian democratic forces.

Among differences of view which became apparent at the conference was that between the French party, which expressed serious reservations about working within the existing framework of the European Communities, and the Italian party, which stressed the possibility of using the Communities' institutions to further working-class interests.

The 1976 Conference. A conference of European Communist parties held in East Berlin on June 29-30, 1976, was attended by 29 party delegations.

These represented (i) the parties of the Soviet bloc (the CPSU, the Communist parties of Bulgaria, Czechoslovakia and Romania, the Socialist Unity Party of the German Democratic Republic, the Hungarian Socialist Workers' Party and the Polish United Workers' Party), (ii) the League of Communists of Yugoslavia; and (iii) West European Communist parties (of Austria, Belgium, Denmark, Finland, France, the Federal Republic of Germany, Greece—the "exterior" party, Ireland, Italy, Luxembourg, the Netherlands, Norway, Portugal, San Marino, Spain, Turkey and the United Kingdom) as well as the Socialist Unity Party of West Berlin, the Cyprus Progressive Party of the Working People, the Swedish Left Communist Party and the Swiss Party of Labour.

The conference adopted a declaration entitled *For Peace, Security, Co-operation and Social Progress in Europe*, which was a compromise involving acceptance of the principles that the declaration must be approved by all participants; must recognize the complete independence of all Communist parties and their right to decide their own policies; and must not criticize or condemn the policies of the Chinese or any other Communist party. (These principles also covered the use of the phrase "international co-operation" in the place of "proletarian internationalism" which was objected to—by a group of parties led by those of France, Italy, Romania, Spain and Yugoslavia—as being associated with the acceptance of Soviet leadership.)

During the debate the concept of "proletarian internationalism" and the condemnation of any criticism of the Soviet Union were supported by the Austrian, West German, Greek, Luxembourg, Norwegian, Portuguese and Turkish representatives.

The declaration adopted by the conference stated in its preamble inter alia:

"The participants in the conference emphasize that their parties, on the basis of a political line worked out and adopted by every party in complete independence in accordance with the socio-economic and political conditions and the specific national features prevailing in the country concerned, are firmly resolved to continue waging a consistent struggle in order to achieve the objectives of peace, democracy and social progress. . . . They state with all clarity that the policy of peaceful coexistence, active co-operation between states irrespective of their social systems, and international détente correspond both to the interests of each people as well as to the cause of progress for the whole of mankind, and in no way mean the maintenance of the political and social status quo in the various countries, but on the contrary create optimum conditions for the development of the struggle of the working class. . . .

"The parties participating in the conference . . . will develop their internationalist, comradely and voluntary co-operation and solidarity on the basis of the great ideas of Marx, Engels and Lenin, strictly adhering to the principles of equality and sovereign independence of each party, non-interference in internal affairs, and respect for their free choice of different roads in the struggle for social change of a progressive nature and for socialism. The struggle of each party for socialism in its own country and its responsibility towards the working class and the people of that country are bound up with mutual solidarity among working people of all countries and all progressive movements and peoples. . . . "

Among its concrete proposals the declaration listed (i) measures to be taken to achieve disarmament and security in Europe; (ii) the removal of impediments to full civil and democratic rights (e.g. in Northern Ireland) and the achievement of independence and territorial integrity for Cyprus; and (iii) settlements leading to peace and security in the Middle East, Indo-China, Latin America and southern Africa.

On the other hand adherence to the concepts of "proletarian internationalism", the "dictatorship of the proletariat" and the leadership of the CPSU was expressed by speakers at a conference of Soviet bloc countries held in Sofia (Bulgaria) on Dec. 15-17, 1976, and attended by party officials from the USSR as well as Bulgaria, Cuba, Czechoslovakia, the German Democratic Republic, Hungary, Mongolia, Poland and Romania. (The concept of the "dictatorship of the proletariat" had been abandoned by the French Communist Party in February 1976 and by the Japan Communist Party in July of that year.)

The 1980 Conference. Convened on the initiative of the French Communist Party and the Polish United Workers' Party, a further conference of European Communist parties was held in Paris on April 28-29, 1980, and devoted to the theme of peace and disarmament. It was attended by delegations of six Soviet-bloc parties (those of Bulgaria, Czechoslovakia, the German Democratic Republic, Hungary, Poland and the Soviet Union) and of 14 West European parties (of Austria, Cyprus, Denmark, Finland, France, the Federal Republic of Germany, Greece, Ireland, Luxembourg, Malta, Norway, Portugal, Turkey and West Berlin), while the Belgian Communist Party and the Swiss Party of Labour sent observers. Among those parties not represented were the Romanian Communist Party, the League of Communists of Yugoslavia and the Italian and Spanish Communist parties.

The principal outcome of the conference was the issuing of an appeal for co-operation between "Communists, Socialists, Social Democrats, Christians and believers of other faiths" to promote peace and disarmament, to which end it was stated that Communists were "ready for any dialogue, for any talks and for any joint action".

The specific aims of such co-operation, said the appeal, would be to prevent the deployment of new US nuclear missiles in Europe as decided by NATO; to work for the earliest possible ratification of the SALT II treaty between the Soviet Union and the United States and the continuation of negotiations on a further reduction of strategic armaments; to seek "decisive progress" at the Vienna talks on mutual and balanced force reductions in Europe (MBFR) and the "establishment of nuclear-free zones in our continent"; to ensure "further progress in the implementation by all states of all the provisions of the Helsinki Final Act [i.e. of the 1975 Conference on Security and Co-operation in Europe], especially through complementing political détente with military détente" to work for "the convocation in Warsaw of a European conference on military détente and disarmament"; to "demand the practical implementation of the decisions of the [1978] UN special disarmament session"; and to ensure that the funds thereby released would be used for development purposes.

The Concept of "Eurocommunism"

At the 1976 Sofia conference Bulgarian representatives in particular attacked as "incorrect" the policies of certain West European Communist parties (notably those of France, Italy and Spain), which had become known as "Eurocommunism".

These parties had in recent years openly stated that they favoured a non-violent road to socialism through co-operation with other parties and the achievement of a parliamentary majority by democratic means and even with the retention of a multi-party system.

In 1972 the French Communist Party entered into an electoral agreement with the Socialist and Left Radical parties (but by October 1978 this agreement had effectively lapsed). In November 1975 the party opted for respecting the people's verdict in all circumstances and for ruling out "categorically all recourse to oppression, totalitarianism and personal rule". However, by January 1980 the party's differences with the CPSU were largely composed as Georges Marchais, the party's secretary general, paid a visit to Moscow.

For the Italian Communist Party (PCI) its then secretary, Palmiro Togliatti, had stated in June 1956 that the Soviet model could not and should no longer be obligatory for other Communist parties, and of the communist movement he had said: "The whole system is becoming polycentric . . . ; we cannot speak of a single guide but rather of progress which is achieved by following paths which are often different." In February 1976 Enrico Berlinguer, the PCI's secretary, declared: "The accession of the working classes to political power can and must be achieved in Italy in a manner fully consistent with democratic institutions, the principles of freedom and the procedures for change embodied in our Constitution." He repeatedly called for the formation of a broadly-based government of "democratic unity" with PCI participation, and the party has sought to come to an understanding with the ruling Christian Democratic Party on a long-term strategy of co-operation. In August 1978 Berlinguer emphasized that Lenin had not excluded "the possibility of a peaceful development of the socialist revolution and of a continuation of a plurality of parties".

For the Spanish party underground leaders called, on Jan. 28, 1976, for a "Spanish road to socialism characterized by democracy and a multi-party system".

The Soviet intervention in Afghanistan in December 1979 was opposed by the Communist parties of Italy, Spain and the United Kingdom, but not by those of France and Portugal. It was also opposed by the parties of Romania and Yugoslavia.

1980 East Berlin Conference

An "international scientific conference" of representatives of 116 Communist parties, revolutionary organizations and national liberation movements, organized by the Socialist Unity Party (SED) of the German

Democratic Republic and the Prague review *Problems of Peace and Socialism*, was held in East Berlin on Oct. 20-24, 1980, on the subject of "the common struggle of the workers' movement and the national liberation movements against imperialism and for social co-operation".

According to Erich Honecker, the General Secretary of the SED, the "three principal revolutionary currents of our time" were "the world socialist system, the workers' movements in capitalist countries and the national liberation movements".

A report by the principal working group of the conference stressed the need "to pursue the struggle against the policy of confrontation followed by imperialism" and to fight for "arms limitation and disarmament", and it denounced in particular "the expansionist and neo-colonialist tendencies of West German imperialism" which was leading the Federal Republic of Germany to support for the nuclear arms race and to the adoption of "a revanchist posture towards the German Democratic Republic and other socialist countries".

At the end of the conference it was admitted (inter alios by Hermann Axen, a member of the Politburo of the SED, and Maxime Granetz, secretary of the central committee of the French Communist Party) that the conference had shown up "differences of conception and of fighting conditions" and also on the role of China.

The Warsaw Treaty Organization

Headquarters of Joint Command: Moscow.

Members: Bulgaria, Czechoslovakia, the German Democratic Republic, Hungary, Poland, Romania and the Soviet Union.

The East European Mutual Assistance Treaty, or Warsaw Pact as it is generally known, is the counterpart, in Communist Eastern Europe, of the North Atlantic Treaty in the West. The 20-year *Treaty of Friendship, Co-operation and Mutual Assistance* was signed in Warsaw on May 14, 1955, by Albania, Bulgaria, Czechoslovakia, the German Democratic Republic, Hungary, Poland, Romania and the Soviet Union. It came into force in the following month.

History

The first move towards a military alliance of the Communist bloc countries in Europe was made at a conference held in Moscow from Nov. 29 to Dec. 2, 1954, and attended by the eight countries listed above. At this conference on "the safeguarding of peace and collective security in Europe", the London and Paris Agreements establishing the Western European Union and providing for West Germany's entry into NATO [see page 103], were condemned as encouraging a revival of German militarism. A declaration published at the end of the conference stated that, if the Paris Agreements were ratified, the countries represented at the Moscow conference would again meet "to adopt measures for safeguarding their security".

On March 21, 1955, agreement was announced between the eight nations on the principles of a mutual defence treaty and the organization of a unified command.

Six days after the Paris Agreements came into force, representatives of the eight nations met again in Warsaw, where they signed a treaty of mutual assistance and decided on the creation of a unified military command for their armed forces with the exception of those of the German Democratic Republic.

The Warsaw Treaty

The preamble to the treaty reiterates the criticism of the Paris Agreements as creating a danger of renewed war through the re-militarization of West Germany.

The principal provisions of the treaty are:

"**Art. 1.** The contracting parties undertake, in accordance with the UN Charter, to refrain in their international relations from the threat or use of force, and to settle their international disputes by peaceful means so as not to endanger international peace and security.

"**Art. 2.** The contracting parties declare their readiness to take part, in a spirit of sincere co-operation, in all international undertakings designed to safeguard international peace and security, and to use all their energies for the realization of these aims. Moreover, they shall work for the adoption, in agreement with other states desiring to co-operate in this matter, of effective measures towards a general reduction of armaments and the prohibition of atomic, hydrogen and other weapons of mass destruction.

"**Art. 3.** The contracting parties shall consult among themselves on all important international questions relating to their common interests. In the interests of organizing their joint defence, and of upholding peace and security, the contracting parties shall immediately consult together whenever, in the opinion of any of them, there has arisen the threat of an armed attack on one or several states that are signatories of the treaty.

"**Art. 4.** In the event of an armed attack in Europe on one or several states that are signatories of the treaty by any state or group of states, each party to this treaty shall, in the exercise of the right to individual or collective self-defence in accordance with Article 51 of the UN Charter, render the state or states so attacked immediate assistance, individually and in agreement with other states parties to this treaty, by all the means it may consider necessary, including the use of armed force. The parties to this treaty shall immediately consult among themselves on the necessary joint measures to be adopted for the purpose of restoring and upholding international peace and security.

In accordance with the UN Charter, the Security Council shall be advised of the measures taken on the basis of this article. These measures shall be discontinued as soon as the Security Council has taken the necessary steps to restore and uphold international peace and security.

"**Art. 5.** The contracting parties have agreed to set up a unified command to which certain elements of their armed forces shall be allocated by agreement among the parties, and which shall function on the basis of jointly defined principles. They shall also take other agreed measures to strengthen their defensive capacity, in order to safeguard the peaceful labour of their peoples, to guarantee the inviolability of their frontiers and territories, and to provide safeguards against possible aggression.

"**Art. 6.** For the purpose of holding the consultations provided for in the present treaty between the states parties thereto, and for considering problems arising out of the implementation of this treaty, a Political Consultative Committee shall be formed in which each state party to this treaty shall be represented by a member of the government, or any other specially appointed representative. This committee may set up any auxiliary organs which may be necessary.

"**Art. 7.** The contracting parties undertake not to participate in any coalitions and alliances, and not to conclude any agreements, the purposes of which would be at variance with those of the present treaty. They declare that their obligations under existing international treaties are not at variance with the provisions of the present treaty.

"**Art. 8.** The contracting parties declare that they will act in a spirit of friendship and co-operation with the object of furthering and strengthening the economic and cultural ties between them, adhering to the principles of mutual respect for their independence and sovereignty, and of non-interference in their internal affairs.

"**Art. 9.** This treaty may be open for accession by other states—irrespective of their social and state systems—who declare their readiness to assist the efforts of the peace-loving states for the purpose of safeguarding the peace and security of nations. . . .

"**Art. 11.** The present treaty shall remain in force for 20 years. For contracting parties which do not, one year before the expiration of that term, give notice of termination of the treaty to the Government of the Polish People's Republic, the treaty shall remain in force for a further 10 years. In the event of the establishment of a system of collective security in Europe and the conclusion for that purpose of a general European treaty concerning collective security, a goal which the contracting parties shall steadfastly strive to achieve, the present treaty shall cease to have effect as from the date on which the general European treaty comes into force."

Formation of Unified Military Command

The decisions of the eight nations relating to the creation of a unified military command were contained in a separate statement declaring inter alia that:

(1) Questions relating to the joint force would be considered by the Political Consultative Committee set up by the Warsaw Treaty.

(2) Ministers of Defence and military leaders would have command of the armed forces of each state allotted to the joint armed forces, and would act as deputies of the Commander-in-Chief.

(3) A General Staff, with its headquarters in Moscow, would include representatives of the general staffs of all the participating countries.

(4) Deployment of the joint armed forces in the territories of member states would be carried out "in accordance with the requirements of mutual defence and by agreement between these states".

(5) The participation of the German Democratic Republic would be examined later.

At the first meeting of the Political Consultative Committee on Jan. 27-28, 1956, it was decided to incorporate contingents of a new East German Army in the joint command of the Warsaw Treaty powers.

Political Consultative Committee

Other important decisions taken at the first meeting of the Political Consultative Committee related to the organization of the committee itself. It was decided that (i) the committee would meet as often as necessary, but at least twice a year (meetings have, in fact, been less frequent); and (ii) two subsidiary bodies—a Permanent Commission to make recommendations on foreign policy, and a Secretariat—should be set up.

Delegations sent by member countries to the Political Consultative Committee generally include the First Secretary of the Party, the Chairman of the Council of Ministers, the Minister of Defence and the Foreign Minister of each country.

The Political Consultative Committee decided in Budapest on March 17, 1969, to endorse new statutes on:

(1) The permanent committee of member-countries' Defence Ministers;

(2) the joint supreme command;

(3) the appointment of deputy supreme commanders from the national general staffs to the joint supreme command;

(4) participation of generals and other

officers from member countries in the various commands of the armed forces in proportion to the member countries' share in the combined forces; and

(5) the establishment of a co-ordinating authority for warfare and types of armament.

Early Developments

Membership. Although the membership of the Warsaw Treaty Organization has not formally changed since the treaty's inception in 1955, one member, Albania, did not participate in the activities of the organization after the severance of relations with the Soviet Union in 1961, and announced its withdrawal from the Warsaw Pact on Sept. 12, 1968, on the ground that by the Soviet invasion of Czechoslovakia on Aug. 20-21, 1968, the Pact had been turned "from a treaty of defence against imperialist aggression into an aggressive treaty against the socialist countries themselves".

Hungary briefly withdrew from the Warsaw Pact on Oct. 31, 1956, at the time of the popular uprising in Hungary, but returned to the organization under the Soviet-oriented Government which replaced the revolutionary government after the insurrection had been put down.

Declarations and Communiqués. A considerable number of declarations and communiqués have been issued by the Political Consultative Committee, embodying the views of the Warsaw Pact Organization. The most significant of these are listed below:

January 1956. A joint declaration, issued after the meeting held on Jan. 27-28, contained the recommendations that neither East nor West Germany should possess atomic weapons, and that NATO and the Warsaw Treaty Powers should sign a collective security treaty.

May 1958. Documents published after the meeting on May 24 included the draft of a proposed non-aggression pact between the Warsaw Treaty Organization and NATO.

August 1961. On Aug. 13 the text of a communiqué was issued in which the member countries of the Warsaw Pact "addressed to the . . . Government of the German Democratic Republic a proposal to establish such control on the borders of West Berlin as would securely block the way for subversive activities against the socialist countries", thus advocating the building of the wall between East and West Berlin.

July 1966. Two important declarations were issued after the meeting of July 4-6:

(1) *Declaration on Strengthening peace and Security in Europe.* This included proposals for the recognition

of peaceful coexistence; for the relaxation of military tension in Europe, towards which all military alliances should be simultaneously dissolved; for the setting-up of nuclear-free zones; for a German peace settlement; and for a general European conference on European co-operation and security.

(2) *Declaration on the Aggression of the USA in Vietnam.*

Developments, 1969-1980

1969 Budapest Meeting. At a meeting held in Budapest on March 17, 1969, the Political Consultative Committee approved a reorganization of the Warsaw Treaty Organization and its military structure, involving the establishment of several new bodies.

(1) A **Committee of Defence Ministers** was to act as a permanent organ and to meet annually, with each member country providing the chairman and the venue in turn, and with the task of considering a report by the Commander-in-Chief of the Joint Armed Forces.

(2) A **Military Council** would function as a consultative committee and be composed of national chiefs of staff or Deputy Defence Ministers with the status of Deputy Commanders-in-Chief of the Joint Armed Forces. This Council was to meet generally twice a year in each member country in turn and with the Commander-in-Chief of the Joint Armed Forces in the chair.

(3) A **Technical Committee of the Joint Armed Forces** was set up at the same time.

As a result of these changes the Joint Command of the Armed Forces (set up in 1955 under the general supervision of the Political Consultative Council) consisted of the Commander-in-Chief, a Chief of Staff and First Deputy Commander-in-Chief, and all the members of the Military Council as Deputy Commanders-in-Chief.

1974 Warsaw Meeting. At a meeting of the Political Consultative Committee in Warsaw on April 17-18, 1974, the participants stated that they were "ready to disband the Warsaw Treaty Organization simultaneously with the disbanding of the North Atlantic Treaty Organization (NATO) or, as an initial step, the liquidation of their military organization". However, they also declared that "as long as the NATO bloc exists and effective disarmament measures have not been implemented, the Warsaw Treaty countries will consider it necessary to strengthen their defences and to develop close co-operation among themselves in the sphere".

1976 Bucharest Meeting. At a further meeting, held in Bucharest on Nov. 25-26, 1976, the Political Consultative Committee set up a Committee of Foreign Ministers as a permanent organ, in parallel with the Committee of Defence Ministers, with consultative functions, its decisions having to be reached by consensus and to be approved by the legislatures of each member state.

A Combined General Staff, set up in 1955 with headquarters in Moscow, and composed of representatives of the organization's seven member states, was given the functions of serving the meetings of both the Military Council and of the Committee of Foreign Ministers, and of planning and evaluating manoeuvres and exercises of the Joint Armed Forces.

At the same time the organization's Joint Secretariat (set up in Moscow in January 1956) was given a higher status by being charged with servicing the Committee of Foreign Ministers and placed under a Soviet director-general.

At the 1976 Bucharest meeting the Political Consultative Committee also adopted a lengthy declaration "for fresh advances in international relaxation, the strengthening of security and the development of co-operation in Europe" as well as a draft treaty designed to promote disarmament and to be submitted to the participants in the 1975 (Helsinki) Conference on Security and Co-operation in Europe [see pages 221-33].

In the declaration it was stated that, following the East Berlin conference of European Communist and Workers' parties in June 1976 [see above], the political atmosphere in Europe was "increasingly being freed of the remnants and vestiges of the cold war". The declaration continued, however: "The cause of strengthening peace in Europe, like universal peace and the process of détente, also encounters big difficulties. There are still forces of reaction, militarism and revanchism which seek to create situations of conflict, spur on the arms race, seek to call in question the sovereignty of states and the inviolability of existing frontiers. . . . These forces provoke intervention in the domestic affairs of states and they would like to dictate to the peoples which internal system must exist in this or that country and which parties can or cannot take part in governmental activities. . . ."

The declaration went on: "In our time peace and security in Europe are indivisible, they cannot be a question of choice. There is no sane alternative to the policy of détente; it is needed equally by all states, irrespective of their social system. This is the firm and immutable point of departure of the Warsaw Treaty member countries in all their foreign policy actions."

In connexion with disarmament, the responsibility for the continuing arms race was laid on "the most aggressive imperialist circles and world reaction", and it was asserted: "If our countries have to take steps to strengthen their armed forces . . . this is done exclusively in the interest of the reliable defence of the peaceful labour of our peoples and to deter the forces of militarism and war."

After reiterating previously-made proposals for general disarmament, including a call for a special session of the UN General Assembly on disarmament, the declaration went on: "The conclusion of a world treaty

on the renunciation of force in international relationships could be a major step forward in strengthening the relaxation of world tensions and world peace." Such a treaty, it was stated, had been submitted for discussion by the United Nations, and the Warsaw Treaty member countries were ready to discuss and to sign it.

Moreover, the participants in the meeting again expressed their readiness to "disband the Warsaw Treaty Organization simultaneously with the disbandment of the North Atlantic Treaty Organization and to abolish their military organizations as the first step". The declaration continued: "They urge all states not to undertake any action that could lead to the expansion of existing closed groupings and military political alliances, or to the establishment of new ones. The simultaneous suspension of Article 9 in the Warsaw Treaty and Article 10 in the North Atlantic Treaty [see page 166], which allow the expansion of the number of participants by the acceptance of new states, could be a practical move in this direction."

The declaration also called for the removal of all remaining "artificial barriers" to the development of mutually profitable economic co-operation between states on the European continent, in particular in the fields mentioned in the Final Act of the Helsinki conference. The participants in the meeting further urged "the restructuring of international economic relationships on a just democratic foundation and on the basis of equality for all states, big and small, socialist and capitalist, industrialized and developing". However, the declaration added: "It has been discovered that certain forces wish to use the development of . . . contacts [between East and West] for purposes that are hostile to understanding and friendship between peoples, and to interfere in the domestic affairs of states. The states participating in the Warsaw Treaty Organization find it necessary to reaffirm that this is a road without a future and that they reject it."

Of co-operation among the socialist states the declaration stated that the Warsaw Treaty member countries reaffirmed "their resolve constantly to strengthen mutual co-operation on the basis of Marxism-Leninism and international solidarity, respect for equality and sovereignty of each state, non-intervention in internal affairs and comradely mutual understanding".

The *draft treaty* contained the following provisions:

Art. 1. All participants of the Helsinki conference would pledge themselves "not to be the first to use nuclear weapons, one against the other, either on land, on the sea, in the air or in outer space".

Art. 2. This commitment would apply "not only to the territory of the states but also to their armed forces in whatever area of the world they may be".

Art. 3. The treaty would be for an unlimited period.

Art. 4. The treaty would be open for signature by any state which signed the Final Act of the Helsinki conference.

Act. 5. The treaty would "enter into force for each of the contracting parties from the time of deposition of its instruments of ratification".

(The NATO Foreign Ministers, however, rejected on Dec. 10, 1976, both the above draft treaty and the proposal for "freezing" the membership of the two military alliances on the ground that they were "a diversionary tactic designed to divert attention from the Soviet Union's poor record in implementing the agreements of the Helsinki conference—notably the provisions for free movement and creating confidence".)

1978 Moscow Meeting. A meeting of the Political Consultative Committee held in Moscow on Nov. 22-23, 1978, unanimously adopted a *Moscow Declaration* on the international situation, which was to be circulated within the United Nations and to be brought to the notice of the participants in the 1975 Helsinki conference (CSCE). The main points of this declaration were as follows:

The declaration stated that discussions at the meeting had centred on "further steps in the struggle to develop the process of détente and disarmament". Significant changes for the better had taken place on the continent of Europe with regard to strengthening security and developing co-operation, and this had been facilitated by the development of relations between the states of the continent in the spirit of the principles contained in the CSCE Final Act and by the general recognition of the existing frontiers between the European states and their inviolability. The trend towards the relaxation of international tension had emerged and had begun to have an impact on the general development of world affairs.

After stating that "the Warsaw Treaty countries attach great importance to attainment of USSR-USA accords on strategic arms limitation" and stressing the "tremendous importance" of the early conclusion of Soviet-US talks on the second agreement on the limitation of strategic offensive arms (SALT II) and the subsequent conclusion of new agreements on a reduction of these arms with the participation of other nuclear powers, the declaration called for the implementation of the following measures: (i) The conclusion of a world treaty on the non-use of force on international relations which would commit all states to renouncing the threat or use of force and would include a ban on the use of nuclear weapons; (ii) the strict observance by all CSCE states of a commitment not to use or threaten force in their relations with one another; (iii) the implementation of a proposal that the CSCE states would commit themselves not to be the first to use nuclear weapons against each other, that the NATO and Warsaw Treaty states should not increase the number of participants in their alliances, that the scale of military exercises by the respective sides in Europe should be limited to the level of 50,000-60,000 men, and that the measures of trust on which agreement was reached at the Helsinki conference should also be applied to the area of the Mediterranean; and (iv) the reinforcement of security guarantees for non-nuclear states, including the renunciation of the use of nuclear weapons against states which did not possess them and did not have them on their own territory, and the renunciation of the deployment of nuclear weapons on the territories of states where there were none at present.

Further, the declaration called on all the states and peoples of the world (i) "to press for holding early negotiations between the five nuclear powers—the USSR, the USA, Britain, France and China—in order to remove nuclear weapons of all types from the arsenals of states and turn nuclear energy to peaceful uses only"; (ii) "to insist firmly that the countries possessing the most considerable military and economic potential, primarily the five powers which are permanent members of the UN Security Council [i.e. the five nuclear powers] . . . , should reach agreement without delay on a reduction of their military budgets by a certain percentage or by magnitudes of the same order, as a first step, for the next three years"; (iii) "to step up the efforts of states and governments with a view to the earliest conclusion of the current talks on the limitation and cessation of the arms race along its main lines, and to pool efforts by all states in the drafting and implementation of disarmament measures"; and (iv) "undeviatingly to pursue the policy of peaceful coexistence".

The declaration also called for an end to the "last vestiges of colonialism" and to national and racial oppression, a restructuring of international economic relations on a just and democratic basis, and the establishment of a "new international economic order".

With regard to human rights, the declaration said that "dangerous trends . . . are engendered by the policy of imperialist circles . . . to try to use the problem of human rights for interference in the internal affairs of socialist and other states and for attacks on the socialist social system"; the socialist countries "reject the slander heaped on them by the ruling classes of states whose peoples have to endure all the hardships of mass unemployment, national and social inequality, racial discrimination, organized crime and moral degradation", and they "do not and will not allow any interference in their internal affairs". The participant countries "stress that they are guided in this respect by concern for the further positive development of international relations and for the removal of the obstacles artificially complicating them".

President Ceausescu of Romania revealed after the meeting that he had refused to agree to Soviet proposals for an increase in defence spending by the individual member countries of the organization and for the integration of each country's national armed forces under a unified command. He later reaffirmed his government's policy of defending the right of each nation "to decide its own destiny without interference from outside". Since the early 1960s Romania had not allowed Warsaw Pact forces to conduct exercises in Romanian territory; it was the only Warsaw Treaty country in which no Soviet troops or advisers were stationed; and since 1969 it had not taken part in Warsaw Pact forces' manoeuvres (except at the level of staff officers).

1979 Budapest Meeting. At a meeting of the Committee of Foreign Ministers in Budapest on May 14-15, 1979, an appeal was launched to all European countries as well as the United States and Canada to convene a general conference with the aim of taking practical measures in order to reduce military forces in Europe. In this context the ministers quoted a paragraph from a "programme for further co-operation between the Soviet Union and France" signed on April 28, 1979, during a visit to Moscow by the French President.

The Ministers also made five specific proposals for (i) the conclusion and implementation of the SALT II agreement and transition to the next stage (SALT III); (ii) the fixing of dates and modalities for talks on ceasing the manufacture of all types of nuclear weapons and for the progressive reduction of stocks of such weapons until their complete elimination; (iii) the definitive prohibition of the use of nuclear weapons; (iv) the conclusion of an agreement on a total and general ban on nuclear weapon tests; and (v) the adoption of measures to strengthen guarantees for the security of non-nuclear countries.

1979 East Berlin Meeting. Meeting in East Berlin on Dec. 5-6, 1979, the Foreign Ministers of the Warsaw Pact countries appealed to NATO not to proceed with the proposed modernization of its long-range theatre nuclear forces (LRTNF)—involving the deployment in Europe of Pershing II launchers and Cruise missiles [see page 181] —as the implementation of this proposal would "destroy the basis for negotiations" and would "signify an attempt by NATO to engage in negotiations from positions of strength which is, as a matter of principle, unacceptable to the Warsaw Treaty states" and "the governments of the NATO countries cannot be unaware of this".

1980 Warsaw Meeting. A meeting of the Political Consultative Committee, held in Warsaw on May 14-15, 1980 (to celebrate the 25th anniversary of the founding of the Warsaw Treaty Organization), and also attended by President Brezhnev of the USSR, issued a statement calling for a world conference on international problems and a lengthy declaration proposing a European conference on disarmament and détente.

The statement proposed the convening in the immediate future of "a top-level meeting of the leaders of states of all the regions of the world" who would focus their attention on "the task of removing the hotbeds of international tension and preventing war"; particular attention should be paid to "the issues of European security and the preservation of peace on the European continent". The statement concluded that such a meeting could be arranged by means of consultations between states, and that "the present situation and the

peril it evokes . . . suggest that it is precisely such a top-level meeting which would provide the safest road to mutual understanding and lasting peace".

The declaration proposed: (i) That as from an agreed date no state or grouping of states in Europe should increase the size of its armed forces in the area defined by the Final Act of the CSCE; (ii) that all the provisions of the Final Act should be strictly observed; (iii) that exchanges of views should be "intensified and deepened" in preparation for the 1980 Madrid follow-up CSCE conference; (iv) that the preparation of a conference on military détente and disarmament in Europe should be accelerated; (v) that efforts should be made to bring about the ratification of the SALT II treaty and to reach swift agreements on the complete prohibition of nuclear weapon tests, radiological weapons and chemical weapons (and on the destruction of stockpiles of the latter), and on the renunciation of the use of nuclear weapons in the territories of non-nuclear states which did not have such weapons on their territory; (vi) that talks should immediately begin on concluding a world treaty on the renunciation of force, on ending the production of nuclear weapons and gradually reducing their stocks until their complete liquidation, on banning the development of new types and systems of weapons of mass destruction, and on the reduction of military budgets, particularly of the major powers; and (vii) that an examination should begin, possibly within a UN framework, of the question of limiting and reducing the level of military presence and activity in the Atlantic, the Indian and Pacific oceans, the Mediterranean and the Persian Gulf.

The participants in the meeting also "stressed the need for a political settlement" of the Afghanistan situation with reliable guarantees for the termination of external interference against that country so that the Soviet Union could commence withdrawing its troops (which had entered that country in December 1979).

Military Strength of Warsaw Pact. According to the Institute of Strategic Studies (in London), the Joint Armed Forces of the Warsaw Treaty Organization numbered (in 1979) a total of 4,763,000 officers and men, of whom the Soviet Union provided 3,658,000 (1,825,000 in the Army, 430,000 in the Navy, 475,000 in the Air Force, 375,000 in the Strategic Rocket Force and 550,000 in an Air Defence Force).

In September 1980 the strength of the Warsaw Pact forces was estimated as 225 active divisions—169 of them being Soviet divisions—with over 55,000 main battle tanks, while the Soviet Air Force was said to include 1,300 MiG-23, MiG-25 and MiG-27 aircraft.

Council for Mutual Economic Assistance (CMEA)

Headquarters: Moscow.

Members: Bulgaria, Cuba, Czechoslovakia, German Democratic Republic, Hungary, Mongolian People's Republic, Poland, Romania, Soviet Union and Vietnam.

Associate Member: Yugoslavia.

History and Membership

The decision to establish a Council for Mutual Economic Assistance (CMEA or Comecon) was made at an economic conference held in Moscow in January 1949 and attended by representatives of Bulgaria, Czechoslovakia, Hungary, Poland, Romania and the Soviet Union. These countries were the founder-members of the CMEA, whose creation was officially announced on Jan. 25, 1949. The purpose of the CMEA would be "the exchange of experience in the economic field, and mutual assistance in regard to raw materials, foodstuffs, machinery, equipment, etc." Each of the participating countries would be equally represented on the Council.

It was further stated that the Council would be open for membership to "other countries in Europe which share its principles and desire broad economic co-operation with the countries already represented in it".

Albania was admitted to membership in February 1949, but left the Council in 1961 as a result of ideological differences. The German Democratic Republic entered in October 1950, and the Mongolian People's Republic in June 1962; Mongolia entered the CMEA under an amendment to the Charter [see below] permitting the admission of non-European countries to membership. Cuba became a full member on July 12, 1972, and Vietnam on June 29, 1978.

Yugoslavia was admitted to associate membership under an agreement concluded on Sept. 17, 1964. By the terms of this agreement, Yugoslavia would be able to share in the work of the CMEA, on a basis of equality and mutual benefit, in the fields of foreign trade, currency and financial relations, ferrous and non-ferrous metallurgy, engineering, the chemical industry, and co-ordination of scientific and technical research. Yugoslavia's participation became effective on April 24, 1965.

Countries admitted as observers are Afghanistan, Angola, Ethiopia, the People's Democratic Republic of Korea, Laos and the People's Democratic Republic of Yemen.

The CMEA Charter

At its 12th session in December 1959, the Council drafted a *Charter*, which was signed on Dec. 14, 1959, and came into force on April 13, 1960. A summary of the document is given below:

In the preamble the signatories state their determination "to continue developing all-round economic co-operation on the basis of the consistent implementation of the international socialist division of labour in the interests of building socialism and communism in their countries and ensuring a lasting peace throughout the world". They also state their "readiness to develop economic relations with all countries, irrespective of their social and state systems".

Art. 1. The purpose of the CMEA is to facilitate, by uniting and co-ordinating the efforts of the Council's member countries, the planned development of the national economy, acceleration of economic and

technical progress in these countries, a rise in the level of industrialization in countries with less developed industries, uninterrupted growth of labour productivity, and a steady advance of the welfare of the peoples in the Council's member countries.

Art. 2 deals with membership of the CMEA. Membership is open to any European country sharing the Council's aims and principles. Any member country may leave the Council with six months' notice. This article was amended at the 16th session of the Council, when admission to membership was extended to non-European countries.

Art. 3 states the functions of the CMEA to be to:
(1) "Organize all-round economic, scientific and technical co-operation of all the Council's member countries in the most rational use of their natural resources and acceleration of the development of their productive forces"; and
(2) "assist the Council's member countries in elaborating and carrying out joint measures for (i) the development of the industry and agriculture of the Council's member countries; (ii) the development of transport . . . ; (iii) the most efficient use of principal capital investments allocated by the Council's member countries for the development of the mining and manufacturing industries and for the construction of major projects which are of interest to two countries or more; (iv) the development of trade and exchange of services between the Council's member countries and between them and other countries; (v) the exchange of scientific and technical achievements and advanced production experience".

Art. 4 states that "recommendations shall be made on questions of economic, scientific and technical co-operation" and on "decisions on organizational and procedural matters". Recommendations and decisions apply only to those members who have declared an interest in the question from which they arise.

Art. 5 names the constituent organs of the Council as the Session of the Council; the Conference of Members' Representatives (since replaced by the Executive Committee); the standing Commissions; and the Secretariat.

Arts. 6, 7, 8 and 9 give details of the composition and functions of the organs of the Council.

The remaining articles deal with the Council's international relations and financial arrangements, and with such matters as the ratification and amending of the Charter.

Organization of the Council

Summit Conferences. Since June 1962 the First or General Secretaries of the Central Committees of the Communist and Workers' Parties and the heads of government of the member countries of the CMEA have met in conference from time to time to discuss the expansion and consolidation of economic co-operation among CMEA countries. At these summit conferences the general lines of the CMEA's work are laid down.

Session of the Council. The supreme permanent organ of CMEA is the Session of the Council, which meets at least once a year in the capital of each member country in turn, the host-country providing the chairman for each session. The programme of work discussed at the summit conferences is here determined in greater detail. Recommendations, which must be passed unanimously, are put into effect by intergovernmental agreements.

Executive Committee. The Executive Committee was set up at the 16th Session of the Council on June 7, 1962. It consists of Deputy Prime Ministers of the CMEA member countries, their deputies and advisers. Meetings are held at least every three months, the function of the Committee being to co-ordinate national economic development plans and to supervise collaboration in scientific and technical research. A branch of the Executive Committee is the Bureau for Common Questions of Economic Planning, in which each CMEA country is represented by the Deputy Chairman of its State Planning Organization.

Secretariat. The Secretariat consists, at present, of the Secretary of the Council and five Deputy Secretaries. It is responsible for preparation of material for the Council, the Committee and the Permanent Commissions, and for the drafting of reports and the compiling of statistics.

Permanent Commissions. Twenty-three Permanent Commissions were set up at various times between 1956 and 1963 to study different aspects of the CMEA's work. All the CMEA member countries are represented on each of the committees and sub-committees of the Permanent Commissions.

The commissions are listed below, together with their date of foundation and present headquarters.

Agriculture	(May 1956; Sofia)
Forestry	(May 1956; Bucharest)
Power	(May 1956; Moscow)
Coal Industry	(May 1956; Warsaw)
Machine Building	(May 1956; Prague)
Oil and Gas	(May 1956; Bucharest)
Ferrous Metals	(May 1956; Moscow)
Non-Ferrous Metals	(May 1956; Budapest)
Chemical Industry	(May 1956; Berlin)
Wood, Cellulose, Paper	(May 1956; Budapest)
Transport	(June 1958; Warsaw)
Construction	(June 1958; Berlin)
Light Industry	(July 1963; Prague)
Food Industry	(July 1963; Sofia)

Created as a single commission in December, 1958

Economic Questions	(1958; Moscow)
Foreign Trade	(May 1959; Moscow)
Peaceful Uses of Atomic Energy	(Sept. 1960; Moscow)
Standardization	(June 1962; Berlin)
Co-ordination of Scientific and Technical Research	(June 1962; Moscow)
Statistics	(June 1962; Moscow)
Finance and Currency	(Dec. 1962; Moscow)
Radio and Electronics Industries	(July 1963; Budapest)
Geology	(July 1963; Ulan-Bator)

The creation of a Permanent Commission for Posts and Telecommunications was decided upon by the Council at its 25th session held in Bucharest on July 27-29, 1971. The Permanent Commission for the Co-ordination of Scientific and Technical Research was at the same time replaced by a Committee for Scientific and Technical Co-operation, and a Committee for Co-operation in the Sphere of Planning was also set up. Permanent commissions have also been set up for health and for civil aviation.

Other permanent bodies created by the Council are a working party for the co-ordination and delivery of finished articles (founded in 1959) and a central dispatcher administration (founded in 1962).

A Standardization Institute was established in 1964, its function being the creation of a progressive standardization of industrial products among the CMEA member countries.

The creation of an International Institute of Economic Problems of the World Socialist System was approved by the CMEA's Executive Committee on July 24, 1970.

CMEA Industrial Organizations

Industrial organizations designed to promote specialization and co-operation in production were set up by CMEA member countries as follows:

(1) Central Control Administration of the United Power Grids of European CMEA Member Countries (CCA), set up in Prague in 1962.

(2) Intermetall, set up in Budapest in 1964 for ferrous metallurgy.

(3) Bearings, established in Warsaw in 1964 for the anti-friction bearings industry.

(4) Computers, formed in Moscow in 1969 for computer engineering, a standardized computer technology and the joint planning of an international industrial complex.

(5) Interchim, founded in Halle (German Democratic Republic) in 1970 for branches of the chemical industry.

(6) Interatominstrument, set up in Warsaw in 1972 for nuclear-technical apparatus construction.

(7) Interatomenergo, established in Moscow in 1973 for nuclear power plant production.

(8) Intertextilmasch, founded in Moscow in 1973 for branches of textile machinery construction.

(9) Interelektro, also founded in Moscow in 1973, for branches of electro-technology.

(10) Assofoto, established in Moscow in 1973 for the photochemical industry.

(11) Interchimvolokno, established in Bucharest in 1973 for the chemical fibres industry.

Other Joint CMEA Bodies

The following joint research institutes and associations have been set up within the framework of the CMEA.

(1) International Centre for Scientific and Technological Information, set up in Moscow in 1969.

(2) Interkosmos, founded in Moscow in 1970 for space research.

(3) Intertalonpribor, formed in Moscow in 1972 for measurement technology.

Joint transport organizations include the Office for Maritime Freight set up in Moscow in 1952 and the OPW established in Prague in 1963 for railway freight transport.

Scientific Co-operation

Joint Institute for Nuclear Research. A preliminary agreement on the establishment of a Joint Institute for Nuclear Research, made on March 26, 1956, was implemented on July 12, 1956, the institute being established at Dubna in the Soviet Union. The members of the institute are Bulgaria, Cuba, Czechoslovakia, the German Democratic Republic, Hungary, the Democratic People's Republic of Korea, the Mongolian People's Republic, Poland, Romania, the Soviet Union and Vietnam. The People's Republic of China, formerly a member, withdrew its scientists in July 1966.

On its inception the institute comprised the former Institute of Nuclear Problems and Electrophysical Laboratory of the Soviet Academy of Sciences. Other sections of the institute, which have come into operation since its establishment, are the laboratory of high energies, which began operating in 1957; the laboratory of neutron physics, equipped with an experimental fast neutron pulse reactor (in operation since 1960); a laboratory of nuclear reactions equipped with a cyclotron for accelerating multicharged ions (also coming into operation in 1960); and laboratories for nuclear problems, theoretical physics and computing and automation. The joint institute also has a computing centre and a radiochemical laboratory.

The supreme authority of the joint institute is the Committee of Government Plenipotentiaries, the members of which are the heads of the atomic energy authorities of the member countries. The committee is responsible for policy and finance. The programme of work is the responsibility of a Scientific Council, while the practical administration is carried out by a management consisting of a director, two vice-directors and an administrative manager.

Other Scientific Centres. Agreements signed in Moscow on April 28, 1971, provided for the establishment of seven new scientific centres to study such matters as new chemical compounds, prevention of pollution, control of weeds and agricultural pests, automated systems for medical institutions, anti-corrosion measures, research in biological physics, and uses of timber.

CMEA Financial Institutions

International Investment Bank. An International Investment Bank, with its seat in Moscow, was set up on July 10, 1970, by seven countries as founder-members (Bulgaria, Czechoslovakia, the German Democratic Republic, Hungary, Mongolia, Poland and the Soviet Union). Romania became a member of the bank on Jan. 12, 1971, Cuba on Jan. 22, 1974, and Vietnam in May 1977.

The bank's highest authority is its Council which meets at least twice a year, on which each member has one vote, and which has to take decisions by unanimous vote. The bank's executive body is its Board, consisting of a chairman and three deputies appointed by the Council.

Starting operations on Jan. 1, 1971, with initial capital subscriptions totalling 175,000,000 roubles (increased by another 175,000,000 roubles in 1972 and rising to a total of 1,071,300 transferable roubles of authorized capital by Jan. 1, 1979), the bank was to concentrate resources for capital construction and for co-ordinated expenditure through the granting of long- and medium-term credits. Membership subscriptions were based on the volume of members' exports in mutual trade turnover, with the Soviet Union providing nearly 40 per cent and the German Democratic Republic about 17.6 per cent of the capital. The bank was also authorized to use loans and investments from third countries.

In 1974 a special fund was set up by the bank for the financing of economic and technical assistance programmes for developing countries.

The bank repeatedly took up credits from Western banks, including a loan, early in 1976, of $600,000,000 from the Dresdner Bank (of the Federal Republic of Germany) for the financing of capital projects; a loan of $500,000,000 granted on June 15, 1977, largely to finance the construction of the natural gas pipeline from Orenburg (Urals) to the Czechoslovak border [see page 207]; and another loan of $500,000,000 granted in September 1978 by a consortium headed by the Dresdner Bank, mainly towards financing the above pipeline.

International Bank for Economic Co-operation. An International Bank for Economic Co-operation, formed by the CMEA's eight member countries with an initial capital of 60,000,000 roubles (to be increased to 300,000,000 roubles within five years) came into being on Jan. 1, 1964.

The bank has a Council consisting of representatives of all its member countries (which are the same as those of the International Investment Bank) and a similarly composed Board.

Its functions are mainly to undertake multilateral settlements on transferable roubles and to grant credits for the financing of foreign trade and other operations of its members.

Co-operation Agreements with Non-Member Countries

Finland. An agreement between the

CMEA and Finland—the first with a non-socialist country—was signed on May 16, 1973. It provided for the establishment of a joint commission, with representatives from all the CMEA members and from Finland, to study the possibilities for the development of economic, scientific and technological co-operation.

Iraq. An agreement with Iraq on multilateral economic, scientific and technical co-operation, signed on July 4, 1975, was the first of its kind to be concluded by the CMEA and a developing country (although Iraq had, since 1973, signed various co-operation agreements with individual CMEA member countries). The agreement was approved at the 30th session of the CMEA in East Berlin on July 7-9, 1976, and ratified on July 23, 1976.

Mexico. A similar agreement was signed with Mexico on Aug. 13, 1975, and likewise approved on July 7-9, 1976, and ratified on July 23, 1976.

CMEA Decisions and Operations

Division of Labour. The work of the CMEA is largely based on the principle of the division of labour. In sessions of the Council from 1956 to 1961 a number of plans were approved for specialization, in various industries, among the CMEA countries. At the session of the Council from Dec. 12-15, 1961, the draft of the "Fundamental Principles of International Socialist Division of Labour" was adopted. The details of the document were published on June 17, 1962. Described as "a planned and consciously moulded process, which takes into consideration the objectively operating economic laws of socialism", the Principles are contrasted with the competitive system of capitalist international division. All later resolutions of the CMEA in the field of the division of labour are based on this document.

"Complex Programme". The Council published on Aug. 7, 1971, a *Complex Programme for the Further Deepening and Improvement of Co-operation and Development of the Socialist Economic Integration of the CMEA Member Countries.*

The purpose of the programme was stated to be "the promotion of the growth of the economic power of the socialist world system and the strengthening of the economic system of each country". Socialist economic integration, however, was to take place on the basis of "complete voluntariness" and would not be linked with the creation of supranational organs. There would be intensified co-operation in planning, with joint forecasts for energy, petrochemicals and automative systems in the period 1971-75, and also in joint research projects in science and technology.

The programme further provided for a new form of trading, i.e. trade in non-quota goods which would not need to be balanced bilaterally but would, for clearing purposes, be counted in the total trade of the respective countries.

The "transferable rouble" (the collective currency used for accounting in the internal CMEA clearing accounts but not transferable otherwise) was to be strengthened so as to attain "real transferability" and be used in clearings with non-CMEA countries, and new parities would be established between the currencies of the member states and in relation to the "transferable rouble".

The proposed increased co-operation was to include the creation of a network of express trains and of long-distance roads, joint shipping enterprises, and the introduction of standardized container transport systems.

The negotiations on the programme during the Council's 25th session in Bucharest, July 27-29, 1971, revealed "serious controversy on questions of integration", and, in particular, strong reservations on any surrender of a country's sovereignty to the CMEA were expressed by Romania.

Further Activities, 1975-80

Oil Prices. It was disclosed in Budapest on March 18, 1975, that the CMEA had agreed that in coming years oil prices would no longer be "determined five years in advance but annually on the basis of five-year average prices in the world markets". This meant that by 1978 prices of Soviet oil would approximate those obtaining in the Western world.

29th CMEA Session. At the 29th session of the CMEA held in Budapest on June 24-26, 1975, a co-ordinated plan for multinational integration was approved with a view to implementing the "complex programme" [see above].

The plan provided mainly for joint investments in developing Soviet raw material resources during 1976-80 at a cost of 9,000 million transferable roubles (then about £6,000 million). The projects included the construction of the natural gas pipeline from the Orenburg fields (in the Urals) to the Czechoslovak border with an annual capacity of 15,000 million cubic metres, and a power transmission line from the Ukraine to Hungary.

The session also decided to draw up a joint long-term co-operation programme for 1976-90 for the raw material, fuel, energy, engineering, farming and food industries.

The Romanian Prime Minister expressed opposition to plans for supranational integration, including the creation of a uniform electrical power system, and he emphasized that his country wanted co-operation based on the co-ordination of national plans rather than a joint plan for integration. The national identity of each economy, he said, should be preserved while co-operation should be improved "in the industrially less developed countries" such as Romania.

Outer Space Agreement. On July 14, 1976, the CMEA member countries signed an agreement on co-operation in exploration and the use of outer space for peaceful purposes.

31st CMEA Session. At the end of the CMEA's 31st session in Warsaw on June 21-23, 1977, it was stated that the socialist countries had become "the world's most dynamic economic force" and that in 1976 the national income of the CMEA member countries had reached nine and a half times the 1948 level (whereas in the industrialized capitalist countries the increase was said to be about three and one-third times).

32nd CMEA Session. The 32nd session, held in Bucharest on June 27-29, 1978, approved long-term target programmes for (i) energy, fuel and raw materials, (ii) machine-building and (iii) agriculture and the food industry for 1981-90. Ten joint projects to be completed under the co-ordinated five-year plan for 1976-80 included the natural gas complex at Orenburg (Urals) and the Soyuz gas pipeline to the Czechoslovak border, which was to reach a maximum capacity of 28,000 million cubic metres in 1980, of which 15,500 million cubic metres would be supplied to the other East European members of the CMEA annually.

Assistance to Developing Countries. In a survey of its activities in 1977, circulated by the CMEA at the 33rd regular session of the UN General Assembly in 1978, the CMEA member countries were stated to have rendered, and to be continuing to render, economic and technical assistance to 78 developing countries in Asia, Africa and Latin America in the construction of a total of 3,560 industrial enterprises and other projects in various fields of these countries' national economies, including 2,685 which had been completed and had gone into service.

Trade and Output Statistics. In connexion with a session of the CMEA's Executive Committee in Moscow on March 30, 1979, it was claimed that, in 1978, trade between CMEA member countries had, in 1978, reached 103,000 million roubles and their foreign trade nearly 174,000 million roubles, and that industrial output in CMEA member countries was twice that of the countries of the European Economic Community.

33rd CMEA Session. The 33rd session of the CMEA held in Moscow on June 26-28, 1979, approved "long-term specific programmes" for satisfying the national requirements of CMEA member countries in manufacturing consumer goods and for

developing transport communications. A total of 14 agreements were signed on the implementation of specific programmes. The final communiqué stated that since the 32nd session the CMEA member countries had concluded 22 agreements on the implementation of "five long-term specific programmes of co-operation and co-ordination of the national economic development plans for 1981-85".

The session also unanimously approved amendments to the CMEA Charter, with the effect that it was no longer necessary for important decisions to obtain the approval of all members; that the statutes provided for mutual consultation on the main aspects of the economic policy of member countries and on the elaboration of long-term co-operation programmes; and that multi-lateral and bilateral co-operation among individual CMEA member countries would be bound up with the overall long-term programmes.

The session further decided to apply to Vietnam special measures, as previously applied to Cuba and Mongolia, to accelerate that country's economic development.

Central European International Bank (CIB). This bank was set up in Budapest in November 1979 by the Hungarian National Bank and six leading banks of member states of the Organization for Economic Co-operation and Development (OECD) (these countries accounting for about 70 per cent of Hungary's foreign trade) with a share capital of US$20,000,000 and a subordinated standby loan of $15,000,000 with the object of financing East-West trade and operations in the CMEA and third-world countries.

1980 Prague Summit. A session of the CMEA held at the level of heads of government in Prague on June 17-19, 1980, approved further extensive programmes.

In a communiqué issued at the end of the session it was emphasized that it was "the invariable striving of CMEA member countries to develop co-operation with other states in the interests of deepening the international division of labour on a just, equitable and mutually beneficial basis" and also that the CMEA was ready "to expand relations of co-operation with countries which are not members of the CMEA and with international economic organizations for the good of peace and progress".

The communiqué also noted that during 1979 there had been a further deepening and improvement of co-operation between the CMEA and Yugoslavia, which was taking part in the work of CMEA bodies in 22 fields of co-operation and was a party to 22 multinational agreements.

The session noted that national income in CMEA countries in 1979 had been 19 per cent higher than in 1975, and industrial output 23 per cent higher; that the average agricultural output in 1976-79 had been 9 per cent higher than in 1971-75; and that the foreign trade turnover of the CMEA countries had increased in 1979 by almost 13 per cent as against 1978 and had reached 196,000 million roubles, of which mutual trade turnover among CMEA members had accounted for 110,000 million roubles and had met the bulk of import needs in respect of key fuels, raw materials, machinery and equipment.

Agreements signed by the participants of the session included one on specialization and co-ordination in the manufacture of computers and another on co-operation in improving oil refining. It was reported that the Soviet Union had undertaken to provide 400,000,000 tons of oil over the next five years. It was also agreed to promote further development of nuclear energy while making a concerted effort to economize on energy and raw material consumption.

The Soviet Prime Minister stated, with reference to a US embargo imposed on trade with the Soviet Union following the latter's intervention in Afghanistan in December 1979: "Such measures may cause some temporary difficulties in the construction of individual projects, but no one has succeeded, and no one will succeed, in preventing us from going forward and im-plementing the plans which we have drafted, even if the US Administration in-cludes all American products in its lists of banned goods."

Upon a request by Afghanistan, this country was admitted to observer status with the CMEA.

Indebtedness to West. According to the UN Economic Commission for Europe, the total debt owed to Western countries by the Soviet Union and East European countries was, at the end of 1979, at least $57,000 million (of which $42,000 million was owed to Western banks and $15,000 million to of-ficial or semi-official creditors), equal to about 4 or 5 per cent of the gross national product of the debtor countries. Eastern bloc receipts of convertible currency during 1979 were said to have reached $44,000 million. On the other hand, the CMEA's countries' overall trade balance with the West moved from a deficit of about $5,000 million in 1978 to a surplus of about $200,000,000 in 1979.

Other Treaties of Communist States

East European Agreements

Prior to the conclusion of the Warsaw Pact the Soviet Union had concluded bilateral agreements with Czechoslovakia, Yugoslavia and Poland, and after 1947 the USSR made similar bilateral agreements with Romania, Hungary and Bulgaria.

Later, the Warsaw Pact was sup-plemented by treaties on the stationing of Soviet troops in East European countries and by bilateral treaties of friendship and mutual assistance concluded among mem-bers of the Warsaw Treaty Organization.

Under the Warsaw Treaty the air defences of the Soviet Union are extended to other East European countries, whose forces are provided with advanced air defence radar systems, surface-to-air missiles and fighter interceptors. Nuclear warheads and weapons, however, are kept in Soviet hands.

Bilateral Agreements of the USSR concluded before 1950

Earlier bilateral treaties between the USSR and East European countries, although not formally abrogated, have been superseded by the Warsaw Pact and new bilateral agreements of 1966.

These were the "treaties of friendship, co-operation and mutual assistance" be-tween the USSR and:

CZECHOSLOVAKIA	..	Dec. 12, 1943
YUGOSLAVIA	.. ..	April 11, 1945, abrogated by the USSR on Sept. 28, 1949
POLAND ..	.. ..	April 21, 1945
ROMANIA	.. ..	Feb. 4, 1948
HUNGARY	.. ..	Feb. 18, 1948
BULGARIA	.. ..	March 18, 1948

An agreement on political co-operation and economic aid concluded with Albania on April 17, 1957 (of unlimited duration) has been inoperative since 1961.

Bilateral Agreements concluded among East European States, all of 20 Years' Duration

		Abrogated
POLAND AND YUGOSLAVIA	March 18, 1946	*by* POLAND *on* Sept. 9, 1949
CZECHOSLOVAKIA AND YUGOSLAVIA	May 9, 1946	*by* CZECHOSLOVAKIA *on* Oct. 4, 1949
ALBANIA AND YUGOSLAVIA	July 10, 1946	*by* YUGOSLAVIA *on* Nov. 13, 1949
POLAND AND CZECHOSLOVAKIA*	March 10, 1947	
BULGARIA AND YUGOSLAVIA	Nov. 27, 1947	*by* BULGARIA *on* Oct. 1, 1949
HUNGARY AND YUGOSLAVIA..	Dec. 8, 1947	*by* HUNGARY *on* Sept. 30, 1949
BULGARIA AND ALBANIA	Dec. 16, 1947	
YUGOSLAVIA AND ROMANIA	Dec. 19, 1947	*by* ROMANIA *on* Oct. 2, 1949
BULGARIA AND ROMANIA*	Jan. 16, 1948	
ROMANIA AND HUNGARY*	Jan. 24, 1948	
CZECHOSLOVAKIA AND BULGARIA*	April 23, 1948	

* Renewed—see below.

BULGARIA AND POLAND	May 29, 1948	
HUNGARY AND POLAND*	June 18, 1948	
BULGARIA AND HUNGARY*	July 19, 1948	
ROMANIA AND CZECHOSLOVAKIA*	July 21, 1948	
POLAND AND ROMANIA*	Jan. 26, 1949	
CZECHOSLOVAKIA AND HUNGARY*	April 16, 1949	

* Renewed—see below.

Treaties on Stationing of Soviet Troops in Four East European Countries

Treaties on the stationing of Soviet troops, in amplification of the Warsaw Pact, were concluded by the USSR in 1956-57 with:

(1) **Poland** on Dec. 17, 1956;
(2) the **German Democratic Republic** on March 12, 1957;
(3) **Romania** on April 15, 1957 (but, as decided by the Political Consultative Committee of the Warsaw Pact in Moscow on April 24, 1958, all Soviet troops were withdrawn from Romania in that year); and
(4) **Hungary** on May 27, 1957.

While the treaty with Hungary was of unlimited duration, the three others were limited to the period during which Soviet troops would be stationed in the country concerned, or until the conclusion of a new agreement by the contracting partners.

The treaties were similar in content, that with Poland specifying inter alia that: (i) The numbers and locations of Soviet troops in Poland would be defined by special agreements between the two countries; (ii) no troop movements outside these locations would be permitted without Polish authorization; (iii) Soviet troops in Poland, and their families, would have to respect Polish law and would be subject to the Polish courts; (iv) persons committing crimes against Soviet military personnel would bear the same responsibility as for crimes committed against the Polish forces; (v) the Soviet Government would pay for any material damage which might be caused by the actions or negligence of Soviet military personnel in Poland; (vi) the Polish Government, in return, could compensate the USSR for damage to Soviet property caused by Polish nationals; (vii) any disputes would be examined by a mixed commission; (viii) the two Governments would appoint representatives to deal with any current problems arising out of the presence of Soviet troops in Poland.

The agreement stressed that "the temporary stay of Soviet troops in Poland can in no way affect the sovereignty of the Polish state and cannot lead to any interference in the domestic affairs of Poland".

1968 Soviet-Czechoslovak Treaty. Following the invasion of Czechoslovakia on Aug. 20, 1968, by troops of the Soviet Union and three other Warsaw Pact member states, a treaty on the "temporary" stationing of Soviet troops in Czechoslovakia was signed in Prague on Oct. 16, 1968, and came into effect on Oct. 18 after ratification by the two countries.

Article 1 of the treaty stated that the Soviet troops would "remain temporarily on the territory of Czechoslovakia in order to ensure the security of the countries of the socialist community against the increasing revanchist strivings of the West German militarist forces".

Bilateral Treaties of Friendship and Mutual Assistance between the USSR and East European States and among the Latter, concluded since 1964

Partners	Date of Signature	Duration (years)	Automatic Extension
USSR AND GERMAN DEMOCRATIC REPUBLIC	June 12, 1964	20	once for 10 years
USSR AND POLAND	April 8, 1965	20	every 5 years
POLAND AND CZECHOSLOVAKIA	March 1, 1967	20	once for 5 years
POLAND AND GERMAN DEMOCRATIC REPUBLIC	March 15, 1967	20	once for 10 years
CZECHOSLOVAKIA AND GERMAN DEMOCRATIC REPUBLIC ..	March 17, 1967	20	once for 10 years
POLAND AND BULGARIA	April 6, 1967	20	every 5 years
USSR AND BULGARIA	May 12, 1967	20	every 5 years
HUNGARY AND GERMAN DEMOCRATIC REPUBLIC	May 18, 1967	20	once for 10 years
BULGARIA AND GERMAN DEMOCRATIC REPUBLIC	Sept. 7, 1967	20	once for 10 years
USSR AND HUNGARY	Sept. 7, 1967	20	every 5 years
BULGARIA AND CZECHOSLOVAKIA	April 26, 1968	20	every 5 years
POLAND AND HUNGARY	May 16, 1968	20	every 5 years
HUNGARY AND CZECHOSLOVAKIA	June 14, 1968	20	every 5 years
ROMANIA AND CZECHOSLOVAKIA	Aug. 16, 1968	20	every 5 years
HUNGARY AND BULGARIA	July 10, 1969	20	every 5 years
USSR AND CZECHOSLOVAKIA	May 6, 1970	20	every 5 years
USSR AND ROMANIA	July 7, 1970	20	every 5 years
POLAND AND ROMANIA	Nov. 12, 1970	20	every 5 years
BULGARIA AND ROMANIA	Nov. 19, 1970	20	every 5 years
HUNGARY AND ROMANIA	Feb. 24, 1972	20	every 5 years
ROMANIA AND GERMAN DEMOCRATIC REPUBLIC	May 12, 1972	20	once for 5 years

The treaties concluded by the German Democratic Republic contain references to (i) rejection of the Federal Republic of Germany's claim to represent the whole of Germany, and (ii) recognition of West Berlin as "an independent political unit" (i.e. not part of the Federal Republic of Germany). Other provisions contained in the various bilateral treaties are: A reference to the principles of peaceful coexistence and those of the UN Charter; guarantees of the post-war frontiers in Europe (including the Oder-Neisse frontier between Germany and Poland and the frontier between East and West Germany); rejection of the 1938 Munich Agreement on Czechoslovakia as "invalid *ab initio*"; a refusal to permit access to nuclear weapons by the Federal Republic of Germany; in the event of an armed attack on either of the contracting parties, immediate assistance, including military aid; and an undertaking to "communicate and consult with one another on all important international problems which concern them".

With reference to the 1970 treaty between the USSR and Romania the two countries' leaders signed, on Nov. 24, 1976, a "statement on the further development of co-operation and fraternal friendship" between the two countries and their Communist parties in "comradely co-operation on the basis of the principles of Marxism-Leninism and proletarian internationalism and equality and in the spirit of mutual trust and respect".

The bilateral treaties concluded by the Soviet Union since 1967, contrary to Article 4 of the Warsaw Treaty, do not limit the obligation of mutual assistance to an attack in Europe but call for all-round military assistance against aggression by "any state or combination of states".

Important Treaties Concluded by German Democratic Republic

Agreement on the Oder-Neisse Frontier. On June 7, 1950, it was announced that agreement had been reached between the Polish and East German Governments on the recognition of the Oder-Neisse line as the permanent frontier between the German Democratic Republic and Poland. This agreement was implemented on July 6, 1950, when a frontier demarcation agreement was signed at the town of Zgorzelec (Görlitz) on the River Neisse.

Soviet-East German Treaty of 1955. By this treaty, which was signed on Sept. 20, 1955, and came into force on Oct. 6, 1955, the USSR recognized the German Democratic Republic as a sovereign state. The main provisions are given below:

Art. 1. Both governments "solemnly confirmed" that their relations were based "on complete equality of rights, mutual respect of sovereignty and non-interference in domestic affairs". In accordance with this principle, the German Democratic Republic was henceforth "free to decide questions concerning its internal and foreign policy, including its relations with the Federal Republic of Germany as well as its relations with other states".

Art. 4. (1) The Soviet forces at present stationed in East Germany under international (i.e. four-power) agreements would continue to be stationed there temporarily with the approval of the Government of the German Democratic Republic, and on conditions to be settled by an additional agreement between the two governments.

(2) Soviet forces stationed in East Germany would not interfere in the internal affairs of the German Democratic Republic or in the social and political life of the country.

Art. 5. Both governments were agreed that it was "their main aim to bring about a peaceful settlement for the whole of Germany by means of appropriate negotiations". To this end they would "make the necessary efforts towards a settlement by a peace treaty and towards the restoration of the unity of Germany on a peaceful and democratic basis".

At the same time it was agreed that the German Democratic Republic would take over responsibility for the control of its frontiers and of lines of communications between the Federal Republic of Germany and West Berlin crossing East German territory.

Soviet-East German Treaty of 1975. The Soviet Union and the German Democratic Republic concluded, on Oct. 7, 1975, a new Treaty of Friendship, Co-operation and Mutual Assistance, which was to be in force for 25 years and would be automatically extended for 10-year periods unless one of the parties expressed, 12 months before the expiry of the current term, its wish to terminate the treaty.

The principal articles of the treaty read as follows:

"**Art. 1.** The high contracting parties will, in accordance with the principles of socialist internationalism, continue to strengthen the relations of eternal and inviolable friendship and fraternal mutual assistance in all spheres. They will systematically and unswervingly develop and deepen all-round co-operation and render each other every assistance and support on the basis of mutual respect of national sovereignty and independence, equality and non-interference in internal affairs.

"**Art. 2.** The high contracting parties will unite their efforts for the effective use of the material and spiritual potential of their peoples and states for the establishment of socialist and communist society and the consolidation of the socialist community. In accord with the principles and aims of socialist economic integration and in order better to meet the material and cultural needs of their peoples, they will strengthen and broaden mutually beneficial bilateral and multilateral economic and scientific-technical co-operation, including co-operation within the framework of the Council for Mutual Economic Assistance. Both sides will continue the long-term co-ordination and harmonization of economic plans, extend specialization and co-operation in production and research, harmonize long-term measures for the development of the most important branches of economy, science and technology, exchange knowledge and experience accumulated in the establishment of socialism and communism, and in the interests of raising the efficiency of social production secure an ever closer co-operation of the national economies of both states.

"**Art. 3.** The high contracting parties will advance co-operation between the organs of state power and the social organizations, develop extensive contacts in the fields of science and culture, education, literature and art, the press, radio, film and television, public health, environmental protection, tourism, physical culture and sports as well as in other fields. They will also develop contact between workers of both countries.

"**Art. 4.** The high contracting parties will advance the further development of fraternal relations between all states of the socialist community to the maximum and always act in the spirit of the strengthening of their unity and cohesion. They declare their willingness to take the necessary measures to protect and defend the historical achievements of socialism and the security and independence of both countries.

"**Art. 5.** The high contracting parties will continue to take all measures incumbent upon them towards the consistent implementation of the principles of peaceful coexistence between states of differing social systems and towards the expansion and deepening of the process of détente in international relations, and will strive to banish war finally from the life of all nations. They will do their utmost to protect international peace and the security of nations against the encroachments of the aggressive forces of imperialism and reaction, to end the arms race, to contribute to general and complete disarmament, finally to abolish colonialism in all forms and manifestations and to support states freed from colonial oppression in the strengthening of their national independence and sovereignty.

"**Art. 6.** The high contracting parties regard the inviolability of state frontiers in Europe as the most important prerequisite for the guarantee of European security and express their firm determination jointly and in alliance with the other participant states of the Warsaw Treaty of Friendship, Co-operation and Mutual Assistance of May 14, 1955, to ensure, in accordance with it, the inviolability of the frontiers of the participant states of this treaty, as they emerged as a result of the 1939-45 war and post-war developments, including the borders between the German Democratic Republic and the Federal Republic of Germany. Both sides will undertake joint efforts to counteract any manifestations of revanchism and militarism, and aspire to the strict observance of treaties concluded with the aim of strengthening European security.

"**Art. 7.** In accordance with the Four-Power Agreement of Sept. 3, 1971 [see page 235], the high contracting parties will maintain and develop their ties with West Berlin on the basis that it is not a constituent part of the Federal Republic and will not be governed by it in the future.

"**Art. 8.** In the event of an armed attack by any state or any group of states on one of the high contracting parties, the other high contracting party will regard this as an attack on itself and will immediately lend it every assistance and support it with all the means at its disposal in the exercise of its right to individual and collective self-defence in accordance with Article 51 of the United Nations Charter. The high contracting parties will immediately inform the UN Security Council of the measures taken on the basis of this article and act in accordance with the provisions of the UN Charter.

"**Art. 9.** The high contracting parties will in all important international questions inform each other, consult each other and act on the basis of their joint position, agreed upon in accordance with the interests of both states.

"**Art. 10.** This treaty does not affect the rights and duties of the high contracting parties under valid bilateral and multilateral agreements. . . ."

The new treaty contained no indication of any termination of either the 1955 treaty on relations between the German Democratic Republic and the Soviet Union or the 1964 Treaty of Friendship, Mutual Assistance and Co-operation concluded for 20 years [see above]. Like other treaties concluded by the Soviet Union with other Communist countries since 1967, the new treaty did not limit the obligation to render military assistance in case of attack to any such attack in Europe. Contrary to the 1955 treaty, the new treaty contained no reference to the reunification of Germany.

Other East German Treaties with Communist States. Treaties with the same provisos as to duration and termination were subsequently concluded by the German Democratic Republic as follows:

(1) With **Hungary** on March 24, 1977;
(2) with **Poland** on May 28, 1977;
(3) with **Bulgaria** on Sept. 14, 1977;
(4) with **Czechoslavakia** on Oct. 3, 1977.

In the treaty with Hungary both sides undertook inter alia to continue their long-term co-ordination and harmonization of economic plans; to act always in the spirit of strengthening unity and cohesion of all states of the socialist community; to expand and deepen the process of détente in international relations and "to contribute to general and complete disarmament"; to guarantee, together with other partners of the Warsaw Treaty Organization, the inviolability of the frontiers between member states, including those between the Federal Republic of Germany and the German Democratic Republic; and to afford each other instant mutual aid, including military assistance, in the event of an armed attack on either side by any country or group of countries.

The treaty with Poland contained, in its preamble, a special reference to the fulfilment by the German Democratic Republic of the provisions of the 1945 Potsdam Agreement [see page 8] and to the Zgorzelec (Görlitz) treaty of 1950 [see page 210] on the demarcation of the frontier between the two countries.

The treaty with Czechoslovakia was followed, on Dec. 3, 1980, by a joint border treaty providing for easier access across the two countries' common border and for increased economic co-operation in view of a shortfall of imports from Poland.

Treaties of friendship and co-operation were signed by the German Democratic Republic with the following Communist countries on the dates stated:

Cuba (for 25 years) on June 1, 1980 (though without any provision for military co-operation);

Mongolia (also for 25 years) on May 6, 1977 (without any provision for mutual assistance in the event of either party being subjected to armed attack by any state or group of states, and replacing earlier treaties of Aug. 22, 1957, and Sept. 12, 1968); and

Vietnam on Dec. 4, 1977.

East German Treaties with Non-Communist States.

Similar treaties were concluded by the German Democratic Republic with other states as follows:

Angola on Feb. 19, 1979 (for 20 years);

Ethiopia on Nov. 15, 1979 (for 20 years), ratified on Aug. 14, 1980, a military co-operation protocol having been signed on May 31, 1979;

Mozambique (for 20 years), providing inter alia for "co-operation in the military sector through bilateral agreements", a military co-operation protocol having been signed by the two sides on May 26, 1979;

Tanzania on May 17, 1964;

the **People's Democratic Republic of Yemen** on Nov. 17, 1979, on the lines of the treaty concluded with Ethiopia.

Treaties and Agreements concluded by Romania

Romania has concluded treaties of friendship and co-operation with other states as follows:

Angola: April 14, 1979, for a 20-year period.

Burundi: April 23, 1979, for an indefinite period (together with several co-operation agreements, including one on the development of mineral resources).

Gabon: April 11, 1979, for an indefinite period (together with several co-operation agreements).

Kampuchea: May 28, 1978 (with the Pol Pot regime).

Mozambique: April 20, 1979, for 20 years (together with a programme of economic co-operation until 1990).

Sudan: April 25, 1979, for an indefinite period.

Vietnam: May 25, 1978 (a declaration on the permanent consolidation of friendship, solidarity and the development of co-operation).

Zaïre: March 19, 1980.

Zambia: April 17, 1979, for an unlimited period.

(In Angola, Mozambique and Zambia agreements were signed, at the same time as the above treaties, on co-operation between the political parties of the respective two sides.)

Other Treaties and Declarations of East European Countries

Treaties or declarations of friendship and co-operation were signed between:

Bulgaria and Angola on Oct. 22, 1978;

Bulgaria and Mongolia on July 23, 1967, and May 5, 1977;

Bulgaria and Vietnam on Oct. 1, 1979;

Bulgaria and the Yemeni Republic on April 4, 1964;

Czechoslovakia and Cambodia (of which Prince

Norodom Sihanouk was then head of state) on Nov. 27, 1960;

Czechoslovakia and Ethiopia on Dec. 3, 1978;

Czechoslovakia and the Yemeni Republic on May 20, 1964;

Hungary and the Yemeni Republic on May 20, 1964;

Poland and Ethiopia on Dec. 12, 1979.

Bilateral Treaties Between the USSR and Asian Communist Countries

Since before World War II the Soviet Union has concluded a number of treaties and agreements with Asian Communist countries.

Treaties with the People's Republic of Mongolia. (i) 10-year treaty of mutual assistance, signed on March 28, 1936; (ii) 20-year treaty of friendship and mutual assistance, signed on Feb. 27, 1946; and (iii) 20-year treaty of friendship, co-operation and mutual assistance, signed on Jan. 15, 1966.

Treaties with the People's Republic of China. The Soviet Union entered into the following agreements with China (although they are now effectively defunct in view of the Sino-Soviet ideological dispute): (i) 30-year treaty of friendship, alliance and mutual assistance, signed on Feb. 14, 1950; and (ii) agreements on political co-operation, signed on Oct. 12, 1954, for five years with automatic extension for further periods of five years.

Treaty with the Democratic People's Republic of Korea. A treaty of friendship, co-operation and mutual assistance was signed on July 6, 1961, for the duration of ten years.

Common Provisions of Above Treaties. These Soviet treaties of friendship and mutual assistance, although they each contain clauses relating to the particular country forming the second party, have certain provisions in common. These are:

(1) Automatic mutual assistance in the event of one of the parties being an object of armed attack.

(2) An agreement not to include any alliance directed against the other party.

(3) An agreement on mutual consultation on all important international problems affecting the common interests of both.

(4) The development and consolidation of economic and cultural ties between the two countries.

Treaty with Vietnam. A treaty of friendship and co-operation between Vietnam and the Soviet Union was signed in Moscow on Nov. 3, 1978, together with six economic agreements.

The treaty provided inter alia that the parties would consult each other on all important international issues affecting their interests, and that in the event of either becoming the object of attack or of threats of attack they would "immediately begin mutual consultations for the purpose of removing that threat and taking appropriate effective measures to ensure the peace and security of their countries"; that they would strengthen their economic, scientific and technical co-operation and co-ordinate their national economic plans; that they would "wage all-out and consistent struggle for the further strengthening of fraternal relations and of unity and solidarity among socialist countries on the basis of Marxism-Leninism and socialist internationalism"; and that they would promote the development of relations between countries with different social systems on the basis of the principles of peaceful coexistence and the process of détente in international relations. The treaty was to remain in force for 25 years and to be automatically extended for another 10 years unless either party wished to end it. Instruments of ratification of the treaty were exchanged in Hanoi on Dec. 13, 1978.

Treaty with Afghanistan. A 20-year treaty of friendship, good-neighbourliness and co-operation between the USSR and Afghanistan was signed in Moscow on Dec. 5, 1978, following the establishment of the Democratic Republic of Afghanistan through the assumption of power by the (communist) People's Democratic Party of Afghanistan in April 1978.

The principal provisions of the 15-article treaty were as follows:

After reaffirming their commitment to the aims and principles of Soviet-Afghan treaties of 1921 and 1931, the two countries agreed to develop and strengthen bilateral co-operation in a wide range of matters on the basis of "equality, national sovereignty, territorial integrity and non-interference in each other's internal affairs" and to aid one another in the "training of national personnel and in planning the development of the national economy".

They pledged that they would respect each other's foreign policies (including "the policy of non-alignment which is pursued by . . . Afghanistan"), would not engage in any military aggression against each other and would consult one another about all issues which might affect the security, independence and territorial integrity of either country; furthermore, in accordance with Article 4, they agreed that "in the interests of strengthening their defence capacity" they would continue to develop military co-operation "on the basis of appropriate agreements concluded between them".

Both sides declared that they would continue their efforts to promote peace and co-operation in all parts of the world and would "actively contribute towards general and complete disarmament, including nuclear disarmament, under effective international control". With regard to Asia, they stated in Article 8 that they would "facilitate the development of co-operation among Asian states and the establishment of relations of peace, good-neighbourliness and mutual confidence among them" and the establishment in the area of an "effective security system . . . on the basis of joint efforts by all countries of the continent".

An agreement on the establishment of a permanent Soviet-Afghan intergovernmental commission of economic co-operation, signed at the same time, had been preceded by the conclusion of numerous trade and co-operation agreements concluded by the two sides since April 1978 and also by a 12-year agreement on economic co-operation, signed in April 1977.

The Soviet-Afghan treaties of 1921 and 1931, referred to above, had been treaties of neutrality and mutual non-aggression, and that of 1931 had been three times extended for a further 10 years (on Dec. 18, 1955; on Aug. 6, 1965; and on Dec. 10, 1975).

Agreements with Laos. Four agreements signed by the USSR with Laos on April 22, 1976, included a trade treaty and a cultural and scientific co-operation agreement. An agreement on economic and technical co-operation between the two countries in 1979-80 was signed in Vientiane on Feb. 10, 1979.

Agreements with Kampuchea. Agreements on Soviet aid, cultural and scientific co-operation and economic and technical co-operation were signed during an official visit to Moscow by the President of the People's Republic of Kampuchea on Feb. 3-11, 1980.

Bilateral Treaties and Agreements between the USSR and African Countries

The Soviet Union has signed 20-year treaties of friendship and co-operation with the following African countries:

(1) **Angola** on Oct. 8, 1976, when the two sides undertook inter alia to develop co-operation in the military sphere "in the interests of strengthening their defence capacity"—while a co-operation agreement was also signed between the Popular Movement for the Liberation of Angola (MPLA) and the Communist Party of the Soviet Union (CSPU).

(2) **Mozambique** on March 31, 1977, this treaty providing in Art. 4 that "in the interests of reinforcing the defence potential" of the two countries they would "continue to develop co-operation in the military sphere on the basis of the relevant military agreements" and in Art. 9 that "in the event of situations arising that threaten peace or lead to an outbreak of war" the two countries would "immediately get in touch with each other in order to co-ordinate their positions in the interests of eliminating the threat that has arisen or of restoring peace" (this treaty being ratified by the Supreme Soviet of the USSR on June 15, 1977).

(3) **Ethiopia** on Nov. 20, 1978, when the two sides stated that they would (i) "develop and deepen the relations of unbreakable friendship and co-operation" in

the political, economic, trade, scientific, technical and cultural spheres "on the basis of equality, non-interference in each other's internal affairs, respect for sovereignty, territorial integrity and the inviolability of borders" and also respecting each other's foreign policies; (ii) consult each other on "important international questions directly involving the interests of the two countries" and in situations which "constitute a threat to or a breach of international peace"; (iii) work "actively" for the complete elimination of colonialism, neocolonialism and racism; (iv) continue to work towards safeguarding and securing international détente and settling "international controversial issues by peaceful means without prejudice to the legitimate rights of states to defend themselves, individually or collectively, in accordance with the UN Charter"; and (v) "continue to co-operate in the military field in the interests of ensuring the defence capacity" of the two countries. Following ratification by both sides, this treaty entered into force in April 1979.

Earlier, an agreement had been concluded in March 1977 for the supply to Ethiopia of Soviet weapons, including MiG fighters, missiles and tanks. A Soviet-Ethiopian trade agreement was signed on July 22, 1977, and on Sept. 3 of that year it was reported that an agreement concluded in July 1977 provided for the supply of Soviet aircraft, tanks and equipment and of 3,000 Soviet and Cuban experts. (The participation of Cuban forces in Ethiopia's armed conflict with Somalia was officially admitted in Cuba on March 14, 1978, as "following an urgent call by the Ethiopian Government to the Cuban Communist Party".)

1978 Addis Ababa Conference. An "international conference of solidarity with the struggle of the African and Arab peoples against imperialism and reaction" opened in Addis Ababa on Sept. 14, 1978, and was attended by representatives of over 200 international and national organizations, political parties and national liberation movements. In a message to the conference President Brezhnev expressed strong Soviet support for the Ethiopian people's "courageous struggle in defence of their revolutionary gains and the sovereignty, unity and territorial integrity of their country" and condemned "the interference by reaction and imperialism in the affairs of African and Arab peoples". The First Vice-President of the Presidium of the Supreme Soviet said in Addis Ababa on Sept. 11, 1978, that the Soviet Union regarded the "national democratic revolution" in Ethiopia as "an important part of the world revolutionary process".

Arms Supply and Co-operation Agreements

The Soviet Union has also agreed to supply arms to Libya and Mali.

Libya. The Soviet Prime Minister disclosed on May 27, 1975, that the USSR had agreed to supply Libya with military equipment worth $800,000,000. At the same time an agreement was signed on "co-operation in the use of atomic energy for peaceful purposes" involving the setting-up in Libya of an "atomic centre" including a nuclear reactor.

Mali. It was announced on July 23, 1976, that the USSR would supply military aid to Mali and that Soviet army experts would advise the country's military authorities on the modernization of its armed forces.

The Soviet Union has further concluded co-operation agreements with Mauritius, the Congo, Guinea-Bissau, Tanzania and Uganda.

Mauritius. An agreement on technical assistance, signed in July 1970, provided for the supply by the Soviet Union of trawlers at reduced cost for the fishing industry of Mauritius.

Congo. Co-operation agreements relating to the economy, technology, agriculture and culture were signed in March 1975.

Guinea-Bissau. Agreements on economic, technical, cultural and scientific co-operation and on trade and air services were signed in Moscow in February 1975, and a fisheries agreement was concluded on April 14, 1975.

Tanzania. Agreements were signed in Dar-es-Salaam on March 25, 1977, on trade and on cultural, scientific and technical co-operation.

Uganda. An agreement on the supply of Soviet military equipment, including long-range aircraft, was said to have been signed on Sept. 28, 1976. An agreement on co-operation in trade and technology was signed on Jan. 25, 1978, and further co-operation agreements were, on May 11, 1978, reported to have been signed between the two countries.

Abrogation of Soviet Treaties with Egypt and Somalia

Two important treaties of friendship and co-operation concluded by the Soviet Union were abrogated in 1976 and 1977 respectively.

Egypt. Such a treaty, concluded with Egypt for 15 years on May 27, 1971, was abrogated by Egypt on March 15, 1976, on the grounds that (as stated by the Egyptian President) the USSR had refused to supply Egypt with arms and to grant a moratorium for Egypt's debts.

Somalia. A similar treaty, which the USSR had signed with Somalia on July 11, 1974, and under which the USSR had not only supplied that country with defence equipment but had also established a naval base in Somalia, was abrogated by the latter on Nov. 13, 1977, after the Somali President had, on Oct. 21 of that year, condemned the Soviet Union for its "all-out armed support of the Ethiopian regime" with which Somalia was then at war.

Agreements between the Soviet Union and Cuba

A number of agreements for economic co-operation between the Soviet Union and Cuba were signed on Dec. 23, 1972. "Extraordinary assistance'' provided by the Soviet Union for Cuba under these agreements included a deferment of payment of Cuba's accumulated debt; new credits for the years 1973-75; payment of special concessionary prices for Cuban sugar, nickel and cobalt; and for capital development.

Under a five-year trade agreement signed for 1976-80 by the Soviet Union and Cuba on Feb. 6, 1976, the volume of trade foreseen in a previous agreement of September 1975 was to be doubled.

A five-year economic and technical co-operation agreement, signed by the two countries on April 14, 1976, included provision for the construction of a Soviet-built nuclear power station in Cuba.

According to US sources quoted in August 1979, Soviet military co-operation with Cuba had included the supply of the following equipment: (i) Up to 20 MiG fighter-bombers received by Cuba between July and November 1978; (ii) a first Soviet submarine and two high-speed torpedo boats delivered to Cuba in February 1979, while submarine facilities were being built at Cienfuegos (on Cuba's south coast); and (iii) 20 An-26 transport aircraft delivered by July 1979 under a 1977 agreement. A Soviet brigade stationed in Cuba in 1979 was described by the US Government as a combat unit and by President Castro of Cuba as a training centre which had been in Cuba since October 1962. (In September 1979 the Soviet Government stated that this training centre would not be enlarged or given additional capabilities; that Soviet personnel in Cuba would not be a threat to the USA or any other nation; and that the Soviet Union would abide by the understanding reached with the USA in 1962 and by its mutually agreed confirmation in 1970, under which the Soviet Union had undertaken, in 1962, not to place any offensive missiles in Cuba and, in 1970, not to establish a military naval base on the island.)

An economic co-operation agreement, signed in Moscow on Oct. 31, 1980, for 1981-85 provided for bilateral trade to be increased by about 50 per cent as against the 1976-80 period, for the extension of economic co-operation beyond 1985, and for the joint preparation of plans for the the general development of the Cuban economy until 1990 and for other fields until the year 2000.

Bilateral Treaties between the USSR and Non-Communist Countries in Europe and Asia

Finland. A Treaty of Friendship, Co-operation and Mutual Assistance between the Soviet Union and Finland was signed on April 6, 1948, and was concluded for 10 years. A protocol extending the treaty for a further 20 years was signed on Sept. 19, 1955, and it is automatically renewable for five-year periods after 1975, unless abro-

gated by one party one year before the date of expiration.

The treaty differs from other treaties of mutual assistance made by the Soviet Union in that the obligation to intervene with military assistance in the event of aggression by a third party is restricted to the USSR. Finland is obliged only to fight any aggression on her own territory.

The main provisions of the treaty are given below:

Art. 1. In the event of Finland or the Soviet Union, across the territory of Finland, becoming the object of military aggression on the part of Germany or any state allied to the latter, Finland, loyal to her duty as an independent state, will fight to repulse the aggression. In doing so, she will direct all the forces at her disposal to the defence of the inviolability of her territory on land, on sea and in the air, acting within her boundaries in accordance with her obligations under the present treaty with the assistance, in case of need, of the Soviet Union or jointly with the latter.

In the cases indicated above, the Soviet Union will render Finland the necessary assistance, in regard to the granting of which the parties will agree between themselves.

Art. 6. The parties undertake to observe the principles of mutual respect for their state sovereignty and independence, as well as of non-interference in the domestic affairs of the other state.

On July 20, 1970, the treaty was extended for another 20 years (i.e. until 1990), and on April 20, 1971, a further treaty was signed in Moscow on economic, technical and industrial co-operation between the two countries.

India. A 20-year treaty of peace, friendship and co-operation between the Soviet Union and India, automatically renewable for five-year periods unless either party gave prior notice of termination, was signed in New Delhi on Aug. 9, 1971.

The treaty included the following articles:

"**Art. 2.** Guided by the desire to contribute in every possible way towards ensuring the lasting peace and security of their peoples, the high contracting parties declare their determination to continue efforts to preserve and strengthen peace in Asia and throughout the world, end the arms race, and achieve general and complete disarmament, covering both nuclear and conventional weapons, under effective international control.

"**Art. 3.** Guided by their devotion to the noble ideal of equality of all peoples and states, irrespective of race or creed, the high contracting parties condemn colonialism and racialism in all their forms and manifestations and reaffirm their determination to strive for their final and complete elimination.

"The high contracting parties will co-operate with other states in achieving these aims and support the just aspirations of the peoples in their struggle against colonialism and racial domination.

"**Art. 4.** The Union of Soviet Socialist Republics respects India's policy of non-alignment and reaffirms that this policy is an important factor for maintaining world peace and international security and for lessening tensions in the world.

"The Republic of India respects the peaceful policy of the USSR aimed at strengthening friendship and co-operation with all peoples.

"**Art. 8.** In accordance with the traditional friendship established between the two countries, each of the high contracting parties solemnly declares that it will not enter into or participate in any military alliances directed against the other party.

"Each high contracting party undertakes to refrain from any aggression against the other party and not to allow the use of its territory for the commission of any act that might inflict military damage on the other high contracting party.

"**Art. 9.** Each high contracting party undertakes to abstain from giving any assistance to any third party that engages in an armed conflict with the other party. In the event of either party being subjected to attack or threat thereof, the high contracting parties shall immediately enter into mutual consultations with a view to eliminating this threat and taking appropriate effective measures to ensure the peace and security of their countries.

"**Art. 10.** Each high contracting party solemnly declares that it will not enter into any commitment, secret or public, with one or more states which is incompatible with the present treaty. Each high contracting party further declares that no commitment exists, nor shall any be entered into between itself or any other state or states, that might cause military damage to the other party."

In a communiqué issued at the time when the treaty was signed the Indian Minister of External Affairs referred to "a heavy burden . . . placed on India by the influx of more than seven million refugees" from East Pakistan (now Bangladesh), and India's "gratitude for the Soviet Union's understanding of the problem", as shown by an appeal by President Podgorny to the President of Pakistan in April 1971.

The treaty was ratified in New Delhi on Aug. 9 and in Moscow on Aug. 13, 1971.

In a joint communiqué issued in New Delhi at the end of a meeting between the Soviet Foreign Minister and India's Minister of External Affairs on April 27, 1977, it was stated: "The two sides expressed their satisfaction with the development of the time-tested relations of traditional friendship and co-operation, of mutual respect and confidence, that have been established between the Soviet Union and India. The determination of both sides was stressed to continue to follow the course towards the further strengthening of equal and mutually beneficial co-operation in the spirit of the Soviet-Indian treaty of peace, friendship and co-operation of August 1971. . . . The two sides noted with satisfaction that the positions of the Soviet Union and India on many important questions are identical or close." The communiqué also said that the two sides were ready to participate with all the states concerned in "efforts leading to the early establishment of the Indian Ocean as a zone of peace" and called for "the elimination of all existing foreign military bases from the Indian Ocean and the prohibition of new ones".

A 15-year economic and trade agreement, providing for far-reaching economic, technical and scientific co-operation between the Soviet Union and India, was signed on Nov. 29, 1973.

Iran. A 15-year treaty on the development of economic and technical co-operation between the Soviet Union and Iran was signed in Moscow on Oct. 12, 1972. A further economic co-operation agreement, signed on Feb. 25, 1975, covered projects with an estimated value of $3,000 million. (For earlier Soviet-Iranian treaties, see pages 6-7.)

Iraq. A 15-year treaty of friendship and co-operation between the Soviet Union and Iraq, automatically renewable for periods of five years, was signed in Baghdad on April 9, 1972.

Art. 1 of the treaty provided for all-round co-operation in the political, economic, trade, scientific, technical and other fields "on the basis of respect for state sovereignty, territorial integrity, and non-interference in one another's internal affairs".

In **Art. 4** both countries condemned "imperialism and colonialism in all their forms and manifestations" and undertook to "continue to wage an undeviating struggle against imperialism and Zionism . . .".

Art. 8 laid down that "in the event of situations which threaten the peace of either of the sides or create a threat to peace or the danger of a violation of peace" both countries would "immediately contact each other with the aim of co-ordinating their positions . . .".

In **Art. 9** the two sides undertook to "continue to develop co-operation in the strengthening of their defence capabilities".

In **Art. 10** each of the two sides declared that it would "not enter into alliances or take part in any groupings of states or actions or undertakings" directed against the other side, and would "not permit the use of its territory for any act capable of doing military harm to the other side".

The treaty came into force after the exchange of ratification documents in Moscow on July 20, 1972.

In December 1978 agreement was reached on the supply to Iraq of Soviet arms "to reinforce the defence capacity of Iraq".

Syria. In a joint communiqué issued at the end of a meeting between the Soviet and Syrian Presidents in Moscow on Oct. 6, 1978, it was recorded that "relevant decisions" had been taken with a view to strengthening Syria's defence capacity, and on Oct. 17, 1979, an agreement was concluded providing for "substantial military aid" to Syria by the USSR, with details still to be worked out.

A protocol on economic, scientific and technical co-operation between the Soviet Union and Syria was signed on May 15, 1980.

A treaty of friendship and co-operation in various fields, including military affairs, was signed in Moscow on Oct. 8, 1980, during a visit by the Syrian President, and the treaty was approved by the Syrian Government on Oct. 13, 1980.

South Yemen. A 20-year treaty of friendship and co-operation between the Soviet Union and the People's Democratic Republic of Yemen was signed in Moscow on Oct. 25, 1979, and ratified by the Soviet Union on Dec. 26, 1979. It stated in regard to military co-operation that the two countries would "act on the basis of the relevant agreements concluded between them for the purpose of strengthening their defence capability"; that each country would fully respect the territorial integrity and independence of the other and would neither "enter into military or other alliances" nor "take part in any grouping of states and undertakings" directed against the other party; and that in the case of situations arising which would "threaten peace or violate international peace" the two countries would contact each other "for the purpose of removing a threat to peace or restoring peace".

At the same time the two sides signed (i) a "plan of contacts" between the two countries' political parties for 1980-83 and (ii) a protocol on economic and technical co-operation.

Other Soviet Agreements with Non-Communist Countries

Europe, Asia and the Pacific

Australia. Agreements on cultural and on scientific and technical co-operation between the Soviet Union and Australia were signed in Moscow on Jan. 15, 1975.

Japan. A number of agreements signed between June 1974 and July 1975 provided for the joint development of natural resources in Siberia and the Soviet Far East, involving inter alia large-scale supplies to Japan of Soviet coal, oil, gas and timber in return for credits to be granted by Japan to the Soviet Union.

An agreement on co-operation between Japan and the Soviet Union in the peaceful uses of atomic energy, signed in November 1977, provided for exchanges of visits by experts and also for regular exchanges of scientific information.

Nepal. Under an agreement on economic and technical co-operation signed on Nov. 19, 1976, the Soviet Union undertook to supply Nepal with machines and other equipment as well as with specialists for the building of factories.

Philippines. An agreement on the expansion of scientific and cultural exchanges between the two countries was signed in Manila early in January 1975. A trade agreement was signed in Moscow on June 2, 1976.

Sweden. An agreement for the supply of 300 tons of enriched uranium by the Soviet Union to Sweden was signed in 1966.

A 10-year agreement on economic, scientific and technical co-operation was signed in Moscow on April 25, 1975.

Switzerland. An agreement on the development of economic, industrial, scientific and technical co-operation was signed on Jan. 12, 1978, and followed by a long-term programme signed on July 9, 1979.

Turkey. An economic and technical co-operation agreement signed on July 9, 1975, provided inter alia for a Soviet credit of $700,000,000 mainly to finance Soviet-built projects and to be repaid with Turkish exports.

Latin America and the Caribbean

Argentina. A 10-year agreement which was initialled in 1974 and came into force on Aug. 11, 1977, provided for increased trade and technical and scientific co-operation between the two countries, with the Soviet Union supplying mainly machinery in exchange for Argentinian meat, wool, grain, citrus fruit, leather, shoes, chemicals and machinery.

Jamaica. The first economic and technical co-operation agreement between the two countries was signed on Dec. 7, 1977 (with the Soviet Union assisting in the construction of a cement plant and carrying out prospecting for nickel, copper and other minerals in Jamaica).

A number of further economic agreements were signed during the Jamaican Prime Minister's first visit to Moscow on April 9-13, 1979, providing inter alia for alumina exports from Jamaica to the Soviet Union, the establishment of a joint fisheries company and a long-term Soviet loan to finance Jamaican imports from the Soviet Union.

Peru. Under an agreement reached in mid-1976 Peru purchased 36 Soviet Su-22 (Su-20) fighter-bombers to be paid for at $250,000,000 over 10 years. (It was, however, officially denied in Peru on Jan. 7, 1977, that the two sides had signed a military treaty.)

Venezuela. Economic co-operation agreements between the two countries were signed in Moscow in November 1976, among them one on oil sales (signed on Nov. 26) to Venezuela's neighbours (including Cuba) against Soviet supplies to Venezuela's more distant customers (e.g. Spain).

Cuban Agreements with African Countries

Angola. In addition to the military support given to Ethiopia [see page 214], Cuba also sent military forces to Angola in November 1975 (upon a unilateral decision by the Cuban Communist Party). During a visit to Angola Dr Castro, the Cuban leader, stated on March 28, 1977, that Cuba would place no limits on its "international duty" to collaborate with Angola and that Cuba's military presence in Angola would be maintained until the Angolan armed forces were organized, trained and equipped. In May 1977 he said that the Cuban presence was "in accordance with a strict international principle and in full agreement with the Luanda Government". Within the framework of an Angolan-Cuban mixed commission bilateral agreements were signed early in November 1977 on a "supplementary contingent" of Cuban civilians to be sent to Angola. By May 1978 the total of Cuban military personnel in Angola was estimated at 21,000.

On Nov. 30, 1978, a total of 35 agreements on co-operation between Cuba and Angola in economic affairs, defence and political assistance were signed in Havana.

Congo. With the Congo, Cuba signed four co-operation agreements, including one relating to foreign affairs, in May 1978.

Mozambique. With Mozambique, Cuba signed, on June 4, 1977, agreements on co-operation in the fields of health, public works, transport, agriculture and fisheries, and on Oct. 21, 1978, an agreement on economic and scientific co-operation.

Treaties concluded by Vietnam

Treaties signed by the Socialist Republic of Vietnam with neighbouring countries in Indo-China have included the following:

Kampuchea. A treaty of peace, friendship and co-operation signed in Phnom-Penh on Feb. 18, 1979, by Vietnam with the Government set up in Cambodia by the "People's Revolutionary Council" (established with Vietnamese support as the provisional Government of the People's Republic of Kampuchea on Jan. 8, 1979) contained the following provisions:

The two sides would develop their traditional solidarity, friendship and co-operation and would assist each other in all fields on the basis of respect for independence, non-interference in internal affairs and equality; assist each other to strengthen their capacity to defend their independence against "all

schemes and acts of sabotage by the imperialist and reactionary forces"; would resolve all differences which might arise between them by peaceful negotiations and would negotiate a treaty delineating the frontier between them on the basis of the present border line; and would pursue a foreign policy of independence, peace, friendship, co-operation and non-alignment, and of friendship and good-neighbourliness with Thailand and the other South-East Asian countries. The treaty was not aimed at opposing any third country, and it would be valid for 25 years and automatically renewed every 10 years unless either party gave a year's notice of its intention to cancel it.

Laos. A treaty of friendship and co-operation signed in Vientiane on July 18, 1977, between Vietnam and the Lao People's Democratic Republic provided inter alia that both sides would "protect and develop the special Vietnam-Laos relationship"; would "co-operate closely in increasing their capability of defending and protecting their independence, sovereignty and territorial integrity"; would "strive to strengthen the militant solidarity and co-operative relations with other fraternal socialist countries"; and would "positively contribute together with the other socialist countries and the international communist movement to intensifying their solidarity and mutual support and assistance"; "strengthen the militant solidarity, lasting co-operation with and mutual assistance to fraternal Cambodia"; and "establish and develop relations of friendship and co-operation with the countries in this area". The treaty would be valid for 20 years and automatically renewed for further 10-year periods unless one of the signatories gave a year's written notice of intention to cancel it.

(In a joint statement issued at the same time the two sides undertook to "do everything in their power to strengthen their militant solidarity and relations of co-operation with the USSR, China and the other fraternal socialist countries" and "strengthen solidarity and mutual support and assistance on the basis of Marxism-Leninism and proletarian internationalism".)

Mongolia. A treaty of friendship and co-operation, concluded for 25 years and automatically renewable every 10 years, was signed in Hanoi on Dec. 3, 1979, between the Socialist Republic of Vietnam and the Mongolian People's Republic. In this treaty it was stated inter alia that the two sides supported "the South-East Asian peoples' aspiration to turn the region into one of peace, independence, freedom, neutrality, stability and prosperity".

Bilateral Treaties and Agreements concluded by the People's Republic of China

Treaties with Asian Neighbours

Since 1950 the People's Republic of China has concluded a number of border treaties, non-aggression pacts, and treaties of friendship with its neighbours in Asia, thus securing and safeguarding its position within Asia.

Such treaties and agreements have been concluded with the following countries:

Burma. (i) Treaty of friendship and non-aggression; and (ii) agreement on the settlement of border problems (both Jan. 28, 1960).

Nepal. (i) Agreement on settlement of border problems (March 21, 1960); (ii) treaty of peace and friendship (April 28, 1960); and (iii) boundary treaty (Oct. 5, 1961).

Afghanistan. (i) Treaty of friendship and non-aggression (Aug. 27, 1960); and (ii) border treaty (Nov. 24, 1963).

Democratic People's Republic of Korea. Treaty of friendship, co-operation and mutual assistance (July 11, 1961).

This treaty is similarly worded to the treaties of mutual assistance made by the USSR with Mongolia, the People's Republic of China and North Korea [see above].

Pakistan. (i) Border treaty, providing for the possibility that, on the settlement of the Kashmir dispute between India and Pakistan, the region covered by the treaty may come under other than Pakistani rule (March 2, 1963); and (ii) protocol on the final demarcation of the frontier (March 26, 1965).

Non-operative Treaties. Other such treaties concluded by China but no longer operative are a treaty of friendship and good-neighbourly relations signed with the Democratic Republic of Vietnam on July 7, 1955; a treaty of friendship and mutual economic aid signed with the Mongolian People's Republic on May 31, 1960; and a treaty of friendship and non-aggression signed with Cambodia on Dec. 19, 1960. A frontier agreement between China and Mongolia was signed on Dec. 26, 1962.

Laos. With Laos an economic and technical co-operation agreement was signed by China on Oct. 3, 1977, involving Chinese aid of about £25,000,000.

Agreements with Communist Countries in Europe

With **Romania**, agreements were signed on Aug. 21, 1979 (during a visit to Romania by Chairman Hua Guofeng of China) on the establishment of an intergovernmental committee for economic and technical co-operation, on regular shipping services and on trade.

As a result of the Sino-Soviet dispute and the break between China and Albania in 1978, China no longer has any other operative treaties of agreements with Communist countries in Europe.

Treaties with Other Countries

Treaties of friendship were concluded by China with the following countries on the dates stated:

(1) **Guinea** (Sept. 13, 1960).
(2) **Indonesia** (April 1, 1961). There have, however, been no diplomatic relations between China and Indonesia since October 1967.
(3) **Ghana** (Aug. 18, 1961).
(4) **Yemeni Republic** (June 9, 1964).
(5) **Congo** (Oct. 2, 1964).
(6) **Mali** (Nov. 3, 1964).
(7) **Tanzania** (Feb. 20, 1965).

These treaties of friendship are all similar in content and wording. The treaty with Tanzania opens with a preamble in which the two parties state their desire to consolidate and develop their friendship and to "fight the forces of imperialism". In the principal article of the treaty they undertake to guide their mutual relations by "the Five Principles of mutual respect for sovereignty and territorial integrity, mutual non-aggression, non-interference in each other's internal affairs, equality and mutual benefit, and peaceful co-existence". (See "Bandung Conference", page 387.) Other provisions are for economic and cultural relations, and for peaceful consultation on any question concerning both parties.

Under subsequent Sino-Tanzanian agreements, China sent to Tanzania (i) some 13,000 technicians to work on the construction of a railway line from Tanzania to the copperbelt in Zambia, as agreed in July 1970, and (ii) military equipment, including tanks and aircraft. China also undertook to build in Tanzania a naval base, for which the foundation stone was laid in May 1971.

The railway line was completed in July 1976, having been financed by an interest-free Chinese loan equivalent to $415,000,000 repayable over a 30-year period from 1983. A technical co-operation agreement signed in July 1976 provided inter alia for some 1,000 Chinese technicians to continue to train indigenous railway staff over a two-year period.

Agreements with Countries in Africa

Chad. An agreement on economic and

technical co-operation between China and Chad was signed in Peking on Sept. 23, 1978.

Congo. Military aid agreements have been signed between the two countries since 1970.

Egypt. Following the abrogation of the Soviet-Egyptian treaty of friendship and co-operation in March 1976 by Egypt [see above], the latter requested China to supply Egypt with military equipment. Under a protocol signed on April 21, 1976, China agreed to supply such equipment and also to erect a munitions factory in Egypt and possibly to send Chinese technicians for the maintenance of Egypt's Soviet-built MiG fighter aircraft. In the same year China was said to have delivered to Egypt, free of charge, 30 MiG engines and other spare parts. In the first half of 1979 Egypt received 40 Shenyang F-6 jet aircraft (the Chinese version of the Soviet MiG 19), while another 40 or 50 were still to be supplied.

Gabon. A technical and economic co-operation agreement was signed in Peking on Oct. 7, 1974.

Madagascar. Two agreements on trade and economic and technical co-operation were signed in Peking on Jan. 19, 1974.

Nigeria. A five-year economic and technical co-operation agreement and a trade agreement were signed in Lagos late in 1972.

Rwanda. An agreement on economic and technical co-operation was signed in Peking on June 10, 1978.

São Tomé and Príncipe. Agreements on trade and economic and technical co-operation were signed in Peking on Dec. 24, 1975.

Seychelles. An agreement on economic and technical co-operation was signed in Peking on May 2, 1978.

Somalia. A technical aid agreement was signed on Oct. 23, 1966, and under an agreement of May 1972 China was to finance and build a 600-mile road between Mogadishu and Hargeisa (in northern Somalia).

Sudan. An agreement on technical and economic co-operation was signed in Peking on June 9, 1977.

Zaïre. The President of Zaïre stated in March 1980 that, in terms of an existing agreement on military co-operation, China would train 3,000 Zaïrean commandos.

Agreements with Countries in Other Regions

Australia. An agreement on co-operation in science and technology was signed and entered into force on May 6, 1980.

Bangladesh. An economic and technical co-operation agreement and a trade and payments agreement were signed by the two countries in Peking on Jan. 4, 1977.

Brazil. A five-year trade agreement signed in Peking on Nov. 9, 1978, provided for the purchase by China of Brazilian iron ore in exchange for Chinese oil.

Canada. During a visit to China by the Canadian Prime Minister on Oct. 10-17, 1973, several agreements were signed, covering inter alia trade and co-operation in science and technology.

Finland. A scientific, technical, industrial and economic co-operation agreement was signed in Helsinki on May 29, 1979.

Malta. In 1972 China granted Malta a loan equivalent to almost £17,000,000 over six years, whereafter a number of Chinese-backed development projects were initiated in Malta, including the construction of a new graving dock capable of accommodating 300,000-ton tankers. An economic and technical aid agreement was signed in Peking on Nov. 6, 1977.

Mexico. Agreements on tourism and cultural relations between the two countries were signed during a visit to China by the President of Mexico on Oct. 24-30, 1978.

Philippines. Under a five-year trade agreement signed in Peking in July 1978, the Philippines were to import 1,200,000 tonnes of crude oil per annum from China as from January 1979 (making the Philippines the second largest importer of Chinese oil after Japan). Among further agreements concluded in July 1979 was an eight-year trade agreement providing for two-way trade between the two countries amounting to $2,000 million.

12. East-West Treaties of 1970-80

This section covers the major East-West treaties and agreements entered into over the past decade, including (i) the Final Act of the 1975 Conference on Security and Co-operation in Europe, (ii) agreements concluded in the first phase of East-West détente in 1970-73, (iii) further US-Soviet agreements of 1974-79, including those relating to strategic arms limitation and limitation of nuclear tests, (iv) other recent Soviet agreements with Western states and (v) major agreements entered into with Western states by the People's Republic of China.

Conference on Security and Co-operation in Europe (CSCE)

1975 Helsinki Conference

The Conference on Security and Co-operation in Europe (CSCE) was held in three stages—respectively (i) in Helsinki on July 3-7, 1973, (ii) in Geneva from Sept. 19, 1973 to July 21, 1975, and (iii) again in Helsinki from July 30 to Aug. 1, 1975. It was attended by representatives of Canada, the United States and 32 countries of Europe—i.e. all except Albania and Andorra (the latter's foreign affairs being handled by France).

A *Final Act* drawn up by officials of the 35 countries (Australia, Belgium, Bulgaria, Canada, Cyprus, Czechoslovakia, Denmark, Finland, France, the German Democratic Republic, the Federal Republic of Germany, Greece, the Holy See, Hungary, Iceland, Ireland, Italy, Liechtenstein, Luxembourg, Malta, Monaco, the Netherlands, Norway, Poland, Portugal, Romania, San Marino, the Soviet Union, Spain, Sweden, Switzerland, Turkey, the United Kingdom, the United States and Yugoslavia) was signed at the third session of the CSCE in Helsinki on Aug. 1, 1975, by representatives of the above 35 participating countries, the majority of the signatories being heads of state or of government.

The *Final Act* comprised four main sections, described as "baskets", on subjects agreed to at the first stage of the CSCE—on questions relating to security in Europe; co-operation in the fields of economics, science, technology and environment; co-operation in humanitarian and other fields; and a follow-up to the conference. In addition the *Final Act* contained a section on questions relating to security and co-operation in the Mediterranean.

The material passages of the *Final Act* were worded as follows:

"BASKET ONE"

Questions Relating to Security in Europe

"The states participating in the Conference on Security and Co-operation in Europe,

"*Reaffirming* their objective of promoting better relations among themselves and ensuring conditions in which their people can live in true and lasting peace free from any threat to or attempt against their security;

"*Convinced* of the need to exert efforts to make détente both a continuing and an increasingly viable and comprehensive process, universal in scope, and that the implementation of the results of CSCE will be a major contribution to this process;

"*Considering* that solidarity among peoples, as well as the common purpose of the participating states in achieving the aims as set forth by the CSCE, should lead to the development of better and closer relations among them in all fields and thus to overcoming the confrontation stemming from the character of their past relations, and to better mutual understanding;

"*Mindful* of their common history and recognizing that the existence of elements common to their traditions and values can assist them in developing their relations, and desiring to search, fully taking into account the individuality and diversity of their positions and views, for possibilities of joining their efforts with a view to overcoming distrust and increasing confidence, solving the problems that separate them and co-operating in the interest of mankind;

"*Recognizing* the indivisibility of security in Europe as well as their common interest in the development of co-operation throughout Europe and among themselves and expressing their intention to pursue efforts accordingly;

"*Recognizing* the close link between peace and security in Europe and in the world as a whole and conscious of the need for each of them to make its contribution to the strengthening of world peace and security and to the promotion of fundamental rights, economic and social progress and well-being for all peoples;

"*Have adopted the following:*

(A) Declaration on Principles Guiding Relations between Participating States

"The participating states,

"*Reaffirming* their commitment to peace, security and justice and the continuing development of friendly relations and co-operation;

"*Recognizing* that this commitment, which reflects the interest and aspirations of peoples, constitutes for each participating state a present and future responsibility, heightened by experience of the past;

"*Reaffirming*, in conformity with their membership in the United Nations and in accordance with the purposes and principles of the United Nations, their full and active support for the United Nations and for the enhancement of its role and effectiveness in strengthening international peace, security and justice, and in promoting the solution of international problems, as well as the development of friendly relations and co-operation among states;

"*Expressing* their common adherence to the principles which are set forth below and are in conformity with the Charter of the United Nations as well as their common will to act, in the application of these principles, in conformity with the purposes and principles of the Charter of the United Nations;

"*Declare* their determination to respect and put into practice, each of them in its relations with all other participating states, irrespective of their political, economic or social systems as well as of their size, geographical location or level of economic development, the following principles, which are all of primary significance, guiding their mutual relations:

"**I. Sovereign Equality, Respect for the Rights Inherent in Sovereignty.** The participating states will respect each other's sovereign equality and individuality as well as all the rights inherent in and encompassed by its sovereignty, including in particular the right of every state to juridical equality, to territorial integrity and to freedom and political independence. They will also respect each other's right freely to choose and develop its political, social, economic and cultural systems as well as its right to determine its laws and regulations.

"Within the framework of international law, all the participating states have equal rights and duties. They will respect each other's right to define and conduct as it wishes its relations with other states in accordance with international law and in the spirit of the present Declaration. They consider that their frontiers can be changed, in accordance with international law, by peaceful means and by agreement. They also have the right to belong or not to belong to international organizations, to be or not to be a party to bilateral or multilateral treaties including the right to be or not to be a party to treaties of alliance; they also have the right to neutrality.

"**II. Refraining from the Threat or Use of Force.** The participating states will refrain in their mutual relations, as well as in their international relations in general, from the threat or use of force against the territorial integrity or political independence of any state, or in any other manner inconsistent with the purposes of the United Nations and with the present Declaration. No consideration may be invoked to serve to warrant resort to the threat or use of force in contravention of this principle.

"Accordingly, the participating states will refrain from any acts constituting a threat of force or direct or indirect use of force against another participating state. Likewise they will refrain from any manifestation of force for the purpose of inducing another participating state to renounce the full exercise of its sovereign rights. Likewise they will also refrain in their mutual relations from any act of reprisal by force.

"No such threat or use of force will be employed as a means of settling disputes, or questions likely to give rise to disputes, between them.

"**III. Inviolability of Frontiers.** The participating states regard as inviolable all one another's frontiers as well as the frontiers of all states in Europe and therefore they will refrain now and in the future from assaulting these frontiers.

"Accordingly, they will also refrain from any demand for, or act of, seizure and usurpation of part or all of the territory of any participating state.

"**IV. Territorial Integrity of States.** The participating states will respect the territorial integrity of each of the participating states.

"Accordingly, they will refrain from any action inconsistent with the purposes and principles of the Charter of the United Nations against the territorial integrity, political independence or the unity of any participating state, and in particular from any such action constituting a threat or use of force.

"The participating states will likewise refrain from making each other's territory the object of military occupation or other direct or indirect measures of force in contravention of international law, or the object of acquisition by means of such measures or the threat of them. No such occupation or acquisition will be recognized as legal.

"**V. Peaceful Settlement of Disputes.** The participating states will settle disputes among them by peaceful means in such a manner as not to endanger international peace and security, and justice.

"They will endeavour in good faith and a spirit of co-operation to reach a rapid and equitable solution on the basis of international law.

"For this purpose they will use such means as negotiation, enquiry, mediation, conciliation, arbitration, judicial settlement or other peaceful means of their own choice including any settlement procedure agreed to in advance of disputes to which they are parties.

"In the event of failure to reach a solution by any of the above peaceful means, the parties to a dispute will continue to seek a mutually agreed way to settle the dispute peacefully.

"Participating states, parties to a dispute among them, as well as other participating states, will refrain from any action which might aggravate the situation to such a degree as to endanger the maintenance of international peace and security and thereby make a peaceful settlement of the dispute more difficult.

"**VI. Non-Intervention in Internal Affairs.** The participating states will refrain from any intervention, direct or indirect, individual or collective, in the internal or external affairs falling within the domestic jurisdiction of another participating state, regardless of their mutual relations.

"They will accordingly refrain from any form of armed intervention or threat of such intervention against another participating state.

"They will likewise in all circumstances refrain from any other act of military, or of political, economic or other coercion designed to subordinate to their own interest the exercise by another participating state of the right inherent in its sovereignty and thus to secure advantages of any kind.

"Accordingly, they will, inter alia, refrain from direct or indirect assistance to terrorist activities, or to subversive or other activities directed towards the violent overthrow of the regime of another participating state.

"VII. Respect for Human Rights and Fundamental Freedoms, including the Freedom of Thought, Conscience, Religion or Belief. The participating states will respect human rights and fundamental freedoms, including the freedom of thought, conscience, religion or belief, for all without distinction as to race, sex, language or religion.

"They will promote and encourage the effective exercise of civil, political, economic, social, cultural and other rights and freedoms all of which derive from the inherent dignity of the human person and are essential for his free and full development.

"Within this framework the participating states will recognize and respect the freedom of the individual to profess and practise, alone or in community with others, religion or belief acting in accordance with the dictates of his own conscience.

"The participating states on whose territory national minorities exist will respect the right of persons belonging to such minorities to equality before the law, will afford them the full opportunity for the actual enjoyment of human rights and fundamental freedoms and will, in this manner, protect their legitimate interests in this sphere.

"The participating states recognize the universal significance of human rights and fundamental freedoms, respect for which is an essential factor for the peace, justice and well-being necessary to ensure the development of friendly relations and co-operation among themselves as among all states.

"They will constantly respect these rights and freedoms in their mutual relations and will endeavour jointly and separately, including in co-operation with the United Nations, to promote universal and effective respect for them.

"They confirm the right of the individual to know and act upon his rights and duties in this field.

"In the field of human rights and fundamental freedoms, the participating states will act in conformity with the purposes and principles of the Charter of the United Nations and with the Universal Declaration of Human Rights. They will also fulfil their obligations as set forth in the international declarations and agreements in this field, including, inter alia, the International Covenants on Human Rights, by which they may be bound.

"VIII. Equal Rights and Self-Determination of Peoples. The participating states will respect the equal rights of peoples and their right to self-determination, acting at all times in conformity with the purposes and principles of the Charter of the United Nations and with the relevant norms of international law, including those relating to territorial integrity of states.

"By virtue of the principle of equal rights and self-determination of peoples, all peoples always have the right, in full freedom, to determine, when and as they wish, their internal and external political status, without external interference, and to pursue as they wish their political, economic, social and cultural development.

"The participating states reaffirm the universal significance of respect for and effective exercise of equal rights and self-determination of peoples for the development of friendly relations among themselves as among all states; they also recall the importance of the elimination of any form of violation of this principle.

"IX. Co-operation among States. The participating states will develop their co-operation with one another and with all states in all fields in accordance with the purposes and principles of the Charter of the United Nations. In developing their co-operation the participating states will place special emphasis on the fields as set forth within the framework of the CSCE, with each of them making its contribution in conditions of full equality.

"They will endeavour, in developing their co-operation as equals, to promote mutual understanding and confidence, friendly and good-neighbourly relations among themselves, international peace, security and justice. They will equally endeavour, in developing their co-operation, to improve the well-being of peoples and contribute to the fulfilment of their aspirations through, inter alia, the benefits resulting from increased mutual knowledge and from progress and achievement in the economic, scientific, technological, social, cultural and humanitarian fields. They will take steps to promote conditions favourable to making these benefits available to all; they will take into account the interest of all in the narrowing of differences in the levels of economic development, and in particular the interest of developing countries throughout the world.

"They confirm that governments, institutions, organizations and persons have a relevant and positive role to play in contributing towards the achievement of these aims of their co-operation.

"They will strive, in increasing this co-operation as set forth above, to develop closer relations among themselves on an improved and more enduring basis for the benefit of peoples.

"X. Fulfilment in Good Faith of Obligations under International Law. The participating states will fulfil in good faith their obligations under international law, both those obligations arising from the generally recognized principles and rules of international law and those obligations arising from treaties or other agreements, in conformity with international law, to which they are parties.

"In exercising their sovereign rights, including the right to determine their laws and regulations, they will conform with their legal obligations under international law; they will furthermore pay due regard to and implement the provisions in the Final Act of the CSCE.

"The participating states confirm that, in the event of a conflict between the obligations of the members of the United Nations under the Charter of the United Nations and their obligations under any treaty or other international agreement, their obligations under the Charter will prevail, in accordance with Article 103 of the Charter of the United Nations.

"All the principles set forth above are of primary significance and, accordingly, they will be equally and unreservedly applied, each of them being interpreted taking into account the others.

"The participating states express their determination fully to respect and apply these principles, as set forth in the present Declaration, in all aspects, to their mutual relations and co-operation in order to ensure to each participating state the benefits resulting from the respect and application of these principles by all.

"The participating states, paying due regard to the principles above and, in particular, to the first sentence of the tenth principle, 'Fulfilment in good faith of obligations under international law', note that the present Declaration does not affect their rights and obligations, nor the corresponding treaties and other agreements and arrangements.

"The participating states express the conviction that respect for these principles will encourage the development of normal and friendly relations and the progress of co-operation among them in all fields. They also express the conviction that respect for these principles will encourage the development of political contact among them which in turn would contribute to better mutual understanding of their positions and views.

"The participating states declare their intention to conduct their relations with all other states in the spirit of the principles contained in the present Declaration.

(B) Matters Related to giving Effect to Certain of the Above Principles

"(i) The participating states,

"*Reaffirming* that they will respect and give effect to refraining from the threat or use of force and convinced of the necessity to make it an effective norm of international life,

"*Declare* that they are resolved to respect and carry out, in their relations with one another, inter alia, the following provisions which are in conformity with the Declaration on Principles Guiding Relations between Participating States [see above]:

"To give effect and expression, by all the ways and forms which they consider appropriate, to the duty to refrain from the threat or use of force in their relations with one another.

"To refrain from any use of armed forces inconsistent with the purposes and principles of the Charter of the United Nations and the provisions of the Declaration on Principles Guiding Relations between Participating States, against another participating state, in particular from invasion of or attack on its territory.

"To refrain from any manifestation of force for the purpose of inducing another participating state to renounce the full exercise of its sovereign rights.

"To refrain from any act of economic coercion designed to subordinate to their own interest the exercise by another participating state of the rights inherent in its sovereignty and thus to secure advantages of any kind.

"To take effective measures which by their scope and by their nature constitute steps towards the ultimate achievement of general and complete disarmament under strict and effective international control.

"To promote, by all means which each of them considers appropriate, a climate of confidence and respect among peoples consonant with their duty to refrain from propaganda for wars of aggression or for any threat or use of force inconsistent with the purposes of the United Nations and with the Declaration on Principles Guiding Relations between Participating States, against another participating state.

"To make every effort to settle exclusively by peaceful means any dispute between them, the continuance of which is likely to endanger the maintenance of international peace and security in Europe, and to seek, first of all, a solution through the peaceful means set forth in Article 33 of the United Nations Charter.

"To refrain from any action which could hinder the peaceful settlement of disputes between the participating states.

"(ii) The participating states,

"*Reaffirming* their determination to settle their disputes as set forth in the Principle of Peaceful Settlement of Disputes [see above];

"*Convinced* that the peaceful settlement of disputes is a complement to refraining from the threat or use of force, both being essential though not exclusive factors for the maintenance and consolidation of peace and security;

"*Desiring* to reinforce and to improve the methods at their disposal for the peaceful settlement of disputes;

"(1) Are resolved to pursue the examination and elaboration of a generally acceptable method for the peaceful settlement of disputes aimed at complementing existing methods, and to continue to this end to work upon the 'Draft Convention on a European System for the Peaceful Settlement of Disputes' submitted by Switzerland during the second stage of the CSCE, as well as other proposals relating to it and directed towards the elaboration of such a method.

"(2) Decide that, on the invitation of Switzerland, a meeting of experts of all the participating states will be convoked in order to fulfil the mandate described in paragraph 1 above within the framework and under the procedures of the follow-up to the conference laid down in the chapter 'Follow-up to the Conference' [see below].

"(3) This meeting of experts will take place after the meeting of the representatives appointed by the Ministers of Foreign Affairs of the participating states, scheduled according to the chapter 'Follow-up to the Conference' for 1977; the results of the work of this meeting of experts will be submitted to governments.

Document on Confidence-building Measures and Certain Aspects of Security and Disarmament

"The participating states,

"*Desirous* of eliminating the causes of tension that may exist among them and thus of contributing to the strengthening of peace and security in the world;

"*Determined* to strengthen confidence among them and thus to contribute to increasing stability and security in Europe;

"*Determined* further to refrain in their mutual relations, as well as in their international relations in general, from the threat or use of force against the territorial integrity or political independence of any state, or in any other manner inconsistent with the purposes of the United Nations and with the Declaration on Principles Guiding Relations between Participating States as adopted in this Final Act [see above];

"*Recognizing* the need to contribute to reducing the dangers of armed conflict and of misunderstanding or miscalculation of military activities which could give rise to apprehension, particularly in a situation where the participating states lack clear and timely information about the nature of such activities;

"*Taking into account* considerations relevant to efforts aimed at lessening tension and promoting disarmament;

"*Recognizing* that the exchange of observers by invitation at military manoeuvres will help to promote contacts and mutual understanding;

"*Having studied* the question of prior notification of major military movements in the context of confidence-building;

"*Recognizing* that there are other ways in which individual states can contribute further to their common objectives;

"*Convinced* of the political importance of prior notification of major military manoeuvres for the promotion of mutual understanding and the strengthening of confidence, stability and security;

"*Accepting* the responsibility of each of them to promote these objectives and to implement this measure, in accordance with the accepted criteria and modalities, as essentials for the realization of these objectives;

"*Recognizing* that this measure deriving from political decision rests upon a voluntary basis;

"*Have adopted the following:*

I

"**Prior Notification of Major Military Manoeuvres.** They will notify their major military manoeuvres to all other participating states through usual diplomatic channels in accordance with the following provisions:

"Notification will be given of major military manoeuvres exceeding a total of 25,000 troops, independently or combined with any possible air or naval components (in this context the word 'troops' includes amphibious and air-borne troops). In the case of independent manoeuvres involving them, these troops will be included in this total. Furthermore, in the case of combined manoeuvres which do not reach the above total but which involve land forces together with significant numbers of either amphibious or air-borne troops, or both, notification can also be given.

"Notification will be given of major military manoeuvres which take place on the territory, in Europe, of any participating state as well as, if applicable, in the adjoining sea area and air space.

"In the case of a participating state whose territory extends beyond Europe, prior notification need be given only of manoeuvres which take place in an area within 250 kilometres from its frontier facing or shared with any other European participating state. The participating state need not, however, give notification in cases in which that area is also contiguous to the participating state's frontier facing or shared with a non-European non-participating state.

"Notification will be given 21 days or more in advance of the start of the manoeuvre or in the case of a manoeuvre arranged at shorter notice at the earliest possible opportunity prior to its starting date.

"Notification will contain information of the designation, if any, the general purpose of and the states involved in the manoeuvre, the type or types and numerical strength of the forces engaged, the area and estimated time-frame of its conduct. The participating states will also, if possible, provide additional relevant information, particularly that related to the components of the forces engaged and the period of involvement of these forces.

"**Prior Notification of Other Military Manoeuvres.** The participating states recognize that they can contribute further to strengthening confidence and increasing security and stability, and to this end may also notify smaller-scale military manoeuvres to other participating states, with special regard for those near the area of such manoeuvres.

"To the same end, the participating states also recognize that they may notify other military manoeuvres conducted by them.

"**Exchange of Observers.** The participating states will invite other participating states, voluntarily and on a bilateral basis, in a spirit of reciprocity and goodwill towards all participating states, to send observers to attend military manoeuvres.

"The inviting state will determine in each case the number of observers, the procedures and conditions of their participation, and give other information which it may consider useful. It will provide appropriate facilities and hospitality.

"The invitation will be given as far ahead as is conveniently possible through usual diplomatic channels.

"**Prior Notification of Major Military Movements.**

In accordance with the final recommendations of the Helsinki consultations [the preparatory talks for the CSCE], the participating states studied the question of prior notification of major military movements as a measure to strengthen confidence.

"Accordingly, the participating states recognize that they may, at their own discretion and with a view to contributing to confidence building, notify their major military movements.

"In the same spirit, further consideration will be given by the states participating in the CSCE to the question of prior notification of major military movements, bearing in mind, in particular, the experience gained by the implementation of the measures which are set forth in this document.

"**Other Confidence-building Measures.** The participating states recognize that there are other means by which their common objectives can be promoted.

"In particular, they will, with due regard to reciprocity and with a view to better mutual understanding, promote exchanges by invitation among their military personnel, including visits by military delegations.

In order to make a fuller contribution to their common objective of confidence-building the participating states, when conducting their military activities in the area covered by the provisions for the prior notification of major military manoeuvres, will duly take into account and respect this objective.

"They also recognize that the experience gained by the implementation of the provisions set forth above, together with further efforts, could lead to developing and enlarging measures aimed at strengthening confidence.

II

"**Questions relating to Disarmament.** The participating states recognize the interest of all of them in efforts aimed at lessening military confrontation and promoting disarmament which are designed to complement political détente in Europe and to strengthen their security. They are convinced of the necessity to take effective measures in these fields which, by their scope and by their nature, constitute steps towards the ultimate achievement of general and complete disarmament under strict and effective international control, and which should result in strengthening peace and security throughout the world.

III

"**General Considerations.** Having considered the views expressed on various subjects related to the strengthening of security in Europe through joint efforts aimed at promoting détente and disarmament, the participating states, when engaged in such efforts, will, in this context, proceed, in particular, from the following essential considerations:

"The complementary nature of the political and military aspects of security; the inter-relation between the security of each participating state and security in Europe as a whole and the relationship which exists, in the broader context of world security, between security in Europe and security in the Mediterranean area; respect for the security interests of all states participating in the CSCE inherent in their sovereign equality; the importance that participants in negotiating fora see to it that information about relevant developments, progress and results is provided on an appropriate basis to other states participating in the CSCE and, in return, the justified interest of any of those states in having their views considered.

"BASKET TWO"

Co-operation in the Field of Economics, of Science and Technology and of the Environment

"The participating states . . . have adopted the following:

1. Commercial Exchanges

"**General Provisions.** The participating states . . . are resolved to promote, on the basis of the modalities of their economic co-operation, the expansion of their mutual trade in goods and services, and to ensure conditions favourable to such development; recognize the beneficial effects which can result for the development of trade from the application of most-favoured-nation treatment; will encourage the expansion of trade on as broad a multilateral basis as possible, thereby endeavouring to utilize the various economic and commercial possibilities; recognize the importance of bilateral and multilateral intergovernmental and other agreements for the long-term development of trade; note the importance of monetary and financial questions for the development of international trade, and will endeavour to deal with them with a view to contributing to the continuous expansion of trade; will endeavour to reduce or progressively eliminate all kinds of obstacles to the development of trade; will foster a steady growth of trade while avoiding as far as possible abrupt fluctuations in their trade;

"Consider that their trade in various products should be conducted in such a way as not to cause or threaten to cause serious injury—and, should the situation arise, market disruption—in domestic markets for these products and in particular to the detriment of domestic producers of like or directly competitive products; as regards the concept of market disruption, it is understood that it should not be invoked in a way inconsistent with the relevant provisions of their international agreements; if they resort to safeguard measures, they will do so in conformity with their commitments in this field arising from international agreements to which they are parties and will take account of the interests of the parties directly concerned; will give due attention to measures for the promotion of trade and the diversification of its structure; note that the growth and diversification of trade would contribute to widening the possibilities of choice of products; consider it appropriate to create favourable conditions for the participation of firms, organizations and enterprises in the development of trade.

"**Business Contacts and Facilities.** The participating states . . . will take measures further to improve conditions for the expansion of contacts between representatives of official bodies, of the different organizations, enterprises, firms and banks concerned with foreign trade, in particular, where useful, between sellers and users of products and services, for the purpose of studying commercial possibilities, concluding contracts, ensuring their implementation and providing after-sales service; will encourage organizations, enterprises and firms concerned with foreign trade to take measures to accelerate the conduct of business negotiations; will further take measures aimed at improving working conditions of representatives of foreign organizations, enterprises, firms and banks concerned with external trade, particularly as follows:

"By providing the necessary information, including information on legislation and procedures relating to the establishment and operation of permanent representation by the above-mentioned bodies; by examining as favourably as possible requests for the establishment of permanent representation and of offices for this purpose, including, where appropriate, the opening of joint offices by two or more firms; by encouraging the provision, on conditions as favourable as possible and equal for all representatives of the above-mentioned bodies, of hotel accommodation, means of communication, and of other facilities normally required by them, as well as of suitable business and residential premises for purposes of permanent representation;

"Recognize the importance of such measures to encourage greater participation by small and medium-sized firms in trade between participating states.

"**Economic and Commercial Information.** The participating states . . . will promote the publication and dissemination of economic and commercial information at regular intervals and as possible, in particular: Statistics concerning production, national income, budget, consumption and productivity; foreign trade statistics drawn up on the basis of comparable classification, including breakdown by product with indication of volume and value, as well as country of origin or destination; laws and regulations concerning foreign trade; information allowing forecasts of development of the economy to assist in trade promotion, for example, information on the general orientation of national economic plans and programmes; other information to help businessmen in commercial contacts, for example, periodic directories, lists, and where possible, organizational charts of firms and organizations concerned with foreign trade;

"Will in addition to the above encourage the development of the exchange of economic and commercial information through, where appropriate, joint commissions for economic, scientific and technical co-operation, national and joint chambers of commerce, and other suitable bodies; will support a study, in the framework of the UN Economic Commission for Europe [ECE], of the possibilities of creating a multilateral system of notification of laws and regulations concerning foreign trade and changes therein; will encourage international work on the harmonization of statistical nomenclatures, notably in the ECE.

"**Marketing.** The participating states . . . will encourage organizations, enterprises and firms concerned with foreign trade to develop further the knowledge and techniques required for effective marketing; will encourage the improvement of conditions for the implementation of measures to promote trade and to satisfy the needs of users in respect of imported products, in particular through market research and advertising measures as well as, where useful, the establishment of supply facilities, the furnishing of spare parts, the functioning of after-sales services, and the training of the necessary local technical personnel; will encourage international co-operation in the field of trade promotion, including marketing, and the work undertaken on these subjects within the international bodies, in particular the ECE.

2. Industrial Co-operation and Projects of Common Interest

"**Industrial Co-operation.** The participating states . . . propose to encourage the development of industrial co-operation between the competent organizations, enterprises and firms of their countries; consider that industrial co-operation may be facilitated by means of intergovernmental and other bilateral and multilateral agreements between the interested parties; note that in promoting industrial co-operation they should bear in mind the economic structures and the development levels of their countries; note that industrial co-operation is implemented by means of contracts concluded between competent organizations, enterprises and firms on the basis of economic considerations; express their willingness to promote measures designed to create favourable conditions for industrial co-operation; recognize that industrial co-operation covers a number of forms of economic relations going beyond the framework of conventional trade, and that in concluding contracts on industrial co-operation the partners will determine jointly the appropriate forms and conditions of co-operation, taking into account their mutual interests and capabilities;

"Recognize further that, if it is in their mutual interest, concrete forms such as the following may be useful for the development of industrial co-operation: joint production and sale, specialization in production and sale, construction, adaptation and modernization of industrial plants, co-operation for the setting up of complete industrial installations with a view to thus obtaining part of the resultant products, mixed companies, exchanges of 'know-how', of technical information, of patents and of licences, and joint industrial research within the framework of specific co-operation projects;

"Recognize that new forms of industrial co-operation can be applied with a view to meeting specific needs; consider it desirable to improve the quality and the quantity of information relevant to industrial co-operation, in particular the laws and regulations, including those relating to foreign exchange, general orientation of national economic plans and programmes as well as programme priorities and economic conditions of the market; and to disseminate as quickly as possible published documentation thereon;

"Will encourage all forms of exchange of information and communication of experience relevant to industrial co-operation, including through contacts between potential partners and, where appropriate, through joint commissions for economic, industrial, scientific and technical co-operation, national and joint chambers of commerce, and other suitable bodies; consider it desirable, with a view to expanding industrial co-operation, to encourage the exploration of co-operation possibilities and the implementation of co-operation projects and will take measures to this end, inter alia, by facilitating and increasing all forms of business contacts between competent organizations, enterprises and firms and between their respective qualified personnel; note that the provisions adopted by the conference relating to business contacts in the economic and commercial fields also apply to foreign organizations, enterprises and firms engaged in industrial co-operation, taking into account specific conditions of this co-operation, and will endeavour to ensure, in particular, the existence of appropriate working conditions for personnel engaged in the implementation of co-operation projects;

"Consider it desirable that proposals for industrial co-operation projects should be sufficiently specific and should contain the necessary economic and technical data, in particular preliminary estimates of the cost of the project, information on the form of co-operation envisaged, and market possibilities, to enable potential partners to proceed with the initial studies and to arrive at decisions in the shortest possible time; will encourage the parties concerned with industrial co-operation to take measures to accelerate the conduct of negotiations for the conclusion of co-operation contracts;

"Recommend further the continued examination—for example within the framework of the ECE—of means of improving the provision of information to those concerned on general conditions of industrial co-operation and guidance on the preparation of contracts in this field; consider it desirable to further improve conditions for the implementation of industrial co-operation projects, in particular with respect to: the protection of the interests of the partners in industrial co-operation projects, including the legal protection of the various kinds of property involved; the consideration, in ways that are compatible with their economic systems, of the needs and possibilities of industrial co-operation within the framework of economic policy and particularly in national economic plans and programmes;

"Consider it desirable that the partners, when concluding industrial co-operation contracts, should devote due attention to provisions concerning the extension of the necessary mutual assistance and the provision of the necessary information during the implementation of these contracts, in particular with a view to attaining the required technical level and quality of the products resulting from such co-operation; recognize the usefulness of an increased participation of small and medium-sized firms in industrial co-operation projects.

"**Projects of Common Interest.** The participating states . . . regard it as necessary to encourage, where appropriate, the investigation by competent and interested organizations, enterprises and firms of the possibilities for the carrying out of projects of common interest in the fields of energy resources and of the exploitation of raw materials, as well as of transport and communications; regard it as desirable that organizations, enterprises and firms exploring the possibilities of taking part in projects of common interest exchange with their potential partners, through the appropriate channels, the requisite economic, financial and technical information pertaining to these projects;

"Consider that the fields of energy resources, in particular, petroleum, natural gas and coal, and the extraction and processing of mineral raw materials, in particular, iron ore and bauxite, are suitable ones for strengthening long-term economic co-operation and for the development of trade which could result; consider that possibilities for projects of common interest with a view to long-term economic co-operation also exist in the following fields: Exchanges of electrical energy within Europe with a view to utilizing the capacity of the electrical power stations as rationally as possible; co-operation in research for new sources of energy and, in particular, in the field of nuclear energy; development of road networks and co-operation aimed at establishing a coherent navigable network in Europe; co-operation in research and the perfecting of equipment for multimodal transport operations and for the handling of containers;

"Recommend that the states interested in projects of common interest should consider under what conditions it would be possible to establish them, and if they so desire, create the necessary conditions for their actual implementation.

3. Provisions concerning Trade and Industrial Co-operation

"**Harmonization of Standards.** The participating states . . . reaffirm their interest to achieve the widest possible international harmonization of standards and technical regulations; express their readiness to promote international agreements and other appropriate arrangements on acceptance of certificates of conformity with international co-operation on standardization, in particular by supporting the activities of intergovernmental and other appropriate organizations in this field.

"**Arbitration.** The participating states . . . recommend, where appropriate, to organizations, enterprises and firms in their countries to include arbitration clauses in commercial contracts and industrial co-operation contracts, or in special agreements; recommend that the provisions on arbitration should provide for arbitration under a mutually acceptable set of arbitration rules, and permit arbitration in a third country, taking into account existing intergovernmental and other agreements in this field.

"**Specific Bilateral Arrangements.** The participating states . . . will consider favourably the conclusion, in appropriate cases, of specific bilateral agreements concerning various problems of mutual interest in the fields of commercial exchanges and industrial co-operation, in particular with a view to avoiding double taxation and to facilitating the transfer of profits and the return of the value of the assets invested.

4. Science and Technology

"**Possibilities for improving Co-operation.** [The participating states] recognize that possibilities exist for further improving scientific and technological co-operation and, to this end, express their intention to remove obstacles to such co-operation, in particular through: the improvement of opportunities for the exchange and dissemination of scientific and technological information among the parties interested in scientific and technological research and co-operation, including information related to the organization and implementation of such co-operation; the expeditious implementation and improvement in organization, including programmes, of international visits of scientists and specialists in connexion with exchanges, conferences and co-operation; the wider use of commercial channels and activities for applied scientific and technological research and for the transfer of achievements obtained in this field while providing information on and protection of intellectual and industrial property rights.

"**Fields of Co-operation.** [The participating states] consider that possibilities to expand co-operation exist within the areas given below as examples, noting that it is for potential partners in the participating countries to identify and develop projects and arrangements of mutual interest and benefit:

"*Agriculture.* Research into new methods and technologies for increasing the productivity of crop cultivation and animal husbandry; the application of chemistry to agriculture; the design, construction and utilization of agricultural machinery; technologies of irrigation and other agricultural land improvement works;

"*Energy.* New technologies of production, transport and distribution of energy aimed at improving the use of existing fuels and sources of hydro-energy, as well as research in the field of new energy sources, including nuclear, solar and geothermal energy;

"*New Technologies, Rational Use of Resources.* Research on new technologies and equipment designed in particular to reduce energy consumption and to minimize or eliminate waste;

"*Transport Technology.* Research on the means of transport and the technology applied to the develop-

ment and operation of international, national and urban transport networks including container transport as well as transport safety;

"*Physics.* Study of problems in high energy physics and plasma physics; research in the field of theoretical and experimental nuclear physics;

"*Chemistry.* Research on problems in electro-chemistry and the chemistry of polymers, of natural products, and of metals and alloys, as well as the development of improved chemical technology, especially materials processing; practical application of the latest achievements of chemistry to industry, construction and other sectors of the economy;

"*Meteorology and Hydrology.* Meteorological and hydrological research, including methods of collection, evaluation and transmission of data and their utilization for weather forecasting and hydrology forecasting;

"*Oceanography.* Oceanographic research, including the study of air/sea interactions;

"*Seismological Research.* Study and forecasting of earthquakes and associated geological changes; development and research of technology of seism-resisting constructions;

"*Research on Glaciology, Permafrost and Problems of Life under Conditions of Cold.* Research on glaciology and permafrost; transportation and construction technologies; human adaptation to climatic extremes and changes in the living conditions of indigenous populations;

"*Computer, Communications and Information Technologies.* Development of computers as well as of telecommunications and information systems; technology associated with computers and telecommunications, including their use for management systems, for production processes, for automation, for the study of economic problems, in scientific research and for the collection, processing and dissemination of information;

"*Space Research.* Space exploration and the study of the earth's natural resources and the natural environment by remote sensing, in particular with the assistance of satellites and rocket probes;

"*Medicine and Public Health.* Research on cardiovascular, tumour and virus diseases, molecular biology, neurophysiology; development and testing of new drugs; study of contemporary problems of paediatrics, gerontology and the organization and techniques of medical services;

"*Environmental Research.* Research on specific scientific and technological problems related to human environment."

Forms and Methods of Co-operation. The document enumerated a wide range of forms and methods by which scientific and technological co-operation should be promoted, including the exchange of publications, exchange of visits, international conferences and seminars, joint programmes, use of commercial channels and more effective use of existing international organizations.

5. Environment

"**Aims of Co-operation.** [The participating states] agree to the following aims of co-operation, in particular:

"To study, with a view to their solution, those environmental problems which, by their nature, are of a multilateral, bilateral, regional or sub-regional dimension; as well as to encourage the development of an interdisciplinary approach to environmental problems; to increase the effectiveness of national and international measures for the protection of the environment by the comparison and, if appropriate, the harmonization of methods of gathering and analysing facts, by improving the knowledge of pollution phenomena and rational utilization of natural resources, by the exchange of information, by the harmonization of definitions and the adoption, as far as possible, of a common terminology in the field of the environment; to take the necessary measures to bring environmental policies closer together and, where appropriate and possible, to harmonize them; to encourage, where possible and appropriate, national and international efforts by their interested organizations, enterprises and forms in the development, production and improvement of equipment designed for monitoring, protecting and enhancing the environment.

"**Fields of Co-operation.** To attain these aims, the participating states will make use of every suitable opportunity to co-operate in the field of environment and, in particular, within the areas described below as examples."

These areas included control of air pollution; water pollution control and fresh water utilization; protection of the marine environment; land utilization and soils; nature conservation and nature reserves; improvement of environmental conditions in areas of human settlement; fundamental research, monitoring, forecasting and assessment of environmental changes; legal and administrative measures.

"**Forms and Methods of Co-operation.** The participating states . . . agree on the following recommendations on specific measures:

"To develop through international co-operation an extensive programme for the monitoring and evaluation of the long-range transport of air pollutants, starting with sulphur dioxide and with possible extension to other pollutants, and to this end to take into account basic elements of a co-operation programme which were identified by the experts who met in Oslo in December 1974 at the invitation of the Norwegian Institute of Air Research;

"To advocate that within the framework of the ECE a study be carried out of procedures and relevant experience relating to the activities of Governments in developing the capabilities of their countries to predict adequately environmental consequences of economic activities and technological development."

6. Co-operation in Other Areas

Development of Transport. The document outlined various ways in which the participating states would seek to develop co-operation in the field of transport, including the simplification of frontier formalities, the harmonization of safety provisions, the elimination of disparities arising from the legal provisions applied to traffic on inland waterways subject to international conventions and the improvement of international rail transport.

Promotion of Tourism. The participating states expressed their intention "to encourage increased tourism on both an individual and group basis", the document specifying a number of ways to achieve this end.

"**Economic and Social Aspects of Migrant Labour.** The participating states . . . are of the opinion that the problems arising bilaterally from the migration of workers in Europe as well as between the participating states should be dealt with by the parties directly concerned in order to resolve these problems in their

mutual interest, in the light of the concern of each state involved to take due account of the requirements resulting from its socio-economic situation, having regard to the obligation of each state to comply with the bilateral and multilateral agreements to which it is party, and with the following aims in view:

"To encourage the efforts of the countries of origin directed towards increasing the possibilities of employment for the nationals in their own territories, in particular by developing economic co-operation appropriate for this purpose and suitable for the host countries and the countries of origin concerned; to ensure through collaboration between the host country and the country of origin the conditions under which the orderly movement of workers might take place, while at the same time protecting their personal and social welfare and, if appropriate, to organize the recruitment of migrant workers and the provision of elementary language and vocational training; to ensure equality of rights between migrant workers and nationals of the host countries with regard to conditions of employment and work and to social security, and to endeavour to ensure that migrant workers may enjoy satisfactory living conditions, especially housing conditions;

"To endeavour to ensure, as far as possible, that migrant workers may enjoy the same opportunities as nationals of the host countries of finding other suitable employment in the event of unemployment; to regard with favour the provision of vocational training to migrant workers and, as far as possible, free instruction in the language of the host country, in the framework of their employment; to confirm the right of migrant workers to receive, as far as possible, regular information in their own language, covering both their country of origin and the host country; to ensure that the children of migrant workers established in the host country have access to the education usually given there, under the same conditions as the children of that country and, furthermore, to permit them to receive supplementry education in their own language, national culture, history and geography; to bear in mind that migrant workers, particularly those who have acquired qualifications, can by returning to their countries after a certain period of time help to remedy any deficiency of skilled labour in their country of origin; to facilitate, as far as possible, the reuniting of migrant workers with their families; to regard with favour the efforts of the countries of origin to attract the savings of migrant workers with a view to increasing, within the framework of their economic development, appropriate opportunities for employment, thereby facilitating the reintegration of these workers on their return home."

Training of Personnel. The document stressed "the importance of the training and advanced training of professional staff and technicians for the economic development of every country" and outlined ways of promoting co-operation in this field.

"BASKET THREE"
Co-operation in Humanitarian and Other Fields
1. Human Contacts

"The participating states . . . express their intention now to proceed to the implementation of the following:

"**(a) Contacts and Regular Meetings on the Basis of Family Ties.** In order to promote further development of contacts on the basis of family ties the participating states will favourably consider applications for travel with the purpose of allowing persons to enter or leave their territory temporarily, and on a regular basis if desired, in order to visit members of their families. Applications for temporary visits to meet members of their families will be dealt with without distinction as to the country of origin or destination; existing requirements for travel documents and visas will be applied in this spirit. The preparation and issue of such documents and visas will be effected within reasonable time limits; cases of urgent necessity—such as serious illness or death—will be given priority treatment. They will take such steps as may be necessary to ensure that the fees for official travel documents and visas are acceptable. They confirm that the presentation of an application concerning contacts on the basis of family ties will not modify the rights and obligations of the applicant or of members of his family.

"**(b) Reunification of Families.** The participating states will deal in a positive and humanitarian spirit with the applications of persons who wish to be reunited with members of their family, with special attention being given to requests of an urgent character—such as requests submitted by persons who are ill or old. They will deal with applications in this field as expeditiously as possible. They will lower where necessary the fees charged in connexion with these applications to ensure that they are at a moderate level. Applications for the purpose of family reunification which are not granted may be renewed at the appropriate level and will be reconsidered at reasonably short intervals by the authorities of the country of residence or destination, whichever is concerned; under such circumstances fees will be charged only when applications are granted.

"Persons whose applications for family reunification are granted may bring with them or ship their household and personal effects; to this end the participating states will use all possibilities provided by existing regulations. Until members of the same family are reunited meetings and contacts between them may take place in accordance with the modalities for contacts on the basis of family ties. The participating states will support the efforts of Red Cross and Red Crescent societies concerned with the problems of family reunification. They confirm that the presentation of an application concerning family reunification will not modify the rights and obligations of the applicant or of members of his family. The receiving participating state will take appropriate care with regard to employment for persons from other participating states who take up permanent residence in that state in connexion with family reunification with its citizens and see that they are afforded opportunities equal to those enjoyed by its own citizens for education, medical assistance and social security.

"**(c) Marriage between Citizens of Different States.** The participating states will examine favourably and on the basis of humanitarian considerations requests for exit or entry permits from persons who have decided to marry a citizen from another participating state. The processing and issuing of the documents required for the above purposes and for the marriage will be in accordance with the provisions accepted for family reunification. In dealing with requests from couples from different participating states, once married, to enable them and the minor children of their marriage to transfer their permanent residence to a state in which either one is normally a resident, the participating states will also apply the provisions accepted for family reunification.

"**(d) Travel for Personal or Professional Reasons.** The participating states intend to facilitate wider travel by their citizens for personal or professional reasons, and to this end they intend in particular: Gradually to simplify and to administer flexibly the procedures for exit and entry; to ease regulations concerning movement of citizens from the other participating states in their territory, with due regard to security requirements. They will endeavour gradually to lower, where necessary, the fees for visas and official travel documents. They intend to consider, as necessary, means—including, in so far as appropriate, the conclusion of multilateral or bilateral consular conventions or other relevant agreements or understandings—for the improvement of arrangements to provide consular services, including legal and consular assistance.

"They confirm that religious faiths, institutions and organizations, practising within the constitutional framework of the participating states, and their representatives can, in the field of their activities, have contacts and meetings among themselves and exchange information.

"**(e) Improvement of Conditions for Tourism on an Individual or Collective Basis.** The participating states consider that tourism contributes to a fuller knowledge of the life, culture and history of other countries, to the growth of understanding among peoples, to the improvement of contacts and to the broader use of leisure. They intend to promote the development of tourism on an individual or collective basis and, in particular, they intend: To promote visits to their respective countries by encouraging the provision of appropriate facilities and the simplification and expediting of necessary formalities relating to such visits; to increase on the basis of appropriate agreements or arrangements where necessary co-operation in the development of tourism, in particular by considering bilaterally possible ways to increase information relating to travel to other countries and to the reception and service of tourists, and other related questions of mutual interest.

"**(f) Meetings among Young People.** The participating states intend to further the development of contacts and exchanges among young people by encouraging: increased exchanges and contacts on a short- or long-term basis among young people, training or undergoing education through bilateral or multilateral agreements or regular programmes in all cases where it is possible; study by their youth organizations of the question of possible agreements relating to frameworks of multilateral youth co-operation; agreements or regular programmes relating to the organization of exchanges of students, of international youth seminars, of courses of professional training and foreign language study; the further development of youth tourism and the provision to this end of appropriate facilities; the development, where possible, of exchanges, contacts and co-operation on a bilateral or multilateral basis between their organizations which represent wide circles of young people working, training or undergoing education; awareness among youth of the importance of developing mutual understanding and of strengthening friendly relations and confidence among peoples.

"**(g) Sport.** In order to expand existing links and co-operation in the field of sport the participating states will encourage contacts and exchanges of this kind, including sports meetings and competitions of all sorts, on the basis of the established international rules, regulations and practice.

"(h) **Expansion of Contacts.** By way of further developing contacts among governmental institutions and non-governmental organizations and associations, including women's organizations, the participating states will facilitate the convening of meetings as well as travel by delegations, groups and individuals.

2. Information

"The participating states . . . express their intention in particular:

"(a) **Improvement of the Circulation of, Access to, and Exchange of Information.** *(i) Oral Information.* To facilitate the dissemination of oral information through the encouragement of lectures and lecture tours by personalities and specialists from the other participating states, as well as exchanges of opinions at round-table meetings, seminars, symposia, summer schools, congresses and other bilateral and multilateral meetings.

"*(ii) Printed Information.* To facilitate the improvement of the dissemination on their territory of newspapers and printed publications, periodical and non-periodical, from the other participating states. For this purpose: They will encourage their competent firms and organizations to conclude agreements and contracts designed gradually to increase the quantities and the number of titles of newspapers and publications imported from the other participating states; these agreements and contracts should in particular mention the speediest conditions of delivery and the use of the normal channels existing in each country for the distribution of its own publications and newspapers, as well as forms and means of payment agreed between the parties making it possible to achieve the objectives aimed at by these agreements and contracts; where necessary, they will take appropriate measures to achieve the above objectives and to implement the provisions contained in the agreements and contracts.

"To contribute to the improvement of access by the public to periodical and non-periodical printed publications imported on the bases indicated above. In particular: They will encourage an increase in the number of places where these publications are on sale; they will facilitate the availability of these periodical publications during congresses, conferences, official visits and other international events and to tourists during the season; they will develop the possibilities for taking out subscriptions according to the modalities particular to each country; they will improve the opportunities for reading and borrowing these publications in large public libraries and their reading rooms as well as in university libraries.

"They intend to improve the possibilities for acquaintance with bulletins of official information issued by diplomatic missions and distributed by those missions on the basis of arrangements acceptable to the interested parties.

"*(iii) Filmed and Broadcast Information.* To promote the improvement of the dissemination of filmed and broadcast information. To this end: They will encourage the wider showing and broadcasting of a greater variety of recorded and filmed information from the other participating states, illustrating the various aspects of life in their countries and received on the basis of such agreements or arrangements as may be necessary between the organizations and firms directly concerned; they will facilitate the import by competent organizations and firms of recorded audio-visual material from the other participating states.

"The participating states note the expansion in the dissemination of information broadcast by radio, and express the hope for the continuation of this process, so as to meet the interest of mutual understanding among peoples and the aims set forth by this conference.

"(b) **Co-operation in the Field of Information.** To encourage co-operation in the field of information on the basis of short- or long-term agreements or arrangements. In particular: They will favour increased co-operation among mass media organizations, including press agencies, as well as among publishing houses and organizations; they will favour co-operation among public or private, national or international radio and television organizations, in particular through the exchange of both live and recorded radio and television programmes, and through the joint production and the broadcasting and distribution of such programmes; they will encourage meetings and contacts both between journalists' organizations and between journalists from the participating states; they will view favourably the possibilities of arrangements between periodical publications as well as between newspapers from the participating states for the purposes of exchanging and publishing articles; they will encourage the exchange of technical information as well as the organization of joint research and meetings devoted to the exchange of experience and views between experts in the field of the press, radio and television.

"(c) **Improvement of Working Conditions for Journalists.** The participating states, desiring to improve the conditions under which journalists from one participating state exercise their profession in another participating state, intend in particular to:

"Examine in a favourable spirit and within a suitable and reasonable time-scale requests from journalists for visas; grant to permanently accredited journalists of the participating states, on the basis of arrangements, multiple entry and exit visas for specified periods; facilitate the issue to accredited journalists of the participating states of permits for stay in their country of temporary residence and, if and when these are necessary, of other official papers which it is appropriate for them to have; ease on a basis of reciprocity procedures for arranging travel by journalists of the participating states in the country where they are exercising their profession, and to provide progressively greater opportunities for such travel, subject to the observance of regulations relating to the existence of areas closed for security reasons; ensure that requests by such journalists for such travel receive, in so far as possible, an expeditious response, taking into account the time-scale of the request;

"Increase the opportunities for journalists of the participating states to communicate personally with their sources, including organizations and official institutions; grant to journalists of the participating states the right to import, subject only to its being taken out again, the technical equipment (photographic, cinematographic, tape recorder, radio and television) necessary for the exercise of their profession; enable journalists of the other participating states, whether permanently or temporarily accredited, to transmit completely, normally and rapidly by means recognized by the participating states to the information organs which they represent the results of their professional activity, including tape recordings and undeveloped film, for the purpose of publication or of broadcasting on the radio or television. The participating states reaffirm that the legitimate pursuit of their professional activity will neither render journalists liable to expulsion nor otherwise penalize them. If an accredited journalist is expelled, he will be informed of the reasons for this act and may submit an application for re-examination of his case."

3. Co-operation and Exchanges in the Field of Culture

This section of the document covered the extension of relations between participating states in the field of culture, the promotion of mutual knowledge, exchanges and dissemination in the field of culture, fuller access to the culture of other participating states, the development of contacts and co-operation and the identification of fields and forms of co-operation. It also stated that the participating states recognized and intended to facilitate the "contribution that national minorities or regional cultures can make to co-operation among them in various fields of culture".

4. Co-operation and Exchanges in the Field of Education

The participating states expressed their intention "to expand and improve . . . co-operation and links in the fields of education and science", in particular by extending relations, promoting access and exchanges, promoting co-operation in the field of science, encouraging the study of foreign languages and promoting the exchange of information of teaching methods.

"BASKET FOUR"

Follow-Up to the Conference

"The participating states . . .

"1. *Declare their resolve*, in the period following the conference, to pay due regard to and implement the provisions of the Final Act of the conference: (*a*) unilaterally, in all cases which lend themselves to such action; (*b*) bilaterally, by negotiations with other participating states; (*c*) multilaterally, by meetings of experts of the participating states, and also within the framework of existing international organizations, such as the ECE and UNESCO, with regard to educational, scientific and cultural co-operation.

"2. *Declare furthermore their resolve* to continue the multilateral process initiated by the conference: (*a*) By proceeding to a thorough exchange of views both on the implementation of the provisions of the Final Act and of the tasks defined by the conference, as well as, in the context of the questions dealt with by the latter, on the deepening of their mutual relations, the improvement of security and the development of co-operation in Europe, and the development of the process of détente in the future; (*b*) by organizing to these ends meetings among their representatives, beginning with a meeting at the level of representatives appointed by the Ministers of Foreign Affairs. This meeting will define the appropriate modalities for the holding of other meetings which could include further similar meetings and the possibility of a new conference.

"3. The first of the meetings indicated above will be held at Belgrade in 1977. A preparatory meeting to organize this meeting will be held at Belgrade on June 15, 1977. The preparatory meeting will decide on the date, duration, agenda and other modalities of the meeting of representatives appointed by the Ministers of Foreign Affairs. . . ."

SECTION ON MEDITERRANEAN

Questions Relating to Security and Co-operation in the Mediterranean

"The participating states,

"*Conscious* of the geographical, historical, cultural, economic and political aspects of their relationship with the non-participating Mediterranean states,

"*Convinced* that security in Europe is to be considered in the broader context of world security and is closely linked with security in the Mediterranean area as a whole, and that accordingly the process of improving security should not be confined to Europe but should extend to other parts of the world, and in particular to the Mediterranean area,

"*Believing* that the strengthening of security and the intensification of co-operation in Europe would stimulate positive processes in the Mediterranean region, and expressing their intention to contribute towards peace, security and justice in the region, in which ends the participating states and the non-participating Mediterranean states have a common interest,

"*Recognizing* the importance of their mutual economic relations with the non-participating Mediterranean states, and conscious of their common interest in the further development of co-operation,

"*Noting* with appreciation the interest expressed by the non-participating Mediterranean states in the conference since its inception, and having duly taken their contributions into account,

"*Declare their intention*: to promote the development of good-neighbourly relations with the non-participating Mediterranean states in conformity with the purposes and principles of the Charter of the United Nations, on which their relations are based, and with the UN Declaration on Principles of International Law concerning Friendly Relations and Co-operation among States [see page 43] and accordingly, in this context, to conduct their relations with the non-participating Mediterranean states in the spirit of the principles set forth in the Declaration of Principles Guiding Relations between Participating States [see above];

"To seek by further improving their relations with the non-participating Mediterranean states to increase mutual confidence, so as to promote security and stability in the Mediterranean area as a whole; to encourage with the non-participating Mediterranean states the development of mutually beneficial co-operation in the various fields of economic activity, especially by expanding commercial exchanges, on the basis of a common awareness of the necessity for stability and progress in trade relations, of their mutual economic interests, and of differences in the levels of economic development, thereby promoting their economic advancement and well-being;

"To contribute to a diversified development of the economies of the non-participating Mediterranean states, whilst taking due account of their national development objectives, and to co-operate with them, especially in the sectors of industry, science and technology, in their efforts to achieve a better utilization of their resources, thus promoting a more harmonious development of economic relations; to intensify their efforts and their co-operation on a bilateral and multilateral basis with the non-participating Mediterranean states directed towards the improvement of the environment of the Mediterranean, especially the safeguarding of the biological resources and ecological balance of the sea by appropriate measures, including the prevention and control of pollution; to this end, and in view of the present situation, to co-operate through competent international organizations and in particular within the UN Environment Programme (UNEP); to promote further contacts and co-operation with the non-participating Mediterranean states in other relevant fields.

"In order to advance the objectives set forth above the participating states also declare their intention of maintaining and amplifying the contacts and dialogue as initiated by the CSCE with the non-participating Mediterranean states to include all the states of the Mediterranean with the purpose of contributing to peace, reducing armed forces in the region, strengthening security, lessening tensions in the region, and widening the scope of co-operation, ends in which all share a common interest, as well as with the purpose of defining further common objectives. The participating states would seek in the framework of their multilateral efforts to encourage progress and appropriate initiatives and to proceed to an exchange of views on the attainment of the above purposes."

Follow-Up Meetings

At the first follow-up meeting of representatives of the CSCE Final Act signatories held in Belgrade from Oct. 4, 1977, until March 9, 1978, over 80 proposals were submitted for improving the implementation of the Helsinki Final Act. However, no consensus was reached on any of the substantive proposals, and this was reflected in the agreed concluding document.

It was nevertheless stated in the document that the representatives had "stressed the political importance of the CSCE and reaffirmed the resolve of their governments to implement fully, unilaterally, bilaterally and multilaterally all the provisions of the Final Act"; that the second follow-up meeting of the CSCE would commence in Madrid on Nov. 11, 1980; and that it was agreed to hold meetings of experts (i) in Montreux (Switzerland) from Oct. 31, 1978, to examine and elaborate a generally acceptable method of peaceful settlement of disputes (as proposed by Switzerland); (ii) in

Bonn from June 20, 1978, to prepare a "Scientific Forum"; and (iii) in Valletta (Malta) from Feb. 13, 1979, on co-operation in the Mediterranean region.

The Montreux conference ended on Dec. 11, 1978, without reaching agreement on three different concepts of settlement procedures (presented respectively by the neutral and non-aligned, the East European and the Western countries) but it agreed on an eight-point basis for the future elaboration of a method of settling international disputes and it recommended that the Madrid follow-up meeting of the CSCE should consider the holding of a further conference of experts on the subject.

The Bonn conference decided to hold a Scientific Forum in Hamburg from Feb. 18, 1980. At this conference a number of Western scientists strongly defended civil liberties and criticized the Soviet Union for violating provisions of the Helsinki Final Act. The conference, attended by some 400 scientists, nevertheless fulfilled its purpose of exchanging scientific knowledge and thus extending scientific co-operation, notably in medicine and the protection of the environment. It agreed on a final document (issued on March 3, 1980), that "respect for human rights and fundamental freedoms by all states" was "one of the bases for a significant improvement in mutual relations and international scientific co-operation".

The Valletta conference, to which Mediterranean countries outside Europe were also invited (of which, however, only Egypt, Israel and Syria attended the conference), was confined to discussing questions of economic, scientific and cultural co-operation, and it ended on March 28, 1979, with the adoption of 23 recommendations on increased co-operation in the region.

East-West Treaties and Agreements, 1970-73

In the pursuit of a policy of negotiation rather than confrontation between Western Governments and those of Communist countries, a number of treaties and agreements designed to increase détente and to normalize relations were concluded in 1970-73.

Federal Republic of Germany and USSR

A treaty on the renunciation of the use of force in relations between the West German and Soviet Governments was signed in Moscow on Aug. 12, 1970. The operative articles of the treaty were as follows:

Art. 1 The Union of Soviet Socialist Republics and

the Federal Republic of Germany regard the maintenance of international peace and the achievement of the relaxation of tension as a major objective of their policies.

They affirm their desire to promote the normalization of the situation in Europe and the development of peaceful relations between all European states, and in so doing proceed from the actual situation existing in this region.

Art. 2. The Federal Republic of Germany and the USSR shall be guided in their mutual relations, as well as in matters concerning the safeguarding of European and international security, by the aims and principles set out in the Charter of the United Nations. Accordingly, they will settle their disputes exclusively by peaceful means and undertake, in accord with Article 2 of the UN Charter, to refrain from the threat of force or the use of force in any matters affecting security in

Europe and international security, as well as in their mutual relations.

Art. 3. In conformity with the foregoing aims and principles set out above, the USSR and the Federal Republic of Germany share the realization that peace in Europe can only be maintained if no one disturbs the present frontiers.

They undertake to respect the territorial integrity of all states in Europe within their existing frontiers.

They declare that they have no territorial claims whatsoever against anybody, and will not assert such claims in the future.

They regard as inviolable now and in the future the frontiers of all states in Europe as they are on the date of the signing of this treaty, including the Oder-Neisse line, which forms the western frontier of the People's Republic of Poland, and the frontier between the Federal Republic of Germany and the German Democratic Republic.

Art. 4. The present treaty between the USSR and the Federal Republic of Germany does not affect any bilateral or multilateral treaties and agreements previously concluded by them.

Art. 5. The present treaty is subject to ratification and shall come into force on the date of exchange of the instruments of ratification, which will take place in Bonn.

The West German Government, also on Aug. 12, 1970, published the following letter sent by the West German Foreign Minister to his Soviet counterpart:

"In connexion with today's signature of the treaty between the Federal Republic of Germany and the Union of Soviet Socialist Republics, the Government of the Federal Republic of Germany has the honour to state that this treaty does not conflict with the political objective of the Federal Republic of Germany to work for a state of peace in Europe in which the German nation will recover its unity in free self-determination."

The West German Government simultaneously advised the Governments of Britain, France and the USA that it had been made clear in the negotiations that the treaty did not affect the rights of the four powers "reflected in the known treaties and agreements" (i.e. the Potsdam Agreements).

The West German Government also advised the Governments of France, the United Kingdom and the USA that its Foreign Minister had declared:

"The question of the rights of the four powers is in no way connected with the treaty which the Federal Republic of Germany and the Union of Soviet Socialist Republics intend to conclude, and is not affected by it."

It added that the Soviet Foreign Minister had declared:

"The question of the rights of the four powers will also not be affected by the treaty which the Union of Soviet Socialist Republics and the Federal Republic of Germany intend to conclude. This is the attitude of the Soviet Government in this matter."

The treaty was ratified in the Federal Republic of Germany on May 23, 1972, and

by the Presidium of the Supreme Soviet on May 31, and it entered into force on June 3, 1972.

An agreement on the development of economic, industrial and technical co-operation between the two countries came into force on May 19, 1973, and long-term perspectives of the above co-operation were agreed on Jan. 18, 1974.

Federal Republic of Germany and Poland

A treaty normalizing relations between the Federal Republic of Germany and Poland was published on Nov. 20, 1970, the two Governments having agreed as follows:

Art. 1. (1) The Federal Republic of Germany and the People's Republic of Poland state in mutual agreement that the existing boundary line, the course of which is laid down in Chapter IX of the decisions of the Potsdam conference of Aug. 2, 1945, as running from the Baltic Sea immediately west of Swinemünde, and thence along the Oder river to the confluence of the western Neisse river and along the western Neisse to the Czechoslovak frontier, shall constitute the western state frontier of the People's Republic of Poland.

[The Polish text defined Poland's western frontier as "running from the Baltic Sea immediately west of Swinoujscie and thence along the Odra river to the confluence of the Lusatian Nysa river and along the Lusatian Nysa to the Czechoslovak frontier."]

(2) They reaffirm the inviolability of their existing frontiers now and in the future and undertake to respect each other's territorial integrity without restriction.

(3) They declare that they have no territorial claims whatsoever against each other and that they will not assert such claims in the future.

Art. 2. (1) The Federal Republic of Germany and the People's Republic of Poland shall in their mutual relations, as well as in matters of ensuring European and international security, be guided by the purposes and principles embodied in the Charter of the United Nations.

(2) Accordingly they shall, pursuant to Articles 1 and 2 of the UN Charter, settle all their disputes exclusively by peaceful means and refrain from any threat or use of force in matters affecting European and international security and in their mutual relations.

Art. 3. (1) The Federal Republic of Germany and the People's Republic of Poland shall take further steps towards full normalization and a comprehensive development of their mutual relations, of which the present treaty shall form the solid foundation.

(2) They agree that a broadening of their co-operation in the sphere of economic, scientific, technological, cultural and other relations is in their mutual interest.

Art. 4. The present treaty shall not affect any bilateral or multilateral international arrangements previously concluded by either contracting party or concerning them.

Art. 5. The present treaty is subject to ratification and shall enter into force on the date of exchange of the instruments of ratification, which shall take place in Bonn.

The treaty was signed in Warsaw on Dec. 7, 1970, by Willy Brandt, the German Federal Chancellor, and Jozef Cyrankiewicz, the President of Poland. It was ratified by the Federal Republic of Germany on May 23, 1972, and by the Polish Council of State on May 26, 1972, and entered into force on June 3, 1972.

Simultaneously with the approval, on May 17, 1972, of this treaty and of that concluded between the German Federal Government and the Soviet Union of Aug. 12, 1970, the parties represented in the *Bundestag* (the West German Lower House of Parliament) adopted, with only five abstentions, a resolution specifying that the treaties did not affect "the [German people's] inalienable right to self-determination" and declaring: "The policy of the Federal Republic of Germany, which aims at a peaceful restoration of national unity within the European framework, is not inconsistent with the treaties." The resolution also reiterated the *Bundestag*'s view that "the final settlement of the German question as a whole" was "still outstanding", but emphasized that the Federal Republic advocated the normalization of relations with the German Democratic Republic.

It was only after agreement on the above resolution that the Opposition (of the Christian Democratic and Christian Social Unions) decided to abstain from voting on the treaties rather than against their approval.

Canada and Soviet Union

A *Protocol on Consultations* signed in Moscow on May 19, 1971, provided for regular consultation between the two countries on "important international problems of mutual interest . . . with the aim of facilitating a relaxation of tension, the development of co-operation, and the strengthening of security", and for such consultation to be held "without delay" in "the event of a situation which, in the opinion of the two Governments, endangers the maintenance of peace or involves a breach of the peace".

Four-Power Agreement on Status of Berlin

Talks between the ambassadors of Britain, France and the United States to the Federal Republic of Germany and the Soviet ambassador to the German Democratic Republic led to the conclusion of an agreement on Berlin, the first part of which was signed on Sept. 3, 1971.

The four powers agreed "to promote the elimination of tension" in the area, to settle disputes solely by peaceful means, and to "respect their individual and joint rights and responsibilities". They declared that transit traffic between West Berlin and the Federal Republic would be "unimpeded", be facilitated so as to take place in the most simple and expeditious manner" and "receive preferential treatment".

The agreement reiterated that the Western sectors of Berlin continued "not to be a constituent part of the Federal Republic of Germany and not to be governed by it".

The Government of the USSR declared: "Communications between the Western sectors of Berlin and areas bordering on these sectors and those areas of the German Democratic Republic which do not border on these sectors will be improved. Permanent residents of the Western sectors will be able to travel to and visit such areas for compassionate, family, religious, cultural or commercial reasons, or as tourists, under conditions comparable to those applying to other persons entering these areas. . . ."

On the status of West Berlin the three Western powers agreed as follows:

"(1) The ties between the Western sectors of Berlin and the Federal Republic of Germany will be maintained and developed, taking into account that these sectors continue not to be a constituent part of the Federal Republic of Germany and not to be governed by it. The provisions of the Basic Law of the Federal Republic of Germany and of the Constitution operative in the Western sectors of Berlin which contradict the above have been suspended and continue not to be in effect.

"(2) The Federal President, the Federal Government, the *Bundesversammlung* (joint session of Parliament), the *Bundesrat* (Upper House), and the *Bundestag* (Lower House), including their committees and *Fraktionen* (parliamentary party groups), as well as other state bodies of the Federal Republic of Germany, will not perform in the Western sectors of Berlin constitutional or official acts which contradict the provisions of Paragraph (1).

"(3) The Government of the Federal Republic of Germany will be represented in the Western sectors of Berlin to the authorities of the three governments and to the Senate by a permanent liaison agency."

On the question of diplomatic representation the three Western powers declared:

"The Governments of the French Republic, the United Kingdom and the United States of America maintain their right and responsibilities relating to the representation abroad of the interests of the Western sectors of Berlin and their permanent residents, including those rights and responsibilities concerning matters of security and status both in international organizations and in relations with other countries.

"The three governments will authorize the establishment of a Soviet consulate-general in the Western sectors of Berlin accredited to the appropriate authorities of the three governments."

In a final *Quadripartite Protocol* the four governments agreed that they would proceed on the basis that the agreements and arrangements concluded between the competent German authorities would enter into force simultaneously with the quadripartite agreement. The protocol was finally signed in West Berlin on June 3, 1972, on which date it entered into force. (For treaty between Federal Republic of Germany and German Democratic Republic signed a week earlier, see below.)

Other Berlin Agreements

Further agreements on Berlin were signed in 1971 as follows:

(1) An agreement on transit traffic between the Federal Republic of Germany and West Berlin, concluded by the West and East German Governments and signed in Bonn on Dec. 17, 1971;

(2) an agreement between the Senate of West Berlin and the German Democratic Republic on "facilitation and improvement of travelling and visiting", signed in East Berlin on Dec. 19, 1971;

(3) an agreement between the Senate of West Berlin and the German Democratic Republic on the "settlement of the question of enclaves by exchange of territories", also signed in East Berlin on Dec. 19, 1971.

France and Soviet Union

In a document laying down *The Principles of Co-operation between the USSR and France*, signed in Paris on Oct. 29, 1971, the two governments declared that their co-operation was based on reciprocity of advantages, was not directed against the interests of any people, and did not affect commitments of either country in respect of third states. In the event of situations creating a threat to peace, both governments would "immediately contact each other with the object of concerting their positions on all aspects of those situations" and on steps which would make it possible to cope with them (as agreed in a protocol signed in Paris on Oct. 13, 1970). Both sides would co-operate closely in Europe, together with other states concerned, "in the maintenance of peace and the pursuit of détente, and in the strengthening of security, peaceful relations and co-operation of all European states, on the basis of unswerving respect for the following principles: Inviolability of the present frontiers, non-interference in internal affairs, equality, independence and renunciation of the use or threat of force". Both parties would also work for "general and complete disarmament, and first of all nuclear disarmament", and "the overcoming of the division of the world into military-political groupings".

United States and Soviet Union

Two agreements signed in Washington on Sept. 30, 1971, were:

(1) An agreement designed to reduce the risk of outbreak of nuclear war, in which both parties undertook to notify each other immediately in the event of an "accidental, unauthorized, or any other unexplained incident involving a possible detonation of a nuclear weapon which would create a risk of outbreak of nuclear war"; "to take necessary measures to render harmless or destroy any such weapon"; and to notify the other "in advance of any planned missile launches" extending "beyond its national territory in the direction of the other party".

(2) An agreement amending an earlier agreement signed in Geneva on June 20, 1963, by the heads of the US and Soviet delegations at the Geneva disarmament conference, known as the "Hot Line" agreement and providing for the establishment of "a direct communications link between the two governments" for use in an emergency, e.g. an abrupt shift in the East-West military balance. Under the 1971 agreement the communications link was improved by the proposed replacement of cable and teleprinter links by a satellite communication system comprising two circuits and a number of ground stations.

Federal Republic of Germany and German Democratic Republic

(1) A *Treaty between the Federal Republic of Germany and the German Democratic Republic (GDR) on Questions of Traffic* was initialled in Bonn on May 12, 1972, and signed on May 26, 1972.

The contracting states undertook "to the greatest possible extent to allow, to facilitate and to organize as expeditiously as possible the traffic in and through their sovereign territories, corresponding to normal international practice on the basis of reciprocity and non-discrimination". Traffic would be subject to the law of the state in which it occurred, as far as the treaty did not provide otherwise.

The treaty included provisions for road and rail traffic and inland navigation. The text was supplemented by protocol notes, which stated that "at the proper time" further discussions on passenger and goods traffic would take place, as well as negotiations on an air traffic agreement. A "Notification of the GDR on Travel Facilitations" stated that at the invitation of the GDR citizens of the Federal Republic would be permitted to visit the GDR.

The treaty was approved by the West German *Bundestag* (Lower House) on Sept. 22, with no opposing votes and with nine abstentions; unanimous approval was given by the *Bundesrat* (Upper House) on Oct. 6. The East German *Volkskammer* approved the treaty on Oct. 16, and the treaty came into force on the following day.

Simultaneously with the traffic treaty a number of new East German travel regulations came into force, setting out conditions under which citizens of the two German states might be permitted to visit the other.

(2) After the signing of the above traffic treaty, the State Secretaries of the Federal Republic of Germany (FRG) and the German Democratic Republic (GDR) succeeded in negotiating the terms of a *Basic Treaty* establishing the basis of relations between the two German states, which was initialled on Nov. 8, 1972, and signed on Dec. 21. The two governments agreed as follows:

Art. 1. The FRG and the GDR will develop normal good-neighbourly relations with each other on the basis of equality of rights.

Art. 2. The FRG and the GDR will let themselves be guided by the aims and principles which are laid down in the Charter of the United Nations, in particular those of the sovereign equality of all states, respect for independence, sovereignty and territorial integrity, the right of self-determination, the protection of human rights, and non-discrimination.

Art. 3. In accordance with the Charter of the United Nations, the FRG and the GDR will solve their differences solely by peaceful means and refrain from the threat of force or the use of force. They affirm the inviolability, now and in the future, of the border existing between them, and pledge themselves to unrestricted repect for each other's territorial integrity.

Art. 4. The FRG and the GDR proceed on the assumption that neither of the two states can represent the other internationally or act in its name.

Art. 5. The FRG and the GDR will promote peaceful relations among the European states and contribute to security and co-operation in Europe. They support the efforts towards a reduction of armed forces and armaments in Europe provided this does not adversely affect the security of the parties concerned. With a view to achieving general and complete disarmament under effective international control, the FRG and the GDR will support efforts serving international security and designed to bring about arms limitation and disarmament, in particular in the field of nuclear arms and other weapons of mass destruction.

Art. 6. The FRG and the GDR proceed from the principle that the sovereign power of each of the two states is confined to its [own] state territory. They respect the independence and sovereignty of each of the two states in its internal and external affairs.

Art. 7. The FRG and the GDR declare their readiness, in the course of the normalization of their relations, to settle practical and humanitarian questions. They will conclude agreements in order—on the basis of this treaty and for their mutual advantage—to develop and promote co-operation in the economic field, science and technology, transport, juridical relations, posts and telecommunications, public health, culture, sport, the protection of the environment and in other spheres. . . .

Art. 8. The FRG and the GDR will exchange permanent representative missions. They will be established at the seat of the respective governments. Practical questions connected with the establishment of the missions will be settled separately.

Art. 9. The FRG and the GDR are agreed that

bilateral and multilateral international treaties and agreements previously concluded by or concerning them are not affected by this treaty.

In a *Supplementary Protocol* it was proposed to set up a commission of representatives of the two governments to "examine and, so far as is necessary, renew or supplement the demarcation of the border existing between the two states" and to "compile the necessary documentation on the line of the border".

In separate declarations on the protocol the Federal Republic stated that questions of nationality had not been settled by the treaty, and the German Democratic Republic stated that it proceeded on the assumption that the treaty would facilitate a settlement of these matters.

The documents were accompanied by a series of exchanges of letters and declarations:

(1) In the course of the normalization of relations after the entry into force of the treaty, the Government of the GDR would take steps for the settlement of questions related to (*a*) problems arising out of the separation of families; (*b*) the improvement of border and tourist passenger traffic; and (*c*) the improvement of non-commercial merchandise traffic.

(2) With the entry into force of the treaty the following improved arrangements would take effect:
Reunion of Families. Married couples would be reunited and parents who were in need of the care of their children could rejoin them, the same applying in the case of grandparents and grandchildren. In special cases the contraction of marriages would be permitted.
Travel Arrangements. These comprised (*a*) an extension of the list of urgent family matters, in the case of which East German citizens might be permitted to pay visits to the Federal Republic of Germany; (*b*) the inclusion of half-brothers and half-sisters having the same mother among those East German citizens entitled to apply for permission to pay visits to the FRG in cases of urgent family matters; (*c*) the extension of the procedure for the issuing of visas in transit traffic between the FRG and West Berlin to other transit traffic by rail and inland navigation; and (*d*) the possibility of breaks in transit journeys (with the exception of Berlin traffic).

(3) At the time of the entry into force of the treaty, four additional border crossing-points on the frontier between the GDR and the FRG would be opened for passenger traffic.

(4) Each side took note that the other would initiate the necessary measures to seek membership of the United Nations; both governments would inform each other of the date of their application.

(5) The Federal Government stated in a declaration that after the reassembly of the *Bundestag* [after the forthcoming general election] it would take steps for the creation of the necessary internal preconditions for application for FRG membership of the United Nations. The leaders of both delegations declared that the above-mentioned reciprocal notification had as its objective that both applications should take place at approximately the same time.

(6) A "declaration on signing" stated that both governments had agreed that in the course of the normalization of relations between the two states they

would consult each other on questions of mutual interest, in particular on those which were of importance for the safeguarding of peace in Europe.

The Basic Treaty between the FRG and the GDR was ratified by the German Federal Parliament on May 25 and by the East German *Volkskammer* on June 13, and came into force at midnight on June 20, 1973.

Talks between the British, French and US ambassadors in the FRG and the Soviet ambassador to the GDR on the maintenance of the rights and responsibilities of the four powers in Germany after the conclusion of the Basic Treaty and the entry of the two German states into the United Nations opened in West Berlin on Oct. 23, 1972.

The text of the joint declaration agreed upon by them and published on Nov. 9, 1972, was worded as follows:

"The Governments of the United Kingdom of Great Britain and Northern Ireland, the French Republic, the Union of Soviet Socialist Republics and the United States of America, having been represented by their ambassadors who held a series of meetings in the building formerly occupied by the Allied Control Council, are in agreement that they will support the applications for membership in the United Nations, when submitted, by the Federal Republic of Germany and the German Democratic Republic, and affirm in this connexion that this membership shall in no way affect the rights and responsibilities of the four powers and the corresponding related quadripartite agreements, decisions and practices."

Article 8 of the Basic Treaty was implemented on March 14, 1974, when documents were signed on the establishment of "permanent representative missions" by the two states in East Berlin and Bonn respectively, with the FRG mission in East Berlin representing also the interests of West Berlin (this being the first occasion on which such a provision was included in any agreement by the FRG with a Warsaw Treaty Organization member state).

United States and USSR

During a visit to Moscow by President Nixon on May 22-29, 1972, a treaty on the limitation of anti-ballistic missile systems, an interim agreement of certain measures with respect to the limitation of strategic offensive arms and six different co-operation agreements were signed by the two sides.

Treaty on the Limitation of Anti-Ballistic Missile Systems

The *Treaty on the Limitation of Anti-Ballistic Missile Systems*, signed on May 26, 1972, was the culmination of over two years of talks on strategic arms limitation (SALT) held between the two Governments. The treaty, also known as SALT I, and concluded for an unlimited duration, consisted of 16 articles, including the following:

Art. 1. (1) Each party undertakes to limit anti-ballistic missile (ABM) systems and to adopt other measures in accordance with the provisions of this treaty.

(2) Each party undertakes not to deploy ABM systems for a defence of the territory of its country and not to provide a base for such a defence, and not to deploy ABM systems for defence of an individual region except as provided for in Article 3 of this treaty.

Art. 2. (1) For the purpose of this treaty an ABM system is a system to counter strategic ballistic missiles or their elements in flight trajectory currently consisting of:

(*a*) ABM interceptor missiles, which are interceptor missiles constructed and deployed for an ABM role, or of a type tested in an ABM mode;

(*b*) ABM launchers, which are launchers constructed and deployed for launching ABM interceptor missiles; and

(*c*) ABM radars, which are radars constructed and deployed for an ABM role, or of a type tested in an ABM mode.

(2) The ABM system components listed in paragraph 1 of this article include those which are: (*a*) operational; (*b*) under construction; (*c*) undergoing testing; (*d*) undergoing overhaul, repair or conversion; or (*e*) mothballed.

Art. 3. Each party undertakes not to deploy ABM systems or their components except that:

(*a*) Within one ABM system deployment area having a radius of 150 kilometres and centred on the party's national capital, a party may deploy: (1) No more than 100 ABM launchers and no more than 100 ABM interceptor missiles at launch sites; and (2) ABM radars within no more than six ABM radar complexes, the area of each complex being circular and having a diameter of no more than three kilometres; and

(*b*) within one ABM system deployment area having a radius of 150 kilometres and containing ICBM silo launchers, a party may deploy: (1) No more than 100 ABM interceptor missiles at launch sites; (2) two large phased-array ABM radars comparable in potential to corresponding ABM radars operational or under construction on the date of signature of the treaty in an ABM system deployment area containing ICBM silo launchers; and (3) no more than 18 ABM radars each having a potential less than the potential of the smaller of the above-mentioned two large phased-array ABM radars.

Art. 4. The limitations provided for in Article 3 shall not apply to ABM systems or their components for development or testing, and located within current or additionally agreed test ranges. Each party may have no more than a total of 15 ABM launchers at test ranges.

Art. 5. (1) Each party undertakes not to develop, test, or deploy ABM systems or components which are sea-based, space-based or mobile land-based.

(2) Each party undertakes not to develop, test or deploy ABM launchers for launching more than one ABM interceptor missile at a time from each launcher, nor to modify deployed launchers to provide them with such a capability, nor to develop, test, or deploy automatic or semi-automatic or other similar systems for rapid reload of ABM launchers.

Art. 6. To enhance assurance of the effectiveness of the limitations on ABM systems and their components provided by this treaty, each party undertakes:

(*a*) Not to give missiles, launchers, or radars, other

than ABM interceptor missiles, ABM launchers, or ABM radars, capabilities to counter strategic ballistic missiles or their elements in flight trajectory, and not to test them in an ABM mode; and

(b) not to deploy in the future radars for early warning of strategic ballistic missile attack except at locations along the periphery of its national territory and oriented outwards.

Art. 8. ABM systems or their components in excess of the numbers or outside the areas specified in this treaty, as well as ABM systems or their components prohibited by this treaty, shall be destroyed or dismantled under agreed procedures within the shortest possible agreed period of time.

Art. 9. To assure the viability and effectiveness of this treaty, each party undertakes not to transfer to other states, and not to deploy outside its national territory, ABM systems or their components limited by this treaty.

Art. 12. (1) For the purpose of providing assurance of compliance with the provisions of this treaty, each party shall use national technical means of verification at its disposal in a manner consistent with generally recognized principles of international law.

(2) Each party undertakes not to interfere with the national technical means of verification of the other party operating in accordance with Paragraph (1) of this article.

(3) Each party undertakes not to use deliberate concealment measures which impede verification by national technical means of compliance with the provisions of this treaty. This obligation shall not require changes in current construction, assembly, conversion or overhaul practices.

After approval by the US Senate, President Nixon ratified the treaty on Sept. 29-30, 1972; the Supreme Soviet of the USSR approved it and President Podgorny ratified it on Sept. 29; and instruments of ratification were exchanged in Washington on Oct. 3, 1972.

At a review of the treaty by the US-Soviet Standing Consultative Commission in November 1977 the two sides agreed that the treaty was operating effectively, had decreased the risk of outbreak of war, facilitated progress in the further limitation and reduction of strategic offensive arms and required "no amendment at this time".

Interim Agreement on Certain Measures with respect to the Limitation of Strategic Offensive Arms

Under the *Interim Agreement*, to be valid for five years, and also signed on May 26, 1972, both parties undertook:

In Article 1, "not to start construction of additional fixed land-based intercontinental ballistic missile (ICBM) launchers after July 1, 1972";

in Article 2, "not to convert land-based launchers for light ICBMs, or for ICBMs of older types deployed prior to 1964, into land-based launchers for heavy ICBMs of types deployed after that time"; and

in Article 3, "to limit submarine-launched ballistic missile (SLBM) launchers and modern ballistic missile submarines to the numbers operational and under con-

struction on the date of signature of this Interim Agreement, and in addition launchers and submarines constucted under procedures established by the parties as replacements for an equal number of ICBM launchers of older types deployed prior to 1964 or for launchers on older submarines''.

A protocol to the Interim Agreement contained the following provisions:

The United States may have no more than 710 ballistic missile launchers on submarines (SLBMs) and no more than 44 modern ballistic missile submarines. The Soviet Union may have no more than 950 ballistic missile launchers on submarines and no more than 62 modern ballistic missile submarines.

Additional ballistic missile launchers on submarines up to the above-mentioned levels—in the United States over 656 ballistic missile launchers on nuclear-powered submarines, and in the USSR over 740 ballistic missile launchers on nuclear-powered submarines, operational and under construction—may become operational as replacements for equal numbers of ballistic missile launchers of older type deployed prior to 1964 or of ballistic missile launchers on older submarines.

The deployment of modern SLBMs on any submarine, regardless of type, will be counted against the total level of SLBMs permitted for the USA and the USSR.

The Interim Agreement also came into force on Oct. 3, 1972.

Soviet-US Co-operation Agreements

The Soviet-US co-operation agreements signed at the same time were:

(1) An *Environmental Protection Agreement* on measures to prevent pollution and to protect environmental quality;

(2) a *Medicine and Public Health Agreement*;

(3) a *Space Co-operation Agreement* providing notably for the first joint space-flight by astronauts of the two countries in 1975 [see page 73];

(4) a *Scientific and Technological Co-operation Agreement*;

(5) an *Agreement on Prevention of Incidents at Sea*, aimed at ensuring safety of navigation by warships and aircraft of the two countries; and

(6) a communiqué announcing the two parties' intention to establish a joint Commercial Commission.

In addition, the two parties issued on May 29, 1972, a statement on the *Basic Principles of Relations between the United States of America and the Union of Soviet Socialist Republics*, in which they expressed their agreement as follows:

(1) They [the USA and the USSR] will proceed from the common determination that in the nuclear age there is no alternative to conducting their mutual relations on the basis of peaceful coexistence. Differences in ideology and in the social systems of the USA and the USSR are not obstacles to the bilateral development of normal relations based on the principles of sovereignty,

equality, non-interference in internal affairs and mutual advantage.

(2) The USA and the USSR attach major importance to preventing the development of situations capable of causing a dangerous exacerbation of their relations. Therefore, they will do their utmost to avoid military confrontations and to prevent the outbreak of nuclear war. They will always exercise restraint in their mutual relations, and will be prepared to negotiate and settle differences by peaceful means. Discussions and negotiations on outstanding issues will be conducted in a spirit of reciprocity, mutual accommodation and mutual benefit.

Both sides recognize that efforts to obtain unilateral advantage at the expense of the other, directly or indirectly, are inconsistent with these objectives. The prerequisites for maintaining and strengthening peaceful relations between the USA and the USSR are the recognition of the security interests of the parties based on the principle of equality and the renunciation of the use or threat of force.

Ineffectual US-Soviet Trade Agreements of 1972

At a session of the US-Soviet Joint Commercial Commission (established under the Soviet-American co-operation agreements of May 1972—see above) held from Oct. 12-16, 1972, a series of agreements was reached covering trade and lend-lease obligations. The trade agreement provided inter alia for most-favoured-nation treatment between the two countries—this, however, being subject to congressional approval, without which the agreement would not enter into force. Under a congressional move known as the Jackson Amendment, led by Senator Henry Jackson, the granting of most-favoured-nation status to the Soviet Union would be made conditional on the removal of restrictions on Jewish emigration from the Soviet Union. The US Ways and Means Committee on Sept. 27, 1973, also voted to deny most-favoured-nation status until this condition was fulfilled.

(A "Jackson Amendment" was also adopted in regard to the ABM treaty [see page 238], in this case President Nixon being urged to seek a future treaty on the limitation of offensive nuclear weapons "which would not limit the United States to levels of intercontinental strategic forces inferior to the limits provided for the Soviet Union".)

Following the passing of a Trade Reform Bill by the US Congress on Dec. 20, 1974, and its enactment on Jan. 3, 1975, the Soviet Government informed the US Government on Jan. 10 of that year that it would not put the 1972 bilateral trade agreement into effect because it considered the US legislation as contravening the agreement and as representing interference in the Soviet Union's domestic affairs (the bill having been amended so as to prevent the US President from granting most-favoured-

nation status to any Communist country unless he certified that that country did not restrict emigration).

Federal Republic of Germany and USSR

A 10-year agreement between the Government of the USSR and the Government of the Federal Republic of Germany on the development of economic, industrial and technical co-operation and a five-year agreement on cultural co-operation were signed on May 19, 1973. The first agreement included provisions for co-operation in the fields of industrial construction and manufacture and for the exchange of patents, licences and technical experts. Both agreements applied to West Berlin in accordance with the 1971 four-power agreement on Berlin [see page 235].

During a visit to the Soviet Union by the German Federal Chancellor on Oct. 28-31, 1974, the first of these agreements was expanded by the conclusion of a supplementary economic co-operation agreement.

Federal Republic of Germany and Czechoslovakia

A treaty normalizing relations between the Federal Republic of Germany and Czechoslovakia and declaring the Munich Agreement of 1938 to be null and void was initialled on June 20, 1973, by the Foreign Ministers of the two states. The text of the treaty is given below.

"The Federal Republic of Germany and the Czechoslovak Socialist Republic;

"In the historic recognition that the harmonious coexistence of the peoples of Europe constitutes a prerequisite for peace;

"In the firm determination once and for all to put an end to the disastrous past in their relations, above all in connexion with the Second World War, which has inflicted immeasurable sufferings on the European peoples;

"Recognizing that the Munich Agreement of Sept. 29, 1938, was imposed on the Czechoslovak Republic by the National Socialist regime under the threat of force;

"In view of the fact that in both countries a new generation has grown up, which has a right to a secure [and] peaceful future;

"With the intention of creating lasting foundations for the development of good-neighbourly relations;

"Endeavouring to strengthen peace and security in Europe;

"Convinced that peaceful co-operation on the basis of the aims and principles of the Charter of the United Nations is in accordance with the wishes of the peoples as well as the interest of peace in the world;

"Have agreed as follows:

"**Art. 1.** The Federal Republic of Germany and the Czechoslovak Socialist Republic consider the Munich Agreement of Sept. 29, 1938, as null and void under the terms of this treaty in regard to their mutual relations.

"**Art. 2.** (1) This treaty does not affect the legal consequences arising with regard to private persons and legal entities from the laws applied in the period Sept. 30, 1938, to May 9, 1945. Excepted from this are the consequences of measures which both contracting parties consider as null and void by reason of their irreconcilability with the fundamental principles of justice.

"(2) This treaty leaves unaffected the citizenship of persons alive and dead resulting from the legal system of each of the two contracting parties.

"(3) This treaty with its declarations on the Munich Agreement does not constitute a legal basis for material claims on the part of the Czechoslovak Socialist Republic and its natural and juristic persons.

"**Art. 3.** (1) The Federal Republic of Germany and the Czechoslovak Socialist Republic are guided in their mutual relations, as well as in questions of guaranteeing security in Europe and in the world, by the aims and principles which are laid down in the Charter of the United Nations.

"(2) Accordingly, in conformity with Articles 1 and 2 of the Charter of the United Nations, they will resolve all their differences by exclusively peaceful means, and in questions which concern European and international security, as well as in their mutual relations, will abstain from the threat of force or the use of force.

"**Art. 4.** (1) In conformity with the foregoing aims and principles the Federal Republic of Germany and the Czechoslovak Socialist Republic reaffirm the inviolability of their common frontier at present and in the future, and reciprocally commit themselves to the unrestricted respect of their territorial integrity.

"(2) They declare that they have no territorial claims of any kind against each other and likewise in the future will not raise any such claims.

"**Art. 5.** (1) The Federal Republic of Germany and the Czechoslovak Socialist Republic will take further steps for the comprehensive development of their mutual relations.

"(2) They are in agreement that an expansion of neighbourly co-operation in the fields of the economy, science, scientific and technological relations, culture, the protection of the environment, sport, traffic and their other relations is in their mutual interest.

"**Art. 6.** This treaty requires ratification and enters into force on the day of the exchange of the ratification documents, which is to take place in Bonn. . . ."

In an exchange of letters the two ministers stated that Article 2 would be extended to cover West Berlin. However, owing to disagreement over the West German claim to represent West Berlin, the signature of the treaty was delayed, but it was eventually signed on Dec. 11, 1973. Despite objections by the *Bundesrat* (Upper House of the West German Parliament) the treaty was finally ratified by the Federal Republic of Germany on June 30, 1974, when the *Bundestag* (Lower House) passed a bill to that effect, and instruments of ratification were exchanged on July 14, 1974.

United States and USSR

During a visit to the USA on June 17-25, 1973, by Leonid Brezhnev, General Secretary of the Communist Party of the Soviet Union (CPSU), a series of agreements between the USA and the Soviet Union was signed, the most important being an agreement on the basic principles of negotiation on the further limitation of strategic offensive arms, and an agreement on the prevention of nuclear war.

(1) The *Agreement on the Basic Principles of Negotiation on the Further Limitation of Strategic Offensive Arms*, signed on June 21, 1973, was worded as follows:

"The President of the United States of America, Richard Nixon, and the General Secretary of the Central Committee of the CPSU, L. I. Brezhnev;

"Having thoroughly considered the question of the further limitation of strategic arms, and the progress already achieved in the current negotiations;

"Reaffirming their conviction that the earliest adoption of further limitation of strategic arms would be a major contribution in reducing the danger of an outbreak of nuclear war and in strengthening international peace and security;

"Have agreed as follows:

"(1) The two sides will continue active negotiations in order to work out a permanent agreement on more complete measures on the limitation of strategic offensive arms, as well as their subsequent reduction, proceeding from the Basic Principles of Relations between the USA and the USSR signed in Moscow on May 29, 1972 [see page 239], and from the Interim Agreement between the USA and the USSR of May 26, 1972, on Certain Measures with Respect to the Limitation of Strategic Offensive Arms [ibid.].

"Over the course of the next year the two sides will make serious efforts to work out the provisions of the permanent agreement on more complete measures on the limitation of strategic offensive arms with the objective of signing it in 1974.

"(2) New agreements on the limitation of strategic offensive armaments will be based on the principles of the American-Soviet documents adopted in Moscow in May 1972 and the agreements reached in Washington in June 1973; and in particular, both sides will be guided by the recognition of each other's equal security interests and by the recognition that efforts to obtain unilateral advantage, directly or indirectly, would be inconsistent with the strengthening of peaceful relations between the USA and the USSR.

"(3) The limitations placed on strategic offensive weapons can apply both to their quantitative aspects as well as to their qualitative improvement.

"(4) Limitations on strategic offensive arms must be subject to adequate verification by national technical means.

"(5) The modernization and replacement of strategic offensive arms would be permitted under conditions which will be formulated in the agreements to be concluded.

"(6) Pending the completion of a permanent agreement on more complete measures of strategic offensive arms limitation, both sides are prepared to reach agreements on separate measures to supplement the existing interim agreement of May 26, 1972.

"(7) Each side will continue to take necessary

organizational and technical measures for preventing the accidental or unauthorized use of nuclear weapons under its control in accordance with the agreement of Sept. 30, 1971, between the USA and the USSR.

(2) The text of the *Agreement on the Prevention of Nuclear War*, signed on June 22, 1973, was as follows:

"The United States of America and the Union of Soviet Socialist Republics, hereinafter referred to as the parties;

"Guided by the objectives of strengthening world peace and international security;

"Conscious that nuclear war would have devastating consequences for mankind;

"Proceeding from the desire to bring about conditions in which the danger of an outbreak of nuclear war anywhere in the world would be reduced and ultimately eliminated;

"Proceeding from their obligations under the Charter of the United Nations regarding the maintenance of peace, refraining from the threat or use of force, and the avoidance of war, and in conformity with the agreements to which either party has subscribed;

"Proceeding from the Basic Principles of Relations between the United States and the USSR signed in Moscow on May 29, 1972;

"Reaffirming that the development of relations between the USA and the USSR is not directed against other countries and their interests;

"Have agreed as follows:

"**Art. 1.** The United States and the Soviet Union agree that an objective of their policies is to remove the danger of nuclear war and of the use of nuclear weapons.

"**Accordingly,** the parties agree that they will act in such a manner as to prevent the development of situations capable of causing a dangerous exacerbation of their relations, as to avoid military confrontations, and as to exclude the outbreak of nuclear war between them and between either of the parties and other countries.

"**Art. 2.** The parties agree, in accordance with Article 1 and to realize the objective stated in that article, to proceed from the premise that each party will refrain from the threat or use of force against other countries, in circumstances which may endanger international peace and security. The parties agree that they will be guided by these considerations in the formulation of their foreign policies and in their actions in the field of international relations.

"**Art. 3.** The parties undertake to develop their relations with each other and with other countries in a way consistent with the purposes of this agreement.

"**Art. 4.** If at any time relations between the parties or between either party and other countries appear to involve the risk of a nuclear conflict, or if relations between countries not parties to this agreement appear to involve the risk of nuclear war between the USA and the USSR or between either party and other countries, the United States and the Soviet Union, acting in ac-

cordance with the provisions of this agreement, shall immediately enter into urgent consultations with each other and make every effort to avert this risk.

"**Art. 5.** Each party shall be free to inform the UN Security Council, the Secretary-General of the United Nations, and the Governments of allied or other countries of the progress and outcome of consultations initiated in accordance with Article 4 of this agreement.

"**Art. 6.** Nothing in this agreement shall affect or impair:

"(*a*) The inherent right of individual or collective self-defence as envisaged by Article 51 of the Charter of the United Nations;

"(*b*) the provisions of the Charter of the United Nations, including those relating to the maintenance or restoration of international peace and security; and

"(*c*) the obligations undertaken by either party towards its allies or other countries in treaties, agreements and other appropriate documents.

"**Art. 7.** This agreement shall be of unlimited duration.

"**Art. 8.** This agreement shall enter into force upon signature."

(3) A 10-year agreement on scientific and technical co-operation in the peaceful uses of atomic energy was signed on June 21, 1973.

This provided for co-operation to be concentrated in the spheres of controlled thermonuclear fission, fast-breeder reactors, and research on the fundamental properties of matter. Under the terms of the agreement a US-Soviet Joint Committee on Co-operation in the Peaceful Uses of Atomic Energy would be established.

(4) Other agreements signed were:

(i) *On June 19*—an agreement on agricultural co-operation; an agreement on transportation; an agreement on studies of the world ocean; a six-year agreement on cultural and scientific exchanges;

(ii) *on June 20*—a convention on taxation (enabling nationals of either country to avoid paying double taxation in the other);

(iii) *on June 22*—a protocol on the establishment of a Soviet trade mission in Washington and a US commercial bureau in Moscow; a protocol on the establishment of a US-Soviet chamber of commerce; and

(iv) *on June 23*—a protocol on co-operation in air traffic.

The agreements on agricultural co-operation, transportation and studies of the world ocean, all for five years, stated that co-operation would be "on the basis of mutual benefit, equality and reciprocity". Each provided for the setting up of a US-Soviet joint committee for its implementation.

Further US-Soviet Agreements, 1974-79

During a further visit to the Soviet Union by President Nixon from June 27 to July 3, 1974, the US President and L. I. Brezhnev

signed (i) a US-Soviet treaty on the limitation of underground nuclear weapon tests and (ii) a protocol to the Treaty on the

Limitation of Anti-Ballistic Missile Systems of May 1972 [see page 238].

Treaty on Limitation of Underground Nuclear Weapon Tests

The full text of this treaty was as follows:

"**Art. I.** (1) Each party undertakes to prohibit, to prevent, and not to carry out any underground nuclear weapon test having a yield exceeding 150 kilotons at any place under its jurisdiction or control, beginning March 31, 1976.

"(2) Each party shall limit the number of its underground nuclear weapon tests to a minimum.

"(3) The parties shall continue their negotiations with a view towards achieving a solution to the problem of the cessation of all underground nuclear weapon tests.

"**Art. II.** (1) For the purpose of providing assurance of compliance with the provisions of this treaty, each party shall use national technical means of verification at its disposal in a manner consistent with the generally recognized principles of international law.

"(2) Each party undertakes not to interfere with the national technical means of verification of the other party operating in accordance with Paragraph 1 of this article.

"(3) To promote the objectives and implementation of the provisions of this treaty the parties shall, as necessary, consult with each other, make inquiries and furnish information in response to such inquiries.

"**Art. III.** The provisions of this treaty do not extend to underground nuclear explosions carried out by the parties for peaceful purposes. Underground nuclear explosions for peaceful purposes shall be governed by an agreement which is to be negotiated and concluded by the parties at the earliest possible time.

"**Art. IV.** This treaty shall be subject to ratification in accordance with the constitutional procedures of each party. This treaty shall enter into force on the day of the exchange of instruments of ratification.

"**Art. V.** (1) This treaty shall remain in force for a period of five years. Unless replaced earlier by an agreement in implementation of the objectives specified in Paragraph 3 of Article I of this treaty, it shall be extended for successive five-year periods unless either party notifies the other of its termination no later than six months prior to the expiration of the treaty. Before the expiration of this period the parties may, as necessary, hold consultations to consider the situation relevant to the substance of this treaty and to introduce possible amendments to the text of the treaty.

"(2) Each party shall, in exercising its national sovereignty, have the right to withdraw from this treaty if it decides that extraordinary events related to the subject-matter of this treaty have jeopardized its supreme interests.

"It shall give notice of its decision to the other party six months prior to withdrawal from this treaty. Such notice shall include a statement of the extraordinary events the notifying party regards as having jeopardized its supreme interests.

"(3) This treaty shall be registered pursuant to Article 102 of the Charter of the United Nations."

A protocol to the treaty said that the two countries had agreed as follows:

"(1) For the purpose of ensuring verification of compliance with the obligations of the parties under the treaty by national technical means, the parties shall, on the basis of reciprocity, exchange the following data:

"(*a*) The geographic co-ordinates of the boundaries of each test site and of the boundaries of the geophysically distinct testing areas therein.

"(*b*) Information on the geology of the testing areas of the sites (the rock characteristics of geological formations and the basic physical properties of the rock—i.e., density, seismic velocity, water saturation, porosity and depth of water table).

"(*c*) The geographic co-ordinates of underground nuclear weapon tests, after they have been conducted.

"(*d*) Yield, date, time, depth and co-ordinates for two nuclear weapons tests for calibration purposes from each geophysically distinct testing area where underground nuclear weapon tests have been and are to be conducted.

"In this connexion the yield of such explosions for calibration purposes should be as near as possible to the limit defined in Article I of the treaty, and not less than one-tenth of that limit.

"In the case of testing areas where data are not available on two tests for calibration purposes, the data pertaining to one such test shall be exchanged, if available, and the data pertaining to the second test shall be exchanged as soon as possible after a second test having a yield in the above-mentioned range. The provisions of this protocol shall not require the parties to conduct tests solely for calibration purposes.

"(2) The parties agree that the exchange of data pursuant to Sub-paragraphs *a, b* and *d* of Paragraph 1 shall be carried out simultaneously with the exchange of instruments of ratification of the treaty, as provided in Article IV of the treaty, having in mind that the parties shall, on the basis of reciprocity, afford each other the opportunity to familiarize themselves with these data before the exchange of instruments of ratification.

"(3) Should a party specify a new test site or testing area after the entry into force of the treaty, the data called for by Sub-paragraphs *a* and *b* of Paragraph 1 shall be transmitted to the other party in advance of use of that site or area. The data called for by Sub-paragraph *d* of Paragraph 1 shall also be transmitted in advance of use of that site or area if they are available; if they are not available, they shall be transmitted as soon as possible after they have been obtained by the transmitting party.

"(4) The parties agree that the test sites of each party shall be located at places under its jurisdiction or control and that all nuclear weapon tests shall be conducted solely within the testing areas specified in accordance with Paragraph 1.

"(5) For the purposes of the treaty, all underground nuclear explosions at the specified test sites shall be considered nuclear weapon tests and shall be subject to all the provisions of the treaty relating to nuclear weapon tests. The provisions of Article III of the treaty apply to all underground nuclear explosions conducted outside of the specified test sites, and only to such explosions."

Protocol to Treaty on Limitation of ABM Systems

A final paragraph of the above treaty stated that the following protocol "shall be considered an integral part of the treaty".

"**Art. I.** (1) Each party shall be limited at any one time to a single area out of the two provided in Article III of the Treaty for Deployment of Anti-Ballistic Missile (ABM) Systems or their Components, and accordingly shall not exercise its right to deploy an ABM system or its components in the second of the two ABM system deployment areas permitted by Article III of the treaty, except as an exchange of one permitted area for the other in accordance with Article II of this Protocol.

"(2) Accordingly, except as permitted by Article II of this Protocol: The United States of America shall not deploy an ABM system or its components in the area centred on its capital, as permitted by Article III (*a*) of the treaty, and the Soviet Union shall not deploy an ABM system or its components in the deployment area of intercontinental ballistic missile (ICBM) silo launchers permitted by Article III (*b*) of the treaty.

"**Art. II.** (1) Each party shall have the right to dismantle or destroy its ABM system and the components thereof in the area where they are presently deployed and to deploy an ABM system or its components in the alternative area permitted by Article III of the treaty, provided that, prior to initiation of construction, notification is given in accord with the procedure agreed to by the Standing Consultative Commission during the year beginning Oct. 3, 1977, and ending Oct. 2, 1978, or during any year which commences at five-year intervals thereafter, those being the years for periodic review of the treaty, as provided in Article XIV of the treaty. This right may be exercised only once.

"(2) Accordingly, in the event of such notice, the United States would have the right to dismantle or destroy the ABM system and its components in the deployment area of ICBM silo launchers and to deploy an ABM system or its components in an area centred on its capital, as permitted by Article III (*a*) of the treaty, and the Soviet Union would have the right to dismantle or destroy the ABM system and its components in the area centred on its capital and to deploy an ABM system or its components in an area containing ICBM silo launchers, as permitted by Article III (*b*) of the treaty.

"(3) Dismantling or destruction and deployment of ABM systems or their components and the notification thereof shall be carried out in accordance with Article VIII of the ABM treaty and procedures agreed to in the Standing Consultative Commission.

"**Art. III.** The rights and obligations established by the treaty remain in force and shall be complied with by the parties except to the extent modified by this Protocol. In particular, the deployment of an ABM system or its components within the area selected shall remain limited by the levels and other requirements established by the treaty.

"**Art. IV.** This Protocol shall be subject to ratification in accordance with the constitutional procedures of each party. It shall enter into force on the day of the exchange of instruments of ratification and shall thereafter be considered an integral part of the treaty."

The above Protocol to the Treaty on the Limitation of ABM Systems was ratified by the US Senate on Nov. 11, 1975, and the relevant instruments of ratification were exchanged in Washington on May 24, 1976.

Explanatory "Fact Sheet"

A "fact sheet" on the ABM Treaty Protocol was released in Moscow on July 3 by the White House Press Secretary, briefly explaining the provisions of the protocol in non-technical language.

"In 1972," the fact sheet recalled, "the United States and the Soviet Union signed an ABM Treaty limiting each side to one ABM site for defence of their national capital and one site for the defence of an ICBM [inter-continental ballistic missile] field. Each side was permitted 100 ABM interceptors at each site. The US has deployed 100 interceptors around a *Minuteman* site at Grand Forks, North Dakota. The Soviets have deployed their ABMs around Moscow. Neither side has initiated construction of the second site permitted under the 1972 ABM Treaty."

It was explained that the Protocol to the ABM Treaty had the following effect:

(1) Each side would be limited to one ABM site for the defence of their national capital (Moscow and Washington) or for the defence of an ICBM field.

(2) Each party would have the right to dismantle its ABM system and components in the area where they were presently deployed, and to deploy an ABM system and its components in the alternative area during the year beginning Oct. 3, 1977, and ending Oct. 2, 1978, and during any year which commenced at five-year intervals thereafter.

(3) The Soviet Union would have the right to dismantle its ABM system centred in its capital and deploy an ABM system in an area containing ICBM silo launchers, at least 1,300 kilometres from Moscow.

(4) The United States would have the right to dismantle the ABM system in the deployment area of ICBM silo launchers and to deploy an ABM system in an area centred on the capital.

(5) Prior notification must be given of the desire to switch ABM defences in accord with procedures agreed to be the SALT Standing Consultative Commission.

Other 1974 US-Soviet Agreements

Also during President Nixon's visit to the Soviet Union, three US-Soviet agreements were signed on June 28, 1974, relating to co-operation in (i) housing and construction, (ii) energy research and (iii) the development of an artificial heart.

A long-term agreement to facilitate economic, industrial and technical co-operation was signed in Moscow on June 29, 1974, and entered into force on the same day.

1974 Agreement to proceed to SALT II

At the end of a meeting in Vladivostok on Nov. 23-24, 1974, President Ford and L.I. Brezhnev agreed that a new agreement should be concluded between the USA and the USSR on the limitation of strategic offensive arms to last until Dec. 31, 1985. The two leaders agreed on the provisions on which further negotiations should be based, in particular that the new agreement should "include the following limitations: (*a*) Both sides will be entitled to have a certain agreed aggregate number of strategic delivery vehicles; (*b*) both sides will be entitled to have a certain agreed aggregate number of ICBMs [intercontinental ballistic missiles] and SLBMs [submarine-launched ballistic missiles] equipped with multiple independently targeted warheads [MIRVs]''. President Ford gave the numbers agreed under (*a*) as up to 2,400 and under (*b*) as up to 1,320 missiles on either side.

1975 US-Soviet Trade and Shipping Agreements

President Ford of the United States announced on Oct. 20, 1975, that two parallel agreements had been concluded on the supply of US grain to the USSR and of Soviet oil to the USA, providing for Soviet purchases, between Oct. 1, 1975, and Sept. 30, 1981, of an annual 6,000,000 tonnes of grain (which might be increased by up to 2,000,000 tonnes per annum unless US grain supplies were not expected to reach 225,000,000 tonnes in the year concerned), and for US purchases of up to 10,000,000 tonnes of crude oil and petroleum products per annum over a period of five years.

A new six-year shipping agreement, effective from Jan. 1, 1976, was signed on Dec. 29, 1975, covering inter alia the fixing of freight charges and the mutual opening of ports to vessels of either country.

1976 US-Soviet Treaty on Limitation of Underground Nuclear Explosions for Peaceful Purposes

A new treaty, signed on May 28, 1976, by President Ford for the United States and L.I. Brezhnev for the Soviet Union, completed and complemented the 1974 treaty on the limitation of underground nuclear weapon tests [see above] which had remained unratified—in which connexion Article IX of the new treaty laid down that both treaties should be ratified simultaneously.

The nine operative articles of the treaty were as follows:

"**Art. I.** (1) The parties enter into this treaty to satisfy the obligations in Article III of the Treaty on the Limitation of Underground Nuclear Weapon Tests and assume additional obligations in accordance with the provisions of this treaty.

"(2) This treaty shall govern all underground nuclear explosions for peaceful purposes conducted by the parties after March 31, 1976.

"**Art. II.** For the purposes of this treaty:

"(*a*) 'Explosion' means any individual or group underground nuclear explosion for peaceful purposes;

"(*b*) 'explosive' means any device, mechanism or system for producing an individual explosion;

"(*c*) 'group explosion' means two or more individual explosions for which the time interval between suc-

cessive individual explosions does not exceed five seconds and for which the emplacement points of all explosives can be interconnected by straight line segments, each of which joins two emplacement points and each of which does not exceed 40 kilometres.

"**Art. III.** (1) Each party, subject to the obligations assumed under this treaty and other international agreements, reserves the right to:

"(*a*) Carry out explosions at any place under its jurisdiction or control outside the geographical boundaries of test sites specified under the provisions of the Treaty on the Limitation of Underground Nuclear Weapon Tests; and

"(*b*) carry out, participate or assist in carrying out explosions in the territory of another state at the request of such other state.

"(2) Each party undertakes to prohibit, to prevent and not to carry out at any place under its jurisdiction or control, and further undertakes not to carry out, participate or assist in carrying out anywhere:

"(*a*) Any individual explosion having a yield exceeding 150 kilotons;

"(*b*) any group explosion:

"(i) having an aggregate yield exceeding 150 kilotons except in ways that will permit identification of each individual explosion and determination of the yield of each individual explosion in the group in accordance with the provisions of Article IV and the Protocol to this treaty;

"(ii) having an aggregate yield exceeding one and one-half megatons;

"(*c*) any explosion which does not carry out a peaceful application;

"(*d*) any explosion except in compliance with the provisions of the Treaty banning Nuclear Weapon Tests in the Atmosphere, in Outer Space and Under Water, the Treaty on the Non-Proliferation of Nuclear Weapons, and other international agreements entered into by that party.

"(3) The question of carrying out any individual explosion having a yield specified in Paragraph (2) (*a*) of this article will be considered by the parties at an appropriate time to be agreed.

"**Art. IV.** (1) For the purpose of providing assurance of compliance with the provisions of this treaty, each party shall:

"(*a*) Use national technical means of verification at its disposal in a manner consistent with generally recognized principles of international law; and

"(*b*) provide to the other party information and access to sites of explosions and furnish assistance in accordance with the provisions set forth in the Protocol to this treaty.

"(2) Each party undertakes not to interfere with the national technical means of verification of the other party operating in accordance with Paragraph (1) (*a*) of this article, or with the implementation of the provisions of Paragraph (1) (*b*) of this article.

"**Art. V.** (1) To promote the objectives and implementation of the provisions of this treaty, the parties shall establish promptly a Joint Consultative Commission within the framework of which they will:

"(*a*) Consult with each other, make enquiries and furnish information in response to such enquiries, to assure confidence in compliance with the obligations assumed;

"(*b*) consider questions concerning compliance with the obligations assumed and related situations which may be considered ambiguous;

"(*c*) consider questions involving unintended interference with the means for assuring compliance with the provisions of this treaty;

"(*d*) consider changes in technology or other new circumstances which have a bearing on the provisions of this treaty; and

"(*e*) consider possible amendments to provisions governing underground nuclear explosions for peaceful purposes;

"(2) The parties through consultation shall establish, and may amend as appropriate, regulations for the Joint Consultative Commission governing procedures, composition and other relevant matters.

"**Art. VI.** (1) The parties will develop co-operation on the basis of mutual benefit, equality and reciprocity in various areas related to carrying out underground nuclear explosions for peaceful purposes.

"(2) The Joint Consultative Commission will facilitate this co-operation by considering specific areas and forms of co-operation which shall be determined by agreement between the parties in accordance with their constitutional procedures.

"(3) The parties will appropriately inform the International Atomic Energy Agency of results of their co-operation in the field of underground nuclear explosions for peaceful purposes.

"**Art. VII.** (1) Each party shall continue to promote the development of the international agreement or agreements and procedures provided for in Article V of the Treaty on the Non-Proliferation of Nuclear Weapons, and shall provide appropriate assistance to the International Atomic Energy Agency in this regard.

"(2) Each party undertakes not to carry out, participate or assist in the carrying out of any explosion in the territory of another state unless that state agrees to the implementation in its territory of the international observation and procedures contemplated by Article V of the Treaty on the Non-Proliferation of Nuclear Weapons and the provisions of Article IV and the Protocol to this treaty, including the provision by that state of the assistance necessary for such implementation and of the privileges and immunities specified in the Protocol.

"**Art. VIII.** (1) This treaty shall remain in force for a period of five years, and it shall be extended for successive five-year periods unless either party notifies the other of its termination no later than six months prior to its expiration. Before the expiration of this period the parties may, as necessary, hold consultations to consider the situation relevant to the substance of this treaty. However, under no circumstances shall either party be entitled to terminate this treaty while the Treaty on the Limitation of Underground Nuclear Weapon Tests remains in force.

"(2) Termination of the Treaty on the Limitation of Underground Nuclear Weapon Tests shall entitle either party to withdraw from this treaty at any time.

"(3) Each party may propose amendments to this treaty. Amendments shall enter into force on the day of the exchange of instruments of ratification of such amendments.

"**Art. IX.** (1) This treaty, including the Protocol which forms an integral part hereof, shall be subject to ratification in accordance with the constitutional procedures of each party. This treaty shall enter into force on the day of the exchange of instruments of ratification, which exchange shall take place simultaneously with the exchange of instruments of ratification of the Treaty on the Limitation of Underground Nuclear Weapon Tests.

"(2) This treaty shall be registered pursuant to Article 102 of the Charter of the United Nations."

The Protocol to the treaty contained details of procedures for on-site inspection.

In a statement signed on May 13 the two parties to the treaty agreed, with reference to Sub-paragraph 2 (*c*) of Article III of the treaty, as follows:

"(*a*) Development testing of nuclear explosives does not constitute a 'peaceful application' and any such development tests shall be carried out only within the boundaries of nuclear weapon test sites specified in accordance with the treaty between the USA and the USSR on the Limitation of Underground Nuclear Weapon Tests;

"(*b*) Associating test facilities, instrumentation or procedures related only to testing of nuclear weapons or their effects with any explosion carried out in accordance with the treaty does not constitute a 'peaceful application'."

However, like the treaty of 1974 on the limitation of underground nuclear weapons tests, this treaty also has remained unratified.

1977 Scientific Co-operation Agreement

An agreement on co-operation in the fields of science and technology between the United States and the Soviet Union was signed in Washington on July 8, 1977, and entered into force on the same day.

Second Strategic Arms Limitation Treaty (SALT II)

The 1972 Interim Agreement between the USA and the USSR, concluded in connexion with the SALT I treaty [see page 238], formally lapsed on Oct. 3, 1977, but both sides undertook to continue to observe its main provisions pending the conclusion of a further strategic arms limitation (SALT II) treaty.

After several years of negotiations such a treaty was eventually signed in Vienna on June 18, 1979, by President Carter for the USA and President Brezhnev for the USSR. The principal provisions of the main SALT II treaty were as follows:

(1) Upon entry into force of the treaty, each side would limit to 2,400 the number of intercontinental ballistic missile (ICBM) launchers, submarine-launched ballistic missile (SLBM) launchers, heavy bombers and air-to-surface ballistic missiles (ASBMs)—i.e. the level agreed by President Ford and L. I. Brezhnev in Vladivostok in November 1974 [see page 244]—and would dismantle or destroy any excess within a period of three to six months; these ag-

gregate numbers would be further reduced to 2,250 for each side in the course of 1981.

(2) Within these aggregates, each side would limit to 1,320 the number of launchers of ICBMs and SLBMs equipped with multiple independently targetable re-entry vehicles (MIRVs), of MIRVed ASBMs and of heavy bombers equipped for cruise missiles capable of a range of over 600 kilometres (about 373 miles); not more than 1,200 might be launchers of MIRVed ICBMs and SLBMs or ASBMs equipped with MIRVs, while within this total the number of launchers of MIRVed ICBMs might not exceed 820.

(3) No more than 10 re-entry vehicles might be placed on any one ICBM or ASBM, nor more than 14 on any one SLBM. Bombers equipped for cruise missiles with a range of over 600 kilometres might not carry more than an average of 28 such missiles.

(4) Neither side might start the construction of additional fixed ICBM launchers, relocate fixed ICBM launchers or convert launchers of light or older types of ICBMs into launchers of heavy or later ICBMs.

(5) Neither side might flight-test or deploy new types of ICBMs, except one new type of light ICBM each, nor might they increase the number of re-entry vehicles on any type of ICBM.

(6) Neither side might develop, test or deploy (i) ICBMs heavier than those currently deployed by either party, (ii) mobile launchers of heavy ICBMs or (iii) fractional orbital missiles; nor might they flight-test or deploy on aircraft MIRVed cruise missiles with a range in excess of 600 kilometres.

(7) The Soviet Union would not produce, test or deploy RS-14 (SS-16) light ICBMs.

(8) The USA and the Soviet Union would seek to conclude a further SALT agreement well in advance of 1985 (the date of expiry of the SALT II treaty).

Under a protocol, which would expire on Dec. 31, 1981, the two sides undertook (i) not to deploy mobile ICBM launchers or to flight-test ICBMs from such launchers; (ii) not to deploy cruise missiles capable of a range in excess of 600 kilometres on sea-based or land-based launchers, nor to flight-test MIRVed cruise missiles capable of such a range from such launchers; and (iii) not to flight-test or deploy ASBMs.

The articles of the treaty were worded as follows:

"**Art. 1.** Each party undertakes, in accordance with the provisions of this treaty, to limit strategic offensive arms quantitatively and qualitatively, to exercise restraint in the development of new types of strategic offensive arms, and to adopt other measures provided for in this treaty.

"**Art. 2.** For the purposes of this treaty:

"(1) Intercontinental ballistic missile (ICBM) launchers are land-based launchers of ballistic missiles capable of a range in excess of the shortest distance between the north-eastern border of the continental part of the the territory of the USA and the north-western border of the continental part of the territory of the USSR, that is, a range in excess of 5,500 kilometres [i.e. about 3,418 miles].

"(2) Submarine-launched ballistic missile [SLBM] launchers are launchers of ballistic missiles installed on any nuclear-powered submarine or launchers of modern ballistic missiles installed on any submarine, regardless of its type.

"(3) Heavy bombers are considered to be:

"(a) Currently, for the USA, bombers of the B-52 and B-1 types and, for the USSR, Tupolev-95 and Myasishchev types;

"(b) in the future, types of bombers which can carry out the mission of a heavy bomber in a manner similar or superior to that of bombers listed in Sub-paragraph (a) above;

"(c) types of bombers equipped for cruise missiles capable of a range in excess of 600 kilometres; and

"(d) types of bombers equipped for ASBMs.

"(4) Air-to-surface ballistic missiles (ASBMs) are any such missiles capable of a range in excess of 600 kilometres and installed in an aircraft or on its external mountings.

"(5) Launchers of ICBMs and SLBMs equipped with multiple independently targetable re-entry vehicles (MIRVs) are launchers of the types developed and tested for launching ICBMs or SLBMs equipped with MIRVs.

"(6) ASBMs equipped with MIRVs are ASBMs of the types which have been flight-tested with MIRVs.

"(7) Heavy ICBMs are ICBMs which have a launch-weight greater or a throw-weight greater than that of the heaviest—in terms of either launch-weight or throw-weight respectively—of the light ICBMs deployed by either party as of the date of signature of this treaty.

"(8) Cruise missiles are unmanned, self-propelled, guided weapon-delivery vehicles which sustain flight through the use of aerodynamic lift over most of their flight path and which are flight-tested from or deployed on aircraft, that is, air-launched cruise missiles, or such vehicles which are referred to as cruise missiles in Sub-paragraph 1 (b) of Article 9.

"**Art. 3.** (1) Upon entry into force of this treaty, each party undertakes to limit ICBM launchers, SLBM launchers, heavy bombers and ASBMs to an aggregate number not to exceed 2,400.

"(2) Each party undertakes to limit, from Jan. 1, 1981, strategic offensive arms referred to in Paragraph 1 of this article to an aggregate number not to exceed 2,250, and to initiate reductions of those arms which as of that date would be in excess of this aggregate number.

"(3) Within the aggregate numbers provided for in Paragraphs 1 and 2 of this article and subject to the provisions of this treaty, each party has the right to determine the composition of these aggregates.

"(4) For each bomber of a type equipped for ASBMs, the aggregate numbers provided for in Paragraphs 1 and 2 of this article shall include the maximum number of such missiles for which a bomber of that type is equipped for one operational mission.

"(5) A heavy bomber equipped only for ASBMs shall not itself be included in the aggregate numbers provided for in Paragraphs 1 and 2 of this article.

"(6) Reductions of the numbers of strategic offensive arms required to comply with the provisions of Paragraphs 1 and 2 of this article shall be carried out as provided for in Article 11.

"**Art. 4.** (1) Each party undertakes not to start construction of additional fixed ICBM launchers.

"(2) Each party undertakes not to relocate fixed ICBM launchers.

"(3) Each party undertakes not to convert launchers of light ICBMs, or of ICBMs of older types deployed prior to 1964, into launchers of heavy ICBMs of types deployed after that time.

"(4) Each party undertakes in the process of modernization and replacement of ICBM silo launchers not to increase the original internal volume of an ICBM silo launcher by more than 32 per cent. Within this limit each party has the right to determine whether such an increase will be made through an increase in the original diameter or in the original depth of an ICBM silo launcher, or in both of these dimensions.

"(5) Each party undertakes:

"(*a*) Not to supply ICBM launcher deployment areas with ICBMs in excess of a number consistent with normal deployment, maintenance, training and replacement requirements;

"(*b*) not to provide storage facilities for or to store ICBMs in excess of normal deployment requirements at launch sites of ICBM launchers;

"(*c*) not to develop, test or deploy systems for rapid reload of ICBM launchers.

"(6) Subject to the provisions of this treaty, each party undertakes not to have under construction at any time strategic offensive arms referred to in Paragraph 1 of Article 3 in excess of numbers consistent with a normal construction schedule.

"(7) Each party undertakes not to develop, test or deploy ICBMs which have a launch-weight greater or a throw-weight greater than that of the heaviest—in terms of either launch-weight or throw-weight respectively—of the heavy ICBMs deployed by either party as of the date of signature of this treaty.

"(8) Each party undertakes not to convert land-based launchers of ballistic missiles which are not ICBMs into launchers for launching ICBMs, and not to test them for this purpose.

"(9) Each party undertakes not to flight-test or deploy new types of ICBMs—that is, types of ICBMs not flight-tested as of May 1, 1979—except that each party may flight-test and deploy one new type of light ICBM.

"(10) Each party undertakes not to flight-test or deploy ICBMs of a type flight-tested as of May 1, 1979, with a number of re-entry vehicles greater than the maximum number of re-entry vehicles with which an ICBM of that type has been flight-tested as of that date.

"(11) Each party undertakes not to flight-test or deploy ICBMs of the new type permitted pursuant to Paragraph 9 of this article with a number of re-entry vehicles greater than the maximum number of re-entry vehicles with which an ICBM of either party has been flight-tested as of May 1, 1979—that is, 10.

"(12) Each party undertakes not to flight-test or deploy SLBMs with a number of re-entry vehicles greater than the maximum number of re-entry vehicles with which an SLBM of either party has been flight-tested as of May 1, 1979—that is, 14.

"(13) Each party undertakes not to flight-test or deploy ASBMs with a number of re-entry vehicles greater than the maximum number of re-entry vehicles with which an ICBM of either party has been flight-tested as of May 1, 1979—that is, 10.

"(14) Each party undertakes not to deploy at any one time on heavy bombers equipped for cruise missiles capable of a range in excess of 600 kilometres a number of such cruise missiles which exceeds the product of 28 and the number of such heavy bombers.

"**Art. 5.** (1) Within the aggregate number provided for in Paragraphs 1 and 2 of Article 3, each party undertakes to limit launchers of ICBMs and SLBMs equipped with MIRVs, ASBMs equipped with MIRVs, and heavy bombers equipped for cruise missiles capable of a range in excess of 600 kilometres to an aggregate number not to exceed 1,320.

"(2) Within the aggregate number provided for in Paragraph 1 of this article, each party undertakes to limit launchers of ICBMs and SLBMs equipped with MIRVs, and ASBMs equipped with MIRVs, to an aggregate number not to exceed 1,200.

"(3) Within the aggregate number provided for in Paragraph 2 of this article, each party undertakes to limit launchers of ICBMs equipped with MIRVs to an aggregate number not to exceed 820.

"(4) For each bomber of a type equipped for ASBMs equipped with MIRVs, the aggregate numbers provided for in Paragraphs 1 and 2 of this article shall include the maximum number of ASBMs for which a bomber of that type is equipped for one operational mission.

"(5) Within the aggregate number provided for in Paragraphs 1, 2 and 3 of this article and subject to the provisions of this treaty, each party has the right to determine the composition of these aggregates.

"**Art. 6.** (1) The limitation provided for in this treaty shall apply to those arms which are:

"(*a*) Operational;

"(*b*) in the final stage of construction;

"(*c*) in reserve, in storage or mothballed;

"(*d*) undergoing overhaul, repair, modernization or conversion.

"(2) Those arms in the final stage of construction are:

"(*a*) SLBM launchers on submarines which have begun sea trials;

"(*b*) ASBMs after a bomber of a type equipped for such missiles has been brought out of the shop, plant or other facility where its final assembly or conversion for the purpose of equipping it for such missiles has been performed;

"(*c*) other strategic offensive arms which are finally assembled in a shop, plant or other facility after they have been brought out of the shop, plant or other facility where their final assembly has been performed.

"(3) ICBM and SLBM launchers of a type not subject to the limitation provided for in Article 5, which undergo conversion into launchers of a type subject to that limitation, shall become subject to that limitation as follows:

"(*a*) Fixed ICBM launchers when work on their conversion reaches the stage which first definitely indicates that they are being so converted;

"(*b*) SLBM launchers on a submarine when that submarine first goes to sea after their conversion has been performed.

"(4) ASBMs on a bomber which undergoes conversion from a bomber of a type equipped for ASBMs which are not subject to the limitation provided for in Article 5 into a bomber of a type equipped for ASBMs which are subject to that limitation shall become subject to that limitation when the bomber is brought out of the shop, plant or other facility where such conversion has been performed.

"(5) A heavy bomber of a type not subject to the limitation provided for in Paragraph 1 of Article 5 shall become subject to that limitation when it is brought out of the shop, plant or other facility where it has been converted into a heavy bomber of a type equipped for cruise missiles capable of a range in excess of 600 kilometres. A bomber of a type not subject to the limitation provided for in Paragraph 1 or 2 of Article 3 shall become subject to that limitation and to the limitation provided for in Paragraph 1 of Article 5 when it is brought out of the shop, plant or other facility where it has been converted into a bomber of a type equipped for cruise missiles capable of a range in excess of 600 kilometres.

"(6) The arms subject to the limitations provided for in this treaty shall continue to be subject to these limitations until they are dismantled, are destroyed, or otherwise cease to be subject to these limitations under procedures to be agreed upon.

"(7) In accordance with the provisions of Article 17, the parties will agree in the Standing Consultative Commission upon procedures to implement the provisions of this Article.

"**Art. 7.** (1) The limitations provided for in Article 3 shall not apply to ICBM and SLBM test and training launchers or to space vehicle launchers for exploration and use of outer space, ICBM and SLBM test and training launchers are ICBM ans SLBM launchers used only for testing or training.

"(2) The parties agree that:

"(*a*) There shall be no significant increase in the number of ICBM or SLBM test and training launchers or in the number of such launchers of heavy ICBMs;

"(*b*) construction or conversion of ICBM launchers at test ranges shall be undertaken only for purposes of testing and training;

"(*c*) there shall be no conversion of ICBM test and training launchers or of space vehicle launchers into ICBM launchers subject to the limitations provided for in Article 3.

"**Art. 8.** (1) Each party undertakes not to flight-test cruise missiles capable of a range in excess of 600 kilometres or ASBMs from aircraft other than bombers or to convert such aircraft into aircraft equipped for such missiles.

"(2) Each party undertakes not to convert aircraft other than bombers into aircraft which can carry out the mission of a heavy bomber as referred to in Subparagraph 3 (*b*) of Article 2.

"**Art. 9.** (1) Each party undertakes not to develop, test or deploy:

"(*a*) Ballistic missiles capable of a range in excess of 600 kilometres for installation on waterborne vehicles other than submarines, or launchers of such missiles;

"(*b*) fixed ballistic or cruise missile launchers for emplacement on the ocean floor, on the seabed, or on the beds of internal waters and inland waters, or in the subsoil thereof, or mobile launchers of such missiles which move only in contact with the ocean floor, the seabed, or the beds of internal waters and inland waters, or missiles for such launchers;

"(*c*) systems for placing into earth orbit nuclear weapons or any other kind of weapons of mass destruction [already banned under the 1966 Outer Space Treaty, whose signatories included the United States and the Soviet Union and which had entered into force

on Oct. 10, 1967—see page 66], including fractional orbital missiles;

"(*d*) mobile launchers of heavy ICBMs;

"(*e*) SLBMs which have a launch-weight greater or a throw-weight greater than that of the heaviest—in terms of either launch-weight or throw-weight, respectively—of the light ICBMs deployed by either party as of the date of signature of this treaty, or launchers of such SLBMs; or

"(*f*) ASBMs which have a launch-weight greater or a throw-weight greater than that of the heaviest—in terms of either launch-weight or throw-weight respectively—of the light ICBMs deployed by either party as of the date of signature of this treaty.

"(2) Each party undertakes not to flight-test from aircraft cruise missiles capable of a range in excess of 600 kilometres which are equipped with multiple independently targetable warheads and not to deploy such cruise missiles on aircraft.

"**Art. 10.** Subject to the provisions of this treaty, modernization and replacement of strategic offensive arms may be carried out.

"**Art. 11.** (1) Strategic offensive arms which would be in excess of the aggregate numbers provided for in this treaty as well as strategic offensive arms prohibited by this treaty shall be dismantled or destroyed under procedures to be agreed upon in the Standing Consultative Commission.

"(2) Dismantling or destruction of strategic offensive arms which would be in excess of the aggregate number provided for in Paragraph 1 of Article 3 shall begin on the date of the entry into force of this treaty and shall be completed within the following periods from that date: four months for ICBM launchers; six months for SLBM launchers; and three months for heavy bombers.

"(3) Dismantling or destruction of strategic offensive arms which would be in excess of the aggregate number provided for in Paragraph 2 of Article 3 shall be initiated no later than Jan. 1, 1981, shall be carried out throughout the ensuing 12-month period, and shall be completed no later than Dec. 31, 1981.

"(4) Dismantling or destruction of strategic offensive arms prohibited by this treaty shall be completed within the shortest possible agreed period of time, but not later than six months after the entry into force of this treaty.

"**Art. 12.** In order to ensure the viability and effectiveness of this treaty, each party undertakes not to circumvent the provisions of this treaty, through any other state or states or in any other manner.

"**Art. 13.** Each party undertakes not to assume any international obligations which would conflict with this treaty.

"**Art. 14.** The parties undertake to begin, promptly after the entry into force of this treaty, active negotiations with the objective of achieving, as soon as possible, agreement on further measures for the limitation and reduction of strategic arms. It is also the objective of the parties to conclude well in advance of 1985 an agreement limiting strategic offensive arms to replace this treaty upon its expiration.

"**Art. 15.** (1) For the purpose of providing assurance of compliance with the provisions of this treaty, each party shall use national technical means of verification at its disposal in a manner consistent with generally recognized principles of international law.

"(2) Each party undertakes not to interfere with the

national technical means of verification of the other party operating in accordance with Paragraph 1 of this article.

"(3) Each party undertakes not to use deliberate concealment measures which impede verification by national technical means of compliance with the provisions of this treaty. This obligation shall not require changes in current construction, assembly, conversion or overhaul practices.

"**Art. 16.** (1) Each party undertakes, before conducting each planned ICBM launch, to notify the other party well in advance on a case-by-case basis that such a launch will occur, except for single ICBM launches from test ranges or from ICBM launcher deployment areas which are not planned to extend beyond its national territory.

"(2) The parties shall agree in the Standing Consultative Commission upon procedures to implement the provisions of this article.

"**Art. 17.** (1) To promote the objectives and implementation of the provisions of this treaty, the parties shall use the Standing Consultative Commission established by the Memorandum of Understanding between the Government of the USA and the Government of the USSR regarding the Establishment of a Standing Consultative Commission of Dec. 21, 1972.

"(2) Within the framework of the Standing Consultative Commission, with respect to this treaty, the parties will:

"(*a*) Consider questions concerning compliance with the obligations assumed and related situations which may be considered ambiguous;

"(*b*) provide on a voluntary basis such information as either party considers necessary to assure confidence in compliance with the obligations assumed;

"(*c*) consider questions involving unintended interference with national technical means of verification, and questions involving unintended impeding of verification by national technical means of compliance with the provisions of this treaty;

"(*d*) consider possible changes in the strategic situation which have a bearing on the provisions of this treaty;

"(*e*) agree upon procedures for replacement, conversion and dismantling or destruction of strategic offensive arms in cases provided for in the provisions of this treaty and upon procedures for removal of such arms from the aggregate numbers when they otherwise cease to be subject to the limitations provided for in this treaty, and, at regular sessions of the Standing Consultative Commission, notify each other in accordance with the aforementioned procedures, at least twice annually, of actions completed and those in process;

"(*f*) consider, as appropriate, possible proposals for further increasing the viability of this treaty, including proposals for amendments in accordance with the provisions of this treaty;

"(*g*) consider, as appropriate, proposals for further measures limiting strategic offensive arms.

"(3) In the Standing Consultative Commission the parties shall maintain by category the agreed data base on the numbers of strategic offensive arms established by the Memorandum of Understanding between the USA and the USSR regarding the Establishment of a Data Base on the Numbers of Strategic Offensive Arms of June 19, 1979 [see below].

"**Art. 18.** Each party may propose amendments to this treaty. Agreed amendments shall enter into force in accordance with the procedures governing the entry into force of this treaty.

"**Art. 19.** (1) This treaty shall be subject to ratification in accordance with the constitutional procedures of each party. This treaty shall enter into force on the day of the exchange of instruments of ratification and shall remain in force through Dec. 31, 1985, unless replaced earlier by an agreement further limiting strategic offensive arms.

"(2) This treaty shall be registered pursuant to Article 102 of the Charter of the United Nations.

"(3) Each party shall, in exercising its national sovereignty, have the right to withdraw from this treaty if it decides that extraordinary events related to the subject matter of this treaty have jeopardized its supreme interests. It shall give notice of its decision to the other party six months prior to withdrawal from the treaty. Such notice shall include a statement of the extraordinary events the notifying party regards as having jeopardized its supreme interests.

"Done at Vienna on June 18, 1979, in two copies, each in the English and Russian languages, both texts being equally authentic."

Protocol to SALT II Treaty

The protocol to the SALT II treaty, valid to Dec. 31, 1981, was worded as follows:

"The USA and USSR, hereinafter referred to as the parties,

"Having agreed on limitations on strategic offensive arms in the treaty,

"Have agreed on additional limitations for the period during which this protocol remains in force, as follows:

"**Art. 1.** Each party undertakes not to deploy mobile ICBM launchers or to flight-test ICBMs from such launchers.

"**Art. 2.** (1) Each party undertakes not to deploy cruise missiles capable of a range in excess of 600 kilometres on sea-based launchers or on land-based launchers.

"(2) Each party undertakes not to flight-test cruise missiles capable of a range in excess of 600 kilometres which are equipped with multiple independently targetable warheads from sea-based launchers or from land-based launchers.

"(3) For the purposes of this protocol, cruise missiles are unmanned, self-propelled, guided weapon-delivery vehicles which sustain flight through the use of aerodynamic lift over most of their flight and which are flight-tested from or deployed on sea-based or land-based launchers—that is, sea-launched cruise missiles and ground-launched cruise missiles respectively.

"**Art. 3.** Each party undertakes not to flight-test or deploy ASBMs.

"**Art. 4.** This protocol shall be considered an integral part of the treaty. It shall enter into force on the day of the entry into force of the treaty and shall remain in force through Dec. 31, 1981, unless replaced earlier by an agreement on further measures limiting strategic offensive arms.

"Done at Vienna on June 18, 1979, in two copies, each in the English and Russian languages, both texts being equally authentic."

Agreed Statements and Common Understandings regarding SALT II Treaty

Agreed statements and common understandings signed by President Carter and L. I. Brezhnev comprised principally definitions of terms used in the treaty and protocol and further details and elaborations of the provisions of the treaty and protocol. The length of these agreed statements and common understandings was approximately twice that of the treaty and protocol themselves, details of the most important being given below.

Art. 2. *Para. 1.* The 177 former US Atlas and Titan 1 ICBM launchers, which were no longer operational and were partially dismantled, should not be considered as subject to the limitations provided for in the treaty.

After the date on which the protocol ceased to be in force, mobile ICBM launchers should be subject to the relevant limitations in the treaty which were applicable to ICBM launchers, unless the parties agreed that mobile ICBM launchers should not be deployed after that date.

Para. 3. Soviet Tupolev-142 aircraft in their current configuration—i.e. for anti-submarine warfare—were considered to be aeroplanes of a type different from types of heavy bombers referred to in Sub-paragraph 3 (*a*) of Article 2.

Not later than six months after entry into force of the treaty, the Soviet Union would give its 31 Myasishchev aeroplanes used as tankers in existence as of the date of the signature of the treaty functionally related observable differences which indicated that they could not perform the mission of a heavy bomber.

The Soviet Tupolev-95 heavy bombers were known in the United States as Bears and the Myasishchev heavy bombers as Bisons.

Para. 5. MIRVed ICBMs and SLBMs as of the date of signature of the treaty were: For the United States Minuteman III light ICBMs, Poseidon C-3 SLBMs and Trident C-4 SLBMs; for the Soviet Union RS-16, RS-18 and RS-20 ICBMs and RSM-50 SLBMs (these Soviet missiles being known in the United States as, respectively, the SS-17 light ICBM, the SS-19 light ICBM, the SS-18 heavy ICBM and the SS-N-18 SLBM).

All ICBM launchers in the Derazhnya and Pervomaysk areas of the Soviet Union were included in the aggregate numbers provided for in Article 5 of the treaty.

Art. 4. *Para. 8.* During the term of the treaty, the Soviet Union would not produce, test or deploy ICBMs of the type designated by the Soviet Union as RS-14 (known to the USA as SS-16)—a light ICBM first flight-tested after 1970 and flight-tested only with a single re-entry vehicle; the Soviet Union would not produce the third stage of that missile, the re-entry vehicle of that missile or the appropriate device for targeting the re-entry vehicle of that missile.

Para. 9. Every ICBM of the one new type of light ICBM permitted to each party under this paragraph should have the same number of stages and the same type of propellant (i.e. liquid or solid) of each stage as the first ICBM of the one new type of light ICBM launched by that party. In addition, after the 25th launch of an ICBM of that type, or after the last launch before deployment began of ICBMs of that type, whichever occurred earlier, ICBMs of the one new type of light ICBM permitted to that party should not be different in any one or more of the following respects: Length, largest diameter, launch-weight or throw-

weight of the missile. A party which launched ICBMs of the one new type of light ICBM permitted under this paragraph should promptly notify the other party of the date of the first launch and of the date of either the 25th or the last launch before deployment began of ICBMs of that type, whichever occurred earlier.

Para. 10. Types of ICBMs and SLBMs equipped with MIRVs had been flight-tested with the maximum number of re-entry vehicles as follows. United States: Minuteman III ICBMs—seven re-entry vehicles; Poseidon C-3 SLBMs—14 re-entry vehicles; Trident C-4 SLBMs—seven re-entry vehicles. Soviet Union: RS-16 ICBMs—four re-entry vehicles; RS-18—six re-entry vehicles; RS-20 ICBMs—10 re-entry vehicles; RSM-50 SLBMs—seven re-entry vehicles. Minuteman III ICBMs had been deployed with not more than three re-entry vehicles; during the term of the treaty the USA had no plans to and would not flight-test or deploy missiles of this type with more than three re-entry vehicles.

Para. 11. Each party undertook not to flight-test or deploy the one new type of light ICBM permitted to each party under Paragraph 9 of Article 4 with a number of re-entry vehicles greater than the maximum number of re-entry vehicles with which an ICBM of that type had been flight-tested as of the 25th launch before deployment began of ICBMs of that type, whichever occurred earlier.

Para. 14. During the term of the treaty no bomber of the B-52 or B-1 types of the USA or of the Tupolev-95 or Myasishchev types of the Soviet Union would be equipped for more than 20 cruise missiles capable of a range in excess of 600 kilometres.

Art. 6. *Para. 6.* The procedures for removal of strategic offensive arms from the aggregate numbers provided for in the treaty which were referred to in this paragraph and were to be agreed upon in the Standing Consultative Committee should include (i) procedures for removal from the aggregate numbers, provided for in Article 5, of ICBM and SLBM launchers which were being converted from launchers of a type subject to the limitation provided for in Article 5 into launchers of a type not subject to that limitation and (ii) procedures for removal from the aggregate numbers provided for in Articles 3 and 5 of bombers which were being converted from bombers of a type subject to the limitations provided for in Article 3 or in Articles 3 and 5 into aeroplanes or bombers of a type not so subject.

Art. 7. *Para. 2.* Current test ranges where ICBMs were tested were located in the United States near Santa Maria (California) and at Cape Canaveral (Florida), and in the Soviet Union in the areas of Tyura-Tam and Plesetskaya. In the future, each party should provide notification in the Standing Consultative Commission of the location of any other test range used by that party to test ICBMs.

Of the 18 launchers of fractional orbital missiles at the test range where ICBMs were tested in the area of Tyura-Tam, 12 launchers should be dismantled or destroyed within eight months of the treaty entering into force and should not be replaced; the other six might be converted after entry into force of the treaty to launchers for testing missiles undergoing modernization; after entry into force of the treaty fractional orbital missiles should be removed and should be destroyed, pursuant to the provisions of Sub-paragraph 1 (*c*) of Article 9, and should not be replaced by other missiles, except in the case of conversion of these six launchers for testing missiles undergoing modernization.

Art. 8. *Para. 1.* For the purposes of testing only, each party had the right, through initial construction or (as an exception to this paragraph) by conversion, to equip for cruise missiles capable of a range in excess of 600 kilometres or for ASBMs no more than 16 aeroplanes, including aeroplanes which were prototypes of bombers equipped for such missiles. None of these 16 aeroplanes might be replaced, except in the event of the involuntary destruction of any such aeroplane or in the case of the dismantling or destruction of any such aeroplane.

Art. 15. *Para. 3.* Each party was free to use various methods of transmitting telemetric information during testing, including encryption, except that, in accordance with the provisions of this paragraph, neither party should engage in deliberate denial of telemetric information, such as through the use of telemetry encryption, whenever such denial impeded verification of compliance with the provisions of the treaty.

Related Understandings and Statements

(1) The following Memorandum of Understanding between the USA and the USSR regarding the Establishment of a Data Base on the Numbers of Strategic Offensive Arms was signed by President Carter and L. I. Brezhnev.

"For the purposes of the Treaty between the USA and the USSR on the Limitation of Strategic Offensive Arms, the parties have considered data on numbers of strategic offensive arms and agree that as of Nov. 1, 1978, there existed the following numbers of strategic offensive arms subject to limitations provided for in the treaty which is being signed today:

	USA	USSR
Launchers of ICBMs	1,054	1,398
Fixed launchers of ICBMs	1,054	1,398
Launchers of ICBMs equipped with MIRVs	550	576
Launchers of SLBMs	656	950
Launchers of SLBMs equipped with MIRVs	496	128
Heavy bombers	574	156
Heavy bombers equipped for cruise missiles capable of a range in excess of 600 kilometres	0	0
Heavy bombers equipped only for ASBMs	0	0
ASBMs	0	0
ASBMs equipped with MIRVs	0	0

"At the time of entry into force of the treaty the parties will up-date the above agreed data in the categories listed in this memorandum.

"Done at Vienna on June 18, 1979, in two copies, each in the English and Russian languages, both texts being equally authentic."

(2) Statements of data on the number of strategic offensive arms as of the date of signature of the treaty were made by both the United States and the Soviet Union, declaring the numbers of arms possessed at June 18, 1979. These showed arms equal to the numbers as of Nov. 1, 1978, except that (i) the USA had only 573 heavy bombers but three heavy bombers equipped for cruise missiles capable of a range in excess of 600 kilometres; and (ii) the Soviet Union had 608 launchers of MIRVed ICBMs and 144 launchers of MIRVed SLBMs.

(3) In a Joint Statement on Principles and Basic Guidelines the two sides agreed to continue negotiations on the further limitation and reduction of strategic arms and to "strengthen verification and to perfect the operation of the Standing Consultative Commission", and they laid down their precise objectives to be pursued in such negotiations.

(4) A written Soviet statement on the TU-22M (Backfire) aircraft, handed to President Carter on June 16, 1979, read as follows:

"The Soviet side informs the US side that the Soviet TU-22M aeroplane, called Backfire in the USA, is a medium-range bomber, and that it does not intend to give this aeroplane the capability of operating at intercontinental distances. In this connexion, the Soviet side states that it will not increase the radius of action of this aeroplane in such a way as to enable it to strike targets on the territory of the USA. Nor does it intend to give it such a capability in any other manner, including by in-flight refuelling. At the same time, the Soviet side states that it will not increase the production rate of this aeroplane as compared to the present rate."

L. I. Brezhnev confirmed that the Soviet Backfire production rate would not exceed 30 per year.

US Deferment of SALT II Ratification

As a result of Soviet intervention in Afghanistan in December 1979, President Carter on Jan. 3, 1980, formally requested the US Senate to delay its consideration of the ratification of the SALT II treaty.

On the following day the US President also announced a number of measures to be taken by the USA against the Soviet Union, including the curtailment of grain sales by 17,000,000 tonnes and the suspension of sales of high technology equipment to the USSR; however, it was officially stated in Washington on April 30, 1980, that the United States would honour the existing five-year US-Soviet grain agreement [see page 245] until its expiry on Sept. 30, 1981.

Further East-West Agreements, 1974-80

Soviet Agreements

France. During a first visit to the Soviet Union by President Giscard d'Estaing of France a joint declaration was signed on Oct. 17, 1975, both sides stating in particular that they were "convinced of the need to prevent the proliferation of nuclear arms . . . and determined to assume the responsibilities incumbent upon them in this respect as nuclear powers" and that they would "display concern to ensure that their supplies of fissile material or equipment to non-nuclear states are used exclusive for the peaceful purposes". [France was not a signatory to the 1968 Nuclear Non-Proliferation Treaty—see page 57.] Co-operation agreements were signed at the same time, covering the fields of energy, civil aviation, the aircraft industry and tourism.

In an exchange of letters dated July 16, 1976, France and the Soviet Union agreed that they would carry out and if possible improve measures to prevent accidental or unauthorized use of nuclear weapons; to notify each other immediately about any incident which might lead to the explosion of combat nuclear devices; and, in the event of an unexplained nuclear incident, to act in such a way as to avoid, as far as possible, its actions being misinterpreted by the other side. [For similar Soviet agreements (i) with the United States in 1971 see page 236; and (ii) with the United Kingdom in 1977 see page 254.]

During a visit to France by President Brezhnev, six documents were signed on June 22, 1977, including three joint statements emphasizing that bilateral talks had taken place "in an atmosphere of great cordiality which accords with the friendly relations and historic ties which exist between the two countries"; stating inter alia that all states should promote détente, which should "not be hampered by considerations of bloc policy"; reaffirming that "respect for human rights and basic freedoms by all states represents one of the fundamental principles for a radical improvement of their relations"; and also reaffirming their determination to prevent the proliferation of nuclear weapons and their "readiness to contribute to improvement of control by the International Atomic Energy Agency".

Three other documents signed at the same time were agreements on co-operation in the economic field, in transportation and in chemistry.

An agreement on relations between the French and Soviet armed forces during the 1977-78 period had been signed earlier by the chiefs of staff of the two countries' armed forces.

During a further visit to Moscow by the French President, seven documents were signed on April 28, 1979—(i) a programme for further co-operation in promoting peace and détente; (ii) a long-term development programme for economic, industrial and technical co-operation for the 1980-90 period; (iii) an economic co-operation agreement for the 1980-85 period; (iv) an agreement on scientific, technical and in-dustrial co-operation in the fields of computer technology and electronics; (v) an agreement on oceanic research; (vi) an agreement on the study of the French and Russian languages in the two countries; and (vii) an exchange of letters extending until December 1990 the agreement on the development of economic, technical and industrial co-operation concluded in 1971 [see page 236].

Germany. An agreement concluded on, and in force from, Oct. 30, 1974, provided for the further development of mutual economic co-operation with the Federal Republic.

During a visit to the Federal Republic of Germany by President Brezhnev of the Soviet Union a long-term economic co-operation agreement was signed on May 6, 1978.

This agreement provided for the further development of co-operation between the Federal Republic and the Soviet Union, in particular in "the creation, expansion and modernization of industrial complexes and enterprises, the joint development of certain types of equipment and other products; the extraction and processing of certain types of raw materials, including the development of minerals on the seabed; co-operation in the field of energy, . . . in banking and insurance, transport and other services", and also in engineering, the chemical industry, electronics and the consumer goods industry. The two sides further agreed to grant medium-term and long-term credits on as favourable terms as possible.

The agreement was concluded for 25 years, with an initial term of 10 years, to "be extended by agreement between the contracting parties for a five-year period each time".

On the basis of the above agreement a "long-term programme of main lines of co-operation" was signed in Moscow on July 1, 1980.

United Kingdom. A 10-year economic, scientific, technical and industrial co-operation agreement between the Soviet Union and the United Kingdom was signed in London on May 6, 1974. In implementation of this agreement a long-term programme for the development of economic and industrial co-operation was agreed upon during a visit to Moscow by a delegation led by Harold Wilson, the UK Prime Minister, on Feb. 13-17, 1975. At the same time a 10-year programme for scientific and technological co-operation was also approved. These programmes were to involve British credit arrangements for the USSR for £950,000,000.

An agreement on co-operation in the field of environmental protection was signed in London on May 21, 1974.

An agreement on Anglo-Soviet co-operation in the scientific, educational and cultural fields was signed in Moscow on Feb. 25, 1977.

On the prevention of any accidental outbreak of nuclear war, similar to those concluded by the Soviet Union with France in July 1976 [see page 253] and with the United States in September 1971 [see page 236] was signed in Moscow on Oct. 10, 1977.

An agreement on relations in the scientific, educational and cultural fields for 1979-91 was signed in London on March 1, 1979.

Belgium. On June 25, 1975, agreements between the two countries were signed in Moscow on environmental protection and co-operation in tourism, while in a joint declaration the two sides expressed their determination "to contribute to the process of international relaxation of tension" and to seek to make this process "irreversible".

Canada. A 10-year agreement to facilitate economic, industrial, scientific and technical co-operation between the two countries was signed in Ottawa on July 14, 1976, and an existing trade agreement was extended for a further five years.

Denmark. A 10-year Soviet-Danish agreement on economic, industrial and technical co-operation was signed in Moscow on Aug. 28, 1975.

Italy. An agreement on scientific and technological co-operation was signed on Feb. 19. 1974, and a long-term agreement on the development and deepening of co-operation in the political, scientific, technical and cultural fields on May 27, 1974.

A joint declaration signed in Moscow on Nov. 20, 1975, provided for the development and deepening of co-operation in the political, economic, scientific, technical and cultural fields, while an economic co-operation agreement for 1975-79 was signed at the same time and notes were exchanged on the application of general principles laid down in a treaty on commerce and maritime navigation signed on Dec. 11, 1948.

Luxembourg. Among agreements signed in Moscow on June 5, 1975, was one on scientific, technical and cultural co-operation between the two countries.

Turkey. With Turkey the Soviet Union signed a number of agreements on June 25, 1978—(i) a "political document on the principles of good-neighbourly and friendly co-operation"; (ii) an agreement on the delimitation of the Black Sea continental shelf; and (iii) a two-year programme of cultural and scientific exchange. Under further agreements concluded at the same time the Soviet Union was to supply Turkey with 3,000,000 tonnes of oil a year from 1979 in exchange for Turkish wheat.

Agreements concluded by Other East European Countries

East European states concluded various co-operation agreements with non-communist countries as follows:

Bulgaria and France. A five-year economic co-operation agreement was signed in Paris on March 19, 1976.

Bulgaria and Federal Republic of Germany. A 10-year agreement on economic, industrial and technological co-operation was signed in Sofia on May 14, 1975.

Bulgaria and Italy. A long-term agreement on the development of economic, industrial, scientific and technical co-operation was concluded on May 27, 1974, and an agreement on economic co-operation in 1975-79 was signed in Rome on June 23, 1975. (An earlier scientific and technical co-operation agreement had been signed on May 30, 1963.)

Bulgaria and United Kingdom. Agreements on the development of economic, industrial, scientific and technological co-operation were signed on May 14, 1974, and an agreement on a programme for the development of this co-operation in 1975.

(For US-Bulgarian agreements, see page 319.)

Czechoslovakia and France. At the conclusion of a visit to France by the Czechoslovak Prime Minister on Nov. 14, 1975, a 10-year trade and technological co-operation agreement was signed, covering in particular co-operation in the motor industry, chemical engineering, machine tools, electronic and energy industries and in farming and food-processing machinery.

Czechoslovakia and Federal Republic of Germany. An agreement on the further development of economic, industrial and technical co-operation was signed and came into force on Jan. 22, 1975.

Czechoslovakia and United Kingdom. A co-operation agreement was signed in 1972.

German Democratic Republic and United Kingdom. An agreement on the development of economic, industrial, scientific and technological co-operation was signed on Dec. 18, 1973.

Hungary and Federal Republic of Germany. An agreement on economic, industrial and technical co-operation was signed in Budapest and came into force on Nov. 11, 1974.

Hungary and Italy. An agreement on the development of economic, industrial and technical co-operation was signed on May 25, 1974, and a joint declaration signed in

Rome on Nov. 12, 1975, provided for the development and deepening of co-operation in the political, economic, scientific, technical and cultural fields.

Hungary and United Kingdom. An economic, industrial and technological co-operation agreement was concluded in 1972, and an agreement on co-operation in medicine and public health was signed in Budapest on Nov. 1, 1978.

Hungary and United States. A trade agreement initialled on March 4, 1978, provided for the granting of most-favoured-nation status to Hungary by the United States and was approved by the US House of Representatives on May 22, 1978.

Poland and France. Agreement was expressed in three documents signed in Warsaw on June 20, 1975, during a visit to Poland by the French President—(i) a declaration on the principles of friendly co-operation between the two countries, providing inter alia for annual political consultation at the level of ministers or their representatives and reserving "a special place" for cultural co-operation; (ii) a declaration on the principles and means of cultural and scientific co-operation, information and human relations between the two countries; and (iii) a five-year economic co-operation agreement. At the same time provision was made for the opening of a French credit line of F7,000 million (then about £800,000) to Poland for the next three years.

Additional co-operation agreements with France were signed on Sept. 14, 1977, during a visit to France by Edward Gierek, the First Secretary of the Polish United Workers' Party.

Poland and Federal Republic of Germany. An agreement on economic, industrial and technical co-operation was signed on Nov. 1, 1974; it came into force on Jan. 15, 1975, and was followed by a long-term programme of such co-operation, which was agreed and came into force on Oct. 9, 1975.

Two agreements and a protocol, initialled in Bonn on Aug. 7, 1975, related to (i) a reciprocal pensions arrangement, under which the FRG would pay Poland, for pension insurance claims arising from World War II, a lump sum of DM1,300 million in three annual instalments; (ii) a long-term credit by the FRG to Poland of DM1,000 million to be paid in three annual instalments in 1975, 1976 and 1977; and (iii) the resettlement in the FRG of between 120,000 and 125,000 ethnic Germans who would be allowed to leave Poland. The agreements were signed in Warsaw on Oct. 9, 1975; effectively ratified by the West German Parliament by March 12, 1976, after the Polish Government had agreed that further emigration of ethnic Germans from Poland beyond the 120,000 to 125,000 would eventually be permitted; and approved by the Polish Council of State on March 15, 1976, whereafter instruments of ratification were exchanged on March 24.

An agreement of June 11, 1976, provided for the further development of co-operation between the two countries in the economic field.

Poland and Italy. An agreement on economic co-operation in 1975-79 was signed in Rome on Oct. 28, 1975.

A visit to Rome by E. Gierek on Nov. 28, 1977, resulted in the signing of (i) a joint political statement in which the two sides inter alia confirmed that "respect for human rights and basic freedoms" was "one of the important foundations for good inter-state relations" and (ii) four economic co-operation agreements.

Poland and United Kingdom. A long-term agreement on the development of economic, industrial, scientific and technical co-operation was signed in London on March 20, 1973, to remain in force until Dec. 31, 1982, and to continue thereafter subject to six months' notice by either side. This agreement extended the tasks of a UK-Polish joint commission established under an economic and trade agreement signed in London on April 21, 1971, and to remain in force until Dec. 31, 1974, subject to mutual agreement on its further extension. A 10-year programme of co-operation under the 1973 agreement was signed in London on Sept. 9, 1975.

During a visit to Poland by the UK Foreign and Commonwealth Secretary on July 13-15, 1975, a declaration on the development of friendly relations between the two countries was signed, laying down the principles of their bilateral relations in conformity with the UN Charter and of their international activities in working for détente and disarmament, with the provision that their Ministers of Foreign Affairs or their representatives should meet at least once a year.

A five-year agreement on economic co-operation was concluded on Dec. 16, 1976.

A convention on co-operation in education, science and culture was signed in London on Nov. 7, 1978.

Poland and United States. With the United States, three joint declarations (on principles of mutual relations, development of co-operation and agricultural trade) and six agreements (inter alia on coal research, health, the environment, science and technology) were signed in Washington between Oct. 8 and 13, 1974.

Romania and France. After the President of Romania (which had had close relations with France since 1964) had first visited France in June 1970, Franco-Romanian agreements were concluded (i) in 1970 (with the state-owned Société nationale industrielle aérospatiale—SNIAS) on the joint production of 50 Alouette helicopters and (ii) in 1974 on the purchase from France of 100 Puma helicopters, part of them to be assembled in Romania under licence from SNIAS.

A long-term agreement on economic, industrial and technical co-operation between France and Romania was signed in Bucharest on July 28, 1975, and new such agreements were concluded on July 24-28, 1978.

At the end of a visit to Romania by the French President, four economic agreements were signed on March 10, 1979, (i) on the adoption by Romania of the French SECAM colour television system; (ii) on the early signing of a contract for 40 Alouette-III helicopters to be supplied to Romania; (iii) on the building of motor vehicles; and (iv) on co-operation in electronics and computer technology.

During a further visit to Paris by President Ceausescu of Romania a nine-page joint declaration was published on July 25, 1980, reaffirming an earlier similar declaration of 1979, noting that trade exchanges between the two countries had been doubled between 1975 and 1979 and stating that a further doubling by 1985 constituted "a realistic target".

Romania and Federal Republic of Germany. A "joint solemn declaration" and eight co-operation agreements were signed on June 29, 1973, during a visit to the Federal Republic by President Ceausescu. In the joint declaration the two sides undertook to intensify their relations of friendship and co-operation in the fields of politics, the economy, industry, science, technology, culture, education and the media and tourism.

During a visit to Romania by the German Federal Chancellor on Jan. 6-7, 1978, agreement was reached (i) on the continued emigration of ethnic Germans from Romania (at the rate of about 11,000 persons a year over the next five years) and (ii) additional credit guarantees to Romania by the Federal Republic.

Romania and United Kindom. A 10-year agreement on economic, industrial and technical co-operation was signed during a visit to Bucharest by Harold Wilson, the UK

Prime Minister, on Sept. 16-18, 1975. A long-term programme for the further development of this co-operation was agreed upon in 1977.

An agreement on co-operation in education, science and culture was signed in London on June 15, 1978.

Romania and United States.* President Ceausescu of Romania signed on Dec. 5, 1973, during a visit to the USA, (i) a joint statement laying down principles for their bilateral relations to be based on the provisions of the UN Charter and expressing their determination "to encourage the expansion of trade as well as industrial, scientific and technical co-operation" and "to develop friendly relations between the two peoples", and (ii) a joint declaration on economic, industrial and technical co-operation, to include most-favoured-nation treatment of Romania by the United States. A US-Romanian trade agreement, signed on April 2, 1975, incorporated the granting of such treatment, which was approved by the US Congress on July 25-28 of that year (subject to the proviso that during the first 18 months the agreement would be under scrutiny in regard to Romania's policy on emigration, as laid down in the 1975 US Trade Reform Act—see page 240). This agreement came into force on Aug. 3, 1975, during a visit to Romania by President Ford.

Agreements between China and Western States

United States. New principles of the relations between the United States and China were agreed upon during a visit to China by President Nixon and laid down in a joint communiqué issued in Shanghai on Feb. 27, 1972. These principles included in particular the provisions that "neither side should seek hegemony in the Asia-Pacific region and each is opposed to efforts by any other country or group of countries to establish such hegemony", and that "neither is prepared to negotiate on behalf of any third party or to enter into agreements or understandings with the other directed at other states".

These principles were reaffirmed in a joint communiqué issued on Dec. 15-16, 1978, to announce the establishment of diplomatic relations between the two countries with effect from Jan. 1, 1979.

Under an agreement which was signed in Peking on March 2, 1979, and entered into force on May 11 of that year, China was to pay the US Treasury $80,500,000 in settlement of some 400 US claims totalling $196,800,000 while the United States would

* See also page 325.

release $80,500,000 of Chinese assets frozen in the USA during the Korean war in 1950.

Under a US-Chinese trade agreement of Jan. 24, 1980, China was granted most-favoured-nation status (as provided for in an agreement initialled in China on May 14, 1979, signed in Peking on July 7, 1979, and approved by the US Congress on Oct. 23, 1979). The trade agreement came into force on Feb. 1, 1980.

Also on Jan. 24, 1980, the US Defence Department announced that it was prepared to sell military equipment (though excluding offensive weapons) to China—this being a reversal of US policy under the rules of the Inter-Allied Co-ordinating Committee for East-West Trade (COCOM, see page 182).

Furthermore it was agreed on the same day (Jan. 24, 1980) in a memorandum of understanding that a ground receiving station would be built in China for data transmitted by the US Landsat-D satellite system (which had possible military applications).

In March 1980 an agreement was signed opening the way for large-scale US assistance in the development of China's hydroelectric industry.

A four-year agreement on US grain supplies to China of 6,000,000 tons per annum was concluded on Oct. 22, 1980.

Canada. A protocol on economic co-operation between the two countries was signed on Oct. 19, 1979.

France. A long-term agreement on the development of economic relations and co-operation (during the seven-year period from 1979 to 1985), signed in Peking on Dec. 4, 1978, by China and France, envisaged trade worth F60,000 million ($13,600 million). Within the framework of the agreement China placed orders for the construction of two 900-MW nuclear reactors by a French subsidiary of a US firm at a cost of F10,000 million. It was officially confirmed in Paris on Oct. 20, 1978, that negotiations had been completed for the sale to China of substantial quantities of French arms, including anti-tank missiles and Crotale anti-aircraft missiles (worth at least $350,000,000), subject to approval by the Inter-Allied Co-ordinating Committee for East-West Trade (COCOM, see page 182).

In an agreement on economic relations between the two countries, signed in Paris on Oct. 17, 1979, it was stated that all useful measures would be taken to develop bilateral economic and commercial relations.

During a visit to China by the French President on Oct. 15-21, 1980, agreement was reached in principle on China's import of complete sets of equipment for nuclear power plants from France and for technical co-operation in this field.

Federal Republic of Germany. Among various agreements concluded by the two countries were one on economic and technical co-operation, signed on Oct. 9, 1978, and another on economic co-operation which was signed and came into force on Oct. 24, 1979.

United Kingdom. An agreement and a protocol on scientific and technological co-operation were signed in London on Nov. 15, 1978.

An agreement on economic co-operation was signed in Peking (Beijing) on March 4, 1979.

13. The Commonwealth

This section covers (i) the membership, structure and historical development of the Commonwealth, (ii) the various regional groupings and organizations which have been created within the Commonwealth framework, (iii) major treaties and agreements concluded by the United Kingdom and (iv) significant treaties and agreements concluded by other Commonwealth member countries.

Structure and Development of the Commonwealth

The Commonwealth is an association of independent sovereign states all of which have been, at some time, British territories. It is neither a formal alliance nor a federation of states since there exists no written Commonwealth constitution and no central political authority. Any former British territory, on attaining independence, may seek membership of the Commonwealth; this is granted only by the unanimous consent of the members.

The head of the Commonwealth is the British monarch, who is recognized, even by those member countries which have their own heads of state, as the symbol of the free association of member nations of the Commonwealth. In those countries which owe allegiance to her as their head of state, the Queen is represented by a Governor-General whom she appoints on the recommendation of the country in question.

One of the principal factors binding together the member nations of the Commonwealth is the use of English Common Law as a basis for most judicial systems. Exceptions are the Canadian province of Quebec, where the judicial system is based on French law; Sri Lanka, where Roman Dutch law is applied (this is also the case in Zimbabwe); and the Moslem countries of Africa and Asia, where Moslem civil law is applied.

Commonwealth Members

The members of the Commonwealth are the United Kingdom, together with its dependent territories, protectorates and protected states, and 43 other independent states. The membership is given in the table below.

Since the merging of the Colonial Office and the Commonwealth Relations Office in August 1966, to form the Commonwealth Office, and its subsequent merger with the Foreign Office to form the Foreign and Commonwealth Office on Oct. 17, 1968, the dependent territories of Britain (listed below) have become the responsibility of this office.

Countries within the Commonwealth

Country	Date of Independence	Political Status
United Kingdom	—	Monarchy
Canada	1867	Monarchy
Australia	1900	Monarchy
New Zealand	1907	Monarchy
India	Aug. 15, 1947	Republic since Jan. 26, 1950
Sri Lanka	Feb. 4, 1948	Republic since May 22, 1972
Ghana	March 6, 1957	Republic since July 1, 1960
Cyprus	Aug. 16, 1960	Republic since Aug. 16, 1960
Nigeria	Oct. 1, 1960	Republic since Oct. 1, 1963
Sierra Leone	April 27, 1961	Republic since April 19, 1971
Tanzania	Dec. 9, 1961	Republic since Dec. 9, 1962 (in union with Zanzibar since April 27, 1964)
Western Samoa ‡	Jan. 1, 1962	Independent State under two Chiefs
Jamaica	Aug. 5, 1962	Monarchy
Trinidad and Tobago	Aug. 31, 1962	Republic since Aug. 1, 1976

Uganda	Oct. 9, 1962	Independent Sovereign State on Oct. 9, 1963. Republic (officially) since Sept. 8, 1967
Malaysia	Sept. 16, 1963	Monarchy*
Kenya	Dec. 12, 1963	Republic since Dec. 12, 1964
Malawi	July 6, 1964	Republic since July 6, 1966
Malta	Sept. 21, 1964	Republic since Dec. 13, 1974
Zambia	Oct. 24, 1964	Republic since Oct. 24, 1964
The Gambia	Feb. 18, 1965	Republic since April 24, 1970
Singapore	Oct. 16, 1965	Republic since Dec. 22, 1965
Guyana	May 26, 1966	Republic since Feb. 23, 1970
Botswana..	Sept. 30, 1966	Republic since Sept. 30, 1966
Lesotho	Oct. 4, 1966	Monarchy*
Barbados..	Nov. 30, 1966	Monarchy
Nauru†	Jan. 31, 1968	Republic
Mauritius..	March 12, 1968	Monarchy
Swaziland	Sept. 6, 1968	Monarchy*
Tonga	June 4, 1970	Monarchy*
Fiji	Oct. 10, 1970	Monarchy
Bangladesh	Dec. 22, 1971	Republic
Commonwealth of the Bahamas	July 10, 1973	Monarchy
Grenada	Feb. 7, 1974	Monarchy
Papua New Guinea	Sept. 16, 1975	Monarchy
Seychelles	June 29, 1976	Republic
Solomon Islands	July 7, 1978	Monarchy
Tuvalu†	Oct. 1, 1978	Monarchy
Commonwealth of Dominica ..	Nov. 3, 1978	Republic
St Lucia	Feb. 22, 1979	Monarchy
Kiribati	July 12, 1979	Republic
St Vincent and the Grenadines†	Oct. 27, 1979	Monarchy
Zimbabwe	April 18, 1980	Republic
Vanuatu	July 31, 1980	Republic

* These monarchies are headed by their own monarchs. All other Commonwealth countries described as monarchies owe allegiance to the British Queen.

† Special member without representation at Commonwealth heads of government conferences.

‡ Western Samoa became a member of the Commonwealth on Aug. 28, 1970.

Pakistan—a Commonwealth member since Aug. 15, 1947, and a Republic since March 23, 1956—withdrew from the Commonwealth on Jan. 30, 1972, in protest against recognition of the independence of Bangladesh (formerly East Pakistan) by Britain, Australia and New Zealand.

BRITISH DEPENDENT TERRITORIES

Associated States. Antigua; St Kitts-Nevis.

Protected State. Brunei.

Colonies with Internal Self-Government. Belize; Bermuda; British Virgin Islands; Cayman Islands; Gibraltar; Montserrat; St Helena and Dependencies; Turks and Caicos Islands.

Other Colonies. Anguilla (formally part of the Associated State of St Kitts-Nevis-Anguilla); British Antarctic Territory; British Indian Ocean Territory; Hong Kong (Colony and Leased Territories); Pitcairn Islands Group.

OTHER DEPENDENCIES

Other dependencies which are members of the Commonwealth are (i) *of Britain*—the Channel Islands and the Isle of Man; (ii) *of Australia*—the Australian Antarctic Territory, Christmas Island, the Cocos (Keeling) Islands, the Coral Sea Islands Territory, the Heard and McDonald Islands and Norfolk Island; and (iii) *of New Zealand*—the Cook Islands, Niue, the Ross Dependency and Tokelau.

Commonwealth Organs

Summit Meetings. Meetings of the heads of government of Commonwealth member countries are held every two years at different capitals in the Commonwealth. These meetings are private and informal, and decisions are taken by consensus (and not by voting). Matters discussed include the international political situation, regional problems (in particular the developments in southern Africa), conflicts affecting Commonwealth members (e.g. Cyprus), economic affairs (with particular reference to assistance for developing Commonwealth countries) and special Commonwealth programmes. A detailed communiqué is issued at the end of each meeting.

Finance Ministers' Meetings. Meetings of Commonwealth Ministers of Finance take place once a year to discuss the world economic situation and to agree on Commonwealth proposals to be made in international economic and financial fora.

Secretariat. The Commonwealth Secretariat was set up in London in July 1965 in pursuance of a recommendation made by the heads of government meeting of July 1964. The Secretariat was to be "a visible symbol of the spirit of co-operation which animates the Commonwealth". Divided into departments dealing with administration, applied studies in government, economic affairs, education, export market development, food production and rural development, information, international affairs, legal matters, medical affairs, youth, and finance and personnel services, the Secretariat is responsible for disseminating

information on questions of common interest; for aiding the various Commonwealth agencies, both official and unofficial, in the promotion of Commonwealth links in all fields; and for preparing and servicing the heads of government and other ministerial meetings.

The Secretariat is headed by a Secretary-General (elected by the heads of government for a five-year term and re-eligible), two Deputy Secretaries-General and two Assistant Secretaries-General.

Commonwealth Organizations

The main Commonwealth organizations active in various fields are listed below.

Commonwealth Fund for Technical Co-operation (CFTC). The CFTC was established in April 1971 to provide technical assistance for economic and social development in Commonwealth developing countries. For the financial year which began

Map 7   African members of Commonwealth

on July 1, 1979, the Fund's provisional budget was fixed at £13,500,000.

Under the CFTC a programme for technical assistance to the Government of Mozambique was set up in April 1976 with an initial target of £1,000,000 (as a sequel to a recommendation by a Commonwealth Sanctions Committee to compensate Mozambique for losses incurred through its participation in sanctions against the then White minority regime in Rhodesia). By November 1977 the Commonwealth Fund for Mozambique had initiated technical assistance and training projects costing £300,000.

Under the aegis of the CFTC an **Industrial Development Unit** (IDU) was set up within the Commonwealth Secretariat in 1980.

Agriculture and Forestry. The Commonwealth Agricultural Bureau—four institutes and 10 bureaux, each concerned with a particular aspect of agricultural science—collects and supplies specialized information on agricultural science for research workers. The organization was founded in 1929.

The bodies concerned with co-operation in the field of forestry are: (i) The Commonwealth Forestry Association, founded in 1921; and (ii) the Standing Committee on Commonwealth Forestry, founded in 1923.

Commonwealth Studies. (i) The Institute of Commonwealth Studies, formed in London in 1949 to promote advanced study of the Commonwealth; and (ii) the Institute of Commonwealth Studies at the University of Oxford.

Communications. (i) The Commonwealth Air Transport Council, formed in London in 1945; (ii) the Commonwealth Telecommunications Organization, with a secretariat known as the Commonwealth Telecommunications Bureau, established in London in 1968; and (iii) Conferences of Commonwealth Postal Administrations, held at various times since 1971.

Education. (i) The Association of Commonwealth Universities, founded in London in 1913 as the Universities Bureau of the British Empire; (ii) the Commonwealth Association of Science and Mathematics Educators (CASME), established in London in 1974; (iii) the Commonwealth Education Conference, held regularly about once in three years since 1959; (iv) the Commonwealth Education Liaison Committee (CELC), founded in 1959; and (v) the League for the Exchange of Commonwealth Teachers, formed in London in 1901.

Health. (i) The Commonwealth Caribbean Health Ministers' Conference; (ii) the Commonwealth Health Ministers' Meeting, held about once in three years; (iii) the Commonwealth Medical Association, formed in London in 1962; (iv) the Commonwealth Regional Health Secretariat for East, Central and Southern Africa, founded in Arusha (Tanzania) in 1974; (v) the Commonwealth Society for the Deaf, London; (vi) the Royal Commonwealth Society for the Blind (at Haywards Heath, Sussex), formed in 1950; and (vii) the West African Health Secretariat (Yaba, Nigeria), founded in 1972 as the Commonwealth West African Health Secretariat, which was joined by Liberia in 1974, when it assumed its present name.

Information and the Media. (i) The Commonwealth Broadcasting Association, formed in London in 1945; (ii) Commonwealth Institute, London, established in 1887 as the Imperial Institute; (iii) the Commonwealth Institute, Scotland (Edinburgh); and (iv) the Commonwealth Press Union, formed in London in 1909.

Law. (i) The Commonwealth Law Ministers' Conference, held about once every two years; (ii) the Commonwealth Legal Advisory Service (c/o British Institute of International and Comparative Law, London); (iii) the Commonwealth Legal Bureau, Auckland (New Zealand); (iv) the Commonwealth Legal Education Association, formed in London in 1971; and (v) the Commonwealth Magistrates' Association, London.

Parliamentary Affairs. (i) The Commonwealth Parliamentary Association, formed in London in 1911; and (ii) the Conference of Speakers and Presiding Officers of Commonwealth Parliaments, Ottawa (Canada), held every two years.

Professions. (i) The Commonwealth Association of Architects, formed in London in 1964; and (ii) the Commonwealth Foundation, established in London in 1965 to administer a fund for promoting interchanges between Commonwealth professional organizations.

Science and Technology. (i) The Commonwealth Advisory Aeronautical Research Council (Teddington, Middlesex), formed in 1946; (ii) the Commonwealth Committee on Mineral Resources and Geology, formed in London in 1948; (iii) the Commonwealth Consultative Space Research Committee, formed in London in 1960; (iv) the Commonwealth Engineers' Council, formed in London in 1946; and (v) the Commonwealth Science Council, formed in London in 1946 for collaboration between Commonwealth government civil science organizations in joint projects.

Sport. The Commonwealth Games Federation (London), which holds games every four years (the first having been held in 1930).

Youth. (i) The Commonwealth Expedition (COMEX), London, for organizing international expeditions; (ii) the Commonwealth Friendship Movement (Brighton, Sussex), formed in 1960 to organize correspondence for the 7-17 age group; (iii) the Commonwealth Youth Affairs Council, London; (iv) the Commonwealth Youth Exchange Council, formed in London in 1970; and (v) the Duke of Edinburgh's Award Scheme (London), enabling young people to gain awards for a programme of activities.

Other Organizations. (i) The British Commonwealth Ex-Services League, London; (ii) the Commonwealth Countries League, formed in London in 1925 to work for equality of status and opportunities between women and men and for mutual understanding throughout the Commonwealth; (iii) the Commonwealth War Graves Commission (Maidenhead, Berks.), formed in 1917 as the Imperial War Graves Commission; (iv) the Joint Commonwealth Societies Council, London; (v) the Royal Commonwealth Society, established in London to promote knowledge and understanding among the peoples of the Commonwealth; (vi) the Royal Over-Seas League, formed in London in 1910 with similar objects; and (vii) the Victoria League for Commonwealth Friendship, formed in London in 1901 to further personal friendship between Commonwealth peoples.

Development of the Commonwealth

The Commonwealth began to evolve with the formation of self-governing dominions. The first of these was the Dominion of Canada, created, under the British North America Act of 1867, out of the provinces of Ontario, Quebec, Nova Scotia and New Brunswick. Additional provinces acceded to the Dominion, in accordance with the provisions of the Act, as follows: Manitoba (1869), British Columbia (1871), Prince Edward Island (1873), Alberta (1905), Saskatchewan (1905) and Newfoundland (1949).

The six self-governing provinces of Australia formed a dominion in 1900 known as the Commonwealth of Australia. New Zealand, which had obtained a unitary form of government in 1876, was designated a dominion in 1907, but did not adopt the principal sections of the Statute of Westminster [see below] until 1947. The

Union of South Africa was formed from four self-governing colonies in 1910. Southern Ireland became in effect a self-governing dominion when the Irish Free State was established in 1921.

An *Imperial Conference of 1926,* adopting a report by an Inter-Imperial Relations Committee, defined the Dominions and Great Britain as "autonomous communities within the Empire, equal in status, in no way subordinate to one another in any aspect of their domestic or external affairs, though united by a common allegiance to the Crown, and freely associated as members of the British Commonwealth of Nations . . . Every self-governing member of the Empire is now the master of its destiny. In fact, if not always in form, it is subject to no compulsion whatever. . . . The British Empire is not founded upon negations. It depends essentially, if not formally, on positive ideals. Free institutions are its lifeblood. Free co-operation is its instrument."

The *Statute of Westminster of 1931* gave effect to the above definition and offered all former colonies the undisputed right to secede from the Commonwealth. Other provisions of the statute are:

(1) The Parliament of Westminster ceases to have the right of revision with regard to the legislation of the Parliaments of the Dominions.

(2) A Dominion possesses full authority to make laws possessing extra-territorial validity.

(3) When there are discrepancies between a Dominion law and an existing law of the United Kingdom, this fact shall not render the Dominion law invalid.

Steps in the gradual decentralization of powers within the Commonwealth were:

(1) The granting of complete independence in 1947 to Burma, Ceylon (later Sri Lanka), India and Pakistan—with Burma seceding from the Commonwealth and the other three states becoming independent members of it.

(2) British recognition of the secession of the Irish Republic in 1949—although citizens of the Republic continued to enjoy in Britain substantially all rights and privileges of British subjects.

(3) The acceptance of India as a Republic in 1949, with the British sovereign being acknowledged as head of the Commonwealth. (The monarchy remained merely a unifying symbol for the Commonwealth, but no longer had valid constitutional significance. Relations among Commonwealth members are no longer based on constitutional law, but on international law—i.e. multilateral treaties which also embrace non-Commonwealth states.)

(4) The Canadian Citizenship Act of 1946 by which Canadians became Canadian citizens first, and British subjects only

by consequence. This act forced the other independent members of the Commonwealth to follow suit by establishing their own citizenships.

South Africa left the Commonwealth in 1961, not because it had become a Republic the previous year, but because its racial policies were at variance with the principles of all other Commonwealth members.

1971 Singapore Declaration. At the Commonwealth conference held in January 1971 in Singapore, a *Declaration of Commonwealth Principles* was unanimously agreed on by the 31 delegations on Jan. 22. The declaration stated inter alia:

". . . We believe in the liberty of the individual, in equal rights for all citizens regardless of race, colour, creed or political belief, and in their inalienable right to participate by means of free and democratic political processes in framing the society in which they live. We therefore strive to promote in each of our countries those representative institutions and guarantees for personal freedom under the law that are our common heritage.

"We recognize racial prejudice as a dangerous sickness threatening the healthy development of the human race and racial discrimination as an unmitigated evil of society. Each of us will vigorously combat this evil within our own nation.

"No country will afford to regimes which practise racial discrimination assistance which in its own judgment directly contributes to the pursuit or consolidation of this evil policy. We oppose all forms of colonial domination and racial oppression and are committed to the principles of human dignity and equality.

"We will therefore use all our efforts to foster human equality and dignity everywhere, and to further the principles of self-determination and non-racialism. . . ."

1973 Ottawa Conference. At the Ottawa conference of Commonwealth heads of government, held from Aug. 2 to 10, 1973, the Prime Minister of Canada, Pierre Trudeau, opened with the following speech on the nature of the Commonwealth:

"Within the Commonwealth we have the opportunity and the means for both communication and understanding. In this forum of discussion each Commonwealth member is equal. None is senior; none is superior. None is distinguished by economic self-sufficiency; none is possessed of all political virtue. In our discussions during the next few days, I have no doubt that we will be able to demonstrate to one another and to the world the advantages of our dissimilarity, the richness of our diversity, the excitement of our variety. We will be able to do so because we are members of an association, not an institution. In this Commonwealth there is no structure to contain us, there are no fetters to chafe us. The Commonwealth is a reflection of its [then] 32 members and of their desire to consult and co-operate with one another. There is no artificial adhesive. Nor is there any voting, any constitution, any flag, any headquarters. This association is neither regional in nature, nor specialized in its interests. The Commonwealth is an organism and this fact guarantees both its vitality and its flexibility. . . .

"None of us in the Commonwealth is so powerful or so self-sufficient that he is able to act independently of the opinion or the assistance of others. None of us disregards the value of consultation and co-operation. We are able in these gatherings of heads of government, and by extension, in those other groupings to which we belong, to ensure that we understand one another's problems and one another's aspirations. That, to me, is the significance of our association. I am not, at this meeting, in search of a new role for the Commonwealth, or indeed any role. The Commonwealth is for many of us our window on the world. Over the years its importance will deepen largely because it has no specific role, but emphasizes instead the value of the human relations. . . ."

1977 Gleneagles Agreement on Apartheid in Sport. At the end of the 21st meeting of the heads of government of Commonwealth countries, held in London on June 8-15, 1977, the participants issued, separately from a final communiqué, a statement on apartheid in sport agreed upon at informal discussions at Gleneagles (Scotland) on June 11-12 and reading as follows:

"The member countries of the Commonwealth, embracing peoples of diverse races, colours, languages and faiths, have long recognized racial prejudice and discrimination as a dangerous sickness and an unmitigated evil and are pledged to use all their efforts to foster human dignity everywhere. At their London meeting, heads of government reaffirmed that apartheid in sports, as in other fields, is an abomination and runs directly counter to the Declaration of Commonwealth Principles which they made at Singapore on Jan. 22, 1971 [see above].

"They were conscious that sport is an important means of developing and fostering understanding between the people, and especially between the young people, of all countries. But they were also aware that, quite apart from other factors, sporting contacts between their nationals and the nationals of countries practising apartheid in sport tend to encourage the belief (however unwarranted) that they are prepared to condone this abhorrent policy or are less than totally committed to the principles embodied in their Singapore Declaration. Regretting past misunderstandings and difficulties and recognizing that these were partly the result of inadequate intergovernmental consultations, they agreed that they would seek to remedy this situation in the context of the increased level of understanding now achieved.

"They reaffirmed their full support for the international campaign against apartheid and welcomed the efforts of the United Nations to reach universally accepted approaches to the question of sporting contacts within the framework of that campaign.

"Mindful of these and other considerations, they accepted it as the urgent duty of each of their governments vigorously to combat the evil of apartheid by withholding any form of support for, and by taking every practical step to discourage, contact or competition by their nationals with sporting organizations, teams or sportsmen from South Africa or from any other country where sports are organized on the basis of race, colour or ethnic origin.

"They fully acknowledged that it was for each

government to determine in accordance with its laws the methods by which it might best discharge these commitments. But they recognized that the effective fulfilment of their commitments was essential to the harmonious development of Commonwealth sport hereafter.

"They acknowledged also that the full realization of their objectives involved the understanding, support and active participation of the nationals of their countries and of their national sporting organizations and authorities. As they drew a curtain across the past they issued a collective call for that understanding, support and participation with a view to ensuring that in this matter the peoples and governments of the Commonwealth might help to give a lead to the world.

"Heads of government specially welcomed the belief, unanimously expressed at their meeting, that in the light of their consultations and accord there were unlikely to be future sporting contacts of any significance between Commonwealth countries or their nationals and South Africa while that country continues to pursue the detestable policy of apartheid. On that basis, and having regard to their commitments, they looked forward with satisfaction to the holding of the [1978] Commonwealth Games in Edmonton [Canada] and to the continued strengthening of Commonwealth sport generally."

1979 Lusaka Conference. At the 22nd meeting of the heads of government of Commonwealth countries, held in Lusaka (Zambia) on Aug. 1-7, 1979, a framework agreement was unanimously approved for a peaceful settlement of Rhodesia's transition to an independent Zimbabwe under Black majority rule, while a strong Commonwealth declaration on racism was also approved.

On the Rhodesian issue the participants of the meeting agreed inter alia that (i) it was "the constitutional responsibility of the British Government to grant legal independence to Zimbabwe on the basis of majority rule"; (ii) "the search for a lasting settlement must involve all the parties to the conflict"; and (iii) "independence on the basis of majority rule requires the adoption of a democratic constitution including appropriate safeguards for minorities", with the government being "chosen through free and fair elections properly supervised under British Government authority and with Commonwealth observers".

Stating that the Commonwealth was "an institution devoted to the promotion of international understanding and world peace, and to the achievement of equal rights for all citizens regardless of race, colour, sex, creed or political belief, and . . . committed to the eradication of the dangerous evils of racism and racial prejudice", the participants of the meeting proclaimed the following *Lusaka Declaration of the Commonwealth on Racism and Racial Prejudice:*

"United in our desire to rid the world of the evils of racism and racial prejudice, we proclaim our faith in the inherent dignity and worth of the human person and declare that:

"(1) The peoples of the Commonwealth have the right to live freely in dignity and equality, without any distinction or exclusion based on race, colour, sex, descent or national or ethnic origin;

"(2) while everyone is free to retain diversity in his or her culture and lifestyle, this diversity does not justify the perpetuation of racial prejudice or racially discriminatory practices;

"(3) everyone has the right to equality before the law and equal justice under the law;

"(4) everyone has the right to effective remedies and protection against any form of discrimination based on the grounds of race, colour, sex, descent, or national or ethnic origin.

"We reject as inhuman and intolerable all policies designed to perpetuate apartheid, racial segregation or other policies based on theories that racial groups are or may be inherently superior or inferior.

"We reaffirm that it is the duty of all the peoples of the Commonwealth to work together for the total eradication of the infamous policy of apartheid which is internationally recognized as a crime against the conscience and dignity of mankind and the very existence of which is an affront to humanity.

"We agree that everyone has the right to protection against acts of incitement to racial hatred and discrimination, whether committed by individuals, groups or other organizations.

"We affirm that there should be no discrimination based on race, colour, sex, descent or national or ethnic origin in the acquisition or exercise of the right to vote; in the field of civil rights or access to citizenship; or in the economic, social or cultural fields, particularly education, health, employment, occupation, housing, social security and cultural life.

"We attach particular importance to ensuring that children shall be protected from practices which may foster racism or racial prejudice. Children have the right to be brought up and educated in a spirit of tolerance and understanding so as to be able to contribute fully to the building of future societies based on justice and friendship.

"We believe that those groups in societies who may be especially disadvantaged because of residual racist attitudes are entitled to the fullest protection of the law. We recognize that the history of the Commonwealth and its diversity require that special attention should be paid to the problems of indigenous minorities. We recognize that the same special attention should be paid to the problems of immigrants, immigrant workers and refugees.

"We agree that special measures may in particular circumstances be required to advance the development of disadvantaged groups in society. We recognize that the effects of colonialism or racism in the past may take desirable special provisions for the social and economic enhancement of indigenous populations.

"Inspired by the principles of freedom and equality which characterize our association, we accept the solemn duty of working together to eliminate racism and racial prejudice. This duty involves the acceptance of the principle that positive measures may be required to advance the elimination of racism, including assistance to those struggling to rid themselves and their environment of the practice.

"Being aware that legislation alone cannot eliminate racism and racial prejudice, we endorse the need to initiate public information and education policies designed to promote understanding, tolerance, respect and friendship among peoples and racial groups.

"We are particularly conscious of the importance

of the contribution the media can make to human rights and the eradication of racism and racial prejudice by helping to eliminate ignorance and misunderstanding between people and by drawing attention to the evils which afflict humanity. We affirm the importance of truthful presentation of facts in order to ensure that the public are fully informed of the dangers presented by racism and racial prejudice.

"In accordance with established principles of international law and, in particular, the provisions of the International Convention on the Elimination of All Forms of Racial Discrimination [of 1965—see page 42], we affirm that everyone is, at all times and in all places, entitled to be protected in the enjoyment of the right to be free of racism and racial prejudice.

"We believe that the existence in the world of apartheid and racial discrimination is a matter of concern to all human beings. We recognize that we share an international responsibility to work together for the total eradication of apartheid and racial discrimination.

"We note that racism and racial prejudice, wherever they occur, are significant factors contributing to tension between nations and thus inhibit peaceful progress and development. We believe that the goal of the eradication of racism stands as a critical priority for governments of the Commonwealth, committed as they are to the promotion of the ideals of peaceful and happy lives for their people.

"We intend that the Commonwealth, as an international organization with a fundamental and deep-rooted attachment to principles of freedom and equality, should co-operate with other organizations in the fulfilment of these principles. In particular the Commonwealth should seek to enhance the co-ordination of its activities with those of other organizations similarly committed to the promotion and protection of human rights and fundamental freedoms."

Commonwealth Regional Groupings

The Colombo Plan

Headquarters: Colombo.

Members within the Area: Afghanistan, Bangladesh, Bhutan, Burma, Fiji, India, Indonesia, Iran, Kampuchea, Korea, Laos, Malaysia, Maldives, Nepal, Pakistan, Papua New Guinea, Philippines, Singapore, Republic of Sri Lanka, Thailand.

Members outside the Area: Australia, Canada, Japan, New Zealand, United Kingdom, United States.

The Colombo Plan for Co-operative Economic and Social Development in Asia and the Pacific was drawn up by a Commonwealth Consultative Committee on South and South-East Asia, and published on Nov. 28, 1950. This plan, originally adopted for a six-year period, was based on detailed development programmes for India, Pakistan, Ceylon, Malaya, Singapore, North Borneo (Sabah), and Sarawak, and formally came into operation on July 1, 1951. Already by February 1951 the scope of the scheme had been widened to include non-Commonwealth countries, and the USA had agreed to join Australia, Canada, New Zealand and the United Kingdom in making available aid within the framework of the Colombo Plan.

Originally known as the Colombo Plan for Co-operative Economic Development in South and South-East Asia, the Plan adopted its present name after the accession of Papua New Guinea in 1976.

Organization. The principal organ of the Colombo Plan is the Consultative Committee, which directs the working of the plan. The committee, consisting of ministers of the member countries, meets annually to discuss the annual reports of the individual members, and to co-ordinate the schemes for aid. The meetings of the committee are also attended by representatives of the Asian Development Bank, the World Bank (IBRD), the International Labour Organization, the UN Economic Commission for Asia and the Far East, the UN Development Programme, the Asian Productivity Organization, the Commonwealth Secretariat and the Colombo Plan Bureau.

The Council for Technical Co-operation in Asia and the Pacific is a consultative organ concerned specifically with the problems of technical co-operation. It is also responsible for the dissemination of information on the Colombo Plan as a whole. The council, which meets in Colombo several times a year, is composed of representatives of the member countries' governments.

The decisions of the Council for Technical Co-operation are executed by the Colombo Plan Bureau. The work of the bureau includes the keeping of records of all technical assistance given and received and of capital aid projects; the provision of information to member governments, in particular on the training facilities, experts and equipment available; and the issuing of progress reports and statistics.

Forms of Aid. Although the bulk of aid within the framework of the Colombo Plan is provided by Australia, Britain, Canada, Japan and the United States, economic co-operation among the other members of the plan is encouraged.

Economic assistance is provided through capital aid in the form of grants and loans for national projects, and through technical aid in the form of experts, facilities for technical training and the supply of special equipment.

By the end of 1977 the total of Colombo Plan aid in the form of capital and technical assistance exceeded US$52,500 million, of which the United States had provided almost three-quarters and the United

Kingdom nearly $3,300 million. Of the total, some $3,000 million had been spent on the training of 130,000 people and on providing the services of 35,000 experts. A number of member countries which had originally been recipients of aid only had themselves become donors, notably India, which had contributed $483,000,000 in capital aid and technical assistance and had thus become the sixth among the major donors (after the United States, Japan, the United Kingdom, Canada and Australia), while other members contributing were Pakistan, the Republic of Korea, Singapore, Thailand, Sri Lanka, the Philippines, Malaysia and Burma.

In 1973 the Colombo Plan launched a Drug Advisory Programme (financed by the United States) with the object of eliminating the causes of drug abuse and remedying its effects in member states.

In 1974 the Plan established a Staff College for Technician Education in Singapore, with all member countries contributing to its operating costs.

Caribbean Community (CARICOM)

Headquarters: Georgetown, Guyana.

Members: Antigua, Barbados, Belize, Dominica, Grenada, Guyana, Jamaica, Montserrat, St Kitts-Nevis-Anguilla, St Lucia, St Vincent and the Grenadines, and Trinidad and Tobago. (The Bahamas are not a member but contribute to the budget of CARICOM's secretariat and attend meetings of various CARICOM institutions.)

The CARICOM was formed on Aug. 1, 1973, under the Treaty of Chaguaramas (Trinidad) signed on July 4, 1973, with the object of achieving economic integration in a Caribbean Common Market, which replaced an earlier Caribbean Free Trade Association (CARIFTA) set up in 1968 by Antigua, Barbados, Dominica, Grenada, Guyana, Jamaica, Montserrat, St Kitts-Nevis-Anguilla, St Lucia, St Vincent and Trinidad and Tobago, and joined by Belize (then British Honduras) in 1971.

The organs of the CARICOM are (i) a heads of government conference, which is the organization's final authority and determines its policies; (ii) a Common Market Council consisting of one minister from each member state and responsible for the development and management of the Common Market and for the settlement of any disputes; and (iii) a secretariat with five divisions (for trade, economics and statistics; sectoral policy and planning; functional co-operation; legal affairs; and general services and administration). There are also a conference of ministers responsible for health, and standing committees of other ministers (responsible for education, labour, foreign affairs, finance, agriculture, mines, industry and transport).

The decision to establish the CARICOM had been reached at a conference of the heads of government of Commonwealth Caribbean countries in Georgetown (Guyana) on April 9-12, 1973, when a Georgetown Accord was signed on the deepening of the integration process within CARIFTA with a view to enabling all member states to share equitably in the benefits of integration. (The CARIFTA members had been grouped as "more developed countries"—MDCs, i.e. Barbados, Guyana, Jamaica, and Trinidad and Tobago—and "less developed countries"—LDCs, i.e. the other CARIFTA member countries.)

At a meeting of the Prime Ministers of Barbados, Guyana, Jamaica and Trinidad and Tobago in Port of Spain (Trinidad) on June 9, 1976, it was agreed inter alia to grant Jamaica short- and long-term loans and credits to alleviate economic difficulties which had arisen in that country, to introduce a common protective policy including quantitative restrictions on imports from outside the region, to encourage further joint industrial projects, and to set up a **Caribbean Food Corporation** in September 1976.

In view of further disparities in the development of CARICOM member states, a **Caribbean Development Facility** (CDF) was set up after a meeting of a Caribbean Group for Co-operation in Economic Development (formed under World Bank auspices) held in Washington in June 1978 and attended by representatives of 31 governments and 16 international and regional agencies. The initial size of the CDF was fixed at US$125,000,000, and at a further meeting of the Group held in Washington in June 1979 aid pledges of $183,000,000 were made for the year commencing on July 1, 1979. Beneficiaries would be all CARICOM member states except Trinidad and Tobago, and also the Bahamas, the Dominican Republic, Haiti, the Netherlands Antilles and Suriname, the principal beneficiaries being Jamaica ($53,000,000) and Guyana ($23,000,000).

Trinidad and Tobago, economically the strongest member of the CARICOM, had during 1978-79 favoured the conclusion of bilaterally agreed arrangements involving financial and economic aid and had not supported economic arrangements between CARICOM member states and third countries nor help to establish or develop institutions or enterprises in competition with Trinidad and Tobago interests. A more balanced picture of CARICOM's internal relations emerged by June 1979, when Guyana announced that its imports from other member states had in 1978 returned to the level of 1976 and Jamaica removed all quota restrictions on intra-regional trade which it had previously imposed. However, no new policy decisions were taken as the heads of government conference was not convened, having held its last meeting in 1976.

Conferences of Heads of Government of Asian and Pacific Commonwealth Member States

A first regional conference of heads of government of Asian and Pacific Commonwealth member countries was held in Sydney (Australia) on Feb. 13-16, 1978, with the principal object of encouraging co-operation for regional development. The participants in the conference acknowledged their collective responsibility for rendering special assistance to the small Commonwealth member states in the region.

A second such conference, held in New Delhi on Sept. 4-8, 1980, expressed its "full support for the independence, sovereignty, territorial integrity and non-aligned status of Afghanistan and other countries of the region". It also called for an opportunity to be afforded to all peoples of the South Pacific "to exercise their right to self-determination" and "commended the desire of Pacific island countries for greater self-reliance through increased mutual co-operation among themselves".

Organization of East Caribbean States (OECS)

At a meeting held in St Lucia in May 1979 by ministers of the seven participants in meetings of the West Indies (Associated States) Council of Ministers (set up on Nov. 1, 1966), it was decided to form an Organization of East Caribbean States (OECS) which would consist of Antigua, Dominica, Grenada, Montserrat, St Kitts-Nevis, St Lucia and St Vincent, and which would be responsible for co-ordination of the member states' foreign policy and relations with international institutions.

The OECS was also given responsibility for (i) the **East Caribbean Currency Authority**, which had been established in 1965 to issue and manage a common currency (the East Caribbean dollar) for Antigua, Barbados, Dominica, Montserrat, St Kitts-Nevis-Anguilla, St Lucia and St Vincent and had been joined by Grenada in 1968, whereas Barbados had withdrawn from it in 1974; (ii) the **East Caribbean Common Market,** which had been established in 1968 and had later become an associate institution of the CARICOM; and (iii) the **East Caribbean Supreme Court,** until 1978 the Supreme Court of Grenada and the West Indies Associated States.

It was also decided that the OECS secretariat and the headquarters of the East Caribbean Supreme Court should be located in St Lucia.

Under a Declaration of St George's, signed at St George's (the capital of Grenada) in July 1979 by the (left-wing) Prime Ministers of Dominica, Grenada and St Lucia, a common position was established by the three governments, calling for free movement of nationals of the three states, the exchange of information on oil exploration and energy matters, the establishment of a regional military force for defence against aggression and the pursuit of policies based on independence and non-alignment.

Major Treaties of the United Kingdom

ANZUK Agreements

In succession to an Anglo-Malaysian Defence Treaty (of Oct. 12, 1957), which was terminated on Oct. 31, 1971, agreements were signed between Australia, Britain and New Zealand to implement as from Nov. 1, 1971, a decision made on April 16, 1971, to set up a joint ANZUK force for the defence of Malaysia and Singapore.

Under these agreements the five Governments decided to establish (1) an Integrated Air Defence System for Malaysia and Singapore under the responsibility of a joint Air Defence Council; (2) a Joint Consultative Council; and (3) continued stationing of Australian, New Zealand and United Kingdom armed forces in Malaysia and Singapore.

The United Kingdom, however, withdrew its ANZUK forces in 1975-76, the last of them leaving Singapore on March 31, 1976.

Important Bilateral Treaties Between Britain and Commonwealth Countries

Britain and Australia. An agreement on the construction of a rocket-testing range in Central Australia (the Woomera range) was announced on May 13, 1947. The cost of maintaining the range, used in a joint British-Australian scheme for the development of guided weapons, is shared by the two governments under an agreement of Sept. 13, 1953.

On April 4, 1955, it was announced that the Australian and British Governments had agreed on the establishment of a new atomic testing ground, to be known as Maralinga, in the South Australian desert.

An agreement concerning nuclear transfers between the two countries, signed on July 24, 1979, entered into force on the same day.

Defence Agreements with Uganda and Kenya. After British troops had helped to put down mutinies in the Uganda and Kenya Armies in January 1964, two new defence agreements were concluded by the British Government on March 3 and March 6, 1964, with the Governments of Uganda and Kenya respectively. The agreements provided for the continuation of British assistance in the command and training of the Uganda and Kenya Armies. Under the agreement with Kenya, Britain was granted training facilities for the Army, overflying and staging rights for the RAF, and port maintenance facilities at Mombasa for the Royal Navy.

The agreement between Britain and Uganda became inoperative by 1975, when Uganda was receiving considerable supplies of Soviet weapons.

UK and Tonga Treaty of Friendship. A treaty of friendship between Britain and Tonga was signed on Aug. 25, 1958, to replace the treaty of 1900 by which Tonga became a British-protected state while remaining self-governing. The treaty provided for greater autonomy for Tonga, which became a sovereign and independent member of the Commonwealth on June 4, 1970.

Britain and Mauritius. A six-year defence agreement signed on March 12, 1968 (when Mauritius attained its independence) provided for joint consultations on any request for assistance by the Government of Mauritius in the event of a threat to the island's internal security and also, inter alia, for the continuation of British facilities on the island.

Britain and Brunei. A treaty of friendship and co-operation, superseding an agreement concluded in 1959 (when Brunei's first written Constitution was promulgated) and amended in 1971 (when Brunei was given full internal self-government, with responsibility for public order) was initialled in London on Sept. 28, 1978, and signed in Brunei on Jan. 7, 1979.

The treaty laid down that by the end of 1983 the Sultanate of Brunei would "assume its full international responsibilities as a sovereign and independent state" and Britain's remaining responsibility for Brunei's defence and external affairs would be terminated. Until that time, however, Britain would keep in Brunei a Gurkha battalion, the costs of which had been met by the Brunei Government since 1968.

Britain and Singapore. An agreement regarding UK assistance for the armed forces of Singapore and the arrangement for a UK force in Singapore, signed on Dec. 1, 1971, was amended on July 26, 1978.

Britain and Tuvalu. At a 1978 constitutional conference it was agreed that Britain's aid to Tuvalu after the latter's achievement of independence would include capital grants for development projects (£2,620,000 for 1978-80), budgetary support (about £875,000 in 1979) and a special development fund (£2,500,000).

British Treaties with Countries outside the Commonwealth

Treaties concluded by the United Kingdom within the NATO framework may be found in the section on the North Atlantic Treaty Organization [pages 164-87] except for those with the USA, which are included in the section on US Defence Treaties [pages 307-17]. A number of other treaties involving Britain, not mentioned elsewhere in this book, are given below.

Anglo-Portuguese Alliance. A treaty of alliance concluded between King Edward III of England and King Ferdinand and Queen Eleanor of Portugal in 1373 provided for "perpetual friendship" between the two countries and mutual assistance "by sea and by land against all men".

This treaty, variously reinforced between 1386 and 1815, was reaffirmed by the Portuguese Government early in World War II and was invoked by the British Government in connexion with a temporary agreement, announced on Oct. 12, 1943, on the use by Britain of facilities in the Azores.

Treaty of Utrecht. Under the Treaty of Utrecht of 1713, which ended the War of the Spanish Succession and by which Spain's power in Europe was greatly reduced, Britain obtained the "full and intire propriety of the Town and Castle of Gibraltar, together with the port fortifications and forts thereunto belonging". However, if Britain should wish to "grant, sell or by any means alienate" ownership of Gibraltar, the treaty stated that Spain should be given first preference to it.

While the provisions of the treaty have not been challenged by Spain, there have been repeated disputes between Britain and Spain, e.g. in 1854 and 1908, when Spain alleged that Britain had moved Gibraltar's frontier farther north, and since 1950 when Britain first granted increased rights of internal government to the people of Gibraltar—the Spanish Government considering the new political institutions in Gibraltar to be incompatible with the Treaty of Utrecht.

The Cyprus Agreements. Agreement on the future of Cyprus was reached in London on Feb. 19, 1959, between the British, Greek and Turkish Governments and representatives of the Greek and Turkish communities in Cyprus. This agreement followed a previous agreement reached in Zürich on Feb. 11, 1959, between the Governments of Greece and Turkey.

The documents embodying these agreements, published on Feb. 23, 1959, included:

(1) A Greco-Turkish declaration on the "Basic Structure of the Republic of Cyprus";

(2) a Treaty of Guarantee between Cyprus on the one hand, and Britain, Greece and Turkey on the other, whereby Britain, Greece and Turkey undertook to recognize and maintain "the independence, territorial integrity and security" of the Republic of Cyprus;

(3) a Treaty of Alliance between Greece, Turkey and Cyprus, whereby the three countries undertook to "co-operate for their common defence" and to "resist any attack or aggression, direct or indirect, against the independence and territorial integrity of the Republic of Cyprus";

(4) a Declaration by the British Government in which it relinquished sovereignty over the island to the Republic of Cyprus, except for two areas [see below].

It was not until July 1960 that the British and Cypriot Governments reached final agreement on the areas of the bases remaining under British sovereignty, the agreement being embodied in the Treaty of Establishment, published on July 7, 1960. This treaty defined the areas of the two bases, Akrotiri and Dhekelia, and gave Britain the right to use 31 defence sites and installations, and 10 training areas and ranges in other parts of the island.

On April 14, 1964, Cyprus unilaterally abrogated the Treaty of Alliance with Turkey.

Following the invasion of Cyprus by Turkish forces on July 20, 1974, new agreements were reached by the Foreign Ministers of Greece, Turkey and the United Kingdom in Geneva on July 30, 1974, on (i) a ceasefire, (ii) the establishment of a security zone with UN participation, (iii) the evacuation and protection by the UN Peacekeeping Force (UNFICYP—see page 22) of Turkish Cypriot enclaves occupied by Greek or Greek Cypriot forces, (iv) an exchange of prisoners of war and (v) implementation "in the shortest possible time" of a UN Security Council resolution of June 20, 1974, calling inter alia for the withdrawal from Cyprus of foreign forces other than those present under international agreements. The three powers, however, reached no agreement on the constitutional future of Cyprus, nor did the new Geneva agreements lead to the withdrawal of Turkish forces from the island.

Britain and Nepal. (1) An agreement on the employment of Gurkha troops in the British Army was signed on Nov. 9, 1947.

(2) A treaty of peace and friendship was signed on Oct. 30, 1950. The treaty, which laid down that each country would acknowledge and respect the independence of the other, replaced an earlier treaty of 1923, which had been made partially invalid through the independence of India and Pakistan.

Britain and Venezuela: Settlement of Territorial Dispute. An agreement on procedure for the settlement of a territorial dispute between Britain and Venezuela, relating to some 60,000 square miles of territory in British Guiana (now Guyana), was signed on Feb. 17, 1966. Guyana became a party to the treaty on attaining independence on May 26, 1966.

Treaties with Countries in the Persian Gulf Area. (1) *Britain-Bahrain.* A treaty of friendship, signed on Aug. 15, 1971, replaced earlier treaties of 1882 and 1892.

(2) *Britain-Qatar.* A treaty of friendship came into force on Sept. 1, 1971, replacing a treaty of 1916 under which Britain had been responsible for Qatar's defence and foreign relations.

(3) *Britain-United Arab Emirates.* A treaty of friendship, concluded on Dec. 2, 1971, replaced earlier 150-year-old treaties with the Trucial Coast sheikhdoms.

Britain and Japan. An atomic energy co-operation agreement was signed on March 6, 1968.

Britain and Pakistan. An atomic energy co-operation agreement was signed on July 26, 1970.

Britain and Thailand. A treaty of commerce and navigation signed in Bangkok on Nov. 23, 1937, was temporarily prolonged by an exchange of notes on Sept. 24-Nov. 15, 1973.

BRITISH AGREEMENTS WITH OTHER COUNTRIES IN EUROPE

Britain and Denmark (then including Iceland). A treaty of peace and commerce was concluded on Feb. 13, 1666, and July 11, 1670, and was revised on Jan. 14, 1814.

Britain and Federal Republic of Germany. A treaty on the delimitation of the continental shelf below the North Sea between the two countries was signed on Nov. 25, 1971, and came into force on Dec. 7, 1972.

Britain, Federal Republic of Germany and Netherlands. Atomic energy co-operation agreements between the three countries were concluded on Nov. 24, 1968, and Dec. 19, 1969.

Britain and Norway. An atomic energy co-operation agreement was signed in March 1968.

Britain and Sweden. A treaty of peace and commerce was signed on Oct. 21, 1661; a treaty of commerce and alliance on Feb. 5, 1766; and a treaty of peace, union and friendship at Örebro on July 18, 1812.

Britain and Switzerland. (1) A treaty of friendship, commerce and reciprocal establishment was signed on Sept. 6, 1855, in force from March 6, 1856, and applied to Liechtenstein on April 26, 1924, and July 14, 1947.

(2) A co-operation agreement on the use of atomic energy for peaceful purposes was signed on Aug. 11, 1964.

Treaties and Agreements concluded by Commonwealth Countries

Australian Treaties

Treaties and Agreements with Other Commonwealth Countries

Australia and India. An agreement on Australian aid in the defence of India with effect from Dec. 1, 1962, was signed in New Delhi on Dec. 3, 1963. It related to the Sino-Indian border conflict at the time.

Australia and New Zealand. An agreement on integrated defence planning and buying of defence equipment was announced on Aug. 28, 1969.

Australia and Papua New Guinea. A treaty on the demarcation of the Torres Strait border between Australia and Papua New Guinea was signed in Sydney (New South Wales) on Dec. 18, 1978. The treaty involved agreement on a seabed resources delimitation line between the two countries to the north of several islands under Australian sovereignty and the recognition of a "protected zone" which included islands on both sides of the above delimitation line and in which the inhabitants would enjoy freedom of movement in pursuit of their traditional way of life, mining and oil drilling would be prohibited for 10 years, and there would be an "equitable division" of fishing rights.

Treaties and Agreements with Non-Commonwealth Countries in South-East Asia and the Pacific

Australia and Indonesia. An agreement on the establishment of seabed boundaries between the two countries was signed in Canberra on May 18, 1971. It was supplemented by a further agreement of Oct. 9, 1972, on such boundaries in the area of the Timor and Arafura Seas. Both agreements came into force on Nov. 8, 1973.

Australia and Japan. (1) An agreement on co-operation in the peaceful uses of atomic energy was signed on Feb. 21, 1972, and came into force on July 28, 1972.

(2) A basic treaty of friendship and co-operation between the two countries was signed in Tokyo on June 16, 1976. Under this treaty the two sides agreed (i) to "endeavour to facilitate, strengthen and diversify mutual understanding and co-operation in . . . the political, economic, labour relations, human rights, legal, scientific, technological, social, cultural, professional, sporting and environmental fields"; (ii) to promote the further strengthening and development of trade on a fair and stable basis, recognizing each other as a "stable and reliable" supplier and market; (iii) to accord to each other's nationals "fair and equitable treatment" with respect to their entry, stay, departure and business and professional activities; and (iv) to review periodically the general operation of the treaty at ministerial level.

Instruments of ratification of the treaty were exchanged in Canberra on July 21, 1977, and the treaty came into force on Aug. 20 of that year.

Australia and Republic of Korea. An agreement concerning co-operation in the peaceful uses of nuclear energy and the transfer of nuclear material was signed and entered into force on May 2, 1979.

Australia and Philippines. An agreement on safeguards for uranium supplied to the Philippines by Australia was signed on Aug. 8, 1978.

Treaties and Agreements with Countries outside the Pacific and South-East Asian Region

Treaties and agreements have been concluded by Australia with countries outside South-East Asia and the Pacific as follows:

Argentina. Treaty of amity, commerce and navigation: Feb. 2, 1825.

Canada. Agreement on co-operation in the peaceful uses of atomic energy: Aug. 5, 1959.

Ecuador. Treaty of amity, commerce and navigation: April 18, 1825.

Ethiopia. Treaty of friendship: May 14, 1897.

Finland. Agreement on the transfer of nuclear material between Australia and Finland: July 20, 1978; entry into force on Feb. 9, 1980.

Federal Republic of Germany. (1) Agreement on scientific and technological co-operation: Aug. 24, 1976; entry into force on Oct. 25, 1976.
(2) Exchange of notes constituting an agreement concerning the launching of two scientific payloads from Woomera for scientific purposes: Feb. 16, 1979.
(3) Agreement for the reciprocal safeguarding of classified material: Nov. 27, 1979.

Jordan. Agreement on co-operation: Oct. 21, 1977; entry into force on Sept. 5, 1978.

Peru. Treaty of friendship, commerce and navigation: April 10, 1850.

Switzerland. Treaty of friendship, commerce and reciprocal establishment: Sept. 26, 1855, with additional convention signed on March 30, 1914.

United States. (1) Agreement on co-operation concerning the civil use of atomic energy: June 22, 1956; entry into force May 28, 1857; amended on Sept. 14, 1960, with effect from March 6, 1961, and on April 11, 1967, with effect from May 5, 1967.
(2) Agreement relating to scientific and technical co-operation: Oct. 16, 1968; extended on July 30, 1973, and on Oct. 10, 1978.
(3) Agreement on the management and operation of a joint geological and geophysical research station at Alice Springs: Feb. 28, 1978.
(4) Interim agreement on peaceful nuclear co-operation: Aug. 4, 1978.

Treaties and Agreements between Other Commonwealth Member States

Bangladesh and Canada. A general agreement concerning development co-operation was signed on Dec. 14, 1979.

Bangladesh and India. (1) A 25-year treaty of friendship and co-operation, signed in Dacca on May 19, 1972, provided inter alia that neither country would participate in any military alliance directed against the other; both would refrain from aggres-

sion against each other; neither would give any assistance to a third party involved in an armed conflict against the other; and, in the event of an attack or threat of attack against either, both parties would immediately enter into consultations in order to take measures to eliminate the threat.
(2) Among other agreements concluded between Bangladesh and India was one (of April 9, 1972) providing for the establishment of a permanent Joint River Commission to formulate plans for flood control, irrigation projects and the linking of power grids, and on April 29, 1972, it was officially announced that complete agreement on these and other matters had been reached.
(3) A border demarcation agreement signed in May 1974, provided for the exchange of 125 Indian enclaves in Bangladesh for 75 Bangladesh enclaves in India without payment of compensation for the additional areas going to Bangladesh. In a joint declaration issued on the same day agreement was announced on economic co-operation between the two countries, with India granting credits for various projects in Bangladesh and also for Indian imports from that country.
(4) An agreement on the division of the Ganges waters at the Farakka barrage (on the Indian side of the two countries' border), which had come into operation on April 21, 1975, was signed on Nov. 5, 1977.

Canada and India. (1) An exchange of notes implementing a statement of principles for co-operative economic development of India took place on Sept. 10, 1951.
(2) A nuclear reactor agreement was concluded on April 28, 1956.
(3) An agreement on the construction of the Kundah hydroelectric projects (under the Colombo Plan—see page 265) was signed on Dec. 29, 1956.
(4) An atomic energy co-operation agreement was signed on Nov. 15, 1963.

Canada and Sri Lanka. An exchange of notes implementing a statement of principles for co-operative development of Ceylon (now Sri Lanka) took place on July 11, 1952.

India and Sri Lanka. (1) An agreement on the demarcation of the boundary between India and Sri Lanka in the waters of the Palk Strait (between the two countries) was signed on June 28, 1974. Under this agreement India recognized Sri Lanka's claim to the (uninhabited) island of Kachchativu (which had been in dispute since 1910).
(2) An agreement on the maritime boundary between the two countries in the Gulf

of Mannar (east of Sri Lanka) and the Bay of Bengal was signed on March 23, 1976, and came into force on May 10 of that year. It supplemented the above agreement on the Palk Strait and recognized each country's economic zone extending to 200 miles from the coastline, or to the median line where these zones overlapped.

Treaties and Agreements of Other Commonwealth Countries with Countries outside the Commonwealth

Bangladesh and Pakistan. A first trade agreement signed in Islamabad on April 30, 1976, provided for most-favoured-nation treatment in trade between the two countries.

Bangladesh and Switzerland. A technical co-operation agreement between the two countries was signed on April 7, 1976.

Canada and Japan. (1) An agreement for co-operation in the peaceful uses of atomic energy, signed on July 2, 1979, provided inter alia for Canadian supplies of uranium to Japan. The agreement was amended on Aug. 22, 1980.

(2) An interim agreement initialled in Tokyo on Jan. 26, 1978, had provided for the resumption of Canadian uranium supplies to Japan, which had been suspended by Canada since Jan. 1, 1977.

Canada and Republic of Korea. An agreement for the purchase of a heavy-water nuclear reactor from Canada was signed by the Republic of Korea on Jan. 26, 1976.

Canada and Pakistan. (1) An agreement on the peaceful uses of atomic energy was signed on May 14, 1959.

(2) An exchange of notes implementing a statement of principles for co-operative economic development of Pakistan took place on Sept. 10, 1951.

Cook Islands and United States. In a treaty signed in June 1980 the United States formally relinquished claims to four northern islands in the Cook Islands group (dating back to 1856), while provisions were also agreed on the overlap area of the respective offshore economic zones of American Samoa and the Cook Islands.

India and Afghanistan. A treaty of peace and friendship, providing for closer commercial, cultural, industrial and agricultural relations between the two countries, was signed on Jan. 4, 1950. Valid in the first instance for five years, the treaty can be terminated by either party at six months' notice.

India and Bhutan. A treaty of "perpetual peace and friendship" was signed on Aug. 8, 1949. It provided, inter alia, that India would not interfere in the internal administration of Bhutan; the Government of Bhutan would be guided by the advice of the Indian Government in its external relations; India would return to Bhutan an area of 32 square miles in the Dewangiri district; and there would be freedom of trade and commerce between the two countries.

India and Burma. An agreement providing for the demarcation of the frontier between India and Burma was signed on March 19, 1967.

India and Egypt. An atomic energy co-operation agreement was signed in September 1962.

India and Federal Republic of Germany. Various agreements concluded between the two countries included (i) an agreement on co-operation in the peaceful uses of nuclear energy and in space research, signed on Oct. 5, 1971, and in force from May 19, 1972; (ii) an agreement on technical co-operation, signed on Dec. 31, 1971, and amended with effect from March 1, 1979; and (iii) an agreement on co-operation in scientific research and technological development, signed on Jan. 30-March 7, 1974.

India and Indonesia. (1) An agreement delimiting the continental shelf boundary between India and Indonesia was signed on Aug. 8, 1974, and came into force on Dec. 17 of that year.

(2) Under an agreement signed in New Delhi on Jan. 14, 1977, the two countries redefined their respective sea boundaries, extending the existing median line 48 nautical miles off the coasts of both the (Indian) Nicobar Islands and Sumatra (established under the 1974 agreement) north-eastwards into the Andaman Sea (towards the Isthmus of Kra) to a possible trijunction point between the waters of India, Indonesia and Thailand, and south-westwards into the Indian Ocean up to a distance of 200 miles from the two countries' respective coasts—with each country exercising sovereignty and exclusive jurisdiction over the continental shelf and the seabed resources within the newly agreed boundaries. Instruments of ratification of this agreement were exchanged on Aug. 15, 1977.

India, Indonesia and Thailand. A trilateral agreement, determining the trijunction point of the seabed boundaries of the three countries in the Andaman Sea (roughly 100 nautical miles from the nearest point of their respective coastlines), was signed in New Delhi on June 22, 1978 (thus complementing the bilateral agreements concluded between the three countries on their common seabed boundaries in the Andaman Sea).

India and Italy. An exchange of notes on economic co-operation took place in New Delhi on Oct. 30, 1975.

India and Maldives. An agreement signed on Dec. 28, 1976, defined the maritime boundary between the two countries as running mainly along the median line between the west coast of India and Maldives and embracing an area extending westwards into the Arabian Sea up to 200 nautical miles from the western atoll of Maldives. It also provided for exclusive jurisdiction over the continental shelf and the exclusive economic zone and their resources for each state on its own side of the boundary.

India and Nepal. (1) A treaty providing for "everlasting peace and friendship" between the Governments of India and Nepal was signed on July 31, 1950. The treaty states, inter alia, that the two countries recognize the "complete sovereignty, territorial integrity and independence" of each other; that Nepal should be free to import from and through Indian territory the arms, ammunition, material and equipment necessary for her security; and that each government would "give, to nationals of the other in its territory, national treatment with regard to participation in the industrial and economic development of such territory . . .".

Cancellation of the arms agreement by Nepal was announced on June 24, 1969.

(2) Two treaties which were signed on March 17, 1978, and came into force on March 25 of that year were (i) a seven-year treaty on transit, providing Nepal and Bangladesh with free access across Indian territory to each other's markets and (ii) a five-year trade treaty (including preferences for a wider range of Nepalese-manufactured goods in Indian markets). At the same time agreement was reached on the control of unauthorized trade between the two countries.

(3) Further co-operation agreements were signed in April and September 1978, involving the promotion of Nepal's industrialization and the construction of a hydro-electric project.

India and Pakistan. (1) *Settlement of Border Disputes.* Agreements were concluded between the Governments of India and Pakistan in September 1958 and October 1959 in regard to a number of border dis-

putes. The latter agreement also laid down "ground rules" governing the conduct of army and police forces on both sides, and principles for provisional demarcation.

(2) *The Indus Waters Treaty.* A treaty settling the long-standing dispute between India and Pakistan regarding the allocation of the waters of the Indus river system was signed on Sept. 19, 1960. Under the treaty, the waters of the three eastern Rivers (Ravi, Beas and Sutlej) are in general allocated to India, those of the three western Rivers (Indus, Jhelum and Chenab) to Pakistan. The treaty states that "both countries recognize their common interest in the optimum development of the rivers, and declare their intention to co-operate by mutual agreement to the fullest possible extent". Provision was made for the setting up of a Permanent Indus Commission, composed of one member appointed by each government and with responsibility for implementing the provisions of the treaty.

(3) *The Tashkent Declaration* was signed at the end of a meeting between Prime Minister Shastri of India and President Ayub Khan of Pakistan, held at Tashkent in Uzbekistan (USSR) on Jan. 4-10, 1966, in an attempt to solve the Indo-Pakistani dispute which had reached a crisis with the outbreak of hostilities over Kashmir in August 1965. Under the declaration India and Pakistan pledged themselves, inter alia, to restore "normal and peaceful relations" between the two countries; to withdraw their armed forces, not later than Feb. 25, 1966, to the positions they held before the outbreak of hostilities; to repatriate captured prisoners of war; to restore diplomatic and economic relations between the two countries; to end hostile propaganda; and to deal with the question of refugees and illegal immigrants.

(4) *The Simla Agreement,* signed on July 3, 1972, and ratified by Pakistan on July 15 and by India on Aug. 1-3, came into effect on Aug. 4, 1972. It was designed to end conflict and confrontation between the two countries after the war which had led to the secession of Bangladesh from Pakistan. The agreement provided in particular for the withdrawal of armed forces to their side of the international border between the two countries, while in Jammu and Kashmir both sides would respect the line of control which had resulted from a ceasefire on Dec. 17, 1971—"without prejudice to the recognized position of either side" on the status of Jammu and Kashmir.

(5) *The 1973 Repatriation Agreement.* An agreement was signed by India and Pakistan on Aug. 28, 1973, in New Delhi on the repatriation of Pakistani prisoners of war and civilian internees held since the

1971 conflict, as well as nationals of Bangladesh in Pakistan and Pakistanis in Bangladesh, with the exception of 195 prisoners of war. It was agreed that no trials of these 195 should take place during the repatriation period, but that on completion of repatriation Bangladesh, India and Pakistan would discuss and settle their fate.

(6) *Agreements on Normalization of Relations.* Agreements on the resumption of trade links between the two countries (which had been severed since the 1965 war) were (i) a protocol on the resumption of shipping services signed on Jan. 15, 1975, and (ii) a trade agreement of Jan. 23, 1975. Agreement on the restoration of air links, rail traffic and diplomatic relations was reached in Islamabad on May 14, 1976.

India and Philippines. A treaty affirming that there should be "perpetual peace and everlasting amity" between the two countries was signed on July 11, 1952. It is to remain in force unless terminated by either side at one year's notice.

India and Portugal. Under an agreement signed in New York on Sept. 24, 1974, Portugal expressed its readiness to relinquish all claims to Portugal's former Indian territories (Goa, Daman, Diu, Dadra and Nagar Haveli), over which India would have full sovereignty while co-operating with Portugal to preserve the Portuguese culture, language and religious monuments in these areas.

India and Switzerland. A technical and scientific co-operation agreement was signed on Sept. 26, 1966.

India and Thailand. An agreement defining the seabed boundary between the two countries in the Andaman Sea, generally on the principle of the median line, was signed in New Delhi on June 22, 1978.

India and Turkey. An agreement on economic and technical co-operation between the two countries was signed in New Delhi on July 13, 1978.

India and the United States. (1) An atomic energy co-operation agreement was signed in July 1963.

(2) An agreement on the establishment of a joint Indo-American commission on economic, commercial, scientific, technological, educational and cultural co-operation was signed on Oct. 28, 1974.

(3) An arms embargo imposed by the United States against both India and Pakistan during their 1965 war was, after being relaxed earlier, finally lifted by the USA on Feb. 24, 1975.

Kiribati and United States. Under a treaty of friendship signed by the Republic of Kiribati and the United States in September 1979, the USA formally relinquished its claim to the eight Phoenix Islands, the five Southern Line Islands and Kiritimati (Christmas) Island in the Northern Line Islands, with the treaty also providing for consultation on any military use of these 14 islands by third parties, and for the use by third parties for military purposes of the facilities constructed by the United States on three of these islands (Enderbury, Kanton and Orona) to be subject to US agreement.

Malaysia and Indonesia. A treaty of friendship between Indonesia and Malaysia and another treaty establishing a boundary through the Straits of Malacca (between Sumatra and the Malay Peninsula) were signed in Kuala Lumpur on March 17, 1970. The treaty of friendship replaced an earlier treaty of April 17, 1959, and formally ended a period of "confrontation" between the two countries.

On Nov. 16, 1971, both governments issued a declaration claiming sovereignty of the Straits, which they no longer considered to be an international waterway.

(While Malaysia had extended its territorial waters limit to 12 nautical miles in August 1969, Indonesia had, in a proclamation issued on Dec. 14, 1957, claimed that all waters "around, between and connecting the islands or part of the islands of the Indonesian archipelago" were "an integral part of the inland waters subject to the absolute sovereignty of Indonesia" and had at the same time fixed the limit of Indonesia's territorial waters at 12 nautical miles "measured from straight base lines connecting the outermost points of the Republic of Indonesia", thus adding about 660,000 nautical square miles to the country's territory and thereby doubling it. This proclamation had, however, been rejected by the principal sea-faring nations of the world.)

Malaysia and Japan. During a visit to Malaysia by the Prime Minister of Japan it was agreed on Aug. 10, 1977, to promote co-operative relations between the two countries in the political, economic and cultural fields, with Japan granting loans to assist Malaysia's economic development plan for 1976-80 (this assistance including a credit equivalent to $80,000,000 for 1977).

Malaysia and Thailand. (1) An agreement on armed forces' co-operation against communist guerrillas in the Thai-Malaysian border region was signed in Bangkok on March 7, 1970.

(2) A border agreement signed in Bang-

kok on March 4, 1977, provided for combined operations by both countries' security forces against communist guerrillas, with these forces being allowed to cross the border for a limited period.

Malta and Italy. For 1980 agreement between these two countries, see page 155.

Papua New Guinea and Indonesia. (1) A border agreement designed to end the frontier problem between Indonesia on the one hand and Australia and Papua New Guinea on the other was signed on Feb. 13, 1974. A further agreement, dealing with the administration of the border between Papua New Guinea and West Irian (Indonesia), was signed on Nov. 13, 1973, and came into force on May 26, 1974. These agreements were replaced by a new one signed on Dec. 17, 1979.

(2) A three-year technical co-operation agreement between Papua New Guinea and Indonesia was signed on June 5, 1979.

Papua New Guinea and Japan. Under an agreement reached on Dec. 8, 1977, Japan undertook to extend loans equivalent to US$15,000,000 for various development projects in Papua New Guinea, with Japan

regarding this agreement as marking "the establishment of a new development co-operation relationship between the two countries".

Sri Lanka and Federal Republic of Germany. An agreement on technical co-operation was signed and came into force on Oct. 13, 1973.

Tonga and Federal Republic of Germany. A treaty of friendly relations and co-operation was signed on June 1, 1977, and came into force on Jan. 2, 1978. An agreement on technical co-operation, signed also on June 1, 1977, came into force on Jan. 31, 1978.

Tuvalu and United States. A treaty of friendship was signed in April 1979, including a renunciation by the United States of any claim (dating back to 1856) to the four southernmost of Tuvalu's nine islands and providing for consultation on security and marine resources.

Western Samoa and Federal Republic of Germany. An agreement on technical co-operation, signed on Dec. 8, 1978, came into force on June 7, 1979.

14. The French Community ("*Communauté*") and Other Francophone Co-operation

Covered in this section are the French Community, its constitution, membership, historical development and related organizations, together with other major multilateral and bilateral co-operation agreements between France and francophone countries.

The French Community ("*Communauté*")

Members: French Republic (including Overseas Departments and Overseas Territories), Central African Republic, Chad, Gabon, Senegal.

Constitution and Membership

The French Union, as defined under the 1946 Constitution of the Fourth Republic of France, was reconstituted as the French Community ("*Communauté*") under the new Constitution of the Fifth Republic, published on Sept. 4, 1958.

Section XII of the Constitution deals with the Community. Its most important provisions are the following:

Art. 77. In the Community established by the present Constitution, the member states enjoy autonomy; they administer themselves and manage their own affairs democratically and freely. There is only one citizenship in the Community. All citizens are equal before the law, whatever their origin, their race or religion. They have the same duties.

Art. 78. The competence of the Community comprises foreign policy, defence, currency, and common economic and financial policy, as well as policy concerning strategic raw materials.

In addition, it comprises (unless excluded by special agreement) control of justice, higher education, the general organization of external and common transport, and telecommunications.

Special agreements may establish other common spheres of competence or regulate the transfer of competences from the Community to one of its members.

Art. 80. The President of the Republic presides over and represents the Community. The organs of the Community are an Executive Council, a Senate, and a Court of Arbitration.

Art. 86. A change in the status of a member state may be requested either by the Republic or by a resolution of the Legislative Assembly of the state concerned which has been confirmed in a local referendum, the organization and supervision of which is carried out by the organs of the Community. The terms of such a change in status are regulated by an agreement approved by the Parliament of the Republic and the Legislative Assembly concerned.

Under the same conditions a member state of the Community may become independent. It then ceases to belong to the Community.

Each overseas territory of France was given the choice of: (i) Becoming a *département* of the French Republic; or (ii) retaining the territorial status it then enjoyed; or (iii) entering the French Community as an autonomous unit.

The Central African Republic, Chad, the Congo, Dahomey (now Benin), Gabon, the Ivory Coast, Madagascar, Mauritania, Niger, Senegal, the Sudan (now Mali) and Upper Volta chose to join the Community.

Early in 1960 the Mali Federation (comprising the Republics of Senegal and the Sudan) and Madagascar decided to ask for full independence while retaining membership in the Community. An amendment to the Constitution, enabling member states to remain in the Community after attaining full independence, was approved by the French National Assembly on May 11, 1960.

Altogether six members of the Community in Africa gained their independence in June and August of 1960. The five remaining members of the old Community—Dahomey, Ivory Coast, Mauritania, Niger and Upper Volta—chose to leave the Community on attaining independence and the Congo and Madagascar withdrew from the Community in 1973. [For dates of independence see table on page 278.] [See also *Conseil de l'Entente*, page 363.]

Development of the Community

The character of the French Community was radically altered by the new, independent status of all its members. This was recognized by the French Government which, on May 18, 1961, agreed upon the creation of new governmental machinery for dealing with the relations of France with French-speaking Africa and Madagascar. The new posts of Minister of Co-operation (to deal with technical assistance), Secretary of State for Political Affairs and Secretary-General for Community, African and Malagasy Affairs were created. The function of the latter was to co-ordinate the activities of the President relating to the countries in question. A Council for African and Malagasy Affairs was also created. The powers exercised by the Community, as laid down in Article 78 of the French Constitution [see above], were transferred to each member country on its attaining independence.

In January 1974 many of the responsibilities of the Secretary-General for Community, African and Malagasy Affairs were transferred to the French Foreign Ministry, and on May 31, 1974, his remaining functions were entrusted to the Minister of Co-operation.

The practical functions of the Community have thus been greatly reduced, its various organs [see above] have fallen into abeyance, and the bond between France and other Community members is now mainly restricted to a co-ordination of foreign policy in certain matters, and to co-operation in the fields of economy and education.

Mutual Defence Agreements

Agreements for co-operation between France and the newly-independent states were signed immediately after the various proclamations of independence. These agreements contained important provisions for mutual military aid. The mutual defence agreement between France and the Mali Federation, which may be taken as typical, stated that France and Mali would assist each other in defence matters; Mali would share with France in the defence of the Community and possibly of other African states; a Franco-Malian defence committee would be set up; Mali would obtain military equipment exclusively from France; and Malian nationals would be free to enlist in the French armed forces.

The defence agreements with the Central African Republic, Chad, the Congo and Gabon were supplemented in 1961, when these four states joined to form, with French co-operation, a "Defence Council of Equatorial Africa".

France also had defence agreements with African countries outside the Community, namely Cameroon, Dahomey, the Ivory Coast, Mauritania, Niger and Togo.

The French military presence in Africa was drastically reduced in the year 1964-65. It was announced on Sept. 29, 1964, that by July 1965 it was intended to reduce the total of French forces in African states and Madagascar to about 6,000 officers and men, from an official total of 27,800 on Oct. 1, 1964. The remaining troops would be regrouped, and there would be four "support points", these being Dakar (Senegal), Abidjan (Ivory Coast), Fort-Lamy (now N'Djaména, Chad) and Diégo-Suarez, Ivato and Antsirabé in Madagascar.

The independence agreements signed by these states included no agreements on their continued membership in the Community.

[For further defence and military co-operation agreements, see pages 280-82.]

Evian Agreements between France and Algeria

After being a member of the French Community—divided into five autonomous territories comprising a total of 13 *départements* (as well as two *départements* of the Saharan territory under the control of the French Minister for the Sahara)— Algeria achieved its independence in 1962 after many years of warfare between French forces and the Algerian National Liberation Front.

On March 18, 1962, after several months of negotiations, a ceasefire agreement between France and the "Provisional Government of the Algerian Republic" was signed at Evian in France, together with a general declaration summarizing the agreements reached on the future of Algeria. The latter agreements included provision for a referendum on self-determination for the people of Algeria (held on July 1, 1962), and outlined the terms of Algerian independence.

Under the provisions concerning Franco-Algerian co-operation, Algeria guaranteed the interests of France and the rights acquired by individuals and organizations, while France, in exchange, undertook to provide technical, cultural and financial assistance to Algeria. Preferential treatment would be applied in certain spheres of trade, and Algeria would be part of the Franc Zone. In the *départements* of the Oases and Sahara the development of subsoil wealth would be carried on under Franco-Algerian co-operation, to be ensured by a technical body for co-operation which would include an equal number of French and Algerian representatives.

The military arrangements laid down in the agreements included the withdrawal of French troops from Algeria, and the leasing to France by Algeria of the naval base of Mers-el-Kébir and the air base of Bou-Sfer for a 15-year period. France was also granted the use of a number of other military areas required by her (including rocket and nuclear-testing installations in the Sahara).

The French Government, however, evacuated the Mers-el-Kébir base on Jan. 31, 1968, and the air base at Bou-Sfer on Dec. 29, 1970.

A convention signed in December 1967 provided for continued Franco-Algerian co-operation.

Bilateral Agreements with France, 1960-64

The table below shows the independence and other bilateral agreements which France concluded with its former African dependencies in the period 1960-64.

	Independence Agreement signed on	Proclamation of Independence	Co-operation and Mutual Defence Agreements signed on
Community Members			
Mali Federation*	April 4, 1960	June 20, 1960	June 22, 1960
Chad	July 12, 1960	Aug. 10, 1960	Aug. 11, 1960
			May 1, 1964
Central African Republic	July 12, 1960	Aug. 12, 1960	Aug. 13, 1960
Gabon	July 15, 1960	Aug. 16, 1960	Aug. 17, 1960
Former Members			
Madagascar	April 2, 1960	June 26, 1960	June 27, 1960
Dahomey	July 11, 1960	Aug. 1, 1960	
Niger	July 11, 1960	Aug. 2, 1960	
Upper Volta	July 11, 1960	Aug. 5, 1960	
Ivory Coast	July 11, 1960	Aug. 6, 1960	
Congo (Brazzaville)	July 12, 1960	Aug. 14, 1960	Aug. 15, 1960
Mauritania	Oct. 19, 1960	Nov. 27, 1960	

* After the secession of Senegal from the Federation of Mali (Aug. 20, 1960) and the subsequent French recognition of Senegal on Sept. 11, 1960, the Republic of Mali declared itself free from all links with France, claiming that the Franco-Malian agreements had been broken by France's recognition of Senegal. Senegal remained within the Community.

The Franc Zone

The Franc Zone provides for the free movement of currency among its members and a guaranteed franc exchange rate. Its members are France (with its Overseas *départements* and Territories, including Mayotte), Benin, Cameroon, the Central African Republic, Chad, the Comoros, the Congo, Gabon, the Ivory Coast, Mali, Niger, Senegal, Togo and Upper Volta.

Mauritania withdrew from the Franc Zone on Feb. 15, 1973, following the Mauritanian Government's decision, first announced on Nov. 28, 1972, to create a national currency. The Malagasy Republic announced its withdrawal from the Franc Zone on May 22, 1973.

The Mali franc became fully convertible on March 29, 1968, following the ratification of Franco-Malian agreements signed in Paris on Dec. 19, 1967, under which France had undertaken to guarantee the Malian franc after a transitional period during which Mali would carry out a monetary and economic reorganization with intensive French technical, economic and financial aid. During a visit to Mali by the French President on Feb. 13-15, 1977, it was agreed that the 1967 monetary agreement would be renewed and that France would give aid to Mali towards railways and road programmes and would take part in mineral exploration.

Other Co-operation between France and Francophone Countries

Central African Countries' Monetary Co-operation

A convention of monetary co-operation was signed with France in 1972 by Cameroon, the Central African Republic, Chad, the Congo and Gabon. The central issuing bank for these countries is the Banque des États de l'Afrique Centrale at Yaoundé (Cameroon).

West African Monetary Union

Members: Benin, the Ivory Coast, Niger, Senegal, Togo and Upper Volta.

The West African Monetary Union (*Union Monétaire Ouest-Africaine*) was established under a treaty which was concluded with France in November 1973 and entered into force in 1974. Its central issuing bank is the Banque Centrale des Etats de l'Afrique de l'Ouest in Dakar (Senegal), founded in 1955 as the Institut d'Emission de l'Afrique de l'Ouest Française et du Togo. Its currency is the CFA (= Communauté Financière Africaine) franc tied to the French franc at the rate of 50 CFA francs to one French franc.

In 1973 the heads of state of the union set up a **West African Development Bank** (Banque Ouest-Africaine de Développement, BOAD) in Lomé (Togo) to promote balanced economic development and integration in West Africa.

Franco-African Conferences

Conferences of the head of state of France and representatives of African states were held from 1973 onwards, and annually from 1975.

First Conference. The first of these conferences, called on the initiative of the President of Niger, took place in Paris on Nov. 13, 1973, under the chairmanship of the French President and was attended by the Presidents of the Central African Republic, Gabon, the Ivory Coast, Niger, Senegal and Upper Volta, the Foreign Ministers of Dahomey (later Benin) and Togo, and the Finance Ministers of the Congo and Mali. It was decided inter alia to hold regular consultations in the future.

Second Conference. The second such conference, held in Bangui (Central African Republic) on March 7-8, 1975, had new participants in the Presidents of Burundi and Rwanda, the Prime Minister of Mauritius and a state commissioner from Zaïre, while the Chief Minister of Seychelles attended as an observer and another observer represented Somalia. The object of the conference was defined by the French President as being the creation of "a new, more equitable economic order" which would require industrialized countries to allocate a fixed percentage of their gross national product to the Third World, which should be added to (and not replaced) by aid from the petroleum-producing countries.

Map 8   African members of Franc Zone

In a final communiqué the participants in the conference expressed their agreement on the need for a thorough reform of the international monetary system and on their wish to follow new guidelines on co-operation, with special account to be taken of the problems of land-locked countries in Africa and of those affected by drought. The participants were also determined to present a united front at a proposed international energy conference, and they stressed that their countries constituted one cultural area and monetary zone, and that they would try to channel Arab oil revenues to the under-developed countries of Africa (through a French fund).

Third Conference. The third conference, held in Paris and Versailles on May 10-11, 1976, had among its participants also ministers from the Cape Verde Islands, Chad, the Comoros, Guinea-Bissau and São Tomé and Príncipe. It was principally concerned with economic problems and decided that an African Solidarity Fund should be set up. In a final communiqué it was stated that "a convergence of views" had been established "on world inflation, the international monetary system, the problem of raw materials, the north-south dialogue and development aid".

The proposed African Solidarity Fund was established under an agreement reached on Dec. 21, 1976, signed by representatives of France, Benin, Burundi, the then Central African Empire, Chad, Gabon, the Ivory Coast, Mali, Mauritania, Niger, Rwanda, Senegal, Togo, Upper Volta and Zaïre, and providing for a fund totalling the equivalent of 100,000,000 French francs (or $20,000,000), of which it was reported that France would contribute one-half.

Fourth Conference. The fourth conference was held in Dakar on April 20-21, 1977, after Guinea-Bissau, the Cape Verde Islands and Seychelles had acceded to the African Solidarity Fund. (Proposals made earlier by the President of Senegal for the conclusion of defence agreements between certain West African states were, however, not discussed at the conference.)

Fifth Conference. The fifth conference took place in Paris on May 22-23, 1978 (the participants including, inter alios, the Presidents of Djibouti and of Zaïre and a representative of the Congo). At this conference the French President clarified his country's policy in regard to military assistance to African states, saying that France had been asked more and more frequently "for military support to poorly-armed countries which are victims of external aggression"; that in each case France's intervention had amounted to "limited technical assistance"; but that the main responsibility for their security rested with the states directly concerned, that "we must not allow the politics of power blocs to play havoc with Africa" and that "in the political domain Africa must remain for the Africans".

After the conference the French President urged the expansion of the West African Economic Community (CEAO—see page 363) to central African countries in the field of defence, with defence and non-aggression agreements to be signed first with Burundi, Rwanda, Gabon and Zaïre, and later with other countries.

(The strength of the principal contingents of French military personnel in African countries or French departments was given as follows in the French press in May 1978: Cameroon 90, Chad 1,800, Djibouti 4,500, Gabon 500, the Ivory Coast 500, Mauritania 100, Mayotte 2,000, Morocco 250, Niger 60, Réunion 2,000, Senegal 1,300, Togo 80 and Zaïre 70.)

Sixth Conference. The sixth conference was held at Kigali (Rwanda) on May 21-22, 1979. Among the observers present at this conference was the Foreign Minister of Liberia. During the session it was announced that France had decided to increase by $50,000,000 its contribution to the African Development Bank [see page 357] and to 12 per cent its share in the African Development Fund [ibid.].

The African participants in this conference asked France to be their spokesman at the European Communities and other industrialized countries, and they endorsed a French call for greater solidarity between European, African and Arab states (the French President having on Feb. 15, 1979, proposed a meeting of leaders of the European Communities, the Organization of African Unity and the Arab League).

Seventh Conference. The seventh conference was held in Nice (France) on May 9-10, 1980, and was attended by representatives of France and 25 African countries (comprising the Presidents of France, Burundi, the Central African Republic, the Comoros, Djibouti, Gabon, Equatorial Guinea, Mali, Niger, Rwanda, Senegal, Sierra Leone, Somalia, Togo and Zaïre; the Prime Minister of Mauritius; ministers from Benin, the Cape Verde Islands, Chad, the Congo, Guinea-Bissau and Morocco; and the Mauritanian ambassador to France).

At the conference the French President again defined his policy as one of "non-interference and solidarity" and of responding to requests for aid.

At the end of the conference the President of Senegal announced that agreement had been reached on the establishment of an "organic community" (comparable to the Commonwealth) with a permanent secretariat to be based in Paris.

Agency for Cultural and Technical Co-operation

This agency (*Agence de Coopération Culturelle et Technique*) was set up, with headquarters in Paris, in 1970, as agreed at an international conference held at Niamey (Niger) on Feb. 17-20, 1969, and attended by representatives of some 30 countries where French was either the official language or widely spoken.

By March 1980 the agency had 23 full members (Belgium, Benin, Burundi, Canada, the Central African Republic, Chad, the Comoros, Djibouti, Dominica, France, Gabon, Haiti, the Ivory Coast, Niger, the New Hebrides—later Vanuatu, Rwanda, Senegal, Seychelles, Togo, Tunisia, Upper Volta, Vietnam and Zaïre), four associate members (Cameroon, Guinea-Bissau, Laos and Mauritania) and two participating governments (New Brunswick and Quebec).

The agency has in particular financed projects in under-developed countries, notably in Benin, Chad, Laos and Vietnam.

Other Agreements between France and Francophone Countries

Mauritius. An agreement on cultural and technical co-operation between France and Mauritius was signed in Port Louis on June 22, 1970.

Mauritania. Three new agreements, covering cultural, technical and economic co-operation between France and Mauritania, were signed on Feb. 15, 1973. Mauritania regarded its 1960 defence agreement with France as void, and no new accord on military matters was reached.

Madagascar. Eight new co-operation agreements between France and the Malagasy Republic were signed on June 4, 1973, replacing those in force since June 27, 1960. An agreement on military co-operation provided for the withdrawal of French ground forces based at Ivato by Sept. 1, 1973; the training of Malagasy units to run the naval installations at Diégo-Suarez; and unlimited French landing and harbouring rights for refuelling and repairs, renewable every year. The withdrawal of all French forces from Madagascar was completed by June 3, 1975.
Three further co-operation agreements were signed in Antananarivo on July 4, 1975.

Congo. New co-operation agreements between France and the Congo were signed in Brazzaville on Jan. 1, 1974, including one on French technical assistance to the Congo's armed forces.

Gabon. A new co-operation agreement between France and Gabon, signed on Feb. 12, 1974, and renewing that of 1960, provided for the partical maintenance of the 1960 defence arrangements and the continued presence in Gabon of a small French force.

Cameroon. A set of co-operation agreements between France and Cameroon, signed on Feb. 21, 1974, covered inter alia technical, cultural, economic, financial and military co-operation.

Senegal. Four separate documents signed on March 29, 1974, comprised a general treaty of friendship and co-operation; an agreement on economic and financial co-operation; a cultural convention; and a military agreement providing for the transfer to Senegal of the French base in Dakar, with France retaining certain facilities, and for the phased reduction of French forces in Senegal from 2,250 to 1,300 men by April 1975.

Benin. An agreement on co-operation in various fields, including military technology, was signed on Feb. 23, 1975, between France and Dahomey (which changed its name to Benin in December 1975).

Togo. New co-operation agreements, to replace earlier ones concluded in 1963, were signed between France and Togo in Lomé on March 23, 1976, covering mainly co-operation in economic, technical and cultural affairs, scientific research and military technology. In September 1975 it had been agreed that France would supply Togo with five training aircraft and two coastal patrol boats and would provide training for Togolese pilots and technicians.

Chad. After the Government of Chad had, on Sept. 28, 1975, accused France of interfering in the country's internal affairs and had demanded the withdrawal of French troops stationed there under the 1964 agreement, the evacuation of all French military bases in Chad was completed by Oct. 27, 1975.
New civil and military agreements signed between France and Chad on March 6, 1976, provided inter alia for co-operation in various fields, including military technology, but they comprised no automatic clause for the defence of Chad in the event of an attack, and it was officially stated at the same time that French military personnel would "not intervene directly" against the rebellion (then in progress in northern Chad). Following these agreements the French military personnel in Chad was said to number only about 300 men. However, in March 1978 more French forces were sent to Chad "to ensure the safety of French nationals" (during the civil war in Chad) and also "to block" any advance by Libyan-backed rebels. During 1979 the number of these French forces was reduced from 2,500 to about 1,100, and at the request of the President of Chad all of them were withdrawn between April 28 and May 16, 1980, after most Europeans had been evacuated from the country.

Djibouti. Seven bilateral agreements— including a treaty of friendship and co-operation, an agreement on economic and financial co-operation and a provisional military protocol—were signed between France and the Republic of Djibouti on June 27, 1977 (when Djibouti achieved independence). (France maintained some 5,000 troops in Djibouti and assisted in the formation of a Djibouti national Army, but it would not intervene militarily unless requested by Djibouti in the event of aggression against it.)

The Comoros. Five agreements signed on Nov. 10, 1978, by France and the Comoros included a treaty of friendship and co-operation, an economic, monetary and financial agreement, a cultural agreement and a military agreement, under which France would supply the Comoros with aid in the event of external aggression and provide technical assistance in the training of the Comoro Army.

Central African Republic. In September

1979 French parachute troops, at the request of opponents of the then Emperor Bokassa, took part in an operation leading to the overthrow of the Emperor and the restoration of the Central African Republic; of the three companies involved, one was withdrawn on Dec. 16, 1979.

A joint plan for the recovery of the Central African Republic's economy was approved by the Governments of France and the Central African Republic in February 1980, and the latter's President asked the French Government on May 16, 1980, to maintain in his country a French army detachment in order to train the forces of the Central African Republic.

15. The Americas

This section deals with treaties, alliances and other agreements concluded by the states of the American continents, covering in particular (i) early manifestations of pan-Americanism and the first regional security arrangements, (ii) the development of the Organization of American States, (iii) other inter-American co-operation agencies and agreements, (iv) the major treaties and agreements concluded by the United States in the fields of defence, economic co-operation and peaceful use of nuclear energy and (v) other important agreements involving American states.

Pan-Americanism and the First Regional Security Arrangements

The Monroe Doctrine

The idea of the unity of interests of the countries of the American continents, or of Pan-Americanism, received its first impetus from the so-called Monroe Doctrine which rejected all interference on American affairs by outside powers.

The doctrine was proclaimed by President James Monroe in a Message to Congress delivered on Dec. 2, 1823, stating inter alia:

"The American continents, by the free and independent condition which they have assumed and maintain, are henceforth not to be considered as subject for future colonization by any European power. . . . We would not view any interposition for the purpose of oppressing" the former colonies in the Americas or "controlling in any other manner their destiny by any European power in any other light than as the manifestation of an unfriendly disposition toward the United States".

The doctrine was restated by President James K. Polk on Dec. 2, 1845, and by other US Presidents later in the 19th century. It was formally recognized by Great Britain after President Theodore Roosevelt had pronounced the following corollary to the doctrine in May 1904: "In the Western Hemisphere the adherence of the United States to the Monroe doctrine may force the United States, however reluctantly, in flagrant cases of such wrongdoing or interference, to the exercise of an international police power."

Earliest Pan-American Organizations

The first manifestation of Pan-Americanism was the **First Congress of American States** convened in Panama City by Simón

Bolívar in 1826 which led to the signing of a *Treaty of Permanent Union, League and Confederation* of Colombia, Central America, Mexico and Peru.

An **International Union of American Republics** was set up at a First International Conference of American States in Washington in 1889-90. The fourth conference of this organization decided in Washington in 1910 to change its name to **Union of American Republics**, and at the fifth conference in Santiago de Chile in 1923 it was decided to adopt the name of **Union of the Republics of the American Continents** and to establish the **Pan-American Union** as its permanent organ. This conference also formulated the *Gondra Treaty* providing for procedures for the peaceful prevention of conflicts.

At the 7th conference of the Union of the Republics of the American Continents in Montevideo in 1933 the United States joined the other member states in signing a convention on the *Rights and Duties of States* declaring explicitly: "No state has the right to intervene in the internal or external affairs of another."

A Conference of American States held in Buenos Aires in December 1936 adopted:

(1) A *Pan American Peace Pact*, providing for consultation in the event of the peace of the American Republics being threatened or in case of war between American nations;

(2) a *Pact for Co-ordination of Treaties*, endorsing and amplifying existing treaties between American states; and

(3) a non-intervention convention named the *'Declaration of Inter-American Solidarity and Co-operation'*.

283

A further conference held in Lima in December 1938 issued the *Declaration of Lima* on inter-American solidarity, under which regular meetings of American Foreign Ministers were agreed upon. A first such meeting, held in Panama on Sept. 23-Oct. 3, 1939, adopted an *Act of Panama* as a multilateral declaration of neutrality (following the outbreak of World War II).

The act contained decisions (i) to establish a committee of experts for the duration of the war to study and make recommendations on problems of neutrality; (ii) to proclaim a neutral zone on the high seas up to 300 miles from the coasts of American Republics; and (iii) to call, in the event of any territory in the Americas belonging to a European state changing sovereignty and thereby endangering American security, for an urgent consultative meeting. (The decision on the 300-mile neutral zone was later invalidated by the doctrine of the freedom of the seas, as embodied in the UN Convention of the High Seas of 1958—see page 48.)

At a further meeting held in Havana on July 21-30, 1940, the Foreign Ministers of the American Republics adopted a *Convention on the Provisional Administration of European Colonies and Possessions in the Americas*.

In this convention it was laid down that, if a non-American state attempted, directly or indirectly, to replace another non-American state in the sovereignty or control over any territory in the Americas, thus threatening the peace of the continent, such territory would automatically be submitted to a provisional administrative regime to be exercised by one or more American states, until such time as the territory would be able to govern itself or be restored to its former status, whenever the latter was compatible with the security of the American Republics.

However, no unanimity on the question of neutrality was maintained among American Republics in subsequent years. When a third meeting of the Republics' Foreign Ministers was held in Rio de Janeiro on Jan. 15-28, 1941, nine Central American and Caribbean states had declared war on the Axis powers, and it was only near the end of the war in 1945 that all American Republics had declared war on Germany and Japan.

Act of Chapultepec

The basis of later alliances between American states is the so-called *Act of Chapultepec* of 1945. This declaration on "reciprocal assistance and American solidarity" was issued on March 3, 1945, during an Inter-American Conference on the Problems of War and Peace", convened by the Pan-American Union.

The declaration of the Act of Chapultepec contained the following provisions:

(1) All sovereign states are juridically equal amongst themselves.

(2) Every state has the right to the respect of its individuality and independence on the part of the other members of the international community.

(3) Every attack against the integrity, territorial inviolability, sovereignty or political independence of an American state shall be considered as an act of aggression against the other states which sign this declaration. Invasion by armed forces of one state into the territory of another, trespassing boundaries established by treaty and marked in accordance therewith, shall constitute an act of aggression.

(4) In the case that acts of aggression occur or that there may be reasons to believe that an aggression is being prepared by any other state against an American state, the states signatory to this declaration will consult amongst themselves in order to agree upon measures they think it may be advisable to take.

(5) This laid down that during the war against the Axis the American nations would, in the event of interference with the war effort of the United Nations, take any or all of the following actions: Recall of diplomatic missions, breaking of diplomatic relations, interruption of economic, financial and commercial relations, breaking off of postal, telegraphic, radio-telephonic, etc., communications, and the use of armed force to prevent or repel aggression.

The signatories were Bolivia, Brazil, Chile, Colombia, Costa Rica, Cuba, the Dominican Republic, Ecuador, Guatemala, Haiti, Honduras, Mexico, Nicaragua, Panama, Paraguay, Peru, the USA, Uruguay and Venezuela. Argentina signed the Act on April 4, 1945.

Treaty of Rio

A mutual defence treaty in pursuance of the Act of Chapultepec was adopted on Aug. 30, 1947, at an inter-American defence conference held at Petropolis near Rio de Janeiro. The treaty—known as the *Treaty of Rio*, or *Inter-American Treaty of Reciprocal Assistance*—was signed on Sept. 2, 1947, by 19 of the 21 American Republics, only Ecuador and Nicaragua—both of which had suffered recent coups d'état—withholding their signatures; Cuba withdrew from the treaty on March 29, 1960.

The treaty came into force on Dec. 3, 1948. Its principal terms are summarized below:

Art. 1. The signatories "formally condemn war and undertake in their international relations not to resort to the threat or use of force in any manner inconsistent with the UN Charter or of this treaty".

Art. 2. Consequently, they "undertake to submit every controversy which may arise between them to methods of peaceful settlement and endeavour to settle such controversies among themselves by means of procedures in force in the inter-American system before referring them to the UN General Assembly or the Security Council".

Art. 3. (1) The signatories "agree that an armed attack by any states against an American state shall be considered as an attack against all the American states", and consequently each of the signatories "undertakes to assist in meeting the attack in exercise of the inherent right of individual or collective self-defence recognized by Art. 51 of the UN Charter".

(2) "On the request of the state or states directly attacked and until the decision of the organ of consultation of the inter-American system", each of the signatories "may determine immediate measures which it may individually adopt in fulfilment of the obligation contained in the preceding paragraph and in accordance with the principle of continental solidarity. The organ of consultation shall meet without delay for the purpose of examining these measures and agreeing upon measures of a collective character that should be adopted".

(3) These provisions shall apply "in case of any armed attack which takes place within the region described in Art. 4 or within the territory of an American state. When an attack takes place outside this area the provisions of Art. 6 shall be applied".

(4) The above measures of self-defence "may be taken until the UN Security Council has taken measures necessary to maintain international peace and security".

Art. 4. This article defines the region to which the treaty refers, which extends from the North Pole to the South Pole, and includes Canada, Alaska, the Aleutians, Greenland, the Falklands, the South Orkneys and Antarctica.

Art. 6. "If the inviolability or the integrity of the territory or sovereignty or political independence of any American state should be affected by an aggression which is not an armed attack or by an intra-continental or extra-continental conflict, or by any other fact or situation that might endanger the peace of America, the organ of consultation shall meet immediately in order to agree on the measures which must be taken in case of aggression to assist the victim of the aggression or, in any case, the measures which should be taken for the common defence and for the maintenance of the peace and security of the continent."

Art. 7. "In the case of a conflict between two or more American states, without prejudice to the right of self-defence in conformity with Art. 51 of the UN Charter", the signatories, "meeting in consultation, shall call upon the contending states to suspend hostilities and restore matters to the *status quo ante bellum*, and shall take in addition all other necessary measures to re-establish or maintain inter-American peace and security and for the solution of the conflict by peaceful means. The rejection of the pacifying action will be considered in the determination of the aggressor and in the application of the measures which the consultative meeting may agree upon."

Art. 8. "The measures on which the organ of consultation may agree will comprise one or more of the following: Recall of chiefs of diplomatic missions, breaking of diplomatic relations, breaking of consular relations, complete or partial interruption of economic relations or of rail, sea, air, postal, telegraphic, telephonic, radio-telephonic or radio-telegraphic communications, and the use of armed force."

Art. 11. "The organ of consultation referred to in this treaty shall be, until a different decision is taken, the meeting of the Ministers of Foreign Affairs of the signatory states."

Art. 20. "Decisions which require the application of the measures specified in Art. 8 shall be binding upon all the signatory states . . . except that no state shall be required to use armed force without its consent."

The Treaty of Rio formed the basis of a series of bilateral treaties of assistance concluded by the USA with Brazil, Chile, Colombia, Cuba, Peru and Uruguay after 1951 (see below under "Defence Treaties of the USA").

Applications of the Treaty of Rio

The Treaty of Rio has been applied in the following disputes and civil conflicts in Latin America:

1948. Dispute between Costa Rica and Nicaragua.
1950. Dispute between the Dominican Republic and Cuba and Guatemala.
     Dispute between Haiti and the Dominican Republic.
1954. Civil war in Guatemala.
1955. Dispute between Costa Rica and Nicaragua.
1957. Border dispute between Honduras and Nicaragua.
1959. Attempted invasion of Panama.
     Attempted coup d'état in Nicaragua.
1960. Dispute between Venezuela and the Dominican Republic.
1962. Events in Cuba caused the treaty to be invoked twice in this year.
1963. Dispute between Haiti and the Dominican Republic.
     Dispute between Venezuela and Cuba.
1964. Dispute between Panama and the USA.
     Venezuelan accusation of aggression by Cuba.
1965. Civil war in the Dominican Republic.

The treaty was amended by the *Protocol of San José*, unanimously approved on July 25, 1975, by the 21 signatories of the treaty. The amendment inter alia expanded the treaty's provisions for dealing with aggression against an OAS member country and defined aggression as "the use of armed force by a state against the sovereignty, territorial integrity or political independence of another state, or in any form incompatible with the UN Charter or the OAS Charter or the present treaty".

The OAS and its Related Structures

Organization of American States (OAS)

Headquarters: Washington, D.C.
Members: Argentina, Barbados, Bolivia, Brazil, Chile, Colombia, Costa Rica, Dominica, Dominican Republic, Ecuador, El Salvador, Grenada, Guatemala, Haiti, Honduras, Jamaica, Mexico, Nicaragua, Panama, Paraguay, Peru, St Lucia,

Suriname, Trinidad and Tobago, USA, Uruguay, Venezuela.

Observers: Austria, Belgium, Canada, Egypt, the Federal Republic of Germany, France, Guyana, Israel, Italy, Japan, the Republic of Korea, the Netherlands, Portugal, Spain and the Vatican (Holy See).

The Organization of American States was formed in 1948 as a regional alliance, under the United Nations, to foster mutual understanding and co-operation among the nations of the Western Hemisphere. The Charter of the OAS was drawn up in treaty form at the ninth Inter-American Conference, held in Bogotá in April 1948, and was signed by 21 American Republics, including Cuba, which was later excluded from the organization [see below]. The Charter gave permanent legal form to the hitherto loosely and indefinitely organized pan-American system.

The organization was joined by Trinidad and Tobago in February 1967, Barbados in October 1967, Jamaica in June 1969, Grenada in May 1974, Suriname in February 1977, and Dominica and St Lucia in May 1979.

OAS CHARTER

A summary of the main provisions of the Charter of the Organization of American States, which entered into force on Dec. 13, 1957, is given on the facing page.

Map 9 Organization of American States (OAS) and Organization of Central American States (OCAS)

286

Chapter 1

Nature and Purposes

Art. 1. The American states "establish the international organization that they have developed to achieve an order of peace and justice, promote their solidarity, strengthen their collaboration, and defend their sovereignty, territorial integrity and independence. The Organization of American States is a regional agency within the United Nations".

Art. 2. All American states ratifying the Charter are members of the Organization.

Art. 3. Any new political entity arising from the union of several member states which, as such, ratifies the Charter shall become a member of the organization, the states forming the new entity forfeiting their separate membership.

Art. 4. The organization has the following aims: (*a*) To strengthen the peace and security of the continent; (*b*) to prevent possible causes of difficulties and ensure the pacific settlement of disputes arising among member states; (*c*) to organize "solidarity action" by those states in the event of aggression; (*d*) to seek the solution of political, juridical and economic problems arising among them; (*e*) to promote by co-operative action mutual economic, social and cultural development.

Chapter 2

Principles

Art. 5. This reaffirms a number of principles, inter alia respect for the "personality and sovereignty of states", for the fulfilment of international obligations derived from treaties and other sources of international law, and for the human rights of the individual without distinction of race, creed, colour, sex or nationality. It also states that the solidarity of the American nations "requires their political organization on the basis of effective exercise of representative democracy"; that "aggression against one American state is aggression against all the others"; that "the spiritual unity of the continent is based on respect for the cultural value of the American countries and demands their close co-operation"; and that "economic co-operation is essential to the common welfare of the continent".

Chapter 3

Fundamental Rights and Duties of States

Arts. 6-19. This section also enunciates various principles, inter alia that states are juridically equal (Art. 6); that each state has "the right to develop its cultural, political and economic life freely and naturally" (Art. 13); that "no state or group of states has the right to intervene in any way, directly or indirectly, for any reason whatever, in the internal or external affairs of any other state" (Arts. 15-16); and that "the American states bind themselves not to use force except in self-defence or in accordance with existing treaties" (Arts. 18-19). Art. 17 stipulates: "The territory of a state is inviolable; it may not be the object, even temporarily, of military occupation or of other measures of force taken by another state. No territorial acquisitions or special advantages obtained either by force or other means of coercion shall be recognized."

Chapter 4

Pacific Settlement of Disputes

Arts. 20-23. All inter-American disputes, before being referred to the Security Council, shall be submitted to one or other of the following peaceful procedures: Direct negotiation, good offices, mediation, investigation and conciliation, judicial procedure, arbitration, and those which the parties may especially agree upon at any time. A special treaty will establish the proper means of settling disputes and determine appropriate procedures.

Chapter 5

Collective Security

Art. 24. "Every act of aggression against an American state shall be considered an act of aggression against the other American states."

Art. 25. If the territorial integrity, sovereignty or political independence of any American state is affected by an armed attack or other act of aggression, or by any extra-continental conflict, or by a conflict between two or more American states, the American states shall apply the measures and procedures established in the special treaties on the subject.

Chapter 6

Economic Co-operation

Art. 26. The member states will co-operate to strengthen their economic structure, develop their agriculture and mining, promote their industry, and increase their trade.

Art. 27. If the economy of an American state is affected by serious conditions that cannot be satisfactorily remedied by its unaided efforts, it may place its economic problems before the Inter-American Economic and Social Council [see below] to seek the most appropriate solution of such problems.

Chapter 7

Social Co-operation

Arts. 28-29. The member states will co-operate to achieve just and decent living conditions for their populations, and affirm the desirability of developing their social legislation of the following bases: "(*a*) All human beings, without distinction as to race, nationality, sex, creed or social condition, have the right to attain material well-being and spiritual growth under circumstances of liberty, dignity, equality of opportunity and economic security; (*b*) work is a right and a social duty . . . to be performed under conditions that ensure life, health and a decent living standard both during working years and in old age or incapacity."

Chapter 8

Cultural Co-operation

Arts. 30-31. The member states agree that (*a*) elementary education shall be compulsory and, when provided by the state, without cost; (*b*) higher education shall be available to all without distinction as to race, nationality, sex, language, creed or social condition. They undertake to facilitate cultural interchange by all media of expression.

Chapters 9-15 (Arts. 32-101) deal with the structure and functions of the organs of the OAS [see below under separate heading]. *Chapter 16* (Art. 102) upholds the rights and obligations of the member states under the United Nations Charter; and *Chapters 17 and 18* (Arts. 103-112) contain miscellaneous provisions covering, inter alia, the diplomatic immunity of OAS officials, and the ratification and entry into force of the Charter.

1948 BOGOTÁ DECLARATIONS

Declaration on European Colonies. A declaration condemning the existence of European colonies in the Western Hemisphere and establishing an inter-American body to study the problem and seek peaceful means of solving it was adopted at the Bogotá conference; the declaration was approved by 17 of the 21 countries represented, those abstaining being the USA, Brazil, Chile and the Dominican Republic.

The declaration considered "that the historical process of emancipation of America will not be completed so long as there remain on the continent peoples and regions subjected to colonial regimes or territories occupied by non-American countries", and described as a "just aspiration" that an end be put to colonialism and to occupation of American territories by extra-continental countries. There would be created, the declaration continued, an "American Commission of Dependent Territories" to centralize the study of the colonial problem, composed of one representative from each member state, and it would be considered to be installed when two-thirds of those representatives had been named. Its site would be Havana and its functions would include study of the "colonial situation" and the seeking of peaceful means for "the abolition of colonialism as well as the occupation of American territories by extra-continental countries". It would submit a report on each territory to the Council, which would inform the member states, the reports being subsequently considered at the first meeting of the Foreign Ministers. "The creation of this Commission," the declaration concluded, "and the exercise of its functions, shall not exclude or limit the rights and actions of interested states in seeking directly and by peaceful means the solution of problems affecting them."

Declaration on Democracy and Communism. Another declaration reaffirming the faith of the American states in democracy and condemning communism was also adopted.

This declaration said inter alia that "the present international situation demands urgent measures to safeguard peace and defend mutual respect among states, proscribing tactics of totalitarian hegemony irreconcilable with the tradition of the American countries and preventing agents at the service of international communism or any totalitarianism from seeking to distort the free world of the peoples of this hemisphere." It reiterated "the faith that the peoples of the New World have placed in the ideal and reality of democracy"; condemned the "interference of any foreign power, or any political organization serving the interests of a foreign power, in the public life of the nations of the American continent"; and promised that the American states would adopt within their respective territories the necessary measures to prevent and uproot activities directed or instigated by foreign governments which tended to subvert their institutions through violence or to promote disorder in their internal political life.

Pact of Bogotá. In fulfilment of Article 23 of the OAS Charter, the Bogotá conference also adopted an *American Treaty on Pacific Settlement* (known as the *Pact of Bogotá*) on procedures for settling disputes (on which reservations were, however, expressed by the United States and also by Argentina, Bolivia, Ecuador, Nicaragua, Paraguay and Peru).

The first special Inter-American Conference—this conference then being the supreme authority of the organization—was held in Washington on Dec. 16-18, 1964, and was limited to establishing, in an *Act of Washington*, procedures for the admission of new members to the organization.

AMENDMENTS TO THE CHARTER

1965 Act of Rio de Janeiro. The *Act of Rio de Janeiro*, embodying suggestions for the amendment of the OAS Charter, was signed by delegates of the 19 American nations (all OAS members except Venezuela) represented at the Second Special Inter-American Conference, held at Rio de Janeiro on Nov. 17-30, 1965. The principal sections of this document are given below.

The Second Special Inter-American Conference:
Reaffirms:
The principles and standards in effect that are embodied in Part One of the Charter of the Organization of American States;
Declares:
(1) That it is essential to forge a new dynamism for the inter-American system and to avoid duplication of efforts and conflicts of jurisdiction among its organs, in order to facilitate co-operation between the American states and obtain a more rational utilization of the resources of the organization;
(2) that it is essential to modify the working structure of the Organization of American States as defined in the Charter; and
Resolves: . . .
(3) To entrust to a Special Committee, composed of representatives of each of the member states, the preparation of a preliminary draft proposal on amendments to the Charter of the organization.
(4) The Special Committee shall use the following guidelines for the amendment of the Charter of the organization:
(*a*) An inter-American conference, as the highest body of the OAS, shall be convened annually at a different location and on a fixed date, for the purposes set forth in Article 33 of the Charter and to approve the programme and budget of the organization, to determine the quotas of the member states, and to co-ordinate the activities of the organs and agencies of the inter-American system.
(*b*) The Meeting of Consultation of Ministers of Foreign Affairs shall be retained in the form established in Article 39 of the Charter.
(*c*) There shall be three Councils directly responsible to the Inter-American Conference, as follows:
(i) The present Council of the organization, which shall be permanent in nature and, in addition to the pertinent powers that may be assigned to it in the Charter of the organization and inter-American treaties and agreements as well as those relative to the maintenance of peace and the peaceful settlement of

disputes, shall be the executive body for the decisions the Inter-American Conference or the Meeting of Consultation does not entrust to the Inter-American Economic and Social Council, to the Inter-American Educational, Scientific and Cultural Council, or to other organs;

(ii) the Inter-American Economic and Social Council (IA-ECOSOC), which shall meet at least once a year and shall have a permanent executive committee with a structure similar to that of CIAP (the Inter-American Committee for the Alliance for Progress—see below, page 293). CIAP shall act as the executive committee of the IA-ECOSOC so long as the Alliance for Progress is in force; and

(iii) the Inter-American Council for Education, Science and Cultures, which shall meet when convoked by the Inter-American Conference and shall have as its duties, in addition to promoting education, science and culture, those assigned to the present Inter-American Cultural Council in Articles 73 and 74 of the OAS Charter. . . . The Inter-American Council for Education, Science and Culture shall have a permanent committee, and its activities in the fields of education and training should be closely co-ordinated, whenever pertinent, with those of the IA-ECOSOC.

(*d*) The Pan-American Union shall continue to function as the central and permanent organ of the OAS and the General Secretariat of the organization, adapting its functions to the needs of the inter-American system.

(*e*) The Secretary-General and the Assistant Secretary-General of the organization shall hold office for five years.

(*f*) The present Inter-American Juridical Committee of Rio de Janeiro shall be maintained as an advisory organ with the structure and functions deemed desirable by the Special Committee, and the situation of the Inter-American Council of Jurists shall be studied.

(*g*) A study shall be made of the advisability of locating the permanent headquarters of all the Councils in one place or having them geographically decentralized, as well as a study of the feasibility of proceeding similarly in the case of the other OAS organs and agencies. ,. . .

(*h*) The provisions of the Act of Washington, signed at the First Special Inter-American Conference on Dec. 18, 1964, regulating the admission of new members, shall be included.

1966 Declaration of Bogotá. The Presidents of Chile, Colombia and Venezuela, and personal representatives of the Presidents of Ecuador and Peru, met at Bogotá on Aug. 14-16, 1966, to consider the question of the reform of the OAS Charter with the emphasis on social and economic development. Those present on Aug. 16 signed the *Declaration of Bogotá*, which reasserted the principle of non-intervention in the internal affairs of American states; called on the rich nations of the world to assist in Latin American development; demanded "greater respect by the United States for the rules of international trade"; and advocated economic integration in the Americas, particularly in the form of closer relations between the Latin American Free Trade Association (LAFTA) and the Central American Common Market [see below].

1967 Protocol of Buenos Aires. At the third special Inter-American Conference held in Buenos Aires in February 1967 the OAS Charter was further amended by the *Protocol of Buenos Aires*, under which the General Assembly of the OAS replaced the Inter-American Conference as the supreme organ of the organization, with the organs of the General Assembly being the three existing councils—(i) the Permanent Council (consisting of one representative of each member state), (ii) the Inter-American Economic and Social Council (IA-ECOSOC), and (iii) the Inter-American Council for Education, Science and Culture. The General Assembly was further assisted by a meeting of consultation of Ministers of Foreign Affairs and by an Inter-American Juridical Committee (of 11 jurists from member states). There were also an Inter-American Commission on Human Rights (of seven members elected for four years) and a General Secretariat (with a Secretary-General and an Assistant Secretary-General).

The Protocol of Buenos Aires came into force on Feb. 27, 1970.

Special Organizations, Agencies and Commissions

The OAS also embraces the following specialized organizations:

(1) **Inter-American Institute of Agricultural Sciences (IAIAS)**, founded in 1942 and based in San José (Costa Rica); its members include Canada.

(2) **Pan-American Health Organization (PAHO)**, founded in 1902 and based in Washington; it acts as a regional organization of the World Health Organization (WHO); and its members include Canada and also France, the Netherlands and the United Kingdom (for their departments and territories in America).

(3) **Inter-American Commission of Women (IACW)**, founded in 1928 and based also in Washington, with the object of extending civil, political, economic, social and cultural rights of women in the Americas.

(4) **Inter-American Children's Institute (IACI)**, based in Montevideo and founded in 1927 to improve the health and living conditions of mothers and children.

(5) **Pan-American Institute of Geography and History (PAIGH)**, based in Mexico, with Canada being one of its members, and with its objects including the opening-up of natural resources available in individual countries of the Americas.

(6) **Inter-American Indian Institute (IAII)**, based in Mexico and founded in 1940; its members are the following OAS member states: Argentina, Bolivia, Brazil, Chile, Colombia, Costa Rica, Ecuador, El Salvador, Guatemala, Honduras, Mexico, Nicaragua, Panama, Paraguay, Peru, the United States and Venezuela.

In addition there are the following special agencies and commissions, all based in Washington:

(1) **Inter-American Defence Board (IADB)**, founded in 1942; it has as one of its institutions an Inter-American Defence College, established in 1962 to provide special education for high-ranking officers of the Latin American armed forces.

(2) **Inter-American Statistical Institute (IASI)**, founded in 1940; Canada is one of its members.

(3) **Inter-American Nuclear Energy Commission (IANEC)**, established in 1959 to assist in the development and co-ordination of research in the peaceful uses of atomic energy.

(4) **Administrative Tribunal**.

(5) **Inter-American Emergency Aid Fund (FONDEM)**.

(6) **Pan-American Highway Congresses**, established in 1925 to promote highway development and progress; they also serve as an advisory body on highways in the American hemisphere.

The Inter-American Economic and Social Council (IA-ECOSOC) established a **Special Development Assistance Fund** in 1965 and an **Inter-American Export Promotion Centre** in 1969.

Protection of American States against Communism

In pursuance of the policies expressed in the Declaration on Communism of 1948 adopted at the Bogotá Conference [see above], further declarations were approved by OAS members as follows:

(1) The *Declaration of Solidarity for Preservation of the Political Integrity of the American States against International Communist Intervention*, presented by John Foster Dulles (then US Secretary of State) and adopted by 17 votes to one, (Guatemala), with Argentina and Mexico abstaining, at the 10th conference of the OAS held in Caracas, March 1-28, 1954.

In its final form the declaration specified that:

(1) The conference condemned the activities of international communism as constituting intervention in American affairs; expressed the determination of the American states "to take the necessary measures to protect their political independence against the intervention of international communism"; reiterated "the faith of the peoples of America in the effective exercise of representative democracy as the best means to promote their social and political progress"; and declared that "the domination or control of the political institutions of any American state by the international communist movement, extending to this hemisphere the political system of an extra-continental power, would constitute a threat to the sovereignty and political independence of the American states . . . and would call for consultation and appropriate action in accordance with existing treaties".

(2) The governments agreed to take the following steps "for the purpose of counteracting the subversive activities of the international communist movement within their respective jurisdictions": (i) To require "the disclosure of the identity, activities and source of funds of those who are spreading propaganda of the international communist movement, or who travel in the interests of that movement, or who act as its agents or on its behalf"; (ii) to exchange information with a view to implementing the resolutions adopted on this subject at inter-American conferences.

(3) "This declaration of foreign policy made by the American Republics in relation to dangers originating outside this hemisphere is designed to protect, and not to impair, the inalienable right of each American state freely to choose its own form of government and economic system, and to live its own social and cultural life."

(2) The *Declaration of Santiago de Chile*, adopted at a meeting of OAS Foreign Ministers at Santiago de Chile on Aug. 14-20, 1959, and laying down the following principles:

"(1) The principle of the rule of law should be assured by the separation of powers and by the control of the legality of governmental acts by competent organs of the state;

"(2) the Governments of the American Republics should be derived from free elections;

"(3) perpetuation in power, or the exercise of power without fixed term and with the manifest intent of perpetuation, is incompatible with the effective exercise of democracy;

"(4) the Governments of the American states should ensure . . . freedom for the individual and social justice based on respect for fundamental human rights;

"(5) the human rights incorporated in the legislation of the various American states should be protected by effective judicial procedures;

"(6) the systematic use of political proscription is contrary to American democratic order;

"(7) freedom of the press, of radio and television, and, in general, of information and expression, are essential conditions for the existence of a democratic regime;

"(8) the American states . . . should co-operate . . . to strengthen and develop their economic structure and achieve just and humane living conditions for their peoples."

(3) The *Declaration of San José*, adopted unanimously (after the withdrawal of the Cuban delegation from the conference) at the meeting of OAS Foreign Ministers in San José (Costa Rica) on Aug. 16-28, 1960.

The declaration contained the following points:

(1) An "emphatic condemnation" of "intervention or the threat of intervention . . . from an extra-continental power in the affairs of the American Republics", coupled with a declaration that "the acceptance of a threat of extra-continental intervention by any American state jeopardizes American solidarity and security".

(2) Rejection of "the attempt of the Sino-Soviet powers to make use of the political, economic or social situation of any American state, inasmuch as any such attempt is capable of destroying hemispheric unity and jeopardizing the peace and security of the hemisphere".

(3) Reaffirmation of "the principle of non-intervention by any American state in the internal or external affairs of other American states", and of the right of each state "to develop its cultural, political and economic life freely and naturally, respecting the rights of the individual and the principles of universal morality. As a consequence, no American state may

intervene for the purpose of imposing upon another American state its ideology or political, economic or social principles".

(4) "The inter-American system is incompatible with any form of totalitarianism and . . . democracy will achieve the full scope of its objectives in the hemisphere only when all the American Republics conduct themselves in accordance with the principles stated in the Declaration of Santiago de Chile [see above]".

(5) A declaration that "all member states (of the OAS) are under obligation to submit to the discipline of the inter-American system, voluntarily and freely agreed upon . . .''.

(6) A declaration that "all controversies between member states should be resolved by the measures of peaceful solution contemplated in the inter-American system".

(7) Reaffirmation of "faith in the regional system" and of "confidence in the Organization of American States, created to achieve an order of peace and justice that excludes any possible aggression, to promote solidarity among its members, to strengthen their collaboration, and to defend their sovereignty, territorial integrity and political independence . . .''.

(4) A resolution dealing with *The Offensive of Communist Governments* in America, approved unanimously, in the absence of the Cuban delegation, at the conference of OAS Foreign Ministers in Punta del Este (Uruguay) held on Jan. 22-31, 1962.

The resolution stated inter alia:

"The Ministers of Foreign Affairs of the American Republics . . . declare that the continental unity and the democratic institutions of the hemisphere are now in danger.

"The ministers have been able to verify that the subversive offensive of Communist governments, their agents and the organizations which they control has increased in intensity. The purpose of this offensive is the destruction of democratic institutions and the establishment of totalitarian dictatorships at the service of extra-continental powers. The outstanding facts in this intensified offensive are the declarations, set forth in official documents of the directing bodies of the international communist movement, that one of its principal objectives is the establishment of Communist regimes in the underdeveloped countries and in Latin America; and the existence of a Marxist-Leninist government in Cuba which is publicly aligned with the doctrine and foreign policy of the Communist powers.

"In order to achieve their subversive purposes and hide their true intentions, the Communist governments and their agents exploit the legitimate needs of the less-favoured sectors of the population and the just national aspirations of the various peoples. With the pretext of defending popular interests, freedom is suppressed, democratic institutions are destroyed, human rights are violated, and the individual is subjected to materialistic ways of life imposed by the dictatorship of a single party. Under the slogan of "anti-imperialism", they try to establish an oppressive, aggressive imperialism, which subordinates the subjugated nations to the militaristic and aggressive interest of the extra-continental powers. By maliciously utilizing the principles of the inter-American system, they attempt to undermine democratic institutions and to strengthen and protect political penetration and aggression. The

subversive methods of Communist governments and their agents constitute one of the most subtle and dangerous forms of intervention in the internal affairs of other countries.

"The ministers . . . alert the peoples of the hemisphere to the intensification of the subversive offensive of Communist governments, their agents and the organizations that they control and to the tactics and methods they employ, and also warn them of the dangers this situation represents to representative democracy, to respect for human rights, and to the self-determination of peoples.

"The principles of communism are incompatible with the principles of the inter-American system.

"Convinced that the integrity of the democratic revolution of the American states can and must be preserved in the face of the subversive offensive of communism, the ministers . . . proclaim the following basic political principles:

"(*a*) The faith of the American peoples in human rights, liberty and national independence as a fundamental reason for their existence, as conceived by the founding fathers who destroyed colonialism and brought the American republics into being.

"(*b*) The principle of non-intervention and the right of peoples to organize their way of life freely in the political, economic and cultural spheres, expressing their will through free elections, without foreign interference. The fallacies of communist propaganda cannot and should not obscure or hide the difference in philosophy which these principles represent when they are expressed by a democratic American country, and when Communist governments and their agents attempt to utilize them for their own benefit.

"(*c*) The repudiation of repressive measures which, under the pretext of isolating or combating communism, may facilitate the appearance or strengthening of reactionary doctrines and methods which attempt to repress ideas of social progress and to confuse truly progressive and democratic labour organizations and cultural and political movements with communist subversion.

"(*d*) The affirmation that communism is not the way to achieve economic development and the elimination of social injustice in America. On the contrary, a democratic regime can encompass all the efforts for economic advancement and all measures for improvement and social progress without sacrificing the fundamental values of the human being. The mission of the peoples and governments of the hemisphere during the present generation is to achieve an accelerated development of their economies and to put an end to poverty, injustice, illness and ignorance as was agreed in the Charter of Punta del Este [see below].

"(*e*) The most essential contribution of each American state in the collective effort to protect the inter-American system against communism is a steadily greater respect for human rights, improvement in democratic institutions and practices, and the adoption of measures that truly express the impulse for a revolutionary change in the economic and social structures of the American Republics."

The conference decided on Jan. 31, 1962, by 14 votes to one (Cuba), with Argentina, Bolivia, Brazil, Chile, Ecuador and Mexico abstaining—i.e. with the bare two-thirds majority required by the OAS Charter—to exclude Cuba from the Inter-American system, and this resolution was ratified by the Council of the OAS of Feb. 14 by 17 votes (including Argentina, Bolivia, and Ecuador) to three (Brazil, Chile and Mexico). Cuba was also excluded "immediately" from the Inter-American Defence Board.

(5) A resolution approved by the OAS Council in Washington on Oct. 23, 1962, by 19 votes to none (with Uruguay abstaining for lack of governmental instructions).

This resolution, inter alia, (i) called for "the immediate dismantling and withdrawal from Cuba of all missiles and other weapons with offensive capability"; and (ii) recommended that the OAS member states, in accordance with Articles 6 and 8 of the Inter-American Treaty of Reciprocal Assistance, should "take all measures, individually and collectively, including the use of armed force, which they may deem necessary to ensure that Cuba cannot continue to receive from the Sino-Soviet powers military material and related supplies which may threaten the peace and security of the continent, and to prevent the missiles in Cuba with offensive capability from ever becoming an active threat to the peace and security of the continent".

(6) A report by the OAS Council, issued on Feb. 24, 1964, indicting the Government of Cuba for "a series of actions . . . openly intended to subvert Venezuelan institutions and to overthrow the democratic Government of Venezuela through terrorism, sabotage, assault and guerrilla warfare".

(7) A resolution adopted by the ninth consultative meeting of American Foreign Ministers in Washington on July 26, 1964, by 15 votes to four (Bolivia, Chile, Mexico and Uruguay) with Venezuela, having brought a charge of aggression against Cuba, taking no part in the vote.

This resolution, based on a report by an investigating committee appointed by the OAS Council in December 1963, inter alia,

(1) declared "that the acts verified by the investigating committee constitute an aggression and an intervention on the part of the Government of Cuba in the internal affairs of Venezuela, which affects all of the member states";

(2) condemned "energetically the present Government of Cuba for its act of aggression and intervention against the territorial inviolability, sovereignty and political independence of Venezuela";

(3) requested member-countries, "in accordance with the provisions of Articles 6 and 8 of the Inter-American Treaty of Reciprocal Assistance, . . . (i) not [to] maintain diplomatic or consular relations with the Government of Cuba", (ii) to "suspend all trade, whether direct or indirect, with Cuba, except in foodstuffs, medicines and medical equipment that may be sent to Cuba for humanitarian reasons", and (iii) to "suspend all sea transportation between their countries and Cuba" except for transportation "necessary for reasons of a humanitarian nature".

Promotion of Economic and Social Co-operation among American States

An inter-American economic conference held under the auspices of the OAS in Buenos Aires from Aug. 15 to Sept. 4, 1957, approved the *Economic Declaration of Buenos Aires*, which expressed the intention of the participating states to increase the volume of mutual trade, to reduce trade barriers, to endeavour jointly to solve the problems of producers of basic raw materials subject to excessive price fluctuations, to take measures to attract foreign capital and stimulate private investment, to establish sound financial and monetary systems in Latin America, and to increase technical co-operation through the OAS.

On Aug. 16, 1958, the Brazilian Government proposed to all Latin American countries a plan known as *Operation Pan-America* for increased economic co-operation with a view to establishing, inter alia, an Inter-American Development Bank and eventually a Latin American Common Market. A conference of Foreign Ministers of the OAS decided in Washington on Sept. 24, 1958, to recommend the establishment of a **Special Commission for Economic Co-operation**, and such a commission was constituted in Buenos Aires from April 28 to May 9, 1959.

1960 Act of Bogotá

At a meeting in Bogotá Sept. 5-12, 1960, the commission approved the *Act of Bogotá*, signed on Sept. 13, 1960, by all American Republics except Cuba and the Dominican Republic which, however, signed it later. Considering it opportune to give further practical expression to the spirit of Operation Pan-America, the act contained the following recommendations:

Measures for Social Development. (1) Modernization and improvement of the legal and institutional systems of land tenure, agricultural credit and taxation; acceleration of projects for land reclamation and improvement, land settlement, and the construction of farm-to market and access roads; and governmental programmes particularly designed to help small farmers.

(2) Expansion and improvement of schemes of housing and community services; strengthening of the existing facilities for mobilizing financial resources for housing, or, if necessary, the creation of new institutions for this purpose; expansion of those industries engaged in house-building; encouragement of pilot projects of "self-help" housing; and the purchase of land for low-cost and industrial housing projects.

(3) Development of all aspects of the educational system, particularly mass education aimed at eradicating illiteracy; instruction in agricultural, technical and scientific subjects; and the training of professional personnel "of key importance to economic development".

(4) Improvement of health services, including the provision of medical services in remote areas, development of health insurance schemes, campaigns for the control or elimination of communicable diseases,

epecially malaria, and the provision of adequate water-supply facilities.

(5) More equitable and effective measures to achieve maximum domestic savings; improvement of fiscal and financial practices; and the allocation of tax revenues to an extent adequate for the above-mentioned measures of social development.

Creation of Special Social Development Fund. The Latin American countries welcomed the decision of the US Government to establish a special inter-American fund for social development, with the Inter-American Development Bank as the primary mechanism for administering the fund.

Measures for Economic Development. (1) Provision of additional domestic and external resources for financing plans and projects of basic economic and industrial development, with special attention to loans on flexible terms and conditions, including repayment in local currency whenever advisable because of balance-of-payments conditions, and the strengthening of credit facilities for small and medium private business, agriculture and industry.

(2) Special attention to the expansion of long-term lending.

(3) Examination of methods to deal with the problem of the instability of exchange earnings in countries relying heavily on exports of primary products.

Alliance for Progress

In a message to Congress on March 14, 1961, President John F. Kennedy declared that the Act of Bogotá marked "an historic turning point in the evolution of the Western Hemisphere", and he requested massive aid to Latin America. The previous day, March 13, he had outlined a broad development plan for Latin America, which he called the **Alliance for Progress**. It contained the following principal provisions:

(1) A "vast new ten-year plan for the Americas" should be initiated, for which, if the Latin American countries were ready to do their part, the USA would help to provide resources "of a scope and magnitude sufficient to make this bold development programme a success".

(2) A ministerial meeting of the Inter-American Economic and Social Council would shortly be convened in order to help each country to formulate its own long-term development plans.

(3) The President would submit to Congress a request for the appropriation of $500,000,000 for aid to Latin America [see above].

(4) Support should be given to all projects of economic integration, such as the Central American Common Market and the free trade areas in South America.

(5) The USA was "ready to co-operate in serious, case-by-case examinations of commodity market problems".

(6) The USA would accelerate its "Food for Peace" emergency programme.

(7) Latin American scientists would be invited to co-operate with the United States in scientific fields, and the USA intended to expand its science teacher training programmes to include Latin American instructors.

(8) Technical training programmes would be expanded, the Peace Corps made available wherever it was needed, and assistance given to Latin American universities, graduate schools and research institutes.

(9) The United States reaffirmed its pledge "to come to the defence of any American nation whose independence is endangered".

(10) "Our friends in Latin America" were invited to "contribute to the enrichment of life and culture in the United States".

First Punta del Este Conference (1961). President Kennedy's proposal for the establishment of an Alliance for Progress was approved by 20 member-countries of the OAS (i.e. all except Cuba) at a conference of the Inter-American Economic and Social Council at Punta del Este (Uruguay) on Aug. 5-17, 1961. The conference also issued (*a*) a *Declaration to the Peoples of America* and (*b*) a *Charter of Punta del Este* setting out the aims, methods, and execution of the Alliance for Progress.

The declaration contained the following operative paragraphs:

"This Alliance is founded on the principles that only under freedom and through the institutions of representative democracy can man best satisfy his aspirations, including those for work, home and land, health and schools. The only system which guarantees true progress is one which provides the basis for reaffirming the dignity of the individual, which is the foundation of our civilization.

"Therefore the countries signing this declaration . . . have agreed to work towards the following goals during the coming years:

"(1) To improve and strengthen democratic institutions through application of the principle of self-determination by the people;

"(2) to accelerate economic and social development to bring about a substantial and steady increase in the average income as quickly as possible, so as to narrow the gap between the standard of living in Latin American countries and that enjoyed in the industrialized countries;

"(3) to carry out housing programmes, both in the city and in the countryside, in order to provide decent homes for the American peoples;

"(4) to encourage, in accordance with the characteristics of each country, programmes of integral agrarian reform leading to the effective transformation, where required, of unjust structures and systems of land tenure and use, with a view to replacing latifundia and dwarf holdings by an equitable system of property so that, supplemented by timely and adequate credit, technical assistance and improved marketing arrangements, the land will become for the man who works it the basis of his economic stability, the foundation of his increasing welfare, and the guarantee of his freedom and dignity;

"(5) to wipe out illiteracy; to extend the benefits of primary education to all Latin Americans; and to provide broader facilities, on a vast scale, for secondary and technical training and for higher education;

"(6) to press forward with programmes of health and sanitation in order to prevent sickness, fight epidemics, and strengthen our human potential;

"(7) to assure workers fair wages and satisfactory working conditions; to establish effective systems of labour-management relations and procedures for consultation and co-operation among government authorities, employers' associations and trade unions in the interests of social and economic development;

"(8) to reform tax laws, demanding more from those who have most, punishing tax evasion severely, and redistributing the national income in order to benefit those who are most in need, while at the same time promoting savings investment and re-investment of capital;

"(9) to maintain monetary and fiscal policies which, while avoiding the calamities of inflation or deflation, will protect the purchasing power of the many, guarantee where posssible price stability, and form an adequate basis for economic development;

"(10) to stimulate private enterprise in order to encourage the development of Latin American countries at a rate which will help them to provide jobs for the growing populations, to eliminate unemployment, and to take their place among the modern industrialized nations of the world;

"(11) to find a rapid and lasting solution to the grave problem created by excessive price fluctuations in the basic exports of Latin American countries on which their prosperity so heavily depends; and

"(12) to accelerate the integration of Latin America so as to stimulate the economic and social development of the continent. This process has already begun through the General Treaty of Economic Integration of Central America and, in other countries, through the Latin American Free Trade Association.

"This declaration expresses the conviction of the nations of Latin America that these profound economic, social and cultural changes can come about only through the self-help efforts of each country. Nonetheless, in order to achieve the goals which have been established with the necessary speed, it is indispensable that domestic efforts be reinforced by essential external assistance.

"The United States, for its part, pledges its efforts to supply financial and technical co-operation in order to achieve the aims of the Alliance for Progress. To this end the USA will provide a major part of the minimum of $20,000 million, principally in public funds, which Latin America will require over the next ten years from all external sources in order to supplement its own efforts. The USA will provide from public funds more than $1,000,000,000 during the twelve months which began on March 13, 1961, when the Alliance for Progress was announced, as an immediate contribution to the economic and social progress of Latin America. The USA intends to furnish development loans on a long-term basis, where appropriate, running up to 50 years and at very low or zero rates of interest.

"For their part, the countries of Latin America agree to devote a rapidly increasing share of their own resources to economic and social development, and to make the reforms necessary to assure that all share fully in the fruits of the Alliance of Progress. The countries of Latin America will formulate comprehensive and well-conceived national programmes for the development of their own economies as the contribution of each one of them to the Alliance for Progress. Independent and highly qualified experts will be made available to Latin American countries in order to assist in formulating and examining national development plans."

Developments in 1963-64. During the following two years, however, the Alliance for Progress failed to achieve many of its objectives. Experts and leaders from the Latin American States criticized the United States for not having lived up to its promises, while US spokesmen placed the blame on the Latin American countries themselves.

The annual report of the Alliance for Progress published on Nov. 11, 1963, showed that the actual growth rate of per capita income in Latin America in 1962 had been between 0.6 and 1 per cent—as against 2.5 per cent aimed at by the Alliance for Progress; this development had been due to a decline in Argentina's gross national product and a fall in Brazil's growth rate.

At a ministerial conference of the Inter-American Economic and Social Council in São Paulo on Nov. 12-16, 1963, President Goulart of Brazil called on the Latin American countries to unite in defence of their common interests in trade and aid, declaring that present trade conditions "represent a continual bleeding of our economies" since "our irreducible needs for imports, combined with falling export receipts, are in large measure responsible for the inflationary process which destroys the values of our national labours". All the Latin American countries, he stressed, were facing the same problem—of "breaking an agrarian structure that is manifestly archaic, in which the barriers of feudalism and intolerable privileges suffocate our effort for development, industrialization and diversification". Deficits in the balance of payments forced the Latin American countries to negotiate loans or to obtain refinancing of debts in conditions which did not meet their interests, and the answer would not be found "in palliatives or false, superficial concessions" by the industrialized capital-exporting countries. "Our objectives," President Goulart declared, "must be the establishment of a new international division of labour, just and remunerative prices for our exports of raw materials, and expansion of our exports of manufactures and semi-manufactures."

A special session of the Inter-American Economic and Social Council in Washington on Jan. 29, 1964, set up an eight-man executive committee to provide new and more dynamic leadership for the Alliance for Progress.

Second Inter-American Conference at Rio (1965). At a second special Inter-American Conference in Rio de Janeiro the US Secretary of State on Nov. 22, 1965, read a message from President Johnson pledging US support for the Alliance for Progress—which had until then totalled $4,000,000,000—beyond 1971, the terminal date agreed at Punta del Este in 1961. In return, the Latin American nations agreed to do more to promote their own economic development.

The conference also adopted the *Economic and Social Act of Rio de Janeiro*, reaffirming the principles and objectives of the Declaration to the Peoples of America and the Charter of Punta del Este [see above].

In *Chapter I*, dealing with "political security and economic and social development", the act declared inter alia:

"To achieve the objectives of the Alliance for Progress, the obligation to co-operate in the solution of economic and social problems is essential, inasmuch as these problems can disturb relations among peoples, limit the opportunities to affirm the dignity of the individual, limit the full exercise of democracy, and endanger the peace and security of the nations."

In *Chapter III* on mutual and external economic and social assistance, the act laid down:

"(13) The member states accept the obligation, within the framework of their constitutional processes and to the extent their resources permit, to help one another and to provide assistance, in the order of need, to the less developed countries of the system, with a view to achieving, on a national and regional level, the social and economic objectives set forth in this act, for the purpose of putting the countries of the hemisphere in a situation of development as soon as possible.

"(14) The member states undertake to avoid adopting policies, actions or measures that might jeopardize the economic and social development of another member state.

"(15) The member states recognize the necessity of co-operating individually and collectively in multinational projects to accelerate the process of Latin American economic integration, particularly those projects originating in the organizations which have that purpose.

"(16) The member states agree to seek the solution of urgent problems that arise when the economic development or stability of any member state is seriously affected by economic or trade measures adopted by other countries, by severe and continuing deficits in their balance of payments resulting from sharp drops in income from foreign sources, or by emergency situations, whatever their origin, that cause a shortage of essential goods and services."

The act further contained provisions for the promotion of foreign trade by, inter alia, eliminating excessive tariffs, trade preferences and other discriminatory practices, and lessening the fluctuations in earnings from export of primary products, and diversifying the export of manufactures and semi-manufactures from developing countries.

In *Chapter V* on "economic integration", the act stated:

"(27) The American states recognize that the economic integration of the developing countries of the hemisphere should be one of the basic objectives of the inter-American system and, for that reason, will orient their efforts and take the measures that are necessary to accelerate the process of integration.

"(28) With the object of strengthening and accelerating integration in all its aspects, special priority must be given to the preparation and execution of multinational projects, and to the financing thereof, and the already existing economic integration agencies should co-ordinate their activities with a view to the earliest possible establishment of the Latin American common market. Likewise, the economic and financial institutions of the region should continue to give their fullest support to the organizations for regional integration.

"(29) Within the framework of mutual assistance, the participation of the comparatively less developed countries in Latin American programmes of multinational economic co-operation should be encouraged, and the smooth, balanced development of Latin American integration promoted, with special importance attached to the needs of those countries and particularly to their infrastructure programmes and programmes for the promotion of new lines of production."

A report issued by the Inter-American Committee on the Alliance for Progress in Washington on March 31, 1967, stated that during 1966 the per capita growth in goods and services in Latin America had been little more than 1 per cent on average, and that economic growth had barely kept ahead of Latin America's increasing population, which was expected to reach 250,000,000 by the end of 1967.

President Johnson asked the US Congress on March 13, 1967, to increase aid to the Alliance for Progress by $1,500,000,000 over the next five years, in addition to the $1,000,000,000 already provided by the USA annually since 1961.

Second Punta del Este Conference (1967). The Punta del Este conference of American Presidents on April 14, 1967, adopted a *Declaration of the American Presidents* embodying an *Action Plan for Latin American Economic Integration and Industrial Development*.

The aims of this plan were defined as follows:

"We, the Latin American Chiefs of State, agree to take action on the following points:

"(A) Beginning in 1970, to establish progressively the Latin American Common Market, which should be substantially in operation within a period of no more than 15 years.

"(B) The Latin American Common Market will be based on the improvement of the two existing integration systems: the Latin American Free Trade Association (LAFTA) and the Central American Common Market (CACM). The two systems will initiate simultaneously a process of convergence by stages of co-operation, by closer ties and integration, taking into account the interests of Latin American countries not yet associated with these systems, in order to provide their access to one of them."

The plan envisaged a system of programmed elimination of duties and other restrictions from 1970 to not later than 1985 within the Latin American Free Trade Area, and of working towards integration in the Central American Common Market countries.

The plan also stated:

"The economic integration of Latin America demands a vigorous and sustained effort to complete and modernize the physical infrastructure of the region. It is necessary to build a land transport network and improve all types of transport systems to facilitate the movement of persons and goods throughout the hemisphere, to establish an adequate and efficient telecommunications system and interconnected power systems, and jointly to develop international watersheds, frontier regions and economic areas that include the territory of two or more countries."

To this end it listed concrete proposals "for immediate implementation", including the completion of the Pan-American Highway.

On international trade conditions the declaration stated inter alia:

"The economic development of Latin America is seriously affected by the adverse conditions in which its international trade is carried out. Market structures, financial conditions, and actions that prejudice exports and other income from outside Latin America are impeding its growth and retarding the integration process. All this causes particular concern in view of the serious and growing imbalance between the standard of living in Latin American countries and that of the industrialized nations, and at the same time calls for definite decisions and adequate instruments to implement the decisions.

"Individual and joint efforts of the member states of the OAS are essential to increase the incomes of Latin American countries derived from, and to avoid frequent fluctuations in, traditional exports, as well as to promote new exports. Such efforts are also essential to reduce any adverse effects on the external earnings of Latin American countries that may be caused by measures which may be taken by industrialized countries for balance-of-payments reasons."

It outlined a programme for overcoming these difficulties, inter alia by "the greatest reduction or the elimination of tariffs and other restrictions" without the more highly developed countries expecting reciprocity.

The plan also listed proposals for the modernization of agricultural activities and for the adjustment of education to the demands of economic, social and cultural development.

OAS Conventions

Major conventions adopted by the OAS are described below.

Latin American Convention on Human Rights. This convention, drawn up in 1969, forbade torture and maltreatment of prisoners, guaranteed freedom of expression and of religion, and provided for the creation of an **Inter-American Court of Human Rights**. It entered into force on July 18, 1978, upon ratification by Grenada (as the eleventh country, the other 10 being Colombia, Costa Rica, the Dominican Republic, Ecuador, El Salvador, Guatemala, Haiti, Honduras, Panama and Venezuela—with Nicaragua ratifying it in September 1979).

The Inter-American Court of Human Rights was accordingly established formally in San José (Costa Rica) on Sept. 3, 1979, with a membership of seven judges. Its mandate was to deal with violations of civil and political rights, but its decisions would not be legally binding and states which had not ratified the 1969 convention would be able to ask the court for an advisory opinion but not to have cases tried by it.

Convention on Kidnapping of Diplomats. A draft convention outlawing the kidnapping of foreign diplomats was approved by the Foreign Ministers of the OAS member states on Feb. 2, 1971, by 13 votes to one (Chile), with Bolivia and Peru abstaining and Barbados absent.

The convention defined criminal acts against persons with diplomatic status as common crimes and not political acts; their perpetrators would therefore not be entitled to political asylum in any country whose government had ratified the convention but would be liable to extradition or trial.

Decisions by OAS General Assembly and Ministerial Meetings

Inaugural Assembly Session. The OAS General Assembly, which normally meets annually to decide on general action and policy, held its first regular session in San José (Costa Rica) in April 1971, when a Canadian initiative for closer co-operation in social and economic development between Canada and the Latin American countries was considered. (Canada was on Feb. 2, 1972, admitted to the OAS as an observer.)

April 1972 Assembly Session. At the second regular session of the General Assembly, which took place in Washington in April 1972, ministers adopted two resolutions (i) condemning all forms of interference in the internal affairs of the 23 OAS member states, in particular "political and economic coercion" and "imported subversion and terrorism" and (ii) undertaking to limit military expenditure by Latin American countries in order that a maximum of financial resources should be devoted to social and economic development. The Assembly endorsed the principle of "ideological pluralism" as advocated by the Foreign Minister of Venezuela, according to which "each nation may realize its own destiny within the framework created by its people's will, their tradition, their temperament and their specific interests", but it did not favour the readmission of Cuba to OAU activities (from which Cuba had been excluded in 1962—see above).

The Assembly also adopted (with the USA abstaining) two resolutions (i) calling on the US Government to prevent large corporations from intervening in the internal affairs of Latin American countries and (ii) urging the US Government to take all possible measures to prevent a fall in prices of vital exports (from Latin American countries) by selling ores, in particular those of zinc, lead, tin and copper, from US strategic reserves.

1974 Declaration of Tlatelolco. In subsequent years the OAS continued to be beset by marked divergencies in the economic interests and policies of the USA and the other OAS member states. At a conference of 24 Foreign Ministers of Latin American and English-speaking Caribbean countries held in Tlatelolco (Mexico) on Feb. 21-23, 1974, with the object of conferring with the US Secretary of State, a *Declaration of Tlatelolco* was agreed to, stating inter alia that "inter-American relations must be sustained on the basis of effective equality between the states" and must be based on "non-intervention, the reduction of the use of force and coercive measures, and on respect for the right of those countries to choose their own political, economic and social systems".

In the declaration the ministers emphasized the need to intensify work on the restructuring of the inter-American system and in particular "to speed up the development of the countries on the Latin American continent and to promote the well-being of all its peoples", while the United States accepted a special responsibility and the most developed nations of the region recognized that special attention would have to be paid to the needs of the less developed. The USA offered to seek congressional approval for legislation relating to generalized tariff preferences for Latin America and the avoidance of new restrictions on market access to the United States for Latin American products. The USA also undertook to maintain present levels of aid "despite rising prices" and to facilitate the flow of new resources to the countries most affected by the rising cost of energy.

Opposition to US Trade Act. A special session of the Permanent Council of the OAS, held on Jan. 20, 1975, expressed overwhelming opposition to the 1975 US Trade Reform Act because of its provisions enabling the US President to exclude from proposed special measures relating to developing countries those states which belonged to producers' cartels—i.e. not only the Organization of Petroleum Exporting Countries (OPEC) but also producer organizations covering coffee, bauxite, copper and bananas. On Jan. 23, 1975, the OAS condemned the US Act as discriminatory and coercive and also as being in conflict with the UN Charter of

the Economic Rights and Duties of States [see page 43].

Relations with Cuba. At a special consultative meeting of OAS ministers held in San José (Costa Rica) on July 29, 1975, a resolution was adopted by 16 votes to three (with two abstentions and with the USA voting in favour) stating that the 21 signatories of the Inter-American Treaty of Reciprocal Assistance would henceforth be free to normalize, or conduct in accordance with national policy and interests, relations with the Republic of Cuba at the level and in the form each state deemed advisable.

Human Rights Issue. At a session of the OAS General Assembly, held in Grenada on June 14-23, 1977, the US Secretary of State declared that US economic aid to and trade with Latin American countries would continue to be linked to observance of human rights by those countries.

On the grounds of alleged human rights violations, the USA had in 1976 limited its military aid to Chile and cancelled that to Uruguay; in February 1977 the US President had decided to reduce US economic aid to Argentina and Uruguay, and this had led to the rejection of various forms of US aid by Argentina, Uruguay, Brazil, El Salvador, Guatemala and Chile. As a result the OAS member states were divided, on this issue, into two major blocs—those opposing the US attitude as constituting interference in their internal affairs (including Argentina, Chile, Brazil, Uruguay, Bolivia, Nicaragua and Paraguay) and those which supported it (notably Venezuela, Costa Rica, Mexico, Colombia and the English-speaking Caribbean countries).

A resolution introduced by the USA, Venezuela, Costa Rica and the Dominican Republic, calling for a strengthening of the resources and the competence of the OAS Human Rights Commission, was approved, on June 18, by 14 states (with eight abstentions and three members being absent from the vote).

Transnational Corporations. At a session of the OAS General Assembly held in Washington from June 21 to July 1, 1978, a *Code of Conduct for Transnational Corporations* was approved by 20 votes to four, with the United States abstaining from voting.

The code, said to be based on the 19th-century Calvo doctrine, laid down that foreign companies (i) must be subject to the exclusive jurisdiction of the host country, (ii) must not serve as instruments of the foreign policy of another state, (iii) must accept the sovereignty of the host country over natural resources and economic activities, and (iv) must not interfere in the host country's internal affairs or its relations with other countries.

The code also stipulated that transnational corporations should operate in a manner such as to produce financial resources for the host country, should supply the host country with the information necessary to ensure that their activities were in accordance with national policies and development programmes, and must refrain from restrictive trade practices and contribute to the scientific and technological capacity of the host country. (In an accompanying document the USA inter alia contested the exclusive jurisdiction of the host country over a foreign company.)

1979 Declaration of La Paz. A session of the General Assembly, held in La Paz (Bolivia) on Oct. 22-31, 1979, unanimously adopted, on Oct. 30, a *Declaration of La Paz*, calling for democracy, respect for human rights, ideological pluralism and disarmament in the region; condemning the use of torture; urging military governments to introduce democratic systems; expressing "deep concern at the heightening of tensions as the result of recent increases in military activity in the Caribbean" (this being a reference to US manoeuvres at the US Guantánamo naval base in Cuba in mid-October); and repudiating "the concept of the region as a sphere of influence of any power" (this concept having earlier been rejected by the Governments of Jamaica, Guyana, Grenada and St Lucia). In connexion with a report to the Assembly by the IA-ECOSOC accusing the USA of having restricted the growth of some developing countries of the region by applying protectionist measures, the declaration urged all OAS member states to refrain from adopting such measures.

Other Inter-American Co-operation Bodies and Agreements

Inter-American Development Bank (IDB)

Headquarters: Washington, D.C.

Members: All members of the Organization of American States and also the Bahamas, Guyana and Canada, as well as (from outside the region) Austria, Belgium, Denmark, Finland, France, the Federal Republic of Germany, Israel, Italy, Japan, the Netherlands, Norway, Portugal, Spain, Sweden, Switzerland, the United Kingdom and Yugoslavia.

The Inter-American Development Bank and a Fund for Special Operations were set up in April 1959. They represented the culmination of prolonged efforts by the Latin American countries for the creation of a development bank backed by the USA, ever since the Marshall Plan was initiated in 1948 for the recovery of Western Europe. Until August 1958, however, the US Government had always opposed such a scheme on the ground that private banks, the World Bank and the US Export-Import Bank were able to provide sufficient credit for sound development projects. The change in US policy was the direct result of a meeting of the Foreign Ministers of the American Republics (then numbering 21) in September 1958.

The Inter-American Development Bank, founded to finance economic and social development projects and to provide technical assistance in member countries, opened with an authorized capital stock of $850,000,000, of which $400,000,000 was to be paid in, the remaining $450,000,000 to be payable on call. The United States provided 37.5 per cent of the payable capital, and 44.5 per cent of that payable on call. By 1979 the paid-in capital amounted to $1,484 million and another $10,538 million was callable.

The IDB also administers funds set up by several donor countries, the largest of these funds being the Social Progress Trust Fund of $525,000,000 established in June 1961 by the United States under the Alliance for Progress programme.

Loans from the capital resources are made for particular economic projects, and are repayable in the currencies lent.

The powers of the IDB are vested in a Board of Governors, on which each member country is represented by one Governor and one alternate. Executive powers are delegated to an Executive Board of 12 Directors, eight of whom are elected by Latin American countries, two by member countries not in the region, one by Canada and one by the USA.

At the bank's 10th anniversary meeting at Punta del Este (Uruguay) on April 22, 1970, its achievements were criticized by the Peruvian Minister of Economic Affairs and Finance as "disheartening and incommensurate with what Latin America expected of economic and social progress", as the disparities in production, income and living standards were "even more marked than at the beginning of the decade".

The Fund for Special Operations opened with a capital of $150,000,000, of which the United States contributed $100,000,000. The fund makes loans on economically and socially useful projects which would not normally be acceptable to a bank. Repayments may be made in local currency. At June 30, 1979, the resources of the fund amounted to $5,906,578,000.

According to the annual report of the IDB presented in Rio de Janeiro on April 14-16, 1980, the gross national product of the region had in 1979 increased by almost 6 per cent (after taking account of inflation), as against an average annual 4.3 per cent for the years from 1975 to 1978 (although there remained wide disparities in per capita income per annum, ranging from $200 in Haiti to $2,100 in Venezuela). The gross national product was said to have risen from $149,000 million in 1960 to $430,000 million (at constant values) in 1979 or to about 8 per cent of the total gross national product of the developed countries, compared with 6 per cent in 1960.

The IDB's President claimed that in the 20 years of the bank's existence more Latin Americans than ever before had attained a higher standard of living and easier access to medical care and to other basic social services, and that Latin America was providing more than half the manufactured goods produced by the Third World, with its population having grown from 200,000,000 to 340,000,000. On the other hand, he said, the gap between the earnings of agricultural workers and those of other workers (the latter having remained five times as high as the former) had continued to grow, as had the gap between average earnings in Latin America and those in the developed countries of the world.

Map 10 Latin American Integration Association (Aladi) and Andean Group

Institute for Latin American Integration

This institute was established in Buenos Aires in 1965 as a permanent department of the IDB with the object of conducting research into problems of the regional integration process, organizing training courses on its various aspects and providing advisory services.

Latin American Integration Association (Aladi)

Aladi—the *Asociación Latinoamericana de Integración*—was established under an agreement signed in Montevideo on Aug. 12, 1980, by Argentina, Bolivia, Brazil, Chile, Colombia, Ecuador, Mexico, Paraguay, Peru, Uruguay and Venezuela, and scheduled to come into force on Jan. 1, 1981, after ratification by the respective signatory countries.

The decision to create Aladi in the place of the Latin American Free Trade Association (LAFTA) had been taken at a meeting of LAFTA's Council of Ministers in Acapulco (Mexico) on June 16-27, 1980. LAFTA had been set up under a Treaty of Montevideo of Feb. 18, 1960, by Argentina, Brazil, Chile, Mexico, Paraguay, Peru and Uruguay and had later been joined by Bolivia, Colombia, Ecuador and Venezuela. It had come into force on Jan. 2, 1962, but its timetable for the gradual reduction of tariff barriers between member countries (to be completed by 1972) fell into arrears; under a Caracas protocol of 1969 the deadline for completion was extended to 1980, but no substantial progress was made towards this goal, largely owing to the disparate level of development among member countries, problems of communications and transport, protectionism, conflicting economic systems and political and economic changes (notably in Brazil and Argentina), and also to the creation of the Andean Group as a subregional grouping within LAFTA [see page 305].

In the new association preferential treatment was to be given by the richer countries to the poorer, and to this end member countries were classified in three groups according to their level of development —(i) less developed (Bolivia, Ecuador, Paraguay); (ii) medium developed (Chile, Colombia, Peru, Uruguay, Venezuela) and (iii) more developed (Argentina, Brazil, Mexico).

A Secretary-General of Aladi was elected on Aug. 12, 1980.

Organization of Central American States (OCAS, or ODECA)

Headquarters: San Salvador.

Members: Costa Rica, El Salvador, Guatemala, Honduras, Nicaragua.

OCAS—the *Organización de Estados Centroamericanos* (ODECA)—was first set up on Oct. 14, 1951, at the end of a conference held in San Salvador on Oct. 10-14, 1951, to discuss measures for common action by the five Central American Republics in regard to problems of mutual interest.

The Charter of San Salvador. The organization came into being with the signing, by the five republics (listed above), of the *Charter of San Salvador*. It was officially stated that the object of the organization would be "to promote by group action the strengthening of the bonds of fraternity among the Central American states, and to serve as an instrument for the study and solution of their common problems"; that periodic meetings of foreign Ministers would be held; that special committees, with representatives from each country, would be set up to study and report on matters of mutual interest; that these bodies would include a committee on economic relations (comprising the Finance Ministers of the five countries), which would report on the possibility of a Central American customs union, and a committee on educational and cultural matters (consisting of the Ministers of Education), which would consider the eventual standardization of educational courses and methods, together with the possibility of establishing a Central American university; and that the organization would have a permanent secretariat with its headquarters in San Salvador.

On Nov. 30, 1961, at a conference of the Foreign Ministers of the organization's member countries, it was decided to prepare for the creation of a common supreme command with an integrated Latin American army; integrated organs for security; a common defence council; and common organs to deal with economic and social matters.

The New Charter. At a meeting of Foreign Ministers of the five member countries held on Nov. 15-17, 1962, and attended also by an observer from Panama, it was provisionally agreed to set up a new Organization of Central American States superseding the organization of the same name which had been set up in October 1951. The Charter of the new organization, known as the *San Salvador Charter* (the same name as the Charter of the previous organization), was formally signed at a further meeting of Foreign Ministers held in Panama City on Dec. 12-14, 1962.

The new San Salvador Charter provided for the setting up of: (i) A Supreme Council of heads of member states; (ii) a Council of Foreign Ministers; (iii) an Executive Council with permanent headquarters in San Salvador; (iv) a Legislative Council comprising three legislators from each member country, to standardize legislation; (v) an Economic Council to pursue ´actively the aim of a common market similar to the European Economic Community; (vi) a Cultural and Educational Council; (vii) a Council of Defence Ministers to maintain collective security; and (viii) a Central American Court of Justice.

The new Charter, which came into force in 1965, was not signed by Panama, because of "international commitments and economic problems". [See also USA-Panama relations, page 318.] In addition to the organs mentioned above, there is a General Secretariat (the Central American Bureau), which serves to co-ordinate the work of the various organs and to prepare information.

Declaration of Central America. On March 18-19, 1963, a meeting between the Presidents of the member countries of OCAS and the Presidents of the USA and Panama took place in San José (Costa Rica). At the end of the meeting a *Declaration of Central America* was issued, in which it was stated:

"The Presidents of the Republics of Central America and Panama are determined to improve the well-being of their peoples, and are aware that such a task demands a dynamic economic and social development programme based on the carefully planned use of human, natural and financial resources. It also depends on important changes of the economic, social and administrative structure, within the framework of the principles that govern our democratic institutions."

The Presidents continued by pledging:

"To accelerate establishment of a customs union to perfect the functioning of the Central American Common Market; to formulate and implement national economic and social development plans, co-ordinating them at the Central American level, and progressively to carry out regional planning for the various sectors of the economy; to establish monetary union and common fiscal, monetary and social policies within the programme of economic integration; to co-operate in programmes to improve the prices of primary export commodities; to complete as soon as possible the reforms needed to achieve the objectives set forth in the Act of Bogotá and the Charter of Punta del Este, especially in the fields of agriculture, taxation, education, public administration and social welfare; to take the above measures with a view to achieving the creation of a Central American economic community which will establish relationships with other nations or regional groups having similar objectives."

El Salvador-Honduras Conflict and Belize Issue

In recent years OCAS has been preoccupied with two problems—(i) the conflict between El Salvador and Honduras, which had led to the severance of their diplomatic relations following the "football" war between them in 1969, and (ii) Guatemala's claim to sovereignty over Belize (the former British Honduras, currently still a British dependence).

In the conflict between El Salvador and Honduras, these two states agreed at a meeting held in San José on June 4, 1970, to the creation of a demilitarized zone along their common frontier, while the three other OCAS member states undertook to police such a zone. However, this agreement was not implemented until after the two Presidents (of El Salvador and Honduras) had on June 14, 1976, agreed on this zone as proposed and a definitive ceasefire agreement, guaranteed by Costa Rica, Guatemala and Nicaragua, had been signed on July 30, 1976. The conflict was, however, settled by a peace treaty signed on Oct. 30, 1980 [see page 332].

The Guatemalan claim to Belize was supported as "legitimate" by the heads of state of Costa Rica, El Salvador, Honduras, Nicaragua and Panama, meeting in Guatemala City on Nov. 3, 1975, and on Aug. 25, 1977, the Foreign Ministers of Costa Rica, El Salvador, Honduras and Nicaragua again expressed their support for Guatemala's Belize policy. These four countries were the only UN member states to vote against a UN General Assembly resolution of Nov. 28, 1977, calling for early independence for Belize. On the other hand the President of Costa Rica agreed, at a meeting held in Bogotá (Colombia) on Aug. 5-6, 1977, with the heads of state of Colombia, Jamaica, Mexico, Panama and Venezuela that "the conflict should be settled by peaceful means prescribed in the OAS and UN Charters with respect for [Belize's] territorial integrity and the principle of self-determination".

Central American Defence Council (CONDECA)

A Central American Defence Council was established on Dec. 14, 1963, with headquarters in Guatemala City, by the Governments of El Salvador, Guatemala, Honduras and Nicaragua. These four governments decided on July 2, 1965, to create a military bloc for the co-ordination of all defence measures against possible communist aggression. CONDECA, which co-operated closely with the US Southern Command, was subsequently joined by Panama, which, however, withdrew from the organization after the assumption of power by Lt. Col. Omar Torrijos Herrera in 1968. Honduras left CONDECA in 1973, and after the overthrow of the Somoza regime in Nicaragua in 1979, only El Salvador and Guatemala were left as CONDECA members. (El Salvador, however, had rejected US military aid in March 1977.)

Central American Common Market (CACM)

Headquarters: Guatemala City.

Members: Costa Rica, El Salvador, Guatemala, Honduras and Nicaragua.

The Ministers of Economy of Costa Rica, Guatemala, Honduras, Nicaragua and El Salvador, meeting in Guatemala City on Feb. 24, 1957, approved in principle two treaties designed to create a free trade area in Central America and a system of regional industries.

A 10-year multilateral trade treaty was designed to eliminate import and export duties on certain products embracing about 49 per cent of inter-Central American trade on the basis of 1955 figures. In its original form the treaty laid down two lists of member countries' products: (i) Those which would have unhindered circulation within the projected free trade zone, and (ii) those that might be subjected to quantitative export and import controls by member countries. To this, the Ministers of Economy added a third classification—viz., products whose tariffs might be lowered gradually over several years to lessen the economic impact of the change. The treaty stated that the five countries would form a customs union after the creation of a free trade zone, "as soon as conditions are propitious".

The second treaty provided for the establishment of regional industries in areas where the most efficient use could be made of local resources and transport, and in such a manner as not to duplicate existing industries. It laid down, inter alia, that the industries concerned would have access to the free trade zone; that conflicting national interests would be resolved by a separate five-nation pact to be signed for every regional industry established; and that such pacts would include the specific amounts of tariff reductions, tax-exemptions, fiscal benefits and subsidies.

A common market for Central America first came into effect on Jan. 8, 1959, when three out of the five countries which had signed the five-nation treaty on the establishment of a free trade area had ratified it. It was brought within the framework of the organization of Central American States in 1960.

On Dec. 13, 1960, representatives of the Governments of El Salvador, Guatemala, Honduras and Nicaragua signed, in Managua, the *General Treaty of Central American Economic Integration*. The 20-year treaty, which came into force in June 1961, established the Central American Common Market, and took precedence over all earlier free trade agreements between the contracting parties. The treaty provided for the immediate removal of internal duties on 95 per cent of product classifications, and

for the abolition of all tariff restrictions by June 1966. Provision was also made for the free movement of labour and capital throughout the treaty area.

Costa Rica entered the common market in 1962, while Honduras withdrew from active participation in December 1970, although it continued to regard itself as a de jure member.

On May 16, 1976, the text of a draft treaty was published in Nicaragua providing for the eventual establishment of a Central American Economic and Social Community (*Comunidad Económica y Social de Centroamérica*) to replace the CACM. According to the draft treaty, all products of the Central American region would circulate duty-free among the member countries and their sale would be liable to restrictions only for health or internal security reasons. It was envisaged that the new community would initially comprise the five CACM member countries and that Panama would have the opportunity of joining at a later date.

CACM TREATIES

The treaties on which the Central American Common Market system of equalization of duties and reduction of tariffs is based are the following:

(1) *Tratado Multilateral de Libre Comercio e Integración Económica Centroamericana*. This was signed in 1958 by El Salvador, Guatemala, Honduras and Nicaragua, and in 1962 by Costa Rica. It provided for the equalization of customs duties between the signatory countries, and for the removal of duties from regionally-produced goods, the latter to be completed by 1972.

(2) *Tratado de Integración Económica Centroamericana*. This was signed in February 1960 by El Salvador, Guatemala and Honduras; Nicaragua signed in December 1960, and Costa Rica in July 1962. When Costa Rica had added her signature in 1962, all five partners signed supplementary agreements establishing uniform duties for some 95 per cent of all goods imported into their countries.

(3) *Tratado de Asociación Económica*. This treaty, between El Salvador, Guatemala and Honduras, was signed in February 1960 and came into force in April 1960. It removed tariffs on groups of commodities in the trade between the three states, to the value of 50 per cent of the total trade. The treaty was valid for 20 years with unlimited extension. A Development and Welfare Fund, with a capital of $5,500,000, was set up under its terms.

(4) *Tratado de Intercambio Preferencial y de Libre Comercio*. This treaty, signed by

Costa Rica, Nicaragua and Panama in 1961 and ratified in 1962, was aimed at speeding up economic integration through tariff reductions between the members.

By 1967 internal tariff dismantlement had been applied to 95 per cent of all items of trade. The rates of a common external tariff had by then entered into force for more than 90 per cent of items of trade.

ORGANIZATION

The principal organ of the CACM is the Central American Economic Council, consisting of the Ministers of Economy of the member countries, which meets every three months. Its other organs are the Executive Council, composed of two government delegates from each of the member countries, and the Permanent Secretariat in Guatemala City.

INSTITUTIONS

There are a considerable number of institutions which now function within the framework of the CACM. The most important of these is the *Banco Centroamericano de Integración Económica* (BCIE). Founded in 1960, the Central American Integration Bank came into operation on Sept. 2, 1961, with a capital of $40,000,000, which by 1972 was raised to $200,000,000. On July 29, 1965, a Central American Integration Fund, to finance regional infrastructure projects, was established when the USA placed a loan of $35,000,000 at the disposal of the members of the bank. Each CACM member also contributed $1,400,000 to the fund. In 1966 Mexico made a loan to the bank of $5,000,000.

A *Camara Centroamericana de Compensación de Monedas* (Central American Clearing House) was set up within the framework of the BCIE to encourage the use of Central American currencies within the area. The clearing house began operations on Oct. 1, 1961.

The *Unión Monetaria Centroamericana*, a union of the central banks of the five Central American Republics, has been effective as a formal union since 1964. Its main organ is the *Consejo Monetaria Centroamericano*.

Other institutions are listed below with their dates of foundation:

(1) *Federación de Cámaras de Comercio del Istmo Centroamericano,* founded 1961.

(2) *Federación de Cámaras y Asociacioned Industriales de Centroamérica,* founded 1960.

(3) *Federación de Asociaciones de Banqueros de Centroamérica y Panamá*, founded 1965.

(4) *Instituto Centroamericano de Investigación y Tecnologia Industrial,* founded 1955.

(5) *Instituto Centroamericano de Administración de Empresas,* founded 1964.

(6) *Instituto Centroamericano de Administración Publica,* founded 1954 (Panama being a member).

(7) *Consejo Superior Universitario Centroamericano,* founded 1948.

(8) *Instituto de Nutrición de Centroamérica y Panama,* founded 1949.

(9) *Corporación Centroamericana de Servicios de Navegación Aerea,* founded 1960.

(10) *Secretaría de Integración Turistica Centroamericana.*

(11) *Comisión Técnica de las Telecomunicaciones de Centroamérica.*

Declaration of Guayana on Venezuelan Aid

Under a Declaration of Guayana, signed in Puerto Ordaz (Venezuela) on Dec. 14, 1974, by the Presidents of Costa Rica, El Salvador, Guatemala, Honduras, Nicaragua and Venezuela and the "supreme leader" of Panama, Venezuela undertook to supply financial aid and investments to the six other countries in order to compensate them for their heavy oil import bills.

Under this agreement the Central American states would purchase Venezuelan oil, paying approximately half the current price to Venezuela and depositing the difference in their central banks in their own currencies; the resulting funds were to be held in interest-bearing accounts at Venezuela's disposal in each country. Venezuela would also contribute between $60,000,000 and $80,000,000 over two years to finance a coffee-stockpiling scheme in Central America, with a multinational coffee organization being created [see page 96], and Venezuela would make a further $60,000,000 available to the Central American Bank for Economic Integration.

Latin American Economic System (SELA)

Headquarters: Caracas.

Members: Argentina, Barbados, Bolivia, Brazil, Chile, Colombia, Costa Rica, Cuba, the Dominican Republic, Ecuador, El Salvador, Grenada, Guatemala, Guyana, Haiti, Honduras, Jamaica, Mexico, Nicaragua, Panama, Paraguay, Peru, Spain, Suriname, Trinidad and Tobago, Uruguay and Venezuela.

SELA (the *Sistema Económico Latinoamericano*) was formed under a treaty signed in Panama on Oct. 18, 1975, to formulate common economic strategies among member states, to encourage the formation of Latin American multinational companies and to develop a code of conduct for transnational companies operating in the region.

Its supreme body is the Latin American Council, which consists of one member from each member country and holds ordinary sessions once a year. It elects the organization's permanent secretary, but it has no powers to make decisions affecting the national policies of member states. SELA has action committees on fertilizer manufacturing (in Mexico City), marine and freshwater products (in Lima, Peru), handicrafts (in Panama City), housing and public works (in Quito, Ecuador), tourism (at San José, Costa Rica), Nicaragua's reconstruction programme (in Managua), technological information (in Rio de Janeiro) and the sale and distribution of highly nutritional food supplements.

At a meeting of the Latin American Council held at Carabellada (Venezuela) on April 3-5, 1978, ministers condemned "restrictions applied by the capitalist countries on raw materials produced by underdeveloped countries" and called for an end to "discriminatory measures by the US foreign trade law".

Spain became a member on SELA under an agreement concluded on Sept. 21, 1979.

At a meeting of the Latin American Council in Lima on April 10-11, 1980, it was decided to create a new financing organization which would make Latin America independent of the International Monetary Fund which (according to the Finance Minister of Peru) was applying credit policies which did not always take due account of the circumstances of the recipient countries.

SELA was granted observer status at the United Nations General Assembly on Oct. 13, 1980.

Latin American Energy Organization (OLADE)

Headquarters: Quito (Ecuador).

Members: Barbados, Bolivia, Brazil, Chile, Colombia, Costa Rica, Cuba, the Dominican Republic, Ecuador, El Salvador, Grenada, Guatemala, Guyana, Haiti, Honduras, Jamaica, Mexico, Nicaragua, Panama, Paraguay, Peru, Suriname, Trinidad and Tobago, Uruguay and Venezuela.

OLADE was formed under a treaty signed by 22 Latin American and Caribbean countries in November 1973 with the object of providing a co-operative (but not a supranational) organization constituting a framework for the integration, conservation, sale, defence and development of oil and other energy resources in the region.

At a ministerial meeting held in Mexico City on Sept. 8-12, 1975, a work programme was approved for the organization's permanent secretariat to (i) establish the basis for a regional inventory of energy resources; (ii)

define general outlines of national energy programmes and a regional energy plan; (iii) draw up national legislation on the transfer of technology; and (iv) study the creation of a financial institution for OLADE. It was also agreed that the oil-exporting member countries (among which Ecuador and Venezuela were members of the Organization of Petroleum Exporting Countries—OPEC, while other significant oil producers included Argentina, Brazil, Colombia, Mexico and Trinidad and Tobago) would establish a $6,000 million loan fund to assist those countries of the region which were experiencing balance-of-payments difficulties.

At another ministerial meeting held in Mexico City on Sept. 5-8, 1978, it was decided to create, as from January 1980, a financing system enabling those Latin American countries which were poor in energy resources to finance their energy research programmes. (This decision was endorsed by Bolivia, Chile, Costa Rica, Cuba, the Dominican Republic, Ecuador, Haiti, Honduras, Jamaica, Panama and Peru but opposed by Brazil, while Venezuela abstained from voting.)

Latin American Parliament

Headquarters: Lima (Peru).

Members: The parliaments of Latin American countries.

At a meeting of representatives of Latin American countries and institutions held in Lima on Dec. 6-11, 1964, it was decided to set up a permanent Latin American Parliament.

The first session of the Parliament was held on July 17-18, 1965, and was attended by delegations from Argentina, Bolivia, Brazil, Chile, Colombia, Ecuador, Guatemala, Panama, Peru, Uruguay and Venezuela. Under the statutes approved at the session, the Latin American Parliament is a permanent unicameral body, meeting in ordinary session once a year and in extraordinary session at the request of a majority of its members.

The functions of the Parliament are to promote Latin American integration in all fields, to protect human rights, to oppose any form of colonialism, and to defend the peace.

River Plate Basin Development

A treaty for the economic integration and joint development of the Rio de la Plata region was signed in Brasília on April 23, 1969, by the Foreign Ministers of Argentina, Bolivia, Brazil, Paraguay and Uruguay. The treaty provided for the establishment of an Inter-governmental Co-ordinating Committee as the permanent body responsible for promoting and co-ordinating assistance from international institutions and for implementing decisions made by the five countries' Foreign Ministers.

However, no full agreement was reached in later years on the exploitation of waters, in particular by means of hydroelectric works, in the region as each of the participating states insisted on retaining its sovereignty over its natural resources and the right to dispose freely of them. (Early in 1977 Argentina revoked an 1857 bilateral treaty with Brazil on river transport in the River Plate basin.)

Andean Group

Headquarters: Lima (Peru).

Members: Bolivia, Colombia, Ecuador, Peru and Venezuela.

Associate Member: Panama.

Observers: Costa Rica, the Dominican Republic, Panama and Spain.

Under the *Cartagena Agreement* signed in Bogotá (Colombia) on May 26, 1969, the Governments of Bolivia, Chile, Colombia, Ecuador and Peru set up an Andean Common Market, in which all internal customs tariffs between the five member countries were to be abolished by 1980. This agreement came into force on Nov. 24, 1969.

The supreme authority of the organization is the Andean Group Commission consisting of one representative from each member country. The Commission's policies are formulated, and their implementation supervised, by a three-member Junta.

The institutional structure of the organization also comprises (i) a Consultative Committee responsible for liaison between the Junta and the member countries, (ii) an Economic and Social Committee, (iii) the Andean Development Corporation, (iv) the Andean Reserve Fund, (v) a Court of Justice, (vi) the Andean Parliament and (vii) the Andean Council of Foreign Ministers (the last three bodies having been set up in 1979 —see also below).

Group Developments

Under Decision 24 taken by the group's Commission in December 1970, foreign investments in the group's five founder member countries were subject to the following conditions: As from July 1971, wholly foreign-owned companies wishing to qualify for preferential treatment in the Andean group market would, within three years, have to sign an agreement to transfer 51 per cent of their shares to local investors over a period of 15 years in Chile, Colombia and Peru, and of 20 years in Bolivia and Ecuador, and such companies would be allowed to repatriate not more than 14 per cent of the invested capital (unless specially exempted from this condition).

In May 1971 the member states agreed on the pooling of their merchant fleets, and in October of the same year agreement was reached on the gradual removal of customs duties as envisaged in the Cartagena Agreement.

In October 1972 Mexico became a working partner in the group, co-operating with it in joint financial and industrial development.

An application by Venezuela for full membership of the group was agreed to on Feb. 13, 1973, and became effective on Jan. 1, 1974. Venezuelan legislation applying the provisions of Decision 24 was published on April 29 of that year, although under special concessions made to Venezuela 450 products were exempted from having to be free of duty by 1985.

Chile formally withdrew from the group on Oct. 30, 1976. Chilean legislation of July 1974 had failed to comply with major conditions laid down in Decision 24. In April 1976 a ministerial conference had ratified a protocol (known as Decision 100) amending the Cartagena Agreement by extending by two years the group's original industrial tariff deadlines and common external tariff programme, but Chile refused to sign this protocol. It subsequently persisted in this refusal even though the group had in August 1976 made special concessions to Chile in an attempt to prevent its defection from the group.

Also on Oct. 30, 1976, Decision 100 was amended by a protocol extending the deadlines by a further year, and at the same time changes in the foreign investment regulations were confirmed, as had been contained in a *Declaration of Sochagota* of Aug. 15, 1976. In particular, the 14 per cent limit on repatriation of profits by foreign companies was raised to 20 per cent; capital from individual member countries was to be treated as national investment within the region as a whole; investments by official international finance organizations were to be treated as "neutral capital" with no restrictive legislation; and foreign companies were to be allowed to increase from 5 to 7 per cent their annual reinvestment in countries in which they operated.

Under the *Arequipa Protocol* signed on April 21, 1978, further amendments were made to the Cartagena Agreement, including the following: (i) In Colombia, Peru and Venezuela the full adoption of the common external tariff would be completed by Dec. 31, 1983 (instead of 1982), and in Bolivia and Ecuador by Dec. 31, 1989 (instead of 1987); and (ii) internal tariffs between Bolivia and Ecuador would be eliminated in 1989 instead of 1988 (although the deadline for the removal of internal tariffs on goods traded between Colombia, Venezuela and Peru remained at 1983).

At a meeting of the heads of state of Bolivia, Colombia, Ecuador, Venezuela and also Panama (not then a member of the group) and the Prime Minister of Peru in Bogotá on Aug. 8, 1978, a *Declaration of Bogotá* was signed in which, inter alia, (i) it was decided to update development programmes in the metal-working and petrochemical industries; (ii) concern was expressed over the situation in less developed Andean nations, notably Bolivia; (iii) greater attention was called to the Andean Development Corporation [see below]; and (iv) it was pointed out that action was needed in facilitating international road transport and implementing joint schemes for border integration.

At a meeting of the Presidents of the group's five member countries in Cartagena on May 26-28, 1978, a *Mandate of Cartagena* was signed, calling for (i) the fostering of greater economic and political co-operation in the 1980s and the encouragement of more subregional development programmes, especially industrial ones; (ii) the promotion of the goals of the Latin American Economic System (SELA, see page 303); (iii) the creation of an Andean judicial tribunal which would seek to resolve problems arising over the interpretation of and compliance with Andean Group decisions; and (iv) the holding of regular summit meetings. It was also agreed to give the private sector of the economy a greater role in planning.

A memorandum of understanding with the United States concerning trade, financing, science and technology, development of industry, agriculture and infrastructure was signed in Washington and entered into force on Nov. 21, 1979.

A consultative Council of Ministers, established under an agreement signed by all Andean Group member states except Bolivia on Nov. 13, 1979, to formulate and co-ordinate the external policy of the region, held its first meeting in Santa Cruz (Bolivia) on Jan. 14-15, 1980, when it declared its support for Bolivia's quest for access to the sea.

A memorandum of understanding on the promotion of mutual relations and the stimulation of Latin American co-operation was signed by the Andean Group and Brazil on Jan. 17, 1980.

In February 1980 it was announced that the target for a common Andean Group customs tariff had been set at about 28 per cent, to be effected by Jan. 1, 1981, with phased approach to this target to be completed by 1983 in Colombia, Peru and Venezuela, and later in Bolivia and Ecuador.

At a meeting in Santa Marta (Colombia) on Dec. 18, 1980, of the heads of state of Colombia, Ecuador, Peru and Venezuela and also those of Costa Rica, the Dominican Republic, El Salvador and Panama and the Prime Minister of Spain, it was decided to grant observer status to Costa Rica and the Dominican Republic. Spain had been made an observer in 1979, and Panama an associate member of the Andean Group in the same year.

Andean Development Corporation and Andean Reserve Fund

The **Andean Development Corporation**, with headquarters in Caracas, was formed in 1968 to act as the development-financing arm of the Andean Group, mainly for industrial development and for the creation of basic services. Its authorized capital was (in 1976) $400,000,000.

The **Andean Reserve Fund**, with headquarters in Bogotá, was established in 1977 and began its operations in July 1978. Its organs are an Assembly consisting of the Ministers of Economy or Finance of the Andean Group's member countries; a Board of Directors comprising the Governors of the member countries' central banks; and an Executive President. Its initial capital was $240,000,000 subscribed by the five member countries, and it was authorized inter alia to invest in the Andean Development Corporation.

Other Organizations for Inter-American Co-operation

(1) A **South Pacific Permanent Commission** was founded by Ecuador, Peru and Chile on Aug. 18, 1952, under a *Santiago Declaration* which established the principle of sovereignty and jurisdiction over adjacent waters up to 200 nautical miles from the coast. On May 7, 1980, Colombia was accepted as a member of the commission.

(2) An **International Regional Organization of Plant Protection and Animal Health** (*Organismo Internacional Regional de Sanidad Agropecuaria—OIRSA*) was set up in 1953 in San Salvador (El Salvador). Its member countries are Costa Rica, El Salvador, Guatemala, Honduras, Mexico, Nicaragua and Panama.

(3) A **Latin American Association of Communications Researchers (ALAIC)** was founded on Nov. 20, 1978, by Chile, Colombia, Peru, Uruguay and Venezuela "to promote a new informational order at an international level".

The 1974 Declaration of Ayacucho

At a meeting of representatives of eight

Latin American countries—Argentina, Bolivia, Colombia, Cuba, Ecuador, Panama, Peru and Venezuela—held in Lima on Dec. 7-9, 1974, to mark the 150th anniversary of the battle of Ayacucho (in which the last of the Spanish royal armies was defeated by South American troops in 1824), the participants signed a *Declaration of Ayacucho* in which they expressed their commitment to the establishment of a permanent state of internal peace and co-operation, to the eventual effective attainment of effective arms limitation and to the dedication of all possible resources to the economic and social development of each country. They condemned the use of nuclear power for other than peaceful purposes and they deplored the "economic dependence" imposed on their continent.

The declaration dealt in particular with the following items:

Latin American Nationalism. The declaration described Latin American nationalism as the awareness of the peoples of their true personality, which was the result of cross-breeding, the fusion of cultures, and common historical, social and economic backgrounds. To strengthen their unity it was necessary, in the present international situation, to solve regional problems without external interference, to act jointly to promote the interests of the nations, and to prevent the prospering in Latin America of policies which might impair the personality of the peoples and the sovereignty of the states.

Inter-State Relations. The signatories reiterated their adherence to the principles of, inter alia: the juridical equality of states; their territorial integrity and right of self-determination; ideological pluralism; respect for human rights; and the renunciation of the threat or use of force or of armed, economic or financial aggression in relations between states.

Economic Questions. The signatories also stated that the concerted efforts of all the nations of Latin America were essential to promote the formation and strengthening of associations between the producer and exporter countries; to obtain the best terms of access for Latin American products to international markets; to obtain the best conditions for the transfer and interchange of technology for their particular needs; to ensure adequate supplies of essential commodities, particularly food; to establish multinational Latin American concerns; and to co-operate in monetary matters, transport and communications.

Other Contents. The declaration also included a pledge to give the fullest understanding to the land-locked position of Bolivia, and condemned the colonial enclaves still existing in Latin America, which were said to constitute a potential threat to peace.

Amazon Co-operation Treaty

A treaty on economic co-operation in the Amazon basin area was signed in Brasília on July 3, 1978, by the Foreign Ministers of Bolivia, Brazil, Colombia, Ecuador, Guyana, Peru, Suriname and Venezuela.

The object of this Amazon Pact was to promote the harmonious development of the Amazon territories of the eight signatory states by joint efforts to their common benefit; to protect the environment; to preserve and make rational use of natural resources; and to maintain full freedom of commercial navigation on the Amazon and other international rivers of the region as guaranteed by each signatory. In particular the treaty provided for the preservation of species of flora and fauna and the maintenance of the ecological balance; co-ordination of health services to fight endemic diseases; increased scientific and technical co-operation; and the establishment of adequate transport and communications facilities. National sovereignty was safeguarded by a number of clauses in the treaty, reserving for each signatory the sovereign right of exploitation and use of its own natural resources with no restrictions other than those established by international law, and stating that "nothing in the treaty can be regarded as having any bearing upon a border dispute or controversy". According to the President of Brazil, the pact's principal aim was to emphasize that the development and preservation of the region was the exclusive responsibility of the Amazon basin countries and to protect the area from "foreign interference".

On Oct. 24, 1980, the parties to the treaty signed a 17-point *Declaration of Belém*, in which it was emphasized that the development of the Amazon region and the conservation of its environment were inseparably linked to each other; that these objectives were the sole responsibility of the Amazon states; and that a programme would be worked out for scientific and technical co-operation in the development and exploration of the region.

Treaties and Agreements of the United States

Defence Treaties of the USA

Many bilateral and multilateral agreements relating to defence have been concluded by the United States with partners throughout the world. Of these a number are direct defence treaties, while others are merely agreements on defence assistance.

BILATERAL TREATIES

The bilateral agreements are listed below in alphabetical order. Where only one date is given, the agreement entered into force immediately after signature.

[*Note.* The (US) Mutual Security Act of 1951 (see also page 184) provided inter alia for the creation of a Mutual Security Agency which would be responsible for developing and administering aid programmes to "sustain and increase military effort, including production, equipment and material in each country, or in groups of countries, which receive US military assistance" and for providing such equipment, materials, commodities, services, financial or other assistance as might be found necessary for carrying out mutual defence programmes.]

Argentina. (1) Agreement relating to a military assistance programme (May 10, 1964).

(2) Armed forces co-operative projects agreement (May 5, 1970).

Australia. (1) Mutual defence assistance agreement (exchange of notes Feb. 1 and Feb. 20, 1951; entry into force Feb. 20, 1951).

(2) Agreement on co-operation regarding atomic information for mutual defence purposes (July 12, 1957; entry into force Aug. 14, 1957).

(3) Agreement to facilitate the interchange of patent rights and technical information for defence purposes (Jan. 24, 1958).

(4) Agreement on a mutual weapons development programme (Aug. 23, 1960).

(5) Agreement relating to the establishment of a United States naval communication station in Australia (signed May 9, 1963; entered into force June 28, 1963; amended on July 12, 1968, with effect from July 1, 1968, and on March 21, 1974).

(6) Agreement relating to the establishment of a joint defence space research facility (Dec. 9, 1966; extended on Oct. 19, 1977).

(7) Agreement relating to the establishment of a joint defence space communications station in Australia (Nov. 10, 1969).

(8) Agreement on the joint operation of the US naval communications station at North-West Cape, Western Australia (Jan. 10, 1974).

(9) Agreement on the establishment in South-West Australia of an OMEGA navigating facility (Sept. 20, 1977).

Austria. (1) Exchange of notes on mutual security agreement (Dec. 14, 1951, and Jan. 5, 1952; entry into force on latter date).

(2) Exchange of notes relating to the purchase by Austria of certain military equipment, materials and services (Aug. 9, 1957).

Barbados. Exchange of notes between the United States and the United Kingdom relating to the assurances required under the (US) Mutual Security Act of 1951 (Jan. 8, 1952; applicable to Barbados March 20, 1952).

Belgium. (1) Mutual defence agreement under the North Atlantic Treaty (Jan. 27, 1950; entry into force March 30, 1950; amended June 19 and 29, 1976. (See also agreements with Denmark, France, Italy, Luxembourg, the Netherlands, Norway and the United Kingdom.)

(2) Exchange of notes relating to the assurances required under the (US) Mutual Security Act of 1951 (Jan. 7, 1952).

(3) Exchange of notes relating to a weapons production programme (April 6 and 22, 1960; entry into force on latter date).

(4) Agreement for co-operation in the use of atomic energy for mutual defence purposes (May 17, 1962; entry into force Sept. 5, 1962).

Benin. Agreement on the furnishing of military equipment, materials and services to Dahomey (now Benin) to help assure its security and independence (exchange of notes June 5 and 13, 1962; entry into force June 13, 1962).

Bolivia. (1) Military assistance agreement (exchange of notes, March 21 and April 22, 1958; entry into force April 22, 1958).

(2) Agreement on the furnishing of defence articles and services to Bolivia (April 26, 1962).

Brazil. (1) Agreement for the establishment of a joint group on emergency supply problems (July 24, 1951).

(2) Military assistance agreement (March 15, 1952; entered into force May 19, 1953; terminated March 11, 1977, except for safeguard clauses).

(3) Exchange of notes on understanding relating to military assistance (Jan. 30, 1964).

Canada*. (1) The Ogdensburg declaration regarding the establishment of a permanent joint board on defence (Aug. 18, 1940).

(2) Protocol concerning the defence of Newfoundland (March 27, 1941).

(3) Joint statement concerning defence co-operation providing for the permanent joint board on defence to continue collaboration for security purposes (Feb. 12, 1947).

(4) Exchange of notes on the establishment of a joint industrial mobilization committee (April 12, 1949).

(5) Exchange of notes relating to economic co-operation for defence (Oct. 26, 1950).

(6) Exchange of notes giving formal effect to a statement of principles for economic co-operation for defence (Oct. 26, 1950).

(7) Exchange of notes regarding the extension and co-ordination of the continental radar defence system (Pine Tree) (Aug. 1, 1951).

(8) Exchange of notes concerning the installation of an oil pipeline from Haines to Fairbanks, Alaska (June 30, 1953).

---

* See also page 185.

(9) Exchange of notes concerning the construction and operation of a loran station at Cape Christian, Baffin Island (May 3, 1954).

(10) Exchange of notes governing the establishment of a distant early warning system in Canadian territory (Dew Line) (May 5, 1955).

(11) Agreement for co-operation regarding atomic information for mutual defence purposes (June 15, 1955, entry into force July 22, 1955; amended May 22, 1959).

(12) Agreement for co-operation on uses of atomic energy for mutual defence purposes (May 22, 1959; entry into force July 27, 1959).

(13) Agreement on the organization and operations of the North American Air Defence Command (NORAD) (May 12, 1958; extended March 30, 1968, May 12, 1973, for two years; May 8, 1975, for five years until May 1980; and on May 12, 1980, for one year).

In 1975 it was decided to extend NORAD by the establishment, in addition to the existing control centre at North Bay (Ontario), of another control centre at Edmonton (Alberta), with the result that all Canadian air space would be controlled from centres located in Canada and manned by Canadian personnel.

(14) Exchange of notes concerning the establishment of a Canada-US committee on joint defence (Aug. 29 and Sept. 2, 1958; entry into force on latter date).

(15) Exchange of notes concerning the establishment in Canada of short-range tactical air navigation facilities at nine sites (TACAN) (May 1, 1959).

(16) Agreement to provide for co-operation in the uses of atomic energy for mutual defence purposes (May 22, 1959).

(17) Exchange of notes concerning the establishment of an integrated communications system to support the ballistic missiles early warning system (July 13, 1959).

(18) Exchange of notes concerning the cost-sharing and related arrangements with respect to planned improvements in the continental air defence system (Sept. 27, 1961).

(19) Exchange of notes concerning the establishment, maintenance and operation of a back-up interceptor control system to strengthen the continental air defence system (Nov. 24, 1965).

(20) Exchange of notes concerning the establishment, operation and maintenance of improved ground-to-air military communications facilities in northern Canada (Dec. 1, 1965).

(21) Exchange of notes revising an agreement of Nov. 15, 1963, providing for joint co-operation on civil emergency planning (Aug. 8, 1967).

(22) Agreement relating to the installation, operation and maintenance of a circuit for narrative record traffic between the defence agencies (Jan. 7 and 19, 1976; entry into force on latter date).

(23) Memorandum of understanding concerning region operations control centre (March 5 and April 11, 1977; entry into force on latter date).

(24) Memorandum of understanding concerning NAVSTAR global positioning system (Aug. 7 and Oct. 5, 1978; entry into force on latter date).

(25) Memorandum of understanding pertaining to co-ordination of co-operative research and development (Feb. 1, 1979).

There are, in addition, a number of agreements between the US and Canada relating to air bases, radar stations and communications facilities in particular regions of Canada.

Chile. Military assistance agreement (April 9, 1952; entered into force July 11, 1952).

Colombia. (1) Military assistance agreement (April 17, 1952).

(2) Agreement on Army, Navy and Air Force advisers (exchange of notes July 13 and Sept. 16, 1955; entry into force Sept. 20, 1955).

(3) Agreement relating to the furnishing of military equipment, materials and services to Colombia (April 3, 1961).

Costa Rica. Agreement on the furnishing of defence articles and services to Costa Rica for the purpose of contributing to its internal security (exchange of notes May 21 and June 18, 1962; entry into force June 18, 1962).

Cuba. Agreement for the lease to the USA of lands in Cuba for coaling and naval stations (Feb. 16 and Feb. 23, 1903; entered into force Feb. 23, 1903).

Under this agreement, confirmed by a treaty of 1934, the United States was granted complete jurisdiction and control over a military base on Guantánamo Bay at the southern tip of Cuba, in return for which the United States would recognize Cuban sovereignty over the area. After the deterioration in US-Cuban relations in 1960, President Eisenhower issued a statement in November of that year, saying that the agreement on the Guantánamo Bay military base could be modified or abrogated only by agreement between the two parties, and that the US Government had no intention of agreeing to modification or abrogation.

Cyprus. Exchange of notes between the United States and the United Kingdom relating to the assurances required under the

(US) Mutual Security Act of 1951, made applicable to Cyprus (Jan. 8, 1952).

Denmark. (1) Mutual defence assistance agreement under the North Atlantic Treaty (Jan. 27, 1950). (See also agreements with Belgium, France, Italy, Luxembourg, the Netherlands, Norway and the United Kingdom.)

(2) Exchange of notes relating to the assurances required by the (US) Mutual Security Act of 1951 (Jan. 8, 1952).

(3) Exchange of notes relating to a weapons production programme (April 12, 1960).

(4) Two agreements concerning the defence of Greenland (the first signed April 27, 1951; and in force June 8, 1951; the second signed and in force Dec. 2, 1960).

Dominican Republic. Military assistance agreement (signed March 8, 1962; entered into force June 10, 1964).

Ecuador. Exchange of notes relating to eligibility for US military assistance and training pursuant to the (US) International Security and Arms Export Control Act of 1976 (Aug. 17 and Sept. 3, 1976; entry into force on latter date).

Egypt. (1) Exchange of notes relating to mutual defence assistance (April 29, 1952).

(2) Agreement concerning the establishment of an early warning system in the Sinai (Oct. 13, 1975).

The conclusion of the Egyptian-Israeli peace treaty [see page 349] was followed by comprehensive US arms supplies to Egypt and by related decisions, as detailed below. (i) In 1979 the US Government proposed to supply $1,500 million in military aid to Egypt over three years. (ii) An agreement on co-operation in the production and assembly of electronic equipment and armoured vehicles was concluded on Oct. 21, 1979. (iii) The US State Department announced on Feb. 25, 1980, that the United States would sell to Egypt 244 M-60 tanks and 40 advanced F-16 fighters, and had agreed in principle to sell F-15 fighters to Egypt later, and by April 1980 this sale was approved by the US Congress. On July 25, 1980, the US Defence Department announced that a further 67 M-60 tanks would be sold to Egypt. (iv) It was announced in Washington on Aug. 26, 1980, that an airfield at Ras Banas (on the Red Sea) would be expanded so as to serve as a launching pad for a US rapid-deployment force (for the Middle East region).

El Salvador. Agreement on the furnishing of defence articles and services to El Salvador to contribute to its internal security (exchange of notes April 10 and 13, 1962; entry into force April 13, 1962).

Ethiopia. (1) Exchange of notes relating to mutual defence assistance (June 12-13, 1952; entry into force on latter date).

(2) Exchange of notes relating to a special programme of facilities assistance (Dec. 26, 1957).

France. (1) Mutual defence assistance agreement under the North Atlantic Treaty (Jan. 27, 1950). (See also agreements with Belgium, Denmark, Italy, Luxembourg, the Netherlands, Norway and the United Kingdom.)

(2) Mutual security agreement (exchange of notes Jan. 5, 1952).

(3) Agreement for co-operation on uses of atomic energy for mutual defence purposes (May 7, 1959; entry into force July 20, 1959).

(4) Exchange of notes relating to a weapons production programme (Sept. 19, 1960).

(5) Agreement for co-operation in the operation of atomic weapons systems for mutual defence purposes (July 27, 1961; entry into force Oct. 9, 1961).

(6) Memorandum of understanding relating to military procurement (Dec. 20, 1961).

(7) General security of information agreement (Sept. 7, 1977).

The Gambia. Exchange of notes between the United States and the United Kingdom relating to the assurances required under the (US) Mutual Security Act of 1951 (Jan. 8, 1952).

Federal Republic of Germany. (1) Exchange of letters relating to the assurances required under the (US) Mutual Security Act of 1951 (Dec. 19 and 28, 1951; entry into force on latter date).

(2) Mutual defence assistance agreement (June 30, 1955; entered into force Dec. 27, 1955).

(3) Agreements on the training of German army and navy personnel (Dec. 12, 1956).

(4) Agreement relating to a weapons production programme (May 27, 1960).

(5) Agreement for co-operation in uses of atomic energy for mutual defence purposes (May 5, 1959; entry into force July 27, 1959).

(6) Agreement relating to the AIM-9L Sidewinder air-to-air missile (Feb. 14, 1974).

(7) Memorandum of understanding relating to co-operative tests for the ROLAND 2 all-weather short-range air defence system (Feb. 18 and 28, 1975; entry into force on latter date).

(8) Memorandum of understanding concerning co-operative development of an advanced surface-to-air missile system (July

16 and 22, 1976; entry into force on latter date).

(9) General security of information agreement (Sept. 7, 1977).

(10) Memorandum of understanding for co-production and sale of the Sidewinder AIM-9L missile system (Oct. 7, 1977; entry into force Oct. 14, 1977).

(11) Memorandum of understanding for co-production and sale of modular thermal imaging systems (MOD FLIR) and their components (Feb. 27 and March 3, 1978; entry into force April 20, 1978; supplement signed March 26, 1979).

(12) Memorandum of understanding concerning the principles governing mutual co-operation in the research and development, procurement and logistic support of defence equipment (Oct. 17, 1978).

Ghana. Mutual defence assistance agreement between the United States and the United Kingdom (Jan. 27, 1950, made applicable to the Gold Coast—now Ghana —on July 19, 1952).

Greece*. (1) Agreement on the use of certain Greek islands for training exercises by the US fleet in the Mediterranean (exchange of notes Feb. 11 and Feb. 21, 1949; entry into force Feb. 21, 1949).

(2) Exchange of notes relating to the assurances required under the (US) Mutual Security Act of 1951 (Dec. 21, 1951 and Jan. 7, 1952; entry into force on latter date).

(3) Agreement concerning military facilities (Oct. 12, 1953; Art. III, Para. 1 partly abrogated Sept. 7, 1956).

(4) Exchange of notes on co-operation in the uses of atomic energy for mutual defence purposes (May 6, 1959; entry into force Aug. 11, 1959).

(5) Exchange of notes on a weapons production programme (Feb. 15, 1960).

(6) Exchange of notes concerning the grant of defence articles and services under the military assistance programme (Aug. 30, 1979).

Guatemala. (1) Exchange of notes providing for the transfer of equipment and material to the Government of Guatemala (July 27 and 30, 1954; entry into force on latter date).

(2) Military assistance agreement (June 18, 1955).

(3) Exchange of notes relating to the furnishing of defence articles and services for the purpose of contributing to its internal security (May 25 and Aug. 2, 1962; entry into force on latter date).

Guinea. Exchange of notes relating to military assistance (June 29, 1965).

Guyana. Exchange of notes between the United States and the United Kingdom relating to the assurances required under the (US) Mutual Security Act of 1951 (Jan. 8, 1952).

Haiti. (1) Military assistance agreement (Jan. 28, 1955; entry into force Sept. 12, 1955).

(2) Exchange of notes relating to the transfer of military equipment, materials and services to Haiti (Sept. 1, 1960).

Honduras. (1) Military assistance agreement (May 20, 1954).

(2) Exchange of notes for performance by members of army and air force missions of duties of military advisory group specified in the above agreement (April 17 and 25, 1956; entry into force April 26, 1956).

(3) Exchange of notes relating to military assistance (Oct. 24, 1962).

Iceland*. (1) Defence agreement pursuant to North Atlantic Treaty (May 5, 1951).

(2) Exchange of notes relating to the assurances required under the (US) Mutual Security Act of 1951 (Jan. 7 and 8, 1952; entry into force on latter date).

(3) Exchange of notes concerning the sale to Iceland of certain military equipment, materials and services (Oct. 4 and Dec. 10, 1954; entry into force on latter date).

(4) Exchange of notes relating to the presence of defence forces in Iceland and setting up an Iceland defence standing group (Dec. 6, 1956).

(5) Exchange of notes relating to the continuation of the defence agreement of May 5, 1951 (Oct. 22, 1974).

(6) Arrangement for Icelandic operation of loran monitor facility at US Naval Station at Keflavik, Iceland (Sept. 9, 1975; effective July 1, 1976).

India. (1) Exchange of notes relating to a military sales agreement (March 7 and 16, 1951; entry into force on latter date).

(2) Exchange of notes concerning an understanding that the assurances contained in the above military sales agreement are applicable to equipment, materials, information and services furnished under the (US) Mutual Security Act of 1954 as amended and such other applicable US laws as might come into effect (April 16 and Dec. 17, 1958; entry into force on latter date).

(3) Exchange of notes supplementing the 1951 military sales agreement (Nov. 14, 1962).

(4) Exchange of notes relating to military assistance (Jan. 13, 1965).

Indonesia. (1) Exchange of notes relating

---

to the sale to Indonesia of military equipment, materials and services (Aug. 13, 1958).

(2) Exchange of notes relating to the furnishing of military equipment, materials and services for a programme of civic action (April 14, 1967).

(3) Exchange of notes relating to the provision by the United States of basic pilot training aircraft (April 9 and 17, 1969; entry into force on latter date).

(4) Exchange of notes relating to the furnishing of combat equipment to Indonesia as additional military assistance (Aug. 18-19, 1970; entry into force on latter date).

(5) Exchange of notes relating to eligibility for US military assistance and training pursuant to the International Assistance and Arms Export Act of 1976 (Aug. 3 and 24, 1976; entry into force on latter date).

Iran. (1) Exchange of notes concerning a mutual defence assistance agreement (May 23, 1950).

(2) Exchange of notes relating to agreement on the continuation of military assistance to Iran (April 24, 1952).

(3) Agreement of co-operation (March 5, 1959).

(4) Exchange of notes relating to the safeguarding of classified information (May 28 and June 6, 1974; entry into force on latter date).

(5) Memorandum of understanding concerning revisions of foreign military sales letters of offer and acceptance between the United States and Iran (Feb. 3, 1979).

Israel. (1) Exchange of notes relating to assurance and economic assistance as authorized in the US Mutual Security Act of 1951 (Dec. 7, 1951).

(2) Exchange of notes relating to mutual defence assistance (July 1 and 23, 1952; entry into force on latter date).

(3) Exchange of notes relating to general procurement arangements for goods and services (July 15 and 20, 1965; entry into force on latter date).

(4) Agreement concerning the establishment and operation of an early warning system in the Sinai (Sept. 1, 1975; entry into force Oct. 13, 1975).

(5) Memorandum of agreement concerning the principles governing mutual co-operation in research and development, scientist and engineer exchange, and procurement and logistic support of selected defence equipment (March 19, 1979).

(6) Agreement concerning construction of airbase facilities and agreement on funding of this construction (April 6, 1979).

(In 1973-74 a total of $2,500 million was made available to Israel by the United States in regular emergency security assistance.

For the 1975-76 fiscal year Israel requested $2,500 million in US military and economic aid, including $1,800 million for prospective Israeli arms purchases, but no final agreement was reached on this figure. In February 1978 the US Secretary of State announced that the US Government proposed to authorize the supply of advance combat aircraft to Israel to the value of $1,900 million.)

Italy*. (1) Exchange of notes on mutual defence assistance agreement (Jan. 27, 1950). (See also agreements with Belgium, Denmark, France, Luxembourg, the Netherlands, Norway and the United Kingdom.)

(2) Exchange of notes relating to the assurances required by the (US) Mutual Security Act of 1951 (Jan. 7, 1952).

(3) Exchange of notes relating to a weapons production programme (July 7, 1960).

(4) Agreement for co-operation on uses of atomic energy for mutual defence purposes (Dec. 3, 1960; entry into force May 24, 1961).

(5) Exchange of notes relating to the safeguarding of classified information (Aug. 4, 1964).

(6) Memorandum of understanding concerning the principles governing mutual co-operation in the research, development, production and procurement of defence equipment (Sept. 11, 1978).

Jamaica. (1) Exchange of notes between the United States and the United Kingdom relating to the assurances required under the (US) Mutual Security Act of 1951 (Jan. 8, 1952).

(2) Exchange of notes relating to the furnishing of defence articles and services to Jamaica (June 6, 1963).

Japan. (1) Mutual defence assistance agreement (March 8, 1954; entry into force May 1, 1954).

(2) Exchange of notes relating to the transfer of military equipment and supplies to Japan (Nov. 19, 1954).

(3) Exchange of notes relating to a programme of aircraft assembly or manufacture in Japan (June 3, 1955).

(4) Exchange of notes relating to a cost-sharing programme for the production and development in Japan of P2V anti-submarine and sea patrol aircraft (Jan. 25, 1958).

(5) Treaty of mutual co-operation and security (Jan. 19, 1960; entry into force June 23, 1960—see page 376).

(6) Various agreements for the production and acquisition of defence equipment,

---

including aircraft as well as Hawk, Nike and Sparrow missiles, concluded since 1960.

Jordan. (1) Exchange of notes relating to the furnishing of defence articles and services to Jordan (Oct. 20, 1976, and Feb. 23, 1977; entry into force on latter date).

(2) Exchange of notes concerning the grant of defence articles and services under the military assistance programme (Aug. 27, 1979; entry into force on the following day).

Kenya. (1) Exchange of notes relating to eligibility for US military assistance and training pursuant to the International Security Assistance and Arms Export Control Act of 1976 (Aug. 10 and 24, 1976; entry into force on latter date).

(2) Agreement initialled on June 26, 1980, providing for mutual and continuing consultation and an "expended relationship" between the two countries in the development of security assistance and economic co-operation.

Republic of Korea. (1) Mutual defence assistance agreement (Jan. 26, 1950).

(2) Exchange of notes relating to the assurances required under the (US) Mutual Security Act of 1951 (Jan. 4 and 7, 1952; entry into force on latter date).

(3) Mutual defence treaty (Oct. 1, 1953; entry into force Nov. 17, 1954).

(4) Memorandum of understanding relating to the establishment of an M-16 rifle production programme in Korea (March 31 and April 2, 1971; entry into force on latter date).

(5) Memorandum of agreement concerning conventional ammunition logistics (Nov. 25, 1974).

Kuwait. (1) Exchange of notes concerning the procurement of defence articles and services by Kuwait and the estabishment of a US liaison office in Kuwait (Feb. 24 and April 15, 1975).

(2) Technical security arrangement (Jan. 18, 1976; amended June 26, 1977).

Lebanon. (1) Exchange of notes relating to the assurances required under the (US) Mutual Security Act of 1951 (Dec. 26, 1951 and Jan. 5, 1952; entry into force on latter date).

(2) Exchange of notes relating to reimbursable military aid (March 6 and 23, 1953; entry into force on latter date).

(3) Exchange of notes on military assistance agreement (June 3 and 6, 1957; entry into force on latter date; amended June 9 and 12, 1958).

Liberia. (1) Exchange of notes relating to mutual defence assistance (Nov. 16 and 19, 1951; entry into force on latter date).

(2) Exchange of notes on an understanding that the assurances contained in the above agreement are applicable to equipment, materials, information and services furnished under the (US) Mutual Security Act of 1954 as amended and such other applicable US laws as may come into effect (April 10 and July 19, 1958; entry into force on latter date).

(3) Agreement of co-operation (July 8, 1959).

(4) Exchange of notes concerning the furnishing of military equipment and materials to Liberia (May 23 and June 17, 1961; entry into force on latter date; amended Jan. 18 and 23, 1962).

Luxembourg. (1) Mutual defence assistance agreement (Jan. 27, 1950; entry into force March 28, 1950; amended Jan. 19 and 31, 1977). (See also agreements with Belgium, Denmark, France, Italy, the Netherlands, Norway and the United Kingdom.)

(2) Exchange of notes relating to the assurances required under the (US) Mutual Security Act of 1951 (Jan. 8, 1952).

Malaysia. (1) Exchange of notes relating to the purchase by Malaya of military equipment, materials and services from the United States (June 30 and July 9, 1958; entry into force on latter date).

(2) Exchange of notes relating to eligibility for US military assistance and training pursuant to the International Security and Arms Export Control Act of 1976 (Feb. 11 and March 14, 1977; entry into force on latter date).

Mali. Exchange of notes on military assistance agreement (May 20, 1961).

Netherlands. (1) Mutual defence assistance agreement (Jan. 27, 1950). (See also agreements with Belgium, Denmark, France, Italy, Luxembourg, Norway and the United Kingdom.)

(2) Agreement relating to the assurances required by the (US) Mutual Security Act of 1951 (Jan. 8, 1952).

(3) Exchange of notes on the stationing of US armed forces in the Netherlands (Aug. 13, 1954; entry into force Nov. 16, 1954).

(4) Exchange of notes on establishing an air defence technical centre, with cost reimbursement contract attached (Dec. 14, 1954).

(5) Agreement for co-operation on uses of atomic energy for mutual defence purposes (May 6, 1959; entry into force July 27, 1959).

(6) Exchange of notes relating to a weapons production programme (March 24, 1960; definitive entry into force Jan. 2, 1962).

(7) Memorandum of understanding con-

cerning principles governing mutual co-operation in research and development, production and procurement of conventional defence equipment (July 25 and Aug. 24, 1978; entry into force on latter date).

New Zealand. (1) Exchange of notes relating to mutual defence assistance (June 19, 1952).

(2) Exchange of notes on an understanding that the assurances contained in the above agreement are applicable to equipment, materials, information and services furnished under the (US) Mutual Security Act of 1954 as amended and such other applicable US laws as may come into effect (March 25, 1960).

Nicaragua. (1) Military assistance agreement (April 23, 1954).

(2) Agreement for the establishment of a loran transmitting station (Sept. 5, 1958).

Niger. Exchange of notes relating to the furnishing of military equipment, materials and services to Niger to help assure its security and independence (May 22 and June 14, 1962; entry into force on latter date).

Norway. (1) Mutual defence assistance agreement (Jan. 27, 1950; entry into force Feb. 24, 1950; amended Nov. 21 and Dec. 1, 1975). (See also agreements with Belgium, Denmark, France, Italy, Luxembourg, the Netherlands and the United Kingdom.)

(2) Exchange of notes relating to a weapons production programme (Feb. 13, 1960; amended April 26 and Sept. 16, 1960).

(3) Exchanges of notes relating to a ship-building programme for the Norwegian Navy (July 6, 1960, and Nov. 29, 1960, entry into force of the latter Jan. 31, 1961).

(4) Exchange of notes relating to the safeguarding of classified information (Feb. 26, 1970).

(5) Memorandum of understanding concerning the principles governing mutual co-operation in the research and development, production and procurement of defence equipment (May 19, 1978).

Pakistan. (1) Exchange of notes relating to transfer of military supplies and equipment to Pakistan (Nov. 29 and Dec. 15, 1950).

(2) Mutual defence assistance agreement (May 19, 1954).

(3) Defence support assistance agreement (Jan. 11, 1955; amended March 11, 1961).

(4) Agreement of co-operation (March 5, 1959).

Panama. (1) Exchange of notes relating to the sale of military equipment, materials and services to Panama (May 20, 1959; operative from April 27, 1959).

(2) Exchange of notes relating to the furnishing of defence articles and services to Panama for the purpose of contributing to its internal security (March 26 and May 23, 1962; entry into force on latter date).

(3) Exchange of notes relating to economic and military co-operation (Sept. 7, 1978).

Paraguay. (1) Exchange of notes concerning the furnishing of assistance to Paraguay for the purpose of increasing the air transport capability of the Paraguayan Air Force (Aug. 25, 1962).

(2) Exchange of notes providing for assistance to increase the road construction and maintenance capability of the Paraguayan Army (Feb. 10, 1964).

(3) Exchange of notes relating to the furnishing of additional military assistance to Paraguay (April 11, 1966).

Peru. (1) Military assistance agreement (Feb. 22, 1952; entry into force April 26, 1952).

(2) Exchange of notes relating to the furnishing of defence articles and services to Peru (Dec. 17 and 20, 1962; entry into force on latter date).

Philippines*. (1) Exchange of notes relating to military assistance (June 26, 1953; entry into force July 5, 1953).

(2) Exchange of notes relating to military assistance (April 27, 1955; amended April 20 1956; June 14, 1957; and April 14, 1958).

(3) Exchange of notes for the establishment of a mutual defence board and the assignment of Philippine liaison officers to US military bases in the Philippines (May 15, 1958).

Portugal†. (1) Mutual defence assistance agreement (Jan. 5, 1951).

(2) Defence agreement regarding use of facilities in the Azores (Sept. 6, 1951; extended and amended Nov. 15, 1957, and June 18, 1979).

(3) Exchange of notes relating to the assurances required by the (US) Mutual Security Act of 1951 (Jan. 8. 1952).

(4) Exchange of notes relating to a weapons production programme (Sept. 26, 1960).

(5) Memorandum of understanding concerning the principles governing mutual co-operation in the research, development, production, procurement and logistic support of defence equipment (Dec. 18, 1978, and March 28, 1979; entry into force on latter date).

(6) Exchange of notes relating to eco-

---

* See also page 376.

† See also page 186.

nomic and military assistance (June 18, 1979).

(7) Exchange of notes concerning the grant of defence articles and services under the military assistance programme (Aug. 14 and 27, 1979; entry into force on latter date).

Saudi Arabia. (1) Exchange of notes relating to the extending of procurement assistance to Saudi Arabia for the transfer of military supplies and equipment (June 18, 1951).

(2) Exchange of notes relating to the construction of certain military facilities in Saudi Arabia (May 24 and June 5, 1965; operative May 24, 1965; extended April 30, July 3 and Aug. 7, 1978).

(3) Agreement on co-operation in the fields of economics, technology, industry and defence (June 8, 1974).

(4) Exchange of notes relating to a US military training mission in Saudi Arabia (Feb. 8 and 27, 1977; entry into force on latter date).

Senegal. Exchange of notes relating to the furnishing of military equipment, materials and services to Senegal for the purpose of assuring its security and supporting its development (July 20, 1962).

Seychelles. Exchange of notes between the United States and the United Kingdom relating to the assurances required under the (US) Mutual Security Act of 1951 (Jan. 8, 1952; applicable to Seychelles on that date).

Solomon Islands. Exchange of notes between the United States and the United Kingdom relating to the assurance required under the (US) Mutual Security Act of 1951 (Jan. 8, 1952; applicable to Solomon Islands on that date).

Somalia. (1) Exchange of notes concerning the furnishing of defence articles and services to Somalia (March 22-23 and April 19 and 29, 1978; entry into force April 29, 1978).

(2) Under an agreement signed on Aug. 21, 1980, the USA was permitted to use the naval and air base at Berbera, on the Gulf of Aden (which had been used by the Soviet Union until November 1977), as well as an airstrip in northern Somalia and port facilities in Mogadishu. In return the United States would grant Somalia arms credits of $20,000,000 in 1980-81 and general aid of $5,000,000 (in addition to $127,000,000 already provided by the USA in economic and refugee aid).

South Africa. Exchange of notes relating to mutual defence assistance (Nov. 9, 1951).

Spain. (1) Mutual defence assistance agreement (Sept. 26, 1953).

(2) Exchange of notes confirming the bilateral arrangements for a facilities assistance programme pursuant to the above mutual defence assistance agreement (April 9 and May 11 and 19, 1954; entry into force May 19, 1954; supplementary agreements: May 25, 1955; Sept. 17, 1956).

(3) Following the expiry, on Sept. 26; 1975, of a 1970 agreement of friendship and co-operation between the United States and Spain, a new treaty of friendship and co-operation, signed on Jan. 24, 1976, allowed the United States the continued use of three air bases in Spain (at Torrejón, Morón and Saragossa), a firing range (at Bárdenas Reales) and a naval base (at Rota, on Spain's southern coast on the Atlantic) for another five years in return for US military and other credits and grants amounting to $1,120 million.

The treaty also provided for the withdrawal of the US Polaris nuclear submarines from Rota by July 1, 1979, and for the supply of substantial numbers of US aircraft, including fighter jets, to Spain.

The treaty was accompanied by seven supplementary agreements—on the functions and organization of a US-Spanish Council established under the treaty and responsible for its implementation; on economic, scientific and technological, and educational and cultural co-operation; on bilateral military co-ordination on facilities; and on co-operation regarding matériel for Spain's armed forces. The agreement on facilities provided inter alia for the phased withdrawal of the US nuclear submarine squadron from Rota between Jan. 1 and July 1, 1979, and it also contained the undertaking that the United States would not store nuclear devices or their components on Spanish soil.

The treaty and its supplementary agreements were ratified by the US Senate on June 21, 1976, and by the Spanish *Cortes* on July 23 of that year, and they came into force on Sept. 21, 1976.

(4) Under a declaration of principles, signed on July 9, 1974, the two countries undertook to continue co-operation in defence matters and to co-ordinate their joint efforts with those of the existing NATO organizations.

Sri Lanka. Exchange of notes relating to the purchase by Ceylon (now Sri Lanka) of certain military equipment, materials and services (Oct. 25 and Nov. 2, 1956; entry into force on latter date).

Suriname. Exchange of notes between the United States and the Netherlands to the assurances required by the (US) Mutual Security Act of 1951 (Jan. 8, 1952).

Sweden. (1) Exchange of notes relating to the procurement of reimbursable military equipment, materials or services (June 30 and July 1, 1952; entry into force on latter date).

(2) Exchange of notes relating to the safeguarding of classified information, equipment, materials or services related to defence (Jan. 30, 1961).

Switzerland. Memorandum of understanding offsetting the amount to be paid by Switzerland for the aircraft and supporting equipment under an F-5 aircraft programme (July 2 and 9, 1975; entry into force on latter date).

Thailand. (1) Agreement respecting military assistance (Oct. 17, 1950).

(2) Exchange of notes relating to the assurances required by the (US) Mutual Security Act of 1951 (Dec. 27 and 29, 1951; entry into force on latter date).

(3) Memorandum of agreement on an integrated communications system (Jan. 10, 1977).

(4) Memorandum of agreement on storage of ammunition in Thailand (March 22, 1977).

[As demanded by Thailand, all US forces (which had in 1969 numbered about 48,000 men) were withdrawn from Thailand by July 20, 1976, except for a 263-strong Military Advisory Group stationed in Thailand under the 1950 defence assistance agreement.]

Tunisia. Exchange of notes relating to a programme of grants of military equipment and material to Tunisia (Oct. 25, 1974; effective July 1, 1974).

Turkey*. (1) Exchange of notes relating to the assurances required by the (US) Mutual Security Act of 1951 (Jan. 7, 1952).

(2) Exchange of notes for co-operation in uses of atomic energy for mutual defence purposes (May 5, 1959; entry into force July 27, 1959).

(3) Exchange of notes concerning the grant of defence articles and services under the military assistance programme (Aug. 15 and 31, 1979; entry into force on latter date).

United Kingdom†. (1) Exchange of notes on an arrangement relating to naval and air bases (Sept. 2, 1940).

(2) Agreement regarding leased naval and air bases (March 27, 1941; amended July 19 and Aug. 1, 1950, with effect from Aug. 1, 1950; and amended with regard to land and facilities on Bermuda on Dec. 5-6, 1978, with effect from the latter date).

(3) Protocol on the defence of Newfoundland (March 27, 1941).

(4) Mutual defence assistance agreement, of which Art. IV is applicable to Brunei, the Falkland Islands, Gibraltar, Belize, Hong Kong, the Leeward Islands, St Helena and

Western Pacific dependencies (Jan. 27, 1950). (See also agreements with Belgium, Denmark, France, Italy, Luxembourg, the Netherlands and Norway.)

(5) Exchange of notes relating to the supply by the United States to the United Kingdom of intermediate-range ballistic missiles (Feb. 22, 1958).

(6) Agreement for co-operation in the uses of atomic energy for mutual defence purposes (July 3, 1958; entry into force Aug. 4, 1958; amended May 7, 1959; Sept. 27, 1968; Oct. 16, 1969; and July 22, 1974).

(7) Exchange of notes relating to the establishment and operation of a ballistic missile early warning station at Fylingdales Moor (Feb. 15, 1960).

(8) Exchange of notes on the setting-up of a missile defence alarm system station in the United Kingdom (July 18, 1961).

(9) Exchange of notes relating to a weapons production programme (June 29, 1962).

(10) Polaris sales agreement (April 6, 1963).

(11) Memorandum of arrangement between the United States, Australia and the United Kingdom to cover re-entry experiments in Australia (Project Sparta) (March 30, 1966).

(12) Memorandum of understanding relating to the principles governing co-operation in research and development, production and procurement of defence equipment (Sept. 24, 1975).

(13) Letter of agreement concerning narrative record telecommunication interface arrangements (Sept. 2 and 21, 1977; entry into force on latter date).

UK Dependencies. (1) Exchange of notes relating to the use of the airfield at Widewake on Ascension Island by the Royal Air Force (Aug. 29, 1962).

(2) Exchange of notes concerning the availability of certain Indian Ocean islands for the defence purposes of both Governments (Dec. 30, 1966; amended June 22 and 25, 1976, to allow for the expansion of the US facility on Diego Garcia, one of the islands in the territory).

(3) Exchange of notes relating to the lease of certain land to the US Navy on the island of Anegada in the British Virgin Islands for use as a drone-launching facility (Feb. 1, 1973).

(4) Exchange of notes relating to the expanded use of Ascension Island (March 30, 1973).

(5) Exchange of notes concerning a US naval support facility on Diego Garcia, British Indian Ocean Territory (Feb. 25, 1976).

(6) Agreement regarding US defence

---

* See also page 186.
† See also page 185.

316

areas and facilities in Antigua (Dec. 14, 1977; entry into force Jan. 1, 1978).

(7) Agreement concerning US defence areas in the Turks and Caicos Islands (Dec. 12, 1979; effective Jan. 1, 1979).

(8) Agreement concerning the turnover of the airfield at Grand Turk Auxiliary Air Base to the Government of the Turks and Caicos Islands and its use by the US Government (Dec. 12, 1979).

Agreements concerning ·the Bahamas. (1) Agreement concerning the establishment of a long-range proving ground for guided missiles—the "Bahamas Long-Range Proving Ground" (July 21, 1950; amended July 17, 1967).

(2) Exchange of notes concerning the extending of the flight-testing range at the Bahamas long-range proving ground (April 1, 1951).

(3) Exchange of notes regarding the establishment by the United States of a high-altitude interceptor range in connexion with the operation of the Bahamas long-range proving ground (Feb. 24 and March 2, 1953; entry into force on latter date).

(4) Agreement concerning the extension of the Bahamas long-range proving ground by the establishment of additional sites on Ascension Island (June 25, 1956; amended July 17, 1967).

(5) Agreement concerning the establishment on the Bahama Islands of a long-range aid to navigation station (June 24, 1960).

(6) Agreement for the establishment of an Atlantic undersea test and evaluation centre in the Bahama Islands (Oct. 11, 1963).

(7) Exchange of notes on an understanding relating to the use of Bahamian organizations, both public and private, of certain land at the US Navy base at Georgetown, Great Exuna Island, Bahamas (June 19, Sept. 12 and Nov. 2, 1972; entry into force on Nov. 2. 1972).

Uruguay. Military assistance agreement (June 30, 1952; entry into force June 11, 1953).

Venezuela. Exchange of notes relating to eligibility for US military assistance and training pursuant to the International Security Assistance and Arms Export Control Act of 1976 (June 16 and 30, 1977; entry into force on latter date).

Yugoslavia. Exchange of notes relating to the purchase by Yugoslavia of military equipment, materials and services (Aug. 25, 1959).

The US Defence Department announced in September 1978 that it had agreed to expand bilateral military co-operation with Yugoslavia in the next few years. (Yugoslavia was reported to have received, since 1948, more than $1,700 million worth of US military aid, but in 1961 President Tito of Yugoslavia had refused to renew an earlier US-Yugoslavia military agreement, and thereafter US military aid had been confined mainly to spare parts.)

Zambia. Exchange of notes relating to the assurances required under the (US) Mutual Security Act of 1951 (Jan. 8, 1952).

Panama Canal Treaties

After 13 years of negotiations between the Governments of the United States and Panama, agreement was reached in principle on Aug. 10, 1977, on the conclusion of (i) a basic treaty between the two countries on the gradual transfer to Panama, to be completed by the year 2000, of the Panama Canal and the Panama Canal Zone (which the USA had leased in perpetuity from the Republic of Panama since 1903) and (ii) a treaty guaranteeing the canal's permanent neutrality.

Basic Treaty. This treaty laid down that upon its entry into force all previous treaties and agreements relating to the canal would be terminated and superseded, among them an Isthmian Canal Convention of Nov. 18, 1903, and a Treaty of Friendship and Co-operation signed on March 2, 1936, as well as a Treaty of Mutual Understanding and Co-operation and related memorandum of Jan. 25, 1955. Under the treaty Panama granted to the USA, "for the duration of this treaty [i.e. until Dec. 31, 1999], the rights necessary to regulate the transit of ships through the Panama Canal, and to manage, operate, maintain, improve, protect and defend the canal", while Panama guaranteed "to the USA the peaceful use of the land and water areas which it has been granted to use for such purposes pursuant to this treaty and related agreements", with Panama participating increasingly in the management, protection and defence of the canal.

The treaty also contained details of the operations, Panama's sovereignty rights (under which Panama would, upon the treaty's entry into force, assume general territorial jurisdiction over the Canal Zone), and the joint defence of the canal. It also provided that Panama would receive exclusively from canal revenues an annual average of $80,000,000 for 23 years, and in addition the USA undertook to make the best possible efforts to arrange, outside the treaty, loan guarantees and credits to Panama totalling $345,000,000, as well as military sales credits of up to $50,000,000 over a 10-year period to improve Panama's ability to assist in the canal's defence.

It was also agreed that during the duration of the treaty no new interoceanic canal would be constructed in the territory of Panama except in accordance with the provisions of the treaty or as otherwise agreed, and that the USA was granted the right to add a third lane of locks to the existing canal.

Neutrality Treaty. The *Treaty on the Permanent Neutrality and Operation of the Canal* contained the following material provisions:

"**Art. 1.** The Republic of Panama declares that the canal, as an international transit waterway, shall be permanently neutral in accordance with the regime established in this treaty. The same regime of neutrality shall apply to any other international waterway that may be built either partially or wholly in the territory of the Republic of Panama.

"**Art. 2.** The Republic of Panama declares the neutrality of the canal in order that both in time of peace and in time of war it shall remain secure and open to peaceful transit by the vessels of all nations on terms of entire equality, so that there will be no discrimination against any nation or its citizens or subjects, concerning the conditions or charges of transit or for any other reason, and so that the canal, and therefore the isthmus of Panama, shall not be the target of reprisals in any armed conflict between other nations of the world. . . .

"**Art. 3.** For purposes of the security, efficiency and proper maintenance of the canal the following rules shall apply:

"(*a*) The canal shall be operated efficiently in accordance with conditions of transit through the canal and rules and regulations that shall be just, equitable and reasonable and limited to those necessary for safe navigation and efficient, sanitary operation of the canal;

(*b*) ancillary services necessary for transit through the canal shall be provided;

(*c*) tolls and other charges for transit and ancillary services shall be just, reasonable and equitable, consistent with the principles of international law; . . .

(*e*) vessels of war and auxiliary vessels of all nations shall at all times be entitled to transit the canal, irrespective of their internal operation, means of propulsion, origin, destination or armament, without being subjected, as a condition of transit, to inspection, search or surveillance. . . .

"**Art. 4.** The United States of America and the Republic of Panama agree to maintain the regime of neutrality established in this treaty, which shall be maintained in order that the canal shall remain permanently neutral, notwithstanding the termination of any other treaties entered into by the two contracting parties.

"**Art. 5.** After the termination of the Panama Canal treaty, only the Republic of Panama shall operate the canal and maintain military forces, defence sites and military installations within its national territory.

"**Art. 6.** (*a*) In recognition of the important contributions of the United States of America and of the Republic of Panama to the construction, operation,

maintenance and protection and defence of the canal, vessels of war and auxiliary vessels of those nations shall, notwithstanding any other provisions of this treaty, be entitled to transit the canal irrespective of their internal operation, means of propulsion, origin, destination, armament or cargo carried. Such vessels of war and auxiliary vessels will be entitled to transit the canal expeditiously.

(*b*) The United States of America, so long as it has responsibilty for the operation of the canal, may continue to provide the Republic of Colombia toll-free transit through the canal for its troops, vessels and materials of war. Thereafter, the Republic of Panama may provide the Republic of Colombia and the Republic of Costa Rica with the right of toll-free transit. . . ."

Under a protocol to the treaty, which was open to signature by all states of the world and would enter into force at the time of deposit of the relevant instrument of accession with the Secretary-General of the Organization of American States, its signatories were able to acknowledge the regime of permanent neutrality of the canal and to agree to observe its rules.

Signature, Ratification and Entry into Force. The two treaties were signed by the US President and the "supreme leader" of Panama on Sept. 7, 1977. They were approved in a referendum held in Panama on Oct. 23, 1977, with about 66 per cent of the valid votes being in favour. They were approved by the US Senate (with the required two-thirds majority) on March 16 and April 18, 1978, respectively. The US Senate, however, also approved a number of amendments and reservations to the neutrality treaty, introduced by opponents to the treaty.

One of these reservations (approved on March 16), inserted at the end of the Senate's resolution of ratification, stated that, notwithstanding the provisions of Article 5 of the treaty [see above], "if the canal is closed or its operations are interfered with, the USA and the Republic of Panama shall each independently have the right to take such steps as it deems necessary . . ., including the use of military force in Panama to reopen the canal or restore the operations of the canal. . . ."

Another reservation (approved on March 15) stated that nothing in the treaty was to preclude Panama and the USA from making any agreement or arrangement between them "to facilitate performance at any time after Dec. 31, 1999, of their responsibilities to maintain the regime of neutrality established in the treaty, including agreements or arrangements for the stationing of any US forces or maintenance of defence sites after that date in the Republic of Panama that Panama and the USA may deem necessary or appropriate".

The US bill implementing the ratification of the treaties was not finally passed by the US Senate until Sept. 25, 1979, and by the House of Representatives until the following day, whereupon the bill was signed by the President on Sept. 27, 1979.

The treaties came into force on Oct. 1,

1979, when the Panama Canal Zone formally ceased to exist as Panama assumed general territorial jurisdiction over it and 11 out of the 14 US military bases in the zone reverted to Panama (although about 40 per cent of the former Canal Zone would remain under effective US control until Dec. 31, 1999).

US Bilateral Co-operation Agreements

Bilateral treaties and agreements on co-operation in various fields have been concluded by the United States with other countries as follows:

Argentina. (1) Treaty of friendship, commerce and navigation (July 27, 1853; entry into force Dec. 20, 1854).

(2) General agreement for a programme of technical co-operation (June 3, 1957).

(3) Exchange of notes relating to a co-operation programme for the optical satellite tracking station at Villa Dolores, Argentina (March 16, 1962).

(4) Agreement for scientific and technical co-operation (April 7, 1972; entry into force Aug. 11, 1972).

Austria. Economic co-operation agreement (July 2, 1948; amended Oct. 21 and Nov. 30, 1949; Feb. 20, 1950; Jan. 16 and March 7, 1951; May 11 and 15, 1951; and Oct. 15 and Dec. 6, 1952).

Bangladesh. (1) Economic, technical and related assistance agreement (May 21, 1974).

(2) Numerous (US) Agency for International Development agreements between 1972 and 1979.

Barbados. (1) Economic co-operation agreement between the United States and the United Kingdom of July 6, 1948, applicable to Barbados (Oct. 26, 1949; amended Jan. 3, 1950; May 25, 1951; Feb. 25, 1953; June 26 and Aug. 20, 1959).

(2) Technical co-operation agreement with the United Kingdom of July 13, 1951, applicable to Barbados (Aug. 14, 1954).

Belgium. (1) Economic co-operation agreements (July 2, 1948; entry into force July 29, 1948; amended Nov. 22 and 29, 1948; June 29, 1950; Sept. 10, 1951; Dec. 11, 1952; and March 5, 1953).

(2) Treaty of friendship, establishment and navigation: Feb. 21, 1961; entry into force Oct. 3, 1963.

Benin. Agreement relating to economic, technical and related assistance (May 27, 1961).

Bolivia. (1) General agreement for tech-

nical co-operation (March 14, 1951; amended Dec. 14, 1951; Jan. 2, 7 and 8, 1952; Aug. 27, 1953; and Jan. 15, 1954).

(2) Agreement providing economic assistance to Bolivia (Nov. 6, 1953; amended Aug. 24 and Nov. 11, 1959).

(3) Numerous agreements by the (US) Agency for International Development between December 1975 and January 1978.

Botswana. Agreement by (US) Agency for International Development (Sept. 19, 1975).

Brazil. (1) Treaty of peace, friendship, commerce and navigation (Dec. 12, 1828; entry into force March 18, 1829; operative Dec. 12, 1928, but all articles were terminated on Dec. 12, 1841, except those relating to peace and friendship).

(2) Agreement relating to the mobilization of productive resources in Brazil (March 3, 1942).

(3) Agreement relating to technical co-operation (Dec. 19, 1950; amended Jan. 8, 1952).

(4) Special services programme agreement (May 30, 1953; extended Dec. 27 and 30, 1963).

(5) Agreement relating to a programme of joint participation in international testing in connexion with experimental communications satellites (Oct. 27, 1961).

(6) Agreement on co-operation for the promotion of economic and social development in the Brazilian North-East (April 13, 1963).

(7) Agreement on a programme of scientific co-operation (Dec. 1, 1971; extended and amended Dec. 27-28, 1976).

(8) Agreement relating to the continued operation of the Doppler geodetic satellite tracking station in Brazil (Feb. 12, 1974).

(9) Agreement relating to the continuation of a collaborative experimental programme in the field of remote sensing surveys of earth resources (May 26, 1976).

(10) Agreement concerning co-operation in launching sounding rockets and balloons for atmospheric research (Jan. 24, 1979).

Brunei. Treaty of peace, friendship, commerce and navigation (June 23, 1850; entry into force July 11, 1853).

Bulgaria. (1) Agreement on exchanges in cultural, scientific, educational, technological and other fields (June 13, 1977; entry into force March 23, 1978).

(2) Programme of cultural, educational, scientific and technological exchanges for 1979-80 (Oct. 26, 1978; effective Jan. 1, 1979).

Burma. Economic co-operation agreement (March 21, 1957; entry into force Oct.

9, 1957; amended Sept. 12, 1959, and June 29, 1960).

Burundi. General agreement for special development assistance (Feb. 13 and 18, 1970; entry into force on latter date).

Cameroon. (1) Agreement providing for the furnishing of economic, technical and related assistance (May 26, 1961; amended Dec. 8, 1961).

(2) (US) Agency for International Development agreements (May 18 and Aug. 30, 1978).

Canada. (1) Exchange of notes on co-operation in intercontinental testing in connexion with experimental communication satellites (Aug. 1 and 23, 1963; entry into force on latter date).

(2) Exchange of notes regarding an experimental communications technology satellite project (April 21 and 27, 1971; entry into force on latter date).

(3) Exchange of notes on a joint programme in the field of experimental remote sensing from satellites and aircraft (May 14, 1971; extended and amended March 19 and 22, 1976).

(4) The Great Lakes Water Quality Agreement on a joint programme for reducing the pollution of Lakes Superior, Huron, Erie, Ontario and Michigan (April 15, 1972).

(5) Agreement concerning liability for loss or damage resulting form certain rocket launches in Canada (Operation Tordo) (Dec. 31, 1974).

(6) Exchange of notes relating to a co-operative programme concerning the development and procurement of a space shuttle attached remote manipulator system (June 23, 1976).

(7) Agreement on the route of a gas pipeline from northern Alaska to link up with existing pipeline networks in both Canada and the United States (Sept. 23, 1977).

(8) Exchange of notes relating to space remote sensing for global crop information (March 31 and April 10, 1978; entry into force on latter date).

(9) Agreement concerning support of US activities at the Canadian National Research Council Space Research (March 19 and Sept. 20, 1979; entry into force on latter date).

Cape Verde. Economic and technical co-operation agreements by the (US) Agency for International Development between June 1975 and May 1978.

Central African Republic. Agreement relating to economic, technical and related assistance (Feb. 10, 1963).

Chad. Economic and technical co-operation agreements by the (US) Agency for International Development between August 1976 and August 1978.

Chile. (1) Treaty of peace, amity, commerce and navigation (May 16, 1932; entry into force April 29, 1834; articles relating to commerce and navigation were terminated on Jan. 20, 1850).

(2) Basic agreement for technical co-operation (Jan. 16, 1951; entry into force July 27, 1951; amended Jan. 8 and Oct. 17, 1952).

(3) (US) Agency for International Development Co-operation agreements (Oct. 23, 1975; Jan. 26, 1976; and Jan. 26 and July 26, 1976).

(4) Exchange of notes concerning a co-operative programme for tracking and receiving radio signals from earth satellites and space vehicles (Feb. 16 and 19, 1959; operative from Dec. 31, 1958).

(5) Memorandum of understanding relating to the installation and use of a Chilean earth resources technology ground station (July 24 and Sept. 8, 1975; entry into force on latter date).

Colombia. (1) General agreement for economic, technical and related assistance (July 23, 1962).

(2) Memorandum of understanding for scientific and technical co-operation in the earth sciences (Dec. 12, 1978, and Jan. 30, 1979; entry into force on latter date).

(3) (US) Agency for International Development agreements concluded between Dec. 24, 1975, and Nov. 29, 1976.

Costa Rica. General agreement for economic, technical and related assistance (Dec. 22, 1961; entry into force Sept. 7, 1962).

Cyprus. (1) Economic co-operation agreement between the United States and the United Kingdom of July 6, 1948, made applicable to Cyprus (July 6, 1948; amended Jan. 3, 1950; May 25, 1951; and Feb. 25, 1953).

(2) General agreement for technical co-operation (June 29, 1961).

Denmark. Economic co-operation agreement (June 29, 1948; entry into force July 2, 1948, applicable to Greenland; amended Nov. 4 and 18, 1948; Feb. 7, 1950; Feb. 2 and 9, 1951; and Nov. 24, 1952).

Djibouti. Economic and technical co-operation agreement by (US) Agency for International Development (Jan. 9, 1978).

Dominican Republic. (1) General agreement for economic, technical and related assistance (Jan. 11, 1962).

(2) Economic and technical co-operation

agreements by (US) Agency for International Development, between Oct. 16, 1974, and April 7, 1977.

Ecuador. (1) Treaty of peace, friendship, navigation and commerce (June 13, 1839; entry into force April 9, 1842; articles relating to commerce and navigation terminated on Aug. 25, 1892).

(2) General agreement for economic, technical and related assistance (April 17, 1962).

(3) Agreement relating to the co-operative programme in Ecuador for the observation and tracking of satellites and space vehicles (Sept. 18, 1975).

Egypt. (1) Arrangements and agreements relating to assistance in the clearance of the Suez Canal and coastal waters areas (April 13 and 25, 1974—entry into force on latter date; June 11, 1974; June 16 and 29, 1975 —entry into force on latter date; and subsequent amendments effective Aug. 21, 1975, and Dec. 17, 1977).

(2) Economic, technical and related assistance agreement (Aug. 16, 1978; entry into force Oct. 15, 1978).

(3) Economic and technical co-operation agreements by the (US) Agency for International Development between Feb. 13, 1975, and Dec. 30, 1979.

(4) Agreement relating to co-operation in the area of technology, research and development (June 6, 1975; definitive entry into force April 14, 1976).

El Salvador. (1) General agreement for economic, technical and related assistance (Dec. 19, 1961; entry into force Jan. 16, 1962).

(2) Economic and technical co-operation agreements by the (US) Agency for International Development (May 3 and Aug. 30, 1978).

Ethiopia. (1) General agreement for technical co-operation (June 16, 1951; extended and amended Dec. 17 and 27, 1951; Jan. 8 and Dec. 24, 1952; March 30, 1953; May 18 and June 12, 1954, April 4 and June 12, 1956).

(2) Exchanges of notes providing for economic assistance to Ethiopia (April 25, 1957).

(3) Economic and technical co-operation agreements by (US) Agency for International Development between Feb. 20, 1975, and Sept. 22, 1978.

France. (1) Economic co-operation agreements, also applicable to French overseas departments and territories (June 28, 1948; entry into force July 10, 1948; amended Sept. 21 and Oct. 8, 1948; Nov. 17 and 20, 1948; Jan. 9, 1950; May 22, 1951; Sept. 25 and 27, 1951; and Sept. 11, 1953).

(2) Exchange of notes on co-operation in intercontinental testing in connexion with experimental communications satellites (March 31, 1961).

(3) Exchange of notes concerning development of satellites and balloon techniques and instrumentation for the study of meteorological phenomena (Project EOLE) (June 16-17, 1966).

(4) Memorandum of understanding concerning a co-operative programme in science and technology (May 30, 1978).

Gabon. Economic and technical co-operation agreement by (US) Agency for International Development (Feb. 21, 1976).

The Gambia. (1) Economic co-operation agreement between the United States and the United Kingdom (July 6, 1948; amended Jan. 3, 1950; May 25, 1951; Feb. 25, 1953; June 26 and Aug. 20, 1959).

(2) Economic and technical co-operation agreements by (US) Agency for International Development (Oct. 26 and 28, 1977; Jan. 12 and Feb. 20, 1978).

Federal Republic of Germany. (1) Economic co-operation agreement (Dec. 15, 1949; definitive entry into force Feb. 6, 1950).

(2) Treaty of amity, commerce and navigation (Oct. 29, 1954; entry into force July 14, 1956; extended Oct. 23, 1979, until Dec. 31, 1981).

(3) Exchange of notes on co-operation in intercontinental testing in connexion with experimental communications satellites (Sept. 5 and 29, 1961; entry into force on latter date).

(4) Agreement on co-operation in the field of magneto-hydrodynamic energy (April 21, 1974).

Ghana. (1) Economic co-operation agreement between the United States and the United Kingdom of July 6, 1948, made applicable to the Gold Coast (now Ghana) (July 6, 1948, amended Jan. 3, 1950; May 25, 1951; and Feb. 25, 1953).

(2) General agreement for technical co-operation (June 3, 1957).

(3) Economic and technical co-operation agreements by (US) Agency for International Development (Sept. 29, 1976; May 24, 1977; and March 31, 1978).

Greece. (1) Agreement on aid to Greece (June 20, 1947).

(2) Economic co-operation agreement (July 2, 1948; entry into force July 3, 1948; amended Dec. 15 and 24, 1949; March 6 and 30, 1951; Oct. 14, 1952; Dec. 2, 1953; April 19, 1963).

(3) Memorandum of understanding for scientific and technological co-operation (Sept. 16, 1978).

(4) A five-year framework agreement on economic, scientific and technological, educational and cultural co-operation (April 22, 1980).

Guatemala (1) Treaty of peace, amity, commerce and navigation (March 3, 1849; entry into force May 13, 1852; articles relating to commerce and navigation terminated Nov. 4, 1874).
(2) General agreement for technical co-operation (Sept. 1, 1954).
(3) Development assistance agreement (Dec. 13, 1954).
(4) Economic and technical co-operation agreements by (US) Agency for International Development (Nov. 3, 1975; April 8, 1976; Sept. 20, 1976; Sept. 14, 1977; May 18, 1978).

Guinea. (1) Exchange of notes providing for the furnishing of economic, technical and related assistance (Sept. 30, 1960).
(2) Economic and technical co-operation agreements by (US) Agency for International Development (Sept. 27, 1977; March 31, 1978; April 14 and June 5, 1978).

Guinea-Bissau. Economic and technical co-operation agreements by (US) Agency for International Development (Nov. 10, 1977; Jan. 8, 1978).

Haiti. (1) Exchange of notes on general agreement for technical co-operation (May 2, 1951; amended Dec. 15, 1951 and Jan. 8, 1952).
(2) Economic and technical co-operation agreements by (US) Agency for International Development (June 29, Sept. 28 and 30, 1976; April 27 and Aug. 30, 1977; March 28, 1978).

Honduras. (1) General agreement for economic and technical co-operation (April 12, 1961; entry into force May 27, 1961).
(2) Economic and technical co-operation agreements by (US) Agency for International Development (Feb. 19, 1975, and Nov. 28, 1977).
(3) Treaty on the cession to Honduras of the Swan Islands, three small islands in the Caribbean which had been under US sovereignty since 1856 (Nov. 22, 1971; entry into force Sept. 1, 1972).

Iceland. (1) Economic co-operation agreement (July 3, 1948; amended: Feb. 7, 1950; Feb. 23, 1951; Oct. 9, 1952; and Oct. 1, 1953).
(2) Exchange of notes concerning special economic assistance to Iceland on a loan basis (June 23, 1959).
(3) Exchange of notes providing for an assistance grant in support of Iceland's economic stabilization programme (Dec. 30, 1960).

India. (1) General agreement for technical co-operation (Dec. 28, 1950).
(2) Agreement relating to the technical co-operation programme (Jan. 5, 1952; extended June 29, 1957).
(3) Agreement to establish a joint commission on economic, commercial, scientific, technological, educational and cultural co-operation (Oct. 28, 1974).
(4) Economic and technical co-operation agreements by (US) Agency for International Development (Aug. 26, 1978, and June 30, 1979).
(5) Memorandum of understanding concerning access by an Indian ground station to Landsat satellites of the (US) National Aeronautics and Space Administration (NASA) and availability to NASA and others of data acquired (Jan. 3, 1978).
(6) Exchange of notes concerning the furnishing of launching and associated services for Indian national satellite system-I spacecraft (July 18, 1978).

Indonesia. (1) Economic co-operation agreement (Oct. 16, 1950).
(2) Exchange of notes relating to continuation of the above agreement (Jan. 5 and 12, 1953; entry into force on latter date).
(3) Agreement relating to the assumption by Indonesia of all responsibilities of the Netherlands incurred under economic and loan agreements of 1948-49 (Feb. 11, 1952).
(4) Economic and technical co-operation agreements by (US) Agency for International Development between June 30, 1975, and Aug. 31, 1978.
(5) Exchange of notes concerning the furnishing of launching and associated services by the (US) National Aeronautics and Space Administration for Indonesian satellites (March 26, 1975).
(6) Exchange of notes concerning the furnishing of launching and associated services for Palapa-B spacecraft (April 11, 1979).

Iran. (1) General agreement for economic co-operation (Dec. 21, 1961).
(2) Memorandum of understanding relating to the installation and use of an Iranian earth resources technology ground station (July 25 and Oct. 29, 1974; entry into force on latter date).
(3) Agreement on technical co-operation (March 4, 1975; entry into force April 5, 1976).

Iraq. General agreement for technical co-operation (April 10, 1951; entry into force June 2, 1951; amended Dec. 18, 1951, and Feb. 21, 1952).

Israel. (1) General agreement for technical co-operation (Feb. 26, 1951; amended June 21, 1954).

(2) Joint fund programme agreement (May 9, 1952; amended Aug. 17, 1952; March 11, 1953; June 21 and 29, 1954; June 10 and July 25, 1958; June 26 and Sept. 24, 1959).

(3) Agreement relating to economic assistance (May 9, 1952).

(4) Exchange of notes relating to special economic assistance (Nov. 25, 1953; amended Jan. 31, 1955).

(5) Agreement establishing the Israel-US Binational Industrial Research and Development Foundation (March 3, 1976; entry into force May 18, 1977).

(6) Economic and technical co-operation agreements by the (US) Agency for International Development between June 27, 1975, and Dec. 12, 1979.

Italy. (1) Agreement concerning assistance to Italy under the US foreign relief programme (July 4, 1947).

(2) Economic co-operation agreement (June 28, 1948; amended Sept. 28 and Oct. 2, 1948; Feb. 7, 1950; May 21, 1951; and Jan. 13, 1953).

(3) Exchange of notes providing for a programme of joint participation in the testing of experimental communications satellites (Nov. 14, 1962).

(4) Exchange of notes concerning co-operation in a scientific experiment for the purpose of launching a scientific satellite into an equatorial orbit (Sept. 5, 1962).

(5) Exchange of notes confirming a memorandun of understanding regarding the launching of NASA satellites from the San Marco range (April 30 and June 12, 1969; entry into force on latter date).

(6) Exchange of notes confirming a memorandum of understanding concerning the furnishing of certain services by NASA for Italian satellites (June 15 and 20, 1970; entry into force on latter date).

Ivory Coast. Agreement providing for economic, technical and related assistance (May 17, 1961).

Jamaica. (1) General agreement for economic, technical and related assistance (Oct. 24, 1963).

(2) Economic and technical co-operation agreements by (US) Agency for International Development (Nov. 13, 1974; Nov. 25 and Dec. 15, 1977; Feb. 28 and March 27, 1978).

Japan. (1) Productivity agreement (April 7, 1955).

(2) Exchange of notes providing for a third-country technical assistance training programme in Japan (March 23, 1960).

(3) Exchange of notes providing for a programme of co-operation in the testing of experimental communications satellites (Nov. 6, 1962).

(4) Exchange of notes relating to the establishment by Japan of a satellite tracking station in Okinawa (Sept. 2, 1968; amended Sept. 25, 1969).

(5) Exchange of notes concerning co-operation in space activities for peaceful purposes (July 31, 1969).

(6) Exchange of notes concerning the furnishing of launching and associated services by NASA for Japanese satellites (May 23, 1975).

(7) Agreement on co-operation in research and development in energy and related fields (May 2, 1979).

Jordan. (1) Exchange of notes relating to economic assistance (June 29, 1957).

(2) General agreement providing for economic, technical and related assistance to Jordan (June 25 and 27, 1957; entry into force: July 1, 1957).

(3) Economic and technical co-operation agreements by (US) Agency for International Development between June 28, 1975, and Jan. 25, 1979.

Kenya. (1) Economic co-operation agreement between the United States and the United Kingdom of July 6, 1948, made applicable to Kenya (July 6, 1948; amended Jan. 3, 1950; May 25, 1951; and Feb. 25, 1953).

(2) Agreement between the United States and the United Kingdom for technical co-operation in respect of the territories for the international relations of which the United Kingdom was responsible (July 13, 1951, applicable to Kenya on July 14, 1961).

(3) Economic and technical co-operation agreements by (US) Agency for International Development (Sept. 11, 1974; Nov. 10, 1975; June 30, 1976; July 1 and 20 and Sept. 30, 1977; and Aug. 29, 1978).

Republic of Korea. (1) Exchange of notes providing for economic, technical and related assistance (Feb. 8, 1961; entry into force Feb. 28, 1961.

(2) Agreement concerning supplemental economic assistance (Oct. 16, 1971).

(3) Economic and technical co-operation agreements by (US) Agency for International Development between Sept. 11, 1974, and Jan. 19, 1977.

Laos. (1) Economic co-operation agreement (Sept. 9, 1951).

(2) Exchange of notes providing for additional direct economic assistance (July 6 and 8, 1955, operative from Jan. 1, 1955).

Lebanon. (1) General agreement for technical co-operation (May 29, 1951; entry into force Dec. 13, 1951).

(2) Technical co-operation programme

agreement (June 26, 1952; amended April 14, 1953; April 30, 1954).

(3) Exchange of notes relating to special economic assistance (June 11 and 18, 1954; entry into force on latter date).

(4) Exchange of notes granting special assistance to Lebanon for budgetary support (Sept. 2 and 3, 1958; entry into force on latter date).

(5) Economic and technical co-operation agreements by (US) Agency for International Development (March 21 and June 22, 1978).

Lesotho. Economic and technical co-operation agreement by (US) Agency of International Development (Aug. 31, 1978).

Liberia. (1) Memorandum of understanding on the joint Liberian-US commission for economic development (Oct. 6, 1955; operative Feb. 3, 1956).

(2) General agreement for technical assistance and co-operation (Oct. 6, 1955; entry into force Feb. 3, 1956).

(3) Economic and technical co-operation agreements by (US) Agency for International Development (Aug. 12, 1977).

Luxembourg. Economic co-operation agreement (July 3, 1948).

Madagascar. (1) Exchange of notes providing for the furnishing of economic, technical and related assistance (June 22, 1961).

(2) Economic and technical co-operation agreement by (US) Agency for International Development (July 25, 1973).

Malawi. Economic and technical co-operation agreement by (US) Agency for International Development (April 29, 1976).

Malaysia. Economic co-operation agreement between the United States and the United Kingdom (July 6, 1948; made applicable to the then Federation of Malaya on July 20, 1948; amended Jan. 3, 1950; May 25, 1951; and Feb. 25, 1953).

Mali. Exchange of notes providing for the furnishing of economic, technical and related assistance (Jan. 4, 1961).

Malta. (1) Economic co-operation agreement between the United States and the United Kingdom (July 6, 1948, applicable to Malta on the same date; amended Jan. 3, 1950; May 25, 1951; and Feb. 25, 1953).

(2) Economic and technical co-operation agreement by (US) Agency for International Development (June 15, 1973).

Mauritania. (1) General agreement for special development assistance (March 23, 1971).

(2) Economic and technical co-operation agreements by (US) Agency for Inter-

national Development (Feb. 26, 1974; May 28, 1976; and April 18, 1978).

Mauritius. Economic co-operation agreement between the United States and the United Kingdom (July 1948; amended Jan. 3, 1950; May 25, 1951; and Feb. 25, 1953).

Mexico. (1) Exchange of notes on general agreement for technical co-operation (June 27, 1951; amended Jan. 21-22, 1952; and April 13, 1954).

(2) Exchange of notes relating to a programme of industrial productivity in Mexico (Feb. 21 and Nov. 15, 1961; entry into force on latter date).

(3) Agreement relating to co-operation in the field of geothermal energy research and development (July 21, 1977).

(4) Agreement on co-operation to improve the management of arid and semi-arid lands and to control desertification (Feb. 16, 1979).

(5) Agreement on natural gas (Sept. 21, 1979).

Morocco. (1) Exchange of notes providing for economic, technical and related assistance (April 1, 1957; entry into force on the following day; amended May 19, 1958).

(2) Memorandum of understanding for technical co-operation in the earth sciences (Aug. 24 and Oct. 7, 1977; entry into force on latter date).

(3) Economic and technical co-operation agreements by (US) Agency for International Development (Nov. 7, 1975; June 14, 1976: and Aug. 14 and 31, 1978).

Mozambique. Economic and technical co-operation agreements by (US) Agency of International Development (Sept. 14, 1976; and Dec. 2, 1977).

Nepal. (1) General agreement for technical co-operation (Jan. 23, 1951; amended Jan. 2 and 8, 1952).

(2) Economic and technical co-operation agreements by (US) Agency for International Development between June 5, 1975, and Aug. 31, 1978.

Netherlands. (1) Economic co-operation agreement applicable to Curaçao; (July 2, 1948; amended Jan. 16 and Feb. 2, 1950; March 7 and April 3, 1951; and Nov. 28, 1952).

(2) General agreement for technical co-operation for Suriname and Netherlands Antilles (Jan. 22, 1954; entry into force April 21, 1954).

New Zealand. (1) Exchange of notes relating to co-operation in scientific and logistical operations in Antarctica (Dec. 24, 1958).

(2) Exchange of notes concerning a

programme of research on aerospace disturbances (May 15, 1963).

(3) Agreement for scientific and technological co-operation (Feb. 27, 1974).

Nicaragua. (1) Exchange of notes on general agreement for economic, technical and related assistance (March 30, 1962; entry into force May 14, 1962).

(2) Economic and technical co-operation agreement by (US) Agency for International Development (Aug. 30, 1978).

Niger. (1) Exchange of notes providing for the furnishing of economic, technical and related assistance (May 26, 1961).

(2) Economic and technical co-operation agreements by (US) Agency for International Development between Sept. 17, 1975, and June 1, 1978.

Nigeria. (1) Economic co-operation agreement between the United States and the United Kingdom (July 6, 1948; made applicable to Nigeria on the same day; amended Jan. 3, 1950; May 25, 1951; and Feb. 25, 1953).

(2) Agreement providing for the establishment and operation of a space vehicle tracking and communications station within the Federation of Nigeria (Oct. 19, 1960; extended and amended April 28 and May 21, 1964).

(2) Memorandum of understanding relating to technical co-operation in geological, water resources, land-use and related studies for the Capital Territory of Nigeria (Feb. 4, 1977).

Norway. (1) Economic co-operation agreement (July 3, 1948; amended Jan. 17, 1950; July 5, 1951; and Jan. 8, 1953).

(2) Exchange of notes relating to the installation, operation and management of a seismic array facility in Norway (June 15, 1968).

Pakistan. (1) Agreement for technical co-operation (Feb. 9, 1951; amended Jan. 8, 1952).

(2) Supplementary agreement for technical co-operation (Feb. 2, 1952; amended March 27 and Dec. 28, 1953; June 24, 1954; and Jan. 18, 1955).

(3) Economic and technical co-operation agreements by (US) Agency for International Development between Oct. 10, 1975, and Nov. 8, 1978.

Panama. (1) General agreement for technical and economic co-operation (Dec. 11, 1961; entry into force March 5, 1962).

(2) Economic and technical co-operation agreements by (US) Agency for International Development between May 6, 1969, and Aug. 23, 1978.

Paraguay. (1) General agreement for

economic, technical and related assistance (Sept. 26, 1961).

(2) Economic and technical co-operation agreements by (US) Agency for International Development (June 30, 1975; Dec. 7, 1976, and Aug. 15, 1977).

Peru. (1) General agreement for technical co-operation (Jan. 25, 1951; entry into force Jan. 15, 1953; amended Jan. 7, 1952; Feb. 21 and 28, 1952; and Jan. 15, 1953).

(2) Economic and technical co-operation agreements by (US) Agency for International Development (Sept. 29, 1976; May 31, June 30 and July 19, 1978).

Philippines. (1) Economic and technical co-operation agreement (April 27, 1951; entry into force May 21, 1951).

(2) Economic and technical co-operation agreements by (US) Agency for International Development between Dec. 23, 1975, and Aug. 18, 1978.

Poland. (1) Agreement on co-operation in science and technology (Oct. 31, 1972).

(2) Agreement on funding of co-operation in science and technology (Oct. 8, 1974).

Portugal. (1) Economic co-operation agreement (Sept. 28, 1948; amended Feb. 14, 1950; May 17, 1951; and March 9 and 18, 1953).

(2) Exchange of letters relating to provision of economic assistance to Portugal (Dec. 9, 1971).

(3) Economic and technical co-operation agreements by (US) Agency for International Development between Feb. 28, 1975, and March 1, 1978.

Romania*. (1) Agreement on co-operation and exchanges in the cultural, educational, scientific and technological fields (Dec. 13, 1974. entry into force Jan. 1, 1975).

(2) Long-term agreement on economic, industrial and technical co-operation (Nov. 21, 1976; entry into force May 5, 1977).

(3) Programme of co-operation and exchanges in educational, cultural, scientific, technological and other fields for the years 1979 and 1980 (Dec. 7, 1978; effective Jan. 1, 1979).

(4) Memorandum of understanding on scientific and technical co-operation (Feb. 27, 1979).

Rwanda. Economic and technical co-operation agreements by (US) Agency for International Development (April 26 and 29, 1977).

St Lucia. (1) Economic co-operation agreement between the United States and

---

* See also page 256.

the United Kingdom of July 6, 1948, applicable to St Lucia (except for Art. IV) on the same date (amended Jan. 3, 1950; May 25, 1951; June 26 and Aug. 20, 1959).

(2) Agreement between the United States and the United Kingdom for technical co-operation in respect of the territories for the international relations of which the United Kingdom was responsible (July 13, 1951; applicable to St Lucia Aug. 14, 1954).

Saudi Arabia. (1) Technical co-operation agreement (Feb. 13, 1975; entry into force May 12, 1975; extended and amended Nov. 25, 1979).

(2) Agreement for technical co-operation in desalination (May 3, 1977; entry into force Aug. 30, 1977).

(3) Numerous project agreements for technical co-operation concluded since 1975.

Senegal. (1) Agreement providing for economic, financial, technical and related assistance (May 13, 1961).

(2) Economic and technical co-operation agreements by (US) Agency for International Development between March 23, 1974, and March 29, 1978.

Seychelles. Agreement relating to the establishment, operation and maintenance of a tracking and telemetry facility on the island of Mahé (due to expire in 1985) (June 29, 1976).

Sierra Leone. (1) Economic co-operation agreement between the United States and the United Kingdom (July 6, 1948, made applicable to Sierra Leone on the same day; amended Jan. 3, 1950; May 25, 1951; and Feb. 25, 1953).

(2) General agreement for a programme of economic, technical and related assistance (May 5, 1961).

Singapore. Economic co-operation agreement between the United States and the United Kingdom (July 6, 1948; amended Jan. 3, 1950; May 25, 1951; and Feb. 25, 1953).

Solomon Islands. As above for Singapore.

Somalia. Economic and technical co-operation agreements by (US) Agency for International Development (June 7, 1976, and Dec. 18, 1977).

Spain. (1) Treaty of friendship and general relations (July 3, 1902; entry into force April 14, 1903; amended as from July 1, 1916, by abrogation of Arts. XXIII and XXIV).

(2) Economic aid agreement (Sept. 26, 1953).

(3) Exchange of notes providing for the

establishment and operation of a tracking and data acquisition station (Jan. 29, 1964; extended and amended Oct. 11, 1965, and June 25, 1969).

(4) Exchange of notes for the continued operation and expansion of the space vehicle tracking and communications station on the island of Gran Canaria (April 14, 1966; extended and amended Jan. 15, 1974).

(5) Exchange of notes providing for a project in Spain to measure winds and temperatures at high altitudes and for continuing other co-operative space research projects (April 14, 1966).

(6) Exchange of notes establishing a joint Spanish-US economic committee to consult with regard to financial and other economic matters of mutual interest (July 15, 1968).

(7) Treaty of friendship and co-operation (Jan. 24, 1976—see page 315).

(8) Agreement in implementation of the above treaty (Jan. 31, 1976; entry into force Sept. 21, 1976).

Sri Lanka. (1) General agreement for technical co-operation (Nov. 7, 1950).

(2) Exchange of notes relating to development assistance programme to Ceylon, now Sri Lanka (April 28, 1956).

Sudan. (1) Exchange of notes providing for economic, technical and related assistance to the Sudan (March 31, 1958).

(2) Economic and technical co-operation agreements by (US) Agency for International Development (May 12, 1977; Aug. 30, 1978; and Dec. 31, 1979).

Suriname. (1) Economic co-operation agreement between the United States and the Netherlands (July 2, 1948; amended Jan. 16, and Feb. 2, 1950; March 7 and April 3, 1951; and Nov. 28, 1952).

(2) General agreement between the United States and the Netherlands for technical co-operation for Suriname and the Netherlands Antilles (Jan. 22, 1954; entry into force April 21, 1954).

Swaziland. (1) General agreement on special development assistance (June 3, 1970).

(2) Economic and technical co-operation agreement by (US) Agency for International Development (Aug. 31, 1978).

Sweden. Economic co-operation agreement (July 3, 1948; entry into force July 21, 1948; amended Jan. 5 and 17, 1950; Feb. 8 and 23, 1951).

Syria. (1) Exchange of notes with the United Arab Republic (UAR) extending to the Syrian region of the UAR application of the general agreement for technical co-operation with Egypt of May 5, 1951, and the economic development programme of Nov. 6, 1954 (April 2, 1960).

(2) Economic and technical co-operation agreements by (US) Agency for International Development between Feb. 27, 1975, and Sept. 12, 1979.

Tanzania. (1) Exchange of notes providing for the furnishing of economic, technical and related assistance (Feb. 8, 1968).

(2) Economic and technical co-operation agreements by (US) Agency for International development (Aug. 12-13, 1975; April 13, 1976; Aug. 15, 1977; Dec. 28-29, 1977; and July 6, 1978).

Thailand. (1) Economic and technical co-operation agreements (June 2, 1977).

(2) Economic and technical co-operation agreements by (US) Agency for International Development (Dec. 11, 1975; March 31 and Sept. 8, 1976; May 31 and Aug. 24 and 29, 1977; and May 4, 1978).

Togo. (1) Exchange of notes providing for economic, technical and related assistance (Dec. 22, 1960).

(2) Economic and technical co-operation agreement by (US) Agency for International Development (Oct. 12, 1977).

Trinidad and Tobago. (1) Economic co-operation agreement between the United States and the United Kingdom (July 6, 1948, applicable to Trinidad and Tobago on March 17, 1949; amended Jan. 3, 1950; May 25, 1951; Feb. 23, 1953; and June 26 and Aug. 20, 1959).

(2) Agreement between the United States and the United Kingdom for technical co-operation in respect of the territories for the international relations of which the United Kingdom was responsible (July 13, 1951, applicable to Trinidad and Tobago on Aug. 14, 1954).

Tunisia. (1) Exchange of notes providing for economic, technical and related assistance (March 26, 1957).

(2) Exchange of notes supplementing the above agreement (Oct. 8, 1958).

(3) Economic and technical co-operation agreements by (US) Agency for International Development (Dec. 29, 1977; Jan. 12, March 24 and Aug. 31, 1978).

Turkey. (1) Agreement on aid to Turkey (July 12, 1947).

(2) Economic co-operation agreement (July 4, 1948; amended Jan. 31, 1950; Aug. 16, 1951; and Dec. 30, 1952).

(3) Economic and technical co-operation agreements by (US) Agency for International Development (Dec. 5, 1978; Nov. 1, 1979; and Jan. 23, 1980).

Uganda. Exchange of notes relating to economic, technical and related assistance

(Dec. 3 and 11, 1971; entry into force on latter date).

United Kingdom. (1) Treaty of amity, commerce and navigation, of which only three articles are still in force (Nov. 19, 1794; entry into force Oct. 28, 1795).

(2) Economic co-operation agreement applicable to Brunei, Channel Islands, Falkland Islands, Western Pacific High Commission territories, Gibraltar, Belize, British Virgin Islands, Hong Kong, Isle of Man and St Helena and Dependencies, and also, except for Art. IV, to Turks and Caicos Islands, Cayman Islands, Antigua, Montserrat and St Kitts, Nevis and Anguilla (July 6, 1948; amended Jan. 3, 1950; May 25, 1951; Feb. 21, 1953; and June 26 and Aug. 20, 1959).

(3) Agreement for technical co-operation in respect of the terrritories for the international relations of which the United Kingdom was responsible, applicable to Antigua, Belize, British Virgin Islands, Montserrat, St Kitts, Nevis and Anguilla, Turks and Caicos Islands and Cayman Islands (July 13, 1951).

(4) Exchange of notes providing for the establishment and operation of a space vehicle tracking and communication station in Bermuda (March 15, 1961; extended and amended Sept. 23, 1963; Jan. 17, 1968).

(5) Exchange of notes on co-operation in intercontinental testing in connexion with experimental communications satellites (March 29, 1961).

(6) Exchange of notes providing for the establishment of a lunar and planetary spacecraft tracking facility on Ascension Island (July 7, 1965).

(7) Exchange of notes providing for the establishment and operation of space vehicle tracking and communications stations in the United Kingdom (Dec. 8, 1966, and Jan. 1, 1967; entry into force on latter date).

(8) Exchange of notes concerning the establishment and operation of a space vehicle tracking and communications station on Antigua (Jan. 17 and 23, 1967; entry into force on latter date).

(9) Exchange of notes confirming a memorandum of understanding concerning the furnishing of launching and associated services by the (US) National Aeronautics and Space Administration for UK satellites (Jan. 17, 1973).

(10) Memorandum of understanding on co-operation in earth sciences and environmental studies (Sept. 21 and 26, 1979; entry into force on latter date).

Upper Volta. (1) Exchange of notes providing for the furnishing of economic, technical and related assistance (June 1, 1961).

327

(2) Economic and technical co-operation agreements by (US) Agency for International Development (June 30 and July 1, 1977; Sept. 9, 1977; and June 8, 1978).

Uruguay. (1) General agreement for a programme of technical co-operation (March 23, 1956; entry into force March 22, 1960).

(2) Economic and technical co-operation agreements by (US) Agency for International Development (Sept. 3 and Dec. 5, 1975).

Venezuela. (1) Treaty of peace, friendship, navigation and commerce (Jan. 20, 1836; entry into force May 31, 1836; articles on commerce and navigation terminated Jan. 3, 1851).

(2) Exchange of notes on general agreement on technical co-operation (Sept. 29, 1952).

Yemen Arab Republic. Economic, technical and related assistance agreement (April 20, 1974).

Yugoslavia. (1) Economic co-operation agreement (Jan. 8, 1952).

(2) Agreement on scientific and technical co-operation (May 18, 1973).

Zaïre. (1) Economic and technical co-operation agreements by (US) Agency for International Development (June 29 and Sept. 30 1976; Jan. 27, 1977; and July 10 and Aug. 9, 1978).

(2) Memorandum of understanding concerning direct access by a Zaïrian ground station to data generated by US earth resources technology satellites (ERTS) and availability to the (US) National Aeronautics and Space Administration of the data so acquired (Jan. 6 and 31, 1975; entry into force on latter date).

Zambia. (1) Economic co-operation agreement between the United States and the United Kingdom of July 6, 1948, made applicable to Northern Rhodesia, now Zambia (July 20, 1948; amended Jan. 3, 1950; May 25, 1951; and Feb. 25, 1953).

(2) Agreement for technical co-operation in respect of the territories for the international relations of which the United Kingdom was responsible of July 13, 1951; made applicable to the Federation of Rhodesia and Nyasaland April 8, 1960.

(3) Economic and technical co-operation agreements by (US) Agency for International Development (Dec. 3, 1976, and March 30, 1978).

Bilateral US Agreements on the Peaceful Use of Nuclear Energy

Agreements on co-operation in the peaceful uses of atomic (or nuclear) energy have been concluded by the United States with the following countries. The dates given are those of the signature and, unless otherwise stated, of entry into force of the agreements. Where no further particulars are given, the agreements refer only to "co-operation in the civil uses of atomic energy".

Argentina. (1) Exchange of notes providing for a grant to assist in the acquisition of certain nuclear resources and training equipment and materials (Sept. 9, 1959, and May 23, 1960; entry into force on latter date).

(2) Exchange of notes providing for equipment to be used in nuclear research and training programme at La Plata University, Argentina (Nov. 8, 1962, and Nov. 30, 1963; entry into force on latter date).

(3) Agreement (June 25, 1969; entry into force July 25, 1969).

Australia. (1) Agreement (June 22, 1956; entry into force May 28, 1957; extended and amended Sept. 14, 1960, and April 11, 1967).

(2) Exchange of notes relating to peaceful nuclear co-operation (Aug. 4 and 7, 1978; entry into force on latter date).

(3) Agreement (July 5, 1979).

Austria. (1) Agreement (July 11, 1969; entry into force Jan. 24, 1970; extended and amended June 14, 1974).

(2) Agreements on research participation and technical exchanges (i) in the US Nuclear Regulatory Commission loss of fluid test (LOFT) research programme and (ii) the US Nuclear Regulatory Commission power burst facility (PBF) research programme (Feb. 25 and March 3, 1977; entry into force on latter date).

Belgium. Arrangements for exchange of technical information in regulatory matters and in co-operation in safety research and in standards development (June 6, 1978).

Brazil. (1) Exchanges of notes providing for grants to assist in the acquisition of nuclear research and training equipment and materials (a) Oct. 20, 1959 and Feb. 27, 1960; entry into force on latter date; (b) Oct. 10, 1960, and March 17, 1962; entry into force on latter date; and (c) Oct. 10, 1962, and March 29, 1963; entry into force on latter date.

(2) Agreement (July 17, 1972; entry into force Sept. 20, 1972).

(3) Arrangement for the exchange of technical information and co-operation in safety research (May 20, 1976).

Canada. (1) Agreement (June 15, 1955; entry into force July 21, 1955; extended and amended June 26, 1956; May 22, 1959; June 11, 1960 and May 25, 1962).

(2) Exchange of notes relating to the application of safeguards on small quantities of natural uranium transferred from Canada to the United States (Jan. 28 and 30, 1969; entry into force on latter date).

(3) Arrangement relating to information in the nuclear field (Aug. 6 and Sept. 8, 1976; entry into force on latter date).

(4) Exchange of notes relating to US-Canadian nuclear co-operation (Nov. 15, 1977). This agreement concerned the application of Canadian non-proliferation controls to Canadian uranium enriched in the United States and subsequently supplied to third countries.

Chile. Exchange of notes providing for a grant for the acquisition of certain nuclear research and training equipment and materials (July 23, 1959, and Feb. 19, 1960; entry into force on latter date).

Colombia. (1) Exchange of notes providing for a grant for the acquisition of nuclear training and research equipment and materials (July 11, 1959 and Jan. 11, 1960; entry into force on latter date).

(2) Exchange of notes continuing in effect safeguards and guarantee provisions of an agreement of April 9, 1962, for civil uses of atomic energy (March 28, 1977).

Denmark. Arrangements for exchange of technical information in regulatory and safety research matters and co-operation in development of safety standards (Oct. 3, 1975).

Egypt. Agreement on co-operation in the construction of a nuclear power station, with US uranium to be supplied (Oct. 3, 1979).

Finland. Agreement (April 8, 1970; entry into force July 7, 1970).

France. (1) Technical exchange arrangement in the field of research on light water reactor safety (Sept. 23 and Oct. 14, 1974; entry into force on latter date).

(2) Agreement in the field of liquid metal-cooled fast-breeder reactors (Jan. 18, 1977).

(3) Protocol relating to the isotopic enrichment of uranium by chemical exchange (Sept. 4, 1979; entry into force Oct. 31, 1979).

(4) Arrangement for the exchange of technical information and co-operation in the regulation of nuclear safety (Oct. 25, 1979).

Federal Republic of Germany. (1) Technical and co-operative arrangement in the field of research and development on reactor safety, applicable also to West Berlin (March 6, 1974).

(2) Technical exchange and co-operative arrangement in the field of management of radioactive wastes (Dec. 20, 1974).

(3) Agreement on research participation and technical exchange in the US Nuclear Regulatory Commission loss of fluid test (LOFT) research programme (June 20, 1975).

(4) Arrangement on co-operation in the field of nuclear facilities safety, applicable also to West Berlin (Oct. 1, 1975).

(5) Agreement for research and development in the field of liquid metal-cooled fast-breeder reactors, applicable also to West Berlin (June 8, 1976).

(6) Agreement in the field of gas-cooled reactor concepts and technology (Feb. 11, 1977).

(7) Agreement on research participation and technical exchange in the US power burst facility (PBF) and heavy section steel technology (HSST) research programmes and the German fuel behaviour and superheat steam reactor (HDR) safety programmes, applicable also to West Berlin (April 26 and May 6, 1977; entry into force on latter date).

(8) Exchange of letters relating to co-operation in the field of nuclear materials safeguards and physical security research and development (Sept. 29, 1977).

Greece. (1) Exchange of notes relating to the applicability of certain provisions of an expired agreement of Aug. 4, 1955, as amended, for co-operation concerning civil uses of atomic energy (Jan. 28, 1977).

(2) Arrangement for the exchange of technical information and co-operation in nuclear safety matters (Oct. 19, 1978).

Guatemala. Exchange of notes providing for a grant to assist in the acquisition of certain nuclear research and training equipment and materials (April 7 and 23, 1960; entry into force on latter date).

India. (1) Exchange of notes providing for a grant of nuclear research equipment in the field of agriculture (April 22 and June 13, 1960; entry into force on latter date).

(2) Exchange of notes providing for a grant for assistance in obtaining materials and equipment for establishing a radiation medicine centre at a Bombay hospital (Jan. 4 and Feb. 1, 1963; entry into force on latter date).

(3) Agreement (Aug. 8, 1963; entry into force Oct. 25, 1963).

Indonesia. Agreement (June 8, 1960; entry into force Sept. 21, 1960; extended and amended Jan. 12, 1966, and June 10, 1970).

Iran. Arrangement for the exchange of technical information and co-operation in nuclear safety matters (April 11, 1977).

Ireland. Exchange of notes providing for a grant to assist in the acquisition of certain nuclear research and training equipment and materials (March 24, 1960; entry into force April 7, 1960).

Israel. (1) Exchange of notes providing for a grant to Israel to assist in the acquisition of certain nuclear research and training equipment and materials (Oct. 19 and Dec. 19, 1960; entry into force on latter date).

(2) Exchange of notes continuing in effect safeguards and guarantee provisions of an agreement of July 12, 1955, as amended, for co-operation concerning civil uses of atomic energy (April 7-8, 1977; entry into force on latter date).

(3) Arrangement for the exchange of technical information and co-operation in nuclear safety matters (May 9 and 19, 1978; entry into force on latter date).

Italy. Arrangement for the exchange of technical information and co-operation in safety research and development and development of standards (May 29, 1975).

Japan. (1) Agreement (Feb. 26, 1968; entry into force July 10, 1968; amended Feb. 24, 1972, and March 28, 1973).

(2) Technical exchange arrangement in the field of regulatory matters (May 18 and 30, 1974; entry into force on latter date).

(3) Agreement on research participation and technical exchange in the US Nuclear Regulatory Commission LOFT research programme (Feb. 23, 1976).

(4) Agreement on research participation and technical exchange in the US power burst facility (PBF) research and the Japanese nuclear safety research reactor (MSRR) programme (March 9, 1976).

(5) Joint determination for reprocessing of special nuclear material of US origin (Sept. 12, 1977).

(6) Agreement in the field of liquid metal-cooled fast-breeder reactors (Jan. 31, 1979).

(7) Agreement extending the period of operation of the reprocessing facility referred to in the joint communiqué of Sept. 12, 1977—see above (Oct. 1, 1979).

Republic of Korea. (1) Exchange of notes providing for a grant to the Government of Korea to assist in the acquisition of certain nuclear research and training equipment and materials (Oct. 14 and Nov. 18, 1960; entry into force on latter date).

(2) Agreement (Nov. 24, 1972; entry into force March 19, 1973).

(3) Arrangement for exchange of tech-

nical information in regulatory and safety research and co-operation in development of safety standards (March 18, 1976).

Lebanon. Exchange of notes providing for a grant to the Government of Lebanon to assist in the acquisition of nuclear research and training equipment and supplies (Sept. 16, 1959).

Netherlands. (1) Agreement for a co-operative research programme on in-pile creep and collapse of zircaloy tubing (Dec. 9 and 24, 1976; entry into force on latter date).

(2) Arrangement for the exchange of technical information on regulatory matters and co-operation in safety research and the development of standards (Oct. 3, 1977).

New Zealand. Exchange of notes providing for a grant to assist in the acquisition of nuclear research and training equipment and materials (March 23, 1960).

Norway. Agreement (May 4, 1967; entry into force June 8, 1967; amended Dec. 23, 1969).

Peru. Exchange of notes providing for a grant to the Government of Peru to assist in the acquisition of nuclear research and training equipment and materials (July 12 and Aug. 22, 1959; entry into force on latter date).

Philippines. Agreement (June 13, 1968; entry into force July 19, 1968).

Portugal. Agreement (May 16, 1974; entry into force June 26, 1974).

Romania. Agreement clarifying certain understandings relating to the supply of enriched uranium to Romania for the TRIGA reactor (Feb. 13, 1978).

South Africa. Agreement (July 8, 1957; entry into force Aug. 22, 1957; extended and amended June 12, 1962; July 17, 1967; and May 22, 1974).

Soviet Union. Agreement (June 21, 1973).

Spain. (1) Agreement (March 20, 1974; entry into force June 28, 1974).

(2) Arrangement for the exchange of technical information and co-operation in nuclear safety matters (Nov. 5, 1979).

Sweden. (1) Agreement (July 28, 1966; entry into force Sept. 15, 1966; amended Oct. 22, 1970, and May 10, 1974). This 30-year agreement provided for the supply of enriched uranium for 11 nuclear reactors to be operative in Sweden by 1980.

(2) Technical exchange and co-operative arrangement in the field of research and development on reactor safety (Nov. 21 and

Dec. 16, 1974; entry into force on latter date).

(3) Agreement concerning a co-operative programme of radioactive waste storage in deep geological formations (June 17 and July 1, 1977; entry into force on latter date).

(4) Arrangement for the exchange of technical information and co-operation in nuclear safety matters (Oct. 30, 1979).

Switzerland. (1) Agreement (Dec. 30, 1965; entry into force Aug. 8, 1966; amended Nov. 2, 1973).

(2) Arrangement for the exchange of technical information and co-operation in the development of standards (Dec. 9, 1974).

(3) Agreement on research participation and technical exchange in the US loss of fluid test programme and the Swiss emergency core cooling systems-reflood programme (June 15 and July 9, 1979; entry into force on latter date).

(4) Agreement on research participation and technical exchange in the US heavy section steel technology programme and the Swiss research programme in fracture mechanics (June 15 and July 9, 1979; entry into force on latter date).

Taiwan. (1) Agreement providing for a grant for the acquisition of nuclear research and training equipment and materials (Oct. 16 and Dec. 2, 1959; entry into force on latter date).

(2) Agreement (April 4, 1972; entry into force June 22, 1972; extended and amended March 15, 1974).

Thailand. Agreement (May 14, 1974; entry into force June 27, 1974).

Turkey. Agreement (June 10, 1955; extended and amended April 27, 1961; June 3, 1965; May 11, 1966; and May 20, 1971).

United Kingdom. (1) Articles of agreement governing collaboration between the authorities of the United States and the United Kingdom in the matter of tube alloys (Aug. 19, 1943).

(2) Arrangement relating to exchange of information on significant matters pertaining to the safety of nuclear installations and on collaboration in the development of regulatory safety (March 13, 1975).

(3) Agreement in the field of liquid metal-cooled fast-breeder reactors (Sept. 20, 1976).

(4) Implementing agreement for collaboration in experimental programmes concerned with safety of nuclear reactors (Dec. 14, 1976).

(5) Arrangement in the field of nuclear safety research and development (July 20 and Aug. 3, 1977; entry into force on latter date).

Venezuela. Agreement (Oct. 8, 1958; entry into force Feb. 9, 1960; extended and amended Nov. 14, 1969).

Yugoslavia. Exchange of notes providing for a grant to assist in the acquisition of certain nuclear research and training equipment and materials (April 19, 1961).

Other Agreements involving American States

Bilateral Agreements in Latin America and the Caribbean

Argentina and Bolivia. Agreements signed in November 1976 provided for the supply to Argentina of 1,400,000 cubic feet of Bolivian gas per day from 1979 onwards.

Argentina and Chile. (1) An arbitration agreement signed in Buenos Aires on April 5, 1972, between Argentina and Chile provided for reference to the International Court of Justice of any bilateral dispute not resolved by direct negotiation. The agreement superseded a 1902 treaty which had provided for arbitration by the British Crown in territorial disputes between the two countries.

(2) A number of co-operation agreements were signed during a visit of the Argentine President to Chile on Nov. 11-13, 1976, covering land transport links, the annual supply by Argentina to Chile of 500,000 tons of wheat during 1977-79 and increased sales of Chilean natural gas to Argentina.

(3) Under an *Act of Puerto Montt* signed by the two countries' Presidents on Feb. 20, 1978, it was agreed to seek to create a "harmonious atmosphere" which might lead to a peaceful solution of the controversies existing between the two sides and subsequently to determining the two nations' respective rights under the legal system. (The Act failed, however, to lead to a settlement of the principal dispute between the two sides, concerning sovereignty over islands in the Beagle Channel (off Tierra del Fuego), which the International Court of Justice had awarded to Chile on May 2, 1977—this award having been rejected by Argentina on Jan. 25, 1978.)

Argentina and Paraguay. A treaty on the construction of a hydroelectric project on the Paraná River (constituting part of the border between the two countries) at the Yaciretá-Agipé falls was signed on Dec. 3,

1973. An agreement on the final specifications of this scheme was, however, not signed until Aug. 30, 1979, when it was agreed that Argentina would pay Paraguay up to $50,000,000 a year in compensation for the flooding of an area in Paraguay by the scheme.

A permanent office for co-operation in investment and industry had been offically opened in Asunción (Paraguay) on June 15, 1974.

Argentina and Peru. At the end of a visit to Peru by Argentina's President on March 3-5, 1977, it was announced that Argentinian technology and equipment would be used to build Peru's first nuclear reactor.

Argentina and Uruguay. A treaty on equal rights in navigation on the River Plate (Rio de la Plata) was signed in Montevideo on Nov. 19, 1973. It provided for freedom of navigation in perpetuity for the vessels of both Argentina and Uruguay on the river; for mutual guarantees for the maintenance of access to the ports of Buenos Aires and Montevideo; and for the use of all shipping lanes by the two countries under conditions of equality. (Under the *Ramírez-Saenz Pena Protocol* of 1910, the frontier between the two countries had been defined as the line of the river's greatest depth—and not the median line as demanded by Uruguay.)

Bolivia and Brazil. An agreement on friendship and co-operation between the two countries, signed by their Presidents during a visit to Brazil by Bolivia's President on Aug. 13-17, 1977, provided inter alia for delivery to Brazil of 240,000,000 cubic feet of natural gas daily for 20 years and of 410,000 tonnes of rolled steel and 100,000 tonnes of urea per annum, in return for which Brazil would invest an estimated $1,000 million for industrial development in Bolivia and for a pipeline to transport the gas.

Brazil and Peru. Agreements were concluded between the two countries on Nov. 5, 1976, on trade, navigation and communications, while a period of "greater rapprochement" was envisaged with "more effective guidelines" to be laid down "for mutual understanding and economic co-operation" between the two sides.

Chile and Peru. Under a 1929 Treaty of Ancón it was agreed that no Chilean territory which had earlier been part of Peru could be surrendered to a third party without Peru's consent. (This related to territory annexed by Chile as a result of the 1879-93 War of the Pacific, through which Bolivia, which had been joined by Peru in fighting against Chile, lost its access to the sea.)

Chile and Uruguay. An agreement on co-operation in the peaceful uses of nuclear energy, including the training of Uruguayan scientists, was signed by the two countries in July 1979.

Colombia and Nicaragua. A Barcenas-Meneses-Esguerra treaty of 1930 provided inter alia for the cession, by Nicaragua to Colombia, of five islands in the Caribbean Sea—Providencia, Quita Sueno, Roncador, San Andrés and Serrana. The treaty was unilaterally abrogated by Nicaragua on Feb. 5, 1980, but Colombia rejected the abrogation and maintained its sovereignty over the islands (which were believed to contain oil reserves).

Colombia and Panama. An agreement was signed on Nov. 20, 1976, on the delimitation of the two countries' marine and submarine territories.

Colombia and Peru. A treaty on the two countries' common boundary was concluded in 1922.

Ecuador and Venezuela. On March 17, 1975, the Presidents of Ecuador and Venezuela signed a 22-point declaration on intensive co-operation between their countries, with Venezuela (i) placing the equivalent of US $23,000,000 in Ecuadorean national bonds on the Venezuelan financial market and (ii) providing capital and technology to finance industrial projects in Ecuador.

El Salvador and Honduras. El Salvador and Honduras agreed to the establishment of a demilitarized zone along their common frontier at a meeting of the Foreign Ministers of five Central American States under OAS auspices at San José (Costa Rica) on June 4, 1970. The OAS had previously mediated in hostilities between the two countries in July 1969) [see also page 301].

A peace treaty between the two countries, signed in Lima (Peru) on Oct. 30, 1980, ended the effective state of war which had existed between them since 1969. It reopened their common border, provided for the resumption of diplomatic relations, committed both parties to the reactivation of the Central American Common Market [see page 301] and demarcated two-thirds of the common frontier, with an undertaking to settle within five years the question of disputed border areas, which formed part of the demilitarized zone. The treaty was ratified by the Constituent Assembly of Honduras at the end of November 1980.

Mexico and El Salvador. An economic and technical co-operation agreement between the two countries was signed in January 1979.

Mexico and Venezuela. A total of 15 agreements covering co-operation between state enterprises in the two countries were signed during a visit of the President of Venezuela to Mexico on March 17-22, 1975.

Trinidad and Tobago and Haiti. A trade agreement signed by the two countries in 1974 was the first of its kind to be concluded between a Commonwealth Caribbean state and Haiti.

Venezuela and Costa Rica. A co-operation and mutual aid agreement was signed between the two countries on Sept. 15, 1978.

Venezuela and Dominica. An economic co-operation agreement was signed between the two countries in Caracas late in January 1979.

Venezuela and Dominican Republic. An economic agreement signed between the two countries in December 1976 involved the purchase of sugar from the Dominican Republic by Venezuela and a Venezuelan loan of $60,000,000 for oil purchases by the Dominican Republic.

Venezuela and Jamaica. A trade agreement concluded in April 1975 included a bilateral arrangement on Jamaican bauxite and alumina to be supplied to Venezuela in return for fertilizer supplies by Venezuela to Jamaica. Early in 1977 a new agreement was signed on intensifying co-operation between the two countries.

Major Agreements between Latin American and Caribbean Countries and Countries outside Latin America

Argentina and United Kingdom. A treaty of amity, commerce and navigation came into force on May 12, 1825.

Brazil and Federal Republic of Germany. (1) A framework agreement on technical co-operation concluded on Feb. 4, 1964, came into force on May 25, 1965. Another framework agreement on co-operation in scientific research and technological development of June 9, 1969, came into force on Aug. 12, 1969.

(2) An agreement approved by the German Federal Cabinet on April 30, 1975, and signed in Bonn on June 27, 1975, provided for the supply to Brazil, over a 15-year period, of eight West German nuclear reactors and for the erection in Brazil of a plant for the retreatment of irradiated fuels and a uranium enrichment plant at a total cost

said to be equivalent to about $5,000 million. The agreement came into force on Nov. 18, 1975.

According to US officials quoted on June 3 of that year, the US Government had persuaded the two sides to sign a special-safeguards treaty with the International Atomic Energy Agency (IAEA), while the Brazilian Foreign Minister pointed out on June 27 that his country had not signed the Treaty of Tlatelolco (on a nuclear-weapon-free zone in Latin America—see page 57) but also explained that Brazil refused to sign the Nuclear Non-Proliferation Treaty because this treaty legalized the possession of atomic weapons by specified countries.

Under an agreement signed by Brazil with the IAEA on Jan. 16, 1976 (to take effect from March 2 of that year), Brazil accepted international inspection and supervision of the reactors and all other installations in the same way as signatories of the NPT were bound to accept.

Notwithstanding attempts by the US Government to force the German Federal Government to abrogate or alter its nuclear agreement with Brazil, the German Federal Chancellor stated on Jan. 25, 1977, that his Government intended to fulfil all its existing treaty obligations, including those with Brazil.

(3) On March 8, 1978, Brazil and the Federal Republic of Germany signed new agreements on co-operation in nuclear research, covering safety precautions for nuclear reactors, protection against radiation, disposal of nuclear waste, research on the vaporization of coal, and studies in metallurgy and welding technology. In a joint declaration signed by the President of Brazil and the German Federal Chancellor on March 10, 1978, the two sides affirmed that they were pursuing "exclusively peaceful" ends in implementing their nuclear agreement, which was based on a policy of "non-proliferation of nuclear weapons", and they agreed to intensify their contacts at all levels, to work towards a just and balanced world economic system, and to expand mutual exchanges in the fields of the economy and industry, science and technology.

(4) On the supply to Brazil of enriched uranium (under a system of strict safeguards) an agreement was formalized by an exchange of notes in Brasília on Sept. 1, 1978, by Brazil, the Federal Republic of Germany, the Netherlands and the United Kingdom (the three latter states being involved as a result of the enriched uranium being supplied by Urenco, a consortium of Dutch, West German and UK interests).

Brazil and Portugal. In a joint communiqué issued at the end of a visit to Brazil by the Portuguese Prime Minister on Dec. 15-18, 1977, the two sides undertook to reactivate trade between them (with the help of a Brazilian credit equivalent to $50,000,000 to finance Portuguese purchases in Brazil), to establish co-operation and friendship with the new Portuguese-speaking states in Africa, and to form joint commissions on economic, scientific and technical co-operation.

Brazil and United Kingdom. A state visit to Britain by the President of Brazil on May 4-6, 1976, ended with the conclusion of economic co-operation agreements covering the supply and financing of about £300,000,000 worth of British capital goods for Brazil.

Colombia and Federal Republic of Germany. (1) A treaty of amity, commerce and navigation, signed with the German Reich on July 23, 1892, and in force from July 12, 1894, was on Dec. 18, 1978, extended until Dec. 31, 1980.

(2) An agreement on technical co-operation, signed on March 2, 1965, came into force on April 26, 1965, and was amended with effect from Aug. 10, 1973.

Colombia and Switzerland. (1) A treaty of friendship, establishment and commerce was signed on March 14, 1908.

(2) A technical and scientific co-operation agreement was signed on Feb. 1, 1967.

Colombia and United Kingdom. A treaty of friendship, commerce and navigation, signed on Feb. 16, 1866, came into force on Oct. 17, 1966, and was prolonged on Dec. 30, 1938.

Costa Rica and United Kingdom. A treaty of friendship, commerce and navigation was signed on Nov. 27, 1849, and came into force on Feb. 20, 1850.

Dominican Republic and Federal Republic of Germany. A treaty of amity, commerce and navigation was signed on Dec. 23, 1957, and came into force on June 3, 1960.

Ecuador and France. Under a contract to purchase 18 French Mirage F-1 aircraft, concluded in November 1977, Ecuador became the first Latin American country to obtain this type of aircraft (although Mirage III or V aircraft were then already in the possession of Peru, Brazil, Argentina, Colombia and Venezuela).

Ecuador and Switzerland. (1) A treaty of friendship, establishment and commerce was signed on June 22, 1888.

(2) A technical and scientific co-operation agreement was signed on July 4, 1969.

Jamaica and Mozambique. It was agreed on Oct. 11, 1977, that the two countries would strengthen their bilateral relations through trade, economic and cultural co-operation.

Mexico and Canada. An agreement on Canadian purchases of Mexican oil to the value of $500,000,000 per annum as from 1980 was concluded on Jan. 12, 1979.

Mexico and France. An industrial and technical co-operation agreement signed on Dec. 11, 1978, and ratified early in February 1979, provided for French purchases of 5,000,000 tonnes of Mexican crude oil per annum for 10 years from Jan. 1, 1980. Economic, scientific and cultural co-operation agreements signed at the same time included one on "scientific and industrial development in the utilization of nuclear energy for exclusively peaceful ends". France also agreed to grant Mexico credits amounting to F1,000 million (or $230,000,000).

Mexico and Japan. Agreements concluded during a visit to Japan by the President of Mexico on Oct. 30-Nov. 4, 1978, included one on Japanese aid for economic and petroleum projects in Mexico.

Mexico and Spain. (1) Agreements on close economic, technical and cultural co-operation between the two countries was reached during a visit to Spain by the President of Mexico on Oct. 8-16, 1977.

(2) Agreements on extradition, air transport and co-operation in industry, energy and minerals were signed on Nov. 21, 1978 (during a visit to Mexico by the Spanish King and Queen).

(3) An agreement in principle was reached on Jan. 11, 1979, on Spanish purchases of 5,000,000 tonnes of Mexican oil per annum for five years from the end of 1979.

Mexico and United States. (1) A border agreement signed on Aug. 21, 1970, settled a dispute caused by repeated changes in the river bed of the Rio Grande (which forms about 1,500 miles of the border between the two countries) and also fixed maritime boundaries in the Gulf of Mexico and the Pacific Ocean up to 12 nautical miles from the coast.

(2) An agreement signed in Washington on Aug. 30, 1973, provided for the construction of a desalination plant for the water entering Mexico in the Colorado River (which flows into the Gulf of California).

(3) A trade agreement (the first since an earlier one of 1942) was signed between the two countries on Dec. 2, 1977.

Paraguay and South Africa. Economic co-operation agreements were signed during a visit to South Africa by the President of Paraguay on April 1-6, 1974, when South Africa agreed to provide technical assistance in oil, gas, bauxite and iron-ore prospecting in Paraguay.

Venezuela and Portugal. (1) During a visit to Portugal by the President of Venezuela on Nov. 29-30, 1976, a credit agreement was signed to assist Portuguese payment for shipments of Venezuelan oil, and Venezuela also agreed in principle to receive refugees from Portugal's former territories in Africa.

(2) During a visit to Venezuela by the President of Portugal in May 1978, agreements were signed on emigration and on economic and industrial co-operation between the two countries.

Venezuela and United Kingdom. (1) A treaty of friendship, commerce and navigation, originally signed on April 18, 1825, with Colombia (of which Venezuela was then an integral part), was applied to Venezuela under a convention of Oct. 29, 1934.

(2) An agreement on economic and industrial co-operation between the two countries was initialled in London on Nov. 23, 1976, and signed in Caracas on Aug. 12, 1977.

Canadian Agreements with European Countries

France. (1) Exchange of notes on exchange of defence science information (May 25, 1962).

(2) Agreement on a wide-ranging programme of industrial and technological co-operation (Oct. 22, 1974).

(Agreements on co-operation between France and the Province of Quebec were signed on Dec. 5, 1974.)

Federal Republic of Germany. (1) Agreement on co-operation in the peaceful uses of atomic energy (Dec. 11, 1957; entry into force Dec. 18, 1957).

(2) Exchange of notes on exchange of defence science information (Aug. 28, 1964).

(3) Agreement on scientific and technological co-operation (April 16, 1971).

Norway. Exchange of notes concerning the organization of a "Canada-Norway defence science information exchange project" (May 24, 1960).

Sweden. Agreement concerning defence research, development and production (Feb. 3, 1975).

Switzerland. Co-operation agreement on the use of atomic energy for peaceful purposes (March 6, 1958; renewed on Dec. 1, 1971).

Dependent Territories in the Americas

United Kingdom

(1) Associated States with full internal autonomy, Britain retaining responsibility for Defence and External Affairs:

Antigua   (since Feb. 27, 1967)

St Kitts-Nevis   (since Feb. 27, 1967)

(2) Colonies with internal self-government, Britain retaining responsibility for Defence, External Affairs and Internal Security:

Belize   (since Jan. 1, 1964)

(3) Colonies with Executive Councils and Legislatures:

Bermuda

British Virgin Islands

Cayman Islands

Falkland Islands (Malvinas)

Montserrat

Turks and Caicos Islands

(4) Colony under direct British rule:

Anguilla   (since July 28, 1971)

France

French Overseas Departments and members of French Community:

French Guiana

Guadeloupe

Martinique

St Pierre and Miquelon

Denmark

Greenland, with a Legislative Council in West Greenland and two members in the Danish Parliament.

Netherlands

Integral parts of the Kingdom of the Netherlands with internal autonomy since Dec. 29, 1954:

Netherlands Antilles (Aruba, Bonaire, Curaçao, Saba, St Eustatius, St Maarten)

United States

Puerto Rico, an autonomous Commonwealth (since 1952), associated with the USA, which retains responsibility for Defence and External Affairs.

Virgin Islands of the USA, governed under the Revised Organic Act of the Virgin Islands of July 22, 1954, with a US-appointed Governor and an elected Legislature.

The 32 Independent States in the Americas

Countries	OAS	Commonwealth	Aladi	SELA	OCAS	Central American Common Market	Andean Group	NATO	Defence Treaty or Military Assistance Agreement with USA
Argentina	☆		☆	☆					☆
Bahamas		☆							
Barbados	☆	☆		☆					
Bolivia	☆		☆	☆			☆		☆
Brazil	☆		☆	☆					☆
Canada		☆						☆	☆
Chile	☆		☆	☆					☆
Colombia	☆		☆	☆			☆		☆
Costa Rica	☆			☆	☆	☆			
Cuba				☆					
Dominica	☆	☆							
Dominican Republic	☆			☆					☆
Ecuador	☆		☆	☆			☆		
El Salvador	☆			☆	☆	☆			
Grenada	☆			☆					
Guatemala	☆			☆	☆	☆			☆
Guyana		☆		☆					
Haiti	☆			☆					☆
Honduras	☆			☆	☆	☆			☆
Jamaica	☆	☆		☆					
Mexico	☆		☆	☆					
Nicaragua	☆			☆	☆	☆			☆
Panama	☆			☆					
Paraguay	☆		☆	☆					☆
Peru	☆		☆	☆			☆		☆
St Lucia	☆	☆							
St Vincent and the Grenadines		☆							
Suriname	☆			☆					
Trinidad and Tobago	☆	☆		☆					
United States	☆							☆	
Uruguay	☆		☆	☆					☆
Venezuela	☆		☆	☆			☆		

16. The Middle East and Islamic States

This section covers the main multilateral and bilateral agreements concluded by Middle East and Islamic states and deals in particular with (i) the Arab League and its related organizations, (ii) co-operation between Islamic states and (iii) other treaties and agreements concluded by Middle East states, notably the 1979 Egyptian-Israeli peace treaty.

The Arab League and its Related Organizations

Seat: Tunis.

Members: Algeria, Bahrain, Djibouti, Iraq, Jordan, Kuwait, Lebanon, Libya, Mauritania, Morocco, Oman, Palestine Liberation Organization, Qatar, Saudi Arabia, Somalia, Sudan, Syria, Tunisia, United Arab Emirates, Yemen (Arab Republic), Yemen (People's Democratic Republic). (The membership of Egypt was suspended in March 1979.)

History

A union of the Arab peoples was envisaged during World War I, when the Arabs rose in revolt against their Turkish rulers. Under the Peace Treaty of 1919, however, the Arab-populated former Turkish territories were split into separate states and, with the exception of the Hedjaz and Yemen, placed under British or French mandate. The Hedjaz was subsequently conquered in 1925 by King Ibn Saud, ruler of Nejd, and his enlarged realm renamed Saudi Arabia in 1932.

Between 1932 and 1946 the British and French mandated territories (Iraq, Lebanon, Syria and Transjordan) succeeded in gaining de facto independence. In 1943 and 1944 a series of bilateral meetings on the formation of an Arab union took place between the various Arab states. This revival of Pan-Arabism differed in its aims from the movement against the Turks during World War I in that it envisaged the mutual co-operation of individual Arab states rather then the formation of a single Arab realm.

A sufficient measure of agreement was reached in these bilateral talks to make possible the convening of a conference of Arab nations. The conference was held at Alexandria from Sept. 25 to Oct. 7, 1944, and was attended initially by delegates from Egypt, Iraq, Lebanon, Syria and Transjordan, and later also by delegates from Saudi Arabia and Yemen and a representative of the Palestinian Arabs. On Oct. 7, 1944, a protocol providing for the establishment of a League of Arab States was signed by the Egyptian, Iraqi, Lebanese, Syrian and Transjordanian delegates.

A Pan-Arab Union Preparatory Committee, formed at the Alexandria conference and consisting of the Foreign Ministers of Egypt, Iraq, Lebanon, Saudi Arabia, Syria and Transjordan, and a Palestinian representative, met on Feb. 14, 1945, to approve and sign a constitution for the proposed Arab League.

The Pact

The *Pact of the Union of Arab States* was finally signed on March 22, 1945, by representatives of Egypt, Iraq, Lebanon, Saudi Arabia, Syria, Transjordan and Yemen. Later adherents to the pact were Libya (March 28, 1953); the Sudan (Jan. 9, 1956); Tunisia and Morocco (Oct. 1, 1958); Kuwait (July 20, 1961); Algeria (Aug. 16, 1962); People's Democratic Republic of Yemen (i.e. South Yemen) (December 1967); Bahrain and Qatar (Sept. 11, 1971); Oman (Sept. 29, 1971); the United Arab Emirates (Dec. 6, 1971); Mauritania (Oct. 13, 1973); Somalia (Feb. 14, 1974); Palestine (represented by the Palestine Liberation Organization, Sept. 9, 1976); and Djibouti (Sept. 3, 1977).

The main provisions of the pact are summarized below:

The League of Arab States. It was laid down that "a

League of Arab States will be formed by those independent Arab countries who wish to join it"; that it would possess a Council on which all member states would be on an equal footing; that the Council would organize periodical meetings to improve and strengthen mutual relations, co-ordinate their political programmes with a view to mutual co-operation, and "safeguard by every possible means their independence and sovereign rights against all aggression"; that decisions of the Council would be binding on all member states (disputes between member states being referred to it for arbitration); that resort to force between member states in settling disputes was forbidden; and that no state would be permitted to follow a policy prejudicial to the League of Arab States as a whole.

Co-operation. The Arab states would co-operate closely on questions of economics and finance (commercial exchanges, customs duties, currency, agriculture and industry), communications (by land, sea and air), cultural matters, social and hygiene questions, and matters relating to nationality, passports and visas, extradition of criminals, etc. For these questions, commissions of exports would be formed, with a co-ordinating committee to direct their work.

Lebanon. The Arab states unanimously affirmed their respect for the independence and sovereignty of Lebanon within its existing frontiers.

Palestine. The declaration on Palestine stated: "The Committee considers that Palestine forms an important integral part of the Arab countries and the rights of the Arabs there cannot be infringed without danger to the peace and security of the Arab world. At the same time it considers that the engagements entered into by Great Britain, which include the cessation of Jewish immigration, the safeguarding of land belonging to the Arabs and the guiding of Palestine along the road to independence, constitute a portion of the rights acquired by the Arabs and that their execution will be a step towards the goal to which they aspire, towards the establishment of peace and security. It proclaims its support of the Palestine cause for the realization of legitimate aspirations and the safeguarding of lawful rights. It sympathizes as deeply as anyone with the Jews for the horrors and sufferings they have endured in Europe through the actions of certain dictatorial

states. But it is careful not to confuse the case of these Jews with Zionism, for nothing would be more arbitrary or unjust than to wish to resolve the question of the Jews of Europe by another injustice of which the Arabs of Palestine, no matter to what religion or confession they belong, would be the victims."

It was also laid down that the Arab League would study means of collaboration with international organizations; that its permanent headquarters would be in Cairo (though the Council could meet in other cities); that the Council would hold biennial meetings (in March and October); that member states could withdraw from the League on one year's notice, or be expelled by unanimous vote for not fulfilling their obligations; and that the Pact could be modified by a two-thirds majority vote.

Organization

The Council is the supreme organ of the Arab League. It is composed of representatives of all the member states, each of which has one vote, and a representative of the Palestinian Arabs. The Council is responsible for the functioning of the League and the realization of its objectives. It meets twice a year; its unanimous decisions are binding on all member states; but majority decisions are binding only on those member states which have accepted them.

The Council is assisted by 14 committees dealing respectively with political, cultural, economic, social, legal and women's affairs, and with communications, information, health and human rights; grouping Arab oil experts and experts on co-operation; and including also two permanent committees (i) for administrative and financial affairs and (ii) for meteorology. There are also an organization for youth welfare and a conference of liaison officers (to co-ordinate activities among commercial attachés at Arab embassies).

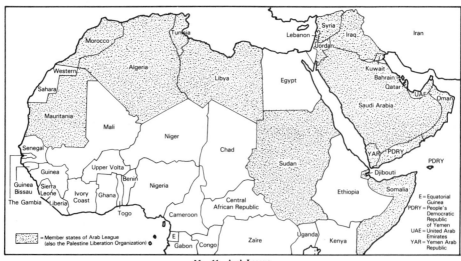

Map 11 Arab League

The other organ of the Arab League is the Secretariat, whose main officers are the Secretary-General, three Assistant Secretaries-General, and an Economic Assistant Secretary. Among the functions of the Secretary-General are the preparation of a draft budget, which he submits to the Council, and the convening of the Council sessions.

Collective Security Pact

On June 17, 1950, a *Collective Security Pact* was signed by Egypt, Syria, Lebanon, Saudi Arabia and Yemen (i.e. the present Yemen Arab Republic). The draft of the pact had been unanimously approved by the Arab League Council on April 13, 1950.

The main provisions of the pact were as follows: (1) An armed attack on one of the signatories would be regarded as aggression against all. In the event of such an aggression, the other signatories would provide, individually or collectively, all military and other aid consistent with existing obligations under the League Charter and Art. 51 of the UN Charter. (2) A permanent Joint Defence Council, consisting of the Foreign Ministers and Defence Ministers of the signatories, would be set up to co-ordinate defensive measures. Its decisions, reached by majority vote, would be binding on all members. (3) A permanent committee composed of the signatories' Chiefs of Staff would draft joint defence plans and give technical advice on measures of collective defence. (4) An economic committee composed of the Ministers of National Economy would carry out economic measures complementary to the military decisions reached. (5) The signatories would give one another priority in the exchange of goods and services, and would co-operate in raising the economic level of the Arab world as a whole, measures envisaged for this purpose including the establishment of an Arab Central Bank and a Bureau of Statistics, the improvement of communications, the joint exploitation of the mineral wealth of the Arab countries, and the modernization of agricultural equipment.

Subsequent signatories to the Collective Security Pact were Iraq on Feb. 2, 1951, Jordan on Feb. 16, 1952, Morocco on June 13, 1961 and Libya, the Sudan, Algeria, Tunisia and Kuwait on Sept. 10, 1964. The pact came into force on Aug. 24, 1952.

Arab League Subsidiary Bodies

In addition to the bodies established under the above Collective Security Pact numerous subsidiary institutions and agencies have been set up by the Arab League, including the following:

(1) The **Council of Arab Economic Unity** (CAEU), with headquarters in Cairo, was set up on June 3, 1957, by a resolution of the Arab Economic Council of the Arab League and became operative on May 30, 1964. Following the suspension of Egypt's membership in 1979 [see page 341], its remaining members were Iraq, Jordan,

Kuwait, Libya, Mauritania, the Palestine Liberation Organization, Somalia, the Sudan, Syria, the United Arab Emirates, the Yemen Arab Republic, and the People's Democratic Republic of Yemen. Its headquarters were moved to Amman (Jordan) in 1979.

(2) Under a resolution adopted by the Council in August 1964, an **Arab Common Market** was to be established in stages between Egypt, Iraq, Jordan and Syria, with customs duties and other taxes on trade between the four countries to be abolished by 1971 and with a full customs union and free movement of capital goods and people to follow later. Libya and the Sudan joined the project in June 1977.

(3) The **Arab League Educational, Cultural and Scientific Organization**, with headquarters in Tunis, was founded in 1964 to promote intellectual unity of the Arab countries through education. Within the organization's framework there are several institutions, among them an Institute for Arab Studies and Research Work, an Arab Literacy and Adult Education Organization, an Institute of Arab Manuscripts and a Permanent Bureau of Arabization (in Rabat, Morocco).

(4) The **Arab Labour Organization**, with headquarters in Baghdad, was established in 1965 to co-ordinate labour conditions throughout the Arab world.

(5) The **Arab Fund for Economic and Social Development**, established in Kuwait in 1968, began its operations in 1972. Its capital is subscribed by the member states of the Arab League, and its object is to participate in the financing of economic and social development projects in the Arab states.

(6) An **Industrial Development Centre for Arab States** (IDCAS), with headquarters in Cairo and later in Tunis, was founded in May 1968 under the auspices of the Arab League. It has 18 member countries —Algeria, Bahrain, Egypt, Iraq, Jordan, Kuwait, Lebanon, Libya, Morocco, Oman, Qatar, Saudi Arabia, the Sudan, Syria, Tunisia, the United Arab Emirates and both Yemen Republics (as well as four associate members—Abu Dhabi, Sharjah, Dubai and Ras Al Khaimah).

(7) The **Arab Bank for Economic Development in Africa**, with headquarters in Khartoum, has as its subscribing countries the members of the Arab League except Djibouti, Somalia and the two Yemen Republics. It was set up under a decision taken at the sixth summit conference of the Arab League in Algiers in November 1973 [see below] to assist in the financing of development projects in African countries and to supply them with technical aid; it began its operations in 1975.

(8) Integrated with the bank is the **Special Arab Assistance Fund for Africa** (originally the Arab Loan Fund for Africa), set up under a resolution adopted in January 1974 by a meeting of Arab Oil Ministers and the Oil Committee of the Organization of African Unity. The fund's object is to provide aid to African countries in serious balance-of-payments difficulties (including those caused by natural disasters and by the rise in oil prices since 1973).

(9) The **Arab Monetary Fund**, with headquarters in Abu Dhabi, was set up under an agreement approved by the Arab Economic Unity Council in Rabat in April 1976, and commenced operations on Feb. 2, 1977. Under its Articles of Agreement the fund was to function both as a fund and as a bank, and it was inter alia to correct balance-of-payments disequilibria among member states; to promote stability of exchange rates and also Arab economic integration; to pave the way for the creation of a unified Arab currency; and to coordinate the monetary policies of member states. In April 1980 the fund's authorized capital was increased to $1,100 million.

(10) There are also an **Arab Postal Union** and an **Arab States Broadcasting Union** (both based in Tunis), an **Arab Telecommunications Union** (based in Baghdad) and a **Civil Aviation Council of Arab States** (based in Rabat).

Arab Summit Conferences

Since 1964 the heads of Arab states have repeatedly met in conference to discuss questions of common political interest.

(1) The first such conference, which took place in Cairo on Jan. 13-16, 1964, styled itself the "Council of the Kings and Heads of State of the Arab League". All 13 Arab League members were represented. A communiqué issued at the end of the conference stated, inter alia, that the meetings had resulted in "unanimous agreement . . . to stop all campaigns by information media, to consolidate relations among the sister Arab states in order to ensure constructive joint co-operation, and to ward off expansionist aggressive ambitions threatening all Arabs alike". It was decided that a meeting of kings and heads of state should be held at least once a year.

(2) At the second Arab summit conference, held at Alexandria on Sept. 5-11, 1964, the organization of the meetings of heads of state was worked out in some detail. It was agreed that a conference of Arab heads of state should be held each year in September. A control commission, meeting monthly, would supervise the implementation of conference decisions.

Every third meeting of this commission would be attended by the Prime Ministers of the Arab countries or their representatives.

Other decisions of the Alexandria conference included the setting up of a unified Arab military command, an Arab Court of Justice, and an Arab council for research into the use of atomic energy for peaceful purposes.

(3) In the course of their third conference, held in Casablanca on Sept. 13-17, 1965, the Arab heads of state signed a "solidarity pact", which was intended to put an end to propaganda attacks by one Arab state against another, and to bind the signatories not to support "subversive movements of any kind" against one another.

(4) The fourth summit conference, scheduled to open in Algiers on Sept. 5, 1966, was indefinitely postponed, after it had been announced that the United Arab Republic (i.e. Egypt) would not take part in a conference with "the reactionary Arab forces". However, it was eventually held in Khartoum from Aug. 28 to Sept. 3, 1967 but was boycotted by the Government of Syria. The conference dealt mainly with the aftermath of the Arab-Israeli war of June 1967. It reached agreement inter alia on the consolidation of Arab military strength, the need to eliminate "all foreign military bases from Arab territory" and "the principles of non-recognition and non-negotiation" in relations with Israel.

(5) The fifth summit conference, held in Rabat (Morocco) on Dec. 21-23, 1969, ended without agreement after President Nasser of the United Arab Republic had failed to obtain general Arab support for his proposal of a mobilization of all Arab resources against Israel.

(6) The sixth summit conference, held in Algiers on Nov. 26-28, 1973, without participation by Iraq and Libya, issued several declarations, including a political declaration in which it was stated that peace in the Middle East could be achieved only after fulfilment of two "paramount and unchangeable" conditions—(i) the evacuation by Israel of all occupied Arab territories and (ii) the re-establishment of the full national rights of the Palestinian people.

In a declaration on Africa it was stated that several decisions taken included (i) the severance by all African countries which had not already done so of diplomatic and other relations with South Africa, Portugal and Rhodesia; (ii) a strict embargo on deliveries of Arab oil to these countries; (iii) intensification of relations with "fraternal" African countries and the creation of an Arab fund for economic, social and technical assistance to these countries; and

(iv) diplomatic and material support for African national liberation movements.

A resolution on Arab oil policy contained the decision "to continue the use of oil as a weapon . . . until the withdrawal from occupied Arab lands is realized and the rights of the Palestinian people are assured", in particular by maintaining an oil embargo against all states supporting Israel.

(7) At the seventh summit conference, held in Rabat on Oct. 26-29, 1974, it was unanimously decided to support the Palestine Liberation Organization (PLO) as "the sole legitimate representative of the Palestinian people" in "carrying out its national and international responsibility within the framework of Arab obligations".

(8) The eighth summit conference was held in Cairo on Oct. 25-26, 1976, when all member countries except Iraq and Libya endorsed an agreement reached in Riyadh (Saudi Arabia) on Oct. 18 of that year by the heads of state of Lebanon, Syria, Egypt, Kuwait and Saudi Arabia and PLO leader on a ceasefire in the civil war in Lebanon. The agreement provided inter alia for the establishment of an Arab security force of 30,000 men to secure observance of the ceasefire.

(9) The ninth summit conference, which took place in Baghdad on Nov. 2-5, 1978, and was attended by all Arab League member states except Egypt, agreed that all Arab countries would give "all forms of support, aid and facilities" to the PLO and that it was "not permitted for any side to act unilaterally in solving the Palestinian question in particular and the Arab-Zionist conflict in general". The conference accordingly rejected the agreements reached between Egypt and Israel at Camp David (USA) and all effects of these agreements [see page 349]. Moreover, it agreed (with only Morocco, Oman and the Sudan dissenting) that, if Egypt proceeded to the signature of a peace treaty with Israel, steps should be taken to remove the headquarters of the Arab League from Cairo and to impose economic sanctions on Egypt. It was also decided to establish a 10-year fund with annual resources of $3,500 million to finance Jordan and Syria as well as the PLO in opposing the Camp David agreements.

Following the signing of the peace treaty between Egypt and Israel on March 26, 1979 [ibid.], Egypt announced on March 27 the "freezing" of its membership of the Arab League, Mahmoud Riad, the League's (Egyptian) Secretary-General, had already announced his resignation from this post on March 22.

A conference of Foreign and Economy Ministers of all Arab League member states except Egypt, Oman and the Sudan, held in Baghdad on March 27-31, 1979, imposed a wide-ranging political and economic boycott (including an oil embargo) by Arab states on Egypt. The measures agreed to by the conference included the withdrawal of Arab ambassadors from Egypt; the suspension of Egypt from the Arab League and all its specialized bodies as well as from a large number of joint Arab projects and undertakings, with effect from the date of Egypt's signing of the peace treaty; the temporary transfer of the Arab League's headquarters from Cairo to Tunis; and the eventual suspension of Egypt's membership of the non-aligned movement, of the Islamic Conference Organization and of the Organization of African Unity. The economic boycott was, however, not to apply to "those private national Egyptian institutions which are confirmed as not to be dealing with the Zionist enemy".

Following this conference, diplomatic relations were broken off by Egypt with all other Arab countries with which it still had such relations, except with Somalia. Organizations which suspended Egypt's membership included the Organization of Arab Petroleum Exporting Countries (OAPEC) and its subsidiary organizations, the Arab Monetary Fund and the Islamic Conference Organization. Saudi Arabia announced on May 14, 1979, that the Arab Military Industries Organization (AMIO), which it had set up in May 1975 with Egypt, the United Arab Emirates and Qatar, would cease to exist as from July 1, 1979.

(10) At the tenth summit conference, held in Tunis on Nov. 19-21, 1979, the measures taken against Egypt were confirmed but no agreement was reached on a framework for a peace initiative which would constitute an alternative to the Egyptian-Israeli peace treaty.

(11) The eleventh summit conference, held in Amman on Nov. 25-27, 1980, showed the Arab League to be in disarray, as the conference was boycotted by six of its members (Syria, Algeria, Lebanon, Libya, the PLO and the People's Democratic Republic of Yemen) and no effective decision was taken on the question of Palestine.

The 15 member countries attending the conference agreed unanimously on the establishment of a long-term economic development fund aimed at reducing the unevenness of wealth among the Arab countries by making available $500,000,000 a year over the next decade from Iraq, Kuwait, Saudi Arabia, the United Arab Emirates and Qatar for financing social and economic projects, improving economic relations between Arab states and raising the standard of living of the less developed Arab countries.

In its final communiqué the conference inter alia called for an end to the war which had broken out in September 1980 between Iraq and Iran and also for recognition of Iraq's right to sovereignty over its territories and waters.

Arab League Measures against People's Democratic Republic of Yemen

A meeting held in Cairo on July 1-2, 1978, by Foreign Ministers and other representatives of 15 of the then 22 member states of the Arab League had decided to declare the Government of the People's Democratic Republic of Yemen (PDRY) guilty of the assassination of the President of the Yemen Arab Republic (on June 24, 1978), to "freeze" political and diplomatic relations with the Government of the PDRY, to suspend economic and cultural relations and to cancel technical aid to the PDRY. (The meeting was unable to expel the PDRY from the Arab League, as had been requested by the Yemen Arab Republic, because this would require unanimous approval by all Arab League member states.)

Multilateral Co-operation between Islamic Countries

Organization of the Islamic Conference

Headquarters: Jeddah (Saudi Arabia).

Members: Afghanistan, Algeria, Bahrain, Bangladesh, Cameroon, Chad, the Comoros, Djibouti, Gabon, The Gambia, Guinea, Guinea-Bissau, Indonesia, Iran, Iraq, Jordan, Kuwait, Lebanon, Libya, Malaysia, Maldives, Mali, Mauritania, Morocco, Niger, Oman, Pakistan, the Palestine Liberation Organization, Qatar, Saudi Arabia, Senegal, Sierra Leone, Somalia, the Sudan, Syria, Tunisia, Turkey, the Turkish Federated State of Cyprus, Uganda, the United Arab Emirates, Upper Volta, the Yemen Arab Republic and the People's Democratic Republic of Yemen. (Egypt's membership was suspended by the 10th conference of the organization's Foreign Ministers held in Fez, Morocco, on May 8-12, 1979.)

The aims of the organization include the promotion of Islamic solidarity among its member states and the consolidation of co-operation among them; the elimination of racial segregation and discrimination and of colonialism in all its forms; and support for the people of Palestine in their struggle to regain their rights and to liberate their land.

The organization has set up the following subsidiary bodies:

(1) The **International Islamic News Agency**, founded in December 1972.

(2) The **Islamic Development Bank**, which was set up in Jeddah in 1974 and began operations in 1975. Its capital is contributed by oil-producing member countries; adhering to Islamic principles, the bank does not grant loans and credits for interest (except at a nominal commission) but takes up equity participation in development projects, while it also finances foreign trade.

(3) Islamic cultural centres in non-Moslem countries.

(4) The **Islamic States Broadcasting Organization**, established in 1975.

(5) The **Islamic Solidarity Fund**, set up in 1977. Contributions to this fund, announced in May 1977, included $15,000,000 from Saudi Arabia, $6,000,000 from Libya and $3,000,000 from the United Arab Emirates.

History of Islamic Co-operation

The Organization of the Islamic Conference was formally established in May 1971, and conferences of the Foreign Ministers of its member countries were held annually thereafter. The formal creation of the Organization marked the culmination of increasing contacts between Islamic countries dating from the mid-1960s.

Early Contacts. A non-governmental Afro-Asian Islamic Organization had been established in Jakarta (Indonesia) in 1965, with delegates from the Soviet Union and China participating; the Chinese Moslems, however, had left this organization in 1966. The first congress of the organization was held by delegates from 25 countries meeting in Bandung (Indonesia) on Oct. 6-10, 1970, when it was decided to change the organization's name to International Islamic Organization, as it included Moslems from outside Africa and Asia. Soviet Moslems were not invited to this congress, which adopted resolutions condemning communism in Moslem countries as "unjust and unlawful" and demanding religious freedom for the Moslem minorities in the Soviet Union and China.

An Islamic summit conference held in Rabat on Sept. 22-25, 1969, was attended by representatives of 25 countries out of 36 invited. Those present included Iran and Turkey but not Iraq and Syria; India was, upon a decision by the conference, admitted as a full member but was subsequently asked to withdraw because the President of Pakistan had refused to attend a conference at which India would be represented.

A first conference of Islamic Foreign Ministers was held in Jeddah on March 23-26, 1970, when it was decided to set up, in Jeddah, a permanent secretariat under a Secretary-General of what was to become the Organization of the Islamic Conference.

The second conference of Foreign Ministers, held in Karachi (Pakistan) on Dec. 26-28, 1970, condemned the Israeli occupation of the territory of three Arab countries as a violation of the UN Charter, and denounced Zionism as a "racial, aggressive and expansionist movement . . . constituting a permanent threat to world peace".

1973 Foreign Ministers' Conference. The fourth conference of the organization's Foreign Ministers, held in Benghazi (Libya) on March 24-27, 1973, decided inter alia to send a mission to the Philippines and to the Vatican with a view to ending the Philippine Government's alleged persecution of Philippine Moslems; however, this and later efforts made in this respect by the organization failed to end the armed confrontation between the (Moslem) Moro National Liberation Front and the Philippine armed forces.

1974 Lahore Summit. An Islamic summit meeting, held in Lahore (Pakistan) on Feb. 22-24, 1974, affirmed the solidarity of the Islamic peoples and issued a *Declaration of Lahore* expressing full support for all Arab countries "to recover, by all means available, all their occupied land" and calling for "the complete Israeli withdrawal from occupied Arab territories and the full restitution of the national rights of the Palestinian people". The meeting also called for the extension of support and solidarity by Moslem countries to each other in their national development efforts and appointed a committee to devise ways and means of inter alia ending the exploitation of developing countries by developed ones and achieving mutual economic co-operation.

1975 Foreign Ministers' Conference. The sixth conference of Foreign Ministers, held in Jeddah on July 12-16, 1975, unanimously decided to seek Israel's expulsion from the United Nations; called on all Moslem states to break off political, economic and cultural relations with Israel and for the recovery of the Arab sector of Jerusalem from Israel; and decided to form a permanent committee to pursue the question of the future of Jerusalem.

1976 Foreign Ministers' Conference. The seventh conference of Foreign Ministers, held in Istanbul on May 12-15, 1976, reaffirmed earlier resolutions on the Middle East and also adopted a resolution on Cyprus, stating that the two communities in that island were "equal partners in an independent and non-aligned Republic of Cyprus" and that the Islamic Turkish community in Cyprus, which would seek a political and peaceful solution on the basis of a federal Constitution, had the right to participate in and address every international meeting at which the Cyprus question was discussed.

1977 Foreign Ministers' Conference. Resolutions adopted at the eighth conference of Foreign Ministers in Tripoli (Libya) on May 16-21, 1977, included (i) a condemnation of France for holding "sham referendums" in Mayotte (in the Comoros) which had resulted in a majority favouring Mayotte's continued status as part of France (and rejecting its adherence to the—Islamic—Republic of the Comoros); and (ii) a call for the establishment of nuclear-free zones in Africa, the Middle East and South-East Asia, and the Indian Ocean.

1978 Foreign Ministers' Conference. At the ninth conference of Foreign Ministers, which ended in Dakar (Senegal) on April 28, 1978, the organization's support for the Palestinian cause was reaffirmed and the United States was condemned for its military and financial aid to Israel and was asked to grant recognition to the Palestine Liberation Organization. The conference also decided to open a permanent bureau of the organization for West Africa in Dakar.

1980 Islamabad Conferences. At an extraordinary meeting of Islamic Foreign Ministers, called on a proposal by Saudi Arabia, held in Islamabad (Pakistan) on Jan. 27-29, 1980, and attended by all member states of the organization except Afghanistan, Guinea-Bissau, Sierra Leone, Syria, the Turkish Federated State of Cyprus, Upper Volta and the People's Democratic Republic of Yemen, the 36 member states represented unanimously approved a resolution which strongly condemned the Soviet Union's intervention in Afghanistan and suspended the latter's membership of the organization.

The resolution inter alia (i) condemned the "Soviet military aggression against the Afghan people" as a flagrant violation of international laws, "an aggression against human rights and a violation of the freedoms of people which cannot be ignored"; (ii) demanded the immediate and unconditional withdrawal of all Soviet troops from Afghanistan; (iii) urged support for the Afghan people and aid for Afghan refugees; and (iv) declared complete solidarity with the Islamic countries neighbouring Afghanistan against any threat to their security and wellbeing.

The meeting also adopted various other resolutions, in particular:

(i) A resolution condemning "the efforts of certain great powers to exert various forms of pressures on the Islamic states, threatening the use of force against them to interfere in their internal affairs and to establish military bases on their territories to protect the interests of those great powers and their strategic plans in the context of the struggle raging between them"; (ii) a resolution on the "increasing tension" between the United States and Iran, affirming "the vital stake of the Islamic Conference in the sovereignty, territorial integrity and political independence" of Iran, expressing the sincere wish that the outstanding problems between the two countries should be solved by peaceful means, and declaring "solidarity with the Moslem people of Iran in choosing whatever system it prefers on the tenets of Islam as a system of social and political life"; and (iii) a resolution condemning "armed aggression" against Somalia, denouncing the presence of "the military forces of the Soviet Union and some of its allies" in the Horn of Africa, calling for the total and unconditional withdrawal of these foreign troops and for the liquidation of foreign bases in the Horn of Africa and the Red Sea, and urging the material and moral strengthening of the Islamic peoples in the Horn of Africa and provision of assistance to refugees in the area, particularly the Eritrean people.

The 11th conference of Islamic Foreign Ministers, held in Islamabad (Pakistan) on May 17-22, 1980, adopted—with objections lodged by Libya, the Palestine Liberation Organization, Syria and the People's Democratic Republic of Yemen—a resolution reaffirming the resolutions approved at the extraordinary session in January 1980 and reiterating the demand for the immediate, total and unconditional withdrawal of all Soviet forces from Afghanistan. The session also appointed a three-member committee (comprising The Gambia, Pakistan and Saudi Arabia) to administer a fund for assistance to Afghan insurgents and refugees, to which the Saudi Arabian Government had contributed $25,000,000.

The session also adopted a resolution calling upon all Moslem nations to guard against efforts to establish foreign military bases on their territories and reaffirming their determination to remain outside the influence of (both Eastern and Western) foreign powers. In another resolution the session denounced "the continued presence of Soviet, Cuban and other troops from outside the continent in the Horn of Africa" and undertook to "support and strengthen the Somali Democratic Republic morally, politically and materially to enable it to withstand foreign pressure and aggression" (with reservations being expressed by Algeria, Libya, Mali, the Palestine Liberation Organization and both Yemens).

Maghreb Permanent Consultative Committee

At a conference held in Tangiers on Nov. 26 and 27, 1964, the Economy Ministers of Algeria, Libya, Morocco and Tunisia decided to establish a permanent joint consultative committee to harmonize economic development plans. Libya withdrew from the committee in 1970, and Mauritania joined it in 1975.

The highest authority of the committee (with headquarters in Tunis) is the conference of Ministers of Economy. There is a permanent committee consisting of a President and a delegate from each of the member countries, and there is also a secretariat.

The committee has set up specialized groups, located in various cities in the member countries, for industrial studies, administrative studies and research, tourism, co-ordination of posts and telecommunications, transport and communications, co-ordination of national accounts and statistics, employment and labour, normalization, insurance and reinsurance, electric energy, and development of stockbreeding.

Maghreb Bilateral Treaties

Treaties concluded by Morocco with Algeria and with Mauritania since 1969 are no longer in force owing to the dispute over the Western Sahara. Other such bilateral treaties are as follows:

(1) A 20-year "treaty of brotherhood, good neighbourliness, and co-operation" between Algeria and Tunisia was signed in Tunis on Jan. 6, 1970. In September 1980 the two Governments agreed on the immediate reactivation of the joint commission established under the 1970 treaty with a view to promoting closer political, economic and cultural relations between the two countries.

(2) At a meeting between the Algerian and Libyan leaders in Tripoli on Dec. 28-29, 1975, it was agreed that "any attack against either of the two revolutions [of Algeria and Libya] will be considered by the other as an attack against itself" and that efforts should be intensified to establish institutional links between the two countries.

(An agreement on a merger between Libya and Tunisia, concluded on Jan. 12, 1974, was not implemented owing to subsequent disagreement by Tunisia. Nevertheless agreement was reached on Oct. 25, 1977, on the co-ordination of industrial development plans and the expansion of transport facilities between the two countries.)

Regional Co-operation for Development (RCD)

Headquarters: Tehran.

Members: Iran, Pakistan, Turkey.

The decision to form a regional co-operation group was made at a meeting of the Foreign Ministers of Iran, Pakistan and Turkey, held in Ankara on July 3-4, 1964. Details of the organization, known as Regional Co-operation for Development (RCD), were worked out at a meeting of the three heads of state on July 20-21, 1964.

Organization. The principal decision-making organ of RCD is the Ministerial Council, consisting of the three Foreign Ministers of the member countries. Meetings are held at least three times a year.

The Ministerial Council is assisted by a Regional Planning Council, consisting of the heads of the planning organizations of the member countries. It is, in turn, assisted by working committees on agriculture, cultural affairs, industry and petroleum, information and tourism, technical co-operation and public administration, trade, and transport and communications.

The Secretariat, which consists of the Secretary-General, three Deputy Secretaries-General and six Directors, was set up in September 1964.

Developments in Co-operation. A considerable number of schemes for co-operation between the three countries of RCD are in operation. They include a Regional Cultural Institute, a tripartite Shipping Conference and a joint Chamber of Commerce and Industry. A tripartite agreement on tourism and bilateral agreements on the abolition of visas for tourists were concluded at the first meeting of the Ministerial Council held in October 1964.

A joint declaration signed by the Shah of Iran, the Prime Minister of Pakistan and the President of Turkey in Izmir (Turkey) on April 22, 1976, provided for increased economic, trade, industrial and cultural co-operation between the three nations and for the establishment of (i) a free trade area through the gradual reduction of tariffs within 10 years and (ii), under a protocol on trade, an RCD investment bank promoting and financing projects of a regional character with participation by the private sector. A *Treaty of Izmir*, implementing the above declaration, was signed in Tehran on March 12, 1977.

Turkish-Pakistani Agreement on "Friendly Co-operation"

An agreement on "friendly co-operation" between Turkey and Pakistan had been signed in Karachi on April 2, 1954. The agreement, which remains valid for consecutive periods of five years if no notice of denunciation is given one year before the end of a five-year period, is open to other countries. It came into force on June 12, 1954.

The main provisions of the agreement are given below:

Art. 1. The contracting parties undertake to refrain from intervening in any way in the internal affairs of each other, and from participating in any alliance or activities directed against the other.

Art. 2. They will consult on international matters of mutual interest and, taking into account international requirements and conditions, co-operate to the maximum extent.

Art. 4. Consultation and co-operation between the contracting parties in the field of defence shall cover the following points:

(*a*) Exchange of information for the purpose of deriving joint benefit from technical experience and progress.

(*b*) Endeavours to meet, as far as possible, the requirements of the parties in the production of arms and ammunition.

(*c*) Studies and determination of the manner and extent of co-operation which might be effected between them, in accordance with Article 51 of the UN Charter, should an unprovoked attack occur against them from outside.

Art. 5. Each contracting party declares that none of the international engagements in force between it and any third state is in conflict with the provisions of this agreement, and that this agreement shall not affect, and cannot be interpreted as affecting, the aforesaid engagements. They undertake not to enter into any international engagement in conflict with this agreement.

A new economic and technical co-operation agreement between the two countries was signed on Nov. 20, 1975.

Other Treaties and Agreements concluded by Middle East States

Agreements Between Arab Countries

Egypt and Other Arab States. An agreement was signed in Cairo on July 19, 1976, by the Finance Ministers of Egypt, Kuwait, Qatar, Saudi Arabia and the United Arab Emirates on the creation of a Gulf Organization for Development in Egypt, with a capital equivalent to $2,000 million.

Egypt and Sudan. In a joint declaration issued in Cairo on Feb. 2, 1974, the Presidents of Egypt and the Sudan announced plans for the co-ordination of their countries' political and economic strategies.

A 25-year joint defence agreement was signed in Alexandria on July 15, 1976; it provided (i) for the two countries to regard an attack on either of them as aggression against both and (ii) for the setting-up of a common defence council and a joint committee of chiefs of staff. The agreement was activated on Jan. 5, 1977, by a declaration of the two countries' Ministers of War.

At a meeting of the Presidents of Egypt, the Sudan and Syria in Khartoum a joint declaration was signed on Feb. 28, 1977, whereby the Sudan joined an Egyptian-Syrian unified political command agreed upon on Dec. 21, 1976 (but since superseded by Syria's rejection of the 1979 Egyptian-Israeli peace treaty—see page 349).

A first joint congress of the Egyptian and Sudanese People's Assemblies (Parliaments) was held in Cairo on Oct. 24-31, 1977, and agreed on a political action programme and economic integration between the two countries.

Gulf States. Agreements were reached between Bahrain, Oman and the United Arab Emirates in December 1978 on the establishment of a unified economic system between the three states. As from March 1, 1979, Bahrain and Kuwait abolished all customs tariffs on goods produced in the other country, and a permanent joint organization was established for the importation of goods "covering all Gulf countries".

Iraq and Saudi Arabia. A 10-year treaty of alliance between the two countries was signed in Baghdad on April 3, 1936. (It was open to accession by other independent Arab countries and was in fact joined by Yemen on April 7 of that year—see below.)

An agreement was concluded on July 2, 1975, on the equal division between Iraq and Saudi Arabia of a neutral zone of about 2,500 square miles to the west of the western end of Kuwait's frontier with the two states. (The frontier between Iraq and Saudi Arabia had been defined by the Treaty of Mohammar in May 1922; the neutral zone had been established later, and in May 1938 Iraq and Saudi Arabia had signed an agreement on its administration.)

Iraq and Syria. A *Charter of Joint National Action* was signed by the Presidents of the two countries during a visit to Baghdad by the Syrian President on Oct. 24-26, 1978. It provided for the creation of a "joint higher political organization" comprising the two heads of state and six other representatives from each side, which was to meet at least every three months and was to form four joint committees to promote co-operation in various fields,

among them a committee for military co-operation consisting of the Foreign and Defence Ministers and the Chiefs of Staff of the two countries and charged with formulating "a joint defence pact providing the groundwork for complete military unity between the two countries". The proposed implementation of the charter was, however, abandoned in the latter part of 1979.

Jordan and Saudi Arabia. On Aug. 29, 1962, it was announced that King Hussein of Jordan and King Saud of Saudi Arabia had concluded agreements on military, political and economic co-operation. The agreements included the establishment of joint Saudi-Jordanian military command. In a communiqué the two countries pledged themselves to work for the achievement of Arab rights in Palestine.

Jordan and Syria. During a visit to Jordan by the Syrian President on June 10-12, 1975, agreement was reached on the creation of a joint high commission to co-ordinate the two countries' policies in the military, political, economic and cultural fields. In August 1975 the two countries established a Joint Supreme Command Council, which was inter alia to approve plans for the co-ordination and integration of their armed forces, and also for an economic policy which would lead to integration and unity of the two countries' economies.

On Jan. 29, 1976, it was announced that the two countries had agreed to co-ordinate their foreign diplomatic representation in countries where only one of them was then maintaining a mission.

By 1980, however, the Governments of Jordan and Syria were openly hostile to each other, partly because of differing attitudes to the Palestinian question, and took opposing sides in the conflict between Iraq and Iran.

Saudi Arabia and Kuwait. An agreement signed in 1942 with the United Kingdom, acting on behalf of Kuwait, provided for friendship and neighbourly relations as well as control of the frontier between Saudi Arabia and Kuwait.

Saudi Arabia and Sudan. An agreement "in principle" on the exploitation of the resources of the Red Sea was reached between the two countries on Jan. 14, 1975. A joint Red Sea Commission was subsequently set up to explore the possibilities of the exploitation of mineral resources.

Saudi Arabia and North Yemen. The *Treaty of Taif*, concluded in May 1934 for a 20-year period to end an armed conflict between Saudi Arabia and Yemen (later the Yemen Arab Republic) provided inter alia for a common foreign policy and mutual support in the event of foreign aggression; in March 1953 it was extended for a further 20 (lunar) years. Another agreement signed in November 1937 provided for the final settlement of the dispute and the delimitation of the two states' common border.

On April 7, 1936, Yemen joined the treaty of alliance concluded by Saudi Arabia with Iraq on April 3 [see above].

Sudan and People's Democratic Republic of Yemen. On March 22, 1977, agreements were signed in Aden on economic and technical co-operation between the two countries and on the establishment of a joint high ministerial council to co-ordinate this co-operation.

Merger of Libya and Syria. The Governments of Libya and Syria announced on Oct. 10, 1980, that their countries were to merge in a unitary state under a single (as yet undefined) leadership with the object of intensifying Arab military confrontation with Israel. The new state was to have full political, economic and military union, and other Arab states were invited to join it. At the conclusion of talks between the two leaderships in December 1980, however, it was disclosed that the countries had agreed only to form a joint "revolutionary leadership" to supervise unification efforts until "the plans for unity and its institutions" had been elaborated.

Agreements between Arab and non-Arab Countries

In addition to entering into a large number of arrangements in the broad sphere of economic co-operation, the following major agreements have been concluded between Arab and non-Arab countries:

Egypt and Switzerland. A treaty of friendship between the two countries was signed on June 3, 1934.

Egypt and United States. Under a joint declaration issued by the Presidents of the United States and Egypt in Cairo on June 14, 1974, the USA undertook to help strengthen the financial structure of Egypt; to play an active part in the restoration of the Suez Canal and the cities damaged in the 1973 Arab-Israeli war; to encourage US private investment in Egypt; to render the greatest possible economic aid to Egypt, subject to congressional approval; and to negotiate an agreement for co-operation in the field of nuclear energy under agreed safeguards, on the conclusion of which "the United States would be prepared to sell nuclear reactors and fuel to Egypt". In

September 1976 the US Congress approved the sale of two such reactors to Egypt.

Iraq and France. Under a nuclear energy co-operation agreement signed on Nov. 18, 1975, France undertook to supply to Iraq (which had in 1968 built a nuclear research centre with Soviet help) a nuclear research centre containing a 70-megawatt Osirak reactor and an 800-kW Isis reactor, which were to be operational by 1981-82. In Iraq these two reactors, both located in a complex near Baghdad, were known as Tamuz-1 and Tamuz-2. In the agreement Iraq undertook to submit the material, equipment and installations received from France to inspection by the International Atomic Energy Agency (IAEA) in accordance with the provisions of the Nuclear Non-Proliferation Treaty, of which Iraq was a signatory (whereas France was not).

In March 1980 France undertook to supply 72 kilogrammes of 93 per cent enriched nuclear fuel to Iraq.

Oman and United Kingdom. A treaty of friendship, commerce and navigation, signed between the two countries on Dec. 20, 1951, came into force provisionally on Jan. 1, 1952, and finally on May 19, 1952.

Oman and United States. An exchange of diplomatic notes on June 4, 1980, provided for co-operation between the two countries in economic development, trade and security "designed to enhance the ability of Oman to develop its economy and to safeguard its territorial integrity and to foster peace and security in the region". (The US State Department explained that under the agreement the USA would obtain land and naval facilities "similar to those enjoyed by other friendly countries" but that the USA would not "seek permission to station any military units in Oman", although it would provide Oman with certain items "appropriate to its defence".)

Saudi Arabia and Federal Republic of Germany. A treaty of friendship concluded on April 26, 1929, between Germany and Hedjaz, Nejd and Dependencies (now Saudi Arabia) and effective from Nov. 6, 1930, was renewed by Saudi Arabia and the Federal Republic of Germany on July 7, 1952, and extended on Oct. 23, 1979, until Dec. 31, 1981.

Saudi Arabia and United Kingdom. In an agreement concluded on May 20, 1927, the United Kingdom recognized the complete independence of the Kingdom of Hedjaz and Nejd and its Dependencies (which assumed the name of Saudi Arabia on Sept. 23, 1932).

Saudi Arabia and United States. A comprehensive economic and military co-operation agreement between the two states was signed in Washington on June 9, 1974, providing for the creation of joint commissions on economic co-operation and on Saudi Arabia's military needs, as well as for joint working groups on economic co-operation between the two countries.

The US Secretary of State announced on Feb. 4, 1978, that the USA would sell to Saudi Arabia (and also to Egypt and Israel) advanced jet warplanes (the total amount involved being $4,800 million, of which $2,500 million would be payable by Saudi Arabia).

Jordan and United States. In a joint statement issued by the US President and the King of Jordan in Amman on June 18, 1974, the US President promised, "in co-operation with the Congress", to play a strong role in maintaining Jordan's military strength. It was also agreed that a joint commission on co-operation in various fields was to be established. On Sept. 5, 1976, it was announced that agreement had been reached on the purchase by Jordan of 14 batteries of Hawk surface-to-air missiles (at a cost of about $540,000,000 financed largely by Saudi Arabia).

Libya, Algeria and Niger. Under an agreement reached in Tripoli on Nov. 20, 1976, by the Presidents of Algeria and Niger and the Libyan leader, a tripartite commission was to be set up to study the possibilities of increased regional co-operation between the three countries, as decided in principle on April 8, 1976.

Libya and Burundi. A 10-year treaty of friendship and co-operation, automatically renewable, was signed in Tripoli on Aug. 24, 1973.

Libya and Cameroon. A treaty of friendship and co-operation was signed in Tripoli on Oct. 29, 1975.

Libya and Chad. In a treaty of friendship signed on June 15, 1980, both parties undertook to "mutually defend each other in the event of one of the two parties being threatened by direct or indirect external aggression" and to "exchange information regarding military plans and plans for internal and external security"; Libya would contribute to the reconstruction of Chad in the sphere of its "economic and military plan"; and Chad would not permit the installation of any "foreign base" or "military, colonialist or imperialist troops on its territory".

Early in January 1981 the two Governments announced their intention to merge their two countries.

Libya and Niger. A defence and security treaty was ratified on March 9, 1974, with provisions for mutual defence against "direct or indirect aggression" and against "internal or external danger" and for "complete co-operation and co-ordination" between the two countries' armed and security forces.

Libya and Togo. A treaty of mutual defence and assistance was announced on Jan. 5, 1976. (On Dec. 24, 1973, it had been decided to set up a joint Libyan-Togolese bank with headquarters in Lomé, Togo.)

Tunisia and Italy. An agreement on the delimitation of the continental shelf on the basis of the median line (as defined in a protocol of Jan. 23, 1975) between the two countries was concluded on Aug. 20, 1971.

Treaties and Agreements concluded by Iran

Iran and Federal Republic of Germany. A treaty of friendship, concluded on Feb. 17, 1929, came into force on Dec. 11, 1930. A treaty of economic and technical co-operation on Nov. 4, 1954, came into force on March 27, 1957.

Iran and Oman. An agreement on the delimitation of the continental shelf between the two countries was signed on May 25, 1975.

Iran and Saudi Arabia. An agreement on the demarcation of the continental shelf between Iran and Saudi Arabia was signed in Tehran on Oct. 24, 1968.

Iran and Switzerland. A treaty of friendship between the two countries was signed on April 25, 1934.

(A "reconciliation" treaty between Iran and Iraq, signed in Baghdad on June 13, 1975, and based on an Algiers agreement of March 6, 1975, on the two countries' common border, was unilaterally abrogated by Iraq on Sept. 17, 1980. This decision was followed by the outbreak of war between Iraq and Iran, with the latter insisting on the reactivation of the treaty.)

1975 Agreement on Western Sahara

An agreement was reached on Nov. 14, 1975, between Spain, Morocco and Mauritania, whereby Spain undertook to hand over control of the then Spanish Sahara (Saguia el Hamra and Rio de Oro) by Feb. 28, 1976, to a provisional administration with the participation of

Morocco and Mauritania. The agreement was approved by the Spanish *Cortes* (Parliament) on Nov. 18, 1975 (but was declared null and void by the Government of Algeria).

Following a change of regime in Mauritania in May 1979, the new Government of that country concluded, on Aug. 5, 1979, a peace agreement with the Algerian-backed Polisario Front (which had conducted an armed struggle against Moroccan and Mauritanian forces) and withdrew its troops from the Western Sahara.

In the peace treaty Mauritania declared that it had no claims, and would not have any, on the territory and would extricate itself from the war, and the Polisario Front declared that it neither had nor would have any territorial claims on Mauritania.

1979 Egyptian-Israeli Peace Treaty

A peace treaty between Egypt and Israel was signed in Washington on March 26, 1979, by President Sadat of Egypt and Menahim Begin, the Israeli Prime Minister, in the presence of President Carter of the USA.

The signing of the treaty was the outcome of protracted negotiations which had been conducted with US participation and had led to the conclusion at Camp David (near Washington, D.C.) on Sept. 17, 1978, of two framework agreements in which the Egyptian President and the Israeli Prime Minister had agreed on certain principles for negotiations between the two sides which would lead to the conclusion of a peace treaty—with this treaty constituting a basis for the eventual peace betwen Israel and all its neighbours.

The Camp David agreements had, however, been rejected by almost all other Arab states and had been followed, in particular, (i) by the signing of a charter of joint national action by the Presidents of Iraq and Syria (in Baghdad on Oct. 26, 1978), providing inter alia for the establishment of a full military union between these two countries [see above] and (ii) by the ninth Arab summit conference held in Baghdad on Nov. 2-5, 1978 [see page 341].

The first five operative articles of the peace treaty read as follows:

"**Art. I.** (1) The state of war between the parties will be terminated and peace will be established between them upon the exchange of instruments of ratification of this treaty.

"(2) Israel will withdraw all its armed forces and civilians from the Sinai behind the international boundary between Egypt and mandated Palestine, as provided in the annexed protocol (Annex I), and Egypt will resume the exercise of its full sovereignty over the Sinai.

"(3) Upon completion of the interim withdrawal provided for in Annex I, the parties will establish normal and friendly relations, in accordance with Article III (3).

"**Art. II.** The permanent boundary between Egypt and Israel is the recognized international boundary between Egypt and the former mandated territory of Palestine as shown on the map at Annex II, without prejudice to the issue of the status of the Gaza Strip. The parties recognize this boundary as inviolable. Each will respect the territorial integrity of the other, including their territorial waters and airspace.

"**Art. III.** (1) The parties will apply between them the provisions of the Charter of the United Nations and the principles of international law governing relations among states in times of peace. In particular:

"A. They recognize and will respect each other's sovereignty, territorial integrity and political independence.

"B. They recognize and will respect each other's right to live in peace within their secure and recognized boundaries.

"C. They will refrain from the threat or use of force, directly or indirectly, against each other and will settle all disputes between them by peaceful means.

"(2) Each party undertakes to ensure that acts or threats of belligerency, hostility or violence do not originate from and are not committed from within its territory, or by any forces subject to its control or by any other forces stationed on its territory, against the population, citizens or property of the other party. Each party also undertakes to refrain from organizing, instigating, inciting, assisting or participating in acts or threats of belligerency, hostility, subversion or violence against the other party, anywhere, and undertakes to ensure that perpetrators of such acts are brought to justice.

"(3) The parties agree that the normal relationship established between them will include full recognition, diplomatic, economic and cultural relations, termination of economic boycotts and discriminatory barriers to the free movement of people and goods, and will guarantee the mutual enjoyment by citizens of the due process of law. The process by which they undertake to achieve such a relationship parallel to the implementation of other provisions of this treaty is set out in the annexed protocol (Annex III).

"**Art. IV.** (1) In order to provide maximum security for both parties on the basis of reciprocity, agreed security arrangements will be established including limited-force zones in Egyptian and Israeli territory, and United Nations forces and observers, described in detail as to nature and timing in Annex I, and other security arrangements the parties may agree upon.

"(2) The parties agree to the stationing of United Nations personnel in areas described in Annex I. The parties agree not to request withdrawal of the United Nations personnel and that these personnel will not be removed unless such removal is approved by the Security Council of the United Nations, with the affirmative vote of the five permanent members [i.e. China, France, the Soviet Union, the USA and the United Kingdom], unless the parties otherwise agree.

"(3) A joint commission will be established to facilitate the implementation of the treaty, as provided for in Annex I.

"(4) The security arrangements provided for in Paragraphs 1 and 2 of this article may, at the request of either party, be reviewed and amended by mutual agreement of the parties.

"**Art. V.** (1) Ships of Israel, and cargoes destined for or coming from Israel, shall enjoy the right of free passage through the Suez Canal and its approaches through the Gulf of Suez and the Mediterranean Sea on the basis of the Constantinople Convention of 1888, applying to all nations. Israeli nationals, vessels and cargoes, as well as persons, vessels and cargoes destined for or coming from Israel, shall be accorded non-discriminatory treatment in all matters connected with usage of the canal.

"(2) The parties consider the Strait of Tiran [at the mouth of the Gulf of Aqaba] and the Gulf of Aqaba to be international waterways open to all nations for unimpeded and non-suspendable freedom of navigation and overflight. The parties will respect each other's right to navigation and overflight for access to either country through the Strait of Tiran and the Gulf of Aqaba."

In the protocol to the treaty Israel undertook to complete its withdrawal from the Sinai (in two phases) not later than three years from the date of exchange of instruments of ratification of the treaty. The protocol also laid down the modalities of this withdrawal.

In an accompanying letter addressed to President Carter the Governments of Egypt and Israel agreed to proceed, within a month after the exchange of instruments of ratification of the peace treaty, to negotiate on implementing the provisions of the framework agreements relating to the West Bank and the Gaza Strip with the object of providing "full autonomy to the inhabitants" of these two areas.

In letters addressed to Egypt and Israel the US Government confirmed that in the event of actual or threatened violation of the treaty the USA would, on request of one or both of the parties, consult with them and "take such other action as it may deem appropriate and helpful to achieve compliance with the treaty"; that the USA would "conduct aerial monitoring as requested by the parties"; and that, if the UN Security Council failed to establish and maintain the arrangements called for in the treaty (through the deployment of UN forces), the US President would "be prepared to take those steps necessary to ensure the establishment and maintenance of an acceptable alternative multinational force".

In a memorandum of understanding signed on March 26, 1979, between the United States and Israel, the USA undertook to give strong support to Israel in certain circumstances, stating in particular: "The United States will provide support it deems appropriate for proper actions taken by Israel in response to . . . demonstrated violations of the treaty of peace. In particular, if a violation of the treaty of peace is deemed to threaten the security of Israel, including, inter alia, a blockade of Israel's use of international waterways, a violation of the provisions of the treaty of peace concerning limitation of forces or an armed attack against Israel, the United States will be prepared to consider, on an urgent basis, such measures as the strengthening of the US presence in the area, the providing of emergency supplies to Israel, and the exercise of maritime rights in order to put an end to the violation."

The Egyptian Government stated subsequently that it would not recognize the legality of this memorandum and considered it null and void, and it listed 16 reasons for rejecting it. Among these reasons were the fact that the US rights referred to in the memorandum had never been mentioned or negotiated with Egypt; that the memorandum could "be construed as an eventual alliance between the United States and Israel against Egypt"; and that it gave the United States "the right to impose a military presence in the region for reasons agreed between Israel and the United States".

The US Secretary of State explained on April 11, 1979, that in connexion with the peace treaty the United States would make available to Egypt and Israel additional financial assistance totalling $4,800 million over three years—approximately $3,000 million for Israel and $1,500 million for Egypt.

The peace treaty was ratified (i) in Israel by the Cabinet on April 1, 1979 (with one cabinet member abstaining from voting) and (ii) in Egypt by the People's Assembly on April 10 (by 328 votes to 15, with one abstention and 16 members being absent) and in a national referendum held on April 19 (by 99.5 per cent of the valid votes cast in a poll of about 90 per cent). The instruments of ratification were exchanged on April 25, 1979 (at a US surveillance post in the Sinai).

The Constantinople Convention on Free Navigation of the Suez Canal

On Oct. 29, 1888, Austria-Hungary, Britain, France, Germany, Italy, the Netherlands, Russia, Spain and Turkey signed the Convention respecting the Free Navigation of the Suez Maritime Canal.

The fundamental provisions of this convention are contained in Articles 1 and 4 as follows:

"The Suez Maritime Canal shall always be free and open, in time of war as in time of peace, to every vessel of commerce or of war, without distinction of flag. . . . The canal shall never be subjected to the exercise of the right of blockade."

"The maritime canal remaining open in time of war

as a free passage, even to ships of war of belligerents . . . , the high contracting parties agree that no right of war, no act of hostility, nor any act having for its object to obstruct the free navigation of the canal, shall be committed in the canal and its ports of access . . . though the Ottoman Empire should be one of the belligerent powers." (In the terms of the convention the legal successor to the Ottoman Empire is Egypt.)

The convention also confirmed and completed the system of international operation embodied by the Universal Suez Canal Company, set up in 1863.

Egypt nationalized the Suez Canal Company in July 1956, an act which was regarded by many users of the canal as a contravention of the 1888 convention.

In April 1957, when the canal was re-opened to navigation, after it had been ob- structed for several months, the Egyptian Government issued a declaration in which it stated its intention to respect "the terms and spirit of the Constantinople Convention and the rights and obligations arising there- from . . .".

The canal was again closed by Egyptian action in the June 1967 Arab-Israeli war and was not re-opened until June 1975. Under the March 1979 Egyptian-Israeli peace treaty [see above], Israeli ships and cargoes were granted the same right of passage in the Suez Canal and its approaches as the vessels of other countries (whereas under the second Egyptian-Israeli disengagement agreement of September 1975 Israel's access to the canal had been confined to non-military cargoes carried by non-Israeli ships).

17. Africa

This section deals with the main international associations, treaties and other agreements entered into by African states, including (i) the Organization of African States, (ii) other continental and regional organizations in Africa and (iii) major treaties and agreements concluded between individual African states.

Organization of African Unity (OAU)

Headquarters: Addis Ababa (Ethiopia).

Members: 50 independent states of Africa (all except South Africa, Bophuthatswana, Transkei and Venda)—see list on page 371.

The Organization of African Unity was constituted at a conference of African heads of state and government in Addis Ababa held from May 23 to 26, 1963.

OAU Charter

Those attending the founding conference signed a Charter of the OAU, the principal provisions of which are as follows:

Establishment

Art. 1. The high contracting parties do by the present Charter establish an organization to be known as the Organization of African Unity.

The organization shall include the continental African states, Madagascar and all the islands surrounding Africa.

Purposes

Art. 2. (1) The organization shall have the following purposes:

(*a*) To promote the unity and solidarity of the African and Malagasy states;

(*b*) to co-ordinate and intensify their co-operation and efforts to achieve a better life for the peoples of Africa;

(*c*) to defend their sovereignty, their territorial integrity and independence;

(*d*) to eradicate all forms of colonialism from Africa; and

(*e*) to promote international co-operation, having due regard to the UN Charter and the Universal Declaration of Human Rights.

(2) To these ends, the member states shall co-ordinate and harmonize their general policies, especially in the following fields:

(*a*) Political and diplomatic co-operation;

(*b*) economic co-operation, including transport and communications;

(*c*) educational and cultural co-operation;

(*d*) health, sanitation, and nutritional co-operation;

(*e*) scientific and technical co-operation; and

(*f*) co-operation for defence and security.

Principles

Art. 3. The member states, in pursuit of the purposes stated in Article 2, solemnly affirm and declare their adherence to the following principles:

(1) The sovereign equality of all member states;

(2) non-interference in the internal affairs of states;

(3) respect for the sovereignty and territorial integrity of each member state and for its inalienable right to independent existence;

(4) peaceful settlement of disputes by negotiation, mediation, conciliation or arbitration;

(5) unreserved condemnation, in all its forms, of political assassination, as well as of subversive activities on the part of neighbouring states or any other states;

(6) absolute dedication to the total emancipation of the African territories which are still dependent;

(7) affirmation of a policy of non-alignment with regard to all blocs.

Institutions

Art. 7. The organization shall accomplish its purposes through the following principal institutions:

(1) The Assembly of Heads of State and Government;

(2) the Council of Ministers;

(3) the General Secretariat;

(4) the Commission of Mediation, Conciliation and Arbitration.

The Assembly of Heads of State and Government

Art. 8. The Assembly of Heads of State and Government shall be the supreme organ of the organization. It shall, subject to the provisions of this Charter, discuss matters of common concern to Africa with a view to co-ordinating and harmonizing the general policy of the organization. It may in addition review the structure, functions and acts of all the organs and any specialized agencies which may be created in accordance with the Charter.

Art. 9. The Assembly shall be composed of the heads of state or government, or their duly accredited representatives, and shall meet at least once a year. At the request of any member state, and upon approval by the majority of the member states, the Assembly shall meet in extraordinary session.

The Council of Ministers

Art. 12. The Council of Ministers shall consist of Foreign Ministers or such other ministers as are designated by the governments of member states.

The Council of Ministers shall meet at least twice a year. When requested by any member state and approved by two-thirds of all member states, it shall meet in extraordinary session.

Art. 13. The Council of Ministers shall be responsible to the Assembly of Heads of State and Government. It shall be entrusted with the responsibility of preparing conferences of the Assembly.

General Secretariat

Art. 16. There shall be an Administrative Secretary-General of the organization, who shall be appointed by the Assembly of Heads of State and Government on the recommendation of the Council of Ministers. The Administrative Secretary-General shall direct the affairs of the Secretariat.

Commission of Mediation, Conciliation and Arbitration

Art. 19. Member states pledge to settle all disputes among themselves by peaceful means and, to this end, decide to establish a Commission of Mediation, Conciliation and Arbitration, the composition and the condition of service of which shall be defined by a separate protocol to be approved by the Assembly of Heads of State and Government.

Specialized Commissions

Art. 20. The Assembly shall establish such Specialized Commissions as it may deem necessary, including the following: (1) Economic and Social Commission; (2) Educational and Cultural Commission; (3) Health, Sanitation, and Nutrition Commission; (4) Defence Commission; (5) Scientific, Technical, and Research Commission.

OAU Institutions

General Secretariat. The OAU's Secretary-General is assisted by five Assistant Secretaries-General—one each for West, Central, North, East and Southern Africa.

Scientific, Technical and Research Commission. The OAU Scientific, Technical and Research Commission (established in Lagos under Art. 20 of the OAU Charter) on Jan. 1, 1965, absorbed the Commission for Technical Co-operation in Africa (CTCA), which had been established in Paris in January 1950.

The CTCA had reconstituted itself in Abidjan (Ivory Coast) Feb. 8-16, 1962, so as to comprise all independent African member states, ending the full membership of Britain, France, and Belgium (which had founded the Commission and were to be invited to participate in the Commission's work at technical level), and excluding Portugal and South Africa.

OAU Liberation Committee. A Co-ordinating Committee for Liberation Movements in Africa was established in 1963 with headquarters in Dar-es-Salaam. Since March 1976 it has consisted of representatives of 21 OAU member states. Its function is to provide financial and military aid to national liberation movements which, on the Liberation Committee's proposal, may be recognized by the OAU as the legitimate representatives of the peoples of territories still to be decolonized.

Assemblies of Heads of State and Government

1964. The second Assembly of Heads of State and Government, held in Cairo on July 17-21, 1964, decided inter alia (i) to make Addis Ababa the seat of the Organization's permanent headquarters; (ii) to approve a protocol providing for mediation, conciliation, and finally, arbitration in disputes between member countries, as well as an undertaking by member states to respect their frontiers as existing at the achievement of independence; and (iii) to set up two permanent commissions—one of African jurists and another on communications.

1965. The third Assembly of Heads of State and Government, held in Accra on Oct. 21-26, 1965, issued a *Declaration on Subversive Activities* containing the following main provisions:

(1) The OAU pledged itself to oppose collectively and firmly, by every means at its disposal, every form of subversion conceived, organized or financed by any foreign power against Africa as a whole or against OAU member states.

(2) The declaration emphasized that member states would tolerate neither subversion by one state against another nor the use of their territory for subversive activity directed from outside Africa against another member state.

(3) All differences between two or more member states should be settled by bilateral or multilateral consultations, on the basis of a protocol of mediation, conciliation and arbitration as laid down in the OAU Charter, and there should be no reaction against a member state by means of a radio or press campaign.

(4) Member states should not give cause for dissension among themselves by fomenting or aggravating racial, religious, linguistic, ethnic or other differences, and should combat all forms of activity of this kind.

(5) In regard to political refugees, the declaration enjoined member states to observe strictly the principles of international law towards all nationals of member states; to try to promote through bilateral or multilateral consultations the return of refugees to their home country with the consent both of the refugees themselves and of their country of origin; and to continue to guarantee the safety of political refugees from dependent territories and support them in their struggle for the liberation of their countries.

It also adopted a resolution on political refugees which recalled the member states' pledge to prevent refugees living in their territories from carrying out by any means whatsoever any acts harmful to the interests of member states; requested all member states never to allow the refugee question to become a source of disagreement among them; appreciated the assistance given to the refugee programmes of African governments by the UN High Commissioner for Refugees (UNHCR); requested African members of the UN Economic and Social Council to seek an increase in African representation on the executive committee of the UNHCR programme on refugees; and requested those member states which had not already done so to ratify the UN convention on refugees and to apply meanwhile the provisions of that convention to refugees in Africa.

1966. The fourth Assembly of Heads of State and Government, held in Addis Ababa on Nov. 5-9, 1966, decided inter alia to replace the Liberation Committee in Dar-es-Salaam by a new committee of 10 members, the executive of which would be placed under the direct control of the OAU Secretariat-General and would be excluded from any initiative of a political nature in its activities.

1967. The fifth Assembly of Heads of State and Government was held in Kinshasa on Sept. 11-14, 1967, without Malawi being represented.

1968. The sixth Assembly of Heads of State and Government, attended by representatives of all 40 member states except Malawi, was held in Algiers on Sept. 13-16, 1968.

1969. The seventh Assembly, at which all 41 member states (including Equatorial Guinea, independent since Oct. 12, 1968) were represented, took place in Addis Ababa on Sept. 6-9, 1969.

1970. The eighth Assembly, held in Addis Ababa from Sept. 1 to 3, 1970, was marked by the reconciliation of the Federal Military Government of Nigeria and the Governments of Gabon, the Ivory Coast, Tanzania, and Zambia, all of which had in 1967 recognized the secessionist regime in "Biafra", since defeated by the Federal Nigerian forces.

1971. The ninth Assembly, which took place in Addis Ababa from June 21 to 23, 1971, was not attended by the Central African Republic and Uganda, the latter being absent in protest against the transfer of the Assembly's venue from Kampala to Addis Ababa as the result of opposition to President Amin of Uganda by several member states. The Assembly adopted, by 28 votes to six, with five abstentions, a declaration rejecting a "dialogue" with the Government of South Africa as suggested by President Houphouët-Boigny of the Ivory Coast.

1972. The 10th Assembly, held in Rabat on June 11-15, 1972, reaffirmed its support for the OAU liberation committee by increasing its budget by 50 per cent and its membership to 15 countries—Algeria, the Congo, Egypt, Ethiopia, Guinea, Libya, Mauritania, Morocco, Nigeria, Senegal, Somalia, Tanzania, Uganda, Zaïre and Zambia. The Assembly also adopted a resolution strongly supporting Egypt's demand for the evacuation by Israel of all Egyptian territory occupied since July 1967.

During the years 1971-72 the OAU was instrumental in achieving reconciliation in a number of disputes between member states, including those between Senegal and Guinea (on Senegal's alleged failure to suppress activities against the Guinean Government), between Guinea and Ghana (over the burial of the late ex-President Kwame Nkrumah), and between rival Angolan liberation movements.

1973. The 11th Assembly was held in Addis Ababa on May 27-29, 1973. In the course of the meeting the disputes between Ethiopia and Somalia and between Uganda and Tanzania were the subject of OAU mediation. An eight-member "good offices committee" was formed to seek ways of reconciling Ethiopia and Somalia in their territorial dispute. In the case of Uganda and Tanzania, whose conflict dated from the previous September, when armed followers of former President Obote of Uganda had invaded Uganda from Tanzania, an agreement was reached, which was signed by the two Presidents on May 28.

Under the terms of the agreement, the Ugandan Government agreed to pay to Tanzania compensation for the deaths of 24 Tanzanian nationals in Uganda; both parties agreed to adhere strictly to the terms of the Mogadishu peace agreement [see below], and in particular to prevent their territories from being used as bases for subversion against each other; the Tanzanian Government assumed responsibility that ex-President Obote would not interfere in Uganda's affairs; and the Ugandan Government would not demand Dr Obote's expulsion from Tanzania.

[The Mogadishu peace agreement, signed on Oct. 5, 1972, provided for the withdrawal of troops from the Ugandan-Tanzanian border and for a cessation of all military activities by the two sides against each other.]

1974. The 12th Assembly was held in Mogadishu (Somalia) on June 12-16, 1974 (with Malawi being represented for the first time in several years). Among resolutions adopted by the Assembly was one confirming acceptance of a loan of US$200,000,000 from Arab League member states and the decision to place this amount in a special account with the African Development Bank (in Abidjan) for subsequent distribution among non-oil-producing African countries in need. The Assembly, however, made no progress towards a solution of the dispute between Ethiopia and Somalia, notwithstanding a private meeting between the two heads of state on June 13.

1975. The 13th Assembly, held in Kampala (Uganda) on July 28-Aug. 1, 1975, elected President Amin of Uganda as President of the OAU (for the customary one-year term), despite strong opposition to President Amin's policies by the Presidents of Botswana, Mozambique, Tanzania and Zambia.

In connexion with the admission of the Comoros to the OAU the Assembly called on France to respect the territorial integrity of the newly-independent state (i.e. with the inclusion of the island of Mayotte which, however, remained under French control).

The Assembly declined to demand the expulsion of Israel from the United Nations (as called for in particular by Libya, whereas in Egypt it was argued that the object should be to pressurize Israel into implementing UN resolutions on the Middle East and not to induce it to renounce its commitment to these UN resolutions).

This session of the Assembly was also addressed by Yassir Arafat, the leader of the Palestine Liberation Organization (PLO), who declared inter alia that there could be no peace in the Middle East without a Palestine; that the PLO was confident of ultimate victory; and that Africa should be given increased Arab aid. He did not, however, refer to the PLO's earlier call for the expulsion of Israel from the United Nations.

The Assembly endorsed a Dar-es-Salaam declaration agreed to at an extraordinary meeting of the OAU Council of Ministers on April 11, 1975, expressing "unqualified support for the freedom fighters" led by the African National Council (ANC) of Rhodesia, and also support for the ANC's efforts to achieve a peaceful change until they were convinced that talks had irretrievably failed. As for South Africa, the declaration stated that the Whites had had "ample time to change their attitude on apartheid" and that armed struggle was the only way left. In two supplementary resolutions to the declaration it was proposed that (i) a special OAU committee, to be appointed from among African members of the UN Council for Namibia, should have special responsibility for facilitating contacts between the South African Government and the South West Africa People's Organization (SWAPO), the national liberation movement recognized by the OAU for Namibia, and (ii) further measures should be taken to isolate the White minority Government in South Africa, including enforcement of sanctions and the denial of port and airport facilities not only to all South African ships and aircraft but also to naval vessels and military aircraft from other countries which used South Africa's facilities.

1976. The 14th regular Assembly was held in Port Louis (Mauritius) on July 2-6, 1976, but was only poorly attended. It approved strong resolutions against the Government of South Africa, including a call for intensified armed struggle (but not mobilization of the armies of Africa's independent countries, as called for by Guinea) and for a possible Arab oil boycott against South Africa. The Assembly also proposed the holding of an OAU emergency summit meeting to discuss the dispute between Algeria and Morocco (supported by Mauritania) over the Western Sahara.

1977. The 15th Assembly, held in Libreville (Gabon) on July 2-5, 1977, was not attended by Benin (formerly Dahomey), whose Government accused that of Gabon of having been involved in an attempted coup by mercenaries who attacked Benin on Jan. 16, 1977.

The Assembly was marked by strong attacks made by several African leaders, notably the President of the Sudan, on Soviet interference in African affairs, and it was overshadowed by numerous disputes among African states during 1976-77 (between Egypt and Libya, Libya and the Sudan, Ethiopia and its neighbours, the member states of the East African Community—which had eventually disintegrated, and Mauritania and Morocco on the one hand and Algeria and the Polisario Front of the Western Sahara on the other, in connexion with which the Government of Morocco had on Feb. 25, 1977, decided to suspend its participation in the OAU temporarily).

On the conflict between Ethiopia and Somalia an OAU eight-member mediation committee set up in 1973 reaffirmed on Aug. 9, 1977, the inviolability of frontiers inherited from the colonial era (in accordance with the UN Charter) and the condemnation of all subversive activities on the part of neighbouring states or other states, and it invited President Bongo of Gabon to take up contact with the two sides with a view to "halting hostilities".

On the question of foreign intervention the Assembly approved a draft resolution submitted by Senegal which (i) appealed to all African states to abstain from having recourse to foreign intervention in internal African problems; (ii) invited OAU member states to prohibit the use of their territory as a base for aggression against another African state; (iii) requested powers outside Africa "to abstain from interfering in the internal affairs of African states" and (iv) recommended member states to reach "a peaceful settlement of their disputes by way of negotiation and mediation". (The resolution referred in particular to Cuban intervention in Angola and to Sudanese support for the insurrection in Eritrea.)

1978. The 16th Assembly took place in Khartoum on July 18-22, 1978, and was attended by representatives of all OAU member states except the Comoros (whose delegation was not admitted on the ground that the existing Comoro Government had been installed with the aid of a White mercenary in May 1978). This session of the Assembly revealed wide differences of opinion on the question of foreign troops and bases in Africa.

At the Council of Ministers' meeting preceding the session, the Foreign Minister of Libya denounced Mauritania, Chad and Zaïre for having invited French troops into their countries, and the Congolese Foreign Minister accused African countries which had made up a pan-African force for intervention in Zaïre (viz. Morocco, Senegal, the Central African Empire, Togo, the Ivory Coast, Gabon and Egypt), calling their action a flagrant violation of the OAU Charter.

After the countries thus accused had defended their actions, the Assembly adopted a resolution in which it (i) condemned the conclusion of military pacts and alliances with non-African powers but reaffirmed the right of each country to choose its own ideological system and to call on any country for assistance if its sovereignty or territorial integrity was threatened; (ii) rejected the idea of an African intervention force which was not formed within the context of the objectives and priorities defined by the OAU and called for the reactivation of the OAU defence committee to consider the establishment of a force supervised by the OAU; (iii) reaffirmed its adherence to the principle of respect for territorial integrity and sovereignty of states and its desire to resort to peaceful ways of settling differences between African states in order not to pave the way for foreign intervention; (iv) condemned the policy of force and intervention in Africa regardless of its source, and opposed all plans to recolonize the continent; (v) demanded that differences between African states should be resolved peacefully and within the African framework; (vi) proclaimed that the maintenance of peace in Africa was the responsibility of Africans alone; (vii) repeated its unanimous strong condemnation of some (unspecified) non-African countries which had resorted to the use of mercenaries to jeopardize the security and independence of African countries; and (viii) reaffirmed the desire to eliminate foreign military bases.

With implied reference to Cuban intervention in Africa, the Assembly also called on the African members of the non-aligned movement to abide by the agreed objectives and principles of the movement, condemned strongly any foreign intervention in the affairs of the African continent and called on all member states to settle their differences within the African framework.

1979. The 17th Assembly was held in Monrovia (Liberia) on July 17-21, 1979. It was attended by representatives of all OAU member states except Chad (which had sent two delegations, neither of which was admitted to the session). This session was again marked by disputes among member states. Tanzania's role in the overthrow of the Amin regime in Uganda in April 1978 was strongly criticized, notably by the Sudan and Nigeria; a resolution calling for a ceasefire and a UN-supervised referendum in the Western Sahara caused the Moroccan delegation to leave the session; and during a speech by the Egyptian President in defence of the 1979 Egyptian-Israeli peace treaty several other Arab delegations also walked out.

In his opening speech President Tolbert of Liberia said on July 16 that as a result of "fratricidal conflicts" there were over 4,000,000 refugees in Africa and that the OAU Charter should be revised by making the provisions concerning the protection of fundamental human rights explicit, and by creating a mechanism for setting up a pan-African force to enable the OAU to respond rapidly to problems which threatened the peace, security and stability of Africa.

Resolutions adopted by the Assembly included one involving approval, in principle, of the establishment of a joint African defence force. It was also announced that a Pan-African News Agency would begin work on Oct. 1, 1979, with headquarters in Dakar and with regional news pools to be set up in the Sudan, Libya, Nigeria, Zaïre and Zambia.

1980. A special conference of the heads of state and government held in Lagos on April 28-30, 1980, adopted a *Lagos Plan of Action* for the implementation of a strategy (previously proposed by Nigeria) for the economic development of Africa, setting out guidelines (i) for 1980-90 on strengthening subregional groupings in central, eastern, northern and southern Africa and (ii) for 1990-2000 on closer integration between such groupings. In a protocol the heads of state and government reaffirmed their commitment to establish, by the year 2000, an African Economic Community.

The proposals were aimed at achieving food self-sufficiency for the continent by 1990; improving communications; harmonizing industrial development so as to increase Africa's share of the world's industrial production from the current estimated 0.6 per cent to 1 per cent by 1985 and to 2 per cent by the year 2000; and expanding inter-African trade, with the elimination of all trade barriers in Africa by 1990.

The 18th Assembly of Heads of State and Government, held in Freetown (Sierra Leone) on July 1-4, 1980, referred the question of the Western Sahara to an ad hoc committee (appointed earlier) which was to convene a meeting of all interested parties within three months. It also called on all OAU member states to contribute to a required budget of $60,000,000 to finance an African peace-keeping force to end the civil war in Chad.

The meeting on the Western Sahara, which took place in Freetown on Sept. 9-12, 1980, formulated a six-point plan for a ceasefire under UN supervision and a referendum under OAU auspices. The Moroccan Foreign Minister, however, stated that the plan would have to be approved by a two-thirds majority of the Assembly of Heads of State and Government (due in Nairobi in July 1981).

Other International Groupings of African States

African Development Bank (AfDB)

Headquarters: Abidjan (Ivory Coast).

Members: All members of the Organization of African Unity except Angola. (Following a 1979 decision by the AfDB to open its capital to non-African countries, by late 1980 France and Switzerland had completed initial procedures for non-regional membership of the bank.)

The decision to set up an African Development Bank was reached by representatives of 32 independent African states and Kenya in Khartoum on Aug. 4, 1963, when the Finance Ministers of 31 of these countries signed an agreement which came into force on Sept. 10, 1964. The bank was formally constituted on Sept. 25, 1964, with its capital being subscribed exclusively by African states, and it began operations in 1966. Loans granted to member countries by the bank totalled $205,720,000 in 1978.

The bank has four associated institutions as follows:

African Development Fund (ADF). This fund was set up in November 1972 on a proposal by the AfDB and under an agreement signed by Belgium, Brazil, Canada, Denmark, Finland, the Federal Republic of Germany, Japan, the Netherlands, Norway, Spain, Switzerland, the United Kingdom and Yugoslavia. The fund began operations on Aug. 1, 1973, with initial resources of about $100,000,000 (its first contributors including Canada, the Federal Republic of Germany and Sweden). The fund was also to administer a Special Swiss Fund for Africa of 12,000,000 Swiss francs (about £2,000,000) set up by the Swiss Government on Sept. 14, 1974. France announced in May 1976 that it would join the ADF.

Nigeria Trust Fund (NTF). This fund was set up under an agreement which was signed by the ADF and the Government of Nigeria in February 1976 and came into force in April of that year. The NTF provides loans for projects in co-operation with other lending institutions.

Société Internationale Financière pour les Investissements et le Développement en Afrique (SIFIDA). SIFIDA was set up in Geneva in November 1970 with the object of promoting the establishment and growth of productive enterprises in Africa.

Africa Reinsurance Corporation (AFRI-CARE). Established under an agreement signed in February 1976 and in force from January 1977, AFRICARE was formally constituted in March of that year with headquarters in Lagos and with the object of fostering the development of the insurance and reinsurance industry in Africa.

Common African and Mauritian Organization (OCAM)

Headquarters: Bangui (Central African Republic).

Members: Benin, the Central African Republic, the Ivory Coast, Mauritius, Niger, Rwanda, Senegal, Seychelles, Togo and Upper Volta.

Superseding the *Union Africaine et Malgache de Coopération Economique* (UAMCE) set up in March 1964 and replacing an earlier *Union Africaine et Malgache* (or Brazzaville Group) of French-speaking African states created in September 1961 by 12 former French territories, OCAM (*Organisation Commune Africaine et Malgache*) was established at Nouakchott (Mauritania) on Feb. 12, 1965, by Cameroon, the Central African Republic, Chad, the Congo (Brazzaville), Dahomey, Gabon, the Ivory Coast, Madagascar, Mauritania, Niger, Senegal, Togo and Upper Volta, which were later joined by Rwanda. While the Congo (Kinshasa)—later Zaïre—was admitted to OCAM on May 26, 1965, and Mauritius on Jan. 20, 1970, several states subsequently withdrew from the organization—Mauritania on June 24, 1965; Zaïre on April 19, 1972; the Congo (Brazzaville) on Sept. 22, 1972; Cameroon, Chad and the Malagasy Republic giving notice of withdrawal on July 1, July 3 and Aug. 4, 1973, respectively; and Gabon withdrawing on Sept. 7, 1976. (The Congo, Mauritania and Gabon, however, continued to participate in various technical agencies of OCAM.) Seychelles was admitted to OCAM on Feb. 9, 1977.

OCAM Charter. A Charter for OCAM was approved by a conference of leaders of the organization's member states in Madagascar on June 25-28, 1966. Defining increased co-operation between member states as the main object of OCAM, the Charter laid down that any African independent and sovereign state accepting the Charter's provisions could be admitted to the organization upon application. It provided for three organs of OCAM, as follows:

(1) The Conference of the Heads of State and Government as the supreme organ of the organization, meeting once a year in ordinary session.

(2) The Council of Ministers, consisting of the Foreign Ministers of member states, meeting once a year in ordinary session, responsible to the conference,

and implementing co-operation between member states as directed by the conference.

(3) The Administrative General Secretariat, appointed for two years by the Conference upon the proposal of the Council of Ministers, with its seat at Yaoundé (Cameroon)—transferred to Bangui in 1974 —and its mandate being renewable.

Aims and Agencies. At its formation, OCAM was characterized by its first President (President Ould Daddah of Mauritania) as "an African grouping which has the aim, within the framework of the OAU, of reinforcing co-operation and solidarity among the African States and Madagascar in order to accelerate their development in the political, economic, social, technical, and cultural spheres".

OCAM has set up the following agencies:

(1) *Bureau africain et mauricien de recherches et d'études législatives* (Libreville, Gabon).

(2) *Centre africain et mauricien de perfectionnement des cadres* (Abidjan).

(3) *Centre interafricain de production de films* (CIPROFILM) (Ouagadougou, Upper Volta).

(4) *Consortium interafricain de distribution cinématographique* (CIDC) (Ouagadougou).

(5) *École inter-états d'ingénieurs de l'équipement rural* (Ouagadougou).

(6) *École inter-états des sciences et médecine vétérinaires* (Dakar).

(7) *Fonds de garantie et de coopération* (Cotonou, Benin).

(8) *Institut africain d'informatique* (Libreville).

(9) *Institut africain et mauricien d'architecture* (Lomé, Togo).

(10) *Institut africain et mauricien de bilinguisme* (Port Louis, Mauritius).

(11) *Institut africain et mauricien de statistique et d'économie appliquée* (Kigali, Rwanda).

(12) *Organisation africaine de la propriété intellectuelle* (OAPI) (Yaoundé, Cameroon).

(13) *Union africaine et mauricienne des banques de développement* (Bangui).

DECISIONS TAKEN AT SUMMIT CONFERENCES

1974 Conference. At the ninth conference of the OCAM member states' heads of state in Bangui on Aug. 10-12, 1974, it

Map 12   Common African and Mauritian Organization (OCAM) and Conseil de l'Entente

was decided inter alia to leave the solution of political problems to the Organization of African Unity and thus to transform OCAM into a "true instrument of economic, cultural and social solidarity and co-operation".

1977 Conference. At the 11th conference of OCAM heads of state and government held in Kigali (Rwanda) on Feb. 9-10, 1977, it was decided to discontinue a sugar agreement which had been in force since 1966 and also to establish a guarantee and co-operation fund (as listed above under agencies) for the strengthening of solidarity among member countries and promoting their economic development.

1979 Conference. At the 12th conference held in Cotonou (Benin) on June 26-27, 1979, it was decided to exclude from OCAM ventures (i) the multinational Air Afrique aviation company, which had been established in June 1961 and from which Cameroon had withdrawn in 1971, Chad in 1972 and Gabon in 1977, and (ii) the Afro-Malagasy Posts and Telecommunications Union (UAMPT) located in Brazzaville.

African Civil Aviation Commission (AFCAC)

An African Civil Aviation Commission open to all member states of the OAU and of the UN Economic Commission for Africa was set up at a meeting of representatives of 32 African countries in Addis Ababa on Jan. 13-18, 1969. With headquarters in Dakar, the commission was to promote the co-ordination and development of African air transport systems and the application of the standards and recommendations of the International Civil Aviation Organization (ICAO).

Concerted Action for Development in Africa (CADA)

The creation of an organization to be known as Concerted Action for Development in Africa (CADA) was agreed upon by representatives of the Governments of Belgium, Canada, France, the Federal Republic of Germany, the United Kingdom and the United States in Paris on Dec. 28, 1979, as a result of a French initiative and on the basis of proposals made by the French President at the third Franco-African conference in May 1976 [see page 280].

The purpose of CADA was to co-ordinate development aid for Africa, in particular for the opening-up of land-locked regions, the development of agricultural resources, or the effects of problems such as drought or tropical diseases—i.e. tasks only partially covered by existing national or international programmes, and this new action was to be "elaborated in close collaboration with the Africans concerned at continental, regional or national levels, in such a way that the projects which are selected for joint action conform to priorities set by the Africans themselves".

Membership of CADA was to be open to other members of the Organization for Economic Co-operation and Development (OECD) and a liaison group of permanent officials was set up in Paris as from Jan. 1, 1980.

Conferences of Heads of State and Government of Countries bordering the Sahara

A conference of heads of state and government of countries bordering the Sahara was held in Bamako (Mali) on March 8-9, 1980, and was attended by the Presidents of Algeria, Chad, Mali, Mauritania and Niger and a member of the General Secretariat of the General People's Congress of Libya.

With a view to "making the subregion a zone of peace, security, stability and co-operation", the participants in the conference adopted several documents, including (i) a programme of economic, technical, cultural and social co-operation and (ii) a political declaration. They also decided that a Ministerial Council would meet every year, and they set up five special commissions to foster development, independence and social progress.

In their political declaration the participants expressed inter alia "absolute support for the struggle of the peoples of Namibia, South Africa, occupied Palestine and the Western Sahara to recover their national rights and for self-determination"; they condemned the 1978 Camp David agreements as aggravating "the violation of the firm rights of the Palestinian people"; they urged "the non-aligned countries to redouble their efforts to lessen tension in the world and to consolidate world peace and security"; and they stressed their determination to work for solidarity among the member states of the Group of 77 [see page 394] in order to bring about the legitimate aspirations of the developing countries.

Earlier meetings between the heads of state of Algeria, Libya and Niger had taken place at Ouargla (Algeria) on April 8, 1976, and in Tripoli on Nov. 23-24, 1976, and the heads of state of Algeria, Chad, Mali and Niger and the Libyan Prime Minister had held a conference in Niamey (Niger) on March 20-21, 1977. The outcome of the Ouargla and Tripoli meetings was the creation of (i) a tripartite commission to study possibilities of increased regional co-operation between the three states concerned and (ii) a Trans-Saharan Road Committee (of which Nigeria became a member in May 1977).

(For Libya's defence agreements with Algeria and Niger see pages 344 and 348.)

Co-operation between former Portuguese Colonies

At the end of a meeting in Maputo (Mozambique) on March 30, 1980, of the Presidents of Angola, Cape Verde, Guinea-Bissau, Mozambique and São Tomé and Príncipe (all former Portuguese territories), a general agreement was signed on co-operation, defining the bases of mutual assistance in the fields of trade, transport, finance, banking and insurance. The five Presidents also decided to meet annually in order to analyse how the agreement was being implemented and to define new guidelines for strengthening the existing relations between the five countries. In the field of foreign policy the five Presidents inter alia expressed their solidarity with "the South African people led by the African National Congress", with the Polisario Front in the Western Sahara, with the Fretilin liberation movement of East Timor (Indonesia) and with the Palestine Liberation Organization.

A first summit conference of the five countries' heads of state had been held in Luanda (Angola) on June 9-10, 1979, when it had been agreed to adopt similar policies for the economic and social development of these countries.

African-Arab Conferences

A first conference of Foreign Ministers from African and Arab countries was held in Cairo on July 9-10, 1975, and was attended by representatives of 23 countries and of the Palestine Liberation Organization (PLO). The participants expressed their desire "to expand and intensify co-operation in trade, mining, industry, agriculture, energy, water resources, transport and communications", and they agreed on the formation of a permanent joint ministerial committee.

A second such conference, held in Dakar on April 19-22, 1976, was attended by 40 ministers and also by representatives of the African Development Bank, the Arab Development Bank and several liberation movements, including the PLO. The conference prepared a draft charter for submission to an Afro-Arab summit meeting to be held in 1977.

This charter provided inter alia for the establishment of direct trade relations between African and Arab countries, with priority to be given to supplying each other's respective markets and mutual preferential treatment to be accorded in trade.

A first conference of heads of state and government of African and Arab states took place in Cairo on March 7-9, 1977, under the joint auspices of the Arab League and the OAU.

It was attended by a total of 60 delegations (from all OAU member states except Malawi and from the 21 members of the Arab League, including the PLO), among them 36 heads of state. Admitted as observers were six national liberation movements—two from Djibouti, SWAPO of Namibia, the South African National Congress and the Pan-Africanist Congress (both from South Africa) and the Patriotic Front of Zimbabwe. The Eritrean Liberation Front was admitted in a semi-official capacity, but the Polisario Front of the Western Sahara was not represented.

During the conference leaders of Arab oil-producing countries announced that they would make grants-in-aid and loans to Black African states. These undertakings included $1,200 million from Saudi Arabia for economic and social development in Africa; $240,000,000 from Kuwait; $76,000,000 from Qatar; and $135,000,000 from the United Arab Emirates.

The conference issued three declarations —including a *Declaration and Action Programme for African-Arab Co-operation,* to be known as the *Cairo Declaration*—and a resolution on the organization and methods of future African-Arab co-operation. The contents of these documents are summarized below.

The "Cairo Declaration". In the Declaration and Action Programme the participants in the conference listed the basic principles of their co-operation as being respect for the sovereignty of all their states, equality among them, permanent sovereignty over their natural resources, the rejection of all aggression and the illegality of forcible occupation or annexation of the land of others, non-interference in the domestic affairs of other states, preservation of mutual interests on the basis of reciprocal treatment and equality, the peaceable settlement of differences, and "joint struggle against hegemony, racialism and exploitation in all their forms".

In this declaration the African and Arab states undertook to co-operate in the fields of politics and diplomacy, economy and finance, trade, education, culture, science, technology and information, with a detailed action programme being outlined for all these fields. It was also decided to establish a permanent joint committee at ministerial level to ensure the implementation of the programme. [For this "standing commission" see below under "Future African-Arab Relations".]

Political Declaration. The political document expressed the participants' commitment to the principles of non-alignment and of peaceful coexistence; called for the establishment of "a just international economic order"; and demanded "the intensification, on an international scale, of the political and economic isolation of Israel, South Africa and Rhodesia as long as these countries have not changed their policies".

The document emphasized the need for an oil embargo, in particular against South Africa (notwithstanding the fact that several states represented at the conference had continued to supply oil to that country), and it also proclaimed support for "the territorial integrity of the Comoros". [Reservations on this declaration had been expressed by Chad, the Congo, Ethiopia and Kenya because it contained no condemnation of "secessionist and counter-revolutionary movements".]

Economic and Financial Co-operation. The Declaration on Economic and Financial Co-operation retraced the development of African-Arab co-operation, which was stated to have increased sevenfold during the past three years, and provided inter alia for (i) encouragement of technical and financial aid for studying the feasibility of development projects and basic structures in Africa and for the financing of such projects; (ii) an expansion of the resources of the Arab Bank for Economic Development in Africa (ABEDA) to enable it to play a greater role; (iii) a strengthening of trade relations between African and Arab countries by mutual preferential treatment; and (iv) encouragement of Arab investment through the creation of a system of investment guarantees in African states. [The development projects to be studied included four sponsored by the UN Economic Commission for Africa which would require total finance of $1,327 million—(i) a trans-African road system of 30,000 kilometres (about 19,000 miles), comprising roads from Algiers to Gao (eastern Mali), from Mombasa (Kenya) to Lagos (Nigeria), from Dakar (Senegal) to N'Djaména (Chad), along the Atlantic coast from Lagos to Nouakchott (Mauritania), from Cairo (via East Africa) to Gaborone (Botswana), and 82 secondary roads of a total length of 47,000 kilometres (28,000 miles) in 40 African countries; (iii) an assessment of Africa's natural resources, in particular of water basins and hydrocarbons; (iii) a pan-African telecommunications network (PANAFTEL), for which 90 per cent of the $250,000,000 required was said to be already available; and (iv) the creation of a computerized data bank (at a cost of $7,000,000).]

Future African-Arab Relations. The resolution on the modalities of African-Arab relations laid down (i) that the Afro-Arab "summit" conference would be held once every three years, and the ordinary meeting of the Afro-Arab Council of Ministers once every 18 months; (ii) that a standing commission would be formed from ministers of the states which were members of the 12-member committees of the OAU and the Arab League, or their representatives, together with the Secretaries-General of the OAU and the Arab League, under the co-chairmanship of the chairmen of these two 12-member committees; (iii) that this standing commission, which would hold ordinary meetings twice a year, would supervise Afro-Arab co-operation and development and would study and direct co-operation in achieving the political, social, technological and economic aims set out in the Declaration and Action Programme; (iv) that working groups and specialized committees would be formed when necessary in a number of fields; (v) that a co-ordinating committee, comprising the chairmen of the two 12-member committees and the two Secretaries-General (of the OAU and the Arab League) and responsible to the standing commission, would co-ordinate the activities of the working groups and supervise the implementation of any decisions taken; (vi) that an ad hoc Afro-Arab court, or arbitration and conciliation commission, would settle any dispute arising; and (vii) that a special fund, financed on a 50-50 basis from the budgets of the OAU and the Arab League, would be established to run the work of the executive organs of Afro-Arab co-operation.

Regional Organizations in Africa

East and Central Africa
Conference of East and Central African States

Heads of state or government of East and Central African states began in 1966 to hold regular conferences to discuss problems of mutual interest.

The first of these conferences, held in Nairobi from March 31 to April 2, 1966, was attended by heads of state, ministers or other representatives of 11 states—Burundi, Congo-Kinshasa (Zaïre), Ethiopia, Kenya, Malawi, Rwanda, Somalia, Sudan, Tanzania, Uganda and Zambia.

The second conference, held in Kinshasa on Feb. 12-14, 1967, was also attended by representatives of the Central African Republic and the Congo (Brazzaville), whereas Ethiopia, Malawi and Somalia were not represented. It issued a "Declaration of Kinshasa" expressing solidarity on African problems and in particular support for the "liberation movement in Africa" and the use of force against the Smith regime in Rhodesia.

The fifth conference, held in Lusaka on April 14-16, 1969, and attended by representatives of 14 countries—i.e. those present at the first conference and also the Central African Republic, Chad and Congo (Brazzaville), issued the "Lusaka Manifesto", defining the 14 states' attitude to "colonialism and racial discrimination . . . practised in southern Africa".

The document contained inter alia the following passages:

"Our stand towards southern Africa involves . . . a rejection of racialism, not a reversal of existing racial domination. . . .

"If peaceful progress to emancipation were possible, or if changed circumstances were to make it possible in the future, we would urge our brothers in the resistance movements to use peaceful methods of struggle, even at the cost of some compromise on the timing of change. But while peaceful progress is blocked by the actions of those at present in power in the states of southern Africa, we have no choice but to give to the peoples of those territories all the support of which we are capable in their struggle against their oppressors. . . .

"The actions of the South African Government are such that the rest of the world has a responsibility to take some action in defence of humanity.

"South Africa should be excluded from the United Nations' agencies and even from the United Nations itself. It should be ostracized by the world community. It should be isolated from world trade patterns and left to be self-sufficient if it can.

"The South African Government cannot be allowed both to reject the very concept of mankind's unity and to benefit by the strength given through friendly international relations."

The seventh conference, held in Mogadishu on Oct. 18-19, 1971, when all 14 countries were represented, approved the "Mogadishu Declaration" condemning any "dialogue" with the Government of South Africa (as had been advocated by President Houphouët-Boigny of the Ivory Coast) and reaffirming support for "armed struggle . . . for the liberation of southern Africa". The conference also adopted a "Declaration on Aggression against Zambia" pledging "all material and other aid" to that country against "aggressive actions on the part of the minority and colonialist regimes in southern Africa".

The eighth conference was held in Dar-es-Salaam on Sept. 7-10, 1972, with 16 countries being represented (i.e. the 14 participants in the previous conference and also Equatorial Guinea and Gabon). The conference adopted a "pledge of solidarity" whereby all member states would grant liberation movements guaranteed access through their territories provided this did not impair national security, and would come to the military assistance of any member state which might be attacked or be subjected to economic pressure by White minority regimes, with aid to be given in particular to Zambia as "the main support base" for the liberation organizations.

At the ninth conference held in Brazzaville on Aug. 31-Sept. 2, 1974, Cameroon was admitted as the 17th member of the conference.

Lake Chad Basin Commission

This commission was set up at a conference held in Chad on May 21-23, 1964, by the heads of state of Cameroon, Chad, Niger and Nigeria. At a further conference held in Lagos on Aug. 20-22, 1968, the heads of state of these four countries signed an agreement on the joint development of the Lake Chad basin, and a quadripartite commission was established under an executive secretary with eight commissioners (two from each of the participating countries), to be located in Chad.

In July 1972 it was decided to create a development fund for the Lake Chad basin and two specialized agencies—for livestock and meat and for agricultural products.

Central African Customs Union (UDEAC)

This union (the *Union Douanière et Économique de l'Afrique Centrale*) was established in Brazzaville on Dec. 8, 1964, and came into force on Jan. 1, 1966, between Cameroon and the members of an earlier Equatorial Customs Union embracing the Central African Republic, Chad, the Congo (Brazzaville) and Gabon, with headquarters at Bangui (Central African Republic). Chad withdrew from the organization on Dec. 31, 1968.

Trade between the four member countries is duty-free, and freedom of movement for nationals of the member states was established in 1972. There is a central issuing bank—the Banque des Etats de l'Afrique Centrale—in Yaoundé (Cameroon) and a development bank—the Banque de Développement des Etats de l'Afrique Centrale—in Brazzaville.

Union of Central African States (UEAC)

The charter of this union (the *Union des États de l'Afrique Centrale*) was signed in Fort Lamy (now N'Djaména) on April 2, 1968, by the Presidents of the Central African Republic, Chad and the Congo (now Zaïre), and on May 7, 1968, the three member states of the UEAC concluded mutual defence and security agreements. On Dec. 8, 1968, however, President Bokassa of the Central African Republic announced that his country would leave the UEAC.

Lakes Tanganyika and Kivu Basin Commission

This development commission was formed in 1975 by Burundi, Rwanda, Tanzania, Zaïre and Zambia under the auspices of the UN Economic Commission for Africa.

Economic Community of the Great Lakes Countries (CEPGL)

This community (the *Communauté Économique des Pays des Grands Lacs*) was established on Sept. 20, 1976, under a convention signed by the Presidents of Burundi, Rwanda and Zaïre at Gisenyi (Rwanda), where the community was to have its permanent secretariat. At the same time the three Presidents signed a treaty of friendship and co-operation between their three countries.

On Dec. 24, 1976, the three Presidents appointed a permanent executive secretary of the community; granted full powers to the community's Council of Ministers to approve an annual budget; and decided to set up a $3,000,000 fund for the community.

On Sept. 8-9, 1977, the three Presidents agreed inter alia on various development programmes designed to lead to regional economic integration, and on the creation of a development bank.

Kagera Basin Organization

In August 1977 Burundi, Rwanda and Tanzania established an Organization for the Management and Development of the Kagera River Basin (straddled by the three countries) with the object of continuing projects begun in 1971 and of developing irrigation, electric power (to enable Burundi to become independent of outside sources for its electricity), navigation and mining in the basin. (The organization was joined by Uganda on May 19, 1981.)

West Africa

Conseil de l'Entente

The *Conseil de l'Entente* (Entente Council) was established by Dahomey (later Benin), the Ivory Coast, Niger and Upper Volta at Abidjan (Ivory Coast) on May 29-30, 1959, as the supreme organ of a union which would involve (i) a customs union; (ii) co-ordination of the four countries' legislation in the spheres of finance, justice, public service, labour, communications and public health; (iii) harmonization of tax legislation; and (iv) the creation of a "Solidarity Fund".

Togo—which had been in a customs union with Dahomey after concluding an agreement on Aug. 20, 1960—became associated with the *Conseil de l'Entente* in 1966.

The four members of the Council achieved full independence outside the French Community in July 1960 and later signed co-operation agreements with France in economic matters and also in defence in April 1961—except in the case of Upper Volta which declined to sign a defence agreement.

The Council has set up a Mutual Aid and Loan Guarantee Fund through which it promotes economic development in the five member countries. By 1978 it was carrying out a rural development programme covering stock-breeding, food production and water supply, with contributions to its cost being received from France, the Netherlands and the United States. The Council also co-operates with the West African Development Bank, the West African Economic Community (CEAO) and the Economic Community of West African States (ECOWAS).

Organization for the Development of the Senegal River (OMVS)

The OMVS (*Organisation pour la mise en valeur du fleuve Sénégal*) was set up in Nouakchott (Mauritania) on March 12, 1972, by the Governments of Mali, Mauritania and Senegal for the joint economic development of the Senegal River and its tributaries. (This organization superseded an earlier Organization of Riparian States of the River Senegal of which Guinea had also been a member, in addition to the above three countries, and which had been disbanded on Nov. 30, 1971.)

At a conference held in Nouakchott in May 1974, a 40-year development plan was adopted with a proposed investment equivalent to about £1,400 million and involving inter alia the construction of two hydroelectric dams within the first seven years, agricultural development to achieve self-sufficiency in food and the elimination of the risk of drought, the building of 232 factories for the processing of agricultural produce, and the exploitation and processing of iron ore and bauxite in Mali and of iron ore in Senegal.

Liptako-Gourma Integrated Development Authority

This authority was formed in 1972 by Mali, Niger and Upper Volta to foster co-operation in the development of the Liptako-Gourma region (straddling the border between Niger and Upper Volta). The authority's main organ is a Ministerial Council.

West African Economic Community (CEAO)

Headquarters: Ouagadougou (Upper Volta).

Members: The Ivory Coast, Mali, Mauritania, Niger, Senegal and Upper Volta.

Observers: Benin and Togo.

The CEAO (*Communauté Économique de l'Afrique de l'Ouest*) was formally set up in April 1973 and came into effect in January 1974, superseding an earlier West African Customs Union (UDEAO) established on June 3, 1966, by Dahomey (Benin), the Ivory Coast, Mali, Mauritania, Niger, Senegal and Upper Volta and in force since Dec. 15, 1966. An agreement to form the CEAO had been signed in Bamako (Mali) on June 3, 1972.

The supreme organ of the CEAO is its Conference of Heads of State, which meets once a year. The CEAO Council of Ministers meets at least twice a year, and there is also a General Secretariat (with several directorates).

The CEAO is a "zone of organized exchanges" with two unique institutions—(i) a regional co-operation tax designed to encourage exchanges within the community and (ii) a community development fund to finance development projects and to compensate for certain types of trade loss.

At the first summit conference of the

CEAO held in Niamey (Niger) on April 7-8, 1975, the member states' leaders solemnly proclaimed their willingness to co-operate with all heads of state of the region to form a larger West African community.

At the end of the second summit conference, held in Dakar on April 8-9, 1976, it was stated that the regional system of customs co-operation had been applied effectively and that this had strengthened preferential development in trade within the CEAO, and that other proposed developments would include the financing of joint exploitation of mineral resources through the CEAO's development fund (which for 1976 had a budget equivalent to about £5,000,000).

At the third summit conference, held in Abidjan (Ivory Coast) on June 8-9, 1977, the heads of state of the six CEAO member countries and of Togo signed an agreement on non-aggression and mutual assistance among their countries, with a permanent secretariat to be set up in Abidjan for supervising the agreement, which was to be open to accession by other countries in the region. It was also decided to establish a $20,000,000 fund to guarantee loans for development projects, in particular in the land-locked member states (Mali, Niger and Upper Volta), with the Ivory Coast contributing $10,000,000, Senegal $6,000,000 and each of the four other member states $1,000,000.

In January 1978 an agreement was signed on co-operation with the *Conseil de l'Entente* [see above].

At the fourth summit conference, held in Bamako on Oct. 27, 1978, an agreement was signed on the free movement of persons and their right to establish residence within the community.

The fifth summit meeting, held in Nouakchott (Mauritania) on Oct. 19-20, 1979, was mainly concerned with a reorganization of the organization's General Secretariat and the adoption of a *Charter of Regional Co-operation,* but it was also pointed out at the conference that the establishment of CEAO organizations and institutions should be in harmony with those of the Economic Community of West African States (ECOWAS) [see below].

On July 26, 1980, a co-operation agreement was signed in Ouagadougou between the CEAO and the Mano River Union [see below].

At the sixth summit meeting, held in Niamey (Niger) with the participation of Togo, it was decided inter alia to extend the freedom of movement of member countries' nationals; to improve the economic development, and in particular the

water supply, of villages; and to convene a committee on the implementation of the non-aggression and mutual assistance agreement with Togo [see above].

Permanent Inter-State Committee on Drought Control in the Sahel (CILSS)

The CILSS (*Comité Inter-Etats pour la Lutte contre la Sécheresse dans le Sahel*) was set up, with headquarters at Ouagadougou (Upper Volta), on Sept. 12, 1973, by the heads of state of Mali, Mauritania, Niger, Senegal and Upper Volta and a representative of the President of Chad. It was later joined by Cape Verde and The Gambia.

The main organs of the CILSS are a Conference of Heads of State and a Council of Ministers. On Feb. 21, 1974, the UN Secretary-General announced the formation of a special UN Sahel Office to work closely with the CILSS in seeking funds for long-range programmes to save the Sahel countries from the effects of the current drought.

With the help of a Club of the Friends of the Sahel (formed in 1976) a working group was set up in March of that year, and this group subsequently drew up a *Sahel Development Plan* (1978-2000) designed to "enable the Sahel states to achieve food self-sufficiency whatever the climatic hazard" and to lead to "self-sustaining development" in these countries. In April 1977 the CILSS Ministerial Council approved preparatory work for this plan.

Mano River Union

The Mano River Union was established, with its secretariat in Freetown (Sierra Leone), under a declaration which was signed by the Presidents of Liberia and Sierra Leone on Oct. 3, 1973, and which provided for co-operation by the two states between which the Mano River forms part of their common boundary.

The achievements of the Mano River Union include the completion of a new bridge across the Mano River in February 1976, the complete liberalization of bilateral trade by the end of 1976, and the harmonization of the two countries' external customs tariffs by October 1977. Among further projects were the construction of (i) a new highway between the two countries' capitals and (ii) a hydroelectric power dam as part of a Mano River Basin Development Project intended to promote industrial development on both sides of the border.

The 1978-79 budget of the Mano River Union totalled $4,980,000, of which the two governments contributed $3,260,000, while the balance was provided by forestry companies operating in both countries and by external aid.

The Republic of Guinea acceded to the Mano River Union on Oct. 3, 1980.

River Niger Commission

This commission was established in 1974 under an Act of Niamey, and with headquarters in Niamey, to co-ordinate navigation and economic development in the Niger River basin. Its members are Benin, Cameroon, Guinea, the Ivory Coast, Mali, Niger, Nigeria and Upper Volta, and its principal organ is its Council of Ministers.

Gambia River Development Organization

This joint development organization was formed by Senegal and The Gambia in 1975.

Economic Community of West African States (ECOWAS)

Headquarters: Lagos.

Members: Benin, Cape Verde, The Gambia, Ghana, Guinea, Guinea-Bissau, the Ivory Coast, Liberia, Mali, Mauritania, Niger, Nigeria, Senegal, Sierra Leone, Togo and Upper Volta.

ECOWAS (or CEDEAO—*Communauté Économique des États de l'Afrique de l'Ouest*) was established in 1976 under the *Treaty of Lagos* signed on May 26 of that year by the heads of state of 15 West African countries (i.e. all current member states except Cape Verde, which did not join ECOWAS until 1977).

The treaty, drawn up as a result of an initiative by Nigeria and Togo, had first been approved in draft form by a meeting of delegates of the 15 countries held in Monrovia (Liberia) in January 1975. By the end of June 1975 it had been ratified by seven states—the minimum required before it could enter into force, but it did not finally become operative until after a further summit meeting held in Lomé

Map 13 Economic Community of West African States (ECOWAS) and West African Economic Community (CEAO)

(Togo) on Nov. 4-5, 1976, when a number of functional protocols were signed.

The treaty's principal objectives, which were to be achieved in stages, were the ending of customs duties and other restrictions on trade between member states; the establishment of a common external customs tariff and commercial policy; and the "harmonization of the economic and industrial policies of member states and the elimination of the disparities in the level of development of member states". The treaty called for the abolition of obstacles to the free movement of people, services and capital, the harmonization of agricultural policies, and the promotion of joint development projects, particularly in the spheres of agriculture (including "agro-industrial" enterprises), transport, communications and energy. Provision was made for the establishment of a community fund for "co-operation, compensation and development", and attention was drawn to the desirability of the harmonization of member states' monetary policies.

The treaty included a timetable for the abolition of barriers to intra-community trade and for the harmonization of external tariffs—the former objective to be fully achieved within 10 years and the latter within 15 years—and proposed that the first step towards the harmonization of economic policy should take the form of a full exchange of information on planned development projects, leading wherever possible to the joint financing of research and feasibility studies.

The principal institutions of the community would be (i) a Supreme Authority of Heads of State, with a rotating chairmanship, to meet at least once a year; (ii) a Council of Ministers, with two representatives from each member state and also with a rotating chairmanship, to meet at least twice a year; (iii) an Executive Secretariat, headed by an executive secretary appointed for a four-year period; (iv) a minimum of four specialized commissions dealing with different aspects of co-operation; and (v) a Community Tribunal which would ensure "the observance of law and justice", would interpret the provisions of the treaty and would settle disputes referred to it.

The treaty also provided that ECOWAS members could belong to other regional or subregional organizations (such as the *Communauté Economique de l'Afrique de l'Ouest*—CEAO), where such membership did "not abrogate from the provisions of the treaty".

At the Lomé summit meeting it was decided that the community's Fund for Co-operation, Compensation and Development (FCCD) should be based in Lomé; that the first Executive Secretary of ECOWAS should come from the Ivory Coast; and that the first managing director of the FCCD should come from Liberia.

It was also agreed that common tariff treatment should be accorded to goods wholly produced by enterprises with headquarters in the community, being at least 51 per cent locally controlled in terms of equity capital and having at least 50 per cent local representation on their boards of directors.

A Trade, Customs, Immigration, Monetary and Payments Commission of ECOWAS was inaugurated in April 1978.

At the third ECOWAS summit meeting, held in Lagos on April 21-22, 1978, it was agreed that as from May 28, 1979, member states should not increase their customs tariffs on goods originating within the community (as a first step towards the elimination of all internal tariff barriers).

The meeting also approved a protocol on non-aggression (which had been discussed by the ECOWAS Council of Ministers in November 1977), under which the heads of state undertook inter alia to refrain from attacking each other and to recognize as definitive the present borders of their territories.

Immediately after the meeting an agreement was signed by Guinea and Nigeria, providing for commercial, agricultural and industrial co-operation between the two countries.

By May 1978 the FCCD had a capital of $20,000,000, of which $6,700,000 had been contributed by Nigeria (by far the strongest partner in ECOWAS).

The fourth ECOWAS summit meeting was held in Dakar on May 28-29, 1979, when it was decided inter alia to set up a commission to study problems connected with mutual defence assistance.

At the fifth ECOWAS summit meeting, held in Lomé on May 27-28, 1980, it was decided that a free trade area for the member states' raw materials (i.e. unprocessed goods) should be established from May 28, 1981, while for the reduction of tariffs on industrial products an eight-year plan was adopted.

The meeting also approved a protocol on the free movement of persons, to come into force after ratification by at least seven member states. (By the end of July 1980 it had been ratified by eight—The Gambia, Ghana, Guinea, Liberia, Niger, Nigeria, Senegal and Togo.) The protocol's provisions, to be implemented over a 15-year period, laid down that in the first stage (which took immediate effect) an ECOWAS citizen had the right to visit any member state other than his own for up to 90 days without visa; in the second stage he would obtain the right of residence; and in the third stage he would have the right to establish a business in another member country.

No consensus was, however, reached at the meeting on a mutual defence agreement as earlier advocated by Senegal and Togo.

Southern Africa

Southern African Development Co-ordination Conference

At a meeting of heads of state and government held in Lusaka (Zambia) on April 1-2, 1980, and attended by leaders from Angola, Botswana, Lesotho, Malawi, Mozambique, Swaziland, Tanzania, Zambia and Zimbabwe, the participants adopted a Lusaka declaration on economic liberation and a programme of action designed to achieve the liberation.

The declaration defined a strategy for closer integration of the nine countries' economies in order to accelerate their development and to reduce their economic dependence on the Republic of South Africa.

The programme of action included proposals for the creation of a southern African transport and communications commission based in Maputo; measures to control foot-and-mouth disease in cattle throughout the region (for which Botswana would be responsible); the preparation of a food security plan for the region (by Zimbabwe); the establishment of a regional agricultural research centre specializing in drought-prone areas; plans for the harmonization of industrialization (to be prepared by Tanzania) and of energy policies (for which Angola would be responsible); sharing of national training facilities within the region (with Swaziland making recommendations in this respect); and studies leading to proposals for the establishment of a southern African development fund (to be undertaken by Zambia).

A first Southern African Development Co-ordination Conference had been held in Arusha (Tanzania) on July 3-4, 1979, and had been attended by ministers from Angola, Botswana, Mozambique, Tanzania and Zambia as well as by representatives of nine Western potential donor countries (Belgium, Canada, Denmark, the Federal Republic of Germany, the Netherlands, Norway, Sweden, the United Kingdom and the United States) and six international organizations. This conference had prepared a draft declaration on "Southern Africa—towards Economic Liberation".

Following the Lusaka meeting of heads of state and government [see above] a second Southern Africa Development Co-ordination Conference was held by the nine states in Maputo (Mozambique) on Nov. 27-28, 1980, to discuss development projects with representatives of potential donor countries and of 17 international organizations.

The conference considered a list of 97 projects estimated to cost a total of $2,000 million, mainly for the improvement of railways, roads, ports and telecommunications, with over 40 per cent of the total to be devoted to railway improvements and port developments in Mozambique. Aid pledged by donors amounted to $650,000,000 over five years, including $380,000,000 from the African Development Bank, $100,000,000 from the European Communities and $50,000,000 from Italy. (It was pointed out by the European Commissioner responsible for development co-operation policy that Community funds provided within the context of the Lomé Convention could not be spent in Angola or Mozambique as they were not signatories of the convention.)

Bilateral Co-operation involving African Countries

Treaties and Agreements between African States*

Angola and Cape Verde. A co-operation agreement between the two countries was signed in Luanda (Angola) on Dec. 15, 1976.

Angola, Mozambique, Tanzania and Zambia. An agreement announced on Nov. 20, 1976 provided for a joint defence strategy against an external attack on any one or several of these four states.

Angola, Zaïre and Zambia. A trilateral non-aggression pact was signed at Ndola (Zambia) on Oct. 12, 1979, by the Presidents of Angola, Zaïre and Zambia. Under this agreement the three Presidents undertook to end any support which they had given to one another's political opponents, and they also declared their readiness to co-operate with each other, especially in the field of transport.

Angola and Zambia. (1) Framework agreements on co-operation between the two countries were signed by their Presidents on Oct. 17, 1978, when relations between them were normalized and they undertook to respect the UN and OAU Charters and the principles of non-aggression, non-interference and respect for each other's territorial integrity.

(2) On May 10, 1979, the Presidents of the two countries agreed at a meeting in Ndola (Zambia) to regard an attack on one of them as an attack on both and to set up a joint security force to repel incursions (from Rhodesia or South Africa).

Cameroon and Ivory Coast. A treaty

---

* For agreements of francophone countries in Africa, see pages 280-82; for agreements of Arab countries in Africa, see pages 344-48; for agreements between African and Communist states, see pages 213-14 and 218-20.

of friendship and co-operation for development of mutual relations was signed during a visit to Cameroon by the President of the Ivory Coast on Feb. 24-March 4, 1978.

Central African Republic and Equatorial Guinea. A 10-year treaty of friendship and co-operation was signed on Jan. 24, 1975.

Central African Republic and Senegal. A 10-year treaty of friendship and co-operation was signed on March 24, 1975.

Egypt and Chad. A treaty of friendship between Egypt and Chad was signed on Feb. 22, 1973.

Egypt and Zaïre. A technical military co-operation agreement was on Feb. 7, 1980, reported to have been signed between the two countries.

Ethiopia and Kenya. (1) A defence agreement, providing for mutual aid in the case of attack by a third party, was concluded between Ethiopia and Kenya in November 1963 and ratified by both countries on Dec. 27, 1963.

(2) A treaty delimiting the entire frontier between both countries was signed in Nairobi on June 9, 1970.

(3) A treaty of friendship and co-operation was signed in Addis Ababa on Jan. 31, 1979, for a period of 10 years and for a further five years thereafter unless one year's notice was given by either party. The treaty contained a reference to the parties' "unwavering opposition to any country or countries which pursue an expansionist policy" (Art. 5) and also stated that they would "continue their co-operation in the political, diplomatic and military fields" and "meet for consultation from time to time" (Art. 6). The treaty also dealt with co-operation in various other fields and envisaged the conclusion of additional agreements on matters of common interest.

The Gambia and Senegal. Agreements concluded upon The Gambia's achievement of independence on Feb. 17, 1965, provided for co-operation between the two countries in foreign affairs, defence and economic matters, and under a treaty of association signed during a visit to The Gambia by the President of Senegal on April 17-20, 1967, a permanent ministerial inter-state committee with an executive secretariat was created.

Guinea and Ivory Coast. A treaty of friendship and co-operation was signed on April 14, 1978.

Guinea and Liberia. A non-aggression and mutual defence treaty was concluded in Monrovia on Jan. 23, 1979.

Guinea and Morocco. Several agreements on economic, scientific, cultural and technical co-operation were signed in Rabat in January 1979, when the heads of state of the two countries agreed to work for the elimination of tension and the installation of détente in the region.

Guinea and Senegal. A treaty of friendship and co-operation was signed on April 14, 1978.

Guinea and Sierra Leone. Under a defence agreement signed on March 26, 1971, Guinean troops were temporarily sent to Sierra Leone to prevent the latter country's Government from being overthrown.

Guinea-Bissau and Algeria. An economic and commercial co-operation agreement was signed in April 1975.

Guinea-Bissau and Republic of Guinea. A treaty of co-operation and friendship was signed in Conakry on Aug. 6, 1974.

Guinea-Bissau and Senegal. A treaty of friendship and co-operation signed in Dakar was ratified by the National Assembly of Senegal on July 4, 1974. A series of 11 co-operation agreements was signed in Bissau on Jan. 8, 1975.

Ivory Coast and Senegal. A treaty of friendship and co-operation between the Ivory Coast and Senegal was signed in Abidjan on Dec. 15, 1971, together with an agreement on the establishment of a joint co-operation commission.

Kenya and Somalia. Under a memorandum of agreement signed at Arusha (Tanzania) on Oct. 28, 1967, Kenya and Somalia agreed to end border fighting (which had been in progress for many months), to restore normal relations, gradually to suspend emergency regulations in force on both sides, and to cease hostile propaganda.

Madagascar and Tanzania. Bilateral agreements signed on June 22, 1973, provided for commercial and cultural links between the two countries.

Mali and Upper Volta. Under an agreement concluded on June 18, 1975, a border dispute between the two countries was settled, and on July 11, 1975, the two countries' Presidents signed a further agreement in which they undertook "definitely to renounce the use of force" in any dispute between them.

Nigeria and Chad. A treaty of friendship, co-operation and mutual assistance, together with an extradition treaty and an agreement on cultural relations, was initialled on Dec. 11, 1972.

Nigeria and Guinea. (1) An agreement on economic, scientific and technical co-operation was signed in Conakry on Feb. 14, 1973.

(2) An agreement on commercial, agricultural and industrial co-operation was signed in Lagos in April 1978.

Nigeria and Mali. A treaty of friendship, co-operation and mutual assistance was signed by the heads of state of Nigeria and Mali on March 3, 1973. It was agreed that a joint commission should be set up to plan for increased co-operation between the two countries. Agreement was also reached on cultural co-operation, a convention on the free movement of persons and goods and the expansion of an existing trade agreement.

South Africa and Mozambique. A railway co-operation agreement was signed on Feb. 26, 1979 (superseding an earlier agreement between Portugal and South Africa), providing for mutual assistance in operating the railway line to and from the ports of Maputo and Matola in Mozambique.

Sudan and Uganda. A mutual defence agreement between the Sudan and Uganda, providing for military aid against aggression by any external enemies, was signed in Khartoum on June 28, 1972.

Tanzania and Mozambique. (1) In an agreement signed in Maputo on Sept. 7, 1975, the heads of state of the two countries agreed on a broad basis of co-operation both ideologically and in the economic fields, with the economies of the two countries to be made complementary while accelerating their development.

(2) New political, military and economic agreements between the two countries were signed in December 1976.

Tanzania and Zimbabwe. Among several agreements signed in Salisbury (Zimbabwe) on Dec. 5, 1980, were a friendship and co-operation agreement and an agreement on economic, technical and scientific co-operation.

Zaïre, Burundi and Rwanda. A mutual security pact between the three countries was signed in Kinshasa on Aug. 30, 1966, and this agreement was reaffirmed on June 12, 1974, when additional provisions were agreed—inter alia on identical treatment of persons declared undesirable in any one of the three countries and on the settlement of refugees (at least 150 kilo-

metres from the border of their country of origin). (For formation of Economic Community of the Great Lakes' Countries, see above.)

Zimbabwe and Mozambique. (1) An agreement was reached on May 23, 1980, on joint military action against armed rebels opposed to the Government of Mozambique.

(2) During a visit to Zimbabwe by the President of Mozambique on Aug. 4-9, 1980, a total of eight agreements were signed on co-operation in the fields of information, tourism, telecommunications, aviation, land transport, energy, trade and banking.

Treaties and Agreements of African States with Non-African Countries*

Treaties and agreements concluded by African states with states outside the continent included the following:

Ethiopia and People's Democratic Republic of Yemen. A 15-year treaty of friendship and co-operation between the two countries was signed on Dec. 2, 1979, together with a six-year "action programme" which would "further strengthen economic, scientific and technical co-operation".

In the treaty the two sides undertook inter alia to work together to "strengthen the unity of the non-aligned movement" (of which they were both members); to continue their efforts to bring about the establishment of a new international economic order; and not to "enter into military alliances or other alliances . . . , join any blocs of states or engage in any actions or measures directed against the other".

On Jan. 17, 1980, the two countries signed a protocol expressing their intention to "continue their co-operation in the political, economic, military and other fields".

Guinea and France. Following the normalization (on July 14, 1975) of relations between France and Guinea (which had been severed in 1958 when Guinea had opted for complete independence outside the French Community), an agreement was concluded in Paris on Jan. 27, 1977, on the final settlement of financial relations between the two countries, entailing the promotion of economic co-operation between them.

---

* For agreements of francophone countries in Africa, see pages 280-82; for agreements of Arab countries in Africa, see pages 344-48; for agreements between African and Communist states, see pages 213-14 and 218-20.

Zaïre and Belgium. A general co-operation agreement was signed between the two countries in Kinshasa on March 28, 1976, together with protocols on economic, technical, scientific and industrial co-operation. At Zaïre's request Belgium later supplied that country with military aid, notably in March 1977 and in May 1978. The President of Zaïre stated in March 1979 that under existing agreements Belgium would train 3,000 Zaïrean infantrymen.

Zaïre and France. A military co-operation agreement signed in May 1974 was not given final approval by the French National Assembly until Nov. 22, 1978. France subsequently rendered military assistance to Zaïre, in particular by providing transport for Moroccan troops in April 1977 and by sending troops and assisting in the dispatch to Zaïre of an African peace-keeping force in May-June 1978. In 1979 France was to train 3,000 Zaïrean paratroopers.

Zaïre and United States. At the request of the Government of Zaïre the USA supplied, in March 1977, limited military assistance to that Government (threatened by an invasion of opponents from Angola) and again in May 1979. US military aid to Zaïre was worth $30,200,000 in 1976-77 and $32,500,000 in 1977-78 (in addition to economic and food aid).

Agreements between Portugal and its Former African Territories

Former Portuguese territories in Africa have concluded agreements with Portugal as follows:

Angola. A three-year agreement on friendship and co-operation was signed in Guinea-Bissau on June 26, 1978; it provided inter alia for technical, economic, financial, educational and cultural exchanges. In a joint communiqué issued at the same time the two heads of state undertook to promote the mutual rapprochement between their countries and to prevent acts of hostility against each other. A trade agreement was signed in Luanda on Jan. 22, 1979.

Cape Verde. A friendship and co-operation agreement was signed on July 5, 1975.

Guinea-Bissau. During a visit to Lisbon by the President of Guinea-Bissau in January 1978 trade, military assistance and technical agreements were signed as well as a treaty granting Portugal preferential fishing rights in Guinea-Bissau's coastal waters.

Mozambique. A treaty on general co-operation, inter alia in the economic, scientific and technological fields, was concluded in October 1975.

São Tomé and Príncipe. Four co-operation agreements (on trade, shipping, emigration and culture) were signed in São Tomé in July 1978. On April 20, 1979, instruments of ratification were exchanged in Lisbon in respect of an agreement on friendship and co-operation and other agreements on scientific, technical and judicial matters, while both countries granted each other most-favoured-nation treatment in trade.

Groupings in Africa
DEPENDENT TERRITORIES
France

French Overseas Department: Réunion.
Territory with special status as a *"collectivité territoriale"*: Mayotte.

South Africa

(1) Namibia (South West Africa), administered by the Government of South Africa as an integral part of the Republic of South Africa under a mandate granted by the League of Nations in 1919. The UN General Assembly decided on Oct. 27, 1966, to terminate South Africa's mandate and to take steps to establish an interim administration to prepare the territory for complete independence.

(2) The following territories (Black "homelands") have, in varying degrees, been granted internal self-government by South Africa: Ciskei, Gazankulu, KaNgwane, KwaZulu, Lebowa, Ndebele and Qwaqwa.

Spain

The towns of Ceuta and Melilla on the North African coast are integral parts of Spain.

United Kingdom

Colonies: British Indian Ocean Territories; St Helena and dependencies (Ascension Island and Tristan da Cunha).

INDEPENDENT COUNTRIES

The independent countries of Africa and their major international links are shown in the table on the facing page.

Three additional countries whose independence is not internationally recognized except by the Republic of South Africa and mutually among themselves are Bophuthatswana, Transkei and Venda, all former Black "homelands" within South Africa.

Among 66 treaties concluded by South Africa with Bophuthatswana, signed on Nov. 15, 1977, and in force since Dec. 6, 1977, is a non-aggression pact between the two countries.

An earlier non-aggression pact between South Africa and Transkei, which had come into force on the latter's achievement of "independence" on Oct. 26, 1976, was abrogated by Transkei on May 10, 1978.

Independent Countries

	OAU	Commonwealth	OCAM	Conseil de l'Entente	Defence Pact with France	West African Monetary Union	Central African Customs Union	West African Economic Community	ECOWAS	Associate of EEC	Arab League	Maghreb Permanent Consultative Committee
Algeria	X									X	X	X
Angola	X											
Benin	X		X	X		X			X	X		
Botswana	X	X								X		
Burundi	X									X		
Cameroon	X				X		X			X		
Cape Verde	X								X	X		
Central African Republic	X		X		X		X			X		
Chad	X				X					X		
Comoros	X									X		
Congo	X				X		X			X		
Djibouti	X				X					X	X	
Egypt	X										S	
Equatorial Guinea	X									X		
Ethiopia	X									X		
Gabon	X				X		X			X		
The Gambia	X	X							X	X		
Ghana	X	X							X	X		
Guinea	X								X	X		
Guinea-Bissau	X								X	X		
Ivory Coast	X		X	X	X	X		X	X	X		
Kenya	X	X								X		
Lesotho	X	X								X		
Liberia	X								X	X		
Libya	X									X	X	X
Madagascar	X									X		
Malawi	X	X								X		
Mali	X							X	X	X		
Mauritania	X							X	X	X	X	
Mauritius	X	X	X							X		
Morocco	X									X	X	X
Mozambique	X											
Niger	X		X	X	X	X		X	X	X		
Nigeria	X	X							X	X		
Rwanda	X		X							X		
São Tomé and Príncipe	X									X		
Senegal	X		X		X	X		X	X	X		
Seychelles	X	X	X							X		
Sierra Leone	X	X							X	X		
Somalia	X									X	X	
South Africa												
Sudan	X									X	X	
Swaziland	X	X								X		
Tanzania	X	X								X		
Togo	X		X	X	X	X			X	X	X	
Tunisia	X									X	X	X
Uganda	X	X								X		
Upper Volta	X		X	X		X		X	X	X	X	
Zaïre	X									X	X	
Zambia	X	X								X		
Zimbabwe	X	X								X		

S = Suspended.

18. South-East Asia and the Pacific Area

This section deals with (i) defence and security agreements of the South-East Asia and Pacific area; (ii) bilateral mutual defence treaties and other agreements concluded by the United States; (iii) intergovernmental organizations and institutions of the region; and (iv) other major agreements concluded by states of the region.

Regional Defence and Security Agreements

Australian-New Zealand Agreement (ANZAC)

After a conference held in January 1944 in Canberra between Australia and New Zealand to discuss their common interests, and in particular joint policy regarding the South-West Pacific region, a joint declaration, the Australian-New Zealand Agreement, 1944 (ANZAC), was signed on Jan. 21.

The two governments agreed that a "regional zone of defence comprising the South-West and South Pacific areas shall be established and that this zone should be based on Australia and New Zealand, stretching through the arch of islands north and north-east of Australia to Western Samoa and the Cook Islands".

In regard to dependent territories, the two governments declared that "the interim administration and ultimate disposal of enemy territories in the Pacific is of vital importance to Australia and New Zealand and that any such disposal should be effected only with their agreement and as part of a general Pacific agreement", and that "no change in the sovereignty . . . of any of the islands of the Pacific should be effected except as the result of an agreement to which they are parties".

In implementation of a further decision of the ANZAC Agreement, a South Pacific Commission was set up on Feb. 6, 1947 [see below].

ANZUS Pact

A tripartite security treaty between Australia, New Zealand and the United States was signed on Sept. 1, 1951, in San Francisco, and came into force on April 29, 1952. The treaty is known as the Pacific Security Treaty or, more usually, the ANZUS Pact. The latter name derives from the initials of the three signatory countries.

The possibility of a pact between Australia, New Zealand and the United States had been discussed in February 1951, when the US President's adviser on foreign affairs, John Foster Dulles, visited the Australian and New Zealand capitals. On April 18, 1951, President Truman announced from Washington that the Australian and New Zealand Governments, in view of the impending re-establishment of peace with Japan (the Japanese peace treaty was signed on Sept. 8, 1951), had suggested to the United States an arrangement between the three countries which would "make it clear that no one of the three would be indifferent to an armed attack upon the others in the Pacific", and which would "establish consultation to strengthen security on the basis of continuous and effective self-help and mutual aid".

THE TREATY

The text of the Pacific Security Treaty was released on July 12, 1951. The preamble ran as follows:

"The parties to this treaty:

"reaffirming their faith in the purposes and principles of the UN Charter and their desire to live in peace with all peoples and governments, and desiring to strengthen the fabric of peace in the Pacific area;

"noting that the United States has already arrangements pursuant to which its armed forces are stationed in the Philippines, and has armed forces and administrative responsibilities in the Ryukyus, and, upon the coming into force of the Japanese peace treaty, may also station armed forces in and about Japan to assist in the preservation of peace and security in the Japan area;

"recognizing that Australia and New Zealand, as members of the British Commonwealth of Nations, have military obligations outside as well as within the Pacific area;

"desiring to declare publicly and formally their sense of unity, so that no potential aggressor could be under the illusion that any of them stand alone in the Pacific area; and

"desiring further to co-ordinate their efforts for

collective defence for the preservation of peace and security pending the development of a more comprehensive system of regional security in the Pacific area; "declare and agree as follows . . .".

The terms of the treaty were contained in 11 articles summarized below:

Art. 1. The parties undertook, in conformity with the UN Charter, to settle by peaceful means any international disputes in which they might be involved, and to refrain in their international relations from the use of force in any manner inconsistent with the purposes of the United Nations.

Art. 2. In order more effectively to achieve the objectives of the treaty, the parties would maintain and develop their individual and collective capacity to resist armed attack "by means of continuous self-help and mutual aid".

Art. 3. The parties would consult together when, in the opinion of any one of them, the territorial integrity, political independence or security of any of them was threatened in the Pacific.

Art. 4. "Each party recognizes that an armed attack in the Pacific area on any of the other parties would be dangerous to its own peace and safety, and declares that it would act to meet the common danger in accordance with its constitutional processes." Any such attack, and all measures taken as a result of such attack, would be reported to the UN Security Council. Such measures would be terminated when the Security Council had taken the necessary steps to restore and maintain international peace and security.

Art. 5. For the purpose of Art. 4, an armed attack on any of the three countries would be deemed to include "an armed attack on the metropolitan territory of any of the parties, or on the island territories under its jurisdiction in the Pacific, or on its armed forces, vessels or aircraft in the Pacific".

Art. 6. The treaty would not affect the rights and obligations of the three countries under the UN Charter, or the responsibility of the United Nations for the maintenance of international peace and security.

Art. 7. The three countries would establish a Council, consisting of their Foreign Ministers or deputies, to consider matters concerning the implementation of the treaty. The Council would be organized so as to be able to meet at any time.

Art. 8. Pending the development of a more comprehensive regional security system in the Pacific, and the development by the United Nations of more effective means to maintain international peace and security, the Council, established under Art. 7, would maintain a consultative relationship with states, regional organizations, associations of states, and other authorities in the Pacific area which were in a position to further the purpose of the treaty and contribute to the security of the area.

Art. 9. The treaty would be ratified by the three countries in accordance with their respective constitutional processes. Instruments of ratification would be deposited with the Australian Government, and the treaty would enter into force as soon as the ratifications of the signatories had been deposited.

Art. 10. The treaty would remain in force indefinitely. Any party to the treaty could cease to be a member of the Council established under Art. 7 one year after notification to the Australian Government.

Art. 11. The treaty, drawn up in the English language, would be deposited in the archives of the Australian Government, which would make copies available to the other signatories.

ORGANIZATION

The Pacific Council. The organ of the ANZUS pact is the Council—known as the Pacific Council—set up under Article 7 of the treaty. It is composed of the Foreign Ministers (or their deputies) of the signatory powers. The Foreign Ministers generally meet once a year, but special Council meetings, attended by the deputies, are held in Washington more frequently. The Council has no permanent staff or funds.

Military Representatives. At the first meeting of the Pacific Council, held in Honolulu on Aug. 4-6, 1952, it was decided to create a military organization. In this organization each of the three signatory countries is represented by a military officer, who attends Council meetings. The military representatives also hold their own meetings from time to time as required by circumstances. Their function is to advise the Council on military co-operation in the Pacific.

AUSTRALIAN-NEW ZEALAND CONSULTATIVE COMMITTEE

The establishment of an Australian-New Zealand consultative committee on defence co-operation was officially announced on July 27, 1972, after the Prime Minister of New Zealand had stated on June 20 that the two countries would come to each other's defence if either of them was attacked with or without the ANZUS Pact.

ANZUS DECISION ON AFGHANISTAN, 1980

Following the Soviet Union's military intervention in Afghanistan in December 1979, it was agreed at a meeting of the UN Secretary of State and the Foreign Ministers of Australia and New Zealand on Feb. 27-28, 1980, to support "the restoration of a truly non-aligned and neutral government in Afghanistan, responsive to the wishes of the Afghan people". It was also agreed that Australia would deploy an aircraft carrier and a task force in the Indian Ocean; that New Zealand would provide air and naval support; and that the USA would increase maritime surveillance, anti-submarine patrolling and military aid to countries in the region.

Australia-New Zealand Free Trade Area

An agreement was signed in Wellington on Aug. 31, 1965, by Australia and New Zealand on the establishment of a limited free trade area. The agreement, covering commodities accounting for some 60 per cent of the value of trade between the two countries, and including forestry and dairy products, was to remain in force for a period of 10 years as from Jan. 1, 1966, and it was extended under an agreement of June 30, 1977.

South-East Asia Collective Defence Treaty

A South-East Asia Collective Defence Treaty was signed in Manila on Sept. 8, 1954, and came into force on Feb. 9, 1955. The treaty was concluded by the Governments of Australia, France, New Zealand, Pakistan, the Philippines, Thailand, the United Kingdom and the United States, which also agreed on the establishment of a South-East Asia Treaty Organization (SEATO) to be headed by the Council provided for in Art. 5 of the treaty [see below]. This organization was, however, dissolved on June 30, 1977, Pakistan having left it in 1972 and France having withdrawn its financial contribution to it in 1974 after ceasing its participation in the organization's military activities in 1967; moreover, the United States as well as the Philippines and Thailand had improved their relations with the People's Republic of China.

The treaty nevertheless remained in force. It was accompanied by (i) a unilateral US declaration in the form of an "understanding" that the pact was directed against communist aggression; (ii) a protocol on Indo-China; and (iii) the "Pacific Charter", a general statement of principles, signed by all the eight contracting parties.

The texts of these documents are given below.

(1) The South-East Asia Collective Defence Treaty

Preamble

"The parties to this treaty: recognizing the sovereign equality of all the parties; retaining their faith in the purposes and principles set forth in the UN Charter, and their desire to live in peace with all peoples and governments; reaffirming that, in accordance with the UN Charter, they uphold the principle of equal rights and self-determination of peoples; declaring that they will earnestly strive by every peaceful means to promote self-government and to secure the independence of all countries whose peoples desire and are able to undertake its responsibilities; intending to declare publicly and formally their sense of unity so that any potential aggressor will appreciate that the parties stand together in the area; and desiring further to co-ordinate their efforts for collective defence for the preservation of peace and security, have agreed as follows:

Articles

"**Art. 1.** The parties undertake, as set forth in the UN Charter, to settle any international disputes in which they may be involved by peaceful means in such a manner that international peace, security and justice are not endangered, and to refrain in their interna-

tional relations from the threat or use of force in any manner inconsistent with the purpose of the United Nations.

"**Art. 2.** In order more effectively to achieve the objectives of this treaty, the parties, separately and jointly, by means of continuous and effective self-help and mutual aid, will maintain and develop their individual and collective capacity to resist armed attack and to prevent and counter subversive acts from without against their territorial integrity and political stability.

"**Art. 3.** The parties undertake to strengthen their free institutions and to co-operate with one another in the further development of economic measures, including technical assistance, designed both to promote economic progress and social well-being and to further the individual and collective efforts of governments towards these ends.

"**Art. 4.** (1) Each party recognizes that aggression by means of armed attack in the treaty area against any of the parties, or against any state or territory which the parties by unanimous agreement may hereafter designate, would endanger its own peace and safety, and agrees that it will, in that event, act to meet the common danger in accordance with its constitutional processes. Measures taken under this paragraph shall be immediately reported to the UN Security Council.

(2) If, in the opinion of any of the parties, the inviolability or integrity of the territory or the sovereignty or political independence of any party in the treaty area, or of any other state or territory to which the provisions of Paragraph (1) of this article from time to time apply, is threatened in any way other than by armed attack, or is affected or threatened by any fact or situation which might endanger the peace of the area, the parties shall consult immediately in order to agree on the measures which should be taken for the common defence.

(3) It is understood that no action on the territory of any state designated by unanimous agreement under Paragraph (1) of this article, or on any territory so designated, shall be taken except at the invitation or with the consent of the government concerned.

"**Art. 5.** The parties hereby establish a Council, on which each of them shall be represented, to consider matters concerning the implementation of this treaty. The Council shall provide for consultation with regard to military and any other planning as the situation obtaining in the treaty area may from time to time require. The Council shall be organized so as to be able to meet at any time.

"**Art. 6.** This treaty does not affect, and shall not be interpreted as affecting in any way, the rights and obligations of any of the parties under the UN Charter or the responsibility of the United Nations for the maintenance of international peace and security. Each party declares that none of the international engagements now in force between it and any other of the parties, or any third party, is in conflict with the provisions of this treaty, and undertakes not to enter into any international engagement in conflict with the treaty.

"**Art. 7.** Any other state in a position to further the objectives of this treaty and to contribute to the security of the area may, by unanimous agreement of the parties, be invited to accede to this treaty. Any state so invited may become a party to the treaty by depositing its instrument of accession with the Philippine Government.

"**Art. 8.** The treaty area is the general area of South-East Asia, including also the entire territories of the Asian parties, and the general area of the South-West Pacific, not including the Pacific area north of 21 degrees 30 minutes North latitude. The parties may, by unanimous agreement, amend this article to include the territory of any state acceding to this treaty in accordance with Article 7, or otherwise to change the treaty area.

"**Art. 9.** (1) This treaty shall be deposited in the archives of the Philippine Government. Copies thereof shall be transmitted by that Government to the other signatories.

"(2) The treaty shall be ratified and its provisions carried out by the parties in accordance with their respective constitutional processes. Instruments of ratification shall be deposited as soon as possible with the Philippine Government, which shall notify all the the other signatories of such deposit.

"(3) The treaty shall enter into force between the states which have ratified it as soon as the instruments of ratification of a majority of signatories shall have been deposited, and shall come into effect with respect to each other state on the date of deposit of its instrument of ratification.

"**Art. 10.** The treaty shall remain in force indefinitely, but any party may cease to be a party one year after notice of denunciation has been given to the Philippine Government, which shall inform the governments of the other parties of each notice of denunciation.

"**Art. 11.** The English text of this treaty is binding on the parties, but when the parties have agreed to the French text thereof and have so notified the Philippine Government, the French text shall be equally authentic and binding."

(2) US 'Understanding'

"The delegation of the United States of America, in signing the present treaty, does so with the understanding that its recognition of the effect of aggression and armed attack, and its agreement with reference thereto in Article 4, Paragraph (1), apply only to communist aggression, but affirms that in the event of other aggression or armed attack it will consult under the provisions of Article 4."

(3) Protocol on Indo-China

"Designations of states and territory as to which the provisions of Articles 3 and 4 are to be applicable— The parties to the South-East Asia Collective Defence Treaty unanimously designate for the purposes of Article 4 of the treaty the States of Cambodia and Laos and the free territory under the jurisdiction of the State of Vietnam.

"The parties further agree that the above-mentioned states and territory shall be eligible in respect of the economic measures contemplated by Article 3. This protocol shall come into force simultaneously with the coming into force of the treaty."

(4) The Pacific Charter

"The delegates, desiring to establish a firm basis for common action to maintain peace and security in South-East Asia and the South-West Pacific, and convinced that common action to this end, in order to be worthy and effective, must be inspired by the highest principles of justice and liberty, do hereby proclaim:

"(1) In accordance with the provisions of the UN Charter, they uphold the principle of equal rights and self-determination of peoples, and will earnestly strive by every peaceful means to promote self-government and to secure the independence of all countries whose peoples desire it and are able to undertake its responsibilities.

"(2) They are each prepared to continue taking effective practical measures to ensure conditions favourable to the orderly achievement of the foregoing purposes in accordance with their constitutional procedures.

"(3) They will continue to co-operate in the economic, social and cultural fields in order to promote higher living standards, economic progress and social well-being in this region.

"(4) As decreed in the South-East Asia Collective Defence Treaty, they are determined to prevent or counter by appropriate means any attempt in the treaty area to subvert freedom or to destroy their sovereignty or territorial integrity."

The Philippine Foreign Minister emphasized on Jan. 24, 1980, that the treaty was "still alive" and that the US President had repeatedly pledged to defend Thailand in case of aggression or invasion under the terms of the treaty.

Bilateral Mutual Defence Treaties of the United States

Basic Content of Treaties

The mutual defence treaties concluded by the USA in the Far East and the Pacific area are all similar in both content and wording. In each, the parties undertake to settle any international dispute in which they may be involved by peaceful means; to consult together at the threat of or in the event of an external armed attack; and to maintain and develop means to deter such an attack. The parties recognize that an armed attack on either would be dangerous to the peace and security of both, and declare their readiness to act to meet the common danger.

The full text of the mutual security treaty between the USA and the Republic of Korea [for further details see below under "USA-Republic of Korea"] is here given as an example:

Preamble

"The parties to this treaty, reaffirming their desire to live in peace with all peoples and governments, and desiring to strengthen the fabric of peace in the Pacific area, to declare publicly and formally their common determination to defend themselves against external armed attack so that no potential aggressor could be under the illusion that either of them stands alone in the Pacific area, and to strengthen their efforts for collective defence for the preservation of peace and security pending the development of a more comprehensive and effective system of regional security in the Pacific area, have agreed as follows:

375

"**Art. 1.** The parties undertake to settle any international disputes in which they may be involved by peaceful means . . . and to refrain in their international relations from the threat or use of force in any manner inconsistent with the purposes of the United Nations, or the obligations assumed by any party towards the United Nations.

"**Art. 2.** The parties will consult together whenever, in the opinion of either of them, the political independence or security of either of the parties is threatened by external armed attack. Separately and jointly, by self-help and mutual aid, the parties will maintain and develop appropriate means to deter armed attack, and will take suitable measures in consultation and agreement to implement this treaty and further its purposes.

"**Art. 3.** Each party recognizes that an armed attack in the Pacific area on either of the parties in territories now under their respective administrative control, or hereafter recognized by one of the parties as lawfully brought under the administrative control of the other, would be dangerous to its own peace and safety, and declares that it would act to meet the common danger in accordance with its constitutional processes.

"**Art. 4.** The Republic of Korea grants, and the United States accepts, the right to dispose US land, air and sea forces in and about the territory of the Republic of Korea as determined by mutual agreement.

"**Art. 5.** This treaty shall be ratified by the Republic of Korea and the United States in accordance with their respective constitutional processes, and will come into force when instruments of ratification have been exchanged.

"**Art. 6.** The treaty shall remain in force indefinitely. Either party may terminate it one year after notice has been given to the other party."

USA-Philippines

The mutual defence treaty between the USA and the Philippines was signed in Washington on Aug. 30, 1951. The treaty, which was intended to reinforce the Pacific security arrangements embodied in the ANZUS pact [see page 372], entered into force on Aug. 27, 1952.

In this treaty it was stated that an armed attack would be deemed to include "an armed attack on the metropolitan territory of either of the parties, or on the island territories under its jurisdiction in the Pacific, or on its armed forces, public vessels or aircraft in the Pacific".

Agreements on Military Bases. On March 14, 1947, an agreement had been signed in Manila by representatives of the USA and the Philippines, providing for the establishment, for a 99-year period, of 23 American military, naval and air bases in the Philippines. Under the agreement, which came into force on March 26, 1947, certain military bases, established before the Philippines' proclamation of independence in July 1946, would be maintained by the USA, while others would pass to the control of the Philippine Government.

In July 1956 the United States affirmed its recognition of the Philippine Govern-

ment's sovereignty over all US bases on Philippine territory. The agreement on military bases was revised by a memorandum signed on Oct. 12, 1959. Among the decisions embodied in the memorandum were the shortening of the leases granted to the USA for military bases from 99 years to 25 years from Oct. 12, 1959, and an agreement that the US Government would consult with the Philippine Government on the operational use of the bases, and before setting up long-range missile sites at American bases.

Under a further agreement signed on Jan. 6, 1979, the USA was allowed continued use of the Clark Field air base and the Subic Bay naval base (as well as two associated facilities) for a further five years and was assured "unhampered military operations involving its forces in the Philippines".

At the same time the principle of Philippine sovereignty over the bases was reaffirmed; Filipino commanders were to be appointed to the bases (which was done on Feb. 16, 1979); the land area of the bases was greatly reduced; and the agreement was to be reviewed every five years. Under the agreement the US Government undertook to exert its "best efforts" to obtain congressional approval for $500,000,000 over the next five years—$300,000,000 in military assistance and sales credits to the Philippines and $200,000,000 in "economic support" assistance—and for granting extra development aid of a further $500,000,000.

USA-Japan

A treaty of mutual co-operation and security between the USA and Japan was signed in Washington on Jan. 19, 1960, and entered into force on June 23, 1960. The treaty, which was concluded after some 18 months of negotiations, replaced the US-Japanese defence pact signed in San Francisco on Sept. 8, 1951.

Under the 1951 treaty the United States had the right to dispose land, air and sea forces in and about Japan, and to use those forces, at the request of the Japanese Government, "to put down large-scale internal riots and disturbances in Japan caused through instigation or intervention by an outside power or powers". The treaty also stated that Japan would not grant, without the prior consent of the United States, any bases, or the right of garrison, or transit of forces, to any third power.

Under the new treaty Japan was no longer treated as the weaker partner, but was placed on an equal footing with the United States.

Treaty Provisions. The most important of the provisions peculiar to this treaty are contained in Articles 2, 6 and 10:

Art. 2. The parties will contribute towards the further development of peaceful and friendly international relations by strengthening their free institutions, bringing about a better understanding of the principles upon which these institutions are founded, and promoting conditions of stability and well-being. They will seek to eliminate conflict in their international economic policies and encourage economic collaboration between them.

Art. 6. For the purpose of contributing to the security of Japan and the maintenance of international peace and security in the Far East, the United States of America is granted the use by its land, air and naval forces of facilities and areas in Japan. The use of these facilities and areas, as well as the status of US armed forces in Japan, shall be governed by a separate agreement, replacing the administrative agreement under Article II of the Security Treaty between the USA and Japan signed at Tokyo on Feb. 28, 1952, on arrangements for the implementation of the 1951 defence pact.

Art. 10. This treaty shall remain in force until, in the opinion of the Governments of the United States and Japan, there shall have come into force such United Nations arrangements as will satisfactorily provide for the maintenance of international peace and security in the Japan area. However, after the treaty has been in force for ten years, either party may give notice to the other party of its intention to terminate the treaty, in which case the treaty shall terminate one year after such notice has been given.

The treaty was clarified by an exchange of notes. In one of the notes the United States agreed to prior consultation with the Japanese Government over (i) any envisaged increase in its forces in Japan; (ii) any essential change in methods of arming and equipping forces (e.g. nuclear weapons); and (iii) the use of Japanese bases for any action outside the treaty area. The treaty area was defined as the territory under Japanese rule at any time. The parties also agreed to consult together in the event of an armed attack or threat of attack against the islands over which Japan claimed residual sovereignty. The principal islands in question were the Ryukyu Islands, the Bonin Islands, Volcano Island and Marcus Island. (For the return of these islands to Japan in 1972 see page 11.)

Subsequent Developments. On the expiry of the first 10 years of the treaty's currency (on which either party could give notice of its intention to terminate the treaty) Japan explicitly, on June 22, 1970, confirmed its intention of continuing to adhere to the treaty.

On Dec. 21, 1970, it was announced that during 1971 the USA would reduce its armed forces personnel to 28,000 and withdraw almost all its combat aircraft from Japan, and on Nov. 30, 1977, the US military authorities returned to Japan the Tachikawa air base (near Tokyo) held by US forces since September 1945.

President Ford of the USA confirmed on Aug. 6, 1975, that the USA would continue to uphold its treaty commitments in Asia and in particular those under the 1960 treaty with Japan "in the event of an armed attack against Japan, whether by nuclear or by conventional forces".

In 1976 a sub-committee for defence co-operation was established in Japan to study "modalities of US-Japanese co-operation, including its military aspects, for the effective attainment of the purposes of the security treaty".

USA-Republic of Korea

The USA-Republic of Korea mutual security treaty was initiated in Seoul on Aug. 8, 1953, shortly after the signing of the armistice at the end of the Korean war. The treaty was formally signed in Washington on Oct. 1, 1953, and entered into force on Nov. 17, 1954. [For the provisions see above.]

1973 Vietnam Peace Agreement

An *Agreement on ending the War and restoring Peace in Vietnam* was signed in Paris on Jan. 27, 1973, by the Foreign Ministers of the USA, North and South Vietnam and the South Vietnamese Provisional Revolutionary Government (PRG). The peace agreement consisted of a preamble and 23 articles under nine chapters, and was accompanied by four protocols dealing in detail with specific matters covered by the agreement.

The salient points of the agreement were as follows:

Chap. I. Article 1 stated: "The United States and all other countries respect the independence, sovereignty, unity and territorial integrity of Vietnam as recognized by the 1954 Geneva Agreements on Vietnam." [These agreements ended the war between France and the *Vietminh* in Indo-China.]

Chap. II. Articles 2 and 3 provided for a ceasefire throughout South Vietnam from midnight on Jan. 27, 1973, and the cessation of all United States military activities against North Vietnam at the same time. The ceasefire would be "durable and without limit of time".

Article 4 stated: "The United States will not continue its military involvement or intervene in the internal affairs of South Vietnam."

Articles 5 and 6 provided for the total withdrawal from South Vietnam of troops, military advisers and personnel, armaments, munitions and war material of the USA and other foreign allies within 60 days of the signing of the agreement, and for the dismantlement of all foreign military bases in South Vietnam.

Chap. III. Article 8 dealt with the return of prisoners of war, which, it was stated, should be "carried out simultaneously with and completed not later than the same day as the troop withdrawal". It also provided for co-operation in the passing of information on military personnel and foreign civilians missing in action and for the locating and care of graves of the dead.

Chap. IV. This chapter covered the exercise of the South Vietnamese people's right to self-determination and contained the following articles:

Art. 9. "The Government of the United States of America and the Government of the Democratic Republic of Vietnam undertake to respect the following principles for the exercise of the South Vietnamese people's right to self-determination:

"(a) The South Vietnamese people's right to self-determination is sacred, inalienable, and shall be respected by all countries.

"(b) The South Vietnamese people shall decide themselves the political future of South Vietnam through genuinely free and democratic general elections under international supervision.

"(c) Foreign countries shall not impose any political tendency or personality on the South Vietnamese people.

Art. 10. "The two South Vietnamese parties undertake to respect the ceasefire and maintain peace in South Vietnam, settle all matters of contention through negotiations, and avoid all armed conflict.

Art. 11. "Immediately after the ceasefire, the two South Vietnamese parties will:

"Achieve national reconciliation and concord, end hatred and enmity, prohibit all acts of reprisal and discrimination against individuals or organizations that have collaborated with one side or the other;

"ensure the democratic liberties of the people: personal freedom, freedom of speech, freedom of the press, freedom of meeting, freedom of organization, freedom of belief, freedom of movement, freedom of residence, freedom of work, right to property ownership, and right to free enterprise.

Art. 12. "(a) Immediately after the ceasefire, the two South Vietnamese parties shall hold consultations in a spirit of national reconciliation and concord, mutual respect and mutual non-elimination to set up a National Council of National Reconciliation and Concord of three equal segments.

"The council shall operate on the principle of unanimity. After the National Council of National Reconciliation and Concord has assumed its functions, the two South Vietnamese parties will consult about the formation of councils at lower levels.

"The two South Vietnamese parties shall sign an agreement on the internal matters of South Vietnam as soon as possible and do their utmost to accomplish this within 90 days after the ceasefire comes into effect, in keeping with the South Vietnamese people's aspirations for peace, independence and democracy.

"(b) The National Council of National Reconciliation and Concord shall have the task of promoting the two South Vietnamese parties' implementation of this agreement, achievement of national reconciliation and concord and ensurance of democratic liberties.

"The National Council of National Reconciliation and Concord will organize the free and democratic general elections provided for in Article 9 (b) and decide the procedures and modalities of these general elections.

"The institutions for which the general elections are to be held will be agreed upon through consultations between the two South Vietnamese parties. The National Council of National Reconciliation and Concord will also decide the procedures and modalities of such local elections as the two South Vietnamese parties agree upon.

Art. 13. "The question of Vietnamese armed forces in South Vietnam shall be settled by the two South

Vietnamese parties in a spirit of national reconciliation and concord, equality and mutual respect, without foreign interference, in accordance with the post-war situation.

"Among the questions to be discussed by the two South Vietnamese parties are steps to reduce their military effectives and to demobilize the troops being reduced. The two South Vietnamese parties will accomplish this as soon as possible.

Art. 14. "South Vietnam will pursue a foreign policy of peace and independence. It will be prepared to establish relations with all countries irrespective of their political and social systems on the basis of mutual respect for independence and sovereignty, and accept economic and technical aid from any country with no political conditions attached.

"The acceptance of military aid by South Vietnam in the future shall come under the authority of the Government set up after the general elections in South Vietnam provided for in Article 9 (b)."

Chap. V. Article 15, on the reunification of Vietnam, stated: "The reunification of Vietnam shall be carried out step by step through peaceful means on the basis of discussion and agreements between North and South Vietnam, without coercion or annexation by either part, and without foreign interference. The time for reunification will be agreed upon by North and South Vietnam.

"Pending the reunification:

"(a) The military demarcation line between the two zones at the 17th parallel is only provisional and not a political or territorial boundary, as provided for in Paragraph 6 of the final declaration of the 1954 Geneva conference.

"(b) North and South Vietnam shall respect the demilitarized zone on either side of the provisional military demarcation line.

"(c) North and South Vietnam shall promptly start negotiations with a view to re-establishing normal relations in various fields. Among the questions to be negotiated are the modalities of civilian movement across the provisional military demarcation line.

"(d) North and South Vietnam shall not join any military alliance or military bloc and shall not allow foreign powers to maintain military bases, troops, military advisers and military personnel on their respective territories, as stipulated in the 1954 Geneva Agreements on Vietnam."

Chap. VI. Articles 16 and 17 provided for the setting up of a four-party joint military commission, consisting of representatives of the four signatories of the agreement, and a two-party military commission representing the two South Vietnamese parties. These commissions would implement the provisions of the agreement concerning the ceasefire, the troop withdrawal and dismantlement of bases, and the return of prisoners of war. Under Article 18 an International Commission of Control and Supervision (ICCS) was to be established immediately after signature of the agreement.

Article 19 stated: "The parties agree on the convening of an international conference within 30 days of the signing of this agreement to acknowledge the signed agreements; to guarantee the ending of the war, the maintenance of peace in Vietnam, the respect of the Vietnamese people's fundamental national rights, and the South Vietnamese people's right to self-determination; and to contribute to and guarantee peace in Indo-China.

"The United States and the Democratic Republic of

Vietnam, on behalf of the parties participating in the Paris Conference on Vietnam, will propose to the following parties that they participate in this international conference: The People's Republic of China, the Republic of France, the Union of Soviet Socialist Republics, the United Kingdom, the four countries of the International Commission of Control and Supervision, and the Secretary-General of the United Nations, together with the parties participating in the Paris Conference on Vietnam.''

Chap. VII. Article 20, which was concerned with Cambodia and Laos, stated:

"(a) The parties participating in the Paris Conference on Vietnam shall strictly respect the 1954 Geneva Agreements on Cambodia and the 1962 Geneva Agreement on Laos [see below], which recognized the Cambodian and the Laos people's fundamental national rights, i.e. the independence, sovereignty, unity and territorial integrity of these countries. The parties shall respect the neutrality of Cambodia and Laos.

"The parties participating in the Paris Conference on Vietnam undertake to refrain from using the territory of Cambodia and the territory of Laos to encroach on the sovereignty and security of one another and of other countries.

"(b) Foreign countries shall put an end to all military activities in Cambodia and Laos, totally withdraw from and refrain from reintroducing into these two countries troops, military advisers and military personnel, armaments, munitions and war material.

"(c) The internal affairs of Cambodia and Laos shall be settled by the people of each of these countries without foreign interference.

"(d) The problems existing between the Indo-Chinese countries shall be settled by the Indo-Chinese parties on the basis of respect for each other's independence, sovereignty and territorial integrity and non-interference in each other's internal affairs.''

Chap. VIII. Articles 21 and 22 were concerned with the relationship between the USA and North Vietnam.

Art. 21. "The United States anticipates that this agreement will usher in an era of reconciliation with the Democratic Republic of Vietnam as with all the peoples of Indo-China. In pursuance of its traditional policy, the United States will contribute to healing the wounds of war and to post-war reconstruction of the Democratic Republic of Vietnam and throughout Indo-China.''

Art. 22. "The ending of the war, the restoration of peace in Vietnam, and the strict implementation of this agreement will create conditions for establishing a new, equal and mutually beneficial relationship between the United States and the Democratic Republic of Vietnam on the basis of respect for each other's independence and sovereignty, and non-interference in each other's internal affairs. At the same time, this will ensure stable peace in Vietnam and contribute to the preservation of lasting peace in Indo-China and South-East Asia.''

Chap. IX. Article 23 provided for the immediate entry into force of the agreement after signature.

The four protocols to the agreement covered the ceasefire, the ICCS, the return of prisoners and the destruction of mines in territorial waters (this last being a bilateral agreement between the USA and North Vietnam).

The treaty's provisions were subsequent-

ly implemented only in part. A ceasefire nominally came into force on Jan. 28, 1973, but fighting continued; no agreement was reached in negotiations between the South Vietnamese Government and the PRG; in December 1973 President Nguyen Van Thieu of South Vietnam rejected the holding of elections because the Communists (he said) did "not want to give up their ambition to attack and annex the South''; peace negotiations and the ceasefire machinery broke down in April-June 1974; and in January 1975 North Vietnam and the United States accused each other of having violated the Paris agreement.

The South Vietnamese forces were finally defeated by Communist forces in April 1975; President Thieu resigned on April 21, saying that the United States had failed to honour a secret commitment to react "violently and immediately'' to a North Vietnamese offensive against the South; Communist forces entered the South Vietnamese capital on April 30; and a provisional revolutionary Government was set up there on May 15, 1975. Following the hold of general elections in the whole of Vietnam on April 25, 1976, the country was proclaimed reunified on July 2, 1976, as the Socialist Republic of Vietnam.

1973 Laos Peace Agreement

A peace agreement between the Government of Laos and the *Pathet Lao* was signed on Feb. 21, 1973. It comprised 12 articles, of which the first laid down the general principles on which the future of Laos should be based.

Art. 1. "(a) The desires of the Lao people to safeguard and exercise their cherished fundamental national rights—the independence, sovereignty, unity and territorial integrity of Laos—are inviolable.

"(b) The declaration on the neutrality of Laos of July 9, 1962, and the 1962 Geneva Agreement on Laos [under which the neutrality of Laos was guaranteed] are the correct bases for the Kingdom of Laos' foreign policies of peace, independence and neutrality. The parties concerned in Laos, the United States, Thailand and other foreign countries must strictly respect and implement this agreement. The internal affairs of Laos must be conducted by the Lao people only, without external interference.

"(c) To achieve the supreme objective of restoring peace, consolidating independence, achieving national concord and restoring national unity, and taking into consideration the present reality in Laos, which has two zones separately controlled by the two sides, the internal problems of Laos must be solved in the spirit of national concord and on the basis of equality and mutual respect, free from pressure or annexation by either side.

"(d) To safeguard national independence and sovereignty, achieve national concord and restore national unity, the people's democratic freedoms must be scrupulously observed, which comprise individual freedom, freedom of religion, speech, press, assembly, establishment of political organizations and associations, candidacy and elections, movement and residence, free enterprise, and the right to ownership of private property. All laws, regulations and institutions contrary to these freedoms must be abolished.''

Articles 2 and 3 provided for a ceasefire throughout Laos from midnight on Feb. 22, 1973, with the cessation of foreign military involvement of any kind. Article 4 dealt with the withdrawal of military personnel and the dissolution of military and paramilitary organizations of foreign countries in Laos within 90 days. Article 5 provided for the return of prisoners of war within the same period.

Articles 6-10 contained provisions for political arrangements.

Art. 6. ''Genuinely free and democratic general elections shall be organized to establish the National Assembly and a permanent National Union Government genuinely representing the people of all nationalities in Laos. The procedures and date of the general elections will be discussed and agreed upon by the two sides. Pending the general elections, the two sides shall set up a new Provisional National Union Government and a National Political Consultative Council within 30 days at the latest after the signing of this agreement, to implement the provisions of the agreement and handle state affairs.

Art. 7. ''The new Provisional National Union Government will be composed of representatives of the Vientiane Government and of the Patriotic Forces [*Pathet Lao*], in equal numbers, and two intellectuals who stand for peace, independence, neutrality and democracy, who will be chosen by common agreement by the two sides. The future Prime Minister will not be included in the two equal numbers of representatives of the two parties.''

Art. 8. The National Political Consultative Council will be an organization of national concord and will be composed of representatives of the Vientiane Government and of the Patriotic Forces in equal numbers, as well as a number of personalities who advocate peace, independence, neutrality and democracy, to be chosen by the two sides by common agreement. It will perform its duties in accordance with the principle of unanimity of the two parties. It has the responsibility to consult with and express views to the Provisional National Union Government on major problems relating to domestic and foreign policies; to support and assist the Provisional National Union Government and the two sides in implementing the agreement in order to achieve national concord; to examine and adopt together the laws and regulations for general elections; and to collaborate with the Provisional National Union Government in holding general elections to establish the National Assembly and the permanent National Union Government.''

Article 9 provided for the neutralization of the towns of Luang Prabang and Vientiane, while Article 10 stated:

''(*a*) Pending the establishment of the National Assembly and the permanent National Union Government . . . the two sides will keep the territories under their temporary control, and will endeavour to implement the political programme of the Provisional National Union Government, as agreed upon by both sides.

''(*b*) The two sides will promote the establishment of normal relations between the two zones, and create favourable conditions for the people to move about, make their living, and carry out economic and cultural exchanges with a view to consolidating national concord and bringing about national unification at an early date.

''(*c*) The two parties take note of the declaration of the US Government that it will contribute to healing the wounds of the war and to post-war reconstruction in Indo-China. The Provisional National Union Government will hold discussions with the US Government in connexion with such a contribution regarding Laos.''

Articles 11 and 12 covered the implementation of the agreement, providing for the setting up by the two sides of a Joint Commission for Implementation of the Agreement and the continued activities of the International Commission for Control and Supervision originally set up under the Geneva Agreements of 1954.

The Laotian Government and the *Pathet Lao* on Sept. 14, 1973, signed an agreement implementing the above peace agreement and aimed at bringing about a coalition Government. The agreement provided for the formation of a provisional national government, headed by Prince Souvanna Phouma and with portfolios equally divided between the two sides, and of a national political consultative council to advise the Government; the neutralization of Vientiane and Luang Prabang and the stationing there of troops and police by both sides; the withdrawal of all foreign troops and advisers within 60 days of the formation of the new Government; and the demarcation of the current ceasefire line with a number of specific points where the armies would particularly avoid confrontation.

After such a coalition Government had been formed in April 1974, however, the *Pathet Lao* gradually extended its influence; in June 1975 elections to a new National Assembly were postponed indefinitely; and in December of that year Laos was proclaimed a People's Democratic Republic under a Government headed by the general secretary of the Lao People's Revolutionary (Communist) Party.

Intergovernmental Organizations and Institutions in the Region

Association of South-East Asian Nations (ASEAN)

Headquarters: Jakarta (Indonesia).

Members: Indonesia, Malaysia, Philippines, Singapore, Thailand.

The Foreign Ministers of Indonesia, Malaysia, the Philippines, Singapore and Thailand signed on Aug. 8, 1967, in Bangkok, a declaration on the establishment of an Association of South-East Asian Nations (ASEAN).

In the preamble to the declaration, stress was laid on the importance of increased regional co-operation and of raising the standard of living in the contracting states. The declaration defined the objectives of ASEAN as being to accelerate economic growth, social progress and cultural development in the region through joint endeavours; to promote regional peace and stability through abiding respect for justice and the rule of law in the relationship among countries of the region and adherence to the principles of the UN Charter; and to promote active collaboration and mutual assistance in matters of common interest, in particular for the greater utilization of their agriculture and industries, expansion of their trade and improvement of transportation and communications. The declaration also emphasized that all military bases of foreign powers existed only on a temporary basis and with the express consent of the countries concerned and could not be used for direct or indirect interference in the national independence and freedom of the region's states, or in their normal development.

The organs of ASEAN are its ministerial conference, which is composed of the Foreign Ministers of the five member countries and which meets annually; a standing committee, which meets when necessary between ministerial meetings; and a secretariat established in 1976.

DEVELOPMENT OF ASEAN

On April 18, 1975, the five ASEAN member countries jointly recognized the Government of Cambodia which had assumed power after the fall of Phnom-Penh (Cambodia's capital) to the (communist) *Khmers Rouges* on the previous day.

At a meeting held on May 13-15, 1975, the ASEAN member countries' Foreign Ministers declared that their countries were ready to enter "into friendly and harmonious relations with each nation in Indo-China" and "to co-operate with these countries in the common task of national development", and that differences in social and political systems should not be an obstacle to the development of constructive and mutually beneficial relations. At this meeting the ministers also decided to expand co-operation with the European Communities, Australia and New Zealand, and they signed an agreement for the facilitation of search for ASEAN member countries' ships in distress and the rescue of survivors of ships' accidents.

On Sept. 4, 1975, it was announced that it had been agreed to set up an ASEAN Council of Petroleum (ASCOPE) for co-operation and mutual assistance in developing oil resources in ASEAN member countries.

At a meeting held at Denpasar, Bali (Indonesia), on Feb. 23-24, 1976, the heads of state and government of the ASEAN member countries signed a *Treaty of Amity and Co-operation in South-East Asia* and a *Declaration of Concord.*

The treaty, consisting of 20 articles grouped in five chapters, laid down binding principles of mutual respect for the independence, sovereignty, equality, territorial integrity and national identity of all nations; the right of every state to lead its national existence

Map 14   Association of South-East Asian Nations (ASEAN)

free from external interference, subversion or co-ercion; non-interference in the internal affairs of one another; settlement of differences or disputes by peaceful means (without the threat or use of force); and effective co-operation among the five countries.

Under the heading "Amity" the parties to the treaty undertook to "endeavour to develop and strengthen the traditional, cultural and historical ties of friendship, good-neighbourliness and co-operation which bind them together" and to encourage and facilitate contact among their peoples.

The treaty expressed the determination of the five parties to "promote active co-operation in the economic, social, cultural, technical, scientific and administrative fields as well as in matters of common ideals and aspirations of international peace and stability in the region". To this end the five nations undertook to "maintain regular contacts and consultations . . . on international and regional matters". The treaty further laid down that "no ASEAN nation shall participate in any activity considered a threat to another member's economic and political stability" and that the signatories should "endeavour to strengthen their respective national as well as the regional prosperity and security based on self-reliance, co-operation and solidarity, for a strong and viable community of nations in South-East Asia".

Intra-regional differences were to be settled through direct friendly negotiations, and to facilitate this the five nations would "constitute a High Council comprising a representative at ministerial level" from each nation. This Council would have powers to "recommend or, upon agreement, even itself form a committee of mediation, inquiry or conciliation" to settle disputes which could not be resolved through direct negotiations. (The Council's decisions would, however, require unanimous agreement of the parties in dispute.) Other nations not parties to the dispute might use their good offices for the amicable settlement of differences. The modes of peaceful settlement of disputes contained in Article 33 (1) of the UN Charter were, however, not excluded.

The *Declaration of Concord* laid down guidelines for ASEAN in the political, economic, social and cultural fields.

It provided for co-operation in the pursuit of political stability in the region as well as in member states individually; for member states to take active steps, individually and collectively, towards the early establishment of a Zone of Peace, Freedom and Neutrality; for economic co-operation by helping each other by "according priority to the supply of the individual country's needs in critical circumstances in respect of basic commodities, particularly food and energy", by the establishment of large-scale ASEAN industrial plants, particularly to meet regional requirements of essential commodities, and by giving priority to "projects which utilize the available materials in the member states, contribute to the increase in food production, increase foreign exchange earnings or save foreign exchange and create employment".

The declaration also envisaged "progress towards the establishment of preferential trade arrangements as a long-term objective" and an acceleration of joint efforts to improve access to markets outside ASEAN for member countries' raw materials and finished products "by seeking the elimination of all trade barriers in those markets, developing new usages for those products and adopting common approaches and actions in dealing with regional groups and individual economic powers".

Furthermore, the declaration called for assistance from ASEAN partners in the event of one member being stricken by natural disasters or major calamities. Members would also study the development of judicial co-operation, including the possibility of an ASEAN extradition treaty. Finally the declaration called for "continuation of co-operation on a non-ASEAN basis between member states in security matters in accordance with their mutual needs and interests".

During their meeting in Bali the South-East Asian leaders made it clear that ASEAN was not intended to be a military organization or pact, or to be an association "against any ideology, economic or political".

At a second meeting of heads of state and government of the ASEAN member countries, held in Kuala Lumpur on Aug. 4-5, 1977, it was emphasized that the ASEAN countries desired "to develop peaceful and mutually beneficial relations with all countries in the region, including Cambodia, Laos and Vietnam", and that in their view the economic and social advancement of the member states of ASEAN was "a fundamental element in ensuring the political stability of the ASEAN region". It was noted that an agreement on ASEAN preferential trading arrangements, signed on Feb. 24, 1977, had been ratified by all member countries; that exchange of preferences on a first batch of 71 products had been agreed upon (this agreement actually coming into force on Jan. 1, 1978); and that progress had been made, inter alia, in the development of an ASEAN submarine cable system, studies on the setting up of an ASEAN regional satellite system, the harmonization and modernization of ASEAN national fleets and the promotion of containerization and joint bulk shipments.

(Additional tariff reductions were agreed to at further ministerial meetings, and by March 1979 a total of 1,326 products were included in the preferential trade arrangements, but the amount of trade affected remained limited.)

Following the overthrow of the Pol Pot regime in Cambodia by Vietnamese forces and its replacement by a "People's Revolutionary Council" in January 1979, the ASEAN member countries' Foreign Ministers, meeting in Bangkok on Jan. 12-13, 1979, issued a statement deploring "the armed intervention threatening the independence, sovereignty and territorial integrity of Cambodia", affirming "the right of the Cambodian people to decide their own future without interference or influence from outside powers", and calling for "the immediate withdrawal of all foreign troops from Cambodian territory".

On the Chinese invasion of Vietnam in February 1979 the ASEAN standing committee, meeting in Bangkok on Feb. 20, 1979, urgently appealed to the conflicting countries to stop all hostile activities against each other and also called for the withdrawal of all foreign troops from areas of conflict in South-East Asia.

An agreement on co-operation in economic development, education, culture and the control of narcotics was signed by ASEAN and the United States on July 2 and Oct. 24, 1979, and entered into force on the latter date.

Asian Development Bank

Headquarters: Pasay City, Manila (Philippines).

Members: To date 43 countries have joined the Bank, of which 29 are regional and 14 non-regional countries.

Regional Members: Afghanistan, Australia, Bangladesh, Burma, Cook Islands, Fiji, Hong Kong, India, Indonesia, Japan, Kampuchea, Kiribati, Republic of Korea, Laos, Malaysia, Maldives, Nepal, New Zealand, Pakistan, Papua New Guinea, Philippines, Singapore, Solomon Islands, Sri Lanka, Taiwan, Thailand, Tonga, Vietnam, Western Samoa.

Non-regional Members: Austria, Belgium, Canada, Denmark, Finland, France, Federal Republic of Germany, Italy, Netherlands, Norway, Sweden, Switzerland, United Kingdom, United States.

On Dec. 4, 1965, 21 countries signed the Charter of the Asian Development Bank, a financial institution set up under the auspices of the United Nations Economic Commission for Asia and the Far East (ECAFE)—since 1974 for Asia and the Pacific ESCAP). The agreement came into force on Aug. 22, 1966.

FUNCTIONS AND ORGANIZATION

The Charter laid down that membership of the Asian Development Bank would be open to members and associate members of ECAFE as well as to other regional countries and non-regional developed countries which were members of the United Nations or any of its specialized agencies.

The Bank now has 12 directors, of whom eight represent Asian or Pacific countries. The Bank's functions are to further investment in development projects within the region, to contribute to the harmonious economic growth of the whole area, to assist Asian member countries in preparing and co-ordinating their development plans, and to provide technical aid for the preparation, financing and execution of individual development projects.

It was laid down that 90 per cent of the bank's capital could be used for "hard" loans (at 5.5 per cent interest for 25-30 years) and 10 per cent for "soft" loans (low-interest and long-term). Member countries such as Australia, Japan and New Zealand, which, though members of ECAFE, were not underdeveloped countries, would not be entitled to draw any loans. A provision in the Charter authorized the bank to administer trust funds for use as "soft" loan money.

The decision-making organ of the bank is the Board of Governors, on which each member country is represented. The executive organ is the Board of Directors.

The bank was inaugurated on Nov. 24, 1966, and began operations on Dec. 19, 1966. By the end of 1978 its authorized capital was $9,407 million, of which $8,741 million had been subscribed.

In June 1974 an **Asian Development Fund** was established to provide a systematic mechanism for mobilizing and administering resources for the bank to enable it to grant loans on concessionary terms. By the end of 1978 the total resources of the fund were $1,839,224.

Mekong River Development Project

An agreement on contributions totalling $22,815,000 for a hydroelectric development project at Nam Ngum (Laos) in the Mekong River area was signed in Washington on May 4, 1966, by Australia, Canada, Denmark, Japan, the Netherlands, New Zealand and the United States.

A further agreement between Thailand and Laos, signed on the same day, provided for cement and power supplies by the former country during construction, and for the repayment by the latter on completion of the dam of funds invested and power consumed.

An agreement providing for the implementation of the Prek Thnot power and irrigation development project on the Lower Mekong River, Cambodia's first multipurpose river scheme, was signed at the UN headquarters in New York on Nov. 13, 1968, by the 10 co-operating governments —Australia, Canada, Western Germany, India, Italy, Japan, the Netherlands, Pakistan, the Philippines and the United Kingdom—and by the Cambodian Government. The 10 governments and the UN Development Programme agreed to contribute $17,745,000 towards the $27,000,000 cost.

Contributions to the cost of the Mekong River Development Project in later years brought the grand total up to US $381,500,000 by December 1978. Work on the project was, however, suspended in 1975 owing to continued unrest and warfare in the Lower Mekong area.

Integrated Rural Development Centre

Under an agreement signed in Kuala Lumpur on July 29, 1978, at an Asian-Pacific ambassadorial conference by Bangladesh, India, Indonesia, Nepal, Pakistan, Papua New Guinea, the Philippines, Sri Lanka, Thailand and Vietnam, an Asian-Pacific integrated rural development centre was set up with effect from March 31, 1979, with the object of strengthening regional co-operation in agriculture in order to raise productivity, income and living standards of farmers.

South Pacific Forum (SPF)

Headquarters: Suva, Fiji.

Members: Australia, the Cook Islands, Fiji, Kiribati, Nauru, New Zealand, Niue, Papua New Guinea, the Solomon Islands, Tonga, Tuvalu, Vanuatu and Western Samoa.

The SPF was formed to provide an opportunity for informal discussions among its members on problems of common interest to them, and its decisions are reached by consensus. It held its first meeting in Wellington (New Zealand) on Aug. 5-7, 1971, with Fiji, New Zealand, Tonga and Western Samoa being represented by their Prime Ministers, Nauru by its head of state, the Cook Islands by their Premier and Australia by its Minister of External Territories.

At a second meeting, held in Canberra on Feb. 23-25, 1972, it was decided to establish a **South Pacific Bureau for Economic Co-operation** at Suva. Under an agreement reached at the third meeting on April 17, 1973, this bureau was finally set up with a committee as its executive board and a secretariat; in 1975 the bureau became the official secretariat of the SPF. The bureau's activities cover trade, transport, communications, agriculture, industrial development, aid and aid co-ordination, the law of the sea, fisheries and seabed resources, the environment and energy.

The bureau has established the following subsidiary organizations: The Pacific Forum Line (a shipping line); the South Pacific Forum Fisheries Agency, with headquarters at Honiara (Solomon Islands); a South Pacific Trade Commission (in Australia); the Association of South Pacific Airlines; and a South Pacific Regional Disaster Fund. It has also co-ordinated the establishment of a South Pacific Regional Environment Programme.

At a meeting held on March 9, 1976, the SPF endorsed the concept of a nuclear-weapon-free zone in the South Pacific and called for the exclusion from the region of land-based nuclear weapons (in particular with regard to the underground testing of such weapons in French Polynesia) but not for any restriction on the movements of nuclear warships and submarines (especially under the ANZUS defence alliance).

At a meeting held in Kiribati on July 15, 1980, a *South Pacific Regional Trade and Economic Co-operation Agreement* (SPARTECA) was signed by most of the SPF members (but not by Fiji). The agreement removed duty on a wide range of goods (but not on exports from Australia or New Zealand to the islands) with the object of making the SPF member countries less dependent on Australia and New Zealand.

South Pacific Commission and Conference

In implementation of the ANZAC agreement [see above], a South Pacific Commission was set up on Feb. 6, 1947, with the aim of promoting the social welfare and economic advancement of island peoples in the region.

A South Pacific Conference is held annually, and countries and territories which took part as full members of the Commission in the 21st conference held in Port Moresby (Papua New Guinea) on Oct. 18-24, 1980, were American Samoa, Australia, the Cook Islands, Fiji, France, French Polynesia, Guam, Kiribati, the Marshall Islands, the Federated States of Micronesia, Nauru, New Caledonia, New Zealand, Niue, Norfolk Island, the Commonwealth of the Northern Mariana Islands, Papua New Guinea, Pitcairn, the Solomon Islands, Tokelau, Tonga, Tuvalu, the United Kingdom, the United States, the US Pacific Islands Trust Territory, Vanuatu, the Wallis and Futuna Islands and Western Samoa.

Other Agreements concluded by South-East Asian and Pacific States

Major Regional Agreements*

Indonesia and Japan. Under an agreement signed on Aug. 13, 1977, Japan's support for Indonesia was greatly increased (a loan for 1977-78 being equivalent to $185,000,000 and further loans and grants being promised).

Indonesia and Philippines. Border co-operation and border control agreements were signed between the two countries on March 11, 1975, with the object of preventing the use of border territory, waters and airspace for illegal activities.

Indonesia and Thailand. An agreement defining the seabed boundary between the two countries in the Andaman Sea was concluded in 1975.

Japan and Republic of Korea. (1) A *Basic Relations Treaty* between Japan and the Republic of Korea was concluded on June 22, 1965. The treaty settled all issues between the two countries after a lapse of 55 years (Korea was a Japanese colony from 1910 until the end of World War II). The treaty, inter alia, provided for the establishment of diplomatic relations; confirmed that "all treaties or agreements concluded between the Empire of Japan and the Empire of Korea on or before Aug. 22, 1910, are null and void"; and confirmed that "the Government of the Republic of Korea is the only lawful Government of Korea".

(2) An *agreement on the joint development of the continental shelf* between Japan and the Republic of Korea was signed in Seoul on Feb. 4, 1974. It provided for the exploration and exploitation of mineral resources, including petroleum and natural gas, in a joint development zone divided into subzones, during specified periods, with the agreement remaining in force for 50 years and further thereafter unless terminated by either party giving three years' advance notice. The agreement was ratified in Korea a few months later but in Japan it was not declared ratified until June 9, 1977. (It was declared null and void on June 13 by the Foreign Ministries of both China and Taiwan, and the Chinese Government declared on June 26, 1978, that it had "inviolable sovereignty" over the continental shelf in the East China Sea and would "never agree" to the Japanese-South Korean agreement.)

Pakistan and Burma. (1) A *treaty of "perpetual peace and friendship"* was signed on June 25, 1952. It provided for mutual co-operation in matters of common concern to both countries, and for periodical meetings of representatives of the two countries.

(2) An *agreement fixing the frontier between Burma and East Pakistan* (now Bangladesh) in the area of the river Naaf was signed on May 9, 1966.

Pakistan and France. An agreement on the purchase by Pakistan of a nuclear reprocessing plant from France (disclosed by the Prime Minister of Pakistan on Feb. 24, 1976) was followed by an agreement between the two states and the International Atomic Energy Agency (IAEA) signed in Vienna on March 18, 1976, under which Pakistan undertook not to use the reprocessing plant or any equipment or material supplied by France for the manufacture of nuclear weapons or any other military purposes.

Philippines and Japan. A treaty of friendship, trade and navigation (superseding an earlier such treaty concluded on Dec. 9, 1960) was signed by the two countries on May 10, 1979. It called for an effort by Japan to correct the trade imbalance between the two countries, granted Japan most-favoured-nation status and pledged the co-operation of the two sides to "contain, control or minimize the effect" of oil and other pollutants on marine and other resources.

Agreements between Regional and Non-regional Countries*

Philippines and Switzerland. A treaty of friendship between the two countries was signed on Aug. 30, 1956.

Thailand and Federal Republic of Germany. A treaty of friendship, commerce and navigation, concluded with the German Reich on Dec. 30, 1937, and put into force on Feb. 26, 1938, was repeatedly extended, most recently on Oct. 23, 1979, until Dec. 31, 1981.

---

* For agreements between Commonwealth countries in the region, see page 271.

* For agreements involving Commonwealth countries, see pages 272-75.

Dependent Territories in the Pacific Area and South-East Asia

Australia

External Territories

Christmas Island (in the Indian Ocean), administered by an Official Representative of the Minister for Territories in Canberra.

Cocos (Keeling) Islands (in the Indian Ocean), administered as above.

Norfolk Island.

France

Overseas Territories

New Caledonia.

French Polynesia (which includes Tahiti).

Wallis and Futuna Islands.

New Zealand

Overseas Territories

Cook Islands, an autonomous state in free association with New Zealand since 1965.

Niue, one of the Cook Islands under separate administration.

Tokelau Islands.

Portugal

Special Territory

Macao (consisting of the Macao peninsula and the two adjacent islands of Taipa and Coloane).

United Kingdom

Colonies

Pitcairn Islands Group, administered by the Governor of Fiji.

Hong Kong (consisting of the island of Hong Kong, Stonecutters Island, the Kowloon Peninsula and the New Territories leased by China to Britain in 1898).

United States of America

(1) *External Territories*

American Samoa, administered by the US Department of the Interior.

Guam, the largest island of the Marianas group [see below]. The island has statutory powers of self-government, and its inhabitants have US citizenship.

(2) *Trust Territory of the Pacific Islands,* administered by the United States under the UN trusteeship system:

(i) Commonwealth of the Northern Mariana Islands.

(ii) Self-governing territories in "free association" with the United States:

Federated State of Micronesia (Caroline Islands of Truk, Yap, Ponape and Kosrae);

Marshall Islands;

Palau (the Republic of Belau from Jan. 1, 1981).

19. The "Third World": Attempts at Achieving Cohesion

This section dealing with various moves by third-world countries to achieve greater political cohesion covers in particular (i) the history and development of the non-aligned movement; and (ii) other groupings of developing countries created to achieve greater international effectiveness in various fields.

History and Development of Non-Aligned Movement

Since the mid-1950s, delegations from countries of Asia, Africa and Latin America have met in conference, from time to time, to define their common attitude with relation to international affairs, and to try to bring about closer solidarity in economic, cultural and political fields. These countries, which represent the less privileged parts of the world, are sometimes referred to as the "Third World" or, since most of them form part of neither the Western (capitalist) bloc nor the Eastern (Communist) bloc, as the "non-aligned" or "uncommitted" nations.

The Bandung Conference

A conference held at Bandung (Indonesia) on April 18-23, 1955, was, as President Sukarno of Indonesia stated in the opening speech, "the first inter-continental conference of the so-called coloured peoples in the history of mankind". It was attended by delegates of the Governments of Afghanistan, Burma, Cambodia, Ceylon (Sri Lanka), the People's Republic of China, Egypt, Ethiopia, the Gold Coast (now Ghana), India, Indonesia, Iran, Iraq, Japan, Jordan, Laos, Lebanon, Liberia, Libya, Nepal, Pakistan, the Philippines, Saudi Arabia, the Sudan, Syria, Thailand, Turkey, North Vietnam, South Vietnam and Yemen (later the Yemen Arab Republic)—as well as many unofficial observers from other countries.

The decision to hold the conference had been made at a conference of the Prime Ministers of Burma, Ceylon, India, Indonesia and Pakistan, held at Bogor (Indonesia) on Dec. 28-29, 1954. The Prime Ministers agreed that an Afro-Asian conference should be held under their sponsorship, and that its basic purpose would

be to make the countries concerned better acquainted with one another's point of view.

Resolutions. The communiqué issued at the end of the Bandung Conference contained resolutions on economic and cultural co-operation; on human rights and self-determination; on problems of dependent peoples: and on world peace and co-operation.

The conference recognized the urgency of promoting economic development in the Asian-African region, and also the desirability of co-operation with countries outside the region. Recommendations were made for, inter alia, the early establishment of a special UN fund for economic development, and the allocation, by the International Bank, of a greater part of its resources to Asian-African countries.

In the cultural field the conference condemned the alleged practice, on the part of colonial powers, of suppressing the national cultures of the peoples of Africa and Asia. This was described as a fundamental denial of the rights of man.

After declaring its full support of the fundamental principles of human rights and of the principle of self-determination of peoples and nations, as set forth in the UN Charter, the conference condemned the policies and practices of racial segregation and discrimination. In a *Declaration on Problems of Dependent Peoples* it was stated that colonialism, in all its manifestations, was an evil which should speedily be brought to an end.

The conference also adopted a *Declaration on World Peace and Co-operation,* in which it agreed that nations should live together in peace with one another as good neighbours, and develop friendly co-operation on the basis of the following principles:

(1) Respect for the fundamental human rights and for the purposes and principles of the UN Charter.

(2) Respect for the sovereignty and territorial integrity of all nations.

(3) Recognition of the equality of all races and nations, large and small.

(4) Abstention from intervention or interference in the internal affairs of other countries.

(5) Respect for the right of each nation to defend itself singly or collectively in conformity with the UN Charter.

(6) Abstention from the use of arrangements of collective defence to serve the particular interests of any of the big powers; and abstention by any country from exerting pressure on other countries.

(7) Refraining from acts or threats of aggression or the use of force against the territorial integrity or political independence of any country.

(8) Settlement of all international disputes by peaceful means such as negotiation, conciliation, arbitration or judicial settlement, as well as other peaceful means of the parties' own choice in conformity with the UN Charter.

(9) Promotion of mutual interest and co-operation.

(10) Respect for justice and international obligations.

The Five Principles. The principles listed above are an extension of the "Five Principles" of peaceful coexistence, or Panch Sila (from the Pali, in which it expresses a Buddhist concept). These principles were first enumerated in an agreement over Tibet —now superseded by China's action in that country—concluded between India and the People's Republic of China in April 1954, where they were given as follows:

(1) Mutual respect for territorial integrity and sovereignty;

(2) mutual non-aggression;

(3) mutual non-interference in each other's internal affairs;

(4) equality and mutual benefit;

(5) peaceful coexistence.

The Non-Aligned Movement

Members: Afghanistan, Algeria, Angola, Argentina, Bahrain, Bangladesh, Benin, Bhutan, Bolivia, Botswana, Burundi, Cameroon, Cape Verde, the Central African Republic, Chad, the Congo, Cuba, Cyprus, Djibouti, Egypt, Equatorial Guinea, Ethiopia, Gabon, The Gambia, Ghana, Grenada, Guinea, Guinea-Bissau, Guyana, India, Indonesia, Iran, Iraq, the Ivory Coast, Jamaica, Jordan, Kampuchea, Kenya, the People's Democratic Republic of Korea, Kuwait, Laos, Lebanon, Lesotho, Liberia, Libya, Madagascar, Malawi, Malaysia, Maldives, Mali, Malta, Mauritania, Mauritius, Morocco, Mozambique, the South West Africa People's Organization (SWAPO)

of Namibia, Nepal, Nicaragua, Niger, Nigeria, Oman, Pakistan, the Palestine Liberation Organization (PLO), Panama, Peru, Qatar, Rwanda, St Lucia, São Tomé and Príncipe, Saudi Arabia, Senegal, Seychelles, Sierra Leone, Singapore, Somalia, Sri Lanka, the Sudan, Suriname, Swaziland, Syria, Tanzania, Togo, Trinidad and Tobago, Tunisia, Uganda, the United Arab Emirates, Upper Volta, Vietnam, the Yemen Arab Republic, the People's Democratic Republic of Yemen, Yugoslavia, Zaïre, Zambia and Zimbabwe; and also Belize with a special status.

Arising out of the Bandung Conference [see above] a movement of non-aligned countries took shape under the guidance of leading Third World statesmen, the most prominent of whom were Jawaharlal Nehru (the first Prime Minister of India), President Sukarno of Indonesia, Gamal Abdel Nasser (Prime Minister and later President of Egypt) and President Tito of Yugoslavia.

A Co-ordinating Bureau, first set up in Algiers in 1973, was in 1976 enlarged from 17 to 25 members, and to 36 members at the Havana conference in August 1979 [see below]. These 36 seats were distributed as follows: *Africa* 17—Benin, Ethiopia, Ghana, Lesotho, Madagascar, Mauritania, Mozambique, Nigeria, Somalia, Togo, Zambia and six other members to be decided by the African group at the United Nations; *Asia* 12—India, Iraq, Jordan, Democratic People's Republic of Korea, Palestine Liberation Organization, Sri Lanka, People's Democratic Republic of Yemen, and as alternate members Afghanistan/Bangladesh, Indonesia/Singapore, Iran/Bhutan and Vietnam/Laos; *Latin America* five—Cuba, Guyana, Jamaica, Panama and as alternate members Peru/Grenada; *Europe* one—Yugoslavia; and one extra seat shared between *Europe and Africa*—Cyprus as alternate member with Uganda.

NON-ALIGNED CO-OPERATION IN THE FIELD OF INFORMATION

A pool of non-aligned news agencies, the creation of which had been decided upon at a meeting in New Delhi on July 8-13, 1976, of delegates from 62 non-aligned countries and 45 representatives of news agencies, began operations in that year, with Tanjug (the Yugoslav news agency) collecting and redistributing (through seven regional centres) news reports among non-aligned countries. Statutes and an action programme for the years until 1982 were adopted for the pool at a conference held in Belgrade on Nov. 22-24, 1979.

The statutes committed the pool to the distribution of "objective, factual, clear, precise and fair" information emanating from reliable national sources and reflecting the principles and objectives of the non-aligned movement. The action programme provided inter alia for comprehensive moral, material and technical aid for the least-developed non-aligned news agencies and for national liberation movements in the training of journalists.

Bodies set up with the object of moving towards a "new international information order" and co-ordinating different sectors of information were an Intergovernmental Council for Co-ordination of Co-operation among Non-Aligned Countries in Information; a Co-ordinating Committee of the News Agencies' Pool; a Committee for Co-operation among Broadcasting Organizations; a Committee of Telecommunications Experts; and a Bureau for Co-ordination among Journalists' Associations.

(The non-aligned countries' endeavours in this field had contributed to the adoption of the 1978 UNESCO declaration on the role of the media—see page 30.)

Conferences of Non-Aligned Countries

1961 Belgrade Conference. A first conference of 25 non-aligned countries took place in Belgrade on Sept. 1-6, 1961. Most of the countries were represented by heads of state or government although, in a few cases, only the Foreign Ministers attended.

The agenda for this conference had been fixed at a preparatory conference held in Cairo on June 5-13, 1961. Items considered included: A general exchange of views on the international situation; the rights of peoples to self-determination; non-interference in the internal affairs of states; the struggle against racial discrimination; general and complete disarmament; peaceful coexistence; and problems of economic development and co-operation.

The Belgrade Conference was attended by delegations from Afghanistan, Algeria, Burma, Cambodia, Ceylon, the Congo (now Zaïre), Cuba, Cyprus, Egypt, Ethiopia, Ghana, Guinea, India, Indonesia, Iraq, Lebanon, Mali, Morocco, Nepal, Saudi Arabia, Somalia, the Sudan, Tunisia, Yemen and Yugoslavia.

At the end of the conference the delegates unanimously adopted a 27-point declaration containing their common views on international problems, and an *Appeal for Peace,* addressed particularly to the USA and the USSR.

The declaration included a demand for all dependent peoples to exercise their right to complete independence, and called for the ending of all armed action and repressive measures against them on the part of colonial powers. It condemned the maintenance of foreign bases in the territories of other countries,

and stated that general, complete and internationally-controlled disarmament was "the most urgent task of mankind". It also stated that efforts should be made "to close, through accelerated economic, industrial and agricultural development, the ever widening gap in the standards of living between the few economically advanced countries and the many economically less developed countries".

1964 Cairo Conference. A second international conference of non-aligned countries took place in Cairo on Oct. 5-10, 1964. A total of 47 countries attended as full participants; in addition to the 25 which attended the Belgrade Conference, delegations were sent by Angola (Government-in-exile), Burundi, Cameroon, Chad, the Congo (Brazzaville), Dahomey (now Benin), Jordan, Kenya, Kuwait, Laos, Liberia, Libya, Malawi, Mauritania, Nigeria, Northern Rhodesia (now Zambia), Senegal, Sierra Leone, Syria, Togo, Uganda and the United Republic of Tanganyika and Zanzibar (now Tanzania). Observers were sent by Argentina, Bolivia, Brazil, Chile, Finland, Jamaica, Mexico, Trinidad and Tobago, Uruguay and Venezuela.

The final communiqué of the conference was entitled *Programme for Peace and International Co-operation.* It included statements on the right to self-determination and independence, on peaceful co-existence and on denuclearization. Neo-colonialism and imperialism, in all forms, were condemned, particularly in South Africa.

1970 Lusaka Conference. A third conference of non-aligned countries was held in Lusaka (Zambia) on Sept. 8-10, 1970, and was attended by representatives of 54 countries, i.e. those represented at the Cairo conference (except Angola's Government-in-exile, Burma, Cambodia, Dahomey, Malawi and Saudi Arabia) and also Botswana, the Central African Republic, Equatorial Guinea, Gabon, Guyana, Jamaica, Lesotho, Malaysia, Rwanda, Singapore, South Yemen, Swaziland and Trinidad and Tobago.

The conference had been preceded by two preparatory meetings in Belgrade (July 8-11, 1969) and Dar-es-Salaam (April 13-17, 1970), and had been further prepared by visits to African states during February 1970 by President Tito of Yugoslavia, who had proposed a "programme of concrete actions to solve the problems which concern the international community as a whole and world peace, such as the liquidation of the vestiges of colonialism, establishment of democratic relations and co-operation on terms of equality, codification of the principles of coexistence, acceleration of the development of the developing countries, disarmament, strengthening of the United Nations and attainment of its universality".

Documents approved by the conference

included the *Lusaka Declaration on Peace, Independence, Co-operation and the Democratization of International Relations,* designed to constitute the *Charter of Non-Alignment.*

This declaration no longer defined non-alignment as "an irreplaceable instrument for the solution of the dangerous contradictions of the contemporary world and the establishment of international relations based upon the principle of active and peaceful coexistence" but rather as "an integral part of the changes in the present structure of the international community in its entirety" and "the product of the anti-colonialist revolution". Instead of "rich" and "poor" countries it distinguished between "oppressors" and "the oppressed", "aggressors" and "victims of aggression". It stated in particular that the immediate danger of a conflict between the super-powers had diminished as the result of their tendency to negotiate, but that this did not contribute to the security of small, medium-sized or developing nations, nor did it prevent the danger of local wars. At the same time the participants in the conference undertook "to continue their efforts to bring about the dissolution of the great military alliances".

1972 Foreign Ministers' Conference. At a conference of Foreign Ministers of non-aligned countries in Georgetown (Guyana) on Aug. 8-12, 1972, a *Declaration of Georgetown* was issued, calling for the extension of the process of détente, which had been successfully intensified in Europe, to all regions of the world, so that all military alliances would be dissolved, all foreign military bases evacuated and new areas of peace declared, especially in the Mediterranean and the Indian Ocean. The declaration also reaffirmed the non-aligned countries' support for African liberation movements and for nationalization policies in Latin American countries, and it called for an end to the war in Indo-China on the basis of peace proposals made by the Communist or pro-Communist forces in Vietnam, Laos and Cambodia, and of the withdrawal of all foreign armed forces from these countries.

1973 Algiers Conference. A fourth conference of non-aligned countries was held in Algiers on Sept. 5-9, 1973, and was attended by 76 full participants, nine observers (i.e. entitled to participate on a consultative basis, but not to vote) and three guests. Also represented at the conference were the United Nations, the Organization of African Unity (OAU), the Arab League, the African, Asian and Latin American Solidarity Organization, and 14 liberation movements recognized by the OAU.

The conference was preceded by meetings of experts on Aug. 27 and of the Ministers of Foreign Affairs on Sept. 1-4, when a definite agenda was decided on and it was agreed to admit to full membership of the non-aligned group Argentina, Bangladesh, Bhutan,

Malta (after an undertaking by Malta to evict foreign military bases upon expiry of the current agreements in 1979), Oman, Peru, Qatar, the Provisional Revolutionary Government of (South) Vietnam and the Cambodian Government-in-exile.

During the conference the Algerian Government made strong efforts to give non-alignment a "new meaning", the Algerian Foreign Minister, M. Abdelaziz Bouteflika, defining the objectives of the conference as "the struggle for economic independence", co-operation on the basis of equality, and action on three fronts— (i) "maximum mobilization of our internal resources"; (ii) the "strengthening of co-operation and trade exchanges . . . between developing and non-aligned countries in general"; and (iii) the "democratization of relations between rich and poor countries". The need for a new appraisal of the idea of non-alignment had also been emphasized by other leaders of states in the "Third World".

At its closing session on Sept. 9 the conference approved:

(1) A political declaration, which inter alia demanded "the immediate and unconditional withdrawal of Israel from all occupied territories", and the recognition of the "inalienable right to independence of the non-aligned countries of Latin America still under colonial domination"; reaffirmed their solidarity with the liberation movements in Africa; and called for the holding of an international conference on disarmament;

(2) an economic declaration, which included a number of proposals for a common posture of non-aligned and other developing countries to be adopted in future trade negotiations;

(3) a number of resolutions on specified subjects, which included a call to boycott Israel, and the recognition of the "legitimacy and legality" of the Cambodian Government-in-exile.

It was decided that the next summit conference of the non-aligned countries should be held in Colombo (Sri Lanka) in 1976.

1975 Dakar Conference on Third-World Strategy on Raw Materials and Economic Development. A conference of representatives of some 110 non-aligned developing countries (which did not include Iran and most of the Middle East oil-producing countries, which had only sent observers) took place in Dakar (Senegal) on Feb. 4-8, 1975.

The conference adopted a motion of solidarity between the developing countries and the member countries of the Organization of Petroleum Exporting

Countries (OPEC). Inter alia the motion expressed the Third World's solidarity with all developing countries which decided "to recover their rights by means of nationalizing their natural resources, by taking control of foreign enterprises operating on their territory, or by fixing the prices of the products which they export".

Among other decisions taken by the conference was (i) one to establish a special fund for the building up of stocks and for ensuring the uninterrupted production of raw materials and basic commodities exported by developing countries, with all countries taking part being called upon to contribute to the fund, and (ii) another to establish a special intergovernmental board representing non-aligned and developing countries which would study the methods and detailed arrangements for the operation of the fund.

The conclusions of the conference were summarized in a *Dakar Declaration* which, although it asked the industrialized countries to assist the developing countries by supplying food, technical aid and credits, called upon the developing countries themselves to take joint action which would make them less dependent upon "imperialism", and which expressed the view that the countries of the Third World would "attain economic emancipation only when they succeed in controlling their resources and natural wealth and thereafter achieve economic development".

1975 Lima Conference. The fifth ministerial conference of non-aligned countries, held in Lima (Peru) on Aug. 25-30, 1975, was attended by ministers from 78 full member countries and nine countries with observer status and representatives of 12 liberation movements admitted as observers.

At the conference its total full membership was raised to 82 by the admission of Panama, the Democratic People's Republic of Korea, the Democratic Republic of (North) Vietnam and the Palestine Liberation Organization—but not of the Republic of Korea (whose application for full membership was rejected on the ground of that country's "close links with the United States"). The conference also admitted eight countries as guests but declined to grant observer status to Guatemala and the Philippines. (The Government of Chile had not been invited and was not represented at the conference.)

It became clear at the conference that the non-aligned movement had transferred its chief concern from the struggle for political liberation to the achievement of a "new international economic order", and this was expressed in the two principal resolutions approved—(i) a *Lima Programme of Mutual Solidarity and Aid* setting out the movement's general political and economic aims, and (ii) a declaration outlining an economic strategy for the non-aligned countries.

The first of these documents declared the international situation to be characterized by the existence of an "unjust international order". In a compromise statement on Israel the document said: "By its continued aggression against the Arab countries and its persistent violation of the UN Charter, Israel has excluded itself from the international community. The time has come for the non-aligned countries to examine other measures against Israel." The document also, inter alia, reaffirmed the right of the Palestinian people to return to their homes and to exercise self-determination; expressed support for the independence and territorial integrity of Cyprus and also for the Moroccan position in regard to the Spanish Sahara; and called for declaring the South Pacific a "zone of peace".

In its declaration on an economic strategy the conference called for "rigorous application of the principles of the new international economic order, in particular the principle of permanent sovereignty over natural resources, as well as the adoption of a common strategy for mutual assistance", especially against political or economic pressure or any attempt to use force or aggression against any member of the non-aligned movement.

The conference also decided to set up six funds as follows:

(1) A solidarity fund for the economic and social development of non-aligned countries, with each of the fund's members contributing the equivalent of 500,000 special drawing rights (SDR), which was expected to produce a basic capital of some SDR 40,000,000;

(2) a special fund for financing buffer stocks of raw materials and primary products by developing countries;

(3) a fund for the development of food production in Third World countries;

(4) another fund for agricultural development;

(5) a special fund for land-locked countries; and

(6) a fund for the post-war reconstruction "of Cambodia, Laos and Vietnam and of the other peoples affected by imperialist aggression".

1976 Colombo Conference. The fifth conference of the heads of state or government of the non-aligned countries was held in Colombo on Aug. 16-19, 1976.

It was preceded by a meeting of Foreign Ministers on Aug. 11-15, which approved the admission of Angola, the Comoros, Maldives and Seychelles as full members of the movement. This meeting was also attended by representatives of 12 countries invited as observers, of seven others as guests (Austria, Finland, the Philippines, Portugal, Romania, Sweden and Switzerland) and of 12 international organizations.

The conference of heads of state or government received goodwill messages from the Soviet Union and China and was addressed by the UN Secretary-General.

Documents approved by consensus were a political declaration, a declaration on economic problems, an action programme for economic co-operation, and various resolutions on economic questions.

In the political declaration the conference reaffirmed the rejection by the non-aligned countries of the idea that world peace could rest in a balance of forces, or that security could be assured by countries associated with blocs and adhering to military alliances with the great powers. Noting that the process of decolonization had reached its "final and decisive phase", the conference called for the withdrawal of France from Mayotte ("an integral part of the Comoros"); reaffirmed the right of self-determination of the people of Puerto Rico, East Timor and Djibouti (then not yet independent); and demanded that sovereignty over Guantánamo (the US base on Cuba), the Panama Canal Zone [see also page 317] and the Malvinas (Falkland Islands) should be restored to their "rightful owners" (i.e. Cuba, Panama and Argentina respectively). The conference also demanded the withdrawal of all foreign troops from the Republic of Korea, the liquidation of foreign military bases and the termination of the UN Command in that country.

In the declaration on economic problems the conference took the view that the most dangerous source of conflict and tension was the growing disparity between "north" and "south" (the developed and the developing countries), and it demanded "full compensation for the exploitations" of the past, criticized the activities of multinational corporations; and issued a warning against foreign investment which might jeopardize the political and economic sovereignty of the non-aligned countries. It advocated the creation of raw materials cartels on the model of OPEC; called for a fundamental restructuring of world trade; suggested the indexation of commodity prices; expressed itself in favour of "adequate solutions" of the debt problem of the poorest of the developing countries; and demanded a reorganization of the world's monetary system because of its current "chaotic currency fluctuations".

In the action programme for economic co-operation the leaders of the non-aligned countries reaffirmed their belief in the "concept of collective reliance on one's own resources" and called for co-operation between non-aligned and other developing countries in the fields of raw materials, trade, currencies and finance, and in other areas. They called on all member countries to sign and ratify the agreement on the creation of a solidarity fund as decided at the Lima ministerial conference in August 1975 [see above].

1978 Belgrade Conference of Foreign Ministers. A conference of Foreign Ministers of the non-aligned countries was held in Belgrade on July 25-30, 1978.

It was attended by representatives of 85 countries and the Palestine Liberation Organization as full members, of 10 states with observer status and of seven guest states (among them the newly admitted Pakistan and San Marino). Certain liberation movements and international organizations were also represented as observers. (The conference declined to grant full membership to Bolivia and also to admit a delegation from the Comoros, the then Government of which had come to power with the aid of a White mercenary and was therefore not regarded as non-aligned.)

The unity of the non-aligned movement was at that time threatened by disagreement over Cuba's endeavours to commit it to an alliance with the "socialist countries" led by the Soviet Union and over numerous bilateral conflicts between non-aligned countries.

Documents adopted by consensus at the conference included a declaration (with both a political and an economic part) and an action programme for economic co-operation.

In the political part of the declaration it was stated that the non-aligned movement had proved to be "an indispensable factor in resolving fundamental international problems in the conditions of existing contradictions and the world's growing interdependence"; that it was committed to "the struggle against imperialism, expansionism, colonialism, neocolonialism, apartheid, racism, including Zionism, exploitation, power politics and all forms of foreign domination and hegemony, in other words the rejection of any form of subjugation, dependence, interference or pressure, be it economic, political or military"; and that it had "rejected resolutely bloc politics, military alliance, as well as any policy tending to divide the world into spheres of domination and influence".

The declaration also stated: "The ministers point with concern to the more and more overt recourse to interference in the internal affairs of independent, particularly non-aligned countries in order to influence their socio-political development [and] their foreign policies, and to circumscribe their independence. . . . Interference is becoming one of the principal forms of attack against the non-aligned movement and the unity of the non-aligned countries." At the same time they reaffirmed "the legitimate right of peoples under colonial domination and foreign occupation to resort to armed struggle for their national liberation and independence".

For the first time in a document issued by the non-aligned movement the declaration contained a section dealing with human rights, stating inter alia that "the issue of human rights cannot be isolated from its national, economic and social context", that "the freedom of the individual is inseparable from the rights of the people" and that "human rights and the fundamental freedoms of the individual and of the people are inalienable".

In the economic part of the declaration it was noted with concern that "the efforts made to date towards the establishment of the new international economic order and the solution of current economic problems" had "not achieved any significant results", and it was reaffirmed that the movement should "continue to maintain and strengthen its solidarity" with the "Group of 77" [see below] in further negotiations.

1979 Colombo Meeting of Co-ordinating Bureau. At the end of a meeting of the movement's Co-ordinating Bureau, held in Colombo on June 6-10, 1979, a declaration was issued which inter alia condemned the Egyptian-Israeli peace treaty [see page 349] as a "partial and selective agreement"; criticized "the important role of the United States in aggravating the situation in the Middle East" and Israel's "expansionist, imperialist policy" of "annexing occupied Palestinian territory, including Jerusalem, and establishing paramilitary Zionist settlements"; expressed the belief that the peace treaty violated the decisions and resolutions of the non-aligned movement and the United Nations; and appealed to the non-aligned countries not to extend any recognition to the treaty.

1979 Havana Conference. The sixth conference of the heads of state or government of the non-aligned countries was held in Havana (Cuba) on Sept. 3-9, 1979.

A meeting of Foreign Ministers held in Havana on Aug. 30-Sept. 1, 1979, approved the admission of seven new full members to the movement (Bolivia, Grenada, Iran, Nicaragua, Pakistan, Suriname and the Zimbabwe Patriotic Front). (The South West Africa People's Organization—SWAPO, regarded as the legitimate representative of the people of Namibia—had been admitted as a full member at a ministerial meeting held in New York on Oct. 2, 1978.) This brought the number of full members of the movement to 95—of which Kampuchea (Cambodia) was excluded from the conference as no consensus could be obtained on the question of its representation, which was claimed by both the *Khmers Rouges* regime of Pol Pot and the Vietnamese-backed People's Revolutionary Council.

The conference of heads of state or government was largely dominated by the threat to its unity arising out of the divergence between Cuba and Yugoslavia over the character of the non-aligned movement.

Cuba, which assumed the presidency of the movement for three years until 1982, had presented the "radical thesis" which identified the socialist bloc led by the Soviet Union as the "natural ally" of the non-aligned countries in the struggle against "imperialism" and for "socialism in the world". Yugoslavia, on the other hand, had (with the support of other member countries of the movement, notably India, Indonesia, Sri Lanka and Tanzania) defended the move-

ment's "anti-bloc" commitment and its opposition to all foreign military intervention, with President Tito stating in his opening address: "The non-aligned movement is an independent, united and autonomous factor in world politics, and such it must remain."

The final declaration of the conference, containing a political and an economic section and adopted by consensus, gave in its political section a redefinition of the principles and objects of the non-aligned movement, as follows:

"Basic Principles: National independence, sovereignty and territorial integrity, sovereign equality and the free social development of all countries; independence of non-aligned countries from great-power or bloc rivalries and influences and opposition to participation in military pacts and alliances arising therefrom; the struggle against imperialism, colonialism, neo-colonialism, racism including Zionism and all forms of expansionism, foreign occupation and domination and hegemony; active peaceful co-existence among all states; indivisibility of peace and security; non-intervention and non-interference in the internal and external affairs of other countries; freedom of all states to determine their political systems and pursue economic, social and cultural development without intimidation, hindrance and pressure; establishment of a new international economic order and development of international co-operation on the basis of equality; the right to self-determination and independence of all peoples under colonial and alien domination and constant support to the struggle of national liberation movements; respect for human rights and fundamental freedoms; opposition to the division of the world into antagonistic military-political alliances and blocs and rejection of outmoded doctrines such as spheres of influence and balance of terror; permanent sovereignty over natural resources; inviolability of legally established international boundaries; non-use of force or threat of use of force and non-recognition of situations brought about by the threat or use of force; and peaceful settlement of disputes.

"Essential Objectives: Preservation of the national independence, sovereignty, territorial integrity and security of non-aligned countries; elimination of foreign interference and intervention in the internal and external affairs of states and the use of the threat of force; strengthening of non-alignment as an independent non-bloc factor and the further spread of non-alignment in the world; elimination of colonialism, neo-colonialism and racism including Zionism and support to national liberation movements struggling against colonial and alien domination and foreign occupation; elimination of imperialistic and hegemonistic policies and all other forms of expansionism and foreign domination; safeguarding international peace and security and the universalization of the relaxation of international tensions; promotion of unity, solidarity and co-operation among non-aligned countries with a view to the achievement of the objectives of non-alignment thus preserving its essential character; ending the arms race, particularly the nuclear arms race, and the achievement of general and complete disarmament under effective international control; the early establishment of the new international economic order with a view to accelerating the development of developing countries, eliminating the inequality between developed and

393

developing countries and the eradication of poverty, hunger, sickness and illiteracy in the developing countries; participation on the basis of equality in solving international issues; establishment of a democratic system of international relations based on the equality of states, respect for and preservation of human rights and fundamental freedoms; the strengthening of the United Nations as an effective instrument for promoting international peace and security, resolving international problems, the struggle against colonialism, neo-colonialism, racism, Zionism, racial discrimination and apartheid and as an important factor in the development of international co-operation and the establishment of equitable economic relations between states; dissolution of great-power pacts and military alliances and interlocking arrangements arising therefrom; withdrawal of foreign military forces and dismantling of foreign military bases; promotion of economic co-operation among the non-aligned and other developing countries with a view to the achievement of collective self-reliance; establishment of a new international order in the field of information and mass media for the purpose of forging new international relations in general; and revival, preservation and enrichment of the cultural heritage of the peoples of non-aligned countries and promotion of cultural co-operation among them.''

The political section also dealt with specific problems.

In regard to Western Sahara the conference deplored Morocco's occupation of the southern part of the territory (previously administered by Mauritania) and expressed the hope that all parties involved would co-operate in implementing the recommendation of the Organization of African Unity calling for a referendum on self-determination for Western Sahara.

The conference also condemned the Egyptian-Israeli peace treaty and any partial settlements or separate treaties relating to the Arab-Israeli conflict, but it deferred a decision on the possible suspension of Egypt from the non-aligned movement. A decision on the question of which regime to recognize in Kampuchea was similarly deferred.

The Government of Burma confirmed, in September 1979, its decision to withdraw from the movement, after its Foreign Minister had criticized ''the manoeuvres of countries tending to align themselves'' and had unsuccessfully called for the formation of a new, genuinely neutral movement.

Other Groupings of Third-World Countries

The ''Group of 77''

This group—set up at the 1964 UN Con-Conference on Trade and Development (UNCTAD) [see page 20] as a pressure group defending the interests of developing countries—had by February 1979 reached a membership of 117 developing countries.

At a special ministerial meeting held in Algiers on Feb. 16-19, 1975, the group drafted a ''platform'' for submission to the UN Industrial Development Organization (UNIDO), proposing that UNIDO should become a UN specialized agency; that UNIDO should eventually assist the needy countries in their efforts to recover their natural resources and in undertaking the processing of these resources in their own territory; that developing countries should have the right to form more raw materials cartels, to nationalize foreign-owned industry and to regulate multinational corporations; that ''selected production capacities'' should be transferred to the developing countries; that help should be given to ''uneconomic and inefficient'' domestic industries to phase themselves out, so that the field would be left open to imports from developing countries (e.g. of textiles); and that the generalized system of preferences should be expanded and improved.

In a ''position paper'' submitted to the UN General Assembly's special session on development and international economic co-operation in September 1975, the group called for adherence to the ''indexation'' principle by tying the prices of raw material exports to the prices of imports from the developed world so as to provide ''insulation from the adverse effects of inflation in developed countries'', and for the developed countries to devote a minimum of 0.7 per cent of gross national product to official development assistance (as had been proposed for the UN Second Development Decade in 1970).

At a ministerial meeting held in Manila on Feb. 2-7, 1976, the group issued a *Declaration of Manila* and a programme of action.

The declaration contained 17 objectives for international co-operation, towards the attainment of which the group's member-states expressed ''their firm conviction to make full use of the bargaining power of the developing countries through joint and united action''. The 17 objectives included action on. An integrated programme on commodities designed to guarantee prices; industrial production and trade; the expansion of the developing countries' total export capacity; ''substantive results'' from the multilateral trade negotiations then being conducted in Geneva [under GATT auspices, on the application of the ''Tokyo round''—see page 41]; reforms in the international monetary system; increased financial assistance; debt-relief; technology transfers; controls on multinational corporations; greater economic co-operation among developing countries themselves; expanded trade with the communist world; special measures to aid the least developed countries (LDC—see page 93), land-locked and island countries and those most seriously affected by the current world economic crisis (MSA—ibid.); greater efforts to improve world food production; and a strengthening of the negotiating function of UNCTAD itself.

An indicative list of 18 commodities to be covered by an integrated programme comprised bananas, bauxite, cocoa, coffee, copper, cotton, hard fibres (e.g. sisal), iron ore, jute, manganese, meat, phosphates, rubber, sugar, tea, timber, tin and vegetable oils.

In the programme of action demands were made for the abolition of customs barriers imposed by developed countries on the entry of manufactured or semi-finished products of the Third World, and an improvement in the generalized system of preferences [see page 91]; an increase in public aid by developed countries (including those of Eastern Europe) to reach by 1980 the target of 0.7 per cent of gross national product, and the introduction of a development tax by these countries; the effective application of measures and methods of indexing prices of basic commodities exported by developing countries to the import prices of articles manufactured in developing countries; a proportion of at least 90 per cent of public development aid to consist of free gifts or interest-free loans not tied to obligatory purchases in the donor country; the cancellation of the public debt of the LDC and MSA countries and the consolidation of other third-world countries' trade debts for 25 years, as well as the creation of "a fund or a bank destined to finance short-term debts of developing countries"; a code of conduct for transfers of technology and the creation of a "multilateral instrument with powers of compulsion"; and a strengthening of the powers of UNCTAD, which should nevertheless retain its links with the UN General Assembly.

At a conference on economic co-operation held in Mexico City on Sept. 13-22, 1976, the group adopted various recommendations, among them one for preparations for studying the possibility of setting up a global system of trade preferences for developing countries only, in order to support their industries, and another for early completion of statutes for a council of raw material producers' associations. (The group agreed on the need to establish its own multinational corporations for the marketing of raw materials and to set up commodity exchanges within the group's own territories.)

At a ministerial meeting held at Arusha (Tanzania) on Feb. 12-16, 1979, an Arusha programme for collective self-help and a framework for negotiations were agreed upon.

The Arusha programme inter alia called for a legally binding code for the transfer of technology, changes in the International Monetary Fund, structural reforms in the international trade and monetary system and large-scale resource transfers to the developing countries.

The meeting also agreed to support a proposal for mandatory direct contributions of $1,000,000 towards the capital of the Common Fund for the financing of buffer stocks of raw materials, then being negotiated under UNCTAD auspices.

Asian-African Legal Consultative Committee

Headquarters: New Delhi.

Members: Bangladesh, Botswana, Cyprus, Egypt, Ethiopia, The Gambia, Ghana, India,

Indonesia, Iran, Iraq, Japan, Jordan, Kenya, Democratic People's Republic of Korea, Republic of Korea, Kuwait, Libya, Malaysia, Mauritius, Mongolia, Nepal, Nigeria, Oman, Pakistan, the Philippines, Qatar, Saudi Arabia, Senegal, Sierra Leone, Singapore, Somalia, Sri Lanka, Syria, Tanzania, Thailand, Turkey, Uganda, the United Arab Emirates and the Yemen Arab Republic.

The committee was founded by the Governments of Burma, Ceylon (Sri Lanka), India, Indonesia, Iraq, Japan and Syria in 1956 with the object of submitting its views on legal matters to the International Law Commission, considering legal problems referred to it by its member-states and promoting Asian-African co-operation in international law. It was granted observer status at the United Nations General Assembly on Oct. 13, 1980.

Afro-Asian People's Solidarity Organization (AAPSO)

1958 Cairo Conference. The decision to set up an Afro-Asian People's Solidarity Organization, a permanent organization to promote and strengthen Afro-Asian solidarity, was taken at an Afro-Asian "solidarity conference" held at non-governmental level in Cairo from Dec. 26, 1957, to Jan. 1, 1958. All those nations which had taken part in the Bandung Conference of 1955 were invited, and invitations also went to Morocco, Nigeria, Somaliland and Uganda. A number of invitations were, however, refused on account of the pro-communist character of the conference, which was organized by a communist-front body known as the Asian Solidarity Committee.

The conference agreed that the Afro-Asian People's Solidarity Organization should have its headquarters in Cairo and meet at least once a year. All Afro-Asian peoples would be represented in it.

1960 Conakry Conference. The second conference of the organization was held on April 11-15, 1960, at Conakry in Guinea. It was attended by delegates from 50 countries, both Communist and pro-Western as well as neutral. In addition to passing a number of resolutions on various current situations, the conference recommended that an Afro-Asian governmental conference similar to the Bandung conference should be convened in the near future. It was also decided to enlarge the steering committee of the conference to 27, and to strengthen African representation on the permanent secretariat.

1963 Moshi Conference. The third conference of the organization took place in Moshi (Tanganyika—now mainland Tanzania)

on Feb. 7-11, 1963. In the opening speech, President Nyerere of Tanganyika gave a warning against the "new colonialism" of the Communist states, whom he accused of using their economic strength to obtain political power in countries of Africa and Asia.

Among the resolutions adopted by the conference were a condemnation of British and French arms supplies to South Africa, and a demand for the release of political prisoners held there. The conference appointed a committee to prepare a conference of representatives from three continents to be held in Havana at the invitation of Dr. Fidel Castro, then Prime Minister of Cuba.

The conference approved the creation of a **Three Continents Solidarity Organization** [see below], based in Havana and with a provisional executive secretariat headed by a Cuban. The conference also approved the formation of a committee to assist the national liberation movements in their struggle against "colonialism".

1965 Winneba Conference. The fourth AAPSO conference, held at Winneba (Ghana) on May 10-16, 1965, was the first to be attended by delegates from Latin America. In a general political resolution the conference accused the United Nations of deviating from the principles of its Charter and of reflecting the will of the "imperialists" instead of that of the people. A general declaration called for the immediate destruction of all nuclear weapons and the means of their production.

The conference decided to expand into a new organization which would embrace Latin America and hold its first conference in Havana in January 1966. It was, however, decided at the Havana Conference [see below], that the existing Afro-Asian Solidarity Organization should not be dissolved, but should continue to be maintained with its headquarters in Cairo.

Further AAPSO Conferences. An AAPSO conference held in Khartoum (Sudan) on Jan. 19-20, 1969, called inter alia on all governments to recognize the national liberation movements of Angola, Guinea-Bissau, Mozambique, Rhodesia, South Africa and South West Africa (Namibia) and denounced the alleged role of the North Atlantic Treaty Organization (NATO) in "colonialist, neocolonialist and racist activities in Africa".

An AAPSO conference which was ended in Tripoli (Libya) on Nov. 12, 1970, and was attended by representatives from 69 countries and international organizations, condemned the United States for its "aggressive policy in South-East Asia and the Middle East", Israel for its "attitude to peace

negotiations" and France for "colonialism" in regard to Djibouti and the Comoros (which were then not yet independent); it denounced arms sales to South Africa and aid given to Portugal by various European states; and it declared its solidarity with "the courageous struggle of the Arab people" and attacked the "imperialist policy of Zionism".

During a further AAPSO conference, held in Cairo on June 10-13, 1972, Iran withdrew in protest against a resolution condemning Iran's occupation of three islands in the Persian Gulf. The conference also recognized the right to self-determination of Bangladesh, which was admitted as a full member of the AAPSO in March 1972.

An AAPSO conference held in Moscow on Sept. 17-19, 1975, was attended by delegates from more than 70 Asian and African countries and from socialist states, and also by representatives of international and regional organizations. In a general declaration issued at the end of the conference the AAPSO called for all-round assistance and support for the newly-independent former Portuguese territories, and stated that the basic principles established in the 1975 Final Act of the Helsinki Conference on Security and Co-operation in Europe extended beyond the boundaries of Europe and could be applied to other continents, which would benefit the economic and social development of the young states and contribute to the elimination of tension and conflict.

Three Continents Solidarity Organization

The first "Solidarity Conference of the Peoples of Asia, Africa and Latin America" took place in Havana between Jan. 3 and 15, 1966. The declared main object of the "Three Continents Conference", as it is generally designated, was "to oppose the world-wide enterprises of imperialism with a global revolutionary strategy".

Over 500 delegates took part in the conference, which had a distinctly communist character. Some represented the governments of Communist countries (including both the Soviet Union and the People's Republic of China); others were representatives of national Communist parties and of other left-wing movements (many of the Latin American delegates belonged to this category); others represented national liberation movements, such as the National Liberation Front of South Vietnam, the *Pathet Lao* of Laos, and the African National Congress of South Africa. Additional delegates represented the Governments of certain non-aligned African countries, including Algeria, Congo (Brazzaville), Egypt and Guinea.

At its final plenary session, the conference adopted a general declaration; a general political resolution; and resolutions on the situation in various countries (Vietnam, Laos, the Dominican Republic, Angola and the Congo-Kinshasa—now Zaïre), on peaceful coexistence, and on the dismantling of military bases in foreign countries.

The general declaration stressed the need for social revolution to aid the "struggle" of the national liberation movements. It also proclaimed the right of the peoples to have recourse to all forms of struggle to achieve complete political independence. In the general political resolution, "colonialism and neocolonialism" were condemned, and the United Nations was accused of allowing itself to be the instrument of "US imperialism".

Latin American Solidarity Organization

On Jan. 18, 1966, delegates representing national revolutionary committees in 27 Latin American and Caribbean countries and territories announced the formation of a Latin American Solidarity Organization, with headquarters in Havana. The organization, which would support revolutionary liberation movements in the Western hemisphere, would co-ordinate its work with that of the Three Continents Organization. A preparatory committee of representatives from Brazil, British Guiana (now Guyana), Colombia, Cuba, Guatemala, Mexico, Peru, Uruguay and Venezuela was given the task of preparing a first "Solidarity Conference of Latin American Peoples", to be held in 1967.

The policy of the Latin American Solidarity Organization was revealed at its first conference, held in Havana from July 31 to Aug. 10, 1967, as one of guerrilla warfare against all Latin American Governments other than that of Cuba, with the aim of seizing power, as Dr. Castro had done in Cuba in 1959, in order to establish communism.

The conference, attended by delegates from 27 countries and by observers (including some from the Government of North Vietnam and from the National Liberation Front of South Vietnam), endorsed resolutions calling for guerrilla warfare, opposition to "servile Pan-Americanism" and the Organization of American States, and support for the Viet Cong and for the Black Power movement among US Negroes. A resolution condemning "certain socialist countries" which gave "credits and technical aid to dictatorships and oligarchies" was adopted in committee—against the wishes of representatives of various South

American Communist parties—by 15 votes to three with nine abstentions. The conference thus gave expression to the quarrel, as President Castro defined it, "between those who want to make revolution and those who in reality only wish to brake it" (i.e., the official Communist parties advocating the use of means other than violence and guerrilla warfare).

Afro-Latin American Solidarity Conference

An Afro-Latin American Solidarity Conference was held in Luanda (Angola) on Dec. 15-19, 1979. In addition to affirming its anti-Zionist attitude in the Arab-Israeli conflict and its support for the People's Republic of Angola and the South West Africa People's Organization (SWAPO) of Namibia, the conference denounced Latin American dictatorships and accused them of maintaining "relations in all fields with the racist and neocolonialist regimes of southern Africa and with Zionist Israel".

Afro-Asian Organization for Economic Co-operation (AFRASEC)

The decision to establish a permanent Afro-Asian Organization for Economic Co-operation was made at the first economic conference of chambers of commerce in African and Asian countries, held in Cairo on Dec. 8-11, 1958. The objectives of the organization were stated to be (i) to supply information on the economic situation in Afro-Asian countries; (ii) to eliminate customs and other trade barriers; (iii) to lay down principles for sound commercial competition; (iv) to promote contact and good understanding between Afro-Asian businessmen.

Among the organs created were a Council, meeting every two or three years, with a permanent Secretariat in Cairo, and a Consultative Committee (consisting of delegates from the People's Republic of China, Egypt, Ethiopia, Ghana, India, Indonesia, Iraq, Japan, Libya, Pakistan and the Sudan), which was given the immediate task of drafting a charter for the organization.

The Consultative Committee decided that only those countries which participated in the Bandung Conference or had since acquired their independence, could become members of the organization. At a conference held in Karachi on Dec. 5-9, 1963, decisions to admit seven more States to full membership of AFRASEC raised the total membership of the organization to 45.

At an AFRASEC conference held in Casablanca (Morocco) on May 16-19, 1966, the majority of the more than 20 countries represented refused to discuss applications for membership made by the Chambers of Commerce of the Soviet Republics of Georgia, Tadzhikistan and Uzbekistan, the opposition to their admission being led by China, on the ground that these republics were part of the Soviet Union which was neither an Asian nor an African country.

At a further conference held in Karachi (Pakistan) in February 1967 a commission was appointed to examine ways and means of creating a kind of common market of member states. No AFRASEC activities have been reported since 1973, however.

Index

A

Aaland Islands Convention (1921), 6
Addis Ababa Conference (on Afro-Arab solidarity), 214
Afghanistan
  bilateral treaties and agreements, 213, 219, 272
  Islamic Conference, suspension of membership (1980), 343
Africa Reinsurance Corporation (AFRICARE), 357
African and Malagasy Coffee Organization (OAMCAF), 96
African-Arab conferences, 360-1
African Development Fund (ADF), 357
African Civil Aviation Commission (AFCAC), 359
African Development Bank (AfDB), 357
African Groundnut Council, 97
African Solidarity Fund, 280
Afro-Asian Islamic Organization, 342
Afro-Asian Organization for Economic Co-operation (AFRASEC), 397-8
Afro-Asian People's Solidarity Organization (AAPSO), 395-6
Afro-Latin American Solidarity Conference, 397
Agency for Cultural and Technical Co-operation, 280
Aggression, UN definition of, 46-7
Albania
  bilateral treaties and agreements, 191, 208
  CMEA (Comecon), membership (1949-61), 203
  Soviet Union, diplomatic break, 191
  Warsaw Treaty Organization, withdrawal (1968), 199
Algeria
  bilateral treaties and agreements, 277-8, 344, 348, 368
  European Communities, trade and co-operation agreement (1976), 145
Alliance for Progress, 293-5
Alps-Adria Regional Economic Grouping, 153
Amazon Co-operation Treaty, 307
American Treaty on Pacific Settlement (1948), 288
Andean Development Corporation, 306
Andean Group, 305-6; map, 299
Andean Reserve Fund, 306
Anglo-Portuguese alliance, 268
Angola
  bilateral treaties and agreements, 212, 213, 218, 367, 370
Antarctic Treaty (1959) and later agreements, 64
Anti-Ballistic Missile Systems, Treaty on the Limitation of (1972), 238-9; protocol (1974), 243-4
ANZAC, 372
ANZUK agreements, 267
ANZUS Pact, 372-3
Arab Bank for Economic Development in Africa, 339
Arab Common Market, 339
Arab Fund for Economic and Social Development, 339
Arab Labour Organization, 339
Arab League, 337-42 (including map); African members, 371

Arab League Educational, Cultural and Scientific Organization, 339
Arab Loan Fund for Africa, 340
Arab Military Industries Organization (AMIO), 341
Arab Monetary Fund (AMF), 340
Arab Postal Union, 340
Arab States, Pact of the Union of (1945), 337-8
Arab States Broadcasting Union, 340
Arab Telecommunications Union, 340
Argentina
  bilateral treaties and agreements, 217, 270, 308, 319, 328, 331-2, 333
  European Communities, nuclear agreement with Euratom, 124; EEC-Argentina trade agreement (1971), 146
ASEAN, see Association of South-East Asian Nations
Asian-African Legal Consultative Committee, 395
Asian and South Pacific Coconut Council, 96
Asian Coconut Community, 96
Asian Development Bank, 383
Asian Development Fund, 383
Asian-Pacific integrated rural development centre, 384
Association of Iron-Ore Exporting Countries (AIOEC), 97
Association of Natural Rubber Producing Countries (ANRPC), 100
Association of South-East Asian Nations (ASEAN), 147, 380-3 (including map)
Atlantic Charter (1941), 13
Australia
  ANZAC, 372
  ANZUK agreements, 267
  ANZUS Pact, 372-3
  bilateral treaties and agreements, 217, 220, 267-8, 270-1, 308, 328, 372, 373-4
  dependent territories, 259, 386
  IAEA-US-Australia, nuclear agreement (1974), 40
Australia-New Zealand free trade area, 373-4
Australian-New Zealand Agreement (ANZAC), 372
Australian-New Zealand consultative committee, 373
Austria
  Austrian State Treaty (1955), 11-12
  bilateral treaties and agreements, 10, 151, 308, 319, 328
  EEC, trade agreement, 147
  IAEA-US-Austria, nuclear agreement (1971), 40
Ayacucho, Declaration of (1974), 306-7

B

Bacteriological weapons, convention against, 61
Bahamas, 317
Bahrain
  bilateral treaties and agreements, 269
Balkan states, co-operation among, 153
Baltic Sea
  environmental protection, 75-6
  fisheries arrangements, 82
Bananas, 95
Bandung Conference (1955), 387-8

399

INDEX

W

War Crimes and Crimes against Humanity, Convention on the Non-Applicability of Statutory Limitations to, 42
Warfare, agreements on the conduct of, 1-4
Warsaw Treaty Organization, 197-202; map, 165
West African Development Bank, 279
West African Economic Community (CEAO), 363-4; map, 365
West African Monetary Union, 278-9, 371
Western European Union (WEU), 103-5
Western Sahara, 348-9
Western Samoa
    bilateral treaties and agreements, 275
Wheat, 102
Wildlife, conventions on protection of, 74
Wine, 102
Women, conventions on the status of, 47-8
World Bank, 31-2
World Food Council (WFC), 24
World Food Programme (WFP), 29
World Health Organization (WHO), 31; membership, 49-54
World Intellectual Property Organization (WIPO), 38; membership, 49-54
World Meteorological Organization (WMO), 37; membership, 49-54
World Tourist Organization (WTO), 23
World War II, peace treaties and other agreements arising from, 8-12

Y

Yalta Conference (1945), 8, 14
Yaoundé Conventions, 141
Yemen, People's Democratic Republic of (South Yemen)
    Arab League sanctions, 342
    bilateral treaties and agreements, 212, 217, 347, 369
Yemen Arab Republic (North Yemen)
    bilateral treaties and agreements, 328, 346-7
Yemeni Republic
    bilateral treaties and agreements, 212, 219
Yugoslavia
    bilateral treaties and agreements, 10, 194, 208, 317, 328, 331
    CMEA (Comecon), associate membership, 203
    EEC, trade and co-operation agreements, 145-6
    EFTA, co-operation, 150
    Soviet Union, break and reconciliation, 188, 194
    Trieste agreements, 10

Z

Zaïre
    bilateral treaties and agreements, 212, 220, 328, 367, 368, 369-70
Zambia
    bilateral treaties and agreements, 212, 317, 328, 367
Zimbabwe
    bilateral treaties and agreements, 369
Zinc, *see* Lead and zinc
Zones of peace, 61-2

409